VOLUME TWO: STATISTICS

UNITED STATES
NAVAL AVIATION
1910 - 2010

ROY A. GROSSNICK
MARK L. EVANS

United States Naval Aviation, 1910-2010 (Volume Two: Statistics)
published as an Uncommon Valor Reprint Edition, January 2016

ISBN-13: 978-1523715565
ISBN-10: 1523715561

This edition is an unabridged reprint of the original book listed below. This edition
has been printed with a new cover and in a slightly smaller page size.

Library of Congress Cataloging-in-Publication Data

Evans, Mark L.
   United States naval aviation 1910-2010 / Mark L. Evans, Roy A. Grossnick. -- 5th ed.
     pages cm
     Includes index.
     ISBN 978-0-945274-86-5 (v. 1 : alk. paper) 1. United States.
Navy--Aviation. 2. United States. Navy--Aviation--Chronology. I. Grossnick, Roy A. II. Naval History &
Heritage Command (U.S.) III. Title.
   VG93.E95 2015
   359.9'409730904--dc23
                          2015002942

United States
Naval Aviation

1910–2010

Volume II
Statistics

Roy A. Grossnick
Mark L. Evans

Naval History and Heritage Command
Department of the Navy
Washington, D.C.

Contents

Part IV: Ships

Part V: Deployments

Part VI: Operations

Part VII: Other Actions

Preface

Naval aviation has celebrated more than 100 years of service to this country. Its story as told in this volume and its companion, the chronology, had its origins in the 1950s. This is the fifth update to the original book, *United States Naval Aviation 1910–1960*, and due to the extensive role naval aviation has played in its country's history, the book is published in two volumes.

This volume provides invaluable facts, figures, and a compilation of data not suitable for a chronological approach. When *United States Naval Aviation 1910–1995* was published, the appendix section had more than doubled in size from the previous edition. Many statistical facts and compilations frequently requested of naval aviation historians were incorporated into that book. The current work further expands the number of chapters. It provides the researcher, Navy study groups, statistical analysis groups, and anyone interested in the topic a more detailed account of specific subjects pertinent to better understanding its history.

To facilitate a better grasp of the various subjects, the chapters have been divided into seven sections covering aircraft, personnel, units, ships, deployments, operations, and other actions. Personnel are key to naval aviation's success, closely followed by technological developments. There are many different functions within naval aviation; this volume attempts to document the multiple aspects, including operational activities, administrative and personnel changes, and the technical evolutions that have kept it in the forefront of the United States' military role in the world.

Compiling statistical information requires the historian to search a very wide range of sources. Over the past 15 years many of those reliable sources have ceased to exist. This drying up of sources resulted when specialized documents were no longer published or compiled within the Navy and from the trend toward computerized data not being maintained or transferred to the Naval History and Heritage Command archives. An exhaustive effort was made to find all possible sources necessary to compile the information presented in these chapters. When records provided conflicting data, I selected the most accurate information after reviewing all possible sources. Professional standards were paramount when conducting this research.

Special recognition is made to the naval aviation historians preceding me who were instrumental in researching and publishing the previous editions of this book: Mr. Adrian O. Van Wyen, Mr. Lee M. Pearson, Dr. William J. Armstrong, and Mr. Clarke Van Vleet. As primary compiler for these chapters, I am fully responsible for any errors of fact or mistakes that may have occurred in this volume.

ROY A. GROSSNICK
Naval Aviation Historian

Acknowledgments

This centennial update of United States Naval Aviation would not be possible without the previous editions covering the periods 1910–1960, 1910–1970, 1910–1980, and 1910–1995. The dedication and professionalism of the authors of these original editions—Adrian O. Van Wyen, Lee M. Pearson, Clarke Van Vleet, Dr. William J. Armstrong, and Major John M. Elliott, USMC (Ret.)—laid the foundation for this new version.

In addition, the extensive revisions and updates to the previous versions' appendices would not have been possible without the generous support of the Naval Historical Foundation. Updating of this primary reference work on naval aviation was facilitated by a generous donation from former CNO Admiral James L. Holloway III, USN (Ret.). His donation to the Naval Historical Foundation enabled an aviation historian to research, write, and update all the chapters of volume II. The Naval Historical Foundation then gifted the completed text to the Naval History and Heritage Command.

A project of this magnitude requires the work of many people. The authors owe a debt of gratitude to historians Dr. Michael J. Crawford, Dr. Timothy L. Francis, Dr. Jeffrey G. Barlow, Dr. Robert J. Schneller Jr., Dr. John D. Sherwood, and Robert J. Cressman of the Naval History and Heritage Command who reviewed chapter manuscripts. Their subject matter expertise, insight, and exacting verification of salient points ensured the historical accuracy and the development of cogent themes.

Additional people outside the command generously reviewed chapter manuscripts. Vice Adm. Robert F. Dunn, USN (Ret.) of the Naval Historical Foundation; Maj. Elliott; Dr. Sarandis Papadopoulos, Secretariat Historian, Department of the Navy; Capt. Edmund T. Wooldridge, USN (Ret.); and Capt. Rosario M. Rausa, USNR (Ret.) examined the voluminous material and provided critical objectivity and analysis.

Other members of the command played a key role by researching information or by providing their extensive background knowledge in specific areas. The then Head, Archives Branch Curtis A. Utz and archivists Dale J. Gordon and John L. Hodges provided an incalculable wealth of specific knowledge of naval aviation and archival sources.

Historian Dr. Regina T. Akers of the command contributed her unparalleled knowledge of diversity issues to ensure a balanced representation of the people who comprise the rich heritage of naval aviation. Then-Art Director Morgan I. Wilbur cheerfully disregarded the repeated interruptions to help with the accurate and comprehensive selection of images. Librarians Glenn E. Helm, A. Davis Elliott, J. Allen Knechtmann, and Linda J. Edwards provided crucial, enthusiastic, and knowledgeable reference support. Former photographic curator Robert Hanshew offered technical expertise that enabled the timely processing of the numerous photographic images.

The extent of the material involved required the assistance of additional people outside the command. Historian and consultant Harold Andrews was an indispensable technical expert, and his lifetime of experience and attentive character facilitated the compilation of multiple entries. Marine Corps historian Annette D. Amerman and Coast Guard historian Scott Price consistently offered immediate and vital assistance. William C. Booth of Aircraft Inventory N8812A provided indispensable support.

A special acknowledgment goes to editors Wendy Sauvageot, James M. Caiella, and Caitlin Conway of the Naval History and Heritage Command. Their keen professionalism, diligent attention to detail, and unique combination of naval aviation knowledge and matchless editorial skills proved invaluable, and every page bears their legacy.

Because an index is the key to making this book a successful reference document, the final thanks go to those who helped with it: Cmdr. Austin W. O'Toole, USNR; Cmdr. Ronald B. Mitchell, USNR (Fleet Historian, Undersea Warfare Operations Det. D); and Byron W. Hurst, Communication and Outreach Division, NHHC.

Glossary

1st MAW	First Marine Aircraft Wing	ALARS	air-launched acoustical reconnaissance
6th FLT	Sixth Fleet		
7th FLT	Seventh Fleet	ALM	Antilliaanse Luchtvaart Maatschappij (airline)
A&R	Assembly & Repair		
A.P.	armor piercing	ALNAV	All Navy
AAF	United States Army Air Forces	ALVRJ	advanced low volume ramjet
AAM	air-to-air missile	AMD	aeronautical maintenance duty
AARGM	Advanced Anti-Radiation Guided Missile	AMO	aviation medical officer
AAS	United States Army Air Service	AMRAAM	advanced medium range air-to-air missile
ABATU	advanced base training unit	ANA	Association of Naval Aviation
ABDA	American-British-Dutch-Australian Command	ANG	Air National Guard
ACC	Air Combat Command	AOCP	aviation officer continuation pay
ACLS	automatic carrier landing system	AOCS	aviation officer candidate school
ACMR	Air Combat Maneuvering Range	ARAPHAHO	merchant ship portable modular aviation facility
ACNO	Assistant Chief of Naval Operations	ARG	amphibious ready group
ACP	aviation continuation pay	ARM	antiradiation missile
ADVCAP	advanced capability	Arowa	Applied Research: Operational Weather Analysis
AED	Aeronautical Engineering Duty		
AEDO	Aeronautical Engineering Duty Officer	ARPA	Advanced Research Projects Agency
Aéronautique Militaire	Army Air Service (France)	ARPS	automatic radar processing system
AESR	active electronically scanned radar	ASM	air-to-surface missile
AEW	airborne early warning	ASMD	antiship missile defense
AEWWINGPAC	Airborne Early Warning Wing, Pacific	ASO	aviation supply office
		ASR	antisubmarine rocket
AFB	Air Force base	ASROC	Anti-Submarine Rocket
AIM	aircraft intermediate maintenance	ASTOVL	advanced short takeoff/ vertical landing
AIM	air-launched aerial intercept guided missile	ASV	surface vessel detection
		ASW	antisubmarine warfare
AIMD	Aircraft Intermediate Maintenance Division	ATARS	Advanced Tactical Airborne Reconnaissance System
AirDet/AIR DET	air detachment	ATC	Air Transport Command
AirLant/AIRLANT	Air Force, Atlantic Fleet or Commander, Air Force, U.S. Atlantic Fleet	ATFLIR	advanced targeting forward looking infrared
		ATG	air task group
AirPac/AIRPAC	Air Force, Pacific Fleet or Commander, Air Force, U.S. Pacific Fleet	ATS	Air Transport Service
		ATU	advanced training unit
		AVG	American Volunteer Group

AWACS	airborne warning and control systems
BAMS	Broad Area Maritime Surveillance
BAMS-D	Broad Area Maritime Surveillance Demonstrator
BRAC	Defense Base Closure and Realignment
BTG	basic training group
BuAer	Bureau of Aeronautics
BuC&R	Bureau of Construction and Repair
BuMed	Bureau of Medicine
BuNav	Bureau of Navigation
BuOrd	Bureau of Ordnance
BuPers	Bureau of Naval Personnel
BuShips	Bureau of Ships
BuWeps	Bureau of Naval Weapons
CAA	Civil Aeronautics Administration
CAA	Civil Aeronautics Authority
CAEWWS	Carrier Airborne Early Warning Weapons School
CAINS	carrier aircraft inertial navigation system
CalTech	California Institute of Technology
CAP	Civil Air Patrol
CAP	combat air patrol
CARDIV	carrier division
CASU	carrier aircraft service unit
CASU(F)	combat aircraft service unit (forward)
CC	Construction Corps
CCR	circulation control rotor
CEC	cooperative engagement capability
CG	commanding general
CGAS	Coast Guard Air Station
CHNAVRSCH	Chief of Naval Research
CIA	Central Intelligence Agency
CIC	combat information center
CincPac/CINCPAC	Commander in Chief, Pacific
CincPacFlt/CINCPACFLT	Commander in Chief, U.S. Pacific Fleet
CINCUS	Commander in Chief, U.S. Fleet
CIWS	Close-In Weapons System (Phalanx)
CJTF	Combined Joint Task Force
CNATRA	Chief of Naval Air Training
CNATT	Center for Naval Aviation Technical Training
CNO	Chief of Naval Operations
CNR	Chief of Naval Research
COD	carrier on-board delivery
COIN	counter insurgency
ComAirLant	Commander, Naval Air Force, U.S. Atlantic Fleet
ComAirPac	Commander, Naval Air Force, U.S. Pacific Fleet
ComFAIR/COMFAIR	Commander, Fleet Air
COMHATWING	Commander, Heavy Attack Wing
COMHSLWINGPAC	Commander, Helicopter Antisubmarine Light Wing, U.S. Pacific Fleet
COMINCH	Commander in Chief, U.S. Fleet
COMINCUS	Commander in Chief, U.S. Fleet
COMLATWING	Commander, Light Attack Wing
COMMATWING	Commander, Medium Attack Wing
COMNAVAIRESFOR	Commander, Naval Air Reserve Force
COMNAVAIRLANT	Commander, Naval Air Force, U.S. Atlantic Fleet
COMNAVAIRPAC	Commander, Naval Air Force, U.S. Pacific Fleet
COMNAVELEX	Naval Electronic Systems Command
COMNAVFOR Somalia	Commander, Naval Forces Somalia
COMNAVSUPFOR	Commander, Naval Support Force
COMOPDEVFOR	Commander, Operational Development Force, U.S. Fleet
COMPATWING	Commander, Patrol Wing
COMSTRKFIGHTWING	Commander, Strike Fighter Wing
CONUS	Continental United States
CTF	Combined Task Force
DARPA	Defense Advanced Research Projects Agency
DASH	Drone Anti-Submarine Helicopter

DCNO	Deputy Chief of Naval Operations	FLIR	forward looking infrared radar
DEW	Distant Early Warning line	FMS	foreign military sales
DICASS	directional command active sonobuoy system	FOB	forward operating base
		FORSCOM	Forces Command
DIFAR	directional frequency analysis and recording	FROG	free rocket over ground
		FTEG	Flight Test and Engineering Group
DMZ	demilitarized zone		
DOD	Department of Defense	FY	fiscal year
DODGE	Department of Defense Gravity Experiment satellite	G.P.	general purpose
		GBU	guided bomb unit
EALS	Electromagnetic Aircraft Launch System	GCA	ground-controlled approach
ECM	electronic countermeasures	Glomb	guided glider bomb
ECMO	electronic countermeasures operator/officer	GMGRU	guided missile group
		GMU	guided missile unit
ECP	Enlisted Commissioning Program	Halon	fire suppression agent
EDO	engineering duty officer	HARM	High Speed Anti-Radiation Missile
EFM	enhanced fighter maneuverability	HATWING	heavy attack wing
ELEX	Naval Electronic Systems Command	HIPEG	high-performance external gun
EOD	explosive ordnance disposal	HTA	heavier-than-air
		HUD	heads-up display
ESG	expeditionary strike group	Huff-Duff	high frequency direction-finder
EW	electronic warfare		
EXCAP	expanded (extended) capability	HVAR	High-Velocity Aircraft Rocket
FAA	Federal Aviation Administration	IBM	International Business Machine Company
FAA	Fleet Air Arm	ICAP	improved capability
FAB	Fleet Air Base	IFF	identification friend or foe
FAC	Federal Aviation Commission	IGY	International Geophysical Year
FAC	forward air controller	IO	Indian Ocean
FAETU	fleet airborne electronics training unit	IOC	initial operational capability
		IR	imaging infrared
FARP	forward arming and refueling point	IR	infrared
FASOTRAGRULANT	Fleet Airborne Specialized Operational Training Group Atlantic	ITALD	Improved Tactical Air Launched Decoy
		JAGM	Joint Air-to-Ground Missile
FAW	fleet air wing	JASSM	Joint Air-to-Surface Standoff Missile
FAWTUPAC	Fleet All Weather Training Unit, Pacific	JATO	jet-assisted takeoff
FBM	fleet ballistic missile	JCM	joint common missile
FEMA	Federal Emergency Management Agency	JCS	Joint Chiefs of Staff
		JDAM	Joint Direct Attack Munition
FEWSG	Fleet Electronic Warfare Support Group	JPALS	Joint Precision Approach and Landing System
FKR	frontoviye krilatiye raketi (frontal rocket)		

JPATS	Joint Primary Aircraft Training System	MCB	Marine Corps Base
		MCM	mine countermeasures
JRB	joint reserve base	MEB	Marine Expeditionary Brigade
JRFB	joint reserve force base		
JSF	joint strike fighter	Med	Mediterranean Sea
JSOW	joint standoff weapon	MEF	Marine Expeditionary Force
JSTARS	Joint Surveillance Target Attack Radar System	MEU	Marine Expeditionary Unit
		MIA	missing in action
KIA	killed in action	MiG	Russian aircraft designed by Artem I. Mikoyan and Mikhail I. Gurevich
LAMPS	Light Airborne Multipurpose System		
Lant/LANT	Atlantic	MIO	maritime interception operations
LANTIRN	low altitude navigation/targeting infrared for night	MIRALC/SLBD	mid-infrared advanced chemical laser/Sea Lite Beam Director
Laser-JDAM	Laser-Joint Direct Attack Munition		
		MIT	Massachusetts Institute of Technology
LCAC	landing craft, air cushion		
LCS	littoral combat ship	MLS	microwave landing system
LDO	limited duty officer	MMA	multimission maritime aircraft
LGB	laser-guided bomb		
LIC	low intensity conflict	MOL	Manned Orbiting Laboratory
LJDAM	Laser Joint Direct Attack Munition		
		MOUT	military operations in urban terrain
Lofti	Low Frequency Transionospheric satellite		
		MRASM	medium range air-to-surface missile
LORAN	Long Range Navigation		
LRAACA	Long-Range Air Antisubmarine Warfare Capable Aircraft	MRBM	medium range ballistic missile
		MRC	major regional conflict
LSO	landing signal officer	MSC	Military Sealift Command
LTA	lighter-than-air	MSO	maritime security operations
LTV	Ling-Temco-Vought Corp.		
MAC	Military Airlift Command	NAA	National Aeronautic Association
MACV	Military Assistance Command, Vietnam	NAAF	Naval Air Auxiliary Facility
		NAAS	Naval Air Auxiliary Station
MAD	magnetic airborne/anomaly detection	NAATSC	Naval Air Advanced Training Subordinate Command
MAG	Marine Aircraft Group	NAB	Naval Air Base
MAGTF	Marine Air-Ground Task Force	NACA	National Advisory Committee for Aeronautics
MATS	Military Air Transport Service		
		NAD	Naval Aviation Depot
MAU	master augmentation unit	NADC	Naval Air Development Center
MAW	Marine Aircraft Wing		
MAWSPAC	Medium Attack Weapons School, Pacific	NADEP	Naval Aviation Depot
		NADS	Naval Air Development Station
MC	Medical Corps		
MCAAS	Marine Corps Auxiliary Air Station	NAEC	Naval Air Engineering Center
MCAF	Marine Corps Air Facility	NAESU	Naval Aviation Electronic Service Unit
MCAS	Marine Corps Air Station		

NAF	Naval Air Facility	NAVCAD	naval aviation cadet
NAF	Naval Aircraft Factory	NAVICP	Naval Inventory Control Point
NAFC	Naval Air Ferry Command	NAVMAT	Naval Material Command
NAILS	Naval Aviation Integrated Logistic Support	NAVPRO	Naval Plant Representative Office
NALCOLANTUNIT	Naval Air Logistics Control Office, Atlantic Unit	NAVRES	Naval Reserve
NAMC	Naval Air Material Center	NAVSEA	Naval Sea Systems Command
NAMO	Naval Aviation Maintenance Office	Navstar	navigation satellite
NAMTC	Naval Air Missile Test Center	NAWC	Naval Air Warfare Center
NAO	naval aviation observer	NAWCAD	Naval Air Warfare Center Aircraft Division
NAOTS	Naval Aviation Ordnance Test Station	NAWCWD	Naval Air Warfare Center Weapons Division
NAP	naval aviation pilot/naval air pilot	NAWS	Naval Air Weapons Station
NAR	Naval Air Reserve	NB	Naval Base
NARF	Naval Air Rework Facility	NERV	Nuclear Emulsion Recovery Vehicle
NARTS	Naval Air Rocket Test Station	NFO	naval flight officer
NARTU	Naval Air Reserve Training Unit	NMC	Naval Material Command
NARU	Naval Air Reserve Unit	NME	National Military Establishment
NAS	Naval Aeronautic Station	NMF	Naval Missile Facility
NAS	Naval Air Station	NNV	national naval volunteers
NASA	National Air and Space Administration	NOB	Naval Operating Base
NASM	National Air and Space Museum	NORAD	North American Air Defense Command
NATB	Naval Air Training Base	NorLant	Northern Atlantic Ocean
NATC	Naval Air Training Center	NorPac	Northern Pacific Ocean
NATC	Naval Air Training Command	NOTS	Naval Aviation Ordnance Test Station
NATEC	Naval Airship Training and Experimental Command	NOTS	Naval Ordnance Test Station
NATMSACT	Naval Air Training Maintenance Support Activity	NR	Naval Reserve/Navy Reserve
NATO	North Atlantic Treaty Organization	NRAB	Naval Reserve Aviation Base
NATOPS	Naval Air Training and Operating Procedures Standardization	NRFC	Naval Reserve Flying Corps
		NRL	Naval Research Laboratory
		NROTC	Naval Reserve Officer Training Corps
NATS	Naval Air Transport Service	NS	Naval Station
NATT	Naval Air Technical Training	NSA	Naval Support Activity
NATTC	Naval Air Technical Training Center	NSAWC	Naval Strike and Air Warfare Center
NAVAIR	Naval Air Systems Command	NSC	National Security Council
NAVAIRSYSCOM	Naval Air Systems Command	NSRB	National Security Resources Board
		NTPS	Naval Test Pilot School
		NVG	night vision goggles

NVN	North Vietnam	RNAS	Royal Naval Air Station
NWC	Naval Weapons Center	ROK	Republic of Korea
OASU	Oceanographic Air Survey	RPG	rocket-propelled grenade
OCS	Officer Candidate School	RPV	remotely piloted vehicle
ODM	operational development model	RVN	Republic of Vietnam
ONR	Office of Naval Research	SAM	surface-to-air missile
OPNAV	Naval Operations	SAR	search-and-rescue
Ops	operations	SCS	sea control ship concept
OSD	Office of the Secretary of Defense	SDB	small diameter bomb
		SEAL	Sea-Air-Land team
OSRD	Office of Scientific Research and Development	SEAPAC	sea activated parachute automatic crew release
P/A	pilotless aircraft	SecDef/SECDEF	Secretary of Defense
Pac/PAC	Pacific	SecNav/SECNAV	Secretary of the Navy
PASU	Patrol Aircraft Service Unit	SEVENTHFLT	Seventh Fleet
Patriot	Phased Array Tracking Intercept of Target missile	SIXTHFLT	Sixth Fleet
		SLAM	Standoff Land Attack Missile
PatSU/Patsu	Patrol Aircraft Service Unit	SLAM-ER	Standoff Land Attack Missile–Expanded Response
PatWing/PATWING	Patrol Wing		
PIMA	planned incremental maintenance availability	SLCM	Sea/Surface Launched Cruise Missile
PLAF	People's Liberation Armed Forces (Viet Cong)	SLEP	Service Life Extension Program
PLAT	Pilot Landing Aid Television system	SoLant/SOLANT	Southern Atlantic Ocean
		SolRad	Solar Radiation (satellite)
PMTC	Pacific Missile Test Center	SoPac/SOPAC	Southern Pacific Ocean
POL	petroleum, oil, lubricants	SPASUR	Navy Space Surveillance System
POW	prisoner of war		
PPI	plan position indicator	SSM	surface-to-surface missile
RAAF	Royal Australian Air Force	STAG	Special Task Air Group
radar	radio detection and ranging	STM	supersonic tactical missile
RAF	Royal Air Force	STOL	short takeoff and landing
RAG	replacement air group	STOVL	short takeoff/vertical landing
RAM	Rolling Airframe Missile		
RAST	recovery assist, securing, and traversing system	STRATCOM	Strategic Command
RCA	Radio Corporation of America	SWIP	System Weapons Integration Program
RDT&E	research, development, test, and evaluation	SWOD	Special Weapons Ordnance Device
retrorocket ASR	rearward-firing antisubmarine rocket	T&E	test and evaluation
		TACAMO	Take Charge and Move Out
REWSON	reconnaissance, electronic warfare, and special operations	TACAN	tactical air navigation system
		TACELWING	Tactical Electronic Warfare Wing
RFC	Royal Flying Corps		
RimPac	Rim of the Pacific Exercise (Joint)	TACGRU	tactical group
		TALD	tactical air launch decoy
RIO	radar intercept officer		
RN	Royal Navy		

TARPS	Tactical Aerial Reconnaissance Pod System	USNR	United States Naval/Navy Reserve
TERCOM	terrain contour matching	USNRF	United States Naval/Navy Reserve Force
TF	task force	USNS	United States Naval Ship
TG	task group	V/STOL	vertical and/or short takeoff and landing
TINS	Thermal Imaging Navigation Set	VAST	versatile avionics shop test
TLAM	Tomahawk land-attack missile	VCNO	Vice Chief of Naval Operations
TOW	tube-launched, optically tracked, wire-command-link	VFAX	advanced experimental fighter aircraft
TRAM	Target Recognition Attack Multisensor	Viet Cong	People's Liberation Armed Forces
TraWing/TRAWING	Training Air Wing	VOD	vertical on-board delivery
TRIM	Trail Road Interdiction Mission	VOR	very-high frequency omni-range direction finder
TU	task unit	VORTAC	very-high frequency omni-range direction finder tactical air navigation system
TWA	Trans World Airlines		
UAS	unmanned aerial systems	VSTOL	vertical/short takeoff and landing
UAV	unmanned aerial vehicle		
UCAS	unmanned combat air system	VT	variable-time (fuze)
UDT	underwater demolition team	VTOL	vertical takeoff and landing
		VTUAV	vertical takeoff and landing tactical unmanned aerial vehicle
UN	United Nations		
USA	United States Army	VTXTS	fixed-wing experimental training aircraft training system
USAAF	United States Army Air Forces		
USAAS	United States Army Air Service	VWS	ventilated wet suit
		WAVES	Women Accepted for Volunteer Emergency Service
USACOM	United States Atlantic Command		
USAF	United States Air Force	WestPac/WESTPAC	Western Pacific Ocean
USCG	United States Coast Guard	WNY	Washington Navy Yard
USMC	United States Marine Corps	WWI	World War I
USN	United States Navy	WWII	World War II

Note: Acronyms or abbreviations for squadron designations, air groups or air wings, aviation ship designations, and aviation ratings may be found in the Vol. II appendices, as will other more specialized acronym meanings.

Chapter 1

Aircraft Designations and Popular Names

Background on the Evolution of Aircraft Designations

Aircraft model designation history is very complex. To fully understand the designations, it is important to know the factors that played a role in developing the different missions that aircraft have been called upon to perform. Technological changes affecting aircraft capabilities have resulted in corresponding changes in the operational capabilities and techniques employed by the aircraft. Prior to WWI, the Navy tried various schemes for designating aircraft.

In the early period of naval aviation a system was developed to designate an aircraft's mission. Different aircraft class designations evolved for the various types of missions performed by naval aircraft. This became known as the Aircraft Class Designation System. Numerous changes have been made to this system since the inception of naval aviation in 1911.

While reading this section, various references will be made to the Aircraft Class Designation System, Designation of Aircraft, Model Designation of Naval Aircraft, Aircraft Designation System, and Model Designation of Military Aircraft. All of these references refer to the same system involved in designating aircraft classes. This system is then used to develop the specific designations assigned to each type of aircraft operated by the Navy. The F3F-4, TBF-1, AD-3, PBY-5A, A-4, A-6E, and F/A-18C are all examples of specific types of naval aircraft designations, which were developed from the Aircraft Class Designation System.

AIRCRAFT CLASS DESIGNATION SYSTEM

Early Period of Naval Aviation up to 1920

The uncertainties during the early period of naval aviation were reflected by the problems encountered in settling on a functional system for designating naval aircraft. Prior to 1920, two different Aircraft Class Designation Systems were used. From 1911 up to 1914, naval aircraft were identified by a single letter indicating the general type and manufacturer, followed by a number to indicate the individual plane of that type-manufacturer. Under this system:

"A" was used for Curtiss hydroaeroplanes

"B" for Wright hydroaeroplanes

"C" for Curtiss flying boats

"D" for Burgess flying boats

"E" for Curtiss amphibian flying boats

This system had been established in 1911 by Capt. Washington I. Chambers, Director of Naval Aviation. The following is a list of the types of aircraft and their designations in existence from 1911–1914:

Aircraft Designation System 1911–1914

A-1	Curtiss hydroaeroplane (originally an amphibian, and the Navy's first airplane)
A-2	Curtiss landplane (rebuilt as a hydroaeroplane)
A-3	Curtiss hydroaeroplane
A-4	Curtiss hydroaeroplane
B-1	Wright landplane (converted to hydroaeroplane)
B-2	Wright type hydroaeroplane
B-3	Wright type hydroaeroplane
C-1	Curtiss flying boat

C-2	Curtiss flying boat
C-3	Curtiss flying boat
C-4	Curtiss flying boat
C-5	Curtiss flying boat
D-1	Burgess Co. and Curtis flying boat
D-2	Burgess Co. and Curtis flying boat
E-1	OWL (Over Water and Land; originally the A-2, it was rebuilt as a short-hulled flying boat for flying over water or land and fitted with wheels for use as an amphibian)

A new Aircraft Class Designation System was established by Capt. Mark L. Bristol, the second Director of Naval Aviation who assumed the position from Capt. Chambers in December 1913. The new system was issued on 27 March 1914 as General Order 88, "Designation of Air Craft." This system changed the original designation of the aircraft to two letters and a number, of which the first letter denoted class; the second, type within a class; and the number the order in which aircraft within the class were acquired. The four classes set up on 27 March 1914 are as follows:

Aircraft Designation System, 1914-1920

Aircraft Classes

"A" for heavier-than-air craft. Within the "A" class:

L stood for land machines

H stood for hydroaeroplanes

B stood for flying boats

X stood for combination land and water (amphibians)

C stood for convertibles (could be equipped as land or water machines)

"D" for airships or dirigibles

"B" for balloons

"K" for kites

Under this new system the A-1 aircraft (the Navy's first airplane) was redesignated AH-1, with the "A" identifying the plane as a heavier-than-air craft and the "H" standing for hydroaeroplane. General Order No. 88 also provided a corresponding link between the old aircraft designations and the new system: "The aeroplanes now in the service" are hereby designated as follows:

A-1 became the AH-1

A-2 became the AH-2

A-3 became the AH-3

B-1 became the AH-4

B-2 became the AH-5

B-3 became the AH-6

C-1 became the AB-1

C-2 became the AB-2

C-3 became the AB-3

C-4 became the AB-4

C-5 became the AB-5

D-1 became the AB-6

D-2 became the AB-7

E-1 became the AX-1

Despite the phrase, "now in the service," the A-1, B-1, and B-2, and probably the D-1 had ceased to exist before the order was issued.

The Early 1920s

In General Order 541, issued in July 1920, two overall types of aircraft were identified and assigned permanent letters, which have remained in effect since that date. Lighter-than-air types were identified by the letter Z and heavier-than-air types were assigned the letter V. Within these two categories, various class letters were assigned to further differentiate the aircraft's operation or construction. Class letters assigned to the Z types were R for rigid, N for nonrigid, and K for kite. By combining the type and class designation, the different airships in the Navy's inventory could be categorized. As an example:

ZR referred to rigid dirigibles (airships)

ZN stood for nonrigid airships

ZK for kite balloons

The class letters assigned to the heavier-than-air vehicles covered a wider range and generally reflected the mission responsibilities of the aircraft classes. Class letters assigned to the V types were:

F	Fighting
O	Observation
S	Scouting
P	Patrol
T	Torpedo
G	Fleet (utility)

By combining the V designation for heavier-than-air vehicles with the class letters, the following aircraft class definitions were assigned in 1920:

VF	Fighting plane
VO	Observation plane
VS	Scouting plane
VP	Patrol plane
VT	Torpedo and bombing plane
VG	Fleet plane (most likely a general utility aircraft)

This class designation system for aircraft has continued to remain a functional system and is still used today. There have been many additions, deletions, and major changes to the system over the years but the concept has remained intact. The current naval aircraft inventory still lists VP and VT aircraft classes. Only VP retains the same definition it was assigned in 1920. The VT designation now refers to training aircraft.

The 1920 designation system established by General Order 541 was modified on 29 March 1922 by Bureau of Aeronautics Technical Note 213. It added the identity of the manufacturer to the aircraft model designation. The aircraft class designations remained the same as those issued by General Order 541 (G.O. 541); however, besides the six aircraft classes listed in the order—VF, VO, VS, VP, VT, and VG—two additional classes were added: VA for training aircraft and VM for Marine expeditionary aircraft.

The mid- to late-1920s

Only a few modifications were made to the Aircraft Class Designation System between 1922 and 1933. The Bureau of Aeronautics, established in July 1921 was thereafter responsible for changes to the system. In response to a Secretary of Navy letter dated 13 February 1923, the Bureau of Aeronautics issued a Technical Note on 10 March 1923 that changed the VA training aircraft designation to VN, dropped the VG designation, and added the VJ designation for transport plane. This was followed by the addition, in 1925, of the VX designation for experimental aircraft, which was dropped from the Aircraft Class Designation list in January 1927. In July 1928, the VM designation was dropped and the VJ designation was changed from transport to general utility aircraft. Two new designations were also instituted, VB for bombing and VH for ambulance. An additional class, VR, was added in July 1930, assigned for transport aircraft. This designation has remained in effect for transports since then.

The 1930s

Similar changes took place in the Aircraft Class Designation System during the early 1930s. By July 1933, there were ten aircraft class designations and this list did not vary much from those identified in the previous ten years. The aircraft class designations identified in July 1933 were:

VB	Bombing
VF	Fighting
VH	Ambulance
VJ	General Utility
VN	Training
VO	Observation
VP	Patrol
VR	Transport
VS	Scouting
VT	Torpedo

A major change was instituted to the designation system on 2 January 1934. Prior to 1934, aircraft classes had been established according to the primary mission the aircraft was to perform. The fact that many aircraft were capable of performing more than one mission was recognized in the revised system by assigning an additional letter to the previous two-letter aircraft class designation. In the new three-letter designation, the first identified the type of vehicle, such as, V for heavier-than-air (fixed-wing) and Z for lighter-than-air. For heavier-than-air, the second letter identified the primary mission of the aircraft, using the same ten letter designations listed in the above paragraph. The third letter indicated the secondary mission of the aircraft class, such as:

F	Fighting
O	Observation
B	Bombing
T	Torpedo
S	Scouting

By assigning these five secondary mission letters to the primary aircraft letter designations, seven new aircraft class designations were established:

VBF	Bombing-Fighting
VOS	Observation-Scouting
VPB	Patrol-Bombing
VPT	Patrol-Torpedo
VSB	Scouting-Bombing
VSO	Scout-Observation
VTB	Torpedo-Bombing

On the eve of WWII, the Model Designation of Airplanes for 1 July 1939 was very similar to what had been identified in 1934. There were 11 primary aircraft class designations and six others that included a secondary mission letter. The 1 July 1939 list included the following designations:

VB	Bombing
VF	Fighting
VM	Miscellaneous
VO	Observation
VP	Patrol
VS	Scouting
VT	Torpedo
VN	Training
VR	Transport (multi-engine)
VG	Transport (single engine)
VJ	Utility
VOS	Observation-Scouting
VPB	Patrol-Bombing
VSB	Scouting-Bombing
VSO	Scouting-Observation
VTB	Torpedo-Bombing
VJR	Utility-Transport

World War II

The designation changes for the aircraft classes and squadron system during WWII and the immediate post-war period are identified in the Model Designation of Naval Aircraft, the Aviation Circular Letters, and in the Navy Department Bulletins.

By mid-1943, many new aircraft class designations had been added to the Model Designation of Naval Aircraft. These included:

VA	Ambulance
VBT	Bombing-Torpedo
VSN	Scout training
VL	Glider
VLN	Training glider
VLR	Transport glider
VH	Helicopter
VHO	Observation helicopter
VD	Drone
VTD	Torpedo and/or target drone
ZN	Nonrigid airship
ZNN	Nonrigid training and/or utility airship
ZNP	Nonrigid patrol and/or scouting airship

As the war progressed, more changes were made to the Model Designation of Naval Aircraft. In July 1944, a major change was instituted for the Aircraft Class Designation System. Naval aircraft were divided into three main types identified by a letter:

V	Fixed-wing vehicle (airplane, glider, and drone)
H	Rotary-wing vehicle (helicopter)
Z	Lighter-than-air vehicle (airship)

The three main types were then each subdivided into classes. Those under the heavier-than-air fixed-wing type included:

VF	Fighter
VF(M)	Fighter (medium or 2-engine)
VSB	Scout Bomber
VTB	Torpedo Bomber
VO/VS	Observation Scout
VPB(HL)	Patrol Bomber (heavy or 4-engine landplane)
VPB(HS)	Patrol Bomber (heavy or 4-engine seaplane)
VPB(ML)	Patrol Bomber (medium or 2-engine landplane)
VPB(MS)	Patrol Bomber (medium or 2-engine seaplane)
VR(HL)	Transport (heavy or 4-engine landplane)
VR(HS)	Transport (heavy or 4-engine seaplane)
VR(ML)	Transport (medium or 2-engine landplane)
VR(MS)	Transport (medium or 2-engine seaplane)
VJ(M)	Utility (medium or 2-engine)
VJ	Utility
VN	Training
VSN	Training
VSN(M)	Training (2-engine)
VK	Drone
VKN	Drone (target training)
VL	Glider
VLN	Glider (training)
VLR	Glider (transport)

The helicopter type (H) had the following classes:

HO	Helicopter (observation)
HN	Helicopter (training)
HR	Helicopter (transport)

The lighter-than-air type (Z) had the following classes:

ZN	Nonrigid airship
ZNN	Nonrigid airship (training)
ZNP	Nonrigid airship (patrol and escort)

This July 1944 change to the Model Designation of Naval Aircraft was still in effect at the close of WWII and only a couple of additions had been made, they included:

VKC   Assault drone

HJ   Utility helicopter

Post–World War II and the late 1940s

On 11 March 1946, a major revision was issued to the Class Designation of Naval Aircraft. Aviation Circular Letter Number 43-46 divided naval aircraft into four types and assigned a letter designation. They were:

V   Heavier-than-air (fixed-wing)

K   Pilotless aircraft

H   Heavier-than-air (rotary-wing)

Z   Lighter-than-air

V type aircraft class designations and primary missions were:

Class	Designation	Primary Mission
VF	Fighter	destroy enemy aircraft in the air
VA	Attack	destroy enemy surface or ground targets
VP	Patrol	search for enemy
VO	Observation	observe and direct ship and shore gunfire
VR	Transport purposes	
VU	Utility	
VT	Training purposes	
VG	Glider	

H type (rotary-wing) class designations and primary missions were:

HH   Air-sea rescue

HO   Observation

HT   Training

HR   Transport

HU   Utility

K type (pilotless aircraft) class designations and primary missions were:

KA   Attack aircraft targets

KS   Attack ship targets

KG   Attack ground targets

KD   Target aircraft

KU   Utility purposes

Z type (lighter-than-air) class designations and primary missions were:

ZP   Patrol and escort

ZH   Air-sea rescue

ZT   Training

ZU   Utility

This order provided that "no changes . . . be made in the model designation of aircraft already produced or in production, except that the mission letter of all BT class aircraft shall be changed to A." Thus, the SB2C and TBF/TBM aircraft remained in use until they were removed from the inventory, while the BT2D and BTM aircraft were redesignated as AD and AM. These aircraft were assigned to the new attack squadrons established in the latter part of 1946.

In 1947 a modification was made to CNO's Aviation Circular Letter No. 43-46 of 11 March 1946 whereby a fifth class designation was added to the naval aircraft types. This was the M type for guided missiles and its class designations and primary missions were:

AAM	Air-to-air
ASM	Air-to-surface
AUM	Air-to-underwater
SAM	Surface-to-air
SSM	Surface-to-surface
SUM	Surface-to-underwater
UAM	Underwater-to-air
USM	Underwater-to-surface
TV	Test vehicle

Two years later, in 1949, the class designations were:

V type (heavier-than-air, fixed-wing) classes

VF	Fighter	Air defense and escort
VA	Attack	Surface and ground attack
VP	Patrol	ASW (antisubmarine warfare) reconnaissance and attack
VO	Observation	Gunfire and artillery spotting
VR	Transport	Air logistic support
VU	Utility	Fleet utility support
VT	Training	Basic and fleet training
VG	Glider	

H type (heavier-than-air, rotary-wing) classes

HH	Air-sea rescue
HO	Observation
HT	Training
HR	Transport
HU	Utility

K type (pilotless aircraft) classes

KD	Aerial target

M type (guided missile) classes

AAM	Air-to-air
ASM	Air-to-surface
AUM	Air-to-underwater
SAM	Surface-to-air
SSM	Surface-to-surface

SUM	Surface-to-underwater
UAM	Underwater-to-air
USM	Underwater-to-surface
TV	Test vehicle

Z type (lighter-than-air) classes

ZP	Patrol and escort
ZH	Search and rescue
ZT	Training
ZU	Utility

The 1950s, 1960s, 1970s, and 1980s

During the early 1950s several changes were made to the V (heavier-than-air fixed-wing) type. The VG glider class was dropped and these classes were added:

| VS | Search | Submarine search and attack (carrier) |
| VW | Warning | Airborne early warning |

In the 1953 the nine classes of the V type were further divided into sub-classes. These were:

VA	Attack		Surface and ground attack
		VA (Int'd)	Interdiction
		VA (GS)	Ground support
		VA (AW)	All-weather and ASW
		VA (W)	Air early warning (AEW) and ASW
		VA (H)	Heavy
		VA (P)	Photographic
VF	Fighter		Air defense and escort
		VF (Int)	Interceptor
		VF (Day)	Day, jet
		VF (Day)(Prop)	Day, reciprocating
		VF (AW)	All-weather, jet
		VF (AW)(Prop)	All-weather, reciprocating
		VF (P)	Photographic, jet
		VF (P)(Prop)	Photographic, reciprocating
		VF (D)	Drone control
		VF (FT)	Flight test
VO	Observation		Gunfire and artillery spotting
VP	Patrol		ASW reconnaissance, mining, and weather
		VP (L)	Landplane
		VP (S)	Seaplane
		VP (MIN)	Mining
		VP (WEA)	Weather
		VP (Q)	Countermeasures
VR	Transport		Air logistic support

		VR (H)	Heavy landplane
		VR (M)	Medium landplane
		VR (S)	Heavy seaplane
		VR (C)	Carrier
VS	Antisubmarine		Submarine search and attack
		VS	Search and attack
		VS (S)	Attack
		VS (W)	Search
VT	Training		Basic, fleet, and primary training
		VT (Jet)	Jet
		VT (ME)	Two-engine, reciprocating
		VT (SE)	One-engine, reciprocating
		VT (E)	Electronic
		VT (Nav)	Navigation
VU	Utility		Fleet utility support
		VU (Gen)	General
		VU (SAR)	Search and rescue
		VU (Tow)	Tow
VW	Warning		Airborne early warning
VW			Air early warning

Between 1953 and 1960 there was only one change in the V class and a few modifications in the sub-classes. The VG class, for in-flight refueling, tanker, was added in 1958. In 1960 the type letter for the heavier-than-air fixed-wing class was still identified as V, however, it was omitted from the acronym for the class designation. The class designations for the heavier-than-air fixed-wing type and their basic mission were as follows:

A	Attack
F	Fighter
G	In-flight refueling tanker
O	Observation
P	Patrol
R	Transport
S	Antisubmarine (for carrier-based aircraft)
T	Training
U	Utility
W	Airborne early warning

The H type classes for 1953 were:

HO	Observation
HR	Transport
HS	Antisubmarine
HT	Trainer
HU	Utility
HC	Cargo

In 1955 a new H type class was added and designated HW for aircraft early warning. This class remained in effect for only a short time and was removed by 1961. The only other change for the H type during the 1950s was the removal of the HC cargo class by 1961.

The Z type classes for 1953 were:

ZP   Patrol

ZT   Trainer

There were several changes to the Z type classes in the 1950s. In 1954 two new classes were added, ZS search and antisubmarine and ZW air early warning. The other changes in 1954 included the dropping of the ZT trainer designation and modifying the ZP designation to patrol and antisubmarine. In 1955 the ZS designation was dropped after being in effect for only a year.

The K type class for 1953 was:

KD   Target

This designation was modified in 1955 to KK Target Drone. Sometime in the latter part of the 1950s, the K type designation was dropped and a new D type was listed as remotely controlled tactical airborne vehicle. Within this type, the class was identified as DS antisubmarine.

The M type for 1953 was modified as follows:

M   Tactical weapon

RV   Research vehicle

A Bureau of Aeronautics Aviation Circular Letter Number 25-51 of 14 July 1951 removed the guided missile type from the naval aircraft types and listed only four types of naval aircraft. They were:

V   Heavier-than-air (fixed-wing)

H   Heavier-than-air (rotary-wing)

Z   Lighter-than-air

K   Target drones

The Bureau of Naval Weapons Instruction 13100.1A "Model Designation of Naval Aircraft", dated 17 May 1961, lists the type letter designations as follows:

V   Heavier-than-air (fixed-wing) [the V is omitted from the aircraft designation]

H   Heavier-than-air (rotary-wing)

Z   Lighter-than-air

D   Remotely controlled tactical airborne vehicle

R   Rotorcycle

The classes within each of these five aircraft type designations were:

V type heavier-than-air (fixed-wing) classes

VA   Attack

VF   Fighter

VG   In-flight refueling tanker

VO   Observation

VP   Patrol

VR   Transport

VS   Antisubmarine

VT	Training
VU	Utility
VW	Airborne early warning

H type heavier-than-air (rotary-wing) classes

HO	Observation
HR	Transport
HS	Antisubmarine
HT	Training
HU	Utility

Z type lighter-than-air classes

ZP	Patrol
ZW	Airborne early warning

D type remotely controlled tactical airborne vehicle class

DS	Antisubmarine

R type rotorcycles class

RO	Observation (equipment)

In 1962 a major change occurred in the model designation for naval aircraft. The Department of Defense (DoD) consolidated the aircraft designation systems of the Navy, Army, and Air Force. A new DoD Directive was established that designated, redesignated, and named military aircraft. Under the new system, the V for heavier-than-air fixed-wing types was dropped completely and a single letter was used to identify the basic mission of the vehicle. The basic mission and associated type symbols were as follows:

A	Attack	Aircraft designed to search out, attack, and destroy enemy land or sea targets using conventional or special weapons. Also used for interdiction and close air support missions.
B	Bomber	Aircraft designed for bombing enemy targets.
C	Cargo/transport	Aircraft designed for carrying cargo and/or passengers.
E	Special Electronic	Aircraft possessing electronic countermeasures (ECM) capability or installation having electronic devices to permit employment as an early warning radar station.
F	Fighter	Aircraft designed to intercept and destroy other aircraft and/or missiles.
H	Helicopter	A rotary-wing aircraft designed with the capability of flight in any plane; e.g., horizontal, vertical, or diagonal.
K	Tanker	Aircraft designed for in-flight refueling of other aircraft.
O	Observation	Aircraft designed to observe (through visual other means) and report tactical information concerning composition and disposition of enemy forces, troops, and supplies in an active combat area.
P	Patrol	Long-range all-weather multi-engine aircraft operating from land and/or water bases, designed for independent accomplishment of antisubmarine warfare, maritime reconnaissance, and mining.

S	Antisubmarine	Aircraft designed to search out, detect, identify, attack, and destroy enemy submarines.
T	Trainer	Aircraft designed for training personnel in the operation of aircraft and/or related equipment, and having provisions for instructor personnel.
U	Utility	Aircraft used for miscellaneous missions such as carrying cargo and/or passengers, towing targets, etc. These aircraft will include those having a small payload.
V	VTOL and STOL	Aircraft designed for vertical takeoff or landing with no takeoff or landing roll, or aircraft capable of takeoff and landing in a minimum prescribed distance.
X	Research	Aircraft designed for testing configurations of a radical nature. These aircraft are not normally intended for use as tactical aircraft.
Z	Airship	A self-propelled lighter-than-air aircraft.

The only type symbol not in use by the Navy from the above listing was the B for bomber aircraft. The O observation aircraft designation was in the naval inventory but was used primarily by the Marine Corps.

Between 1962 and 1990 there were only two modifications to the listing of basic mission and aircraft type symbols in DoD's *Model Designation of Military Aircraft, Rockets and Guided Missiles*. These changes involved the addition of the letter R for reconnaissance and the deletion of the Z type for airships. The basic mission for the R type was an aircraft designed to perform reconnaissance missions.

Even though a consolidated DoD directive was issued on aircraft designations for the Navy, Air Force, and Army in 1962, the Navy continued to publish a listing of naval aircraft classes and sub-classes that differed slightly from the DoD directive. However, the Navy did follow the new procedures for designating its aircraft, as an example, the AD-5 Skyraider aircraft designation was changed to A-1E. The December 1962 issue of the "Allowances and Location of Naval Aircraft" lists the following classes and sub-classes for fixed-wing aircraft (note the continued use of "V" as part of the class designation and the failure to change the VG class designation for air refueler to K, as listed by the DoD instruction):

VF	Fighter	
	VF FB	Fighter-bomber
	VF P	Photo reconnaissance
VA	Attack	
	VA L	Light Attack
	VA LP	Light Attack (Prop)
	VA M	Medium Attack
	VA H	Heavy Attack
	VA P	Photo Reconnaissance (long range)
	VA Q	ECM Reconnaissance (long range)
	VA QM	Tactical ECM
	VA QMP	Tactical ECM (Prop)
VS	ASW (carrier based)	
VP	ASW Patrol	
	VP L	ASW Patrol (land based)
	VP S	ASW Patrol (sea based)
VW	Airborne early warning	
	VW M	AEW Medium (carrier based)

	VW H	AEW Heavy (land based)
VR	Transport	
	VR H	Heavy transport
	VR M	Medium transport
	VR C	Carrier transport
VG	Air refueler, heavy	
VT	Trainer	
	VT AJ	Advanced jet trainer
	VT BJ	Basic jet trainer
	VT SJ	Special jet trainer
	VT AP	Advanced prop trainer
	VT BP	Basic prop trainer
	VT PP	Primary prop trainer
	VT SP	Special prop trainer
VK	Drone	
	VK D	Drone control

The only change to this listing occurred in 1965 with the addition of the VO class for observation. Between 1965 and 1988 there was no change to the aircraft class listing in the "Allowances and Location of Naval Aircraft." However, there were numerous changes in the listing for the sub-classes. The final publication of the "Allowances and Location of Naval Aircraft" was March 1988.

On 2 May 1975, the Navy selected a derivative of the YF-17 as the winner of the Navy's VFAX competition for a new multimission fighter attack aircraft. The VFAX was designed to replace two aircraft in the Navy's inventory, the F-4 Phantom II and the A-7 Corsair II. This program was reinstituting an old Navy policy, whereby, multimission requirements for attack and fighter, be incorporated into a single aircraft. Fighter and light attack missions had previously been assigned to various types of aircraft, particularly in the period prior to WWII and also in the 1950s. The Navy was now reverting to an old policy and designing a plane with a dual capacity as a fighter and an attack aircraft to meet new multimission requirements.

The VFAX aircraft was initially assigned the F-18A designation. A new model designation F/A (strike fighter) was established and assigned to the aircraft in the late 1970s. The Navy accepted its first F/A-18 Hornet on 16 January 1979. The F/A designation was identified as a sub-class and listed under the VF class in the Navy's "Allowances and Location of Naval Aircraft." Under the DoD model designation listing the F/A-18 designation is listed under both the A and F symbol designations as A-18 and F-18.

The 1990s

The following is a list of the Naval Aircraft Class and Sub-classes used in the 1990s:

VF	Fighter	
	VF FA	Strike Fighter
	VF FB	Fighter
	VF P	Photo Reconnaissance
VA	Attack	
	VA L	Attack, light
	VA M	Attack, medium
	VA H	Attack, heavy
	VA P	Attack, photo reconnaissance
	VA Q	Attack, electronic countermeasures
	VA QM	Attack, tactical electronic countermeasures

VS	Sea Control (was Antisubmarine until 1993)	
	VS	ASW carrier based
VP	Patrol	
	VP L	Patrol, land based
VW	Warning	
	VW A	AEW medium, carrier based
VR	Transport	
	VR H	Transport, heavy
	VR M	Transport, medium
	VR C	Transport, cargo, carrier based
VG	In-flight Refueling	
VO	Observation	
	VO L	Observation
VQ	Reconnaissance	
	VQ	Reconnaissance
VU	Utility	
	VU L	Utility
	VU S	Utility, search and rescue
VT	Training	
	VT AJ	Training, advanced jet
	VT SJ	Training, special jet
	VT PP	Training, primary prop
	VT SP	Training, special prop
H	Rotary-Wing	
	H F	Rotary-Wing, fighter
	H A	Rotary-Wing, attack
	H S	Rotary-Wing, ASW
	H H	Rotary-Wing, heavy
	H M	Rotary-Wing, medium
	H L	Rotary-Wing, light
	H T	Rotary-Wing, trainer
	H R	Rotary-Wing, transport
VK	Drones	
	VK D	Drones
	VK K	Drones jet

The Post-2006 Period

The publication "Allowance and Location of Naval Aircraft" was discontinued by the Navy Department and, with it, the end of publishing the Naval Aircraft Classes and Sub-classes. Consequently the DoD publication "Model Designation of Military Aerospace Vehicles" (DoD 4120.15-L) is now the defacto source for aircraft designations, known as MDS (aircraft Mission Design Series). The following lists of symbols are used to create the aircraft designators:

Status Prefix Symbols

G	Permanently Grounded	Aircraft permanently grounded (may be used for ground training).

J	Special test (Temporary)	Aircraft in special test programs by authorized organizations, on bailment contract with a special test configuration, or with installed property temporarily removed to accommodate a test.
N	Special test (Permanent)	Aircraft in special test program by authorized activities or on bailment contract where the configuration changes so drastically that returning to the original operational configuration is impractical or uneconomical.
X	Experimental	Aircraft in a development or experimental stage.
Y	Prototype	A model suitable for evaluation of design, performance, and production potential.
Z	Planning	Aircraft in the planning or predevelopment state.

Modified Mission Symbols

A	Attack	Aircraft modified to find, attack, and destroy enemy targets using conventional or special weapons. This symbol also describes aircraft used for interdiction and close air support missions.
C	Transport	Aircraft modified to carry personnel, cargo, or both.
D	Director	Aircraft modified for controlling drone aircraft or missiles.
E	Special Electronic Installation	Aircraft modified with electronic devices for one or more of the following missions:

    (1) Electronic countermeasures

    (2) Airborne early warning radar

    (3) Airborne command and control, including communications relay

    (4) Tactical data communications link for all non-autonomous modes of flight.

F	Fighter	Aircraft modified to intercept and destroy other aircraft or missiles.
H	Search and Rescue	Aircraft modified for search and rescue missions.
K	Tanker	Aircraft modified to refuel other aircraft in flight.
L	Cold Weather	Aircraft modified for operation in Arctic and Antarctic regions, includes skis, special insulation, and other equipment for extreme cold-weather operations.
M	Multimission	Aircraft modified to perform several different missions.
O	Observation	Aircraft modified to observe (through visual or other means) and report tactical information concerning composition and disposition of forces.
P	Patrol	Long-range all-weather multi-engine aircraft that operate from land or water bases modified for independent antisubmarine warfare, maritime reconnaissance, and mining.
Q	Drone	An aerospace vehicle modified for remote or automatic control.
R	Reconnaissance	Aircraft modified for photographic or electronic reconnaissance missions.
S	Antisubmarine	Aircraft modified to find, identify, attack, and destroy enemy submarines.
T	Trainer	Aircraft modified for training purposes.
U	Utility	Aircraft modified to perform multiple missions such as battlefield support, localized transport, and special light missions.
V	Staff	Aircraft modified to provide support for the President or Vice President of the United States.

| W | Weather | Aircraft modified and equipped for meteorological missions. |

Basic Mission Symbols

A	Attack	Aircraft designed to find, attack, and destroy enemy land or sea targets using conventional or special weapons. This symbol also applies to aircraft used for interdiction and close air support missions.
B	Bomber	Aircraft designed for bombing enemy targets.
C	Transport	Aircraft designed primarily to carry personnel, cargo, or both.
E	Special Electronic Installation	Aircraft designed for one or more of the following missions:
		(1) Electronic countermeasures
		(2) Airborne early warning radar
		(3) Airborne command and control, including communications relay
		(4) Tactical data communications link for all non-autonomous modes of flight.
F	Fighter	Aircraft designed to intercept and destroy other aircraft or missiles. Includes multipurpose aircraft also designed for ground support missions such as interdiction and close air support.
L	Laser	Vehicle designed for employing a high-energy laser weapon.
O	Observation	Aircraft designed to observe (through visual or other means) and report tactical information concerning composition and disposition of forces.
P	Patrol	Long-range all-weather multi-engine aircraft operating from land or water bases designed for independent antisubmarine warfare, maritime reconnaissance, and mining.
R	Reconnaissance	Aircraft designed for photographic or electronic reconnaissance missions.
S	Antisubmarine	Aircraft designed to find, detect, identify, attack, and destroy enemy submarines.
T	Trainer	Aircraft designed for training purposes.
U	Utility	Aircraft designed to perform multiple missions such as battlefield support, localized transport, and special light missions. Included are aircraft designed for small payloads.
X	Research	Aircraft designed for testing highly experimental configurations. These aircraft are not generally intended for use as operational aircraft.

Vehicle Type Symbols

D	UAV Control Segment	Vehicles designed to control or direct UAVs.
G	Glider	Engine or engineless fixed-wing aircraft flown by using air currents to keep it aloft.
H	Helicopter	Rotary-wing aircraft (deriving lift from a rotating lifting surface).
Q	Unmanned Aerial Vehicle	An unmanned aircraft that uses aerodynamic forces for lift, autonomously or remotely piloted, expendable or recoverable, and can carry a lethal or nonlethal payload.
S	Spaceplane	Aircraft designed to travel above the earth's atmosphere and return to earth in support of space operations.

V	VTOL and STOL	Aircraft designed to take off and land vertically or in a very short distance.
Z	Lighter-Than-Air Vehicle	Nonrigid or semi-rigid aircraft that achieves its primary lift through use of hot gases or lighter-than-air gases (includes blimps and balloons).

Note: During the period of 2000–2010 the Navy quit using or no longer had basic mission aircraft with the following designations:

VA	Attack
VF	Fighter
VO	Observation
VS	Antisubmarine

The F/A-18 aircraft fell into the category of VA and VF but was identified as a multimission aircraft with the designation strike fighter.

Aircraft Designation List

The Aircraft Designation Listings have been divided into four separate lists to help clarify the different designation systems used by the Navy. They are:

- 1911–1922 Designation Systems (there were three separate systems during this period)
- 1922–1923 Designations
- 1923–1962 Navy System
- 1962 to Present DoD Designation System.

Column headings within each of these vary. However, if the popular name (official name assigned by the Navy) or common name (name usually assigned by the manufacturer) was known it is included in each of the listings. The popular or common name may not always apply to all the specific aircraft model designations. The primary emphasis for the Aircraft Designation Listings is to provide a composite list of all the aircraft designations the Navy has had in its inventory. It should also be noted, some aircraft in these listings were not assigned bureau numbers, especially in the case of experimental aircraft. Others were one-of-a-kind models, and some were acquired through a means other than the usual ordering via aircraft production contracts, these include foreign aircraft acquired for evaluation. A separate listing—Naval Aircraft Redesignated in 1962—has been added to help clarify the redesignations that occurred in 1962.

1911–1922 Designation Systems

Within this time frame there were three separate designation systems. The three separate columns identify those systems. Column three (Other Designation Systems or Popular Name) covers the period 1917–1922 during which there was no standard designation system. During WWI the Navy generally adopted whatever designations were assigned by the developer or manufacturer.

1911 Designation System	1914 Designation System	Other Designation Systems, Popular or Common Name	Manufacturer or other Source
A-1	AH-1	Triad	Curtiss
A-2/E-1	AX-1	OWL (Over-Water-Land, also called Bat Boat)	Curtiss
A-3	AH-3		Curtiss
A-4	AH-2		Curtiss
B-1	AH-4		Wright
B-2	AH-5		Wright
B-3	AH-6		Wright
C-1	AB-1		Curtiss

1911 Designation System	1914 Designation System	Other Designation Systems, Popular or Common Name	Manufacturer or other Source
C-2	AB-2		Curtiss
C-3	AB-3		Curtiss
C-4	AB-4		Curtiss
C-5	AB-5		Curtiss
D-1	AB-6		Burgess & Curtis
D-2	AB-7		Burgess & Curtis
E-1	AX-1	OWL (Over-Water-Land, also called Bat Boat)	Curtiss (1913)
	DN-1	(Navy's first LTA vehicle, D stood for dirigible and N for non-rigid)	Connecticut Aircraft Company
	AH-7		Burgess-Dunne
	AH-8		Curtiss
	AH-9		Curtiss
	AH-10		Burgess-Dunne
	AH-11		Curtiss
	AH-12		Curtiss
	AH-13		Curtiss
	AH-14		Curtiss
	AH-15		Curtiss
	AH-16		Curtiss
	AH-17		Curtiss
	AH-18		Curtiss
	AH-19	Martin S	Martin
	AH-20	Thomas HS	Thomas Brothers
	AH-21	Thomas HS	Thomas Brothers
	AH-22		Martin
	AH-23		Wright
	AH-24	Sturtevant S	Sturtevant
	AH-25		Burgess
	AH-26		Burgess
	AH-27		Burgess
	AH-28		Burgess
	AH-29		Burgess
	AH-30		Curtiss
	AH-31		Burgess
	AH-32		Curtiss
	AH-33		Curtiss
	AH-34		Curtiss
	AH-35		Curtiss
	AH-36		Curtiss
	AH-37		Curtiss
	AH-38		Curtiss
	AH-39		Curtiss
	AH-40		Curtiss
	AH-41		Curtiss
	AH-42		Curtiss
	AH-43		Curtiss
	AH-44		Curtiss
	AH-45		Curtiss

1911 Designation System	1914 Designation System	Other Designation Systems, Popular or Common Name	Manufacturer or other Source
	AH-46		Curtiss
	AH-47		Curtiss
	AH-48		Curtiss
	AH-49		Curtiss
	AH-50		Curtiss
	AH-51		Curtiss
	AH-52		Curtiss
	AH-53		Curtiss
	AH-54		Curtiss
	AH-55		Curtiss
	AH-56		Curtiss
	AH-57		Curtiss
	AH-58		Curtiss
	AH-59		Curtiss
	AH-60		Curtiss
	AH-61	D-1	Gallaudet
	AH-62	R-3	Curtiss
	AH-63		Paul Schmitt, Paris
	AH-64		Curtiss
	AH-65	R-3	Curtiss
		18-T Kirkham Fighter	Curtiss
		AR-1	Morane-Saulnier
		Avorio Prassone	Italian Govt.
		C-1	Fokker, Netherlands
		C-1F	Boeing
		Camel (F-I)	Sopwith, from Army
		Caproni Ca-44	Caproni, Italy
		CR-1,-3	Curtiss
		CS-1	Curtiss
		CS-II	Dornier
		CT	Curtiss
		D-1	Gallaudet Aircraft Corp.
		D-1	Dornier, Swiss Agent
		D-4	Gallaudet Aircraft Corp.
		D-7 or D.VII	Fokker
		DH-4	Dayton-Wright, from Army
		DH-4B/4B-1	NAF and Army
		DH-9A	British Govt.
		DN-1	Connecticut Aircraft Co.
		Donne Denhaut	French Govt.
		DT-1,-2	Douglas, NAF, LWF
		E-1 (M Defense)	Standard, from Army
		EM-1,-2	G. Elias & Brothers
		EO-1	G. Elias & Brothers
		F Boat	Curtiss, Alexandria (Briggs)
		F-5/F-5L	Curtiss, Canadian Aeroplanes Ltd., and NAF
		F-6	NAF

1911 Designation System	1914 Designation System	Other Designation Systems, Popular or Common Name	Manufacturer or other Source
		FT-1	Fokker, Netherlands
		Gastite Kite	Goodrich
		GS-1,-2 Gnome Speed Scout	Curtiss
		H-12,-12L	Curtiss
		H-16	Curtiss, NAF
		H-4-H	Standard
		HA-1,-2	Curtiss
		HB-2	Levy-Lepen
		HD-1,-2	Hanriot
		Heinkel Seaplane	Casper Werke, Germany
		HPS-1	Handley Page
		HS-1,-1L	Curtiss, Boeing, Loughead, LWF, Gallaudet, Standard
		HS-2L	Curtiss, Boeing, NAF, Gallaudet, Standard, Loughead, LWF
		HS-3	Curtiss, NAF
		HT-2	Burgess
		JL-6	Junkers-Larsen
		JN-4	Curtiss
		JN-4B	Curtiss
		JN-4H	From Army
		JN-4HG	From Army
		JN-6H	From Army
		JN-6HG-I	From Army
		K Boat	Austrian Govt.
		K-4 (variant of NO-1)	J. V. Martin
		KF-1 (also known as KIV)	J. V. Martin
		L-2	Curtiss
		L-3	Longren
		Le Pen Seaplane	From Abroad
		LePere	From Army
		LS-1	Loening Aeronautical Engineering Co.
		M-3 Kitten	Loening Aeronautical Engineering Co.
		M-8	Loening Aeronautical Engineering Co.
		M-8-0 (M-80)	Loening Aeronautical Engineering Co.
		M-8-1 (M-81)	NAF (Loening design)
		M-8-1S (M-81S)	Loening
		M2O-1	Martin
		M.5	Macchi
		M.8	Macchi
		M.16	Macchi
		MB-3	Thomas Morse
		MB-7	Thomas Morse
		MBT/MT	Martin
		MF Boat	Curtiss and NAF
		MO-1	Martin
		MS-1	Martin

1911 Designation System	1914 Designation System	Other Designation Systems, Popular or Common Name	Manufacturer or other Source
		MT/MBT	Martin
		Model 10	Alexandria Aircraft
		Model 39-A, -B	Aeromarine Plane & Motor Co.
		Model 40F	Aeromarine Plane & Motor Co.
		Model 700	Aeromarine Plane & Motor Co.
		N-1	NAF
		N-9, -9H	Curtiss, Burgess
		N-10 (2 reworked N-9)	Curtiss
		NC-1, 2, 3, 4	Curtiss
		NC-5 to -10	NAF
		Nieuport 28	From Army
		Night Bomber	Sperry
		NO-1	NAF
		NW-1, -2	Wright
		O-SS	British
		Panther	Parnall
		Paul Schmitt Seaplane	Paul Schmitt, Paris
		PT-1,-2	NAF
		R-3	Curtiss
		R-6,-6L	Curtiss
		R-9	Curtiss
		S-4B	Thomas Morse
		S-4C	Thomas Morse Scout
		S-5	Curtiss
		S-5 (not the same aircraft as Curtiss S-5)	Thomas Morse
		SA1	NAF
		SA2	NAF
		SC-1, -2	Martin
		SE-5	From Army
		SH-4	Thomas-Morse
		Sopwith Baby	Sopwith
		Sopwith Camel	Sopwith
		Sopwith Pup	Sopwith
		Sopwith 1½ Strutter	Sopwith
		SS-Z-23	British Admiralty
		ST-1	Stout Metal Airplane Co.
		Swift	Blackburn Aeroplane Co.
		Tellier Flying Boat	French Govt.
		TF Boat	NAF
		TG-1,-2,-3,-4,-5	NAF
		TS-1	NAF and Curtiss
		TS-2,-3	NAF
		TR-2 (TS-3 A6449 redesignated, one of a kind)	NAF
		TR-3,-3A	NAF (Rebuilt TS-2)
		TW-3	Wright
		U-1	Caspar, Germany

1911 Designation System	1914 Designation System	Other Designation Systems, Popular or Common Name	Manufacturer or other Source
		U-2	Burgess
		USXB-1	Dayton Wright, from Army
		VE-7,-7F	Lewis & Vought and NAF
		VE-7G,-7GF	NAF
		VE-7H	NAF
		VE-7S,-7SF,-7SH	NAF
		VE-9,-9H	Chance Vought
		Zodiac-Vedette	French Govt.
		Viking IV	Vickers
		VNB-1	Boeing
		WA	Dayton-Wright
		WP-1	Wright
		WS Seaplane	Dayton-Wright
		XDH-60 Moth	De Havilland
		XS-1	Cox-Klemin
		Exp. Seaplane	NAS Pensacola
		Glider	Am. Motorless
		Hydroaeroplane	Pensacola and Curtiss
		Richardson Seaplane	Washington Navy Yard
		Seaplane	Aeromarine
		Seaplane	DWF, Germany
		Seaplane	Farman
		Seaplane	Loening
		Seaplane	Standard
		Seaplane	Wright
		Seaplane	Wright-Martin

1922–1923 Designations

Original Navy Designation	Other Designation, Popular or Command Name	Manufacturer or other Source
BR		Bee Line
HN-1,-2		Huff-Daland
HO-1		Huff-Daland
NM		NAF

1923–1962 Navy System

Post-1962 DoD Designation	Original Navy Designation	Popular or Common Name, other Designation and Miscellaneous Data	Manufacturer or Source
	AE-1	(L-4)(HE-1)	Piper
A-1	AD-1 thru -7	Skyraider (XBT2D-1)	Douglas
	A2D-1	Skyshark	Douglas
A-3	A3D-1, -2	Skywarrior	Douglas
A-4	A4D-1, -2, -5	Skyhawk	Douglas
	AF-2, -3	Guardian (XTB3F-1)	Grumman
A-6	A2F-1	Intruder	Grumman
F-4	AH	Phantom II	McDonnell
A-2	AJ-1, -2	Savage	North American
A-5	A3J-1 thru -3	Vigilante	North American

Post-1962 DoD Designation	Original Navy Designation	Popular or Common Name, other Designation and Miscellaneous Data	Manufacturer or Source
	AM-1	Mauler (XBTM-1)	Martin
	AU-1	Corsair (XF4U-6)	Vought
		B-314	Boeing
		Bulldog IIA	Bristol
	BD-1, -2	Havoc (A-20)	Douglas
	BG-1		Great Lakes
	XB2G-1		Great Lakes
	BM-1, -2	(XT5M-1)	Martin
	BT-1		Northrop
	XBT-2	(SBD-1)	Northrop/Douglas
	XBTC-2		Curtiss
	XBY-1		Consolidated
	XB2Y-1		Consolidated
	XBFC-1	(XF11C-1)	Curtiss
	BFC-2	Goshawk (F11C-2)	Curtiss
	BF2C-1	(F11C-3)	Curtiss
	XBTC-1	Cancelled	Curtiss
	XBTC-2		Curtiss
	XBT2C-1		Curtiss
	BTD	Destroyer	Douglas
A-1	XBT2D-1	Skyraider (AD-1)	Douglas
	XBTK-1	(BK-1 original designation, changed before first aircraft completed)	Kaiser-Fleetwings
	XBTM-1	Mauler (AM-1)	Martin
	CS-1, -2		Curtiss
	SC-1, -2	(CS-1)	Martin
	D-558-1	Skystreak	Douglas
	D-558-2	Skyrocket	Douglas
	XDH-80	Puss Moth	De Havilland
QH-50D,-50C	DSN	DASH	Gyrodyne
	F-5L		NAF
	XFA-1		General Aviation
	F2A-1 thru -3	Buffalo	Brewster
	F3A-1	Corsair (F4U)	Brewster
	FB-1 thru -5		Boeing
	F2B-1		Boeing
	F3B-1		Boeing
	F4B-1 thru -4		Boeing
	XF5B-1		Boeing
	XF6B-1		Boeing
	XF7B-1		Boeing
	XF8B-1		Boeing
	F2C-1	(F2C-1 a paper designation for R2C-1, never used as F2C-1)	Curtiss
	F4C-1		Curtiss
	F6C-1 thru -4	Hawk	Curtiss
	F6C-6	Hawk	Curtiss
	XF6C-5 thru -7		Curtiss
	F7C-1	Seahawk	Curtiss

Post-1962 DoD Designation	Original Navy Designation	Popular or Common Name, other Designation and Miscellaneous Data	Manufacturer or Source
	XF8C-1	Falcon	Curtiss
	F8C-1, -3	Falcon (OC)	Curtiss
	F8C-4, -5	Helldiver (O2C)	Curtiss
	XF8C-2, -4	Helldiver	Curtiss
	XF8C-7, -8	Helldiver (O2C)	Curtiss
	XF9C-1, -2		Curtiss
	F9C-2	Sparrowhawk	Curtiss
	XF11C-1	(XBFC-1)	Curtiss
	XF11C-2	Goshawk (XBFC-2)	Curtiss
	XF11C-3	(XBF2C-1)	Curtiss
	F11C-2	Goshawk (BFC-2)	Curtiss
	XF13C-1 thru -3		Curtiss
	XF14C-2		Curtiss
	XF15C-1		Curtiss
	XFD-1		Douglas
	FD-1	Phantom (FH-1)	McDonnell
	XF2D-1	Banshee (F2H)	McDonnell
F-10	F3D-1, -2	Skyknight	Douglas
F-6	F4D-1	Skyray	Douglas
	F5D-1	Skylancer	Douglas
	FF-1, -2		Grumman
	F2F-1		Grumman
	F3F-1 thru -3		Grumman
	XF4F-3 thru -6, -8	Wildcat	Grumman
	F4F-3, -3A, -4, -7	Wildcat (FM)	Grumman
	XF5F-1	Skyrocket	Grumman
	XF6F-3, -4, -6	Hellcat	Grumman
	F6F-3, -5	Hellcat	Grumman
	F7F-1 thru -4	Tigercat	Grumman
	F8F-1, -2	Bearcat	Grumman
	F9F-2 thru -5	Panther	Grumman
F-9	F9F-6 thru -8	Cougar	Grumman
	XF10F-1	Jaguar	Grumman
F-11	F11F-1	Tiger (F9F-9)	Grumman
	XFG-1/XFG2G-1		Eberhart
	FG-1	Corsair (F4U)	Goodyear
	F2G-1, -2	(FG/F4U)	Goodyear
	XFH-1		Hall
	FH-1	Phantom	McDonnell
F-2	F2H-1 thru -4	Banshee (F2D)	McDonnell
F-3	F3H-1, -2	Demon	McDonnell
F-4	F4H-1	Phantom II	McDonnell
	FJ-1, -2	Fury	North American
F-1	FJ-3, -4	Fury	North American
	XFJ-1, -2		Berliner-Joyce
	XF2J-1		Berliner-Joyce
	XF3J-1		Berliner-Joyce
	XFL-1	Airabonita	Bell

Post-1962 DoD Designation	Original Navy Designation	Popular or Common Name, other Designation and Miscellaneous Data	Manufacturer or Source
	F2L-1	Airacobra (XTDL-1)	Bell
	FM-1, -2	Wildcat	General Motors
	FO-1	Lightning (P-38)	Lockheed
	XFR-1	Fireball	Ryan
	FR-1	Fireball	Ryan
	XF2R-1		Ryan
	XFT-2		Northrop
	F2T-1	Black Widow (P-61)	Northrop
	FU-1		Vought
	XF2U-1		Vought
	XF3U-1	(SBU)	Vought
	XF4U-1, -3 thru -5	Corsair	Vought
	F4U-1 thru -5, -7	Corsair (AU/FG/F3A/F2G)	Vought
	XF5U-1		Vought
	F6U-1	Pirate	Vought
	F7U-1 thru -3	Cutlass	Vought
F-8	F8U-1, -2	Crusader	Vought
	F8U-3	Crusader III	Vought
	F2W-1		Wright
	F3W-1	Apache	Wright
	XFY-1	Pogo	Consolidated
F-7	F2Y	Sea Dart (Never used in F-7 designation)	Convair
	GB-1, -2	Traveler (JB)	Beech
	GH-1 thru -3	Nightingale (NH)	Howard
	GK-1	Forwarder (JK)	Fairchild
	GQ-1	Reliant	Stinson
C-130	GV-1	Hercules (R8V)	Lockheed
	HE	(L-4)(AE)	Piper
	XHL-1		Loening
	XHJH-1		McDonnell
	XHJP-1		Piasecki
	XHJS-1		Sikorsky
	HNS-1	Hoverfly	Sikorsky
	XHOE-1		Hiller
H-43	HOK-1		Kaman
	HOS-1		Sikorsky
	HO2S-1		Sikorsky
	HO3S-1		Sikorsky
	XHO3S-3		Sikorsky
H-19	HO4S-3	(HRS)	Sikorsky
	HO5S-1		Sikorsky
H-46	HRB-1		Vertol
	XHRH-1	Order cancelled	McDonnell
	HRP-1, -2	Rescuer (Flying Banana)	Piasecki
H-19	HRS-1 thru -3	(HO4S)	Sikorsky
H-37	HR2S-1	Mojave	Sikorsky
	HSL-1	Model 61	Bell
H-34	HSS-1	Sea Bat	Sikorsky

Post-1962 DoD Designation	Original Navy Designation	Popular or Common Name, other Designation and Miscellaneous Data	Manufacturer or Source
H-3	HSS-2	Sea King	Sikorsky
	HTE-1, -2	UH-12A	Hiller
	HTK-1		Kaman
H-13	HTL-1 thru -7	Did not use Sioux	Bell
H-43	HUK-1	Did not use Huskie	Kaman
H-2	HU2K-1	Seasprite	Kaman
H-13	HUL-1	Did not use Sioux	Bell
	HUM-1	MC-4A	McCulloch
H-25	HUP-1 thru -3	Retriever	Piasecki (Vertol)
H-34	HUS-1	Seahorse	Sikorsky
H-52	HU2S-1		Sikorsky
	XJA-1	Super Universal	Fokker
	JR-1 thru -3	(RR)	Ford
	JA-1	Norseman	Noorduyn
	JB-1	Traveler (GB)	Beech
	JD-1	Invader	Douglas
	JE-1		Bellanca
	JF-1 thru -3	Duck	Grumman
	J2F-1 thru -5	Duck	Grumman
	J2F-6	Duck	Columbia
	XJ3F-1	G-21	Grumman
	J4F-1, -2	Widgeon	Grumman
	JH-1		Stearman-Hammond
	JK-1		Fairchild
	J2K-1	Coast Guard only	Fairchild
	XJL-1		Colombia
	JM-1, -2	Marauder	Martin
	JO-1, -2	Model 12A	Lockheed
	XJO-3		Lockheed
	XJQ-1, -2	(XRQ/R2Q)	Fairchild
	J2Q-1	Coast Guard (R2Q)	Fairchild
	XJW-1	UBF	Waco
	JRB-1 thru -4	Voyager/Expediter	Beech
	JRC-1	Bobcat	Cessna
	JRF-1 thru -6	Goose, G-21	Grumman
	XJR2F-1	Albatross (UF/UH-16)	Grumman
	JRM-1 thru -3	Mars (XPB2M)	Martin
	JRS-1		Sikorsky
	JR2S-1	VS-44A	Vought Sikorsky
	XLBE-1	Glomb	Pratt-Read (Gould)
	LBP-1	Glomb	Piper
	LBT-1	None acquired (XLBE-1)	Taylorcraft
	LNE-1		Pratt-Read (Gould)
	XLNP-1		Piper
	XLNR-1		Aeronca
	LNS-1		Schweizer
	XLNT-1		Taylorcraft
	XLRA-1		Allied

Post-1962 DoD Designation	Original Navy Designation	Popular or Common Name, other Designation and Miscellaneous Data	Manufacturer or Source
	XLR2A-1		Allied
	XLRN-1		NAF
	XLRQ-1		Bristol
	LRW-1		Waco
	XLR2W-1		Waco
		M-130, PanAm owned	Martin
		Me-108B	Messerschmitt
		Me-262S	Messerschmitt
	NB-1 thru –4	Model 21	Boeing
	XN2B-1	Model 81	Boeing
	N2C-1, -2	Fledgling	Curtiss
L-4	NE-1, -2	Grasshopper	Piper
	NH-1	Nightingale (GH)	Howard
	NJ-1		North American
	XNK-1		Keystone
	XNL-1		Langley
	N2M-1		Martin
	N2N-1		NAF
	N3N-1 thru –3	Yellow Peril	NAF
	NP-1		Spartan
	XNQ-1		Fairchild
	XNR-1		Maxon
	NR-1	Recruit	Ryan
	NS-1		Stearman
	N2S-1 thru –5	Kaydet/Caydet	Stearman/Boeing
	NT-1		New Standard
	N2T-1	Tutor	Timm
	NY-1 thru –3	(PT-1)	Consolidated
	N2Y-1		Consolidated (Fleet Aircraft Inc.)
	XN3Y-1		Consolidated
	XN4Y-1	(PT-11)	Consolidated
	O2B-1	DH-4B metal fuselage	Boeing
	OC-1, -2	Falcon (F8C-1, -3)	Curtiss
	XOC-3		Curtiss
	O2C-1, -2	Helldiver (F8C-5)	Curtiss
	XO3C-1	(SOC)	Curtiss
	OD-1		Douglas
	XO2D-1		Douglas
O-1	OE-1, -2	Bird Dog	Cessna
	XOJ-1		Berliner-Joyce
	OJ-2		Berliner-Joyce
	XOK-1		Keystone
	OL-1 thru –9		Loening Aeronautical Engineering Company
	XO2L-1		Loening
	O2N-1	None accepted (XOSN-1)	NAF
	OO	Schreck FBA	Viking
	XOP-1, -2		Pitcairn

Post-1962 DoD Designation	Original Navy Designation	Popular or Common Name, other Designation and Miscellaneous Data	Manufacturer or Source
	O2U-1 thru -4		Vought
	O3U-1, -2	(O3U-2 redes. SU-1) -3, -4, -6 (O3U-4 redes. SU-2, -3)	Vought
	XO3U-5, -6		Vought
	XO4U-1, -2		Vought
	XO5U-1		Vought
	OY-1	Sentinel (L-5) Stinson V-76	Convair (Stinson, Vultee, Consolidated)
	XOZ-1		Penn Acft. Syndicate
	XOSE-1, -2		Edo
	XOSN-1		NAF
	OS2N-1	Kingfisher (OS2U)	NAF
	XOSS-1		Stearman
	OS2U-1 thru -3	Kingfisher	Vought
		(P-59)	Bell
		(P-63)(L-39)	Bell
	PB-1	Flying Fortress (B-17)	Boeing
	P2B-1, -2	Superfortress (B-29)	Boeing
	PD-1	(PN-12)	Douglas
	P2D-1		Douglas
	XP3D-1		Douglas
	UF-1	Albatross (XJR2F/UH-16)	Grumman
	PH-1 thru -3		Hall
	XP2H-1		Hall
	PJ-1, -2	FLB, Coast Guard	North American
	PK-1	(PN-12)	Keystone
	PM-1, -2	(PN-12)	Martin
	XP2M-1		Martin
	P3M-1, -2	(XPY-1)	Martin
	P4M-1	Mercator	Martin
P-5	P5M-1, -2	Marlin	Martin
P-6	XP6M-1	Seamaster (never used in P-6 designation)	Martin
P-6	P6M-2	Seamaster (never used in P-6 designation)	Martin
	PN-7 thru -12		NAF
	P2N	Never used in this designation (NC boats)	NAF
	P3N		NAF
	XP4N-1, -2		NAF
	PO-1	Constellation	Lockheed
	PO-2	Warning Star (WV)	Lockheed
	XPS-1, -2	(XRS-2)	Sikorsky
	PS-3	(RS-3)	Sikorsky
	XP2S		Sikorsky
	PV-1, -3	Ventura	Lockheed
	PV-2	Harpoon	Lockheed
P-2	P2V-1 thru -7	Neptune	Lockheed
P-3	P3V-1	Orion	Lockheed
	XPY-1	Admiral (P3M-1, -2)	Consolidated
	P2Y-1 thru -3		Consolidated
	XP3Y-1	(PBY)	Consolidated

Post-1962 DoD Designation	Original Navy Designation	Popular or Common Name, other Designation and Miscellaneous Data	Manufacturer or Source
	XP4Y-1	Model 31	Consolidated
QP-4B	P4Y-2	Privateer (PB4Y-2)	Consolidated
	XP5Y-1	(R3Y)	Convair
	XPBB-1		Boeing
	PB2B-1, -2	Catalina	Boeing
	PBJ-1	Mitchell (B-25)	North American
	PBM-1 thru -3, -5	Mariner	Martin
	XPB2M	Mars (JRM)	Martin
	PBN-1	Nomad	NAF
	PBO-1	Hudson	Lockheed
	XPBS-1		Sikorsky
	PBY-1 thru -6A	Catalina	Consolidated
	XPB2Y-1	Coronado	Consolidated
	PB2Y-2 thru -5	Coronado	Consolidated
	PB4Y-1	Liberator (B-24)	Consolidated
	PB4Y-2	Privateer	Consolidated
	XPTBH-2		Hall
	R2C-1, -2	(F2C-1 paper designation for R2C-1, never used)	Curtiss
	R3C-1 thru -4		Curtiss
	RA-1 thru -4	(TA)	Atlantic
	RB-1	Conestoga	Budd
	RC-1	Kingbird	Curtiss
	R4C-1	Condor	Curtiss
C-46	R5C-1	Commando (may not have been used under C-46 designation)	Curtiss
	RD-1 thru -4	Dolphin	Douglas
	R2D-1	DC-2	Douglas
	R3D-1 thru -3	DC-5	Douglas
C-47	R4D-1 thru -7	Skytrain	Douglas
C-117	R4D-8	Skytrain	Douglas
C-54	R5D-1 thru -5	Skymaster	Douglas
C-118	R6D-1	Liftmaster, DC-6A	Douglas
	XRE-1 thru -3	Skyrocket	Bellanca
	RG-1		Romeo Fokker, Italy
	XRK-1	Envoy	Kinner
C-3	RM-1	Model 4-0-4 (VC-3A)	Martin
	XRO-1	Altair	Detroit/Lockheed
	XR2O-1	Electra	Lockheed
	XR3O-1	Electra	Lockheed
	R4O-1	Model 14	Lockheed
	R5O-1 thru -6	Lodestar	Lockheed
	XR6O-1	Constitution	Lockheed
C-121	R7O-1	Constellation	Lockheed
	R2Q-1	(J2Q) Coast Guard	Fairchild
	XR3Q-1	Reliant	Stinson
C-119	R4Q-1, -2	Packet	Fairchild
	RR-4, -5	(JR)	Ford
	RS-1 thru -3, -5	(PS)	Sikorsky

Post-1962 DoD Designation	Original Navy Designation	Popular or Common Name, other Designation and Miscellaneous Data	Manufacturer or Source
	RT	Delta	Northrop
	R6V-1	Constitution	Lockheed
C-121	R7V-1	Constellation	Lockheed
	R8V-1G	Hercules	Lockheed
	RY-1 thru -3		Consolidated
	XR2Y-1		Convair
	R3Y-1, -2	Tradewind	Convair
C-131	R4Y-1, -2	Convair Liner	Convair
	ROE-1		Hiller
	RON-1	(HOG-1)	Gyrodyne
	SC-1, -2	Seahawk	Curtiss
	XS2C-1	Shrike	Curtiss
	XS3C-1		Curtiss
	SDW-1	(DT)	Dayton-Wright
	XSE-2		Bellanca
	SF-1	(FF-1)	Grumman
	XSG-1		Great Lakes
	XSL-1		Loening
	XS2L-1		Loening
	XSS-2		Sikorsky
	SU-1 thru -3	Corsair (O3U)	Vought
S-2	S2F-1 thru -3	Tracker	Grumman
	XS2U-1W	Cancelled (XWU-1)	Vought
	XSBA-1	(SBN)	Brewster
	SB2A-1 thru -4	Buccaneer	Brewster
	XSBC-1	(XF12C-1)	Curtiss
	XSBC-2 thru -4		Curtiss
	SBC-3, -4	Helldiver	Curtiss
	SB2C-1 thru -5	Helldiver (SBF/SBW)	Curtiss
	XSB2C-6		Curtiss
	SBD-1 thru -6	Dauntless	Douglas
	XSB2D-1	Destroyer	Douglas
	SBF-1, -3, -4	Helldiver (SB2C/SBW)	Fairchild Aircraft Ltd., Canada
	SBN-1	(XSBA)	NAF
	SBU-1, -2		Chance Vought
	SB2U-1 thru -3	Vindicator	Vought-Sikorsky, Chance Vought
	XSB3U-1		Vought-Sikorsky
	SBW-1, -3 thru -5	Helldiver (SB2C/SBF)	Canadian Car & Foundry
	SNJ-1 thru -7	Texan	North American
	XSN2J-1		North American
	SNB-1, -2	Kansan	Beech
C-45	SNB-5	Navigator	Beech
	SNC-1	Falcon	Curtiss
	SNV-1, -2	Valiant	Vultee
	SOC-1 thru -4	Seagull	Curtiss
	XSO2C-1		Curtiss
	SO3C-1 thru -3	Seamew	Curtiss

Post-1962 DoD Designation	Original Navy Designation	Popular or Common Name, other Designation and Miscellaneous Data	Manufacturer or Source
	XSOE-1		Bellanca
	SON-1	(SOC-3)	NAF
	XSO2U-1		Vought
	TB-1		Boeing
	T2D-1		Douglas
	XT3D-1		Douglas
	TG-1, -2		Great Lakes
	T3M-1, -2		Martin
	T4M-1		Martin
	XT5M-1	(BM)	Martin
	XT6M-1		Martin
	XTN-1		NAF
	XT2N-1		NAF
	TA-1 thru -3	(RA)	Atlantic
	XTE-1		Edo
	TE-2		Edo
C-1	TF-1	Trader	Grumman
	XTF-1W	Tracer (WF-2)	Grumman
T-2	XT2J-1, -2	Buckeye	North American
T-2	T2J-1	Buckeye	North American
T-39	T3J-1		North American
T-33	TO-1, -2	Shooting Star (TV)	Lockheed
	TT-1	Pinto	Temco
T-33	TV-1, -2	Shooting Star (TO)	Lockheed
T-1	T2V-1	Seastar	Lockheed
	TBD-1	Devastator	Douglas
	XTB2D-1		Douglas
	TBF-1	Avenger (TBM)	Grumman
	XTBF-2, -3	Avenger (TBM)	Grumman
	XTB3F-1	Guardian (AF)	Grumman
	XTBG-1		Great Lakes
	TBM-1 thru -4	Avenger (TBF)	General Motors
	XTBU-1	Seawolf (TBY)	Vought
	TBY-2	Seawolf (XTBU)	Consolidated
	TDC-1, -2	(PQ-8) drone	Culver
	TD2C-1	(PQ-14) drone	Culver
	XTD3C	(PQ-15) drone	Culver
	XTD4C-1	(XUC) drone	Culver
	TDD	(OQ-2A) drone	Radioplane
	TD2D	Katydid, drone	McDonnell
	TD3D	(OQ-16) drone	Frankfort
	TD4D	(OQ-17) drone	Radioplane
	XTDL-1	(P-39Q) drone	Bell
	TDN-1	Drone	NAF
	TD2N	Gorgon	NAF
	TD3N	Gorgon	NAF
	TDR-1	Drone	Interstate
	XTD2R-1	Drone	Interstate

Post-1962 DoD Designation	Original Navy Designation	Popular or Common Name, other Designation and Miscellaneous Data	Manufacturer or Source
	XTD3R-1	Drone	Interstate
	TS-1		Curtiss
	XUC	(XTD4C)	Culver
U-1	UC-1	Otter	De Havilland
U-16	UF-1, -2	Albatross (XJR2F)	Grumman
U-11	UO-1	Aztec	Piper
	UO-1	(not the same as Piper UO-1)	Vought
E-1	WF-2	Tracer	Grumman
E-2	W2F-1	Hawkeye	Grumman
	XWU-1	Cancelled (XS2U-1W)	Vought
	WV-1	Constellation	Lockheed
EC-121	WV-2, -3	Warning Star	Lockheed

Note:

- The list does not include all X model designations.
- Aircraft designations in parentheses are a cross reference to a similar model or a redesignation of that aircraft. Parentheses are also used to identify Army Air Corps/Air Force designations. Civilian model designations are not placed in parentheses.
- The designations T-28B/C, T-34B, and C-130BL were used by the Navy prior to the change to the DoD Designation System in 1962.

How to Read the 1923 to 1962 Aircraft Model Designations for U.S. Naval Aircraft

There have been several systems to designate U.S. naval aircraft. However, the most common system covered the period 1923 to 1962 and consisted of four major elements:

- Aircraft Type/Class
- Manufacturer Type Sequence
- Manufacturer
- Modification

In the beginning there were just two classes: heavier-than-air (fixed-wing) identified by the letter V and lighter-than-air identified by the letter Z. The letter H for heavier-than-air (rotary-wing) was added with the introduction of the helicopter in the 1940s. Late in 1945 the letter K was added for pilotless aircraft, making four distinct types. In March 1946 the type/class designation was separated into two distinct headings of Type and Class. The letter V was omitted in the model designation, but H, K, and Z were used where applicable. The letter X was added as a prefix designating an experimental model.

In designating the first model of a class produced by a given manufacturer, the first number (1) is omitted in the Manufacturer Type Sequence position, but is shown in the Modification Sequence position. Thus, in the VJ class, the first utility aircraft produced by Grumman Aircraft Corporation was the JF-1. When a major modification was instituted for the JF-1 without changing the character of the model, that modification changed the designation to JF-2. The second modification changed the designation to JF-3. The second utility aircraft built by Grumman was designated the J2F-1 and successive modifications to this aircraft became J2F-2, J2F-3, etc. It must be remembered that the aircraft Modification Sequence Number is always one digit higher than the actual modification number. The basic designation could be expanded to show additional characteristics, as demonstrated below:

Suffix letters came into a more general use during the period of rapid expansion immediately prior to U.S. entry into WWII. Unfortunately, the use of suffix letters was not strictly defined and the same letter was frequently used to denote several different characteristics causing considerable confusion. By the time the system was abandoned, it was necessary to know the aircraft in question rather than relying on the suffix letter to tell the specific characteristics being identified.

The following lists provide all of the letter designations necessary to understand the system:

Table 1. Type/Class Designation		
Type/Class	**Meaning**	**Period**
A	Attack	1946–1962
A	Ambulance	1943–1946
B	Bomber	1931–1946
BT	Bomber Torpedo	1942–1946
D	Target Drone	1946–1947
F	Fighter	1922–1962
G	Glider	1946–1962
G	Transport, Single Engine	1939–1946
G	In-Flight Refueling Tanker	1960–1962
H	Hospital	1929–1942
H	Air-Sea-Rescue	1946–1962
J	Utility	1931–1946
J	Transport	1928–1931
JR	Utility Transport	1935–1946
K	Drone	1945–1962
L	Glider	1941–1945
M	Marine Expeditionary	1922–1925
N	Trainer	1922–1946
O	Observation	1922–1962
OS	Observation Scout	1935–1945
P	Patrol	1922–1962
P	Pursuit	1923
PB	Patrol Bomber	1935–1946
PT	Patrol Torpedo	1922
PT	Patrol Torpedo Bomber	1937–1938
R	Transport	1931–1962
R	Racer	1923–1928
S	Scout	1922–1946
SB	Scout Bomber	1934–1946
SN	Scout Trainer	1939–1946
SO	Scout Observation	1934–1946
T	Torpedo	1922–1935
T	Transport	1927–1930
T	Training	1946–1962
TB	Torpedo Bomber	1936–1946
TD	Target Drone	1942–1946
U	Utility	1946–1962

Table 2. Special Purpose Suffix		
Suffix	Meaning	Example
A	Target towing and photography	JRF-1A
A	Nonfolding wings and no carrier provisions	SB2C-1A
A	Armament on normally unarmed aircraft	J2F-2A
A	Arresting gear normally on noncarrier planes	SOC-3A
A	Amphibious version	PBY-5A
A	Land-based version of carrier aircraft	F4F-3A
A	Built for the Army Air Force	SBD-3A
B	Special armament version	PB4Y-2B
B	British lend-lease version	JRF-6B
C	Carrier operating version of a noncarrier aircraft	SNJ-2C
C	British-American standardized version	PBM-3C
C	Equipped with two .50-cal. machine guns	TBF-1C
C	Cannon armament	F4U-1C
D	Drop tank configuration	F4U-1D
D	Special search radar	TBM-3D
E	Special electronic version	SB2C-4E
F	Converted for use as a flagship	PB2Y-3F
G	Air-sea-rescue version	TBM-5G
H	Hospital version	SNB-2H
H	Air-sea rescue version	PB2Y-5H
J	Target towing version	TBM-3J
K	Target drone version	F6F-5K
L	Search light version	P2V-5L
M	Weather reconnaissance version	PB4Y-2M
N	Night operating version (all weather)	F6F-5N
P	Photographic version	SBD-2P
Q	Countermeasure version	TBM-3Q
R	Transport version	PBM-3R
S	Antisubmarine version	P5M-2S
T	Training version	R4D-5T
U	Utility version	PBM-3U
W	Special search version	PB-1W
Z	Administrative version	R4D-5Z

Letter	Manufacturer	Period
	Table 3. Manufacturer's Designation	
A	Aeromarine Plane and Motor Co.	1922
A	Atlantic Aircraft Corp. (American Fokker)	1927–1930
A	Brewster Aeronautical	1935–1943
A	General Aviation Corp. (ex-Atlantic)	1930–1932
A	Noorduyn Aviation, Ltd. (Canada)	1946
B	Beech Aircraft Co.	1937–1962
B	Boeing Aircraft Co.	1923–1962
B	Budd Manufacturing Co.	1942–1944
C	Cessna Aircraft Corp.	1943–1951
C	Culver Aircraft Corp.	unknown–1946
C	Curtiss Aeroplane and Motor Co.	1922–1946
C	Curtiss-Wright Corp.	1948–1962
C	De Havilland Aircraft of Canada	1955–1962
D	Douglas Aircraft Co.	1922–1967
D	McDonnell Aircraft Corp.	1942–1946
D	Radioplane Co.	1943–1948
D	Frankfort Sailplane Co.	1945–1946
DH	De Havilland Aircraft Co. Ltd. (England)	1927–1931
DW	Dayton-Wright Airplane Co.	1923
E	Bellanca Aircraft Corp.	1931–1937
E	Cessna Aircraft Co.	1951–1962
E	Edo Aircraft Corp.	1943–1962
E	G. Elias & Brothers	1922–1924
E	Gould Aeronautical Corp.	1942–1945
E	Hiller Aircraft Corp.	1948–1962
E	Piper Aircraft Corp.	1941–1945
E	Pratt-Read	1942–1945
F	Fairchild Aircraft, Ltd. (Canada)	1942–1945
F	Columbia	1943–1944
F	Grumman Aircraft Engineering Corp.	1931–1962
G	Gallaudet Aircraft Corp.	1929–1935
G	Globe Aircraft Corp.	1946–1948
G	Goodyear Aircraft Corp.	1942–1962
G	Great Lakes Aircraft Corp.	1929–1935
H	Hall Aluminum	1928–1945
H	Howard Aircraft Co.	1941–1944
H	Huff, Daland & Co.	1922–1927
H	McDonnell Aircraft Corp.	1946–1962
H	Stearman-Hammond Aircraft Corp.	1937–1939
J	Berliner/Joyce Aircraft Co.	1929–1935
J	North American Aviation	1937–1962
K	Fairchild Aircraft Corp.	1937–1942
K	Kaman Aircraft Corp.	1950–1962
K	Kaiser Cargo Inc. Fleetwings Div.	1948–1962
K	Keystone	1927–1930
K	Kinner Airplane & Motor Corp.	1935–1936
L	Bell Aircraft Corp.	1939–1962

Table 3. Manufacturer's Designation		
Letter	Manufacturer	Period
L	Columbia	1944–1946
L	Grover Loening, Inc.	1923–1933
L	Loening Aeronautical Engineering Corp.	1922–1932
M	General Motors Corp. (Eastern Aircraft Div.)	1942–1945
M	Glenn L. Martin Co.	1922–1962
N	Gyrodyne Company of America	1955–1962
N	Naval Aircraft Factory	1922–1948
N	Naval Air Development Station	1948–1962
O	Lockheed Aircraft Corp.	1931–1962
P	Pitcairn Autogyro Co.	1931–1932
P	Piasecki Helicopter Corp.	1946–1955
P	Vertol Aircraft Corp.	1955–1962
P	Spartan Aircraft Co.	1940–1941
Q	Bristol Aeronautical Corp.	1941–1943
Q	Fairchild Engine and Airplane Co.	1928–1962
Q	Stinson Aircraft Corp.	1934–1936
R	Aeronca Aircraft Corp.	1942–1946
R	Ford Motor Co.	1927–1932
R	Interstate Aircraft and Engineering Corp.	1942–1962
R	Radioplanes Co.	1948–1962
R	Ryan Aeronautical Co.	1948–1962
S	Schweizer Aircraft Corp.	1941
S	Sikorsky Aviation Corp.	1928–1962
S	Sperry Gyroscope Co.	1948–1962
S	Stearman Aircraft Co.	1934–1945
T	Taylorcraft Aviation Corp.	1942–1946
T	Tempco Aircraft Corp.	1955–1962
T	New Standard Aircraft Corp.	1930–1934
T	The Northrop Corp.	1933–1937
T	Northrop Aircraft Inc.	1944–1962
T	Timm Aircraft Corp.	1941–1943
U	Lewis & Vought, Chance Vought, Vought-Sikorsky	1922–1962
V	Vultee Aircraft Inc.	1943–1945
V	Lockheed Aircraft Corp.	1942–1962
W	Canadian Car and Foundry Co., Ltd.	1942–1945
W	Waco Aircraft Corp.	1934–1945
W	Willys-Overland Co.	1948–1962
W	Wright Aeronautical Corp.	1922–1926
X	Cox-Klemin Aircraft Corp.	1922–1924
Y	Consolidated Aircraft Corp.	1926–1954
Y	Convair Division (General Dynamics Corp.)	1954–1962
Z	Pennsylvania Aircraft Syndicate	1933–1934

A basic company name has been used in some of the above entries even though the company may have undergone restructuring.

Naval Aircraft Redesignated in 1962

In 1962 a standardized system for designation of U.S. aircraft went into effect. The following is a list of naval aircraft that were redesignated in 1962:

Old Designation	New Designation	Popular Name
Attack		
A-1		
AD-5	A-1E	Skyraider
AD-5W	EA-1E	Skyraider
AD-5Q	EA-1F	Skyraider
AD-5N	A-1G	Skyraider
AD-6	A-1H	Skyraider
AD-7	A-1J	Skyraider
A-2		
AJ-1	A-2A	Savage
A-3		
A3D-1	A-3A	Skywarrior
A3D-1Q	EA-3A	Skywarrior
A3D-2	A-3B	Skywarrior
A3D-2Q	EA-3B	Skywarrior
A3D-2P	RA-3B	Skywarrior
A3D-2T	TA-3B	Skywarrior
A-4		
A4D-1	A-4A	Skyhawk
A4D-2	A-4B	Skyhawk
A4D-2N	A-4C	Skyhawk
A4D-5	A-4E	Skyhawk
A-5		
A3J-1	A-5A	Vigilante
A3J-2	A-5B	Vigilante
A3J-3	A-5C	Vigilante
A-6		
A2F-1	A-6A	Intruder
A2F-1H	EA-6A	Intruder
Fighters		
F-1		
FJ-3	F-1C	Fury
FJ-3D	DF-1C	Fury
FJ-3M	MF-1C	Fury
FJ-3D2	DF-1D	Fury
FJ-4	F-1E	Fury
FJ-4B	AF-1E	Fury
F-2		
F2H-3	F-2C	Banshee
F2H-4	F-2D	Banshee

Old Designation	New Designation	Popular Name
F-3		
F3H-2	F-3B	Demon
F3H-2M	MF-3B	Demon
F3H-2N	F-3C	Demon
F-4		
F4H-1F	F-4A	Phantom II
F4H-1	F-4B	Phantom II
F4H-1P	RF-4B	Phantom II
F-6		
F4D-1	F-6A	Skyray
F-7		
YF2Y-1	YF-7A	Sea Dart
F-8		
F8U-1	F-8A	Crusader
F8U-1D	DF-8A	Crusader
F8U-1KD	QF-8A	Crusader
F8U-1P	RF-8A	Crusader
F8U-1T	TF-8A	Crusader
F8U-1E	F-8B	Crusader
F8U-2	F-8C	Crusader
F8U-2N	F-8D	Crusader
F8U-2NE	F-8E	Crusader
F-9		
F9F-5KD	DF-9E	Cougar
F9F-6	F-9F	Cougar
F9F-6D	DF-9F	Cougar
F9F-6K	QF-9F	Cougar
F9F-6K2	QF-9G	Cougar
F9F-7	F-9H	Cougar
F9F-8	F-9J	Cougar
F9F-8B	AF-9J	Cougar
F9F-8P	RF-9J	Cougar
F9F-8T	TF-9J	Cougar
F-10		
F3D-1	F-10A	Skyknight
F3D-2	F-10B	Skyknight
F3D-2M	MF-10B	Skyknight
F3D-2Q	EF-10B	Skyknight
F3D-2T2	TF-10B	Skyknight
F-11		
F11F-1	F-11A	Tiger
F-111		
TFX	F-111B	

Old Designation	New Designation	Popular Name
Patrol		
P-2		
P2V-4	P-2D	Neptune
P2V-5F	P-2E	Neptune
P2V-5FD	DP-2E	Neptune
P2V-5FE	EP-2E	Neptune
P2V-5FS	SP-2E	Neptune
P2V-6	P-2F	Neptune
P2V-6M	MP-2F	Neptune
P2V-6T	TP-2F	Neptune
P2V-6F	P-2G	Neptune
P2V-7	P-2H	Neptune
P2V-7S	SP-2H	Neptune
P2V-7LP	LP-2J	Neptune
P-3		
YP3V-1	YP-3A	Orion
P3V-1	P-3A	Orion
P-4		
P4Y-2K	QP-4B	Privateer
P-5		
P5M-1	P-5A	Marlin
P5M-1S	SP-5A	Marlin
P5M-1T	TP-5A	Marlin
P5M-2	P-5B	Marlin
P5M-2S	SP-5B	Marlin
Antisubmarine		
S-2		
S2F-1	S-2A	Tracker
S2F-1T	TS-2A	Tracker
S2F-1S	S-2B	Tracker
S2F-2	S-2C	Tracker
S2F-2P	RS-2C	Tracker
S2F-3	S-2D	Tracker
S2F-3S	S-2E	Tracker
Airborne Early Warning		
E-1		
WF-2	E-1B	Tracer
E-2		
W2F-1	E-2A	Hawkeye
Observation		
O-1		
OE-1	O-1B	Bird Dog

Old Designation	New Designation	Popular Name
OE-2	O-1C	Bird Dog

Helicopters		
H-1		
HU-1E	UH-1E	Iroquois

H-2		
HU2K-1	UH-2A	Seasprite
HU2K-1U	UH-2B	Seasprite

H-3		
HSS-2	SH-3A	Sea King
HSS-2Z	VH-3A	Sea King

H-13		
HTL-4	TH-13L	Sioux
HTL-6	TH-13M	Sioux
HTL-7	TH-13N	Sioux
HUL-1	UH-13P	Sioux
HUL-1M	UH-13R	Sioux

H-19		
HRS-3	CH-19E	
HO4S-3	UH-19F	

H-25		
HUP-2	UH-25B	Retriever
HUP-3	UH-25C	Retriever

H-34		
HSS-1L	LH-34D	Seahorse
HUS-1	UH-34D	Seahorse
HUS-1Z	VH-34D	Seahorse
HUS-1A	UH-34E	Seahorse
HSS-1	SH-34G	Seahorse
HSS-1F	SH-34H	Seahorse
HSS-1N	SH-34J	Seahorse

H-37		
HR2S-1	CH-37C	Mojave

H-43		
HUK-1	UH-43C	
HOK-1	OH-43D	

H-46		
HRB-1	CH-46A	Sea Knight

H-50		
DSN-1	QH-50A	DASH
DSN-2	QH-50B	DASH

Old Designation	New Designation	Popular Name
DSN-3	QH-50C	DASH

Bombers		
JD-1	UB-26J	Invader
JD-1D	DB-26J	Invader

Utility		
U-1		
UC-1	U-1B	Otter

U-6		
L-20A	U-6A	Beaver

U-11		
UO-1	U-11A	Aztec

U-16		
UF-1	HU-16C	Albatross
UF-1L	LU-16C	Albatross
UF-1T	TU-16C	Albatross
UF-2	HU-16D	Albatross

Cargo/Transport		
C-1		
TF-1	C-1A	Trader
TF-1Q	EC-1A	

C-45		
SNB-5P	RC-45J	
SNB-5	TC-45J	

C-47		
R4D-5	C-47H	Skytrain
R4D-5Q	EC-47H	Skytrain
R4D-5L	LC-47H	Skytrain
R4D-5S	SC-47H	Skytrain
R4D-5R	TC-47H	Skytrain
R4D-5Z	VC-47H	Skytrain
R4D-6	C-47J	Skytrain
R4D-6Q	EC-47J	Skytrain
R4D-6L	LC-47J	Skytrain
R4D-6S	SC-47J	Skytrain
R4D-6R	TC-47J	Skytrain
R4D-6Z	VC-47J	Skytrain
R4D-7	TC-47K	Skytrain

C-54		
R5D-1Z	VC-54N	Skymaster
R5D-2	C-54P	Skymaster
R5D-2Z	VC-54P	Skymaster
R5D-3	C-54Q	Skymaster

Old Designation	New Designation	Popular Name
R5D-3Z	VC-54Q	Skymaster
R5D-4R	C-54R	Skymaster
R5D-5	C-54S	Skymaster
R5D-5Z	VC-54S	Skymaster
R5D-5R	C-54T	Skymaster
C-117		
R4D-8	C-117D	Skytrain
R4D-8L	LC-117D	Skytrain
R4D-8Z	VC-117D	Skytrain
R4D-8T	TC-117D	Skytrain
C-118		
R6D-1	C-118B	Liftmaster
R6D-1Z	VC-118B	Liftmaster
C-119		
R4Q-2	C-119F	Packet
C-121		
R7V-1	C-121J	Constellation
WV-2	EC-121K	Warning Star
WV-2E	EC-121L	Warning Star
WV-2Q	EC-121M	Warning Star
WV-3	WC-121N	
C-130		
GV-1U	C-130F	Hercules
GV-1	KC-130F	Hercules
C-130BL	LC-130F	Hercules
C-131		
R4Y-1	C-131F	Convair Liner
R4Y-2	C-131G	Convair Liner
C-140		
UV-1	C-140C	Jet Star
Training		
T-1		
T2V-1	T-1A	Seastar
T-2		
T2J-1	T-2A	Buckeye
T2J-2	T-2B	Buckeye
T-28		
T-28A	T-28A	Trojan
T-28B	T-28B	Trojan
T-28BD	DT-28B	Trojan
T-28C	T-28C	Trojan

Old Designation	New Designation	Popular Name
T-33		
TV-2	T-33B	Shooting Star
TV-2D	DT-33B	Shooting Star
TV-2KD	DT-33C	Shooting Star
T-34		
T-34B	T-34B	Mentor
T-39		
T3J-1	T-39D	Sabreliner
Airship		
ZPG-2W	EZ-1B	Reliance
ZPG-2	SZ-1B	
ZPG-3W	EZ-1C	

DoD Designation System, 1962 to Present

In the following list the primary emphasis is on new aircraft model designations accepted after the Navy adopted the Department of Defense aircraft designation system in 1962. Aircraft that were in service and redesignated under the DoD Designation System will only have the primary designation (basic mission) listed. As an example, the AD-6 and AD-7 were redesignated A-1H and A-1J respectively. However, only A-1, the primary designation, will be listed instead of all the model variations. The modified mission designations will normally not be listed. Hence, designations such as RC-45J or TC-45J will not always be listed, however, the basic mission designation C-45 will be. Only officially designated popular names are placed in this list. A more comprehensive list of pre-1962 aircraft designations will be found in the **1923–1962 Navy System** list.

Post-1962 DoD Designation	Original Navy Designation Before 1962	Popular Name Only, other Designations and Miscellaneous Data	Manufacturer or Source
A-1 (series)	AD	Skyraider	Douglas
EA-1E		Skyraider	Douglas
A-2	AJ	Savage	North American
A-3A/B	A3D	Skywarrior	Douglas
EA-3B		Skywarrior	Douglas
KA-3B		Skywarrior	Douglas
EKA-3B		Skywarrior	Douglas
NA-3B		Skywarrior	Douglas
RA-3B		Skywarrior	Douglas
ERA-3B		Skywarrior	Douglas
NRA-3B		Skywarrior	Douglas
TA-3B		Skywarrior	Douglas
UA-3B		Skywarrior	Douglas
A-4 (series)	A4D	Skyhawk	Douglas
NA-4E/F/M		Skyhawk	Douglas
OA-4M		Skyhawk	Douglas
EA-4F		Skyhawk	Douglas
TA-4B/E/F/J		Skyhawk	Douglas
NTA-4J		Skyhawk	Douglas
A-5	A3J	Vigilante	North American
RA-5C		Vigilante	North American
A-6A/B/C/E/F	A2F	Intruder	Grumman

Post-1962 DoD Designation	Original Navy Designation Before 1962	Popular Name Only, other Designations and Miscellaneous Data	Manufacturer or Source
EA-6A	A2F-1Q	Intruder	Grumman
NA-6A/E		Intruder	Grumman
KA-6D		Intruder	Grumman
EA-6B		Prowler	Grumman
JA-6B		Intruder	Grumman
A-7A/B/C/E		Corsair II	Vought
NA-7C/E		Corsair II	Vought
EA-7L		Corsair II	Vought
TA-7C		Corsair II	Vought
AV-8A/TAV-8A		Harrier	Hawker-Siddeley
AV-8C		Harrier	British Aerospace
AV-8D		Harrier	British Aerospace
AV-8B/TAV-8B		Harrier II	McDonnell Douglas/Boeing
NAV-8B		Harrier II	McDonnell Douglas
NTAV-8B		Harrier II	McDonnell Douglas
A-12A		Avenger II	McDonnell Douglas
F/A-18A/B/C/D		Hornet	McDonnell Douglas/Boeing
F/A-18E/F		Super Hornet	Boeing
EA-18G		Growler	Boeing
NFA-18A/C/D		Hornet	McDonnell Douglas
RFA-18A		Hornet	McDonnell Douglas
TFA-18A		Hornet	McDonnell Douglas
EB-47E		Stratojet	Boeing
NB-47E		Stratojet	Boeing
C-1A	TF-1	Trader	Grumman
C-2A		Greyhound	Grumman
VC-3A	RM	Model 404	Martin
TC-4C		Academe	Grumman
UC-8A		Buffalo, DHC-5	De Havilland
C-9B		Skytrain II, DC-9	McDonnell Douglas
UC-12B/F/M		Huron	Beech
NC-12B		Huron	Beech
RC-12F/M		Huron	Beech
TC-12B		Huron	Beech
TC-18F			Boeing
C-20D		Gulfstream III	Gulfstream Aerospace
C-20G		Gulfstream IV	Gulfstream Aerospace
EC-24A	DC-8		McDonnell Douglas
C-26B/D			Fairchild
UC-27A		F-27F	Fokker (Fairchild-built)
C-28A		Model 404	Cessna
UC-35C/D		Encore	Cessna
C-37A/B		Gulfstream	Gulfstream
C-40A		Clipper	Boeing
C-45H/J	SNB-5	Navigator	Beech
C-47	R4D	Skytrain	Douglas
C-54	R5D	Skymaster	Douglas

Post-1962 DoD Designation	Original Navy Designation Before 1962	Popular Name Only, other Designations and Miscellaneous Data	Manufacturer or Source
C-117D	R4D-8	Skytrain	Douglas
NC-117D		Skytrain	Douglas
TC-117D		Skytrain	Douglas
C-118B	R6D	Liftmaster	Douglas
C-119	R4Q	Packet	Fairchild
C-121	R7V	Constellation	Lockheed
EC-121	WV	Warning Star	Lockheed
NC-121K		Warning Star	Lockheed
C-130F/T	GV/R8V	Hercules	Lockheed
DC-130A		Hercules	Lockheed
EC-130G/Q		Hercules	Lockheed
KC-130C/F/R/T		Hercules	Lockheed Martin
KC-130J		Super Hercules	Lockheed Martin
LC-130F/R		Hercules	Lockheed
NC-130H		Hercules	Lockheed Martin
C-131F/G/H	R4Y	Samaritan	Convair
NKC-135A		Stratotanker	Boeing
UC-880		Convair 880	Convair
E-1B	WF	Tracer	Grumman
E-2A/B/C	W2F	Hawkeye	Grumman
TE-2A/C		Hawkeye	Northrop Grumman
YE-2C		Hawkeye	Grumman
E-6		Hermes (redesignated Mercury)	Boeing
E-6A		Mercury	Boeing
F-1 (series)	FJ	Fury	North American
F-2 (series)	F2H	Banshee	McDonnell
F-3 (series)	F3H	Demon	McDonnell
F-4A/B/C/J/N/S	F4H	Phantom II	McDonnell
QF-4B		Phantom II	McDonnell Douglas
RF-4B		Phantom II	McDonnell Douglas
EF-4J		Phantom II	McDonnell Douglas
YF-4J		Phantom II	McDonnell Douglas
F-5E/F/N		Tiger II	Northrop
F-6 (series)	F4D	Skyray	Douglas
F-8 (series)	F8U	Crusader	Vought
RF-8G		Crusader	LTV
DF-8L		Crusader	LTV
F-9 (series)	F9F	Cougar	Grumman
F-10 (series)	F3D	Skyknight	Douglas
F-11 (series)	F11F	Tiger	Grumman
F-14A/A+/B/C/D		Tomcat	Grumman
NF-14A/B/D		Tomcat	Grumman
F-16A/N		Fighting Falcon	General Dynamics
TF-16		Fighting Falcon	General Dynamics
YF-17			Northrop
F/A-18A/B/C/D		Hornet	McDonnell Douglas
TF-18A		Hornet	McDonnell Douglas

Post-1962 DoD Designation	Original Navy Designation Before 1962	Popular Name Only, other Designations and Miscellaneous Data	Manufacturer or Source
F/A-18E/F		Super Hornet	Boeing
F-21A		Kfir	Israel Aircraft Industries
F-35B/C		Lightning II	Lockheed Martin
F-86H		Sabre	North American
QF-86F/H		Sabre	North American
F-111B			Grumman/General Dynamics
AH-1G/S		Cobra	Bell
AH-1J/T/W		Sea Cobra	Bell
AH-1Z		Viper	Bell
JAH-1T		Sea Cobra	Bell
MH-1W			Bell
NAH-1Z			Bell
HH-1K/N		Iroquois	Bell
UH-1C/D/E/H/L/M/N	HU-1	Iroquois	Bell
UH-1Y		Venom	Bell
NUH-1E/N		Iroquois	Bell
TH-1E/F/L		Iroquois	Bell
H-2	HU2K	Seasprite	Kaman
HH-2D		Seasprite	Kaman
SH-2D/F/G		Seasprite	Kaman
YSH-2E/G		Seasprite	Kaman
UH-2C		Seasprite	Kaman
H-3	HSS-2	Sea King	Sikorsky
HH-3A		Sea King	Sikorsky
SH-3A/D/G/H		Sea King	Sikorsky
NSH-3A		Sea King	Sikorsky
UH-3A		Sea King	Sikorsky
NVH-3A		Sea King	Sikorsky
YSH-3J		Sea King	Sikorsky
CH-3B		Sea King	Sikorsky
OH-6A/B		Cayuse	Hughes
TH-6B			McDonnell Douglas
H-13	HTL/HUL	Sioux	Bell
H-19	HRS-3	Chickasaw	Sikorsky
H-I9	HO4S-3	Chickasaw	Sikorsky
H-25	HUP	Retriever	Piasecki (Vertol)
H-34	HSS-1	Sea Bat	Sikorsky
H-34	HUS	Seahorse	Sikorsky
H-37	HR2S	Mojave	Sikorsky
H-43	HOK	Huskie	Kaman
H-46	HRB	Sea Knight	Boeing Vertol
CH-46A/D/E/F		Sea Knight	Vertol
HH-46A		Sea Knight	Vertol
NCH-46A		Sea Knight	Vertol
UH-46A/D		Sea Knight	Vertol
QH-50D, -50C	DSN	DASH	Gyrodyne
H-51		L-186, tri-service evaluation	Lockheed

Post-1962 DoD Designation	Original Navy Designation Before 1962	Popular Name Only, other Designations and Miscellaneous Data	Manufacturer or Source
H-52	HU2S	Coast Guard	Sikorsky
CH-53A/D		Sea Stallion	Sikorsky
CH-53E		Super Stallion	Sikorsky
JCH-53E		Super Stallion	Sikorsky
YCH-53E		Super Stallion	Sikorsky
MH-53E		Sea Dragon	Sikorsky
NMH-53E			Sikorsky
RH-53D		Sea Stallion	Sikorsky
NRH-53D		Sea Stallion	Sikorsky
TH-57A/B/C		Sea Ranger	Bell
OH-58A		Kiowa	Bell
CH-60S		Seahawk	Sikorsky
SH-60B/F		Seahawk	Sikorsky
NSH-60B/F		Seahawk	Sikorsky
YSH-60B		Seahawk	Sikorsky
SH-60R		Seahawk	Sikorsky
NSH-60R		Seahawk	Sikorsky
HH-60H/J		Seahawk	Sikorsky
MH-60R/S		Seahawk	Sikorsky
YMH-60R		Seahawk	Sikorsky
MH-60S		Seahawk	Sikorsky
UH-60L		Black Hawk	Sikorsky
VH-60D/N		Nighthawk	Sikorsky
YCH-60		Black Hawk	Sikorsky
HH-65A/B/C		Dolphin, Coast Guard	Aerospatiale
UH-72A		Lakota	EADS North America
O-1A/B/C/G	OE	L-19A	Cessna
O-2A			Cessna
P-2	P2V	Neptune	Lockheed
DP-2E/H		Neptune	Lockheed
EP-2H		Neptune	Lockheed
NP-2H		Neptune	Lockheed
SP-2H		Neptune	Lockheed
P-3A/B/C	P3V	Orion	Lockheed
EP-3A/B/J		Orion	Lockheed
NP-3A/C/D		Orion	Lockheed
RP-3A/D		Orion	Lockheed
TP-3A		Orion	Lockheed
UP-3A/B		Orion	Lockheed
NUP-3A		Orion	Lockheed
WP-3A		Orion	Lockheed
VP-3C		Orion	Lockheed
QP-4B	PB4Y-2K	Privateer	Consolidated
P-5	P5M	Marlin	Martin
P-8A		Poseidon	Boeing
S-2 (series)	S2F	Tracker	Grumman
ES-2D		Tracker	Grumman

Post-1962 DoD Designation	Original Navy Designation Before 1962	Popular Name Only, other Designations and Miscellaneous Data	Manufacturer or Source
TS-2A		Tracker	Grumman
US-2A/B/C/D		Tracker	Grumman
YS-2G		Tracker	Grumman
S-3A/B		Viking	Lockheed
KS-3A		Viking	Lockheed
ES-3A		Shadow	Lockheed
NS-3A		Viking	Lockheed
US-3A		Viking	Lockheed
T-1	T2V	Seastar	Lockheed
T-2A/B/C	T2J	Buckeye	North American
DT-2B		Buckeye	North American
YT-2B		Buckeye	North American
T-6A		Texan II	Raytheon/Beech
T-28A/B/C	T-28	Trojan	North American
T-29B/C		Flying Classroom	Convair/General Dynamics
T-33A	TO/TV	Shooting Star	Lockheed
QT-33A		Shooting Star	Lockheed
T-34B/C	T-34	Mentor	Beech
NT-34C		Mentor	Beech
YT-34C		Mentor	Beech
T-38A/B		Talon	Northrop
QT-38A		Talon	Northrop
T-39D/G/N	T3J	Sabreliner	North American/Boeing
CT-39E/G		Sabreliner	North American/Boeing
T-41B		Mescalero	Cessna
T-42A		Cochise	Beech
T-44A		King Air 90	Beech
T-45A/B/C		Goshawk	McDonnell Douglas/Boeing
T-47A		Cessna Citation II	Cessna
U-1	UC	Otter	De Havilland
NU-1B		Otter	De Havilland
U-3A/B		Model 310	Cessna
U-6A		Beaver, L-20A	De Havilland
U-8D/F/G		Seminole	Beech
U-9D		Aero Commander	Aero Design
U-11A	UO	Aztec	Piper
U-16	JR2F/UF	Albatross	Grumman
HU-16E		Albatross	Grumman
U-21A		Ute	Beech
HU-25A/B/C		Guardian	Dassault-Breguet
RU-38A		(for Coast Guard)	Schweizer Acft
OV-1A/B/C		Mohawk	Grumman
XV-6A		Kestrels	Hawker-Siddeley
OV-10A/D		Bronco	North American
YOV-10D		Bronco	North American
XFV-12A		Prototype of a high performance V/STOL fighter, never operational.	Rockwell International

Post-1962 DoD Designation	Original Navy Designation Before 1962	Popular Name Only, other Designations and Miscellaneous Data	Manufacturer or Source
AV-16A		Joint proposal in 1973 for an advanced version of the AV-8.	McDonnell Douglas/Hawker-Siddeley
V-22		Osprey	Bell/Boeing
HV-22A/B			Bell/Boeing
MV-22A/B		Osprey	Bell/Boeing
SV-22A			Bell/Boeing
X-22A			Bell
X-25A			Bensen
X-26A			Schweizer
X-26B		QT-2PC	Lockheed/Schweizer
X-28A			Pereira
X-29A			Grumman
X-31A			Rockwell/DASA
X-45A			Boeing
X-46A			Boeing
X-47A/B			Northrop
X-49A			Sikorsky/Piasecki
MZ-3A			American Blimp
SZ-1A			Airships Ind.
YEZ-2A		Operational development model airship.	Westinghouse Airships Inc.

How to Read the DoD Aircraft Model Designations

The Navy system had worked well for 40 years, however, Congress decreed in 1962 that there should only be one system to designate military aircraft in the United States. The new system was based on that of the Air Force and the aircraft manufacturer was no longer identified. While there were relatively few changes to Air Force aircraft designations, the Navy made a complete change. Aircraft models all started with the numeral 1, except for those aircraft on hand which were used by both services, in which case the existing Air Force designation applied. Thus, the FJ-3 became the F-1C, while the SNB-5P became the RC-45J. It must be emphasized that the placement of the dash is critical to distinguish aircraft under the new system from those under the previous Navy system. For example, the F4B-4 was a Boeing biplane fighter of the mid 30s, while the F-4B is an early version of the 1960s Phantom II.

The new system consisted of a Status Prefix Symbol (letter), a Basic Mission Symbol (letter), a Design Number (numeral), a Modified Mission Symbol (letter), a Series letter, and a Type Symbol (letter). A Design Number was assigned for each basic mission or type. New design numbers were assigned when an existing aircraft was redesigned to an extent that it no longer reflected the original configuration or capability. A Series Letter was assigned to each series change of a specific basic design. To avoid confusion, the letters "I" and "O" were not used as series letters. The Series Letter was always in consecutive order, starting with "A."

A typical designation was as follows:

This was the Y/FJ -4B under the Navy system and the YAF-1E under the new DoD system.

Status Prefix Symbols	
Letter	Title
G	Permanently Grounded
J	Special Test, Temporary
N	Special Test, Permanent
X	Experimental
Y	Prototype
Z	Planning

Basic Mission Symbols	
Letter	Title
A	Attack (currently not used by Navy)
B	Bomber (not used by Navy)
C	Transport
E	Special Electronic Installation
F	Fighter (currently not used by Navy)
F/A	Strike Fighter
L	Laser (not used by Navy)
O	Observation
P	Patrol
R	Reconnaissance
S	Antisubmarine
T	Trainer
U	Utility
X	Research

Modified Mission Symbols	
Letter	Title
A	Attack (currently not used by Navy)
C	Transport
D	Director
E	Special Electronic Installation
F	Fighter (currently not used by Navy)
H	Search/Rescue/Medevac
K	Tanker
L	Cold Weather
M	Multi-mission
O	Observation (currently not used by Navy)
P	Patrol
Q	Drone
R	Reconnaissance
S	Antisubmarine
T	Trainer
U	Utility
V	Staff
W	Weather

Vehicle Type Symbols	
Letter	Title
D	UAV Control Segment
G	Glider
H	Helicopter
Q	Unmanned Aerial Vehicle
S	Spaceplane
V	Vertical Takeoff and Landing (VTOL)/Short Takeoff and Landing (STOL)
Z	Lighter-than-Air Vehicle

Alphabetical Listing of Popular Names

The official assignment of names to naval aircraft began 1 October 1941 when a Navy Department press release reported that the Secretary issued orders assigning names "for popular use" to a number of in-service and developmental aircraft. This decision was first acknowledged in the April 1942 edition of the "Model Designation of Naval Aircraft (SH-3AF)" published by the Bureau of Aeronautics. A War Department Press Release of 4 January 1943 distributed a consolidated list of names for Navy and Army aircraft, thus beginning interservice coordination on aircraft names. This latter press release pointed out that the practice of naming aircraft had long been in effect in England, "In order that the general public may get a better idea of the character of military aircraft and more easily identify the combat planes mentioned in press dispatches from the battlefields of the world. . . ."

Prior to October 1941, manufacturers on occasion chose to use names for an aircraft model or a series of models; thus, the Curtiss Company used the name Helldiver for aircraft which they built as naval dive bombers from the late 1920s. The October 1941 action officially assigned the name Helldiver to the latest member of the family, the SB2C. Vought choose to use the name Corsair for a series of carrier-based aircraft, which included the O2U and the O3U/SU; in October 1941 the Navy officially assigned the name Corsair to Vought's new fighter, the F4U.

Although assignment of aircraft names was coordinated by the Army and Navy from 1943, each service had developed its own model designation system independently. The result was that the U.S. military forces used two separate model designation systems. Moreover, when the Navy used an Army Air Forces aircraft, it assigned a designation based upon its own system; thus, the Army Air Force's B-24 became the PB4Y-1 in Navy service while such trainers as the Army Air Force's AT-6 and PT-13/-17 were the Navy SNJ and N2S.

On 19 August 1952, the Joint Aircraft Committee of the Munitions Board took an initial step to eliminate multiple designations by establishing the policy that original model designations would generally be retained by the second service in the event of cross-service procurement of aircraft, thus the North American Trojan which was used as a trainer by the Air Force retained the Air Force designation T-28 when procured for naval service. Designations of aircraft already in service were not changed at that time.

On 18 September 1962, the Department of Defense issued a uniform model designation system and directed its immediate adoption. The new system, adapted from the Air Force model designation system, assigned a basic mission letter followed by a number which indicated the sequential relationship of aircraft designed for the mission. Thus, the Navy AD was redesignated A-l. To avoid compounding the confusion, the new system, insofar as was possible, correlated the new designation of naval aircraft with the older designation; thus, the F9F became the F-9 and the F8U became the F-8. By the same token, the three in-service patrol planes, the P2V, the P3V, and P5M were redesignated P-2, P-3, and P-5 even though the designation P-l was not assigned.

To summarize the foregoing, the Navy developed an aircraft model designation system in the early 1920s and used it until 1962 when it was replaced by a Department of Defense unified system. The official assignment of names to naval aircraft did not begin until 1941; interservice coordination began in 1943, thus, the system for naming aircraft has changed little since the practice became official more than 70 years ago.

In compiling the listing for popular names, one of the thorniest difficulties was the problem of distinguishing between what the official records said and what has long been accepted as fact. For example, few aviation historians believe that the SB2C-5 was ever assigned the name Hellcat, yet it does appear in the Bureau of Aeronautics' Model Designation of Naval Aircraft. Because this particular case is so extraordinary, there seemed ample reason to consider it an error; therefore, the SB2C-5 does not appear in this listing as a Hellcat. Others were equally questionable and were accordingly omitted. However, when sufficient doubt was present, the designation and its name were included here. As a result, some of the information in this listing will raise the eyebrows of those readers who are familiar with the popular names of naval aircraft.

Within the Alphabetical Listing of Popular Names the column headings are:

- **Popular Names**—The popular names the Navy assigned to its aircraft are listed alphabetically. Cross-references are given when different names were assigned to different models of the same basic aircraft. In a few cases two different names were assigned to identical aircraft models. These are cross-referenced here. Also in rare instances entirely different aircraft have the same name, if so, the name is listed twice.

- **Original Navy Designation, pre-1962**—The original designation was the first designation under which the Navy accepted the aircraft. Basic designations are listed unless specific models were assigned different names. The Navy never officially assigned a name to the designation in parentheses. They are listed because they were the original designations of the aircraft to which the Navy later assigned a name under a new designation.

- **Redesignation to the Post-1962 DoD Designation**—In 1962 the Department of Defense standardized its system of aircraft designations. Most naval aircraft, however, retained the same popular name. Basic designations are listed unless specific models were assigned different names. They are included because they are the redesignations of aircraft to which the Navy had previously assigned a name under its original designation. New aircraft acquired after 1962 and the new post-1962 aircraft designation are listed in this column.

Popular Names	Original Navy Designation, pre-1962	Redesignation to the Post-1962 DoD Designation System or New Post-1962 Designation
Academe		TC-4C
Aero Commander		U-9
Albatross	JR2F/UF	U-16
Avenger	TBF TBM	
Avenger II		A-12 (never acquired)
Aztec	UO	U-11
Banshee	F2H	F-2
Bearcat	F8F	

Popular Names	Original Navy Designation, pre-1962	Redesignation to the Post-1962 DoD Designation System or New Post-1962 Designation
Beaver		U-6
Bird Dog	(OE)	O-1
Black Hawk		UH-60L
Black Widow	F2T	
Bobcat	JRC	
Bronco		OV-10
Buccaneer	SB2A	
Buckeye	T2J	T-2
Buffalo	F2A	
Buffalo		UC-8A
Catalina	PBY PB2B PBN	
Caydet (also Kaydet)	N2S	
Cayuse		OH-6A/B
Chickasaw	(HO4S-3)	H-19
	(HRS-3)	H-19
Clipper		C-40A
Cobra		AH-1
Cochise		T-42A
Commando	R5C	
Condor	R4C-1	
Conestoga	RB	
Constellation (See Warning Star)	PO WV-1	
R70/R7V		C-121
Constitution	R60/R6V	
Convair Liner	R4Y	C-131
Coronado	PB2Y	
Corsair	F4U FG F3A AU F2G	
Corsair II		A-7
Cougar	F9F-6,-7,-8	F-9
Crusader	F8U	F-8
Crusader III	F8U-3	
Cutlass	F7U	
DASH	(DSN)	QH-50
Dauntless	SBD	
Demon	F3H	F-3
Destroyer	(SB2D) BTD	
Devastator	(XTB2D-1) TBD	
Dolphin		H-65
Duck	(JF) J2F	
Encore		UC-35D
Excalibur	JR2S	
Expediter	JRB-1 thru -4	C-45

Popular Names	Original Navy Designation, pre-1962	Redesignation to the Post-1962 DoD Designation System or New Post-1962 Designation
Falcon	SNC	
Fighting Falcon		F-16A/N, TF-16
Fireball	FR	
Flying Classroom		T-29
Flying Fortress	PB-1G, -1W	
Forwarder	GK	
Fury	FJ	F-I
Goose	JRF	
Goshawk		T-45
Grasshopper	NE	
Greyhound		C-2
Growler		EA-18G
Guardian	AF	
Guardian	HU-25	
Gulfstream		C-37A/B
Gulfstream III		C-20D
Gulfstream IV		C-20G
Harpoon	PV-2	
Harrier		AV-8A
Harrier II		AV-8B
Havoc	BD	
Hawkeye	W2F	E-2/TE-2C
Hellcat	F6F	
Helldiver	SB2C SBC-3, -4 SBW SBF	
Hercules	GV	C-130
Hermes		E-6 (changed to/See Mercury)
Hornet		F/A-18
Hoverfly	HNS-1	
Hudson	PBO	
Huron		UC-12/RC-12
Huskie	(HOK) (HUK)	H-43
Intruder	A2F	A-6
Invader	JD	B-26
Iroquois		UH-1/TH-1/HH-1
Jaguar	F10F	
Kansan	SNB-1	
Kaydet (See Caydet)	N2S	
Kfir		F-21A
Kingfisher	OS2U OS2N	
Kiowa		OH-58A
Lakota		UH-72A
Liberator	PB4Y-1/P4Y-1	
Liberator Express	RY-1	
Liftmaster	R6D	C-118

Popular Names	Original Navy Designation, pre-1962	Redesignation to the Post-1962 DoD Designation System or New Post-1962 Designation
Lightning II		F-35
Lodestar	R5O	
Mako Shark		MH-68A (CG)
Marauder	JM	
Mariner	PBM	
Marlin	P5M	P-5
Mars	PB2M JRM	
Mauler	(BTM-1), AM	
Mentor	T-34	T-34
Mercator	P4M	
Mercury (See Hermes)		E-6A
Mescalero		T-41B
Mitchell	PBJ	
Mohawk	OV-1A/B/C	
Mojave	(HR2S)	H-37
Navigator	SNB-2C, -5	C-45
Neptune	P2V	P-2
Nighthawk		VH-60
Nightingale	GH, NH	
Norseman	JA	
Orion	P3V	P-3
Osprey		V-22A/MV-22B
Otter	UC	U-1
Packet	R4Q	C-119
Panther	F9F-2, -4, -5	DF-9
Phantom	FD, FH	
Phantom II	F4H	F-4
Pinto	TT-1	
Pirate	F6U	
Poseidon		P-8A
Privateer	PB4Y-2, P4Y-2	QP-4B
Prowler		EA-6B
Puss Moth	XDH-80	
Recruit	NR	
Reliance	ZPG-2W	EZ-1
Rescuer	HRP	
Retriever	HUP	H-25
Sabre	(F-86)	QF-86
Sabreliner	(T3J)	T-39
Samaritan		C-131
Savage	AJ	A-2
Sea Bat	(HSS-1)	H-34
Sea Cobra		AH-1J/T/W
Sea Dart	F2Y	F-7
Sea Dragon		MH-53
Seafarer	ZPG-2	SZ-1
Seagull (not official)	SOC, SO3C	

Popular Names	Original Navy Designation, pre-1962	Redesignation to the Post-1962 DoD Designation System or New Post-1962 Designation
Seahawk	SC	
Seahawk		SH-60/HH-60/CH-60/MH-60
Seahorse	(HUS)	H-34
Sea King	(HSS-2)	H-3
Sea Knight	(HRB)	H-46
Seamaster	P6M	
Seamew	SO3C	
Sea Ranger	XPBB-1	
Sea Ranger		TH-57
Seasprite (also Sea Sprite)	HU2K	H-2
Sea Stallion		CH-53/RH-53
Sea Star	T2V	T-1
Sea Wolf (also Seawolf)	TBY	
Seminole		U-8
Sentinel	OY	
Shadow		ES-3A
Shooting Star	TV, TO	T-33
Sioux	(HTL), HUL	H-13
Skyhawk	A4D	A-4
Skyknight	F3D	F-10
Skylancer	F5D	
Skymaster	R5D	C-54
Skyraider	(BT2D), AD	A-1
Skyray	F4D	F-6
Skyrocket	D-558-2	
Skyshark	A2D	
Skytrain	R4D-1, -5, -6, -7 R4D-8	C-47 C-117
Skytrain II		C-9
Skystreak	D-558-1	
Skytrooper	R4D-2,-3,-4	
Skywarrior	A3D	A-3
Stratojet		EB-47E
Stratotanker		NKC-135A
Super Hercules		KC-130J
Super Hornet		F/A-18E/F
Superfortress	P2B-1	
Super Stallion		CH-53E/RH-53/MH-53E
Talon		T-38
Texan	SNJ	
Texan II		T-6A
Tiger	F11F	F-11
Tiger II		F-5E/F/N
Tigercat	F7F	
Tomcat		F-14
Tracer	WF	E-1
Tracker	S2F	S-2
Trader	TF-1	C-1

Popular Names	Original Navy Designation, pre-1962	Redesignation to the Post-1962 DoD Designation System or New Post-1962 Designation
Tradewind	R3Y	
Traveler	GB	
Trojan	T-28	T-28
Tutor	N2T	
Ute		U-21A
Valiant	SNV	
Venom		UH-1Y
Ventura	PV-1, -3	
Vigilante	A3J	A-5
Viking		S-3
Vindicator	SB2U	
Viper		AH-1Z
Volunteer	ZSG-1	
Warning Star (See Constellation)	WV	EC-121
White Hawk		VH-60N
Widgeon	J4F	
Wildcat	F4F FM	

CHAPTER 2

Combat Aircraft Procured

The following tables contain key dates relating to development, procurement, and service use of combat types of airplanes obtained in quantities sufficient to equip a squadron. "Combat type" excludes trainers, transports, and utility types; however, models originally obtained for such purposes and later reported as being utilized for combat missions are included—e.g., the VE-7 and VE-9. Noncombat configurations of combat aircraft, such as TA-4E and PB2Y-3R, are also included. The term "quantities sufficient to equip a squadron" is somewhat elastic; through the 1920s (and 1930s for patrol planes) aircraft are included if as few as nine were obtained. Other than that, the table is limited to aircraft of which at least 18 were purchased.

The complete tabulation consists of five tables: attack planes, fighter planes, patrol and early warning planes, observation planes, and WWI aircraft. Attack and patrol planes each include a number of specific missions identified in the heading of the table. Aircraft did not always lend themselves to the above divisions; for example, a fighter-bomber can be either a fighter or an attack plane. Arbitrary judgments, necessary to place such aircraft in one table, are reflected in designations and cross-references under alternate designations.

WWI aircraft were listed in a separate table because of the lack of data on first flight, contract date, etc., and in order to show shipments overseas.

Description Of Column Headings

Designation—Basic designations and redesignations are included and arranged alphabetically. If aircraft were procured from the Army/Air Force, their designations are also listed.

First Contract—This shows the date of the first contractual commitment for delivery of an airplane. If the first aircraft was ordered by amendment to a design contract, the date of the amendment is used. Letters of Intent and even telegraphic orders are treated as contracts. If a contract date could not be established, an estimate, shown as "(est)", was made from available data. The use of a year followed by a number (as 1922-2), shows that the contract was made in the quarter (in this example, the second) of the calendar year. For cross-service procurement, the date of the Navy's commitment to the Army or Air Force is shown. For WWII Army Air Force bombers, the date of the policy decision that the Navy would procure such aircraft is shown.

First Flight—Refers to first flight of first aircraft, generally an "X" model. Frequently the date of first flight was estimated (shown as "[est]") usually from date of delivery for Navy flight tests. If documentation permitted, specific dates are given; otherwise the month and year are shown. No first flight date is given for aircraft which were in operation with the Army or the Air Force or commercially before they were delivered to the Navy.

Number Accepted, Manufacturer, and *Models Accepted*—These columns are keyed to each other and show model designations and gross acceptances for Navy, for other services, and for allies—whether lend-lease, military assistance programs, or (more recently) military sales in which the Navy served as the agent of the procuring government—are shown in parentheses and included in the overall totals. For aircraft still in production, number accepted is total as of 31 December 2010.

In general, the manufacturer can be readily identified although the following may have become obscure: LWF for Lowe, Willard, and Fowler; NAF for Naval Aircraft Factory; and B/J for Berliner/Joyce. No attempt was made to indicate corporate history except in the use of the family spelling "Loughead" as well as the better-known "Lockheed," and in distinguishing between the Northrop subsidiary of Douglas and the Douglas Company. Thus Vought includes Lewis and Vought, the independent Chance Vought Corporation, the Vought and Vought-Sikorsky divisions of United Aircraft Corporation, the later independent Vought company, and the present Vought Aeronautics Division of Ling-Temco-Vought. McDonnell and Douglas are treated as separate entities.

For aircraft redesignated while in production, both old and new designations are shown (P3V-1/P-3A), indicating that aircraft were accepted under both designations.

Squadron Delivery and Last Report in squadron or inventory—These give the date when the first combat type unit received basic aircraft and similarly gives the date of the last report that such a unit had the aircraft in its custody. Thus these columns show the span of aircraft service life in combat units of the U.S. Navy and identify the first and last squadron to have custody of the aircraft. The occasional assignment of a single experimental aircraft to a combat unit is omitted; this sometimes occurred a year or more in advance of actually equipping the first squadron. For purposes of this table, combat units are defined as squadrons attached to the Atlantic or Pacific Fleet, including replacement training squadrons but excluding utility, transport, and experimental and evaluation squadrons. Thus units of the training commands and naval reserve are omitted as generally are the pre–WWII District squadrons. If squadron data is incomplete, the ships, or stations to which the unit was attached are given. Particularly, for late WWII and the early post-war years, the final squadrons with a particular aircraft could not be identified beyond the fact that they were in the Atlantic or Pacific Fleets.

A variety of sources were utilized in compiling the service history. Correspondence, individual aircraft history cards, and the monthly status report compiled by the Bureau of Aeronautics, or Deputy Chief of Naval Operations (Air). From 1926 until 1941 this report was titled, "Monthly Report, Status of Naval Aircraft," it then became "Monthly Status of Naval Aircraft"; in 1948, "Location of Naval Aircraft"; and in 1951, "Allowances and Location of Naval Aircraft." Initial assignment data is believed to be exact. The data in "Last Report," are approximate; they were drawn almost entirely from the above reports, and there is uncertainty as to the currency of the data supporting any particular issue. In addition, data within the report were, at times, a month out of phase with the issue date. Unfortunately all of these primary sources are no longer produced and some of the data for the columns listed may no longer be available.

Since the squadron organization did not come into being until after WWI, the table for WWI aircraft shows assignment to stations and final withdrawal from inventory.

Description—This column shows the number of wings and crew provision as a single entry, i.e., B/2 means biplane, two place. Variations in size of crew are shown in parentheses; fighters were single place, unless otherwise indicated. Other notes on equipment and structure are included to indicate basic technological advances. When mission data is shown it generally reflects a change in military requirements.

The standard engine nomenclature is used: R for radial air-cooled (generally followed by a number indicating displacement); J for jet; T for turboprop; O for horizontally opposed; all others were in-line or Vee-type, generally liquid-cooled. Standard power terminology is used: horsepower for propeller drives and pounds thrust for jet units. The practice on turboprops has varied. Sometimes the horsepower absorbed by the propeller and the residual thrust in pounds are both given; at others, the two are combined in equivalent shaft horsepower "eshp." Identifying nomenclature for engine manufacturers was adapted from standard practice as follows:

AL, Allison; ACM, Aircooled Motors; AIR, AiResearch; AM, Aeromarine; BO, Boeing; CAM, Curtiss Aeroplane & Motor Co.; CO, Continental; FR, Franklin; GE, General Electric; LA, Lawrance; Lib, Liberty; LY, Lycoming; PKD, Packard; P&W, Pratt & Whitney Aircraft; RA, Ranger; WAC, Wright Aeronautical Corporation; WE Westinghouse; WR, Warner.

Attack Series Includes Dive Bomber (VB), Torpedo Planes (VT), Torpedo Bombers (VTB), Scout Bomber (VSB), Carrier Scouts (VS), and Carrier ASW (VS)									
Designation	First Contract	First Flight	Last Delivery	Number Accepted	Manufacturer	Models Accepted	Squadron Delivery	Last Report*	Description
A-I	(Redesignation of AD)								
A-2	(Redesignation of AJ)								
A-3	9/29/49	10/28/52	1/61	282	Douglas	XA3D-1; A3D-1, -2, -2P, -2Q, -2T; A-3B; KA-3B, EKA-3B, RA-3B, EA-3B	3/31/56 VAH-1	3/91 KA-3B	M/3 (7in -2Q; 8 in -2T). Swept wing; 2 P&W J57, 9,500# to 10,500#
A-4	9/13/52	6/22/54	2/27/79	2,876 (294)	Douglas	XA4D-1; A4D-1, -2, -2N, -5; A-4A, -4C, -4E, -4F, -4G, -4H, -4K, -4KU, -4M, -4N; TA-4E, -4F/J, -4H, -4J, -4K, -4KU; EA-4F	9/27/56 VA-72	3/94 A-4M	M/1 (2 in TA versions). Modified delta wing; WAC J65, 7,700# or P&W J52, 7,500 to 8500#
A-5	8/29/56	8/31/58	11/5/70	156	North American	A3J-1; A-5A, -5B; RA-5C	6/61 VAH-3	3/81 RA-5C	M/2. Supersonic; 2 GE J79, 17,000#
A-6	3/26/59	4/1960	1/31/92	890	Grumman	A2F-1, A-6A, -6E, EA-6A, -6B, KA-6D, YA-6F	2/63 VA-42	3/97 VA-75	M/2. 2 P&W J52, 8,500#, EA-6B 4 crew, 2 Pratt & Whitney J52-P-408 engines, 10,400#

Designation	First Contract	First Flight	Last Delivery	Number Accepted	Manufacturer	Models Accepted	Squadron Delivery	Last Report[a]	Description
A-7	3/19/64	9/27/65	10/86	1,491 (498)	Vought	A-7A, -7B, -7D, -7C, -7E, -7H; EA-7L	10/13/66 VA-147	6/92 A-7E	M/1. Developed from F-8; P&W TF-30 (non-afterburning)
F/A-18 (Also listed in the Fighter Series)	5/75	11/78		1,441	McDonnell Douglas/ Boeing	F/A-18A, -18B, -18C, -18D, -18E, -18F, EA-18G	1/7/83 VMFA-314		M/1 (2). 2 F404GE-402, F/A-18D and F/A-18F are 2 seat, EA-18G 2 crew, 2 GE F414-GE-400 turbofan engines
AV-8	12/22/69		4/23/96	494† (58)	Hawker Siddeley/ McDonnell Douglas/ Boeing	AV-8A, TAV-8A, AV-8B, -8C, TAV-8B, EAV-8A for Spain	1/27/71		M/1 (2 in TA version). V/STOL aircraft. One RR F402-RR-401, 21,500#
AD	7/6/44	3/18/45	3/57	3,180 (20)	Douglas	XBT2D-1, -1W, -1P, -1Q, -1N; XAD-1W, -2; AD-1, -1Q, -2, -2Q, -3, -3Q, -4B, -4N, -4Q, -4W, -5, -5W, -5N, -6, -7; EA-1F	12/6/46 VA-19A	12/31/71 EA-1F	M/1 (2 in -5; 2 to 4 in -Q, -W, -N, and -S). First successful USN aircraft orginally designed as both dive bomber and torpedo plane; WAC R-3350, 2700 to 3,150 hp
A3D	(Redesignated A-3)								
A4D	(Redesignated A-4)								
AF	2/19/45	12/46	4/53	389	Grumman	XTB3F-1,-1S, -2S; AF-2W, -2S, -3S	10/18/50 VS-25	8/31/55 VS-37	M/3. ASW attack (S) and search (W); P&W R-2800, 2300 hp; also WE 19XB, 1,600 in XTB3F-1
A2F	(Redesignated A-6)								
AJ	6/24/46	7/3/48	6/54	143	North American	XAJ-1; AJ-1, -2, -2P	9/13/49 VC-5	1/31/60 VAP-62, VCP-61, AJ-2P	M/3. First heavy attack; 2 P&W R-2800, 2300 hp and J33, 4,600#
A3J	(Redesignated A-5)								
AM	1/14/44	8/26/44	10/49	152	Martin	XBTM-1; AM-1, -1Q	3/1/48 VA-17A	10/1/50 VC-4, AM-1Q	M/1 (2 in-1Q). P&W R-4360, 3,310 hp
BF2C	12/16/32	5/11/33 est	10/34	28	Curtiss	XF11C-3; BF2C-1	11/34 VB-5B	2/29/36 VB-5B, BF2C-1	B/1. WAC R-1820, 700 hp
AU	(Designation for last U.S. Navy production version of F4U)								
BFC	(Redesignation XF11C-1, -2)								
BG	6/13/32	6/33 est	11/35	61	Great Lakes	XBG-1; BG-1	10/24/34 VT-1S	6/30/41 VMS-6, BG-1	B/2. 1000# dive bomber; P&W R-1535, 700 hp
BM	6/18/28	5/29 est	1/33	34	Martin	XT5M-1; XBM-1; BM-1, -2	10/24/32 VT-1S	9/30/38 VCS-5, BM-2	B/2. First "heavy" 1000# dive bomber; P&W R-1690, 625 hp
				1	NAF				

Designation	First Contract	First Flight	Last Delivery	Number Accepted	Manufacturer	Models Accepted	Squadron Delivery	Last Report*	Description
BT			10/20/38	54	Northrop	XBT-1; BT-1; XBT-2	4/38 VB-5	1/43 PAC	M/2. 1000# dive bomber; P&W R-1535-94, 825 hp
BTD	6/30/41	4/8/43	10/45	30	Douglas	XSB2D-1; BTD-1; XBTD-2	(Not assigned to Fleet Squadrons)		M/1 (2 in SB2D). WAC R-3350, 2100 hp; also WE 19B Jet, 860# in XBTD-2
BT2D	(Initial designation for AD)								
BTM	(Initial designation for AM)								
CS	6/22 est	11/23 est	1/26	8	Curtiss	CS-1, -2. SC-1, -2	3/1/24 VS-3	12/19/27 VT-2, SC-2	B/2. Conv't 3-in-1—torpedo, scout & bomber; steel tube fuselage & tail; WAC T-2 or T-3, 525 or 625 hp
				75	Martin				
DT	1921	11/21 est	1924-2	41	Douglas	DT-1, -2	12/12/22	4/1/28	B/1 (2 in -2). Conv't; torpedo; welded steel tube forward fuselage and horizontal tail; fuselage skin partially aluminum; folding wings; Lib. 400 or 450 hp; WAC T-3, 650 hp in -4
				6	NAF	DT-2, -4			
				20	LWF	DT-2			
				11	Dayton-Wright	DT-2			
MBT	(Original version of Martin Bomber, See MT)								
MT	9/30/19	2/4/20	8/20	10	Martin	MT; MBT	8/20 LANT and PAC	6/2/28 VO-8M, MT	B/3. Land, folding wing on some aircraft; 2 Lib. 400 hp
PT	1921	7/21 est	7/22	33	NAF	PT-1, -2	3/22 VT-1	7/23 VT-1, PT-2	B/2. Lib. 400 hp
S-2	6/30/50	12/4/52	12/67	1,120 (63)	Grumman	XS2F; S2F-1, -2, -3, -2D; S2F-3S/S-2E	2/54 VS-26	3/84 S-2E	M/4. ASW; 2 WAC R-1820, 1,525 hp
S-3	8/69	1/21/72	9/77	187	Lockheed	S-3A, -3B	2/20/74 VS-41	3/09 VS-22	M/4. ASW aircraft. 2 GE TF-34-GE-2, 9,000#
SBA	(Prototype for SBN)								
SB2A	4/4/39	6/17/41	2/44	771 (468)	Brewster	XSB2A-1; SB2A-1, -2, -3, -4	1/31/43 VMF(N)-531	11/30/43 VMF(N)-532, SB2A-4	M/2. Used for training, WAC R-2600, 1700 hp
SBC	6/30/32	6/14/34	4/41	258	Curtiss	XSBC-3, -4; SBC-3, -4	7/17/37 VS-5	6/1/43 VMSB-151, SBC-4	B/2. P&W R-1535, 825 hp in -3; WAC R-1820, 1950 hp in -4
SB2C	5/15/39	12/18/40	10/45	5,516 (1)	Curtiss	XSB2C-2, -5, -6; SB2C-1, -1A, -1C, -3, -4, -4E, -5	12/15/42 VS-9	6/1/49 VA-54, SB2C-5	M/2 (XSB2C-2, sea). WAC R-2600, 1,700 to 1,900 hp; P&W R-2800, 2,100 hp in -6
				834 (26)	CanCar	SBW-1, -1B, -3, -4, -4E, -5			

Designation	First Contract	First Flight	Last Delivery	Number Accepted	Manufacturer	Models Accepted	Squadron Delivery	Last Report*	Description
				300	Fairchild	SBF-1, -3, -4E			
SBD	11/18/34	8/35 est	8/44	5,321 (338)	Douglas	SBD-1, -2, -3. -3A, -4, -4A, -5, -5A, -6	4/11/38 VB-5	9/30/45 PAC, SBD-6	M/2. "All metal," stressed skin; WAC R-1820, 1,000 hp in SBD-1, -2, -3; 1,200 hp in -5 & -6
				55	Northrop	XBT-1, -2, BT-1			
SB2D	(Redesignated to BTD)								
SBF	(SB2C manufactured by Fairchild of Canada)								
SBN	10/15/34	3/36	3/42	30	NAF	SBN-1	8/41 VT-8	12/31/41 VT-8, SBN-1	M/2. Used for training; WAC R-1820, 950 hp; 725 hp in XSBA-1
				1	Brewster	XSBA-1			
SBW	(SB2C manufactured by Canadian Car and Foundry [CanCar])								
SBU	6/30/32	6/33 est	8/37	126	Vought	XF3U-1; XSBU-1; SBU-1, -2	11/20/35 VS3B	4/30/41 VS-41, SBU-1	B/2. P&W R-1535, 700 hp
SB2U	10/11/34	1/4/36	7/41	170	Vought	XSB2U-1,- 3; SBU-1,- 2, -3	12/20/37 VB-3	2/28/43 VB-9, SB2U-1	M/2. -3 Conv't; 1st folding wing dive bomber; P&W R-1535, 835 hp
SC	(CS manufactured by Martin in 1920s)								
SC	(Battleship and cruiser aircraft, WWII, See Observation series)								
SF	6/9/31	8/19/32	12/34	35	Grumman	XSF-1; SF-1; XSF-2	3/30/34 VF2B	1/31/36 VS-3B, SF-1	B/2. Retractable landing gear; same basic airframe as FF; WAC R-1820, 700 hp
S2F	(Redesignated S-2)								
SU	(O3U converted to carrier scout, See Observation series)								
TBD	6/30/34	4/15/35	11/39	130	Douglas	XTBD-1; TBD-1	10/5/37 VT-3	8/31/42 VT-4, TBD-1	M/3. P&W R-1830, 850 hp
TBF	4/8/40	8/7/41	9/45	2,290 (458)	Grumman	XTBF-1, -2, -3; TBF-1, -1B, -1C	3/25/42 VT-8	10/31/54 VS-27, TBM-3E	M/3. WAC R-2600, 1,700 hp; 1,800 hp in -3
				7,546 (526)	Eastern	XTBM-3, -4, TBM-1, -1C, -3, -3E			
TB3F	(Prototype for AF)								
TBM	(TBF manufactured by Eastern Aircraft Division, General Motors Corp.)								
TBU	(Produced as TBY)								

Designation	First Contract	First Flight	Last Delivery	Number Accepted	Manufacturer	Models Accepted	Squadron Delivery	Last Report*	Description
TBY	4/22/40	12/22/41	9/45	180	Consolidated	TBY-2	4/45 VT-97	3/31/45 PAC, TBY-2	M/3. P&W R-2800, 2,100 hp; 1850 hp in XTBU-1
				1	Vought	XTBU-1			
T2D	(Initial designation for P2D, See Patrol series)								
TG	(T4M as manufactured by Great Lakes Aircraft Corp.)								
T3M	1925	7/26 est	1927	124	Martin	T3M-1, -2	9/7/26 VT-1	7/30/32 VP-3S, T3M-2	B/3. Conv't; WAC T-3, 575 hp; PKD 3A-2500, 770 hp in -2
T4M	6/30/27	5/27 est	12/31	103	Martin	XT4M-1; T4M-1	8/9/28 VT-2B	3/31/38 VT-6, TG-2	B/3. Conv't; generally carrier based; P&W R-1690, 525 hp; WAC R-1820, 575 hp in -2
				50	Great Lakes	TG-1, -2			
T5M	(Initial prototype for BM)								
T2N	(Similar to T5M, included with BM)								

* Dates in this column through 1969 refer to squadrons. After 1969 these dates refer to the inventory unless a squadron is listed.
† Includes 26 remanufactured from AV-8A to AV-8B and aircraft for Italy and Spain, including the EAV-8A.

Designation	First Contract	First Flight	Last Delivery	Number Accepted	Manufacturer	Models Accepted	Squadron Delivery	Last Report*	Description
F-1	(Redesignation of FJ-3 and -4)								
F-2	(Redesignation of F2H-3 and -4)								
F-3	(Redesignation of F3H-3)								
F-4	10/18/54	5/27/58	12/29/71	4,261 (3,057)	McDonnell	F4H-1; F-4A, -4B, -4C, -4D, -4E, -4G,- 4J, -4K, -4M, -4N, -4S; RF-4B, -4C; YF-4K, -4M	12/60 VF-121	12/89 F-4S	M/2. Mach 2 plus; all missile; 2 GE J79, 17,000#
F-5	Acquired from U.S. Air Force and Swiss Air Force surplus			46	Northrop	F-5E, -5F, -5N	9/77 NFWS		M/2 for F-5F and -N. Mach 1.5; AIM-9, M39 20mm gun, F-5F and -N has 2 turbojet GE J85-GE-21C, 5,000# each
F-6	(Redesignation of F4D)								
F-8	6/29/53	3/25/55	1/65	1,264 (42)	Vought	XF8U-1; F8U-1, -1P, -2, -2N, -3 -2NE/F-8E; F-8E; F-8E (FN); F-8J	3/57 VF-32, VC-3	8/82 F-8J	M. Variable incidence wing; supersonic; P&W J57, 15,000# to 18,000#
F-9	(Redesignation of F9F-5 through 8)								

Designation	First Contract	First Flight	Last Delivery	Number Accepted	Manufacturer	Models Accepted	Squadron Delivery	Last Report*	Description
F-10	(Redesignation of F3D)								
F-11	(Redesignation of F11F)								
F-14	2/3/69	12/21/70	7/10/92	679 (78)	Grumman	F-14, -14B, -14A+, -14D	1/14/73 VF-1	9/22/06 VF-31	M/2. Mach 2 plus. 2 P&W TF-30-P-44, up to 20,000#
F-16N	Developed by U.S. Air Force			28	General Dynamics	F-16N, TF-16N, F-16A	4/87 NFWS		M/2. Mach 2 plus; 2 P&W F110, 20,000#
F/A-18 (Also listed in the Attack Series)	5/75	11/78		1,441	McDonnell Douglas/ Boeing	F/A-18A, -18B, 18C, -18D, -18E, -18F, EA-18G	1/7/83 VMFA-314		M/1. FA-18D & -F are 2 seat, EA-18G 2 crew. Mach 2 plus. 2 GE F414-GE-400, 16,000#
F-35	10/25/01	12/15/06		6 Not yet delivered	Lockheed Martin	F-35B, -35C			M/1. Type of engine varies with model, F-35B or F-35C
F2A	6/22/36	12/37	4/42	503 (340)	Brewster	XF2A-1; F2A-1, -2, -3	12/8/39 VF-3	9/30/42 VMF-112, F2A-2; VMF-211, F2A-3	M/1. Midwing, cantilever monoplane; WAC R-1820, 950 to 1,200 hp
F-21A				37	Israel	F-21A	3/85 VF-43	8/26/87	M/1. Mach 2 plus. GE J79-GE-J1E, 30mm cannon, missile, bombs, rockets
F3A	(F4U manufactured by Brewster)								
FB	1925	11/25 est	1/27	43	Boeing	FB-1, -2, -3, -5	12/25/25 VF-2	6/30/30 VF-6M, FB-5	B. Carrier, -2 & -5; conv't, -3; radio, -5; CAM D-12, 410 hp in -1 and -2. PKD 1A-1500, 525 hp in -3 and -5
F2B	1926	12/26 est	2/28	33	Boeing	F2B-1	12/2/27 VF-1B	5/31/35 VN-5D8, F2B-1	B. Conv't; P&W R-1340, 410 hp
F3B	6/30/27	6/27 est	1/29	74	Boeing	F3B-1	10/17/27 VF-1B	4/28/33 VF-2B, F3B-1	B. P&W R-1340, 410 hp
F4B	11/28/28	6/28 est	1/33	188†	Boeing	F4B-1, -2, -3, -4	8/8/29 VB-1B	10/10/42 VJ-5, F4B-4	B. P&W R-1340, 450 hp in -1; 500 hp in -2 to -4
F6C	1925	7/25 est	6/27	75	Curtiss	F6C-1, -3, -4	9/30/25 VF-2	10/31/32 VF-10M, F6C-4	B. Conv't carrier, -2 to -4; CAM D-12, 400 hp in -1 to -3; P&W R-1340, 410 hp in -4
F7C	6/30/27	6/27 est	1/29	18	Curtiss	XF7C-1; F7C-1	12/28/28 VF-5M	3/31/33 VF-9M, F7C-1	B. P&W R-1340, 450 hp
F8C	(For F8C-1, -3 See OC in Observation series; F8C-3 became OC-2)								
F8C-2	3/15/28	11/28	11/31	124	Curtiss	XF8C-2, -4, -7; F8C-4, -5; O2C-1, -2	8/30 VF-1B	7/31/38 VMJ-1, O2C-1	B/2. 500# dive bomber; P&W R-1340B, 450 hp; WAC R-1820, 575 hp in O2C-2

Designation	First Contract	First Flight	Last Delivery	Number Accepted	Manufacturer	Models Accepted	Squadron Delivery	Last Report*	Description
F9C	6/30/30	2/12/31	9/32	8	Curtiss	XF9C-1, -2; F9C-2	9/32 *Akron* Unit	1/31/35 *Macon* Unit, F9C-2	B. Skyhook; droppable under-carriage; metal monocoque fuselage; WACR-975, 400 hp
F11C	4/16/32	3/20/32	5/33	29	Curtiss	XF11C-1, -2; F11C-2 redesignated BFC-2	3/22/33 VF-1B	5/31/38 VB-6, BFC-2	B. WAC R-1820, 600 hp
F12C	(XF12C-1 monoplane successively modified to XS4C-1 and XSBC-1 and then crashed; it was replaced by XSBC-2 biplane, which became XSBC-3)								
FD	(Original designation for FH)								
F3D	4/3/46	3/23/48	10/53	268	Douglas	XF3D-1; F3D-1, -2, -2M	2/51 VC-3	5/31/70 EF-10B	M/2. Jet night-fighter; 2 WE J34, 3,250#, 3400# in -2
F4D	12/16/48	1/25/51	12/58	421	Douglas	XF4D-1; F4D-1, F-6	4/16/56 VMF-115, VC-3	2/29/64 VMF-115, F4D-1, F-6	M. Modified delta wing; tailless; WE J40, 13,700# in XF4D-1; P&W J57, 16,000#
FG	(F4U manufactured by Goodyear)								
FF	4/2/31	12/21/31	11/33	28	Grumman	XFF-1; FF-1, -2	6/21/33 VF-5B	3/31/36 VF-5B, FF-1	B/2. Metal monocoque fuselage; retractable landing gear; WAC R-1820, 600 hp
F2F	11/2/32	10/9/33	8/35	56	Grumman	XF2F-1; F2F-1	2/19/35 VF-2B	9/30/40 VF-2, F2F-1	B. P&W R-1535, 650 hp
F3F	10/15/34	3/20/35	5/39	164	Grumman	XF3F-1, -2, -3; F3F-1, -2, -3	4/3/36 VF-5B	10/31/41 VMF-111, VMF-211, F3F-2	B. P&W R-1535, 700 hp in -1; WAC R-1820, 950 hp in -2 and -3
F4F	7/28/36	9/2/37	5/45	1,978 (431)	Grumman	XF4F-2/3; -4, -5, -6, -8; F4F-3, -3A -4, -7	12/5/40 VF-4	11/30/45 PAC, FM-2	M. Folding wings on F4F-4/FM-1, P&W R-1830, 1,050 to 1,200 hp; WAC R-1820,1350 hp in -5 and -8/FM-1, -2
				5,927 (651)	Eastern	FM-1, -2.			
F6F	6/30/41	6/26/42	11/45	12,275 (1,182)	Grumman	XF6F-1/-3, -4, -6; F6F-3, -3E, -3N, -5, -5N	1/16/43 VC-4, VF-9	8/31/53 VC-4, F6F-5N	M. P&W R-2800, 2,000 hp to 2,325 hp
F7F	6/30/41	11/3/43	11/46	364	Grumman	XF7F-1, -2; F7F-1, -1N, -2N, -3, -3N, -4N	1/44 VMF(N)-531	3/31/54 VJ-62, F7F-3N/-4N	M. (2-place in -2N, -3N). Tricycle landing gear; 2 P&W R-2800, 2,400 hp; 2,100 hp in -4
F8F	11/27/43	8/31/44	5/49	1,263	Grumman	XF8F-1, -1N, -2, F8F-1,-1B, -1N,-2,-2N, -2P	5/21/45 VF-19	1/31/53 VF-921, VF-859, F8F-2	M. Medium altitude interceptor; P&W R-2800, 2750 hp; 2,500 hp in -2

Designation	First Contract	First Flight	Last Delivery	Number Accepted	Manufacturer	Models Accepted	Squadron Delivery	Last Report*	Description
F9F-2/-5	12/16/46	11/21/47	12/52	1,388	Grumman	XF9F-2, -3; F9F-2,- 3, -4, -5, -5P	5/8/49 VF-51	10/31/58 VAH-7, F9F-5	M. Straight wing; P&W J42, 5,750# in -2; J48, 7,000# in -5; AL J33, 5,400# in -3; 6,500# in -4
F9F-6/-8	3/2/51	9/20/51	12/59	1,985	Grumman	F9F-6, -6P, -7, -8,- 8P, -8T	11/52 VF-32	2/29/60 VFP-62, F9F-8P	M. (2 place in -8T). Swept wing; P&W J48, 7,250# in -6,- 8; AL J33, 6,250# in -7
F11F	4/27/53	7/30/54	12/58	201	Grumman	F9F-9; F11F-1, -1F	3/8/57 VA-156	4/30/61 VF-33, VF-111. F11F-1	M. Supersonic; WAC J65, 10,500#; GE J79, 14,350# in -1F
FH	1/7/43	1/26/45	5/48	61	McDonnell	XFD-1; FD-1/ FH-1	7/23/47 VMF-122	7/1/50 VMF-122, FH-1	M. First USN all jet; tricycle landing gear; 2 WE J30, 1,560#
F2H	3/2/45	1/11/47	8/53	894	McDonnell	XF2H-1; F2H-1, -2, -2N, -2P, -3, -4	3/49 VF-171	9/30/59 VAW-11, F2H-3/-4	M. Pressurized cabin; ejection seat; 2 WE J34, 3,150#; 3,250# in -3 and -4
F3H	9/30/49	8/7/51	11/59	519	McDonnell	XF3H-1; F3H-1, -1N, -2, -2N, -2M; F-3B, -3C; MF-3B	3/7/56 VF-14	8/31/64 VF-161, F-3B	M. Sparrow missile: I in -2M, III in -2; WE J40, 13,700 and 10,900# in -1 and -1N; AL J71, 14,400#
F4H	(Redesignated F-4)								
FJ	1/1/45	9/11/46	4/48	33	North American	XFJ-1; FJ-1	11/18/47 VF-5A	10/1/49 VF-51, FJ-1	M. Straight wing; power boost control; GE TG-180 in XFJ-1; AL J35 (TG-180), 4,000# in FJ-1
FJ-2/-4	2/10/51	12/27/51	5/58	1,115	North American	XFJ-2, -2B; FJ-2, -3, -3M, -4, -4B; F-1C, -1E	1/54 VMF-122	9/30/62 VA-216, F-1E	M. Swept wing; GE J47, 6,000# in -2; WAC J65, 7,800#
FR	2/11/43	6/25/44	11/45	69	Ryan	XFR-1, FR-1	3/45 VF-66	6/30/47 VF-1E, FR-1	M. Combination jet-propeller; tricycle gear; WAC R-1820, 1,400 hp; plus GE I-16, 1,610#
FU	(Single seat fighter-trainer version of UO, 20 aircraft converted from UO-3, delivered January–July 1927)								
F3U	(Original XF3U-1 was replaced by XSBU-1 after original acceptance; it was later reaccepted under different serial number.)								
F4U	6/30/38	5/29/40	1/53	7,829 (1,067)	Vought	XF4U-1, -3, -4, -5; F4U-1, -1C, -1D, -2, -4, -4B, -4C, -4P, -5, -5N, -5NL, -5P, -7; AU-1	10/3/42 VF-12	12/31/55 VC-4, F4U-5N	M. Inverted gull wing; 20MM cannon in -1C, -4B, -5 and in subsequent -2, night fighter; P&W R-2800, 2,000 hp to 2,700 hp
				735 (430)	Brewster	F3A-1			

Fighter Series

Designation	First Contract	First Flight	Last Delivery	Number Accepted	Manufacturer	Models Accepted	Squadron Delivery	Last Report*	Description
				4,006 (989)	Goodyear	FG-1, -1D			
F6U	12/29/44	10/2/46	2/50	33	Vought	XF6U-1; F6U-1	VX-3	3/52	M. Skin of dural-balsa sandwich; afterburning, WE J34, 4,100#
F7U	6/25/46	9/48	12/55	307	Vought	XF7U-1; F7U-1, 3, -3M, -3P	4/54 VF-81	11/30/57 VA-66, F7U-3	M. Swept wing; tailless; 2 WE J34, 4,900# in -1; J46, 5,800# in -3
F8U	(Redesignated F-8)								
MB-3	1921		1/22	11	Thomas Morse	MB-3	Quantico 3/22	Quantico 11/23	B. WAC H, 300 hp. Land
TS	1921	4/22 est	10/23	34	Curtiss	TS-1	12/22 Langley	5/31/27 VF-1, TS-1	B. Conv't; LA J-1, 200 hp in -1; AM U-8-D, 210 hp in -2; WAC E-2, 180 hp in -3
				9	NAF	TS-1, -2, -3			
VE-7	1920	5/20 est	1924	60	Vought	VE-7, -7SF	7/20 GITMO	5/1/28 VT-6D-14, VE-7	B/2 (SF, single place). Land; -7H, Sea; WAC E-2, 180hp. See Observation series
				69	NAF	VE-7, -7G, -7GF, -7H, -7SF			

' Dates in this column through 1969 refer to squadrons. After 1969, these dates refer to the inventory unless a squadron is listed.
† Omits 23 F4B-4A obtained from Army 12/39 and 1 F4B-4 built from spares 6/34.

Patrol And Early Warning Series

Designation	First Contract	First Flight	Last Delivery	Number Accepted	Manufacturer	Models Accepted	Squadron Delivery	Last Report*	Description
A-29	(See PBO)								
B-24	(See PB4Y-1)								
B-25	(See PBJ)								
B-34	(See PV)								
EC-121	(See WV)								
E-I	6/15/56	12/17/56	12/61	88	Grumman	WF-2	11/59 VAW-12	3/31/78 E-1B	M/4. Carrier parasol radome; 2 WAC R-1820, 1,525 hp
E-2	3/12/59	10/21/60		253 (14)	Northrop Grumman	W2F-1; E-2A -2B, -2C, -2D; TE-2C	1/64 VAW-11		M/5. Carrier; 2 position parasol rotodome; 4 vertical tails; 2 AL T56, 4,050 eshp., E-2D has 2 Rolls-Royce T-56-A-427 turboprop, 5100 shp each
E-6	Commercial 707-320	1989		16	Boeing	E-6A, -6B	8/3/89 VQ-3		M/22. 4 CFM-56-2A-2 high bypass turbofans
EC-130				18 EC-130Q	Lockheed	C-130G, EC-130Q	12/26/63 VR-1 and VR-21, C-130Gs forerunner of EC-130Q	5/26/92 VQ-4	See C-130 specifications

Designation	First Contract	First Flight	Last Delivery	Number Accepted	Manufacturer	Models Accepted	Squadron Delivery	Last Report*	Description
P-2	2/19/43	5/17/45	9/62	1,036 (193)	Lockheed	XP2V-1, -2; P2V-2, -3, -3W, -4,- 5, -6, -6B, -7, -7U, -7S; SP-2H	3/47 VP-ML-2	4/82 SP-2H	M/7-9. Land; 2 WAC R-3350, 3,090 to 3,700 hp; also in -7, 2 WE J34, 3,400#
P-3	2/2/59		11/30/90	610 (36)	Lockheed	YP3V-1; P3V-1/P-3A, -3B, -3C, -3F; YP-3C; RP-3A, -3D; WP-3D; EP-3E	8/22/62 VP-8		M/12. Land; 4 AL T56, 4,500 to 4,900 eshp. EP-3E has a crew of 24 and 4 Allison T-56-A-14 turboprop engines at 4,600 shp each
P-4	(Redesignation of P4Y-2)								
P-5	6/26/46	4/30/48	12/60	239 (21)	Martin	XP5M-1; P5M-1, -2	4/23/52 VP-44	10/31/67 VP-40, SP-5B	M/7. Boat: long hull; faired step; 2 WAC R-3350, 3,250 hp
P-8	circa 2005–2006	4/25/09		On order	Boeing	P-8A			M/9. 2 CFM 56-76-7B engines with 27,300 # thrust each
PB2B	(PBY-5 manufactured by Boeing of Canada, Vancouver, B.C.)								
PBJ	7/7/42		6/45	706	North American	PBJ-1, -1C, -1D -1G, -1H, -1J	2/43 VMB-413	1/31/46 PAC, PBJ-1J	M/4-5. Land; 2 WAC R-2600, 1,700 hp
PBM	6/30/37	2/18/39	3/49	1,366	Martin	XPBM -1 -2, -3, 3C, -3D, -3R, -3S, -5, -5A; PBM-1, -3C, -3D, -3R, -3S, -5, -5E,-5G	9/1/40 VP-55	7/31/56 VP-50, PBM-5S2	M/7-9. Boat: (-5A, amphibian); WAC R-2600, 1,600 to 1,900 hp; 2 P&W R-2800, 2,100 hp in -5
PBN	(PBY manufactured by Naval Aircraft Factory; longer bow)								
PBO	9/41		10/41	20	Lockheed	PBO-1	10/29/41 VP-82	10/31/42 VP-82, PBO-1	M/5. 1st USN land type patrol; 2 WAC R-1820, 1,000 hp
PBY	10/28/33	3/35	9/45	2,387 (636)	Consolidated	XP3Y-1; XPBY-5A; PBY-1, -2, -3,- 4, -5, -6A, OA-10, -5B, -6A	10/5/36 VP-11F	6/1/49 VP-32, PBY-6A	M/5-8. Boat (-5A & -6A, OA-10 & -10B, amphibian); 2 P&W R-1830, 900 to 1,200 hp
				290 (270)	Boeing	PB2B-1, -2			
				155 (137)	NAF	PBN-1			
				230 (230)	Vickers	PBV-1A, OA-10B			
PB2Y	7/23/36	12/17/37	9/44	176 (33)	Consolidated	XPB2Y-1, -3; PB2Y-2, -3, -3B	12/31/40 VP-13	11/30/45 PAC, PB2Y-3/-5	M/9-10. Boat; 4 P&W R-1830, 1,200 hp
				41	Rohr	PB2Y-3R			
PB4Y-1	7/7/42		1/45	977‡	Consolidated	PB4Y-1, P4Y-1	10/42 VP-51	5/31/56 VJ-62 P4Y-1P	M/6-11. Land; twin tail; 4 P&W R-1830, 1,200 hp
PB4Y-2	5/3/43	10/43	10/45	739‡	Consolidated	PB4Y-2, P4Y-2	8/44 VB-200	6/30/54 VW-3, P4Y-2S	M/11. Land; single tail; 4 P&W R-1830, 1,200 hp

Designation	First Contract	First Flight	Last Delivery	Number Accepted	Manufacturer	Models Accepted	Squadron Delivery	Last Report*	Description
						Patrol And Early Warning Series			
PD	12/29/27	5/29 est	6/30	25	Douglas	PD-1	7/10/29 VP-7B	10/31/36 VP-6F PD-1	B/4. Boat; aluminum alloy with fabric covered wings; 2 WAC R-1750, 525 hp
P2D	7/25	1/27/27	6/32	30	Douglas	T2D-I, P2D-I	5/25/27 VT-2	2/28/37 VP-3F, P2D-1	B/3. Twin float; duralumin and fabric; 2 WAC R-1820, 575
PH	12/29/27	11/29 est	7/32	10	Hall	XPH-1, PH-1	6/24/32 VP-8S	5/19/37 VP-8F, PH-1	B/5. Boat; lightweight metal structure with fabric covered wings; 2 WAC R-1820, 575 hp
PK	11/30/29	3/31 est	12/31	18	Keystone	PK-1	9/23/31 VP-1B	7/30/38 VP-1, PK-1	B/5. Boat; twin tail; 2 WAC R-1820 575 hp
PM	5/31/29	7/30 est	10/31 est	55	Martin	PM-1, -2	8/21/30 VP-8S	4/30/38 VP-16, PM-1	B/5. Boat; 2 WAC R-1820, 575 hp
P3M	2/28/28	12/28 est	5/31	9	Martin	P3M-1, XPY-1	4/29/31 VP-10S	5/31/38 VP-15, P3M-2	M/4-5. (1st monoplane patrol); 2 or 3 P&W R-1340, 450 hp
				1	Consolidated				
P4M	7/6/44	9/20/46	9/50	21	Martin	XP4M-1, P4M-1	6/28/50 VP-21	5/31/60 VQ-1, P4M-1	M/9. Land; 2 P&W R-4360, 3,250 hp and 2 AL J33, 4,600#
P5M	(Redesignated P-5)								
PO-1W	(Initial designation for WV, the Airborne Early Warning version of the Lockheed Constellation)								
PV	7/7/42		12/45	2,162	Lockheed	PV-1 -2, -2C, -2D, -3	10/42 VP-82	8/1/48 VP-ML-3, PV-2	M/4. Land; 2 P&W -2800, 2,000 hp
P2V	(Redesignated P-2)								
P3V	(Redesignated P-3)								
PY	(Prototype for P3M)								
P2Y	5/26/31	3/26/32	5/35	47	Consolidated	XP2Y-1; P2Y-1, -2, -3	2/1/33 VP-10S	3/31/41 VP-43, P2Y-3	Sesquiplane/5. Enclosed cabins (2 or 3 in XP2Y-1) WAC R-1820, 575 to 700 hp
P3Y	(Initial designation of PBY)								
P4Y	(Redesignation of PB4Y-1 and -2)								
PT	(Torpedo plane manufactured by Naval Aircraft Factory, See Attack series)								
WF	(Redesignated E-1)								
W2F	(Redesignated E-2)								

Patrol And Early Warning Series

Designation	First Contract	First Flight	Last Delivery	Number Accepted	Manufacturer	Models Accepted	Squadron Delivery	Last Report*	Description
WV	9/28/48		9/58	152	Lockheed	PO-1W; WV-2,-3	7/52	3/31/79 EC-121K	M/26–31. Land; vertical fin and belly radomes; 4 WAC R-3350, 2,500–3,250 hp

* Dates in this column through 1969 refer to squadrons. After 1969, these dates refer to inventory unless a squadron is listed.
† Transport versions of PB4Y-1, 3 RY-1, and 5 RY-2, not included in totals.
‡ Transport versions of PB4Y-2, 33 RY-3, of which three were for U.K., not included in totals.

Observation Series

Designation	First Contract	First Flight	Last Delivery	Number Accepted	Manufacturer	Models Accepted	Squadron Delivery	Last Report*	Description
M-8	1919	8/19 est	3/21	17	Loening	M-8, M-80, M-81-S, M-81	8/20† LANT	7/21 PAC, M-81	1st USN production monoplane; M-8 and M-80, land; M-81, conv't; M-80, 2-place reconnaissance; M-81, 1-place fighter or 2-place; Hispano Suiza, 300 hp
				36	NAF				
MO	1922	12/22 est	1/24	36	Martin	MO-1	2/21/23 VO-2	Prior to 1/26	M/3. Conv't; aluminum frame; CAM D-12, 300 hp
O2B	1924	3/25 est	1925	30	Boeing	O2B-1	4/25 Quantico	2/28/29 VO-9M, O2B-1	B/2. Land; DH-4B with steel tube fuselage; Lib., 400 hp
O-1	(Redesignation of OE)								
OC	6/30/27	12/27 est	1928	27	Curtiss	F8C-1, -3; OC-1, -2	1/21/28 VO-7M	9/35 VJ-7M, OC-2	B/2. Land; Marine obs. and attack; P&W R-1340, 410 hp
O2C	(Redesignation for F8C-5, See Fighter Series)								
OE	6/51 est		8/1/67	97 (4)	Cessna	OE-1, -2; O-1G	11/51 VMO-1, VMO-6	3/31/70 O-1C, O-1G	M/2. Land; CO O-470, 265 hp
OJ	6/28/29	5/31 est	12/34	40	B/J	XOJ-1; OJ-2	3/33 VS-6B	2/29/36 VS-5B, OJ-2	B/2. Conv't; P&W R-985, 400 hp
OL	1924	5/25 est	3/32	84	Loening	OL-1, -2, -3, -6, -8	2/26 Quantico	7/38 NRAB Oakland	B/2–3. Amph; PKD 1500, 400 to 525 hp; Lib., 400 hp in -2; P&W R-1340, 450 hp in -8 and -9
				26	Keystone	OL-9			
OS2N	(OS2U manufactured at NAF)								
OS2U	3/22/37	5/38 est	11/42	1,218 (154)	Vought	XOS2U-1; OS2U-1, -2, -3	8/16/40 VO-4	5/31/46 PAC, OS2U-3	M/2. Conv't; P&W R-985, 450 hp
				300	NAF	OS2N-1			
O2U	1926	11/26 est	2/30	291	Vought	O2U-1,- 2, -3, -4	12/17/27 VO-7M	4/30/36 VB-2B, O2U-2	B/2. Conv't; P&W R-1340, 450 hp
O3U	1/18/30	6/30 est	7/35	330	Vought	O3U-1, -2, -3, -6; XO4U-2; XO3U-6; SU-1, -2, -3, -4	7/15/30 VO-3B	3/42 VJ-3	B/2. Conv't; amph. or land; P&W R-1340, 450 hp

Designation	First Contract	First Flight	Last Delivery	Number Accepted	Manufacturer	Models Accepted	Squadron Delivery	Last Report*	Description
OV-1O	10/15/64	7/16/65	1977	356 (239)	North American	OV-1OA, -10B, -10D	2/23/68 HML-267	4/94 VMO-4, OV-10D	M/2. Light Armed Reconnaissance Aircraft (LARA) for Counter-insurgency (COIN) missions; 2 Air T76, 715 shp
OY	11/1/43		8/45	306	Consolidated	OY-1, -2	1/44 VMO-1, -2, 3-, -4	11/30/54 VMO-1, OY-2	M/2. Land; LY O-435, 185 hp
SC	(CS design, manufactured by Martin in 1920s, See Attack Series)								
SC	3/31/43	2/16/44	10/46	577	Curtiss	XSC-1A, -1A, -2; SC-1, -2	10/12/44 *Alaska* (CB 1)	10/1/49 HU-2, SC-1	M/1. Sea; WAC R-1820, 1,300 hp
SOC	6/19/33	4/34 est	8/39	259	Curtiss	XO3C-1; XSOC-1, SOC-1, -2, -3	11/12/35 VS-5B	11/30/46 LANT, SOC-1	B/2. Sea; P&W R-1340, 550 hp
				44	NAF	SON-1			
SO3C	5/9/38	10/6/39	1/44	794 (250)	Curtiss	XSO3C-1; SO3C-1, -2, -2C, -3	7/42 VCS-12	3/31/44 VS-46, SO3C-3	M/2. Conv't; RA V-770, 520 hp
SON	(SOC-3 manufactured by the Naval Aircraft Factory)								
SU	(O3U converted to carrier-based scout)								
UO	1922	19/22 est	16/27 est	163 (2)	Vought	UO-1, -4, FU-1	6/14/24 *Tennessee* (BB 43)	12/31/29 VS-8A, VO-6M, UO-1	B/2. Conv't; LA/ WAC R-790 (J-1 to J-5) 200 to 220 hp
VE-7	(See Fighter Series. Of the 129 total, 70 were VE-7SF fighters; 39 were VE-7 and VE-7H trainers; 20 were VE-7G observation planes)								
VE-9	1922	6/22 est	7/23	21	Vought	VE-9, VE-9H	6/22 *Nevada* (BB 36)	10/30/30 Navy Mission Rio de Jeneiro, Brazil, VE-9	B/2. Land; -9H, Sea; WAC E-3 180 hp

* Dates in this column through 1969 refer to squadrons. After 1969 these dates refer to the inventory unless a squadron is listed.
† Estimated date.

Designations	First Order (Fiscal Year)	Delivery (D) or First Flight (F)	Number Accepted	Manufacturer	Models Accepted*	Delivery Continental		Delivery For Overseas Shipment		Service History Withdrawal from Inventory			Description
						Date	Destination	Date	Destination	Date	Location	Model	
DH-4	1918	5/24/18 (D)	333	Dayton-Wright	DH-4, -4B	6/4/18	Miami	5/24/18		10/31/26	Dahlgren	DH-4B-2	B/2. Land; bomber & fighter; British design; USN obtained from U.S. Army; two syn. Marlin guns, 2 flex Lewis guns; Lib., 360 hp
F-5	1918	7/15/18 (F)	30	Canadian Aeroplanes	F-5L	10/4/18	Hampton Roads	10/12/18	Pauillac	1/31	Hampton Roads	F-5L	B/4. Boat; ASW; British F-5 adapted to American manufacture; 5 Lewis guns, 4-230# bombs; 2 Lib., 360 hp
			60	Curtiss	F-5L								
			137	NAF	F-5L								
H-12	1917	3/17 (D)	20	Curtiss	H-12	1/17/18	Hampton Roads		United States Only	7/17/20		H-12	B/2-4. Boat; training or ASW; 2-160# (Mk IV) bombs, Lewis gun, radio; 2 CAM V2-3, 200 hp or 2 Lib., 300 hp
H-16	1918	2/1/18 (D)	124	Curtiss	H-16	2/18	Hampton Roads	3/18	England	5/30	NAF	H-16	B/4. Boat; ASW; was 1st aircraft built at NAF; radio, 5 Lewis guns, 4-230# bombs; 2 Lib., 360 hp
			150	NAF	H-16		Pensacola						
HS	1918	10/21/17 (F) (with Lib. engine)	678	Curtiss	HS-1, -2L, -3L	1/14/18	Hampton Roads	3/25/18	Pauillac	9/28	Hampton Roads	HS-2L	B/3. Boat; pusher; ASW; some aircraft delivered as HS-1, and converted to HS-2 with 25% greater wing area; Lewis gun, 2-230# (160# in HS-1) bombs; Davis gun or radio in some machines; Lib., 360 hp
			250	LWF	HS-2L								
			80	Standard	HS-2L								
			60	Gallaudet	HS-2L								
			25	Boeing	HS-2L								
			2	Loughead	HS-2L								
NC	1918	10/4/18 (F)	4	Curtiss	NC-1 thru -4	5/2/19	Rockaway			5/20/24		NC-10	B/5. ASW; boat; 3 Lib., 360 or 400 hp; NC-TA (Trans-Atlantic type) had 3 tractor and 1 pusher, Lib. 400 hp
			6	NAF	NC-5 thru -10								
R	1916	11/16 est (D)	200	Curtiss	R-3, -5, -6, -6L, -9	6/20/17	Pensacola	1/18	Azores	9/26	Pearl Harbor	R-6L	B/2. Twin Float; Curtiss, 200 hp, trainer, but used for ASW; R-9 fitted for Lewis gun and small bombs; R-6L with Lib., 360 hp) used as torpedo plane

* Excludes aircraft erected from spares at the Naval Aircraft Factory and various air stations, even when Bureau Numbers were assigned.

CHAPTER 3

Transport and Training Aircraft Procured

In basic organization and concept this table generally follows the table on combat aircraft (Chapter 2); the major difference is that this includes only the major/primary transport and training aircraft used by the Navy since the beginning of WWII. Service history data is somewhat broader because of aircraft assignment to shore stations in some cases rather than squadrons. The descriptive data is generally self-explanatory. For explanation of engine nomenclature, *See* discussion of combat aircraft.

Transport and Training Aircraft Data

Transport Aircraft									
Designation	**First Contract**	**First Flight**	**Last Delivery**	**Number Accepted**	**Manufacturer**	**Models Accepted**	**Base or Squadron Delivery**	**Last Report***	**Description†**
Boeing-314	(Acquired Feb 1942 from Pan AM)			5	Boeing	Boeing 314		End of WWII	M. Flying boat, four WAC R-2600, 1,600 hp each
GV/C-130	6/30/59	6/13/61		187	Lockheed Martin	C-130F, C-130T, C-130G; LC-130F, LC-130B, LC-130R; KC-130; EC-130Q, EC-130E; DC-130A; HC-130R; KC-130J; NC-130H	VMGR-352		M/7 crew. In-flight refueling and transport. Four AL T56-A-16, 4,910 eshp each
JRB/C-45	6/12/40	10/27/40	10/10/44	209	Beech	JRB-1, JRB-2, JRB-3, JRB-4	NAS Anacostia	9/69	M/2 crew. Six passengers, two P&W R-985, 450 hp each
JRC	4/21/43	1943‡	12/20/43	67	Cessna	JRC-1		5/47	M/2 crew. Four or five passenger, two Jacobs R-775, 450 hp each
JRF	4/24/39	11/29/39	12/18/45	256	Grumman	XJ3F-1; JRF-1, JRF-3, JRF-4, JRF-5, JRF-6B	VJ-1	12/58	M/2 or 3 crew. Four to seven passengers, amphibian two P&W R-985, 450 hp each
JRM	6/27/44	11/1/45	4/4/47	5	Martin	JRM-1	VR-2	1/57	M. Flying boat, four WAC R-3350-8, 2,300 hp each
J4F	6/10/42	2/28/44		131	Grumman	J4F-1, J4F-2	NAS New York	8/48	M/2 crew. Three passenger amphibian, two RA L-440, 200 hp each
RY	3/14/44	10/12/45		47	Convair	RY-1, -2, -3	MarFair West	3/49	M/3 crew. 44 passengers, four P&W R-1830-94, 1,350 hp each
R3Y	9/26/50	2/25/52	11/28/56	11	Convair	XP5Y-1; R3Y-1, R3Y-2	VR-2	1/72	M. Nose loading door for vehicles, flying boat, four AL XT40-A-4, 5,500 eshp each
R4D/C-47	9/16/40	2/9/42	5/31/45	609	Douglas	R4D-1 thru R4D-7	BAD-1 (Marine Corps)	11/83	M/3 crew. 27 passengers, two P&W R-1830-92, 1,200 hp each
R4D-8/C-117				100	Douglas	R4D-8	NAS Norfolk 12/51	China Lake 1982	M/3. 30 passengers, Two WAC R-1820-20, 1,475 hp each, converted from earlier R4D versions
R4Q/C-119	4/22/48	9/1/50	25/5/53	99	Fairchild	R4Q-1, R4Q-2	VMR-252	5/75	M/5 crew. 44 passenger, two WAC R-3350-36WA, 3,400 hp each

Transport Aircraft									
Designation	First Contract	First Flight	Last Delivery	Number Accepted	Manufacturer	Models Accepted	Base or Squadron Delivery	Last Report*	Description†
R4Y/C-131	7/26/54	8/31/55	30/12/57	39	Convair	R4Y-1, R4Y-1Z, C-131H	Hq Marine Corps Flt. Sect.	3/88	M/4 crew. 44 passengers, two P&W R-2800-52W, 2,500 hp each
R5C	6/1/48	3/19/43	7/6/45	130	Curtiss	R5C-1	VMJ-3	8/56	M/4 crew. 50 troops, two P&W R-2800-51, 2,000 hp each
R5D/C-54	7/31/42	2/22/43	5/31/45	194	Douglas	R5D-1, R5D-2, R5D-3, R5D-4	VR-1	7/73	M/4 crew. 30 passengers, four P&W R-2000-7, 1,350 hp each
R5O	11/13/39	6/12/42	10/5/43	95	Lockheed	XR5O-1; R5O-1, R5O-2, R5O-3, R5O-4, R5O-5, R5O-6	NAS Jacksonville	6/50	M/2 crew. Four to seven passengers, two WAC R-2800-40, 1,200 hp each
R6D/C-118	8/18/50	6/6/52	27/5/53	65	Douglas	R6D-1, R6D-1Z	VR-3	10/83	M/4 crew. Four P&W R-2800-52W, 2,500 hp each
R7O/R7V	9/26/50	3/11/52‡	5/28/54	55	Lockheed	R7V-1, R7V-1P; R7V-2	VR-7	9/74	M. Accommodates 72 troops, four WAC R-3350-91, 3,250 hp each
C-1				87	Grumman	C-1A (TF-1)	VR-22	4/85	M/2. Accommodates 9 passengers. Designed as COD aircraft. Two WR-1820-82, 1,525 hp each
C-2			2/6/90	39	Grumman	C-2A	VRC-50		M/3. Accommodates 39 passengers. Designed as COD aircraft. Two AL T56-A-8B, 4,050 shp each
C-9				16	McDonnell Douglas	C-9, C-9B (DC-9)	VR-30 NAS Alameda		M. Accommodates 107 passengers. P&W JT8-D-9, 14,500#
C-12				90	Beech/Hawker Beechcraft	UC-12B, -12F, -12M, -12W			M/2 crew. Light passenger and cargo, 2 Pratt & Whitney PT6A-60A engines, each deliver 1050 shaft hp
C-20			12/13/94	7	Gulfstream	C-20D, C-20G	NAF Washington		M/5. Accommodates 14 passengers, two RR Spey Mk 511-8, 11,400# each
C-26B	1998 From other military services			7	Fairchild	C-26D, RC-26D, EC-26D			M/2 crew & 19 passengers. 2 Allied Signal (Garrett) TPE-331 12UAR turboprop engines
UC-35	Accepted 11/99			13	Cessna	UC-35C, UC-35D			M/2 crew & 7 passengers. 2 Pratt & Whitney JT15D-5D
C-37A Gulfstream V	Deployed 2005			4	Gulfstream	C-37A, C-37B			M/3–4 crew & 5–8 passengers. 2 Rolls Royce BR 710-A1 turbofan engines
C-40A	Accepted 4/01			8	Boeing	C-40A	CNARF 5/01		M/4 crew & 121 passengers. 2 CFM56-7 SLST engines
C-45 (See JRB)									
C-47 (See R4D)									
C-54 (See R5D)									
C-117 (See R4D-8)									
C-118 (See R6D)									
C-119 (See R4Q)									
C-130 (See GV)									
C-131 (See R4Y)									

Designation	First Contract	First Flight	Last Delivery	Number Accepted	Manufacturer	Models Accepted	Squadron Delivery	Last Report*	Description†
									Training Aircraft
JN-4		5/10/17	4/11/23	216	Curtiss	JN-4A, -4B, -4H, -6H, -4HG	Marine Advance Base Force, Philadelphia	4/27	B/2. Land; flight and gunnery trainer; 1 Wright-Hispano, 150 hp
N-9		11/16/15	10/28/18	531	Curtiss	N-9H	Miami	8/28	B/2. Water; single float; primary trainer; CAM OXX-6, 100 hp; -9H Hispano-Suiza A 150 hp
NB	2/11/23	1/21/23‡	11/23/25	93	Boeing	NB-1, -2, -3, -4	*Langley* (CV 1)	12/31	B/2. Land, conversion; primary and gunnery trainer; 1 .30 cal. machine gun on Scarff ring; Law J-1, 200 hp; Wright-Hispano E-4, 180 hp
NE		3/16/42	8/9/45	250	Piper	NE-1, -2	NRAB Anacostia	12/47	M/2. Land; primary trainer; CO O-170, 65 hp
NH		1/15/43	3/7/44	205	Howard	NH-1	NAS Atlanta	11/47	M/4. Instrument trainer; P&W R-985 400 hp
NJ		11/16/37	8/28/38	40	North American	NJ-1	NAS Pensacola	8/44	M/2. Basic trainer; fixed under carriage, P&W R-1340-6, 500 hp
NR		8/4/41	10/8/41	100	Ryan	NR-1	NAS Jacksonville	9/43	M/2. Primary trainer; all metal; Kinner R-440-3, 125 hp
NY		5/18/26	2/21/30	292	Consolidated	NY-1, -2, -2A, -3	Pensacola	12/37	B/2. Land, converted; primary trainer; steel tube fuselage, wooden wings; WAC R-790-8, 220 hp
NS				61	Stearman	NS-1		11/44	B/2. Land; primary trainer WAC R-790-8, 200 hp
N2C		7/10/29	12/20/30	54	Curtiss	N2C-1, -2	NRAB Squantum	5/38	B/2. Land; used mainly in reserve training; 1 WAC R-790-8, 200 hp; R-760-94, 240 hp
N2S		9/30/40	3/4/44	3,700	Stearman	N2S-1, -2, -3, -5	NAS Anacostia	6/50	B/2. Land trainer; the most prevalent trainer in WWII; CO R-670-4, 240 hp
N2T		4/16/42	10/11/42	262	Timm	N2T-1	NAS Pensacola	8/44	M/2. Land, primary trainer, plastic bonded plywood construction; CO R-670-4, 229 hp
N3N		10/26/36	1/23/42	998	NAF	N3N-1, -2, -3	NAS Pensacola	10/59	B/2. Land, converted; primary trainer; all fabric covered; WAC R-760-2, 235 hp
SNC				305	Curtiss	SNC-1		10/44	M/2. Land; primary trainer; WAC R-974, 420 hp, all metal retractable landing gear
SNJ		11/8/39	8/27/45	4,024	North American	SNJ-1 thru -6	NAS Pensacola	6/68	M/2. Land; basic trainer; first trainer with retractable landing gear and covered cockpits; 1 P&W R-1340, 550hp
SNV		8/5/41	2/28/44	2,000	Vultee	SNV-1, -2	NAS Corpus Christi	4/46	M/2. Land; basic trainer; retractable landing gear; P&W R-985, 450 hp
T-1 (*See* T2V)									
T-2 (*See* T2J)									
T-6		7/98		109	Raytheon	T-6A, 6B	NAS Pensacola, 11/02		M/2. All-purpose jet trainer. 1 Pratt & Whitney Canada PT-6A-68 turboprop engine, 1,100 hp
T-28		9/26/49‡	10/29/57	1,175	North American	T-28B, T-28C	NATC Patuxent River	4/82	M/2. Land; the first of the standardized trainers for USAF and Navy; WAC R-1820-86, 1425 hp
T-33 (*See* TO/TV)									
T-34		1948‡	6/18/84	423	Beech	T-34A, T-34B, T-34C	NAS Pensacola	10/93	M/2. Land; primary trainer, CON O-470-13, 225 hp
T-39 (*See* T3J)									

Training Aircraft									
Designation	**First Contract**	**First Flight**	**Last Delivery**	**Number Accepted**	**Manufacturer**	**Models Accepted**	**Squadron Delivery**	**Last Report***	**Description†**
T-44				66	Beech	T-44A, 44B			M/2. Land; turboprop pilot training, two 550 shp P&W PT6A-34B engines
T-45		4/80		225	McDonnell Douglas/ Boeing	YT-45A, T-45A, T-45C			M/2. Land; jet trainer; RR F405-RR401 turbofan engine with 5,527 pounds thrust
TO/TV		1944‡	9/29/48	50	Lockheed	TO-1/TV-1	Undetermined	10/57	M/1. Land; advanced jet trainer; AL J33-A-20, 5,200#
TO/TV/T-33		3/22/48‡	1960	698	Lockheed	TO-2/ TV-2/T-33	Muroc	7/74	M/2. Land
TT		3/26/56‡	1957	14	Temco	TT-1	NAAS Saufley Field	10/60	M/2. Land; primary jet trainer; CON J69, 920#
T2J/T-2		2/10/58‡	12/18/74	519	North American	T2J-1; T-2A, -2B, -2C	NATC Patuxent River	6/94	M/2. Land; all-purpose jet trainer; 2 GE 085-GE-4, 2,950# each
T2V/T-1		12/26/57	2/14/58	150	Lockheed	T2V-1/T-1A	NAS Pensacola	7/72	M/2. Land; deck-landing, advanced jet trainer; AL J33-A-24, 6,100#
T3J/T-39				81	North American/ Boeing	T3J-1/T-39D, -39N; CT-39A, -39E, -39G	NAS Pensacola		M/2. Land; twin-jet radar trainer, two 3,000 lb P&W J60P-3

* The dates in this column refer to either a squadron or the Navy's aircraft inventory. If only a date is listed then it refers to the inventory unless a squadron is listed.

† M-monoplane, B-biplane

‡ Aircraft already developed and in operation by Army Air Corps/Air Forces or a commercial entity before being acquired by the Navy.

CHAPTER 4

Helicopters and Tiltrotor V/STOL Aircraft Procured

In basic organization and concept this table generally follows that on combat aircraft; the major difference is that this includes practically all helicopters with which the Navy was involved. Because of the helicopter's capability for tethered flight and low-altitude free flight, first flight data was not always available and was sometimes of uncertain meaning. Because of this, first acceptance was used as being somewhat analogous to first flight of a fixed-wing aircraft. Service history data is somewhat broader than for fixed-wing aircraft to accompany the wider scope of models covered, assignment to experimental squadrons (VX) is reported for models that were not later assigned to operational units. Marine Helicopter Experimental squadron (HMX) is considered to be an operational squadron. The descriptive data is generally self-explanatory. For explanation of engine nomenclature, *See* discussion of combat aircraft (Chapter 2).

Naval Helicopter Data									
Designation	First Contract	First Acceptance	Final Acceptance	Number Accepted	Manufacturer	Models Accepted	Squadron Delivery	Last Report*	Description
DSN	(Redesignated QH-50, *See* H-50)								
H-I	6/14/62	2/64		1,153	Bell	AH-1G,-1J, -1T, -1W, -1Z; TH-1E, -1L; UH-1E, -1L -1N, -1R, -1Y; HH-1K	3/64 VMO-1		Rotor 44' D & tail rotor; observation. One crew; 4 pass., LYT53, 1,150 hp
H-2 (Redesignation of HU2K)									
H-3 (Redesignation of HSS-2)									
H-12 (Hiller and Navy designation for HTE prototype)									
H-13 (Redesignation of HTL)									
H-I9 (Redesignation of HRS-3 and HO4S-3)									
H-23 (Army and Air Force designation and Navy redesignation for HTE)									
H-25 (Redesignation of HUP-2)									
H-34 (Redesignation of HUS and HSS-I)									
H-37 (Redesignation of HR2S)									
H-43 (Redesignation of HUK and HOK)									
H-46	9/29/61	5/62	1/31/77	624	Boeing	HRB-1/ CH-46A, -46D, -46F; UH-46A, -46D	6/64 HMM-265		Tandem rotors, 50' D; assault transport; 3 crew; 17 passenger, 2 GE T58, 1,250 hp
H-50	12/31/58	3/60	10/20/69	633 (1)	Gyrodyne	DSN-1, -3; QH-50C, -50D	1/23/63 *Buck* (DD 761)	1/31/71 QH-50C/D	Coaxial rotors, 20' D; ASW drone; BO T50, 300 hp in QH-50C
H-51				2	Lockheed	XH-51A			Prototype, tri-service evaluation, P&W PT6A turboshaft, 500 shp, rigid rotor 35' D, 2 crew
H-53	2/7/63	5/64		736	Sikorsky	CH-53A, -53D, -53E; HH-53B, -53C; RH-53D; MH-53E	11/2/66 HMH-463		Rotor 72' D and tail rotor; assault transport; 38 passenger or 4 ton; 2 GE T64, 2,850 hp

Designation	First Contract	First Acceptance	Final Acceptance	Number Accepted	Manufacturer	Models Accepted	Squadron Delivery	Last Report*	Description
H-57	1968	10/10/68		140	Bell	TH-57A, -57B, -57C	11/10/68 HT-8		Trainer, 5 place; rotor 33'4'' D and tail rotor 5'5''; -57C powered by 1 Allison 250-C-20J Gas turbine, 317 shp
H-58	From Army			14	Bell	OH-58A, -58C	Naval Test Pilot School		Rotor 35'4'', training, 2 crew, 1 Allison T63-A-700 turboshaft, 317 shp (236 kW)
H-60	2/78	3/31/80		1,222	Sikorsky	SH-60B, -60F, -60R; HH-60A, -60S, -60J, -60H; UH-60A, -60L; YCH-60; VH-60A, -60N; CH-60, -60S; MH-60S, -60R	9/28/83 HSL-41		LAMPS MK III, ASW, anti-surface warfare, surveillance, communications relay, combat search and rescue, naval gunfire support and logistics support, rotor 53'7'' D and tail rotor. 3 crew. 2 GE-401T700, 1,284 hp each
H-72	10/08	8/26/09		5	EADS North America	UH-72A	Naval Test Pilot School		Rotor 36.1' and tail rotor 6.4', light utility & training, 2 crew plus 8 passengers, 2 Turbomeca Arriel 1E2 tuboshaft engines providing 550kW of take-off power and 516kW continuous power

XHCH-1 (Prototype for ship-to-shore crane, Bureau Numbers 138654-138656 cancelled)

HJD (Initial designation of HJH, *See* XHJH-1)

XHJH-1	3/1946	3/25/49	3/25/49	1	McDonnell	XHJD-1			Prototype, twin rotor with 2 R-985s, use for research and development

HJP (XHJP-1 was prototype for HUP-1)

HJS	11/1947			2	Sikorsky	XHJS-1			Prototype for utility-rescue, 3 crew, R-9 520 hp
HNS	2/20/43	10/43	12/44	68	Sikorsky	HNS-1	11/43 NAS New York	12/31/47 VX-3, HNS-1	Rotor 38' D plus tail rotor; 1st USN helo. WR R-550, 2,00 hp
HOE	11/11/53	6/23/55	6/23/55	3	Hiller	HOE-1	NATC R&D Pax River	4/1957 NATC R&D Pax River	Utility, rotor-tip ramjets, 2 crew
HOK (H-43†)	6/26/50	4/53	12/57	83	Kaman	HOK-1	4/12/56 VMO-1	5/31/65 VMO-2, OH-43D	Side-by-side rotors, 47' D; utility, 2 place; CO R-975, 525 hp
HOS	3/20/43	9/44	1/46	3 102	Sikorsky Nash-Kelvinator	XHOS-1 HOS-1	10/44 NAS New York	1/31/48 VX-3, HOS-1	Rotor 38' D and tail rotor; utility, 2-place; FR 0-435, 235 hp
HO2S	6/22/43	12/45	12/45	44	Sikorsky	HO2S-1	2/46 NAS New York	5/31/46 CGAS Eliz. City, HO2S-1	Rotor 48' D and tail rotor; utility and rescue; 2 crew, 2 passenger; P&W R-985, 450 hp

Designation	First Contract	First Acceptance	Final Acceptance	Number Accepted	Manufacturer	Models Accepted	Squadron Delivery	Last Report*	Description
HO3S	9/27/46	11/46	1/50	92	Sikorsky	HO3S-1	12/47 VU-7	11/30/54 HU-1, HO4S-3	Rotor 48' D and tail rotor; utility, 4-place; P&W R-985, 450 hp
HO4S-3 (H-19†)	4/28/50	8/50	1/58	129	Sikorsky	HO4S-1, -2, -3, -3G	12/27/50 HU-2	12/31/60 HU-4, HO4S-3	Rotor 53' D and tail rotor; ASW, observation and rescue; crew 2 or 3. P&W R-1340, 600 hp; WAC R-1300, 800 hp in -3
HO5S	6/30/50	2/52	2/53	79	Sikorsky	HO5S-1	7/1/52 VMO-1	6/30/57 VMO-1, HO5S-1	Rotor 33' D and tail rotor; observation, liaison and utility; 5 place; ACM O-425, 245 hp
HRB (Initial designation for H-46, See H-46)									
HRH				0	McDonnell	XHRH-1 cancelled			Heavy assault, BuNo. 133736-133738 cancelled
HRP	2/1/44	6/47	12/50	82	Piasecki	XHRP-1; HRP-1	4/48 HU-2	2/28/53 HS-3, HRP-1	Tandem rotors 41' D; 1st tandem configuration; 2 crew, 8 passenger, P&W R-1340, 600 hp
HRS-3 (H-19†)	8/2/50	3/51	11/57	271	Sikorsky	HRS-1, -2, -3	4/7/51 HMR-161	2/28/69 HC-5, CH-19E	Rotor 53' D and tail rotor; assault transport; 2 crew, 10 passenger; P&W R-1340, 600 to 800 hp
HR2S (H-37†)	5/9/51	10/53	2/59	59	Sikorsky	HR2S-1, -1W	3/20/57 HMR(M)-461	3/31/66 HMH-462 CH-37C	Rotor 72' D and tail rotors; assault transport; 2 crew, 20 passenger; 2 P&W R-2800, 2,100 hp
HSL	6/28/50	10/53	10/56	51	Bell	XHSL-1, HSL-1		9/59	Tandem rotors, 51'6" D; ASW search or attack; 2 or 3 crew; P&W R-2800, 1,900 hp
HSS-1 (H-34†)	6/30/52	2/54	4/66	385	Sikorsky	XHSS-1, HSS-1, SH-34J	8/55 HS-3	3/31/74 UH-34D	Rotor 56' D and tail rotor ASW; 2 to 4 crew; WAC R-1820, 1,525 hp
HSS-2 (H-3†)	12/24/57	3/59	11/26/75	396	Sikorsky	HSS-2/ SH-3A, SH-3D, HSS-2Z/ VH-3A, -3D; CH-3B, -3E	6/61	5/96	Rotor 59' D and tail rotor; all weather ASW, "seaworthy hull", 4 crew, 2 GE T58, 1,050 hp
HTE (H-12/ H-23†)	4/17/50	5/50	8/51	108	Hiller	UH-12A; HTE-1, -2	1/19/51 HTU-1	10/31/52 HTU-1, HTE-2	Rotor 35' D and tail rotor; training and utility, 3 place; FR O-335, 200 hp in HTE-2
HTK	9/5/50	11/51	10/53	29	Kaman	HTK-1	1/28/53 HU-2	11/31/55 HU-2, HTK	Side-by-side rotors, 40' D; trainer and general utility, 3 place; LYO-435, 255 hp
HTL (H-13†)	6/20/46	2/47	7/59	187	Bell	HTL-1, -2, -3, -4, -5, -6, -7	4/48 HU-2	6/30/73 UH-13P	Rotor 35' D and tail rotor; trainer and general utility; 2 or 3 place; ACM O-325, 178-200 hp, LY O-435, 240 hp in -7
HU (Redesignated H-1, See H-1)									

Designation	First Contract	First Acceptance	Final Acceptance	Number Accepted	Manufacturer	Models Accepted	Squadron Delivery	Last Report*	Description
HUK (H-43†)	12/27/56	5/58	12/58	24	Kaman	HUK-1	8/1/58 HU-2	4/30/65 VMO-2, UH-43C	Side by side rotors, 50' D; cargo and rescue; 2 crew, 3 passenger; P&W R-1340, 600 hp
HU2K (H-2†)	11/29/57	4/59	4/28/93	256	Kaman	HU2K-1/ UH-2A, -2B; SH-2F, -2B	12/18/62 HU-2	6/94	Rotor 44' D and tail rotor; 2 crew, 4 passenger; GE T58, 1,050 hp; tandem engines prototyped in a -2B
HUL	4/2/55	11/55	3/59	30	Bell	HUL-1, -1G	1/7/57 HU-2	6/30/73 UH-13P	Rotor 37' D and tail rotor; transport and utility; 1 crew, 3 passenger, LY O-435, 240 hp
HUP-2 (H-25†)	2/8/46	1/49	6/54	476	Piasecki	XHJP-1; HUP-1, -2,- 2S, H-25A	1/11/51 HU-2	8/31/64 VU-1, HU-1, UH-25B	Tandem rotors, 35' D; ASW and utility; 3 crew, 4 passenger, CO R-975, 550 hp
HUS (H-34†)	10/15/54	1/57	12/30/68	549	Sikorsky	HUS-1/ UH-34D; HUS-1A, -1G, -1Z; CH-34A, -34C	2/5/57 HMR(L)- 363	3/31/74 UH-34D	Rotor 56' D and tail rotor; cargo transport; 2 crew, 12 passenger or 2 ton of cargo; WAC R-1820, 1,525 hp
K-225	9/26/49	3/50	6/50	3	Kaman	K-225 (K-5)	6/20/50 NAS Patuxent River	5/55	Side by side rotors 40' D; LY O-435, 225 hp. K-5 was first turbine powered helo; BO-502 turbine, 175 hp

R-4 (HNS-1 obtained from Army, YR-4 and YR-4B; Sikorsky model VS-316A)

R-5 (HO2S obtained from Army)

R-6 (HOS-1 obtained from Army, R-7A and B)

* Dates in this column through 1969 refer to squadrons. After 1969, these dates refer to inventory unless a squadron designation is listed.
† This is the new designation assigned the helicopter in 1962.

Designation	First Contract	First Acceptance	Final Acceptance	Number Accepted	Manufacturer	Models Accepted	Squadron Delivery	Last Report	Description
V-22	6/7/96*	5/24/99†		129	Bell-Boeing	MV-22B	2006, VMM-263		Rotor/Wingspan 84'8'', combat assault and assault transport, 3 crew and 24 troops, 2 Rolls-Royce Liberty AE1107C engines, each deliver 6,200 shp

* First Lot Contract for Fleet MV-22: 7 Jun 1996 (N00019-96-C-0054 [Basic])
† First Acceptance of Lot 1 First Fleet MV-22 Aircraft DD250 Date: 24 May 1999 (BuNo. 165433)

CHAPTER 5
Drones and Missiles Procured

Pilotless Aircraft/Drones/Targets			
New and Old Model Designation	**Manufacturer**	**Popular Name**	**Description**
—	Bristol Siddeley Corp/LTV	Jindivik	Guided missile target drone
—	—	Glimps	ASW pilotless plane, released from blimps, never used
AQM-34B/KDA-1	Ryan	Firebee	Subsonic target drone
AQM-34C/KDA-4	Ryan	Firebee	Subsonic target drone
AQM-37A/KD2B-1	Beech	Challenger	Air-launched supersonic target missile
AQM-37C	Beech	Jayhawk	Supersonic missile target
AQM-38B/RP-78	Northrop Ventura	—	Army contract, missile target
AQM-81B	Teledyne Ryan	Firebolt	Navy modified AQM-81A target missile
AQM-127	LTV Corp.	SLAT	Supersonic low-altitude target
BQM-6C/KDU-1	Chance Vought	—	BuAer managed, target drone version of Regulus I
BQM-34E/KDA series	Ryan	Firebee II	Navy version of BQM-34A, supersonic target drone
BQM-34S	Ryan	Firebee II	Upgraded BQM-34E with integrated target control
BQM-34T	Ryan	Firebee II	BQM-34E modified with transponder set and autopilot
BQM-74C	Northrop	Chukar III	Recoverable, remotely controlled, gunnery target
BQM-74E	Northrop	—	Subscale, subsonic aerial target drone
BQM-126A	Beech	—	Variable-speed target missile
CQM-10A	NAVAIR	BOMARC	Converted Air Force weapon system to missile target
F.B./N-9	—	Flying Bomb	N-9 configured as a Flying Bomb
F.B.	Sperry-Curtiss	Flying Bomb	
F.B.	Witteman-Lewis	Flying Bomb	
KAQ	Fairchild Engine & A/c Co.	—	Pilotless aircraft
KAY	Consolidated Vultee A/c Co.	—	Ship-to-air pilotless aircraft
KDA-1 (BQM-34 series)	Ryan	Firebee I	Target aircraft
KDB (See MQM-39A)	Beech	—	
KDC-1	Curtiss-Wright Corp.	—	Mid-wing monoplane target, not procured
KDD-1 (See KDH-1)	McDonnell	Katydid	
KDG-1	Globe	Snipe	Mid-wing monoplane for gunnery practice
KDG-2	Globe	Snipe	Similar to KDG-1 except for 24-volt system
KDH-1/TD2D-1/KDD-1	McDonnell	Katydid	Remotely controlled aerial target
KDM-1	Martin	Plover	High-wing air launched, development of PTV-N-2
KDR-1/TD4D-1	Radioplane	Quail	Similar to TD3D-1, Army model OQ-17
KDR-2	Radioplane	Quail	Similar to KDR-1 except structural changes
KDT-1	Temco	—	Solid propellant rocket-powered drone
KDU-1	—	—	Target drone for guided missile evaluation firings
KD2C-1	Curtiss-Wright Corp.	Skeet	Pilotless aircraft target drone
KD2G-1	Globe	Firefly	Mid-wing, all metal, twin tail, monoplane target
KD2G-2	Globe	Firefly	Similar to KD2G-1
KD2N-1	NAMU	—	High mid-wing monoplane, canard design
KD2R-1	Radioplane	Quail	Wooden wings, metal monocoque fuselage target drone
KD2R-2	Radioplane	Quail	Similar to KD2R-1 except 28-volt radio and stabilized
KD2R-2E	Radioplane	Quail	KD2R-2 modified system for test at NAMTC
KD2R-3	Radioplane	Quail	Similar XKD2R-4 except engine and C-2A stabilization

Pilotless Aircraft/Drones/Targets			
New and Old Model Designation	**Manufacturer**	**Popular Name**	**Description**
KD2U	Chance Vought Corp.	—	Regulus II conversion to supersonic drone
KD3G-1	Globe	Snipe	Same as KDG-1 except for engine
KD3G-2	Globe	Snipe	Same as KD3G-1 with radio control receiver 28-volt
KD4G-1	Globe	Quail	High all-metal wing gunnery trainer
KD4G-2	Globe	Quail	Similar to KD4G-1 except engine and higher speed
KD4R-1	Radioplane	—	Rocket propelled target drone
KD5G-1	Globe	—	High-wing and twin-tail aircraft target
KGN/KUN	NAMU	—	High-wing monoplane, canard design target drone
KGW/KUW	—	—	Pilotless aircraft
KSD/KUD	—	—	Pilotless aircraft
KU2N-1/KA2N-1	NAMU	—	High mid-wing monoplane, canard design, liquid rocket
KU3N-1/KA3N-1	NAMU	—	High mid-wing monoplane, conventional, liquid rocket
KU3N-2/KA3N-2	NAMU	—	Similar to KU3N-1
KUD-1/LBD-1/KSD-1/ BQM-6C	McDonnell	Regulus I	BuAer managed, target drone version of Regulus I
KUM	Glenn Martin Company	—	Pilotless aircraft for testing ramjet power plant
KUN-1/KGN-1	NAMU	—	High-wing monoplane, canard design target drone
LBE-1	Gould/Pratt-Read & Co.	Glomb	Expendable bomb-carrying guided assault glider
LBP	Pratt-Read & Co.	Glomb	Was scheduled for development
LBT-1	Taylorcraft	Glomb	Expendable bomb-carrying guided glider
LNS-1	Schweizer	Glomb	Glider test vehicle for Glomb
LNT-1	NAF	Glomb	Assault glider, television controlled
LRN-1	NAF	Glomb	Large explosive carrying glider
LRW-1	—	Glomb	Test vehicle for Glomb
MQM-8	Bendix Aerospace	Vandal/Vandal ER	Reconfigured Talos for simulating cruise missile
MQM-15A/KD2U-1	Chance Vought	Regulus II	BuAer program, Regulus II conversion to target drone
MQM-36A/KD2R-5	Northrop Ventura	—	Small propeller driven target drone
MQM-39A/KDB-1	Beech	—	
MQM-61A	Beech	—	
MQM-74C	Northrop	Chukar II	Turbojet, remotely controlled drone, target training
RP-78	Northrop Ventura	—	Army contract, missile target
TD2C-1	Culver	Turkey	Target drone for aircraft and antigunnery training
TD2D-1/XTD2D-1	McDonnell	—	Remotely controlled aerial target, resojet powered
TD2N-2/TD3N-1	NAF/NAMU	—	Target aircraft
TD2R	Interstate	—	Assault drone, program dropped
TD3C-1	Culver	—	Target drone for aircraft and antiaircraft training
TD3D-1	Frankfort Sailplane Co.	—	Target drone, similar to TDD-3, Army model OQ-16
TD3N-1	NAF	—	Target aircraft
TD3R-1	Interstate	—	Torpedo carrying remote-controlled assault drone
TD4D-1	Radioplane	—	Target drone, Army model OQ-17
TDC-2	Culver Air	—	Target drone
TDD-1/2/3	Radioplane/Globe	Denny	Remotely controlled aerial target, gunnery practice
TDD-4	Radioplane/Globe	Denny	Same as TDD-3 except for engine
TDN	NAF	—	WWII assault drone
TDR	Interstate	—	WWII assault drone
XBDR-1	Interstate	—	WWII jet-powered, television-directed assault drone
XBQ-3	Fairchild Corp.	—	Assault drone, Army Air Corps controllable bomb

Pilotless Aircraft/Drones/Targets			
New and Old Model Designation	**Manufacturer**	**Popular Name**	**Description**
XKD3C-1	Curtiss	—	Similar to KD2C-2 with engine change, no rudder
XKD6G-1	Globe	—	Similar to KD2G-2, except for engine, new fuselage
XKD6G-2	Globe	—	Similar to KD6G-1, except for engine
XQM-40A/KD6G-2	Globe Corp.		
XUC-1K	Culver	—	XUC-1 aircraft converted to target drone
YAQM-128A	TBD	—	Air-launched, supersonic subscale aerial target
YBQM-126A	TBD/Beechcraft	—	Supersonic subscale target
ZBQM-90A	TBD	—	High-altitude, supersonic aerial target

Note: The above list does not include aircraft modified for use as drones or towed targets.

Unmanned Aerial Vehicles (UAV)/Unmanned Combat Aerial Vehicles (UCAV)/Remotely Piloted Vehicles (RPV)			
New and Old Model Designation	**Manufacturer**	**Popular Name**	**Description**
Buster UAV	Mission Technologies Inc.	Buster	A small low-audible biplane UAV that carries an electro-optical sensor payload
BQM-145A	Teledyne Ryan	Peregrine	Reconnaissance drone
BQM-147A	RPV Industries	—	Remotely/automatically piloted vehicle
DSN/QH-50C	Gyrodyne	Dash	Remotely controlled ASW helicopter
MQ-4C/RQ-4B/BAMS UAS	Northrop Grumman	Global Hawk	Provides persistent maritime ISR
MQ-8A	Northrop Grumman	Fire Scout	RQ-8A evolution toward an increased, multi-functional role and will provide critical situational awareness, intelligence, surveillance, reconnaissance, and targeting data
MQ-9A	General Atomics	Reaper	Surveillance
RPV/RQ-2A	AAI Corp	Pioneer	Remotely piloted vehicle with television camera
RQ-4A/BAMS-D	Northrop Grumman	Global Hawk	Maritime and littoral intelligence, surveillance, and reconnaissance mission
RQ-8A	Northrop Grumman	Fire Scout	Surveillance
RQ-15A	DRS Technologies Inc.	Neptune	Surveillance and dropping of small payloads
STUAS	Insitu Inc.		Under development. Mission expectations are to provide intelligence coverage, surveillance, reconnaissance, and communications relay
X-47B/UCAS-D	Northrop Grumman		Unmanned combat aircraft/aerial vehicle. A tailless fighter-sized unmanned aircraft capable of providing persistent, penetrating surveillance, and penetrating strike capability in high-threat areas. Still undergoing testing

Aircraft Configured as Drones/Flying Bombs, Early Period to 1945	
Designation	**Comments**
BG-1	Pre-WWII aircraft configured as radio controlled drone
F4B	Configured as a drone
F4U	Configured as a drone
F6F	Configured as a drone
JH-1	Modified aircraft, Stearman Hammond
N-9 F.B.	Experiments to convert an N-9 training plane into a flying bomb, 1917
N2C	1937, first successful pilotless aircraft flight
NT	Modified training plane, New Standard Aircraft Corp
O2U	Configured as a drone
O3U	Configured as a drone
PB4Y	Project Anvil, radio & television controlled PB4Y loaded with torpex, flown out of England against a German target, one attack flown with limited success

Aircraft Configured as Drones/Flying Bombs, Early Period to 1945	
Designation	Comments
PBJ	Configured as a drone
SB2C	Configured as a drone
SBD	Configured as a drone
SBU	Configured as a drone
SF-1	Configured as a drone
SNB	Configured as a drone
SNV	Configured as a drone
SO3C	Matson Navigation Company converted the SO3C planes into target drones
Sperry-Curtiss F.B.	Flying Bomb developed from a Curtiss Company Speed Scout plane, WWI
TBM	Configured as a drone
TG-2	NAF converted a TG-2 into a radio-controlled plane capable of carrying a torpedo; experiments conducted by VU-3
VE-7H	1924 experiment with radio-controlled VE-7
Witteman-Lewis F.B.	BuOrd contract with company to design a flying bomb more successful than Sperry-Curtiss F.B., airframe similar to Speed Scout, tests conducted 1919–1921

Air-to-Ground/Air-to-Surface Missiles			
New and Old Model Designation	Manufacturer	Popular Name	Description
—	BuOrd/BuAer/Zenith/G.E.	Pelican/Dryden Bomb	Glide bomb, terminated late 1944
2.75-inch Rocket	NOTS/NWC China Lake	Mighty Mouse/FFAR	Folding-fin aircraft rocket (FFAR), numerous Mks and Mods for this series
5-inch Rocket	—	HVAR/Holy Moses	Aircraft rocket, developed during WWII, numerous Mks and Mods for this series
30.5-inch Rocket	NOTS/NWC China Lake	BOAR	Bombardment Aircraft Rocket, a stand-off weapon
AGM-12A/ASM-N-7	Martin/Maxson	Bullpup	Tactical air-to-surface short-range radio-controlled
AGM-12B/ASM-N-7A	Martin/Maxson	Bullpup	Upgraded AGM-12A, radio-link command guidance
AGM-12C/ASM-N-7B	Martin	Bullpup	Upgraded AGM-12B
AGM-45A/ASM-N-10	Texas Instruments/Sperry Farragut	Shrike	Tactical missile used to destroy radar targets, developed by NOTS
AGM-45B	Texas Instruments/Sperry Farragut	Shrike	Upgraded AGM-45A
AGM-53A/ASM-N-11	North American/Rockwell/NWC	Condor	Long-range, electro-optical guided missile, cancelled
AGM-53B	North American/Rockwell/NWC	Condor	Upgraded AGM-53A with EMI capability, not completed
AGM-65E/F/G	Hughes	Maverick	Navy version of AGM-65; TV-, laser- or IR-guidance
AGM-78A/B/C/D	General Dynamics	Standard ARM	Tactical, antiradiation missile, upgrades listed
AGM-83A	NWC	Bulldog	Used parts of AGM-12A, laser guided
AGM-84A/C/D	McDonnell Douglas/Boeing	Harpoon	Air-to-surface missile designed to destroy ships, upgrades listed
AGM-84E SLAM	McDonnell Douglas	Harpoon/SLAM	Standoff land-attack missile variant of Harpoon
AGM-84K	Boeing	SLAM-ER	Standoff land-attack missile variant of the AGM-84A/C/E
AGM-86B	—	ALCM	Air-launched cruise missile, See AGM-109L Tomahawk
AGM-87A	NWC/G.E.	FOCUS I/FOCUS II	Sidewinder AIM-9B modified for air-to-surface use
AGM-88A/B/C	NWC/Texas Instruments/Ford Aero	HARM	Antiradiation missile used against surface radar, upgrades listed
AGM-88E	Alliant Techsystems	AARGM	HARM (AGM-88A/B/C) was the predecessor. Air-to-ground missile employed for destruction of enemy air defenses
AGM-109C	General Dynamics	MRASM	Medium-range missile, never completed development

Air-to-Ground/Air-to-Surface Missiles

New and Old Model Designation	Manufacturer	Popular Name	Description
AGM-109L	General Dynamics	Tomahawk	Medium-range, air-launched, land/sea attack missile
AGM-114B	Rockwell	Hellfire	Helicopter missile, with various capabilities
AGM-114E	U.S. Army Missile Command	Hellfire	AGM-114B modified with digital autopilot
AGM-114K	Lockheed Martin	Hellfire	Variant of AGM-114B
AGM-114M	Lockheed Martin	Hellfire	Variant of AGM-114B, for military operations in urban terrain (MOUT) targets
AGM-114N	Lockheed Martin	Hellfire	Variant of AGM-114B, for use against MOUT targets
AGM-114P	Lockheed Martin	Hellfire	Variant of AGM-114B, for high-altitude launch trajectories
AGM-114Q	Lockheed Martin	Hellfire	Variant of AGM-114B, training version
AGM-114R	Lockheed Martin	Hellfire II	Variant of AGM-114B
AGM-119B	Norsk Forsvarsteknologi	Penguin Mk-2	AGM-119A, with modified warhead, fuze, rocket motor
AGM-122	NWC China Lake/Motorola	Sidearm	Sidewinder antiradiation missile, built from AIM-9C and designed to attack radar-directed air defense systems, variations of AGM-122 developed
AGM-123A	NWC	Skipper	Modified laser-guided bomb, with Shrike rocket motor
AGM-136A	Northrop Corp.	Tacit Rainbow ARM	Antiradiation missile, long range, terminated
AGM-154A	Raytheon	JSOW	Joint Standoff Weapon, air-to-surface for use against fixed and relocateable soft targets
AGM-154B	Raytheon	JSOW	Effective against mobile area targets
AGM-154C	Raytheon	JSOW	Blast/fragmentation/penetrator effective against fixed-point and hardened tactical targets
AQM-41A/AUM-N-2	Fairchild	Petrel/Kingfisher C	Air-to-underwater/surface tactical guided missile
ASM-2/ASM-N-2	Nat'l Bureau of Standards	Bat-0	Glider operational missile
ASM-N-2A	Nat'l Bureau of Standards	Bat-1	Similar to ASM-N-2
JDAM	Boeing	JDAM	Joint Direct Attack Munition, guided air-to-surface weapon
SLAM-ER	Boeing	SLAM-ER	Long-range, air-launched precision land- and sea-attack cruise missile
XASM-N-4/XASM-4	Eastman/BuOrd	Dove	Stand-off delivery missile, never operational
XASM-N-5	NADC	Gorgon V	Glide offensive missile
XASM-N-8/XASM-8/XM-17	Temco Aircraft Corp.	Corvus	Air-to-surface attack missile, never operational
XAUM-2	Bureau of Standards	Petrel/Kingfisher C	
XAUM-N-4/XAUM-4	Bureau of Standards	Diver/Kingfisher D	
XAUM-N-6/XAUM-6	Bureau of Standards	Puffin/Kingfisher F	
XSUM-N-2	National Bureau of Standards (NBS)	Grebe/Kingfisher E	Member of the Kingfisher missile projects
YAGM-114B	Rockwell	Hellfire	Navy version of AGM-114A, antiarmor missile

Note: The above list does not include training missiles, i.e. ATMs, CATMs, or DATMs.

Surface-to-Surface/Surface-to-Ship Missiles and Special Category Rockets

New and Old Model Designation	Manufacturer	Popular Name	Description
—	—	Albatross	Ship-to-ship missile
—	Aerojet-General Corp.	Aerobee-Hi	Similar to Aerobee, a vertical sounding rocket
—	Applied Physics Lab	Triton	Program cancelled in 1957
—	BuAer/BuOrd/NBS/NAOTS	Regal	Experimental program, air-launched Regulus
—	Consolidated-Vultee	Old Rippy	Automatic FM homing, pulse-jet, ship-to-ship

Surface-to-Surface/Surface-to-Ship Missiles and Special Category Rockets

New and Old Model Designation	Manufacturer	Popular Name	Description
RGM-6A/SSM-8/SSM-N-8	Chance Vought	Regulus I	BuAer managed program
RGM-6B/SSM-N-8A	Chance Vought	Regulus I	BuAer managed program
RGM-15A/SSM-N-9	Chance Vought/LTV Aerospace	Regulus II	Surface-to-surface missile developed by BuAer
RIM-7	BuWps/Raytheon	Seaspar/Sea Sparrow	Sparrow III used in a surface-to-surface or SAM mode
RTV-N-8/RTV-8/XASR-1	BuOrd/Douglas Aircraft Co.	Aerobee	A liquid-fueled rocket for upper atmosphere research
RTV-N-15	NADC	Pollux	Also known as Gorgon IIC, See CTV-N-2, test vehicle
XSSM-N-6/XSSM-6/PA-VII	Grumman	Rigel	Missile fired from surface ship against land targets
XSSM-N-9	Applied Physics Lab	Lacrosse	

Note: Surface-to-surface missiles designed primarily for ship-based operations, such as the Taurus, Talos, Tartar, Terrier, and Standard Missile have not been included in the above list.

Surface-to-Air and Special Launch Test Missiles or Rockets

New and Old Model Designation	Manufacturer	Popular Name	Description
—	—	Arrow Shell	See Zeus (XSAM-N-8)
—	NADS	Gorgon IIB	High mid-wing monoplane, canard design, turbojet
—	NAMU	Gorgon IIIB	Conventional airframe with turbo jet, eliminated
CTV-2/CTV-N-2/KGN-1/KUN-1	NADC	Gorgon IIC	Monoplane canard design, pulse jet, ship-to-shore
CTV-4/CTV-N-4/KA2N-1	NADC	Gorgon IIA	Monoplane, canard design with rocket, also KU2N-1
CTV-8/RTV-6/XPM	Navy/Applied Physics Lab	Bumblebee	Program led to development of Tartar, Terrier, Talos, and Typhon. Typhon was cancelled
CTV-N-6/KA3N-1/KU3N-1	NADC	Gorgon IIIA	High mid-wing monoplane, conventional design, rocket
CTV-N-9/KAQ-1/XSAM-2	Fairchild	Lark	Ship-to-air guided missile, used wing flaps
CTV-N-9a/b/c	Fairchild	Lark	Ship-to-air guided missile, test vehicle
CTV-N-10/KAY-1/XSAM-4	Consolidated Vultee Aircraft	Lark	Ship-to-air, variable incidence wings (test vehicle)
KAN-1	NAMU	Little Joe	Ship-launched, use against aircraft suicide attacks
KAN-2	NAMU	Little Joe	Similar to KAN-1, never operational
KUD-1/RTV-2 (See RTV-N-2)	—	Gargoyle	
KUW-1 (See NTV-N-2)	USAF procurement	Loon	Test vehicle
LTV-N-2/LTV-2/KGW-1	Willys-Overland/AAF	Loon	Similar to German V-1, Launching Test Vehicle
PTV-N-2/PTV-2/KUM-1	Martin	Gorgon IV	Vehicle for testing subsonic ramjet engine
RTV-N-2/LBD-1/KSD-1	McDonnell	Gargoyle	Low-wing monoplane V-tail, aerial bomb
RTV-N-4/KA3N-2/KU3N-2	NADC	Gorgon III-C	Similar to CTV-6, dual rockets, conventional design
TD2N/KDN-1	NAMU	Gorgon	Monoplane, conventional design, turbo jet
TD3N-1/KD2N-1	NADS	Gorgon	Canard, resojet power plant, similar to Gorgon IIC
XSAM-6 (See XSAM-N-6)	—	Bumblebee	
XSAM-N-6	Navy/Applied Physics Lab	Triton/Bumblebee II	Program cancelled
XSAM-N-8	NOL	Zeus	

Air-to-Air Missiles			
New and Old Model Designation	**Manufacturer**	**Popular Name**	**Description**
—	—	Lady Bug	Short-range adaption of German X-4
—	NELC/Hughes Aircraft	Brazo/Pave ARM	Antiradiation missile
AAM-N-3	Douglas	Sparrow II	Production version of YAAM-N-3
ADM-141A	Brunswick Defense Corp.		Air-launched decoy to create a false radar image
ADM-141B	Brunswick Defense Corp.		Air-launched decoy that dispenses chaff
AEM-54A	Hughes	Phoenix	AIM-54A with telemetry evaluation kit
AEM-54B	Hughes	Phoenix	AIM-54A, telemetry equipment, missile flight evaluations
AIM-7A/AAM-N-2/KAS-1	Sperry	Sparrow I	Short range beam-rider missile
AIM-7B/AAM-N-3	Douglas	Sparrow II	Cancelled
AIM-7C/AAM-N-6	Raytheon	Sparrow III	Semi-active radar homing, CW seeker radar homing, mid range
AIM-7D/E/F/M/AAM-N-6A/B	Raytheon	Sea Sparrow/ Sparrow III	Supersonic launch version, upgrades listed
AIM-7P	Raytheon		Upgraded AIM-7
AIM-9A/AAM-N-7	Philco	Sidewinder I	
AIM-9B/AAM-N-7	Philco/General Electric	Sidewinder 1A	1A supersonic, homing weapon, passive infrared
AIM-9C/AAM-N-7	Motorola	Sidewinder 1C-SARAH	Semi-active radar guided
AIM-9D/AAM-N-7	Philco/Raytheon	Sidewinder 1C-IRAH	IR upgraded AIM-9B, infrared homing radar guiding
AIM-9G	Raytheon	Sidewinder	Upgraded AIM-9D
AIM-9H	Raytheon (GCG only)	Sidewinder	Upgraded AIM-9G with solid-state guidance control
AIM-9J	Philco	Sidewinder	Upgraded AIM-9E
AIM-9L/M/N/P/S	Raytheon	Sidewinder	Upgrades listed
AIM-9R	NWC	Sidewinder	Cancelled
AIM-9X	Raytheon	Sidewinder	Upgrade
AIM-54A/AAM-N-11/AIM-54C	Hughes	Phoenix	Long-range, tactical, air-to-air missile, upgrades listed
AIM-120A	Raytheon	AMRAAM	Advanced medium-range, beyond visual range combat
AIM-120C	Raytheon	AMRAAM	Improved AIM-120A
AIM-120D	Raytheon	AMRAAM	Improved AIM-120C
XAIM-95A	NWC China Lake	Agile	Short-range, for aerial combat, cancelled

Note: The above list does not include training versions or electronic monitoring designations, i.e. ATMs, CAEMs, and DATMs.

Experimental or Prototype Air-to-Air Missiles			
New and Old Model Designation	**Manufacturer**	**Popular Name**	**Description**
RAAM-N-2A	Sperry	Sparrow I	Converted AAM-N-2 Sparrow I, R&D test missile
RAAM-N-2B	Sperry	Sparrow IA	Converted AAM-N-2, R&D test missile
XAAM-N-4/RV-N-16	Martin	Oriole	Long-range antiaircraft, active radar seeker
XAAM-N-5	MIT/BuOrd	Meteor	
XAAM-N-10	Bendix Aviation Corp.	Eagle/Missileer	Long-range air-to-air high-performance missile
XAIM-54C	Hughes	Phoenix	Experimental AIM-54C with digital technology
YAAM-N-3	Douglas	Sparrow II	Preproduction version of XAAM-N-3
YAIM-7F	Raytheon	Sparrow	Improved version of AIM-7E
YAIM-7G	Raytheon	Sparrow	Similar to YAIM-7F, with modifications

Experimental or Prototype Air-to-Air Missiles

New and Old Model Designation	Manufacturer	Popular Name	Description
YAIM-54C	Hughes	Phoenix	Prototype AIM-54C
YAIM-120A	Hughes		Prototype AIM-120A
ZAIM-9K	Raytheon	Sidewinder	Upgraded AIM-9H

Guided Weapons, Air-to-Ground

New and Old Model Designation	Manufacturer	Popular Name	Description
2-inch FFAR	NOTS	Gimlet	Air-launched rocket development
5-inch FFAR	NOTS China Lake	Zuni	Aircraft rocket, replaced the HVAR/Holy Moses
AGM-62A	NWC/Martin Marietta	Walleye I Mk 1	An electro-optical glide weapon, passive homing
—	NWC/Martin Marietta	Walleye I Mk 22	Similar to Walleye I, with RF data link
—	NWC/Martin Marietta	Walleye II Mk 5/ Fat Albert	Similar to Walleye I, with larger warhead
—	NWC/Martin Marietta	Walleye II Mk 13	Similar to Walleye II, with RF data link
—	NWC	Paveway II	Laser-guided bomb

How to Read Missile Designations
Missile Designations (Pre-1962). Alphabetical Symbols Used in Missile Designations

Pilotless Aircraft/Target Drones (Type K)	Test Vehicles (Type TV)		Tactical Weapons–Guided Missiles (Type M)	
KD	CTV	Control	AAM	Air-to-Air
	LTV	Launch	ASM	Air-to-Surface
	PTV	Propulsion	AVM	Air-to-Underwater
	RTV	Reasearch	SAM	Surface-to-Air
			SSM	Surfacce-to-Surface

Test Vehicles

Tactical Weapon–Guided Missile

Pilotless Aircraft/Target Drone Designation

Note: Prior to 1962, normal man-carrying aircraft configured as a drone used the original aircraft designation with a K at the end of the designation; i.e. F6F-5K.

Status Prefix

C	Captive	Vehicle designed for carry on a launch platform, but incapable of being fired
D	Dummy	Non-flyable vehicle used for training
J	Special Test (Temporary)	Vehicle in special test programs by authorized organizations, on bailment contract with a special test configuration, or with installed property temporarily removed to accommodate tests
N	Special Test (Permanent)	Vehicle in special test programs by authorized activities or on bailment contract whose configuration changes so drastically that returning to its original operational configuration is beyond practical or economical limits
X	Experimental	Vehicle in a development or experimental stage
Y	Prototype	Vehicle suitable for evaluation of design, performance, and production potential
Z	Planning	Vehicle in the planning or predevelopment stage

Launch Environment

A	Air	Vehicle launched in the air by another vehicle
B	Multiple	Vehicle capable of being launched from more than one environment
C	Coffin	Vehicle stored horizontally or at less than a 45-degree angle in a protective enclosure (regardless of structural strength) and launched from the ground level
F	Individual	Vehicle hand-carried and launched by combat personnel
G	Surface	Vehicle launched from a runway or the ground
H	Silo Stored	Vehicle vertically stored—but not launched from—below ground level
L	Silo Launched	Vehicle launched vertically from below ground level
M	Mobile	Vehicle launched from a ground vehicle or movable platform
P	Soft Pad	Vehicle partially protected or unprotected in storage and launched from ground level
R	Ship	Vehicle launched from a surface vessel (ship or barge)
S	Space	Vehicle launched from an aerospace vehicle that operated outside the earth's atmosphere
U	Underwater	Vehicle launched from a submarine or other underwater device

Basic Mission

C	Transport	Vehicle designed to carry personnel; cargo; command, control, and communications equipment; or weapons systems
D	Decoy	Vehicle designed or modified to confuse, deceive, or divert enemy defenses by simulating an attack vehicle
E	Electronic/ Communications	Vehicle designed or modified with electronic equipment for communications, countermeasures, electronic-radiation sounding, or other electronic recording or relay missions
G	Surface Attack	Vehicle designed to destroy enemy land or sea targets
I	Aerial/Space Intercept	Vehicle designed to intercept aerial/space targets in defensive or offensive roles
L	Launch Detection/ Surveillance	Vehicle designed for the systematic observation of aerospace for the purpose of detecting, tracking, and characterizing objects, events, and phenomena associated with satellites and in-flight missiles, including intrusion detection
M	Scientific/Calibration	Vehicle designed for the collection, evaluation, analysis, and interpretation of scientific and technical information
N	Navigation	Vehicle designed to provide data for navigation purposes
Q	Drone	Aerospace vehicle remotely or automatically controlled
S	Space Support	Vehicle designed to ensure maintainability of space control and support of terrestrial forces. Includes activities such as launching and deploying space vehicles, maintaining and sustaining space vehicles while in orbit, and recovering space vehicles if required
T	Training	Vehicle designed or permanently modified for training purposes
U	Underwater Attack	Vehicle designed to detonate underwater and to destroy submarines or other underwater targets
W	Weather	Vehicle designed to observe, record, or relay meteorological data

Vehicle Type

B	Booster	A primary or auxiliary propulsion system used as a source of thrust for a satellite, missile, or aerospace vehicle. A booster system may consist of one or more units

K	Pilotless Aircraft	An unmanned vehicle under remote controlled flight
M	Guided Missile	An unmanned vehicle that flies in and above the atmosphere and an external or internal guidance system controls its flight path trajectory
N	Probe	Non-orbital, instrumented vehicle designed to penetrate the aerospace environment. Commonly used for collection of meteorological data
R	Rocket	Vehicle propelled by an engine that derives its thrust from ejection of hot gases generated by liquid or solid propellants carried in the vehicle. A rocket has no guidance (internal or external) after launch
S	Satellite	Vehicle placed in various orbits to collect, transmit various types of data for multiple purposes

Missile Designation

Note: After 1962, normal man-carrying aircraft configured as a drone would use the original design preceded by the letter Q, i.e. QF-86D.

Chapter 6

Aircraft on Hand

1911–1918					
1 July	Total HTA inventory	Seaplanes*	Flying boats	Landplanes	LTA Airships
1911	1†	1			
1912	3	3			
1913	6	4	2		
1914	12	6	6		
1915	15	9	6		
1916	17	14	3		
6 Apr 1917	54	45	6	3	1
11 Nov 1918	2,107	695	1,170	242	1

* Pontoon type, referred to as hydroaeoplanes through 1916.
† The Curtiss Triad which made its first flight in the hands of a naval officer on 1 July; the plane was formally accepted on 9 August.

1920–1965 Navy and Marine Corps Combined. Including those assigned to the Air Reserve and In Storage									
			HTA Types*					LTA Types†	
1 July	HTA Inventory	Combat	Transport and Utility‡	Observation§	Training	Miscellaneous°	Helicopter#	Rigid	Blimp
1920		1,205							16
1921		1,134							16
1922	1,234	780			454				10
1924	700	530			170			1	1
1925	860	491	134		188	47		2	1
1926	888	600			282	6		1	1
1927	886	599			284	3		1	1
1928	851	605			217	29		1	2
1929	1,038	664	7		205	162		1	2
1930	1,081	734	12		303	32		1	3
1931	1,204	776	14		300	114		1	3
1932	1,234	909	17		246	62		2	4
1933	1,380	863	38		176	303		2	3
1934	1,347	950	43		157	197		2	2
1935	1,456	1,041	67		170	178		1	2
1936	1,655	1,100	90		166	319		1	4
1937	1,637	972	113		161	393		1	4
1938	2,050	1,284	125		268	373		1	5
1939	2,098	1,316	150		262	370		1	8
1940	1,741	1,194	152		363	32			6
1941	3,432	1,774	183		1,444	31			7
1942	7,058	3,191	461		3,378	28			16
1943	16,691	8,696	878		7,021	96			78
1944	34,077	22,116	1,939		9,652	364	6		146
1945	40,939	29,125	2,897		8,370	520	27		139
1946	24,269	14,637	2,864		5,725	1,006	37		93
1947	17,629	11,181	1,288	413	3,941	779	27		66

1920–1965 Navy and Marine Corps Combined. Including those assigned to the Air Reserve and In Storage									
	HTA Types*							LTA Types†	
1 July	HTA Inventory	Combat	Transport and Utility‡	Observation§	Training	Miscellaneous#	Helicopter‡	Rigid	Blimp
1948	15,198	9,899	1,295	299	3,109	545	51		56
1949	14,159	9,372	1,272	144	3,118	150	103		59
1950	14,149	9,422	1,193	126	3,092	203	113		58
1951	13,636	8,713	775	101	3,527	357	163		58
1952	14,163	8,742	971	136	3,567	371	376		59
1953	15,327	8,818	1,250	194	3,700	704	661		50
1954	16,209	8,829	1,276	237	3,762	1,381	724		47
1955	17,116	8,884	1,299	217	3,679	2,361	676		61
1956	16,458	7,961	1,239	233	3,519	2,752	754		51
1957	14,725	7,591	1,287	164	3,341	1,521	821		54
1958	13,464	7,408	1,307	160	3,008	648	933		42
1959	13,007	7,030	1,355	150	3,027	468	977		37
1960	12,253	6,074	1,320	135	2,925	800	999		18
1961	12,667	6,305	1,285	129	2,769	1,147	1,032		14
1962	13,041	6,420	1,600		2,561	1,210	1,250		13
1963	12,438	6,265	1,639		2,290	970	1,274		
1964	11,851	5,420	1,727		2,149	1,290	1,265		
1965	11,386	5,127	1,681	20	2,305	968	1,285		

* As determined by model designation.

† Includes *Los Angeles* under Rigids while in non–flying status 1932–39, and the metal clad ZMC-2 under blimps, 1930–38.

‡ Includes assault transport helicopters after 1961.

§ Included under combat through 1946; thereafter VO and HO.

Has different meanings at different times, but generally includes experimental and obsolete aircraft, those awaiting disposition, on loan, and other categories officially considered "nonprogram" aircraft.

‡ Total on hand; also counted in pertinent columns under HTA types.

1966–2010							
30 June	Total Aircraft Inventory*	Total Operating Inventory†	Combat	Transport/ Utility	Observation	Training	Miscellaneous 1966–98, Tilt Rotor 1999ff *	Rotary-Wing
1966	9,509	6,485	3,163	489		1,678	3,110	1,069
1967	9,399	6,591	3,160	543	14	1,679	2,884	1,119
1968	9,326	6,962	3,362	561	36	1,876	2,300	1,191
1969	9,192	6,984	2,964	614	111	2,180	2,110	1,213
1970	8,646	6,528	3,043	549	91	1,741	1,979	1,243
1971	7,974	6,059	2,793	353	80	1,465	2,007	1,276
1972	7,836	5,658	2,663	445	63	1,369	2,223	1,073
1973	7,444	5,590	2,697	416	78	1,286	1,909	1,058
1974	7,509	5,279	2,817	402	71	1,314	1,776	1,129
1975	7,526	4,915	2,747	377	52	1,204	2,012	1,134
1976	6,836	4,931	2,344	323	63	1,067	1,952	1,087
30 Sep								
1977	6,593	4,698	2,346	268	61	879	1,943	1,096
1978	6,359	4,512	2,219	249	53	907	1,895	1,036
1979	6,390	4,463	2,207	213	55	916	1,975	1,024
1980	6,300	4,436	2,164	219	74	884	1,913	1,046
1981	6,225	4,474	2,156	221	79	908	1,803	1,058

1966–2010								
30 June	Total Aircraft Inventory*	Total Operating Inventory†	Combat	Transport/Utility	Observation	Training	Miscellaneous 1966–98, Tilt Rotor 1999ff *	Rotary-Wing
1982	6,130	4,534	2,223	199	79	908	1,645	1,076
1983	6,178	4,469	2,418	219	78	1,004	1,230	1,229
1984	6,230	4,437	2,348	214	80	1,028	1,339	1,221
1985	5,396	4,462	2,067	183	73	845	1,004	1,224
1986	5,389	4,474	2,112	137	81	849	993	1,217
1987	5,433	4,421	2,093	131	77	816	1,106	1,210
1988	5,424	4,174	1,945	188	68	740	1,253	1,230
1989	5,972	4,572	2,588	217	72	931	774	1,390
1990	5,895	4,766	2,550	212	57	915	722	1,439
1991	4,629	4,578	2,146	204	36	866		1,377
1992	4,684	4,403	2,235	211	43	797		1,398
1993	4,704	4,134	2,276	220	36	772		1,400
1994‡	4,514	3,868				617		
1995‡	4,406	3,811				632		
1996‡	4,228	3,574				626		
1997‡	4,124	3,523				619		
1998‡	4,084	3,421				640		
1999‡	4,047	3,392				656	1	
2000‡	4,055	3,434				662	8	
2001‡	4,089	3,566				671	7	
2002‡	4,079	3,461				686	7	
2003‡	4,048	3,454				680	7	
2004‡	3,837	3,346				664	11	
2005‡	3,727	3,022				647	28	
2006‡	3,698	3,037				644	42	
2007‡	3,729	3,045				657	54	
2008‡	3,745	3,025				646	67	
2009‡	3,784	3,049				658	85	
2010‡	3,860	3,111				673	104	

Note: Category changes from Miscellaneous to Tilt Rotor in 1999.

* Figures include aircraft in the pipeline, inactive aircraft, and non-program aircraft but do not include the inactive aircraft inventory. Figures drawn from NavSo P-3523 generated by the Office of the Navy Comptroller. Financial & Statistical Reports Branch.

† Total operating inventory accounts for only operational aircraft in the reporting and physical custody of the operating unit to which assigned. Figures drawn from the Naval Aviation Summary reports (OpNav Notice C3100) and beginning in 1994 from the Aircraft Inventory & Readiness Reporting System (AIRRS) database.

‡ Extracted from Aircraft Inventory & Readiness Reporting System (AIRRS) data using Active Aircraft Status Codes as of 30 September of each year. The Total Aircraft Inventory does not include the inactive aircraft inventory numbers. Note: Combat numbers include antisubmarine, attack, fighter, patrol, and warning aircraft. Transport/Utility numbers include in-flight refueling, utility, and transport aircraft.

CHAPTER 7

Naval Aircraft Bureau (Serial) Numbers

Serial number and bureau number are synonymous terms for the identifying number assigned to individual naval aircraft. The earliest system was a letter-number combination, which segregated the aircraft by manufacturer (or designer) and general type. As this scheme developed, the letter "A" was used with Curtiss hydroaeroplanes, "B" for Wright-type hydroaeroplanes, "C" for Curtiss flying boats, "D" for Burgess flying boats, and "E" for Curtiss amphibian flying boats. Sequential numbers beginning with 1 were assigned to each set of aircraft.

That scheme was replaced by AH numbers which were assigned aircraft in service. A system of construction numbers was then initiated to identify aircraft on order. The two coexisted for some 15 months when the service numbers were abandoned (*See* 27 Mar 1914, 10 Feb 1916, and 19 May 1917, Vol. I chronology entries).

Construction numbers began with A-51 and, as serial numbers or bureau numbers, ran through A-9206 after which the letter "A" was dropped although sequential numbering continued through 9999. A second series of four-digit numbers began with 0001 and ran through 7303. The last number in this series was assigned in December 1940. Beginning in 1941 a series of five-digit numbers, beginning with 00001 was adopted and numbers were assigned through 99999, with 99991–100000 cancelled. A six-digit numbering system was then added beginning with 100001 and is still in use.

To summarize, the five major numbering systems are as follows:

1. A-51 to A-9206

2. 9207 to 9999 (the A prefix was dropped)

3. 0001 to 7303

4. 00001 to 100000 (99991–100000 were cancelled)

5. 100001 to present (still in use but with many modifications)

There are several major exceptions to the assignment of numbers in the six-digit numbering system. In the 1960s a block of six-digit numbers, beginning with 00, were assigned to the DASH vehicle (Drone Antisubmarine Helicopter). The original designation for the unmanned helicopter was DSN. Production models of the DSN were designated QH-50C and QH-50D. All of these had six-digit bureau numbers that began with 00. The double zeros were part of the bureau number. These numbers obviously do not fit into the regular six-digit numbering system that began with 100001. Documentation has not been found that explains why the normal numbering system was not employed for these aircraft.

The other major exception to the normal sequential assignment of bureau numbers in the six-digit system involves numbers beginning with 198003 and ranging up to 999794. This group is not sequentially assigned. Almost all of the aircraft in this group were acquired by the Navy from the Army, Air Force, or other organizations, not directly from the manufacturer. There appears to be no logical sequence or reasoning for the assignment of these numbers. It is believed that some numbers may have been derived by modifying the Air Force aircraft numbering system. However, this is only conjecture since there is no verification documentation.

Aside from the very sizable overlap stemming from the numbering schemes, the same number was never used on more than one aircraft. During the planning and contracting processes, however, numbers were often assigned to aircraft that were never obtained. Sometimes, but by no means always, these cancelled numbers were reassigned to other aircraft.

The basic sources used in compiling the following list include a master "Serial List of Designating Numbers for Naval Aircraft" prepared by the aircraft records office in the Bureau of Aeronautics. It was typed on twelve 17 1/2-inch by 21 1/2-inch pages and numbered consecutively 0 through 11. It was probably put in that form in 1935 when the first significant handwritten changes appeared. Page 0 covered the pre-1916 schemes and pages 1 through 11 began with A-51 and ran through all four-digit serials. For later aircraft, primarily those in the six-digit system, the bureau number listing was compiled by using the "List of Serial Numbers Assigned Navy Aircraft" developed by the Aviation Statistics Office of DCNO (Air) and by reviewing the Aircraft History Card microfilm collection.

The compilations have been cross-checked against that in William T. Larkins, *U.S. Navy Aircraft 1921–41*; a compilation made by William H. Plant, Librarian, Naval Air Systems Command; and a more comprehensive listing compiled by Jack Collins, a historian and specialist in bureau numbers. Monthly and quarterly reports on the status of aircraft production, Aircraft History Cards, and the Aircraft Strike Listing were used in reconciling discrepancies.

One problem is that interpretations do not show in the final list. In addition, the compiler makes no claim to infallibility in transcribing long lists of numbers and, as a result, may have unwittingly introduced errors not in the original compilations.

The Early Designation Systems are as follows:

The First System from 1911–1914

A-1	Curtiss hydroaeroplane (originally an amphibian)
A-2	Curtiss landplane, rebuilt as hydroaeroplane. It was again rebuilt as a short-hulled flying boat variously described as OWL for over-water-land or as a Bat boat, and was fitted with wheels for use as an amphibian. This was recorded in the aircraft log for 25 November 1913: "title by order of Captain Chambers [was] changed [to] E-1."
A-3	Curtiss hydroaeroplane, received summer of 1912
A-4	Curtiss (or Curtiss-type) hydroaeroplane
B-1	Wright landplane, converted to hydroaeroplane
B-2	Wright-type hydroaeroplane, built from spares, October 1912
B-3	Wright-type hydroaeroplane, built from spares, October 1913
C-1	Curtiss flying boat
C-2	Curtiss flying boat
C-3	Curtiss flying boat
C-4	Curtiss flying boat
C-5	Curtiss flying boat
D-1	Burgess Co. & Curtis flying boat
D-2	Burgess Co. & Curtis flying boat
E-1	OWL or short hulled amphibious flying boat (*See* A-2)

The Second Designation System, 1914–1916

AH designations

General Order No. 88 of 27 March 1914 listed the corresponding designations between the above designations and the new system: "The aeroplanes now in the service are hereby designated as follows:

New Designation	Old
AH-1	A-1
AH-2	A-2
AH-3	A-3
AH-4	B-1
AH-5	B-2
AH-6	B-3
AB-1	C-1
AB-2	C-2
AB-3	C-3
AB-4	C-4
AB-5	C-5
AB-6	D-1

New Designation	Old
AB-7	D-2
AX-1	E-1"

Despite the phrase, "now in the service," the A-1, B-1, B-2, and probably the D-1 had ceased to exist before the order was issued. Other records show AH-2 as redesignation for A-4.

The designation of follow-on aircraft was as follows:

AH-7	Burgess-Dunne hydroaeroplane
AH-8	Curtiss hydroaeroplane
AH-9	Curtiss hydroaeroplane
AH-10	Burgess-Dunne hydroaeroplane
AH-11	Curtiss hydroaeroplane
AH-12	Curtiss hydroaeroplane
AH-13	Curtiss hydroaeroplane
AH-14	Curtiss hydroaeroplane
AH-15	Curtiss hydroaeroplane
AH-16	Curtiss hydroaeroplane
AH-17	Curtiss hydroaeroplane
AH-18	Curtiss hydroaeroplane

The following listings are the five major post-1916 aircraft numbering systems:

Bureau Number	Aircraft Type	Manufacturer	Miscellaneous Notes
A-51	Seaplane	Wright	
A-52	Seaplane	Paul Schmitt	Paris
A-53	Seaplane	DWF, German	
A-54–56	Hydro-pusher	Burgess Co.	
A-57–58	Seaplane	Thomas Bros.	AH-20, AH-21
A-59	Seaplane	Gallaudet	D-1 (AH-61)
A-60–65	Hydroaeroplane	Curtiss	
A-66–67	R-3	Curtiss	AH-65, AH-62
A-68–69	Seaplane	Martin	AH-19, AH-22
A-70–75	Tractor Seaplane	Burgess	AH-25 to -31
A-76–81	Seaplane	Sturtevant	A-76 was AH-24
A-82	Richardson	Wash. Navy Yard	Seaplane
A-83–84	Hydroaeroplane	Pensacola	Curtiss type from spares
A-85–90	Seaplane	Curtiss	
A-91	Seaplane	Standard	
A-92	Seaplane	Standard	Twin engine, Cancelled
A-93	JN Twin Tractor	Curtiss	Seaplane
A-94–95	BC-2, BC-3	Goodyear	Kite Balloon
A-96–125	N-9	Curtiss	
A-126–127	Seaplane	Farman	A-127 Cancelled
A-128–133	Seaplane	Sturtevant	
A-134–136	SH-4	Thomas-Morse	Seaplane

Bureau Number	Aircraft Type	Manufacturer	Miscellaneous Notes
A-137–139	H-4-H	Standard	
A-140–141	Seaplane	Thomas Bros.	Twin tractor, Cancelled
A-142–144	Seaplane	Aeromarine	
A-145–146	Flying Boat	Curtiss	Cancelled
A-147–148	Seaplane	Pacific Aero.	Boeing
A-149–150	Speed Scout	Curtiss	Seaplane
A-151	BC-4	Goodyear	Kite Balloon
A-152	H-12	Curtiss	Flying Boat
A-153–154	Seaplane, experimental	NAS Pensacola	A-154 Cancelled
A-155–156	HT-2 Seaplane	Burgess	Speed Scout
A-157–159	JN-4B	Curtiss	
A-160–161	Kite Balloon	Goodyear	
A-162–197	R-6	Curtiss	
A-198	JN, Twin Engine	Curtiss	
A-199–200	Speed Scout	Burgess	Cancelled
A-201–234	N-9	Curtiss	
A-235–243	B Class Airship	Goodyear	
A-244–248	B Class Airship	Goodrich	
A-249–250	B Class Airship	Connecticut Acft	
A-251	Free Balloon	Connecticut Acft	
A-252–275	Unknown	Unknown	Cancelled
A-276–287	Kite Balloon	Goodyear	
A-288–290	Seaplane	Wright-Martin	
A-291–293	L-2, Triplane	Curtiss	
A-294–295	Unknown	Unknown	Cancelled
A-296–297	Seaplane	General/Verville	Cancelled
A-298–299	Unknown	Unknown	Cancelled
A-300–301	Seaplane	Gallaudet	Cancelled
A-302–341	R-6	Curtiss	
A-342–371	N-9	Curtiss	
A-372–373	Kite Balloon	Goodyear	
A-374–379	HT-2	Burgess	Speed Scout
A-380–385	U-2 Seaplane	Burgess	
A-386–387	F-Boat	Curtiss	
A-388–389	JN-4	Curtiss	
A-390–393	F-Boat	Curtiss	
A-394	Sopwith	British	Seaplane
A-395–406	SH-4 Seaplane	Thomas-Morse	
A-407	Sopwith	British Admiralty	Seaplane
A-408	F-Boat	Curtiss	
A-409–438	N-9	Burgess	
A-439–441	Seaplane	Aeromarine	
A-442–444	Seaplane	Loening	Lawrance two-cylinder engine
A-445–449	GS-2 Gnome	Curtiss	Gnome Speed Scout
A-450–649	39 A and B	Aeromarine	Seaplanes

Bureau Number	Aircraft Type	Manufacturer	Miscellaneous Notes
A-650–699	Type C	Boeing	Seaplane
A-700	Kite Balloon	Goodyear	
A-701	Kite Balloon	Goodrich	
A-702–726	Kite Balloon	Goodyear	
A-727–751	Kite Balloon	Goodrich	
A-752–756	F Boat	L. S. Thompson	
A-757–762	S-5	Thomas-Morse	
A-763–764	Caquot M	British Gov't	Kite Balloon
A-765–783	H-12	Curtiss	
A-784–799	H-16	Curtiss	
A-800–815	HS-1	Curtiss	A-815 Cancelled
A-816–817	Caquot P	French Gov't	Kite Balloon
A-818–867	H-16	Curtiss	
A-868	GS-1, Gnome	Curtiss	Speed Scout
A-869–872	Sopwith Baby	British Gov't	Seaplane
A-873–891	R-9	Curtiss	
A-892–893	R-6	Curtiss	
A-894	R-9	Curtiss	
A-895	R-6	Curtiss	
A-896–909	R-9	Curtiss	
A-910	R-6	Curtiss	
A-911–918	R-9	Curtiss	
A-919–920	R-6	Curtiss	
A-921–924	R-9	Curtiss	
A-925	R-6	Curtiss	
A-926–955	R-9	Curtiss	
A-956	R-6	Curtiss	
A-957	R-9	Curtiss	
A-958–959	R-6	Curtiss	
A-960–962	R-9	Curtiss	
A-963–966	R-6	Curtiss	
A-967–969	R-9	Curtiss	
A-970	R-6	Curtiss	
A-971–975	R-9	Curtiss	
A-976	R-6	Curtiss	
A-977–990	R-9	Curtiss	
A-991	R-6	Curtiss	
A-992–993	R-9	Curtiss	
A-994	R-6	Curtiss	
A-995–997	JN-4	Curtiss	
A-998	Kite Balloon	Goodrich	
A-999–1028	N-9	Burgess	
A-1029–1030	O-SS Dirigible	British	
A-1031–1048	H-16	Curtiss	
A-1049–1098	H-16	NAF	
A-1099–1398	HS-1, -1L, -2L	LWF	50 Cancelled

Bureau Number	Aircraft Type	Manufacturer	Miscellaneous Notes
A-1399–1548	HS-1, -2L	Standard	Last 70 Cancelled
A-1549–2207	HS-1, -1L, -2L	Curtiss	
A-2208–2214	Free Balloon	Goodyear	
A-2215–2216	Free Balloon	Connecticut Acft	
A-2217–2276	HS-2L	Gallaudet	
A-2277	Flying Boat	Curtiss	
A-2278	Dunkirk Fighter	Curtiss	
A-2279–2280	F Boat	Wrigley	
A-2281	F Boat	Mitchell	
A-2282–2283	Davis Gun capable	NAF	
A-2284	Unknown	Unknown	Cancelled
A-2285–2290	N-9	Curtiss	
A-2291–2294	NC-1 to NC-4	Curtiss	
A-2295–2344	F Boat	Curtiss	
A-2345–2350	MF Boat	Curtiss	
A-2351–2650	N-9	Burgess	
A-2651–2652	F Boat	Alexandria Acft	Briggs
A-2653–2654	D-4	Gallaudet	Light bomber
A-2655–2664	Type R	Goodyear	Caquot Kite Ballons, 2659–2664 to British Admiralty
A-2665–2929	Type R and M	Goodyear	Caquot Kite Balloons, 180 R and 10 M, 2845–2929 Cancelled
A-2930–3204	Type R and M	Goodrich	Caquot Kite Balloons, 81 R and 10 M, 3021–3204 Cancelled
A-3205–3234	JN-4H		From Army
A-3235–3244	Gnome, Speed Scout	Thomas-Morse	From Army
A-3245–3324	DH-4	Dayton-Wright	From Army
A-3325–3326	Kirkham Fighter	Curtiss	
A-3327	F Boat	Alexandria/Briggs	
A-3328–3332	F Boat	Am. Trans-Oceanic Co. Curtiss	
A-3333–3382	F-5	Canadian Aeroplanes Ltd.	3363–3382 Cancelled
A-3383	Balloon	Goodrich	Gastite Kite
A-3384–3458	DH-4	From Army	Dayton-Wright
A-3459–3558	H-16	NAF	
A-3559–4035	F-5	NAF	137 accepted; 343 cancelled: 3616–3658, 3684–3782, 3801–3858, 3881, 3883–3935, 3941–4008, 4014–4035
A-4036–4037	F-6	NAF	
A-4038	F-5	NAF	
A-4039–4078	H-16	Curtiss	
A-4079–4108	F Boat	Curtiss	
A-4109	E-1 Dirigible	Goodyear	
A-4110–4111	Dunkirk Fighter	Curtiss	(HA)
A-4112–4117	JN-4B	Curtiss Exhibition Co.	
A-4118	C Class	Goodyear	Dirigible
A-4119	C Class	Goodrich	Dirigible

Bureau Number	Aircraft Type	Manufacturer	Miscellaneous Notes
A-4120	C Class	Goodyear	Dirigible
A-4121	C Class	Goodrich	Dirigible
A-4122–4123	C Class	Goodyear	Dirigible
A-4124–4125	C Class	Goodrich	Dirigible
A-4126–4127	C Class	Goodyear	Dirigible
A-4128–4217	JN-4HG	From Army	Hispano-Suiza engine
A-4218–4227	E-1 (M Defense)	Standard	From Army
A-4228–4229	HS-2	Loughead	
A-4230	Tellier	French Gov't	Flying Boat
A-4231–4255	HS-2L	Boeing	
A-4256–4280	Unknown	Boeing	Cancelled
A-4281–4340	F-5	Curtiss	
A-4341–4342	N-1	NAF	
A-4343	F Boat	Carolina Acft Co.	Experimental, rejected
A-4344–4346	Unknown	Carolina Acft Co.	Cancelled
A-4347	C-1F	Boeing	
A-4348	F-1 Dirigible	Goodyear	
A-4349–4402	F Boat	Curtiss	
A-4403–4449	MF Boat	Curtiss	
A-4450	D-1	Goodyear	Airship
A-4451	D-2	Goodrich	Airship
A-4452–4453	D-3, D-4	Goodyear	Airship
A-4454	D-5	Goodrich	Airship
A-4455–4469	D Class	Goodrich	Airship, 5 cancelled
		Goodyear	Airship, 10 cancelled
A-4470–4819	F-5L	Curtiss	Cancelled
A-4820–5019	N-9	Burgess	Cancelled
A-5020–5021	R type, reduced	Goodyear	Caquot Kite Balloon
A-5022–5023	R type, reduced	Goodrich	Caquot Kite Balloon
A-5024	F Boat	Alexandria	
A-5025–5028	P type	Goodyear	Caquot Kite Balloon
A-5029	Kite Balloon	Goodyear	Experimental
A-5030–5039	N-1	NAF	Cancelled
A-5040–5089	Model 40 F Boat	Aeromarine	
A-5090–5239	Unknown	Aeromarine	Cancelled
A-5240	M type	British Admiralty	Caquot Kite Balloon
A-5241–5242	Avorio Prassone	Italian Gov't	Kite Balloon
A-5243	Night Bomber	Sperry	
A-5244–5246	Unknown	Sperry	Cancelled
A-5247–5256	Model 10 F Boat	Alexandria Acft	
A-5257	B-20 Airship	Goodyear	
A-5258	F Boat	Curtiss	
A-5259–5458	F-5L	NAF	Cancelled
A-5459–5462	HS-3	Curtiss	
A-5463	Kite Balloon	Goodyear	
A-5464–5465	B-17, B-18	Goodyear	Airship cars rebuilt

Bureau Number	Aircraft Type	Manufacturer	Miscellaneous Notes
A-5466	Airship car	Goodyear	
A-5467	B-19 Airship car	Goodyear	
A-5468	Airship	Goodyear	
A-5469	M-3 Cat	Loening	Seaplane
A-5470–5471	JN-6HG-1	From Army	
A-5472	Astra-Torres	French Gov't	Airship
A-5473–5482	Kite Balloon	British Gov't	
A-5483–5562	MF Boat	NAF	
A-5563	SS-Z-23	British Admiralty	Airship, former O-SS A-1030
A-5564–5569	HS-2	NAS Miami	From spares
A-5570–5571	SA-1	NAF	For "Ship's Airplanes"
A-5572–5573	SA-2	NAF	
A-5574–5575	Macchi	Italian Gov't	
A-5576–5579	TF Boat	NAF	Tandem-engine fighting patrol plane
A-5580	NS-1	British Gov't	North Sea dirigible
A-5581–5586	JN-6HG-1	From Army	
A-5587	O-1 Dirigible	Italian Gov't	
A-5588–5589	SE-5	From Army	
A-5590–5591	HS-3	NAF	
A-5592–5593	Vedette-Zodiac	French Gov't	Dirigible
A-5594–5605	Free Balloon	Connecticut Acft	
A-5606	LS Seaplane	Loening	
A-5607–5608	LS Seaplane	Loening	Cancelled
A-5609–5611	LB Flying Boat	Loening	
A-5612–5614	AS Seaplane	Aeromarine	
A-5615–5619	HS-2	NAS	Hampton Roads, from spares, one cancelled, apparently 5619
A-5620–5629	Hanriot	French Gov't	
A-5630	HS-2	LWF	Formerly A-1171 rebuilt
A-5631	M-8 Airplane	Loening	
A-5632–5635	NC-5 to -8	NAF	
A-5636	Seaplane	Paul Schmitt	Paris
A-5637–5646	M-80 Airplane	Loening	
A-5647–5649	Tellier	From Abroad	5649 Cancelled
A-5650–5651	Le Pen Seaplane	From Abroad	
A-5652–5653	Donne Denhaut	From Abroad	
A-5654	Caproni	From Abroad	
A-5655–5656	Pup	From Abroad	Sopwith
A-5657	Le Pen Seaplane	From Abroad	
A-5658–5659	Camel (F-1)	From Abroad	Sopwith
A-5660	1 1/2 Strutter	From Abroad	1A2 Sopwith
A-5661–5680	VE-7	Lewis & Vought	
A-5681–5700	VE-7G, -7GF	NAF	
A-5701–5710	M-81	NAF	Loening design
A-5711–5712	MBT	Martin	
A-5713–5720	MT	Martin	

Bureau Number	Aircraft Type	Manufacturer	Miscellaneous Notes
A-5721–5724	Camel (F-1)	From Army	Sopwith
A-5725–5728	1 1/2 Strutter	From Army	1A2 Sopwith
A-5729–5730	Camel	From Army	Sopwith
A-5731–5733	Unknown	Unknown	Cancelled
A-5734–5750	1 1/2 Strutter	From Army	Sopwith
A-5751–5752	Panther	G. Parnall & Son	UK
A-5753–5755	AP Type	Connecticut Acft	Kite Balloon
A-5756–5757	D-11 Seaplane	Gallaudet	Cancelled
A-5758–5760	D-9 Seaplane	Gallaudet	Cancelled
A-5761–5786	M-81 Airplane	NAF	
A-5787	HS-2L	NAS Key West	From spares
A-5788–5793	M-81-S	Loening	
A-5794–5805	Nieuport 28	From Army	
A-5806–5807	K Type Boat	Austrian Gov't	
A-5808	HS-2L	NAS Anacostia	From spares
A-5809–5814	DH-4B	From Army	
A-5815–5829	Caproni	Caproni	Cancelled
A-5830–5833	JN-6H	From Army	
A-5834–5839	DH-4B	From Army	
A-5840–5842	K-4	J. V. Martin	Gallaudet, subcontractor
A-5843–5854	D-7	Fokker	5849–5854 Cancelled
A-5855–5858	S-4C Scout	Thomas-Morse	From Army
A-5859	JN-6H	War Department	
A-5860–5866	Free Balloon	Goodyear	
A-5867–5869	JL-6	Junkers-Larsen	
A-5870–5884	DH-4B	From Army	
A-5885–5886	NC-9, -10	NAF	
A-5887–5889	C-1	Fokker	Netherlands
A-5890–5898	CT Seaplane	Curtiss	5891-5898 Cancelled
A-5899–5901	ST Airplane	Stout	Rejected
A-5902–5904	ST Airplane	Stout	Cancelled
A-5905–5911	EM-2 Seaplane	G. Elias & Bros.	
A-5912–5941	VE-7-SF	Lewis & Vought	
A-5942–5955	VE-7-SF	NAF	
A-5956–5971	VE-7	NAF	
A-5972	D-6 Airship	Goodyear	
A-5973	H-1 Airship	Goodyear	Towing Airship (T-1)
A-5974–5975	USXB-1	Dayton Wright	From Army
A-5976–5981	Morane Saulnier	Morane Saulnier	
A-5982–6001	DH-4B	From Army	
A-6002–6004	Exp. Ship plane	Curtiss	Cancelled
A-6005–6007	Macchi M-16	S.A.N.M., Italy	
A-6008–6010	Fokker FT	Netherlands Acft Co.	
A-6011–6020	VE-7SF	NAF	
A-6021–6030	VE-7SF	Lewis & Vought	
A-6031–6033	DT Seaplanes	Davis-Douglas Co.	

Bureau Number	Aircraft Type	Manufacturer	Miscellaneous Notes
A-6034–6048	PT	NAF	
A-6049–6054	Seaplane	Austrian Gov't	
A-6055	Dornier CS-2	Van Berkel	
A-6056–6057	Swift	Blackburn Aeroplane Co.	
A-6058	Dornier D-1	Swiss Agent	
A-6059	Giant Boat	NAF	Cancelled
A-6060–6070	MB-3	Thomas-Morse	From Army
A-6071	MB-7	Thomas-Morse	From Army
A-6072	SV Airplane	Stout	
A-6073	Viking IV	Vickers	Amphibian Boat
A-6074–6076	Free Balloon	Connecticut Acft	
A-6077–6079	Unassigned		
A-6080–6081	CR Racer	Curtiss	
A-6082	WA Amphibian	Dayton-Wright	
A-6083	WS Seaplane	Dayton-Wright	
A-6084	WD Seaplane	Dayton-Wright	Cancelled
A-6085–6095	DT-2	Dayton-Wright	Reassigned from WA-WS-WD
A-6096–6102	WA-WS-WD		Cancelled
A-6103–6110	F Type	Goodyear	Kite Balloon
A-6111–6112	J Class Airship	Goodyear	
A-6113–6192	DH-4B	From Army	
A-6193–6246	JN-4H	From Army	
A-6247	JN-4H	Parris Island Marine Base	From spares
A-6248–6270	TS Airplane	Curtiss	
A-6271–6288	JN-4H	From Army	
A-6289–6290	BS-1 Boat	NAF	Cancelled
A-6291–6292	BS-2 Boat	NAF	Cancelled
A-6293–6294	BS-3 Boat	NAF	Cancelled
A-6295–6299	BS	NAF	Cancelled
A-6300–6304	TS-1	NAF	
A-6305–6315	TS-1	Curtiss	
A-6316–6325	JN-4	NAF	Cancelled
A-6326–6343	PT-2	NAF	
A-6344–6346	TG-1	NAF	
A-6347–6348	TG-2	NAF	
A-6349–6351	HN-1	Huff-Daland	
A-6352–6401	DH-4	From Army	
A-6402–6404	HPS-1	Handley Page	Cancelled
A-6405–6422	DT-2	Davis-Douglas Co.	
A-6423–6428	DT-2	NAF	
A-6429–6430	BR-1	Bee Line Acft Co.	
A-6431–6433	NO-1	NAF	
A-6434–6435	Heinkel seaplane submarine type	Caspar-Werke	Germany
A-6436–6444	VE-7H	NAF	

Bureau Number	Aircraft Type	Manufacturer	Miscellaneous Notes
A-6445	Racing Balloon	NAF	
A-6446–6447	TS-2	NAF	
A-6448–6449	TS-3	NAF	
A-6450–6451	NM-1	NAF	6451 Cancelled
A-6452–6454	M2O-1	Martin	
A-6455–6460	MO-1	Martin	
A-6461–6464	VE-9H	Vought	
A-6465–6481	VE-9	Vought	
A-6482–6499	UO-1	Vought	
A-6500–6505	CS-1	Curtiss	
A-6506	HS-2L	NAS Coco Solo	From spares
A-6507–6513	HS-2L	NAF	From spares
A-6514	DH-4B	NAF	From spares
A-6515–6520	XS-1	Cox-Klemin	
A-6521–6526	MS-1	Martin	
A-6527	Free Balloon	NAF	
A-6528–6542	N-9	NAS Pensacola	From spares
A-6543–6544	NW-1, -2	Wright	
A-6545	JN-4H	Port-au-Prince	From spares
A-6546–6551	UO-1	Vought	
A-6552	Libelle	Dornier	Cancelled
A-6553–6556	HS-2L	NAS San Diego	From spares
A-6557–6559	F-5L	NAS Hampton Roads	From spares
A-6560–6562	HO-1	Huff-Daland	
A-6563–6582	DT-2	Douglas	
A-6583–6602	DT-2	LWF	
A-6603–6615	UO-1	Vought	
A-6616–6617	PN-7	NAF	
A-6618–6632	N-9	NAS Pensacola	From spares
A-6633–6662	MO-1	Martin	
A-6663–6688	NO-1	LWF	6684–6688 Cancelled
A-6689–6690	F4C-1	Curtiss	
A-6691–6692	R2C-1	Curtiss	
A-6693–6695	N2N-1	NAF	
A-6696	JL-6 Junkers	Larson	
A-6697	F-5L	NAS San Diego	From spares
A-6698–6700	Free Balloon	Goodyear	
A-6701–6703	HN-2	Huff-Daland	
A-6704–6705	VE-9W	Vought	Cancelled
A-6706–6729	UO-1	Vought	
A-6730	TW-3	Wright	
A-6731–6732	CS-2	Curtiss	
A-6733–6742	N-9	NAS Pensacola	From spares
A-6743–6744	F2W-1	Wright	
A-6745–6747	L-3	Longren	
A-6748	WP-1	Wright	

Bureau Number	Aircraft Type	Manufacturer	Miscellaneous Notes
A-6749–6798	NB-1, NB-2	Boeing	
A-6799	PN-8	NAF	
A-6800	N2M-1	Martin	
A-6801–6835	SC-1	Martin	
A-6836–6857	NB-1	Boeing	
A-6858–6877	UO-1	Vought	
A-6878	PN-8	NAF	
A-6879–6880	OL-1	Loening	
A-6881	PB-1	Boeing	
A-6882–6883	OB-1	Boeing	Cancelled
A-6884–6897	FB-1, 2, 3	Boeing	From Army
A-6898–6927	O2B-1	Boeing	From Army
A-6928–6967	SC-2	Martin	
A-6968–6976	F6C-1	Curtiss	
A-6977	LePere	From Army	
A-6978–6979	R3C-1	Curtiss	
A-6980–6983	OL-2	Loening	
A-6984–7023	UO-1	Vought	
A-7024–7026	TB-1	Boeing	
A-7027	TN-1	NAF	
A-7028–7029	PN-10	NAF	
A-7030	OL-2	Loening	
A-7031–7050	UO-1	Vought	
A-7051–7053	T2D-1	Douglas	
A-7054	R3C-1	Curtiss	
A-7055–7058	OL-3	Loening	
A-7059–7064	OL-4	Loening	
A-7065–7088	T3M-1	Martin	
A-7089–7090	FB-3	Boeing	
A-7091–7100	N-9	NAS Pensacola	Reconstructed
A-7101–7127	FB-5	Boeing	
A-7128–7162	F6C-3	Curtiss	
A-7163–7202	NY-1	Consolidated	
A-7203–7204	OD-1	From Army	
A-7205–7220	NY-1	Consolidated	
A-7221–7222	O2U-1	Vought	
A-7223	F3W-1	Wright	
A-7224–7323	T3M-2	Martin	
A-7324–7334	OL-6	Loening	
A-7335	OL-7	Loening	
A-7336–7350	OL-6	Loening	
A-7351–7360	NY-1	Consolidated	
A-7361–7380	FU-1	Vought	
A-7381	R Type	From Army	Kite Balloon
A-7382	J-3 Airship	Goodyear	TC Type, from Army
A-7383	PN-10	NAF	

Bureau Number	Aircraft Type	Manufacturer	Miscellaneous Notes
A-7384	PN-12	NAF	
A-7385	F2B-1	Boeing	
A-7386–7389	Free Balloon	Goodyear	
A-7390–7392	Kite Balloon	Goodyear	
A-7393–7423	F6C-4	Curtiss	
A-7424–7455	F2B-1	Boeing	
A-7456–7525	NY-2	Consolidated	
A-7526	XJR-1	Ford	
A-7527	PN-11	NAF	
A-7528–7560	O2U-1	Vought	
A-7561–7563	TA-1	Atlantic Fokker	
A-7564	DH-60 Moth	DeHavilland	
A-7565	RO-1	Italian Gov't	Romeo Fokker
A-7566	XT4M-1	Martin	
A-7567–7586	O2U-1	Vought	
A-7587–7595	T2D-1	Douglas	
A-7596–7649	T4M-1	Martin	
A-7650–7652	XN2C-1	Curtiss	
A-7653	XF7C-1	Curtiss	
A-7654–7670	F7C-1	Curtiss	
A-7671–7672	F8C-1	Curtiss	
A-7673	XF8C-2	Curtiss	
A-7674–7691	F3B-1	Boeing	
A-7692	XF2U-1	Vought	
A-7693–7707	NY-2	Consolidated	
A-7708–7763	F3B-1	Boeing	
A-7764–7795	NY-2	Consolidated	
A-7796–7831	O2U-1	Vought	
A-7832–7851	OL-8	Loening	
A-7852–7899	T4M-1	Martin	
A-7900–7940	O2U-1	Vought	
A-7941–7943	XNK-1	Keystone	
A-7944	XFG-1	Eberhart	
A-7945–7948	F8C-1	Curtiss	
A-7949–7962	F8C-3	Curtiss	
A-7963–7969	OC-2	Curtiss	
A-7970–7977	NY-2	Consolidated	
A-7978	XJQ-1	Fairchild	
A-7979–8003	PD-1	Douglas	
A-8004	XPH-1	Hall	
A-8005	XPS-1	Sikorsky	
A-8006	PN-11	NAF	
A-8007–8008	TA-2	Atlantic	
A-8009	XFH-1	Hall	
A-8010	XN2B-1	Boeing	
A-8011	XPY-1	Consolidated	

Bureau Number	Aircraft Type	Manufacturer	Miscellaneous Notes
A-8012	XJA-1	Atlantic	Cancelled
A-8013–8017	NY-2	Consolidated	
A-8018	TA-2	Atlantic	
A-8019	XN2Y-1	Consolidated	
A-8020–8050	N2C-1	Curtiss	
A-8051	XT5M-1	Martin	
A-8052	XT2N-1	NAF	
A-8053–8068	NK-1	Keystone	
A-8069–8088	OL-8	Loening	
A-8089–8090	XPS-2	Sikorsky	
A-8091–8127	O2U-2	Vought	
A-8128–8156	F4B-1	Boeing	
A-8157	TA-2	Atlantic	Cancelled
A-8158–8172	NY-2	Consolidated	
A-8173–8182	NY-1	Consolidated	
A-8183–8192	NY-2	Consolidated	
A-8193–8272	O2U-3	Vought	
A-8273–8274	JR-2	Ford	
A-8275–8276	XHL-1	Loening	
A-8277–8281	Free Balloon	Meadowcraft	
A-8282	ZMC-2 Airship	Acft Dev. Corp.	
A-8283	XN3Y-1	Consolidated	
A-8284–8287	PS-3	Sikorsky	
A-8288	XFJ-1	Berliner-Joyce	
A-8289–8313	PM-1	Martin	
A-8314	XF8C-4	Curtiss	
A-8315–8356	O2U-4	Vought	
A-8357	XOK-1	Keystone	Cancelled
A-8358	XP2M-1	Martin	
A-8359	XOJ-1	Berliner-Joyce	
A-8360–8400	NY-1	Consolidated	
A-8401–8410	NY-2	Consolidated	
A-8411	XT6M-1	Martin	
A-8412–8420	P3M-1	Martin	
A-8421–8447	F8C-4	Curtiss	
A-8448–8450	F8C-5	Curtiss	
A-8451–8456	O2C-1	Curtiss	
A-8457	JR-3	Ford	
A-8458–8475	TG-1	Great Lakes	
A-8476	Free Balloon	Goodyear	
A-8477–8481	PM-1	Martin	
A-8482	XP4N-1	NAF	
A-8483–8484	XP4N-2	NAF	
A-8485	Bulldog	Bristol	
A-8486	XJQ-2	Fairchild	
A-8487–8506	NY-3	Consolidated	

Bureau Number	Aircraft Type	Manufacturer	Miscellaneous Notes
A-8507–8524	PK-1	Keystone	
A-8525	XO2L-1	Loening	
A-8526–8545	N2C-2	Curtiss	
A-8546	Glider	Am. Motorless Av. Co.	
A-8547–8582	O3U-1	Vought	
A-8583–8588	NT-1	New Standard	
A-8589–8597	O2C-1	Curtiss	
A-8598–8599	JR-3	Ford	
A-8600–8605	N2Y-1	Fleet Acft Corp	
A-8606	XO2L-1	Loening	
A-8607	Bulldog	Bristol	
A-8608–8609	C-3	Goodyear	Kite Balloon
A-8610–8612	Free Balloon	Goodyear	
A-8613–8639	F4B-2	Boeing	
A-8640	XF5B-1	Boeing	
A-8641	XO4U-1	Vought	
A-8642	XP2S-1	Sikorsky	
A-8643	XBN-1	NAF	Cancelled
A-8644–8661	P2D-1	Douglas	
A-8662–8686	PM-2	Martin	
A-8687–8695	PH-1	Hall	
A-8696	XSL-1	Loening	
A-8697–8728	TG-2	Detroit/Great Lakes	
A-8729	XP2H-1	Hall	
A-8730	XT3D-1	Douglas	
A-8731	XF9C-1	Curtiss	
A-8732	XFA-1	Fokker	
A-8733–8747	OL-9	Keystone	
A-8748–8790	F8C-5/O2C-1	Curtiss	Redesignated O2C-1
A-8791–8809	F4B-2	Boeing	
A-8810–8839	O3U-1	Vought	
A-8840	RR-4	Ford	
A-8841	RA-4	Fokker	Cancelled
A-8842–8844	RS-1	Sikorsky	
A-8845	XF8C-7	Curtiss	
A-8846	RC-1	Curtiss	
A-8847–8849	O2C-2	Curtiss	
A-8850	XOP-1	Pitcairn	Autogiro
A-8851–8871	O3U-1	Vought	
A-8872–8875	O3U-2/SU-1	Vought	Redesignated SU-1
A-8876	XRD-1	Douglas	
A-8877	DH-80	DeHavilland	Called Puss Moth
A-8878	XFF-1	Grumman	
A-8879–8890	BM-1	Martin	
A-8891–8911	F4B-3	Boeing	
A-8912–8920	F4B-4	Boeing	

Bureau Number	Aircraft Type	Manufacturer	Miscellaneous Notes
A-8921	XBY-1	Consolidated	
A-8922–8923	RS-3	Sikorsky	
A-8924–8927	Free Balloon	Goodyear	
A-8928–8937	O3U-2	Vought	
A-8938	XRE-1	Bellanca	
A-8939	XP2Y-1	Consolidated	
A-8940	XSF-1	Grumman	
A-8941–8970	O2C-1	Curtiss	
A-8971	XS2L-1	Loening	
A-8972	XSS-2	Sikorsky	
A-8973	XF2J-1	Berliner-Joyce	
A-8974	XSG-1	Great Lakes	
A-8975	XF6B-1	Boeing	
A-8976–8977	XOP-1	Pitcairn	Autogiro
A-8978	XFN-1	NAF	Cancelled
A-8979–8985	OL-9	Keystone	
A-8986–9007	P2Y-1	Consolidated	
A-9008	XP2Y-2	Consolidated	
A-9009–9053	F4B-4	Boeing	
A-9054	XRO-1	Detroit/Lockheed	
A-9055	RS-3	Sikorsky	
A-9056–9061	F9C-2	Curtiss	
A-9062–9076	O3U-2	Vought	
A-9077–9121	SU-2	Vought	
A-9122–9141	SU-3	Vought	
A-9142–9169	O3U-3	Vought	
A-9170–9185	BM-2	Martin	
A-9186	XSE-2	Bellanca	Cancelled
A-9187–9204	OJ-2	Berliner-Joyce	
A-9205–9206	RR-5	Ford	

A-prefix dropped

Bureau Number	Aircraft Type	Manufacturer	Miscellaneous Notes
9207	XRE-2	Bellanca	
9208–9211	OL-9	Keystone	
9212	XBM-1	Martin	
9213	XF11C-2	Curtiss	
9214–9217	BM-1	Martin	
9218	XJF-1	Grumman	
9219	XF11C-1	Curtiss	
9220	XBG-1	Great Lakes	
9221	XB2Y-1	Consolidated	
9222	XF3U-1/XSBU-1	Vought	
9223	XFD-1	Douglas	
9224	XF3J-1	Berliner-Joyce	

Bureau Number	Aircraft Type	Manufacturer	Miscellaneous Notes
9225*	XSBC-3	Curtiss	
9226–9263	F4B-4	Boeing	
9264	XF9C-2	Curtiss	
9265–9268	F11C-2	Curtiss	
9269	XF11C-3	Curtiss	
9270–9282	F11C-2	Curtiss	
9283–9329	O3U-3	Vought	
9330	XO3U-6	Vought	
9331–9340	F11C-2	Curtiss	
9341	RE-3	Bellanca	
9342	XF2F-1	Grumman	
9343	XF13C-1	Curtiss	
9344–9345	Kite Balloon	Air Cruisers, Inc	
9346	XFL-1	Grover Loening Inc	Cancelled
9347–9349	RD-2	Douglas	
9350–9376	FF-1	Grumman	
9377	XS2C-1	Curtiss	
9378	XF7B-1	Boeing	
9379–9398	SU-4	Vought	Cancelled
9399	XO5U-1	Vought	
9400	XFT-2	Northrop	
9401–9402	Glider	Franklin	
9403–9411	OJ-2	Berliner-Joyce	
9412	XO2D-1	Douglas	
9413	XO3C-1	Curtiss	
9414–9433	SU-4	Vought	
9434–9455	JF-1	Grumman	
9456–9458	XN4Y-1	Consolidated	From Army
9459	XP3Y-1	Consolidated	
9460–9492	SF-1	Grumman	
9493	XSF-2	Grumman	
9494–9520	BG-1	Great Lakes	
9521–9522	XJW-1	Waco	
9523–9527	JF-1	Grumman	
9528–9533	RD-3	Douglas	
9534–9550	BG-1	Great Lakes	
9551–9571	P2Y-3	Consolidated	
9572–9583	OJ-2	Berliner-Joyce	
9584–9585	R4C-1	Curtiss	
9586–9612	BF2C-1	Curtiss	
9613	XP3D-1	Douglas	
9614–9617	PS-2	Franklin	Glider
9618–9619	P2Y-3	Consolidated	
9620–9622	R2D-1	Douglas	
9623–9676	F2F-1	Grumman	
9677–9717	NS-1	Stearman	

Bureau Number	Aircraft Type	Manufacturer	Miscellaneous Notes
9718	XR3Q-1	Stinson	
9719	F4B-4	Quantico	From spares
9720	XTBD-1	Douglas	
9721	XPTBH-2	Hall	
9722	XB2G-1	Great Lakes	
9723	XTBG-1	Great Lakes	
9724	XSOK-1	Kreider-Reisner	
9725	XSB2U-1	Vought	
9726	XSBA-1	Brewster	
9727	XF3F-1	Grumman	
9728	XSOE-1	Bellanca	
9729–9744	O3U-6	Vought	
9745	XBT-1	Northrop	
9746†	XF3U-1	Vought	
9747–9749	XRK-3	Kinner	
9750–9833	SBU-1	Vought	
9834	XSB3U-1	Vought	
9835–9839	JF-3	Grumman	
9840–9855	BG-1	Great Lakes	
9856–9990	SOC-1	Curtiss	
9991	XN3N-1	NAF	
9992	Free Balloon	Air Cruisers Inc	
9993–9994	R2D-1	Douglas	
9995	XPBS-1	Sikorsky	
9996	XSBF-1	Grumman	
9997	F2F-1	Grumman	
9998	XR2K-1	Fairchild	For NACA
9999	G-1 Airship	Goodyear	

The beginning of the second series of four-digit numbers

Bureau Number	Aircraft Type	Manufacturer	Miscellaneous Notes
0001–0016	O3U-6	Vought	
0017–0101	N3N-1	NAF	
0102–0161	PBY-1	Consolidated	
0162–0190	J2F-1	Grumman	
0191–0210	NS-1	Stearman	
0211–0264	F3F-1	Grumman	
0265	XN3N-2	NAF	
0266	JF-2	Grumman	From Coast Guard
0267	XR2O-1	Lockheed	
0268–0381	TBD-1	Douglas	
0382	PM-2	NAS Norfolk	From spares
0383	XF4F-3	Grumman	
0384	PM-2	FAB Coco Solo	From spares and hull of 8480
0385	XOSN-1	NAF	

Bureau Number	Aircraft Type	Manufacturer	Miscellaneous Notes
0386–0425	SOC-2	Curtiss	
0426–0450	N3N-1	NAF	Cancelled
0451	XF2A-1	Brewster	
0452	XF3F-2	Grumman	
0453	XPB2Y-1	Consolidated	
0454–0503	PBY-2	Consolidated	
0504–0506	JRS-1	Sikorsky	
0507–0589	SBC-3	Curtiss	0582 modified to XSBC-4
0590–0626	BT-1	Northrop	
0627	XBT-2	Northrop	
0628–0643	BT-1	Northrop	
0644–0723	N3N-1	NAF	
0724	ME-108b	Bayerische Flugzeugwerke	
0725	C-620 Le Simoun	Caudron	
0726–0778	SB2U-1	Vought	
0779	XSB2U-3	Vought	
0780–0794	J2F-2	Grumman	
0795	JE-1	Bellanca	
0796	XPBM-1	Martin	
0797–0799	Free Balloons	Air Cruisers	
0800	JK-1	Fairchild	
0801	JB-1	Beech	
0802–0841	SBU-2	Vought	
0842–0907	PBY-3	Consolidated	
0908–0909	JH-1	Stearman-Hammond	
0910–0949	NJ-1	North American	From Army
0950	XSO2C-1	Curtiss	
0951	XOS2U-1	Vought	
0952–0966	N3N-1	NAF	
0967–1047	F3F-2	Grumman	
1048–1051	JO-2	Lockheed	
1052	XOSS-1	Stearman	
1053	JO-1	Lockheed	
1054–1063	JRS-1	Sikorsky	
1064–1146	SOC-3	Curtiss	
1147–1190	SON-1	NAF	
1191–1194	JRS-1	Sikorsky	
1195–1209	J2F-2	Grumman	
1210	L-1 Airship	Goodyear	
1211	K-2 Airship	Goodyear	
1212	S-2	S.A.I., Italy	
1213–1244	PBY-4	Consolidated	
1245	XPBY-5A	Consolidated	
1246	PBM-1	Martin	
1247	XPBM-2	Martin	

Bureau Number	Aircraft Type	Manufacturer	Miscellaneous Notes
1248–1266	PBM-1	Martin	
1267	XJO-3	Lockheed	
1268–1325	SBC-4	Curtiss	
1326–1383	SB2U-2	Vought	
1384	XJ3F-1	Grumman	
1385	XSO3C-1	Curtiss	
1386–1396	F2A-1	Brewster	
1397–1439	F2A-2	Brewster	
1440	XSO2U-1	Vought	
1441	XR4O-1	Lockheed	
1442	XF5F-1	Grumman	
1443	XF4U-1	Vought	
1444–1470	F3F-3	Grumman	
1471–1473	Free Balloon	Goodyear	
1474–1504	SBC-4	Curtiss	
1505–1519	TBD-1	Douglas	
1520	XPB2M-1R	Martin	
1521	XN5N-1	NAF	
1522–1551	SBN-1	NAF	
1552–1567	SNJ-1	North American	
1568–1587	J2F-3	Grumman	
1588	XFL-1	Bell	
1589–1595	GB-1	Beech	From Army
1596–1631	SBD-1	Douglas	
1632	XSB2A-1	Brewster	
1633–1637	PB2Y-2	Consolidated	
1638	XPB2Y-3	Consolidated	
1639–1670	J2F-4	Grumman	
1671–1673	JRF-1A	Grumman	
1674–1677	JRF-1	Grumman	
1678–1679	JRF-1A	Grumman	
1680	JRF-1	Grumman	
1681–1734	OS2U-1	Vought	
1735–1755	SBD-1	Douglas	
1756–1757	XNR-1	Maxson	Radio controlled
1758	XSB2C-1	Curtiss	
1759–1808	N3N-3	NAF	
1809–1843	SBC-4	Curtiss	
1844–1845	F4F-3	Grumman	
1846–1847	XF4F-5	Grumman	
1848–1896	F4F-3	Grumman	.
1897	XF4F-4	Grumman	
1898–1900	GB-1	Beech	
1901–1903	R3D-1	Douglas	1901 Cancelled
1904–1907	R3D-2	Douglas	
1908–2007	N3N-3	NAF	

Bureau Number	Aircraft Type	Manufacturer	Miscellaneous Notes
2008–2043	SNJ-2	North American	
2044–2100	SB2U-3	Vought	
2101	XR5O-1	Lockheed	
2102–2188	SBD-2	Douglas	
2189–2288	OS2U-2	Vought	
2289–2455	PBY-5	Consolidated	
2456–2488	PBY-5A	Consolidated	
2489–2511	F4B-4A	Boeing	From Army
2512–2538	F4F-3	Grumman	
2539–2540	XTBF-1	Grumman	2539 crashed prior to acceptance
2541	JO-2	Lockheed	
2542	XTBU-1	Vought	
2543–2547	JRB-1	Beech	
2548–2572	SNJ-2	North American	
2573–3072	N3N-3	NAF	
3073–3130	OS2U-2	Vought	
3131–3143	R4D-1	Douglas	From Army
3144	XPBB-1	Boeing	
3145–3394	N2S-1	Stearman	
3395–3519	N2S-3	Stearman	
3520–3644	N2S-2	Stearman	
3645–3845	NP-1	Spartan	
3846–3855	JRF-4	Grumman	
3856–3874	F4F-3	Grumman	
3875–3969	F4F-3A	Grumman	3875-3904 Cancelled
3970–4057	F4F-3	Grumman	
4058–4098	F4F-4	Grumman	
4099–4198	NR-1	Ryan	From Army
4199–4248	SBC-4	Curtiss	
4249–4250	R5O-1	Lockheed	
4251	BD-1	Douglas	From Army
4252–4351	N2S-3	Stearman	
4352–4517	N3N-3	NAF	
4518–4691	SBD-3	Douglas	
4692–4706	R4D-1	Douglas	From Army
4707–4708	R4D-2	Douglas	From Army
4709–4710	JRB-1	Beech	From Army
4711–4725	JRB-2	Beech	From Army
4726–4729	JRB-1	Beech	From Army
4730–4879	SO3C	Curtiss	
4880–5029	SO3C-2	Curtiss	
5030–5262	F4F-3	Grumman	
5263–5283	F4F-7	Grumman	
5284–5289	OS2U-3	Vought	
5990–6289	OS2U-3	Vought	Cancelled
6290–6439	SNC-1	Curtiss	

Bureau Number	Aircraft Type	Manufacturer	Miscellaneous Notes
6440–6454	JRF-5	Grumman	
6455–6754‡	PBM-3	Martin	
6755–7024	SNJ-3	North American	From Army
7025–7028	K Type Airship	Goodyear	
7029–7030	L Type Airship	Goodyear	
7031	XF4F-6	Grumman	
7032–7034	GK-1	Fairchild	
7035–7042	BD-2	Douglas	
7043–7242	PB2Y-3,-3R	Consolidated	
7243–7302	PBY-5A	Consolidated	
7303	R5O-2	Lockheed	
7304–9999	Unassigned		

The beginning of the five-digit series

Bureau Number	Aircraft Type	Manufacturer	Miscellaneous Notes
00001–00004	SB2C-1	Curtiss	
00005	XSB2C-2	Curtiss	
00006–00200	SB2C-1	Curtiss	
00201–00370	SB2C-1C	Curtiss	
00371–00372	JF-2	Grumman	
00373–00392	TBF-1	Grumman	
00393	XTBF-2	Grumman	
00394–00658	TBF-1	Grumman	
00659–00802	J2F-5	Grumman	
00803–00882	SB2A-2	Brewster	
00883–01004	SB2A-3	Brewster	00943–01004 Cancelled
01005	XSB2A-1	Brewster	
01006–01007	R5O-3	Lockheed	
01008–01215	SB2C-1C	Curtiss	01209–01215 Cancelled
01209–01212	XFO-1	Lockheed	P-38
01213–01215	XF15C-1	Curtiss	
01216–01515	OS2N-1	NAF	
01516–01623	F2A-3	Brewster	
01624–01646	GB-2	Beech	
01647	JF-2	Grumman	
01648–01649	R4D-1	Douglas	
01650–01673	PBM-3C	Martin	
01674–01728	PBM-3S	Martin	
01729–01730	ZNP-K-7, -8	Goodyear	K Class Airship
01731–01770	TBF-1	Grumman	
01771–01976	SNJ-3	North American	
01977–01990	R4D-1	Douglas	
01991–02152	F4F-4	Grumman	
02153–02156	F4U-1	Vought	
02157	XF4U-3	Vought	

Bureau Number	Aircraft Type	Manufacturer	Miscellaneous Notes
02158–02736	F4U-1	Vought	
02737–02746	PB2Y-3R	Consolidated	
02747–02790	OY-1	Consolidated	02789–02790 Cancelled
02789–02790	XP4M-1	Martin	
02791–02946	PBN-1	NAF	02802 Cancelled
02947	R3O-2	Lockheed	
02948–02977	PBY-5A	Consolidated	
02978	V-173	Vought	
02979–02980	LNS-1	Schweizer	
02981	XF6F-4	Grumman	
02982	XF6F-3	Grumman	
02983–03182	SNV-1	Vultee	
03183	XF14C-2	Curtiss	
03184	XF14C-1	Curtiss	Cancelled
03185–03384	SBD-3	Douglas	
03385–03544	F4F-4	Grumman	
03545–03548	Free Balloon	Lakehurst	
03549–03550	XF7F-1	Grumman	
03551–03552	XSB2D-1	Douglas	
03553–03742	SNB-2	Beech	03563–03742 Cancelled
03563–03742	PBM-4E	Martin	Cancelled
03563–03712	PBV-1A	Vickers	Cancelled
03713–03742	JRF-5	Grumman	Cancelled
03743–03744	XSB3C-1	Curtiss	Cancelled
03745–03801	PBB-1	Boeing	Cancelled
03802–03841	F4U-1	Vought	
03842–03861	PBO-1	Lockheed	
03862–04148	SB2C-2	Curtiss	Cancelled
03862–04025	OY-1	Consolidated	04021–04025 Cancelled
04149–04198	SO3C-2	Curtiss	
04199–04348	SO3C-3	Curtiss	04290–04348 Cancelled
04349–04358	JRF-5	Grumman	
04359–04379	ZNPK	Goodyear	
04380–04389	LNS-1	Schweizer	
04390–04395	GH-1	Howard	
04396–04398	JR2S-1	Sikorsky	Cancelled
04399–04420	PBY-5A	Consolidated	
04421–04424	Free Balloon	Lakehurst	
04425–04514	PBY-5	Consolidated	
04515–04774	F3A-1	Brewster	
04775–04958	F6F-3	Grumman	
04959–04961	BTD-1	Douglas	
04962	XBTD-2	Douglas	
04963	BTD-1	Douglas	
04964	XBTD-2	Douglas	
04965–04971	BTD-1	Douglas	

Bureau Number	Aircraft Type	Manufacturer	Miscellaneous Notes
04972–05045	PBY-5A	Consolidated	
05046–05050	R5O-4	Lockheed	
05051–05072	R4D-1	Douglas	
05073–05084	R4D-3	Douglas	
05085–05234	SNC-1	Curtiss	
05235–05434	N2S-3	Stearman	Boeing
05435–05526	SNJ-3	North American	
05527–05674	SNJ-4	North American	
05675–05874	SNV-1	Vultee	
05875–05876	N2T-1	Timm	
05877–06491	TBF-1	Grumman	
06492–06701	SBD-3	Douglas	
06702–06991	SBD-4	Douglas	
06992–06999	R4D-3	Douglas	
07000–07003	R4D-4	Douglas	
07004	JRF-1	Grumman	
07005–08004	N2S-3	Stearman	Boeing
08005	R3D-3	Douglas	
08006–08028	GH-1	Howard	
08029	GH-2	Howard	
08030–08123	PBY-5A	Consolidated	
08124–08549	PBY-5	Consolidated	
08550–08797	F3A-1	Brewster	
08798–09047	F6F-3	Grumman	
09048–09392	BTD-1	Douglas	09063–09392 Cancelled
09063	SNJ-4	North American	
09064	P-51H	North American	From USAF
09085–09095	XBT2D-1	Douglas	XAD-1
09096	XBT2D-1P	Douglas	
09097	XBT2D-1	Douglas	
09098–09099	XBT2D-1N	Douglas	
09100–09106	XBT2D-1	Douglas	
09107	XBT2D-1W	Douglas	XAD-1W
09108	XAD-2	Douglas	
09109	XBT2D-1Q	Douglas	
09110–09351	AD-1	Douglas	
09352–09392	AD-1Q	Douglas	09387–09392 Cancelled
09393–09692	OS2U-3	Vought	
09693–09752	SBD-5A	Douglas	
09753–09764	Free Balloon	Lakehurst	
09765	GB-2	Beech	Misc. acquisition
09766	GB-1	Beech	Misc. acquisition
09767	JRF-4	Grumman	Misc. acquisition
09768	GB-1	Beech	Misc. acquisition
09769–09770	GH-1	Howard	Misc. acquisition
09771	JRB-2	Beech	Misc. acquisition

Bureau Number	Aircraft Type	Manufacturer	Miscellaneous Notes
09772	GB-1	Beech	Misc. acquisition
09773–09774	GB-2	Beech	Misc. acquisition
09775	GH-1	Howard	Misc. acquisition
09776–09778	GB-1	Beech	Misc. acquisition
09779	GH-1	Howard	Misc. acquisition
09780	GB-1	Beech	Misc. acquisition
09781	GH-1	Howard	Misc. acquisition
09782	JRF-1	Grumman	Misc. acquisition
09783	YKS-6	Waco	Misc. acquisition
09784	YKS-7	Waco	Misc. acquisition
09785	CH400	Bellanca	Misc. acquisition
09786	Stinson	Stinson	Misc. acquisition
09787–09788	GK-1	Fairchild	Misc. acquisition
09789	J4F-2	Grumman	Misc. acquisition
09790–09797	GK-1	Fairchild	Misc. acquisition
09798–09799	GQ-1	Stinson	Misc. acquisition
09800	GB-1	Beech	Misc. acquisition
09801–09802	ZNN-L	Goodyear	L Class Airships
09803	R2Y-1	Consolidated	
09804	A-30	Martin	From UK
09805–09816	J4F-2	Grumman	
09817–10316	SNJ-4	North American	
10317–10806	SBD-4	Douglas	
10807–11066	SBD-5	Douglas	
11067–11646	F3A-1	Brewster	11294–11646 Cancelled
11294–11646	AT-19	Stinson	Reverse Lend-Lease
11647–11648	XLRA-1	Allied Aviation	
11649–11650	XLRH-1	Snead	Cancelled
11651–11654	XLRQ-1	Bristol	11653–11654 Cancelled
11655–12227	F4F-4	Grumman	
12228–12229	XF4F-8	Grumman	
12230–12329	F4F-3	Grumman	
12330–12353	GB-2	Beech	
12354–12389	SNB-2	Beech	
12390–12392	JR2S-2	Sikorsky	
12393–12404	R4D-1	Douglas	
12405–12446	R4D-5	Douglas	
12447–12453	R5O-4	Lockheed	
12454–12491	R5O-5	Lockheed	
12492–12991	SNV-1	Vultee	
12992	XF2G-1	Goodyear	
12993–13470	FG-1D	Goodyear	
13471–13472	XF2G-1	Goodyear	
13473–14690	FG-1D	Goodyear	
14691–14695	XF2G-1	Goodyear	
14696–14991	FG-1D	Goodyear	

Bureau Number	Aircraft Type	Manufacturer	Miscellaneous Notes
14992–15951	FM-1	Eastern	
15952–16791	FM-2	Eastern	
16792–17091	TBM-1C	Eastern	
17092–17248	R4D-5	Douglas	
17249–17291	R4D-6	Douglas	
17292–17391	TDN-1	NAF	
17392–17455	F4U-1	Vought	
17456–17515	F4U-1A	Vought	
17516	XF4U-3	Vought	
17517–18121	F4U-1A	Vought	
18122–18191	F4U-1	Vought	
18192–18307	SB2C-1C	Curtiss	
18308	XSB2C-5	Curtiss	
18309–18598	SB2C-1C	Curtiss	
18599–18619	SB2C-3/3E	Curtiss	
18620–18621	XSB2C-6	Curtiss	
18622–19710	SB2C-3	Curtiss	
19711–21191	SB2C-4/4E	Curtiss	
21192–21231	SBW-1	C. C. & F.	
21232	SBW-5	C. C. & F.	Cancelled
21232	PBY-5A	Consolidated	
21233–21645	SBW-3	C. C. & F.	
21646–21741	SBW-4E	C. C. & F.	
21742–22006	BT2D-1/1Q	Douglas	Cancelled
22007–22856	SO3C-3/4	Curtiss	22057–22856 Cancelled
22257–22295	AM-1	Martin	
22296	AM-1Q	Martin	
22297–22345	AM-1	Martin	
22346–22355	AM-1Q	Martin	
22356–22856	AM-1	Martin	Cancelled
22453–22458	HTL-1	Bell	There was no 22455
22857–23656	TBM-3/3E	Eastern	
23657–23756	GB-2	Beech	
23757–23856	SNB-2C	Beech	
23857–24140	TBF-1	Grumman	
24141	XTBF-3	Grumman	
24142–24340	TBF-1	Grumman	
24341	XTBF-3	Grumman	
24342–24520	TBF-1	Grumman	
24521–25070	BM-1	Eastern	
25071–25174	TBM-1C	Eastern	
25175	XTBM-3	Eastern	
25176–25520	TBM-1C	Eastern	
25521	XTBM-3	Eastern	
25522–25699	TBM-1C	Eastern	
25700	XTBM-3	Eastern	

Bureau Number	Aircraft Type	Manufacturer	Miscellaneous Notes
25701–25720	TBM-1C	Eastern	
25721–26195	F6F-3/3N	Grumman	
26196–26425	NE-1	Piper	
26426	LNS-1	Schweizer	Cancelled
26427–27851	SNJ-4	North American	
27852	XP4Y-1	Consolidated	
27853–27856	XTDN-1	NAF	
27857–27858	XTDR-1	Interstate	
27859–27958	TDR-1	Interstate	
27959	R5O-3	Lockheed	
27960–28058	N2S-4	Stearman	
28059–28829	SBD-5	Douglas	
28830	XSBD-6	Douglas	
28831–29213	SBD-5	Douglas	
29214–29375	SB2A-4	Brewster	
29376–29550	NH-1	Howard	
29551–29668	SNB-2C	Beech	29665–29668 Cancelled
29665–29666	XTD3C-1	Culver	
29667–29668	P-80A	Lockheed	From Army
29669–29698	NE-2	Piper	29689–29698 Cancelled
29689	P-80A	Lockheed	From Army
29690	P-80B	Lockheed	From Army
29691–29722	Unknown	Unknown	Cancelled
29723–29922	PV-1	Lockheed	
29923–30146	N2S-4	Stearman	Boeing
30147	R4D-1	Douglas	
30148–30150	R5O-5	Lockheed	
30151	J4F-2	Grumman	
30152–30196	ZNP-K	Goodyear	K Class Airship, K-30 to K-74
30197–30296	AE-1	Piper	HE-1
30297–30298	XF14C-3	Curtiss	Cancelled
30299–31398	TBY-2	Consolidated	30368–30370, 30481–31398 Cancelled
30368	XHJS-1	Sikorsky	
30369	TBY-2	Consolidated	
30370	XHJS-1	Sikorsky	
30481–30542	AT-19	Stinson	From UK
30543–31398	Unknown	Unknown	
31399	XBTC-1	Curtiss	Cancelled
31400	XBTC-2	Curtiss	Cancelled
31399–31400	XJL-1	Columbia	
31401–31402	XBTC-2	Curtiss	
31403–31502	LRA-1	Allied	Cancelled
31503–31504	XLR2A-1	Allied	
31505–31506	XLNE-1	Pratt, Read & Co.	
31507–31585	LNE-1	Pratt, Read & Co.	
31586–31635	LRH-1	Snead	Cancelled

Bureau Number	Aircraft Type	Manufacturer	Miscellaneous Notes
31636–31685	SBF-1	Fairchild	
31686–31835	SBF-3	Fairchild	
31836–31935	SBF-4E	Fairchild	
31936–32085	PB4Y-1	Consolidated	
32086	XPB4Y-2	Consolidated	
32087–32094	PB4Y-1	Consolidated	
32095–32096	XPB4Y-2	Consolidated	
32097–32335	PB4Y-1	Consolidated	
32336–32385	GH-2	Howard	
32386	XPB3Y-1	Consolidated	Cancelled
32386	XTDC-2	Culver	
32387–32636	N2T-1	Timm	
32637–32786	J2F-6	Grumman	
32787–32936	GH-2	Howard	32867–32936 Cancelled
32867–32936	GB-2	Beech	32916–32936 Cancelled, from UK
32937–32986	J4F-2	Grumman	
32987–32991	SNC-1	Curtiss	
32992–33066	GB-2	Beech	
33067–33466	PV-1	Lockheed	From Army
33467–33514	ZNP-K	Goodyear	Cancelled
33515–33614	TDR-1	Interstate	33532–33614 Cancelled
33532–33534	XF6U-1	Vought	
33535–33614	J2F-6	Grumman	
33615–33714	AM-1/1Q	Martin	Cancelled
33615–33621	R4D-4R	Douglas	
33622–33714	TDR-1	Interstate	
33715–33814	LRQ-1	Bristol	33715–33814 Cancelled
33815–33820	R4D-4	Douglas	
33821–33870	AM-1/1Q	Martin	33821–33870 Cancelled
33821–33870	TO-1	Lockheed	TV-1/P-80C
33871–33920	TD3R-1	Interstate	33881–33920 Cancelled
33921	XTD3R-1	Interstate	
33922	XTD2R-1	Interstate	
33923–33924	XTD3R-1	Interstate	
33925–33951	PV-3	Lockheed	
33952–33957	J4F-2	Grumman	
33958–33959	XF5U-1	Vought	33959 Cancelled
33960–34059	PBY-5A	Consolidated	
34060–34094	JRF-5	Grumman	
34095–34096	XSC-1	Curtiss	
34097–34101	N2S-4	Stearman	Boeing
34102–34105	TBM-1C	Eastern	
34106	PB-1W	Boeing	From Army, B-17G
34107–34111	N2S-4	Stearman	Boeing
34112–34113	JK-1	Fairchild	
34114	PB-1W	Boeing	From Army, B-17G

Bureau Number	Aircraft Type	Manufacturer	Miscellaneous Notes
34115–34134	LNE-1	Pratt, Read & Co.	
34135–34584	SNV-1	Vultee	
34585	J4F-2	Grumman	Misc. acquisition
34586–34997	PV-1	Lockheed	
34998–35047	PBJ-1C	North American	
35048–35096	PBJ-1D	North American	
35097	PBJ-1G	North American	
35098–35193	PBJ-1D	North American	
35194–35195	PBJ-1J	North American	
35196–35202	PBJ-1D	North American	
35203–35249	PBJ-1J	North American	
35250–35297	PBJ-1H	North American	
35298–35300	XSC-1	Curtiss	
35301	SC-1	Curtiss	
35302	XSC-1A	Curtiss	
35303–35797	SC-1	Curtiss	
35798–35921	PBN-1	NAF	Cancelled
35798–35920	PBJ-1J	North American	
35921	JRF-4	Grumman	
35922–35949	SBD-5	Douglas	
35950	SBD-6	Douglas	
35951–36421	SBD-5	Douglas	
36422–36424	XLNR-1	Aeronca	
36425–36427	XLNP-1	Piper	
36428–36430	XLNT-1	Taylorcraft	
36431–36432	XLRN-1	NAF	Cancelled
36433–36932	SBD-5	Douglas	
36933–36934	XTB2D-1	Douglas	
36935–37034	J2F-6	Grumman	
37035–37064	PV-2C	Lockheed	
37065–37534	PV-2	Lockheed	
37535–37623	PV-2D	Lockheed	37551–37623 Cancelled
37551	HRP-1	Piasecki	
37624–37634	PV-2D	Lockheed	
37635–37636	XTDR-1	Interstate	Cancelled
37637–37638	AT-19	Stinson	Cancelled
37639–37648	LRW-1	Waco	
37649	VKS-7	Stinson	
37650–37659	Unknown	Unknown	Cancelled
37660–37710	R4D-1	Douglas	37681–37710 Cancelled
37711–37770	J4F-2	Grumman	
37771–37831	JRF-5	Grumman	
37832–37851	Unknown	Unknown	Cancelled
37852–37853	RS-5	Sikorsky	From Pan Am
37854–37855	RS-4	Sikorsky	From Pan Am
37856–37967	N2S-4	Stearman	Boeing

Bureau Number	Aircraft Type	Manufacturer	Miscellaneous Notes
37968–37969	XHRP-1	Piasecki	37968 Cancelled
37970–37972	D-558-1	Douglas	
37973–37975	D-558-2	Douglas	
37976–37977	XHJP-1	Piasecki	
37978–37987	N2S-4	Stearman	Boeing
37988–38437	N2S-3	Stearman	Boeing
38438–38732	N2S-5	Stearman	38611–38732 Cancelled Boeing
38733–38979	PB4Y-1	Consolidated	
38980–39012	PBJ-1J	North American	
39013–39032	RY-2	Consolidated	39018–39032 Cancelled
39033–39055	HNS-1	Sikorsky	39053–39055 Cancelled, from Army
39053–39055	XFJ-1	North American	
39056	XNL-1	Langley Aviation	
39057–39095	R4D-5	Douglas	
39096–39098	R4D-6	Douglas	
39099	R4D-7	Douglas	
39100	R4D-6	Douglas	
39101–39108	R4D-7	Douglas	
39109	R4D-6	Douglas	
39110–39136	R4D-5	Douglas	39112–39136 Cancelled
39112–39128	R5D-4	Douglas	
39137–39181	R5D-1	Douglas	
39182–39191	N2T-1	Timm	
39192–39291	SNB-2	Beech	
39292–39491	RB-1	Budd	39309–39491 Cancelled
39318–39468	P2V-2	Lockheed	39369–39468 Cancelled
39469–39491	Unknown	Unknown	Most likely not used
39492–39611	R5C-1	Curtiss	
39612–39646	R5O-6	Lockheed	
39647–39712	FR-1	Ryan	
39713–39714	XF2R-2	Ryan	Cancelled
39715–39746	FR-1	Ryan	Cancelled
39747–39748	JRF-5	Grumman	
39749–39998	SNB-1	Beech	
39999–43137	F6F-3/3N/3E	Grumman	
43138–43637	N2S-5	Stearman	Boeing
43638–44037	SNJ-5	North American	
44038–44187	SNV-2	Vultee	
44188–44227	PB2B-1	Boeing	Canada
44228–44312	PB2B-2R	Boeing	Canada 44295–44312 Cancelled
44313–44314	XBTK-1	Kaiser	
44315	JRB-4	Beech	
44316–44317	XOSE-1	Edo	
44318	XHJD-1	McDonnell	
44319	LRW-1	Waco	From Army
44320–44354	LBT-1	Taylorcraft	Cancelled

Bureau Number	Aircraft Type	Manufacturer	Miscellaneous Notes
44355–44554	TDC-2	Culver	
44555–44704	JRB-4	Beech	44685–44704 Cancelled
44705–44904	P4Y-1	Consolidated	Cancelled
44905–44920	NH-1	Howard	
44921–44922	GH-3	Howard	
44923–44934	NH-1	Howard	
44935–44937	GH-3	Howard	
44938	NH-1	Howard	
44939	GH-3	Howard	
44940	NH-1	Howard	
44941–45204	GH-3	Howard	45050–45204 Cancelled
45205–45274	PBM-3D	Martin	
45275–45276	XPBM-5	Martin	
45277–45404	PBM-3D	Martin	
45405–45444	PBM-5	Martin	
45445–45644	TBM-1C	Eastern	
45645	XTBM-3	Eastern	
45646–46444	TBM-1C	Eastern	
46445	HNS-1	Sikorsky	
46446–46448	XHOS-1	Sikorsky	
46449	TDC-1	Culver	
46450–46638	PBY-5A	Consolidated	
46639–46698	PBY-6A	Consolidated	
46699–46723	HNS-1	Sikorsky	46701–46723 Cancelled
46724	PBY-6A	Consolidated	
46725–46737	PB4Y-1	Consolidated	
46738–46837	FM-1	Eastern	
46838–47437	FM-2	Eastern	
47438–47637	TBF-1	Grumman	
47638–48123	TBF-1C	Grumman	
48124	PBM-3D	Martin	
48125–48163	PBM-3S	Martin	
48164–48223	PBM-3D	Martin	
48224–48228	B-314	Boeing	From Pan Am
48229	JRF-5	Grumman	
48230–48231	M-130	Martin	From Pan Am
48232–48234	XFR-1	Ryan	
48235–48236	XFD-1	McDonnell	
48237–48238	XP2V-1	Lockheed	
48239–48242	ZNP-M	Goodyear	M Class Airship, M-1 to M-4
48243–48245	SOC-3A	Curtiss	
48246–48251	JRB-4	Beech	
48252–48451	PBY-5A	Consolidated	
48452–48651	Unknown	Unknown	Cancelled
48452–48453	Free Balloon	Lakehurst	
48652–48939	PV-1	Lockheed	

Bureau Number	Aircraft Type	Manufacturer	Miscellaneous Notes
48940–49359	F3A-1	Brewster	Cancelled
49360–49659	PV-1	Lockheed	
49660–49762	F4U-1	Vought	
49763	XF4U-4	Vought	
49764–50300	F4U-1	Vought	
50301	XF4U-4	Vought	
50302–50359	F4U-1	Vought	
50360–50659	F4U-1D	Vought	
50660–50689	JRF-5	Grumman	Cancelled
50690–50739	R5C-1	Curtiss	50730–50739 Cancelled
50740–50839	R4D-6	Douglas	
50840–50849	R5D-1	Douglas	
50850–50868	R5D-2	Douglas	
50869–50888	R5D-3	Douglas	50879–50888 Cancelled
50879–50888	XBT2C-1	Curtiss	50888 Cancelled
50889	R5D-2	Douglas	Cancelled
50889–51022	J4F-2	Grumman	Cancelled
51023–51094	SNB-1	Beech	
51095–51199	SNB-2C	Beech	
51200–51293	SNB-2	Beech	
51294–51349	SNB-2C	Beech	
51350–51676	SNJ-4	North American	
51677–52049	SNJ-5	North American	
52050–52549	SNV-2	Vultee	
52550–53049	N2S-5	Stearman	52627–53049 Cancelled Boeing
52750–52761	F2T-1N	Northrop	P-61B from Army
53050–53949	TBM-3E	Eastern	
53950–54049	JRB-4	Beech	Cancelled
54050–54599	SBD-5	Douglas	
54600–55049	SBD-6	Douglas	
55050–55649	FM-2	Eastern	
55650–55771	N2S-4	Stearman	Boeing
55772–55783	JRC-1	Cessna	
55784–56483	F4U-1	Vought	
56484–56683	NH-1	Howard	Cancelled
56484–56663	R5D-3	Douglas	56550–56663 Cancelled
56684–57083	FM-2	Eastern	
57084–57656	F4U-1D	Vought	
57657–57659	F4U-1C	Vought	
57660–57776	F4U-1D	Vought	
57777–57791	F4U-1C	Vought	
57792–57965	F4U-1D	Vought	
57966–57983	F4U-1C	Vought	
57984–57986	XF8B-1	Boeing	
57987–57999	Unknown	Unknown	Cancelled
57987	P-51	North American	From Army

Bureau Number	Aircraft Type	Manufacturer	Miscellaneous Notes
57988–57989	R5D-1	Douglas	
57990–57991	JD-1	Douglas	
57992–57994	JA-1	Noorduyn	From Army
57995–57998	HO3S-1	Sikorsky	
57999	JA-1	Noorduyn	
58000–58999	F6F-5/5N	Grumman	
59000–59348	PBM-5/5E	Martin	
59349	XPBM-5A	Martin	
59350–59924	PB4Y-2	Consolidated	59554 Cancelled
59925	PB4Y-2B	Consolidated	
59926	PB4Y-2	Consolidated	
59927	PB4Y-2S	Consolidated	
59928	PB4Y-2M	Consolidated	
59929–59937	PB4Y-2	Consolidated	
59938	PB4Y-2M	Consolidated	
59939–59944	PB4Y-2	Consolidated	
59945	PB4Y-2M	Consolidated	
59946–59948	PB4Y-2	Consolidated	
59949	PB4Y-2M	Consolidated	
59950–59954	PB4Y-2	Consolidated	
59955–59969	PB4Y-2M	Consolidated	
59970–60009	PB4Y-2	Consolidated	
60010–60035	SBW-1B	C. C. & F.	
60036–60209	SBW-4E	C. C. & F.	
60210–60459	SBW-5	C. C. & F.	60210, 60296–60459 Cancelled
60460-60507	OY-1	Consolidated	
60508–60581	Unknown	Unknown	Cancelled
60582–62314	N2S-5	Stearman	60582–61036, 61905–62314 Cancelled
62315–62914	Unknown	Unknown	Cancelled
62915–62929	F4U-4B	Vought	
62930	F4U-4P	Vought	
62931–62949	F4U-4B	Vought	
62950	F4U-4P	Vought	
62951–62969	F4U-4B	Vought	
62970	F4U-4P	Vought	
62971–62989	F4U-4B	Vought	
62990	F4U-4P	Vought	
62991–63009	F4U-4B	Vought	
63010	F4U-4P	Vought	
63011–63029	F4U-4B	Vought	
63030	F4U-4P	Vought	
63031–63049	F4U-4B	Vought	
63050	F4U-4P	Vought	
63051–63069	F4U-4B	Vought	
63070	F4U-4P	Vought	
63071–63914	F4U-4B/P	Vought	63072–63914 Cancelled

Bureau Number	Aircraft Type	Manufacturer	Miscellaneous Notes
63915–63991	PB4Y-1	Consolidated	63960–63991 Cancelled
63960–63961	YP-59A	Bell	From Army
63992	PBY-5	Consolidated	
63993–64441	PBY-6A	Consolidated	64100, 64108–64441 Cancelled
64100	P-59B	Bell	From Army
64108–64109	P-59B	Bell	From Army
64442–64496	JRC-1	Cessna	
64497–65396	TDR-1	Interstate	64569–65396 Cancelled
64569–64576	XOSE-1	Edo	Cancelled
64577–64896	SB2C-5	Curtiss	Cancelled
64943–64992	PBJ-1J	North American	
64993–65285	SB2C-4/4E	Curtiss	
65286	XSB2C-5	Curtiss	
65287–65396	SB2C-4	Curtiss	Cancelled
65287–65396	PB4Y-1	Consolidated	
65397–65732	SB2C-5	Curtiss	Cancelled
65733–65889	Unknown	Unknown	Cancelled
65890–66244	F6F-3	Grumman	
66245–66394	PB4Y-2	Consolidated	66325–66394 Cancelled
66325–66361	JRF-6B	Grumman	
66395–66594	JRB-4	Beech	66472–66594 Cancelled
66595–66794	JM-1	Martin	
66795–67054	PB4Y-2	Consolidated	Cancelled
67055–67254	FG-1D	Goodyear	67100–67254 Cancelled
67255–67754	FG-4	Goodyear	Cancelled
67100–67383	SNB-2	Beech	67130–67154 Cancelled
67755–67796	Unknown	Unknown	Cancelled
67797–67799	RY-1	Consolidated	
67800–67806	XLNT-1	Taylorcraft	
67807–67831	J4F-2	Grumman	Cancelled
67832–68061	PBV-1A	Vickers	Canso A, PBY-5A type
68062–69538	TBM-3	Eastern	
69539–69739	TD2C-1	Culver	
69740–69989	F7F-3	Grumman	Cancelled
69990–69991	LRW-1	Waco	
69992–70187	F6F-5	Grumman	
70188	XF6F-6	Grumman	
70189–70912	F6F-5/5N/5P	Grumman	
70913	XF6F-6	Grumman	
70914–72991	F6F-5/5N/5P	Grumman	
72992–73116	PB2B-1	Boeing	
73117–73498	TBM-1C	Eastern	
73499–75158	FM-2	Eastern	
75159–75182	OY-1	Consolidated	
75183–75207	JM-1	Martin	
75208–75209	XOSE-2	Edo	Cancelled

Bureau Number	Aircraft Type	Manufacturer	Miscellaneous Notes
75210–75213	XOSE-1	Edo	
75214–75215	XOSE-2	Edo	
75216–75217	XTE-1	Edo	
75218–75588	SB2C-1A	Curtiss	
75589–75688	HOS-1	Sikorsky	75625–75688 Cancelled
75625–75628	OSE-2	Edo	
75629–75632	TE-2	Edo	
75689–75724	HO2S-1	Sikorsky	75691–75724 Cancelled
75725–75726	XNQ-1	Fairchild	
75727–75728	HNS-1	Sikorsky	
75729–75730	HOS-1	Sikorsky	
75731–75738	HO2S-1	Sikorsky	Cancelled
75739–76138	TD2C-1	Culver	
76139–76148	FG-1	Goodyear	
76149–76449	FG-1D	Goodyear	
76450	FG-3	Goodyear	
76451–76739	FG-1	Goodyear	
76740–76759	JRB-3	Beech	
76760–76779	JRB-4	Beech	
76780–76818	SB2C-1A	Curtiss	
76819–76823	JRM-1	Martin	
76824	JRM-2	Martin	
76825–76838	JRM-1	Martin	Cancelled
76839–77138	PB4Y-2	Consolidated	Cancelled
77137–77138	PB-1W	Boeing	From Army
77139–77224	JD-1	Douglas	
77225–77244	PB-1W	Boeing	From Army
77245–77257	PB-1G	Boeing	From Army
77258	PB-1W	Boeing	From Army
77259–80258	F6F-5/5N/5P	Grumman	
80259–80260	F7F-1N	Grumman	
80261	XF7F-2N	Grumman	
80262–80293	F7F-1N	Grumman	
80294–80358	F7F-2N	Grumman	
80359–80547	F7F-3	Grumman	
80548	F7F-4N	Grumman	
80549–80608	F7F-3N	Grumman	
80609–80620	F7F-4N	Grumman	
80621–80758	F7F	Grumman	Cancelled
80621–80622	JD-1	Douglas	From UK
80759–80763	XF4U-4	Vought	
80764–82177	F4U-4	Vought	
82178–82189	F4U-1C	Vought	
82190–82259	F4U-1D	Vought	
82260–82289	F4U-1C	Vought	
82290–82369	F4U-1D	Vought	

Bureau Number	Aircraft Type	Manufacturer	Miscellaneous Notes
82370–82394	F4U-1C	Vought	
82395–82434	F4U-1D	Vought	
82435–82459	F4U-1C	Vought	
82460–82539	F4U-1D	Vought	
82540–82582	F4U-1C	Vought	
82583–82632	F4U-1D	Vought	
82633–82639	F4U-1C	Vought	
82640–82739	F4U-1D	Vought	
82740–82761	F4U-1C	Vought	
82762–82854	F4U-1D	Vought	82853–82854 Cancelled
82853–82854	XJR2F-1	Grumman	
82855–82857	XF2M-1	Goodyear	Cancelled
82855–82857	PB-1G	Boeing	From Army
82858–83126	SB2C-4/4E	Curtiss	
83127	XSB2C-5	Curtiss	
83128–83751	SB2C-5	Curtiss	
83752–83991	TD2C-1	Culver	
83992–84054	Unknown	Unknown	Cancelled
83992–84027	PB-1W	Boeing	83999–84027 Cancelled From Army
84028–84029	P2B-1S	Boeing B-29	From Army
84030–84031	P2B-2S	Boeing B-29	From Army
84032	JRB-3	Beech	
84055–84056	XTSF-1/XTB2F-1	Grumman	Cancelled
84057–84589	PV-2D	Lockheed	84065–84589 Cancelled
84590–84789	PBM-5	Martin	
84790–84818	JRF-5	Grumman	
84819–85093	SNJ-5	North American	
85094–85095	XLR2W-1	Waco	
85096–85135	JRB-4	Beech	
85136–85160	PBM-5	Martin	
85161–85162	XBTM-1	Martin	
85163–85164	XR6O-1	Lockheed	
85165–85264	LBP-1	Piper	Cancelled
85265–85289	LBT-1	Taylorcraft	
85290–85292	XLBE-1	Pratt, Read & Co.	
85293–85389	LBE-1	Pratt, Read & Co.	Cancelled
85390	XHRP-1	Piasecki	Cancelled
85391–85458	GB-2	Beech	Cancelled
85459–86296	TBM-3E	Eastern	86293–86296 Cancelled
86293	JRB-4	Beech	
86294	JRB-3	Beech	
86295–86296	JRB-4	Beech	
86297–87719	FM-2/2P	Eastern	86974–87719 Cancelled
87720–87762	JRF-5	Grumman	87752–87762 Cancelled
87752	JRB-3	Beech	
87753	RB-4	Beech	

Bureau Number	Aircraft Type	Manufacturer	Miscellaneous Notes
87754–87759	R5D-3	Douglas	
87763–87787	LNT-1	Taylorcraft	
87788–88453	FG-1D	Goodyear	
88454–88458	F2G-1	Goodyear	
88459–88871	F2G-2	Goodyear	88464–88871 Cancelled
88872–89071	PBJ-1H	North American	
89072–89081	JD-1	Douglas	
89082–89085	P2V-1	Lockheed	
89086	XP2V-2	Lockheed	
89087–89096	P2V-1	Lockheed	
89097–89119	XTB2D-1	Douglas	Cancelled
89120–90019	SB2C-5	Curtiss	89466–90019 Cancelled
89466–89492	JRB-5	Beech	
89493	JRB-1	Beech	
89494	JRB-5	Beech	
90020–90131	RY-3	Consolidated	90060–90131 Cancelled
90060–90061	XF2L-1	Bell P-63	Cancelled
90132–90384	R2Y-1	Consolidated	Cancelled
90132–90271	PB4Y-1	Consolidated	
90385–90395	R5D-2	Douglas	
90396–90415	R5D-4	Douglas	
90416–90436	Unknown	Unknown	Cancelled
90437–90459	F8F-1	Grumman	
90460–90461	XF8F-1	Grumman	
90462–90483	PB4Y-1	Consolidated	
90484–90503	XBTK-1	Kaiser	90487–90503 Cancelled
90504–90506	XTB3F-1	Grumman	
90507–90531	JM-2	Martin	90522–90531 Cancelled
90522–90523	JRB-2	Beech	
90532–90581	JRB-4	Beech	
90582–91106	SNJ-5	North American	91102–91106 Cancelled
91102–91103	F2L-1K	Bell	
91104	R4D-1	Douglas	
91105	R5D-1	Douglas	
91106	Mosquito	De Havilland	From UK
91107–92006	TBM-3E	Eastern	91753–92006 Cancelled
91962–91993	JM-2	Martin	
91994–92006	R5D-3	Douglas	92004–92006 Cancelled
92007–93301	FG-1D	Goodyear	92702–93301 Cancelled
93302–93651	SC-1	Curtiss	93368–93651 Cancelled
93652–94751	F6F-5	Grumman	94522–94751 Cancelled
94752–95048	F8F-1	Grumman	
95049	XF8F-2	Grumman	
95050–95329	F8F-1	Grumman	
95330	XF8F-2	Grumman	
95331–96751	F8F-1	Grumman	95499–96751 Cancelled

Bureau Number	Aircraft Type	Manufacturer	Miscellaneous Notes
96752–97295	F4U-4	Vought	
97296	XF4U-5	Vought	
97297–97363	F4U-4	Vought	
97364	XF4U-5	Vought	
97365–97414	F4U-4	Vought	
97415	XF4U-5	Vought	
97416–97531	F4U-4	Vought	
97532–97672	TBM-3	Eastern	Cancelled
97673–97675	XTBM-4	Eastern	
97676–98601	TBM-4	Eastern	Cancelled
98602–98605	PBM-5E	Martin	
98606	PBM-5N	Martin	
98607–98615	PBM-5E	Martin	
98616	XP5M-1	Martin	
98617–99073	PBM-5	Martin	Cancelled
99074–99077	J4F-2	Grumman	Misc. acquisition
99078	JRF-4/G-21A	Grumman	Misc. acquisition
99079	GK-1	Fairchild	Misc. acquisition
99080	PBY-4	Consolidated	American Export
99081–99084	B-314	Boeing	From Pan Am
99085–99088	AT-19	Stinson	From Pan Am
99089	Waco	Waco	From Pan Am
99090–99092	Electra	Lockheed	From Pan Am
99093–99095	Lodestar	Lockheed	From Pan Am
99096–99097	Speedster	Rearwin	From Pan Am
99098	Pilgrim	Pilgrim	From Pan Am
99099	DC-3A	Douglas	From Pan Am
99100–99823	Unknown	Unknown	Cancelled
99824–99857	R4D-7	Douglas	
99858–99860	XF2H-1	McDonnell	
99861–99990	R4D-6	Douglas	Cancelled
99991–100000	Unknown	Unknown	Cancelled

The beginning of the six-digit series

Bureau Number	Aircraft Type	Manufacturer	Miscellaneous Notes
000001	A-1	Navy and IAS	Replica, Navy's 1st acft
001009–001023	DSN-3/QH-50C	Gyrodyne	DSN-3 redesig. QH-50C
001024–001027	QH-50C	Gyrodyne	
001029–001041	QH-50C	Gyrodyne	
001043–001049	QH-50C	Gyrodyne	
001051	QH-50C	Gyrodyne	
001053–001192	QH-50C	Gyrodyne	
001193–001196	QH-50D	Gyrodyne	
001197–001293	QH-50C	Gyrodyne	
001295–001307	QH-50C	Gyrodyne	

Bureau Number	Aircraft Type	Manufacturer	Miscellaneous Notes
001309–001314	QH-50C	Gyrodyne	
001316–001327	QH-50C	Gyrodyne	
001329–001340	QH-50C	Gyrodyne	
001342–001347	QH-50C	Gyrodyne	
001349–001358	QH-50C	Gyrodyne	
001360–001362	QH-50C	Gyrodyne	
001365	QH-50C	Gyrodyne	
001367–001375	QH-50C	Gyrodyne	
001377–001381	QH-50C	Gyrodyne	
001382	QH-50D	Gyrodyne	
001383–001385	QH-50C	Gyrodyne	
001386–001493	QH-50D	Gyrodyne	
001495–001571	QH-50D	Gyrodyne	
001572	QH-50C	Gyrodyne	
001573–001613	QH-50D	Gyrodyne	
001615–001758	QH-50D	Gyrodyne	
002743–002744	X-25A	Bensen	
100001–102000	F8F-1	Grumman	Cancelled
102001–102275	PV-2D	Lockheed	Cancelled
102276–102575	PBM-5	Martin	Cancelled
102576–104575	TBM-4	Martin	Cancelled
104576–105175	FR-2	Ryan	Cancelled
105176–106875	F4U-4	Vought	Cancelled
106876–107875	FG-4	Goodyear	Cancelled
107876–108225	SB2C-5	Curtiss	Cancelled
108226–109272	F6F-5N	Grumman	Cancelled
109273–111148	F3M-1	Eastern	Cancelled
111149–111348	PBY-6A	Consolidated	Cancelled
111349–111748	F6F-5	Grumman	Cancelled
111749–111848	FD-1	McDonnell	111809–111848 Cancelled
111809–111828	HRP-1	Piasecki	
111829–111833	HRP-2	Piasecki	
111834–111848	HRP-1	Piasecki	Cancelled
111849–111948	SC-1	Curtiss	Cancelled
111949–112528	SNJ-6	North American	112360–112528 Cancelled
112529–114528	F8F-1	Grumman	Cancelled
114529–115728	F4U-4	Vought	Cancelled
115729–116728	FG-4	Vought	Cancelled
116729–117728	F7F-3	Grumman	Cancelled
117729–118928	TBM-4	Eastern	Cancelled
118929–119528	TBY-3/4	Consolidated	Cancelled
119529–119778	SC-2	Curtiss	119539–119778 Cancelled
119779–119978	PBY-6A	Consolidated	Cancelled
119979–120338	TD2C-1	Culver	
120339–120341	XFJ-1	North American	Cancelled

Bureau Number	Aircraft Type	Manufacturer	Miscellaneous Notes
120339–120340	XTD4C-1/XUC-1K	Culver	
120342–120441	FJ-1	North American	120372–120441 Cancelled
120442–120474	OY-1	Consolidated	
120475–121414	PBY-6A	Consolidated	Cancelled
121415–121438	OY-1	Consolidated	Cancelled
121439–121440	Unknown	Unknown	Cancelled
121441–121444	Me 262	Messerschmitt	
121445–121446	Ar 234	Arado	
121447	Do 335	Dornier	
121448	Me 262 S	Messerschmitt	
121449–121450	XSN2J-1	North American	
121451–121454	P4M-1	Martin	
121455–121456	XP5Y-1	Consolidated	
121457–121459	XF3D-1	Douglas	
121460–121462	XAJ-1	North American	
121463–121522	F8F-1	Grumman	
121523–121792	F8F-2	Grumman	
121793–121803	F4U-5	Vought	
121804	F4U-5P	Vought	
121805–121815	F4U-5	Vought	
121816	F4U-5N	Vought	
121817–121831	F4U-5	Vought	
121832–121833	F4U-5N	Vought	
121834–121851	F4U-5	Vought	
121852–121853	F4U-5N	Vought	
121854–121871	F4U-5	Vought	
121872–121874	F4U-5N	Vought	
121875–121890	F4U-5	Vought	
121891–121893	F4U-5N	Vought	
121894–121911	F4U-5	Vought	
121912–121915	F4U-5N	Vought	
121916–121931	F4U-5	Vought	
121932–121935	F4U-5N	Vought	
121936	F4U-5P	Vought	
121937–121951	F4U-5	Vought	
121952–121955	F4U-5N	Vought	
121956–121957	F4U-5P	Vought	
121958–121972	F4U-5	Vought	
121973–121976	F4U-5N	Vought	
121977–121978	F4U-5P	Vought	
121979–121994	F4U-5	Vought	
121995–121998	F4U-5N	Vought	
121999–122002	F4U-5P	Vought	
122003–122014	F4U-5	Vought	
122015–122018	F4U-5N	Vought	
122019–122022	F4U-5P	Vought	

Bureau Number	Aircraft Type	Manufacturer	Miscellaneous Notes
122023–122036	F4U-5	Vought	
122037–122040	F4U-5N	Vought	
122041–122044	F4U-5	Vought	
122045–122048	F4U-5P	Vought	
122049–122057	F4U-5	Vought	
122058–122061	F4U-5N	Vought	
122062–122065	F4U-5P	Vought	
122066	F4U-5	Vought	
122067–122086	PBM-5A	Martin	
122087–122152	F8F-1B	Grumman	
122153–122166	F4U-5	Vought	
122167–122206	F4U-5P	Vought	
122207–122209	P4M-1	Martin	
122210–122365	AD-2	Douglas	
122366–122372	AD-2Q	Douglas	
122373	AD-2QU	Douglas	
122374–122387	AD-2Q	Douglas	
122388–122393	AM-1Q	Martin	
122394–122437	AM-1	Martin	
122438–122467	P2V-2	Lockheed	When some of these were stricken, the bureau numbers were reissued
122447–122451	F2L-2	Bell	Cancelled
122452–122461	HTL-1	Bell	These numbers had been used by P2V-2s and when they were stricken were reissued
122468–122471	PBM-5A	Martin	
122472–122474	XF7U-1	Vought	
122475	XF9F-2	Grumman	
122476	XF9F-3	Grumman	
122477	XF9F-2	Grumman	
122478–122507	F6U-1	Vought	
122508–122529	HO3S-1	Sikorsky	
122530–122559	F2H-1	McDonnell	
122560–122589	F9F-2	Grumman	
122590–122601	AJ-1	North American	
122602–122613	PBM-5A	Martin	
122614–122708	F8F-2	Grumman	
122709–122728	HO3S-1	Sikorsky	
122729–122852	AD-3	Douglas	
122853	AD-4	Douglas	
122854–122876	AD-3Q	Douglas	
122877–122905	AD-3W	Douglas	
122906–122907	AD-3E	Douglas	
122908–122909	AD-3N	Douglas	
122910–122911	AD-3S	Douglas	
122912–122922	AD-3N	Douglas	
122923–122951	P2V-3	Lockheed	
122952–122963	HTL-2	Bell	

Bureau Number	Aircraft Type	Manufacturer	Miscellaneous Notes
122964–122987	P2V-3	Lockheed	
122988–122989	XA2D-1	Douglas	
122990–123015	F2H-1	McDonnell	
123016–123083	F9F-3	Grumman	
123084	XF9F-4	Grumman	
123085	XF9F-5	Grumman	
123086–123087	F9F-3	Grumman	123087 Cancelled
123088–123116	AF-2S	Grumman	Even BuNos
123089–123117	AF-2W	Grumman	Odd BuNos
123118–123143	HO3S-1	Sikorsky	
123144–123203	F4U-5N/5NL	Vought	
123204–123299	F2H-2	McDonnell	
123300–123313	F2H-2N	McDonnell	
123314–123396	F2H-2	McDonnell	123383–123396 Cancelled
123397–123740	F9F-2	Grumman	123714–123740 Cancelled
123741–123770	F3D-1	Douglas	123769–123770 Cancelled
123771–124005	AD-4	Douglas	
124006	XAD-5	Douglas	
124007–124036	AD-4	Douglas	Cancelled
124037–124075	AD-4Q	Douglas	
124076–124127	AD-4W	Douglas	
124128–124156	AD-4N	Douglas	
124157–124186	AJ-1	North American	124185–124186 Cancelled
124187–124209	AF-2W	Grumman	Odd BuNos
124188–124210	AF-2S	Grumman	Even BuNos
124211–124267	P2V-4	Lockheed	
124268–124291	P2V-3W	Lockheed	
124292–124323	PF-1	Grumman	Cancelled
124324–124333	R4Q-1	Fairchild	124332–124333 Cancelled
124334–124353	HO3S-1	Sikorsky	
124354–124361	P2V-3W	Lockheed	124360–124361 Cancelled
124362–124373	P4M-1	Martin	
124374–124379	UF-1	Grumman	
124380–124414	F6U-1	Vought	Cancelled
124415–124434	F7U-1	Vought	124429–124434 Cancelled
124435–124436	XF10F-1	Grumman	
124437–124438	PO-1W	Lockheed	
124439–124440	XA2J-1	North American	
124441–124503	F4U-5N	Vought	
124504–124522	F4U-5NL	Vought	
124523	F4U-5N	Vought	
124524–124560	F4U-5NL	Vought	
124561–124569	HTL-3	Bell	
124570–124585	TO-2	Lockheed	
124586–124587	XF4D-1	Douglas	
124588–124594	HUP-1	Piasecki	

Bureau Number	Aircraft Type	Manufacturer	Miscellaneous Notes
124595–124664	F3D-2	Douglas	
124665	XAU-1	Vought	
124666–124709	F4U-5NL	Vought	
124710–124724	F4U-5N	Vought	
124725–124760	AD-4NL	Douglas	
124761–124777	AD-4W	Douglas	
124778–124848	AF-2S	Grumman	Even BuNos
124779–124849	AF-2W	Grumman	Odd BuNos
124850–124864	AJ-1	North American	
124865–124909	P2V-4	Lockheed	
124910–124914	P5M-1	Martin	124914 never received by Navy
124915–124929	HUP-1	Piasecki	
124930–124939	TO-2	Lockheed	
124940–125071	F2H-2	McDonnell	
125072–125079	F2H-2P	McDonnell	
125080–125152	F9F-5	Grumman	
125153–125225	F9F-4	Grumman	
125226–125313	F9F-5	Grumman	
125314–125321	F9F-5P	Grumman	
125322–125409	F7U-2	Vought	Cancelled
125410–125411	F7U-3	Vought	Cancelled
125412–125413	XA3D-1	Douglas	
125414–125443	F9F-5	Grumman	
125444–125445	XF3H-1	McDonnell	
125446	K-225	Kaman	
125447–125476	F9F-5	Grumman	
125477–125478	K-225	Kaman	
125479–125488	A2D-1	Douglas	125485–125488 Cancelled
125489–125499	F9F-5	Grumman	
125500–125505	F2H-2	McDonnell	
125506–125515	HO4S-1	Sikorsky	
125516–125527	HO5S-1	Sikorsky	
125528–125531	HOK-1	Kaman	
125532	UH-12/HTE-1	Hiller	
125533–125648	F9F-5	Grumman	
125649–125679	F2H-2	McDonnell	
125680–125706	F2H-2P	McDonnell	
125707–125741	AD-4N	Douglas	
125742–125764	AD-4NA	Douglas	
125765–125782	AD-4W	Douglas	
125783–125882	F3D-2	Douglas	
125883–125892	F3D-3	Douglas	Cancelled
125893–126256	F9F-5	Grumman	
126257–126264	F9F-6	Grumman	
126265–126290	F9F-5P	Grumman	

Bureau Number	Aircraft Type	Manufacturer	Miscellaneous Notes
126291–126350	F2H-3	McDonnell	126294–126295, 126306, 126310, 126313, 126327, 126330, 126331, 126333–126335, 126337, 126339, 126343, 126346–126347 to Canada
126351–126353	F2H-4	McDonnell	
126354–126489	F2H-3	McDonnell	126361, 126381–126382, 126390, 126392, 126400, 126402–126403, 126414–126415, 126422, 126428–126429, 126434, 126443–126444, 126446, 126449, 126454, 126464, 126,469, 126488 to Canada
126490–126511	P5M-1	Martin	
126512–126513	WV-2	Lockheed	
126514–126573	P2V-6	Lockheed	126548–126573 Cancelled
126574–126582	R4Q-1	Fairchild	
126583–126626	TV-2/TO-2	Lockheed	
126627–126669	F9F-5	Grumman	
126670–126672	XF9F-6	Grumman	
126673–126695	F2H-2P	McDonnell	
126696–126705	HO5S-1	Sikorsky	
126706–126715	HUP-1	Piasecki	
126716–126719	ZP2N-1	Goodyear	126717–126719 Cancelled
126720–126737	AF-2S	Grumman	
126738–126755	AF-2W	Grumman	
126756–126821	AF-2S	Grumman	
126822–126835	AF-2W	Grumman	
126836–126875	AD-4W	Douglas	
126876–126902	AD-4N	Douglas	
126903–126925	AD-4NA	Douglas	
126926–126946	AD-4N	Douglas	
126947–126969	AD-4NA	Douglas	
126970–126987	AD-4N	Douglas	
126988–127010	AD-4NA	Douglas	
127011–127018	AD-4N	Douglas	
127019–127085	F3D-2	Douglas	
127086–127215	F9F-2	Grumman	
127216–127470	F9F-6	Grumman	
127471–127472	F9F-5P	Grumman	
127473–127492	F9F-6P	Grumman	
127493–127546	F2H-3	McDonnell	
127547–127693	F2H-4	McDonnell	
127694–127695	F2H-3P	McDonnell	Cancelled
127696–127719	P5M-1	Martin	
127720–127782	P2V-5	Lockheed	
127783–127843	HRS-1	Sikorsky	127843 Cancelled
127844–127853	AD-4	Douglas	
127854–127860	AD-4B	Douglas	
127861–127865	AD-4	Douglas	
127866–127872	AD-4B	Douglas	

Bureau Number	Aircraft Type	Manufacturer	Miscellaneous Notes
127873–127879	AD-4	Douglas	
127880–127920	AD-4N	Douglas	
127921–127961	AD-4W	Douglas	
127962–128042	A2D-1	Douglas	Cancelled
128043–128054	AJ-2P	North American	
128055–128294	F9F-6	Grumman	
128295–128310	F9F-6P	Grumman	
128311–128322	F10F-1	Grumman	128312–128322 Cancelled
128323–128326	WV-2	Lockheed	
128327–128422	P2V-5	Lockheed	
128423–128432	R6D-1	Douglas	
128433	R6D-1Z	Douglas	
128434–128444	R7V-1	Lockheed	
128445–128449	R3Y-1	Consolidated	
128450	R3Y-2	Consolidated	
128451–128478	F7U-3	Vought	
128479–128600	HUP-2	Piasecki	
128601–128620	HO5S-1	Sikorsky	
128621–128636	HTL-4	Bell	
128637–128652	HTE-1	Hiller	
128653–128660	HTK-1	Kaman	
128661–128722	TV-2/TO-2	Lockheed	
128723–128744	R4Q-1	Fairchild	
128745–128856	F2H-3	McDonnell	Cancelled
128857–128886	F2H-2	McDonnell	
128887–128916	HTL-4	Bell	
128917–128936	AD-4	Douglas	
128937–128943	AD-4B	Douglas	
128944–128970	AD-4	Douglas	
128971–128978	AD-4B	Douglas	
128979–129016	AD-4	Douglas	
129017–129049	HRS-2	Sikorsky	
129050–129132	F2H-3/3P	McDonnell	Cancelled
129133–129136	XHSL-1	Bell	
129137–129138	XS2F-1	Grumman	
129139–129153	YS2F-1	Grumman	
129154–129168	HSL-1	Bell	
129169–129184	HTE-1	Hiller	
129185–129195	AJ-2P	North American	
129196–129242	AF-2S	Grumman	
129243–129257	AF-3S	Grumman	
129258–129299	AF-2W	Grumman	
129300–129317	HTK-1	Kaman	
129318–129417	AU-1	Vought	
129418–129544	FJ-2	North American	Cancelled
129418–129522	HUP-2	Piasecki	Numbers reused, then cancelled

Bureau Number	Aircraft Type	Manufacturer	Miscellaneous Notes
129545–129676	F7U-3	Vought	
129677	F7U-3M	Vought	
129678–129697	F7U-3	Vought	
129698–129744	F7U-3M	Vought	
129745–129756	F7U-3P	Vought	
129757–129791	HTE-2	Hiller	
129792–129799	Unknown	Unknown	Cancelled
129800–129842	HOK-1	Kaman	
129843–129941	HSL-1	Bell	129878–129941 Cancelled
129942–129977	HTL-5	Bell	
129978–130100	HUP-2	Piasecki	130086–130100 Cancelled
130101–130137	HO5S-1	Sikorsky	
130138–130205	HRS-2	Sikorsky	
130206–130264	HRS-3	Sikorsky	
130265–130351	P5M-1	Martin	130307–130351 never accepted
130352	YA3D-1	Douglas	
130353–130363	A3D-1	Douglas	
130364–130388	AF-3S	Grumman	
130389–130404	AF-2W	Grumman	
130405–130421	AJ-2	North American	
130422–130425	AJ-2P	North American	
130426–130462	F3D-2	Douglas	Cancelled
130463–130739	F3D-3	Douglas	Cancelled
130740–130751	F4D-1	Douglas	
130752–130919	F9F-7	Grumman	
130920–131062	F9F-6	Grumman	
131063–131251	F9F-8	Grumman	
131252–131255	F9F-6P	Grumman	
131256–131378	F10F-1	Grumman	Cancelled
131379–131386	F10F-1P	Grumman	Cancelled
131387–131389	WV-2	Lockheed	
131390–131392	WV-2Q	Lockheed	
131393–131399	WV-2	Lockheed	Cancelled
131400–131543	P2V-5	Lockheed	
131544–131550	P2V-6	Lockheed	
131551–131566	P2V-6M	Lockheed	
131567–131620	R6D-1/C-118B	Douglas	From Air Force
131621–131629	R7V-1	Lockheed	
131630–131631	R7V-2	Lockheed	
131632–131659	R7V-1	Lockheed	
131660–131661	R7V-2	Lockheed	
131662–131719	R4Q-2	Fairchild	
131720–131724	R3Y-2	Consolidated	
131725–131888	TV-2/TO-2	Lockheed	131878 From Air Force
131889–131918	UF-1/1T	Grumman	
131919–131926	ZP4K-1	Goodyear	

Bureau Number	Aircraft Type	Manufacturer	Miscellaneous Notes
131927–132226	FJ-2	North American	132127–132226 Cancelled
132227–132391	AD-4B	Douglas	
132392–132476	AD-5	Douglas	
132477	AD-5N	Douglas	
132478	AD-5	Douglas	
132479	AD-5S	Douglas	
132480–132636	AD-5N	Douglas	
132637–132728	AD-5	Douglas	132687–132728 Cancelled
132729–132792	AD-5W	Douglas	132731–132792 Cancelled
132793–133042	A2D-1	Douglas	Cancelled
133043–133328	S2F-1	Grumman	133043–133044 Cancelled
133043–133044	WF-1	Grumman	Numbers reused, then cancelled
133329–133388	S2F-2	Grumman	
133389–133488	F3H-1	McDonnell	Cancelled
133489–133544	F3H-1N	McDonnell	
133545–133568	F3H-2N	McDonnell	
133569	F3H-2M	McDonnell	
133570–133622	F3H-2N	McDonnell	
133623–133638	F3H-2M	McDonnell	
133639	XZP4K	Goodyear	
133640–133651	P2V-5	Lockheed	Australia
133652–133731	F4U-7	Vought	France
133732–133735	XHR2S-1	Sikorsky	
133736–133738	XHRH-1	McDonnell	Cancelled
133739–133753	HO4S-3	Sikorsky	UK
133754–133755	XFJ-2	North American	
133756	XFJ-2B	North American	
133757–133776	AD-5W	Douglas	
133777–133779	HO4S-3	Sikorsky	Netherlands
133780–133781	XS2U-1W/XWU-1	Vought	Cancelled
133782–133816	OE-1	Cessna	L-19A, from Air Force
133817–133818	HUM-1	McCulloch	MC-4
133819–133832	F4U-7	Vought	France
133833–133843	AU-1	Vought	
133844–133853	HO4S-3	Sikorsky	Cancelled
133854–134004	AD-5	Douglas	133930–134004 Cancelled
134004	JRB-4	Beech	
134005–134018	AD-4B	Douglas	Cancelled
134019–134034	ZSG-4	Goodyear	134025–134034 Cancelled
134035–134072	AJ-2	North American	
134073–134075	AJ-2P	North American	
134076–134233	AD-5	Douglas	Cancelled
134234–134244	F9F-8	Grumman	
134245–134433	F9F-6	Grumman	Cancelled
134434–134437	HUP-2	Piasecki	
134438–134445	A2D-1	Douglas	Cancelled

Bureau Number	Aircraft Type	Manufacturer	Miscellaneous Notes
134446–134465	F9F-6P	Grumman	
134466–134637	AD-6	Douglas	
134638–134663	P2V-6	Lockheed	France
134664–134676	P2V-5	Lockheed	134664–134670 Cancelled Netherlands
134668–134670	XHSS-1	Sikorsky	
134677–134691	HUP-2	Piasecki	Cancelled
134692–134717	SNB-5	Beech	134692–134697 to Netherlands, 134698–134717 to France
134718–134723	P2V-5	Lockheed	Netherlands
134724–134743	HTE-2	Hiller	UK
134744–134973	F4D-1	Douglas	
134974–135053	AD-5N	Douglas	
135054	AD-5Q	Douglas	
135055–135138	AD-5N	Douglas	Cancelled
135139–135222	AD-5W	Douglas	
135223–135406	AD-6	Douglas	
135407–135444	A3D-1	Douglas	
135445–135448	ZP2N-1	Goodyear	
135449–135476	P5M-1	Martin	135449–135451 Cancelled
135477–135543	P5M-2	Martin	
135544–135621	P2V-7	Lockheed	135565, and odd BuNos 135571–135577 and 135581–135617 to Canada
135622–135717	HSL-1	Bell	Cancelled
135718–135745	HUP-2	Piasecki	Cancelled
135746–135761	WV-2	Lockheed	
135762–135773	YF2Y-1	Consolidated	135766–135773 Cancelled
135774–136162	FJ-3	North American	
136163–136392	F4D-1	Douglas	Cancelled
136393–136747	S2F-1	Grumman	
136748–136782	TF-1	Grumman	
136783	TF-1Q	Grumman	
136784	TF-1	Grumman	
136785	TF-1Q	Grumman	
136786	TF-1	Grumman	
136787–136788	TF-1Q	Grumman	
136789–136792	TF-1	Grumman	
136793–136886	TV-2	Lockheed	
136887–136911	OE-1	Cessna	
136912–136963	F7U-3	Vought	Cancelled
136964–136965	F7U-3P	Vought	Cancelled
136966–137032	F3H-2N	McDonnell	
137033–137095	F3H-2M	McDonnell	
137096–137131	F3H-1	McDonnell	Cancelled
137132–137155	F3H-2P	McDonnell	Cancelled
137156–137215	F3H-1	McDonnell	
137216–137245	F10F-1	Grumman	Cancelled
137246–137485	SNJ-8	North American	Cancelled

Bureau Number	Aircraft Type	Manufacturer	Miscellaneous Notes
137486–137491	ZS2G-1	Goodyear	
137492–137632	AD-6	Douglas	
137633	Not assigned	Not assigned	
137634–137635	XF2Y-1	Consolidated	137635 Cancelled
137636–137637	T-28A	North American	
137638–137810	T-28B	North American	
137811	XZS2G-1	Goodyear	
137812	XA4D-1	Douglas	
137813–137831	A4D-1	Douglas	
137832	ZPG-2W	Goodyear	
137833–137835	HTK-1	Kaman	
137836–137845	HRS-3	Sikorsky	
137846–137848	P5M-2	Martin	
137849–137858	HSS-1	Sikorsky	
137859–137886	F3H-1	McDonnell	Cancelled
137887–137890	WV-2	Lockheed	
137891–137898	WV-3	Lockheed	
137899–137933	UF-1	Grumman	
137934–138097	TV-2	Lockheed	
138098–138102	HOK-1	Kaman	
138103–138367	T-28B	North American	
138368–138417	A2U-1	Vought	Cancelled
138418–138431	HR2S-1	Sikorsky	138425–138431 Cancelled
138432–138459	HO4S-3	Sikorsky	Cancelled
138460–138493	HSS-1	Sikorsky	
138494–138529	HO4S-3	Sikorsky	
138530–138534	F2Y-1	Consolidated	Cancelled
138535–138568	AD-5W	Douglas	Cancelled
138569–138576	HSL-1	Bell	Cancelled
138577–138601	HO4S-3	Sikorsky	
138602	HTK-1K	Kaman	
138603–138645	F11F-1	Grumman	
138646–138647	F11F-1F	Grumman	
138648–138650	XFY-1	Consolidated	
138651–138653	HOE-1	Hiller	
138654–138656	XHCH-1	McDonnell	Cancelled
138657–138658	XFV-1	Lockheed	
138659	XR4D-8	Douglas	
138660–138819	F3H-1	McDonnell	Cancelled
138820	R4D-8	Douglas	
138821–138822	XP6M-1	Martin	
138823–138898	F9F-8	Grumman	
138899–138901	XF8U-1	Vought	138901 Cancelled
138902–138976	A3D-2	Douglas	
138977–139016	TV-2	Lockheed	
139017–139029	HSS-1	Sikorsky	

Bureau Number	Aircraft Type	Manufacturer	Miscellaneous Notes
139030–139207	F4D-1	Douglas	
139208–139209	F5D-1	Douglas	
139210–139278	FJ-3	North American	
139279–139280	XFJ-4	North American	
139281–139323	FJ-4	North American	
139324–139423	FJ-3	North American	Cancelled
139424–139530	FJ-4	North American	
139531–139555	FJ-4B	North American	
139556–139605	AD-5W	Douglas	
139606–139821	AD-6	Douglas	
139822–139867	A2U-1	Vought	Cancelled
139868–139917	F7U-3M	Vought	
139918	ZPG-2W	Goodyear	
139919–139970	A4D-1	Douglas	
139971–140001	HOK-1	Kaman	
140002–140052	T-28B	North American	
140053–140077	T-28C	North American	
140078–140102	OE-2	Cessna	
140103–140120	S2F-2	Grumman	140103 Cancelled
140121–140139	HSS-1	Sikorsky	
140140–140150	P5M-2	Martin	
140151–140160	P2V-7	Lockheed	
140161–140310	A2U-1	Vought	Cancelled
140311–140313	R7V-1	Lockheed	
140314–140325	HR2S-1	Sikorsky	
140326–140377	JD-1	Douglas	From Air Force
140378	R4Y-1Z	Consolidated	
140379–140413	F11F-1P/F9F-9P	Grumman	Cancelled
140414–140429	HSL-1	Bell	Cancelled
140430–140443	P2V-7	Lockheed	
140444–140446	F8U-1	Vought	
140447–140448	XF8U-2	Vought	
140449–140666	T-28C	North American	
140667–140956	T-34B	Beech	
140957	KH-15	Kellett	For ONR, test vehicle
140958–140961	HRS-3	Sikorsky	Spain
140962–140986	P2V-7	Lockheed	140968, 140970 to Japan
140987–140992	SNB-5	Beech	From Army
140993–141028	R4Y-1	Consolidated	
141029	HRS-3	Sikorsky	
141030–141229	F9F-8	Grumman	
141230	HRS-3	Sikorsky	
141231–141251	P2V-7	Lockheed	141244, 141245 to Japan
141252–141260	P5M-2	Martin	141259–141260 Cancelled
141261–141288	UF-1	Grumman	
141289–141333	WV-2	Lockheed	

Bureau Number	Aircraft Type	Manufacturer	Miscellaneous Notes
141334–141335	ZPG-2W	Goodyear	
141336–141362	F8U-1	Vought	
141363	F8U-1P	Vought	
141364–141443	FJ-3M	North American	
141444–141489	FJ-4B	North American	
141490–141558	TV-2	Lockheed	
141559–141563	ZPG-2	Goodyear	
141564–141570	ZS2G-1	Goodyear	
141571–141602	HSS-1	Sikorsky	
141603–141645	HR2S-1	Sikorsky	141618–141645 Cancelled
141646–141647	HR2S-1W	Sikorsky	
141648–141666	F9F-8	Grumman	
141667	YF9F-8T	Grumman	
141668–141727	F9F-8P	Grumman	
141728–141980	F11F-1	Grumman	141885–141980 Cancelled
141981–142009	F11F-1P	Grumman	Cancelled
142010	XAD-7	Douglas	
142011–142081	AD-7	Douglas	
142082–142141	A4D-2	Douglas	
142142–142235	A4D-1	Douglas	
142236–142255	A3D-2	Douglas	
142256	YA3D-2P	Douglas	
142257	A3D-2Q	Douglas	
142258	A3D-2W	Douglas	Cancelled
142259–142260	F4H-1	McDonnell	
142261–142268	T2V-1	Lockheed	
142269–142348	F-84 (drone)	Republic	From Air Force
142349–142357	F5D-1	Douglas	142351–142357 Cancelled
142358–142363	UF-1	Grumman	142363 Cancelled
142364–142372	HUL-1	Bell	
142373–142396	HTL-6	Bell	
142397–142399	T2V-1	Lockheed	
142400–142407	A3D-2	Douglas	
142408–142415	F8U-1	Vought	
142416–142423	A4D-2	Douglas	
142424–142427	UC-1	DeHavilland	
142428	UF-1L	Grumman	
142429	UF-1G	Grumman	
142430–142436	HRS-3	Sikorsky	Spain
142437–142532	F9F-8T	Grumman	
142533–142541	T2V-1	Lockheed	
142542–142545	P2V-7	Lockheed	
142546–142629	AD-7	Douglas	Cancelled
142630–142665	A3D-2	Douglas	
142666–142669	A3D-2P	Douglas	
142670–142673	A3D-2Q	Douglas	

Bureau Number	Aircraft Type	Manufacturer	Miscellaneous Notes
142674–142953	A4D-2	Douglas	
142954–143013	F9F-8T	Grumman	
143014–143049	TV-2	Lockheed	
143050–143133	AD-7	Douglas	Cancelled
143134–143147	HUL-1	Bell	
143148–143171	HTL-6	Bell	
143172–143183	P2V-7	Lockheed	
143184–143230	WV-2	Lockheed	
143231	Not issued	Not issued	
143232–143366	F11F-1	Grumman	Cancelled
143367–143387	F11F-1P	Grumman	Cancelled
143388–143392	F4H-1F	McDonnell	
143393–143400	F5D-1	Douglas	Cancelled
143401–143402	XF12F-1	Grumman	Cancelled
143403–143492	F3H-2	McDonnell	
143493–143676	FJ-4B	North American	143644–143676 Cancelled
143677–143821	F8U-1	Vought	
143822–143827	P6M-1	Martin	
143828–143863	HR2S-1	Sikorsky	Cancelled
143864–143960	HSS-1	Sikorsky	
143961–143983	HUS-1	Sikorsky	
143984–144116	T-34B	Beech	
144117–144216	T2V-1	Lockheed	
144217–144218	XT2J-1	North American	
144219–144222	T2J-1	North American	
144223–144236	TT-1	Temco	
144237–144238	ZPG-2	Goodyear	Cancelled
144239–144241	ZS2G-1	Goodyear	
144242–144243	ZPG-3W	Goodyear	
144244–144258	HRS-3	Sikorsky	
144259–144261	UC-1	DeHavilland	
144262–144267	P2V-7	Lockheed	Cancelled
144268–144270	HRS-3	Sikorsky	Spain
144271–144376	F9F-8	Grumman	
144377–144426	F9F-8P	Grumman	
144427–144606	F8U-1	Vought	144462–144606 Cancelled
144607–144625	F8U-1P	Vought	
144626–144629	A3D-2	Douglas	
144630–144654	HUS-1	Sikorsky	
144655–144662	HUS-1A	Sikorsky	
144663–144665	OE-1	Cessna	144665 Cancelled
144666–144668	HRS-3	Sikorsky	Spain
144669–144674	UC-1	DeHavilland	
144675–144692	P2V-7	Lockheed	144685–144692 to France, 144675–144680 to Japan
144693–144695	HTL-3	Bell	

Bureau Number	Aircraft Type	Manufacturer	Miscellaneous Notes
144696–144731	S2F-1	Grumman	
144732–144734	P2V-7	Lockheed	144733–144734 Cancelled
144735–144824	T2V-1	Lockheed	144765–144824 Cancelled
144825–144847	A3D-2P	Douglas	
144848–144855	A3D-2Q	Douglas	
144856–144867	A3D-2T	Douglas	
144868–145061	A4D-2	Douglas	
145062–145146	A4D-2N	Douglas	
145147–145156	A4D-3	Douglas	Cancelled
145157–145158	YA3J-1	North American	
145159–145201	F5D-1	Douglas	Cancelled
145202–145306	F3H-2	McDonnell	
145307–145317	F4H-1F	McDonnell	
145318–145415	F8U-1	Vought	
145416–145545	F8U-1E	Vought	
145546–145603	F8U-2	Vought	
145604–145647	F8U-1P	Vought	
145648–145659	F8U-1T	Vought	Cancelled
145660–145669	HSS-1	Sikorsky	
145670–145712	HSS-1N	Sikorsky	
145713–145836	HUS-1	Sikorsky	145813–145836 Cancelled
145837–145854	HTL-7	Bell	
145855–145875	HR2S-1	Sikorsky	
145876–145899	P6M-2	Martin	145880–145899 Cancelled
145900–145923	P2V-7	Lockheed	
145924–145956	WV-2	Lockheed	145942–145956 Cancelled
145957–145961	WF-2	Grumman	
145962–145963	R4Y-2	Consolidated	
145964–145976	R4Y-2/2T	Consolidated	Cancelled
145977–145990	R4Y-2S	Consolidated	Cancelled
145991–145995	R4Y-2Q	Consolidated	Cancelled
145996	T2J-1	North American	
145997	XT2J-2	North American	
145998–146015	T2J-1	North American	
146016–146057	TF-1	Grumman	
146058–146237	T2V-1	Lockheed	Cancelled
146238–146293	T-28C	North American	
146294–146295	ZS2G-1	Goodyear	
146296–146297	ZPG-3W	Goodyear	
146298–146302	HRS-3	Sikorsky	
146303	WF-2	Grumman	
146304–146327	HUK-1	Kaman	
146328–146339	F3H-2	McDonnell	
146340–146341	F8U-3	Vought	
146342–146425	F9F-8T	Grumman	
146426–146430	UF-2	Grumman	Germany

Bureau Number	Aircraft Type	Manufacturer	Miscellaneous Notes
146431–146438	P2V-7	Lockheed	Japan/France
146439	HRS-3	Sikorsky	Spain
146440–146445	P5M-2	Martin	France
146446–146447	A3D-2P	Douglas	
146448–146459	A3D-2Q	Douglas	
146460–146693	A4D-2N	Douglas	Cancelled
146694–146708	A3J-1	North American	146703–146708 Cancelled
146709–146816	F3H-2	McDonnell	146741–146816 Cancelled
146817–146821	F4H-1F	McDonnell	
146822–146905	F8U-1P	Vought	146902–146905 Cancelled
146906–147034	F8U-2	Vought	
147035–147077	F8U-2N	Vought	147073–147077 Cancelled
147078–147084	F8U-1P	Vought	Cancelled
147085–147100	F8U-3	Vought	147088–147100 Cancelled
147101–147136	HR2S-1	Sikorsky	Cancelled
147137–147146	HSS-2	Sikorsky	
147147–147201	HUS-1	Sikorsky	
147202–147205	HU2K-1	Kaman	
147206–147207	XP6Y-1	Consolidated	Cancelled
147208–147262	WF-2	Grumman	147242–147262 Cancelled
147263–147265	W2F-1	Grumman	
147266–147269	OF-1	Grumman	Cancelled
147270–147429	F9F-8T	Grumman	
147430–147530	T2J-1	North American	
147531–147538	S2F-3	Grumman	147538 Cancelled
147539–147542	P5M-2	Martin	France
147543–147547	T-34B	Beech	For MAP
147548	E-18S	Beech	For MAP
147549–147561	S2F-1	Grumman	
147562–147571	P2V-7	Lockheed	France
147572–147573	GV-1	Lockheed	
147574	UC-1	DeHavilland	UK
147575–147576	P5M-2	Martin	
147577	S2F-1	Grumman	
147578–147581	HUL-1	Bell	
147582–147630	HUP-3	Vertol	For MAP
147631–147635	HSS-1N	Sikorsky	
147636–147647	S2F-1	Grumman	147646–147647 Cancelled
147648–147668	A3D-2	Douglas	
147669–147849	A4D-2N	Douglas	
147850–147863	A3J-1	North American	
147864–147867	A2F-1	Grumman	
147868–147895	S2F-3	Grumman	
147896–147925	F8U-2N	Vought	
147926–147945	P5M-2	Martin	147938–147945 Cancelled
147946–147971	P2V-7	Lockheed	

Bureau Number	Aircraft Type	Manufacturer	Miscellaneous Notes
147972–147983	HU2K-1	Kaman	
147984–148032	HSS-1N	Sikorsky	
148033–148052	HSS-2	Sikorsky	
148053–148122	HUS-1	Sikorsky	
148123–148146	WF-2	Grumman	
148147–148149	W2F-1	Grumman	
148150–148239	T2J-1	North American	
148240–148245	UF-2	Grumman	
148246–148249	GV-1	Lockheed	
148250–148251	OE-1	Cessna	L-19E, for MAP
148252–148275	F4H-1F	McDonnell	
148276	YP3V-1	Lockheed	
148277	HUL-1	Bell	47G-2, for MAP
148278–148303	S2F-1	Grumman	
148304–148317	A4D-2N	Douglas	
148318–148321	UV-1L/C-130BL	Lockheed	
148322–148323	L-20	DeHavilland	Philippines
148324–148329	UF-2	Grumman	Japan
148330–148336	P2V-7	Lockheed	
148337–148362	P2V-7S	Lockheed	
148363–148434	F4H-1	McDonnell	
148435–148614	A4D-2N	Douglas	148613–148614 Cancelled
148615–148626	A2F-1	Grumman	148619–148626 Cancelled
148627–148710	F8U-2N	Vought	
148711–148716	W2F-1	Grumman	
148717–148752	S2F-3	Grumman	
148753–148802	HUS-1	Sikorsky	
148803–148805	HUS-1Z	Sikorsky	
148806–148822	HUS-1	Sikorsky	
148823–148882	T2J-1	North American	Cancelled
148883–148889	P3V-1	Lockheed	
148890–148899	GV-1	Lockheed	
148900–148923	WF-2	Grumman	
148924–148933	A3J-1	North American	
148934–148963	HSS-1N	Sikorsky	
148964–149012	HSS-2	Sikorsky	
149013–149036	HU2K-1	Kaman	
149037–149049	S2F-1	Grumman	FMS
149050–149069	UO-1	Piper	
149070–149081	P2V-7	Lockheed	Australia
149082–149087	HSS-1N	Sikorsky	Italy
149088	HUP-3	Piasecki	
149089–149130	P2V-7	Kawasaki/Lockheed	Japan
149131–149133	HSS-1N	Sikorsky	Netherlands
149134–149227	F8U-2NE	Vought	
149228–149256	S2F-3	Grumman	

Bureau Number	Aircraft Type	Manufacturer	Miscellaneous Notes
149257–149275	S2F-3S	Grumman	
149276–149299	A3J-1	North American	
149300–149305	A3J-2	North American	
149306–143317	A3J-3P	North American	
149318–149402	HUS-1	Sikorsky	
149403–149474	F4H-1	McDonnell	
149475–149486	A2F-1	Grumman	
149487–149646	A4D-2N	Douglas	
149647–149666	A4D-5	Douglas	
149667–149678	P3V-1	Lockheed	
149679–149738	HSS-2	Sikorsky	
149739–149786	HU2K-1	Kaman	
149787	GV-1U	Lockheed	
149788–149789	GV-1	Lockheed	
149790	GV-1U	Lockheed	
149791–149792	GV-1	Lockheed	
149793–149794	GV-1U	Lockheed	
149795–149796	GV-1	Lockheed	
149797	GV-1U	Lockheed	
149798–149800	GV-1	Lockheed	
149801	GV-1U	Lockheed	
149802–149804	GV-1	Lockheed	
149805	GV-1U	Lockheed	
149806–149816	GV-1	Lockheed	
149817–149819	W2F-1	Grumman	
149820–149821	UV-1	Lockheed	Cancelled
149822–149824	UF-1	Grumman	FMS
149825–149835	P5M-2	Martin	
149836–149837	UF-1	Grumman	
149838–149839	HUL-1M	Bell	
149840	HSS-1N	Sikorsky	Chile
149841–149842	HSS-1N	Sikorsky	Netherlands
149843–149844	S2F-1	Grumman	
149845–149892	S2F-3	Grumman	
149893–149934	HSS-2	Sikorsky	
149935–149958	A2F-1	Grumman	
149959–150138	A4D-5	Douglas	
150139–150186	HU2K-1	Kaman	
150187–150190	R4D-6	Douglas	
150191–150192	L-20A	DeHavilland	
150193–150194	HO4S-3	Sikorsky	
150195–150264	HUS-1	Sikorsky	
150265–150278	HRB-1	Vertol	
150279–150283	P2V-7S	Lockheed	
150284–150355	F8U-2NE	Vought	
150356–150405	T-28A	North American	

Bureau Number	Aircraft Type	Manufacturer	Miscellaneous Notes
150406–150493	F4H-1	McDonnell	
150494–150529	P3V-1	Lockheed	
150530–150541	W2F-1	Grumman	
150542–150551	T3J-1	North American	
150552–150580	HUS-1	Sikorsky	
150581–150600	A4D-2N	Douglas	
150601–150603	S2F-3	Grumman	
150604–150609	P3V-1	Lockheed	
150610–150617	HSS-2Z	Sikorsky	
150618–150620	HSS-2	Sikorsky	
150621–150623	HU2K-1U	Kaman	
150624–150653	F4H-1	McDonnell	
150654–150683	F8U-2NE	Vought	
150684–150690	GV-1	Lockheed	
150691	HUS-1Z	Sikorsky	Indonesia
150692–150716	T-28A	North American	S. Vietnam
150717–150729	HUS-1	Sikorsky	
150730–150732	HSS-1N	Sikorsky	Chile
150733–150807	CH-34	Sikorsky	Germany
150808–150819	HSS-1N	Sikorsky	Germany
150820	HUS-1	Sikorsky	Cancelled
150821–150822	HSS-1N	Sikorsky	
150823–150842	A3J-3P	North American	
150843–150932	F8U-2NE	Vought	
150933–150968	HRB-1	Vertol	
150969–150992	T3J-1	North American	
150993–151021	F4H-1	McDonnell	
151022–151261	A4D-5	Douglas	151198–151261 Cancelled
151262–151263	XH-51A	Lockheed	
151264–151265	UF-2	Grumman	SA-16B, Thailand
151266–151299	UH-1E	Bell	
151300–151335	HU2K-1U	Kaman	
151336–151347	T3J-1	North American	151344–151347 Cancelled
151348	L-20A	DeHavilland	
151349–151396	P3V-1	Lockheed	
151397–151519	F4H-1	McDonnell	
151520–151521	X-22A	Bell	
151522–151557	HSS-2	Sikorsky	
151558–151594	A2F-1	Grumman	
151595–151612	A2F-1Q	Grumman	151601–151612 Cancelled
151613–151614	CH-53A	Sikorsky	
151615–151634	RA-5C	North American	
151635–151637	SH-3A	Sikorsky	Cancelled
151638–151685	S-2E	Grumman	
151686–151701	CH-53A	Sikorsky	
151702–151725	E-2A	Grumman	

Bureau Number	Aircraft Type	Manufacturer	Miscellaneous Notes
151726–151728	RA-5C	North American	
151729–151731	SH-34J	Sikorsky	Germany
151732–151775	F-8E(FN)	Vought	151774–151775 Cancelled, France
151776–151779	O-1C	Cessna	L-19E, S. Korea
151780–151827	A-6A	Grumman	
151828–151839	EA-6A	Grumman	Cancelled
151840–151887	UH-1E	Bell	
151888–151891	C-130G	Lockheed	
151892–151901	T-41A	Grumman	TC-4B Cancelled
151902–151905	UH-46A	Vertol	
151906–151961	CH-46A	Vertol	
151962–151969	RA-5C	North American	Cancelled
151970–151974	F-111B	Grumman	
151975–151983	RF-4B	McDonnell	
151984–152100	A-4E	Douglas	
152101	A-4F	Douglas	
152102–152103	TA-4E	Douglas	
152104–152138	SH-3A	Sikorsky	
152139	YSH-3D	Sikorsky	
152140–152187	P-3A	Lockheed	
152188	SH-34G	Sikorsky	Germany
152189–152206	UH-2B	Kaman	
152207–152331	F-4B	McDonnell	
152332–152379	S-2E	Grumman	
152380–152381	SH-34J	Sikorsky	Germany
152382–152391	T-2B	North American	
152392–152415	CH-53A	Sikorsky	
152416–152439	UH-1E	Bell	
152440–152475	T-2B	North American	
152476–152489	E-2A	Grumman	
152490–152495	UH-46A	Vertol	
152496–152553	CH-46A	Vertol	
152554–152579	CH-46D	Vertol	
152580–152582	YA-7A	Vought	
152583–152646	A-6A	Grumman	
152647–152685	A-7A	Vought	
152686	UH-34D	Sikorsky	FMS
152687–152689	C-118B	Douglas	
152690–152713	SH-3D	Sikorsky	
152714–152717	F-111B	Grumman	
152718–152765	P-3B	Lockheed	
152766–152785	E-2A	Grumman	Cancelled
152786–152797	C-2A	Grumman	
152798–152845	S-2E	Grumman	
152846–152878	TA-4F	Douglas	
152879–152885	YOV-1OA	North American	

Bureau Number	Aircraft Type	Manufacturer	Miscellaneous Notes
152886–152890	P-3B	Lockheed	New Zealand
152891–152964	A-6A	Grumman	152955–152964 Cancelled
152965–153070	F-4B	McDonnell	
153071–153088	F-4J	McDonnell	
153089–153115	RF-4B	McDonnell	
153116–153133	UH-34D	Sikorsky	
153134–153273	A-7A	Vought	
153274–153313	CH-53A	Sikorsky	
153314–153403	CH-46D	Vertol	
153404–153413	UH-46D	Vertol	
153414–153442	P-3B	Lockheed	
153443	YP-3C	Lockheed	
153444–153458	P-3B	Lockheed	
153459–153531	TA-4F	Douglas	
153532–153537	SH-3D	Sikorsky	Spain
153538–153555	T-2B	North American	
153556–153558	UH-34D	Sikorsky	
153559–153608	S-2E	Grumman	Australia, 153583–153594 Cancelled
153609–153610	H-23G	Hiller	
153611–153616	P-2H	Kawasaki/Lockheed	Japan
153617–153622	SH-34J	Sikorsky	Italy
153623–153642	F-111B	Grumman	Cancelled
153643–153659	T-28B	North American	
153660–153690	TA-4F	Douglas	
153691–153694	C-118B	Douglas	
153695–153704	UH-34D	Sikorsky	FMS
153705–153739	CH-53A	Sikorsky	
153740–153767	UH-1E	Bell	
153768–153911	F-4J	McDonnell	
153912–153950	F-4B	McDonnell	153916–153950 Cancelled
153951–154044	CH-46D	Vertol	
154045	UH-34D	Sikorsky	FMS
154046–154099	A-6B	Grumman	Cancelled
154100–154123	SH-3D	Sikorsky	
154124–154171	A-6A	Grumman	
154172–154286	A-4F	Douglas	154218–154286 Cancelled
154287–154343	TA-4F	Douglas	
154344–154360	A-7A	Vought	
154361–154573	A-7B	Vought	154557–154573 Cancelled
154574–154613	P-3B	Lockheed	154606–154613 Cancelled
154614–154657	TA-4F	Douglas	
154658–154729	T-28C	North American	
154730–154749	TH-1E	Bell	
154750–154780	UH-1E	Bell	
154781–154788	F-4J	McDonnell	
154789–154844	CH-46D	Vertol	

Bureau Number	Aircraft Type	Manufacturer	Miscellaneous Notes
154845–154862	CH-46F	Vertol	
154863–154884	CH-53A	Sikorsky	
154885–154886	CH-53G	Sikorsky	
154887–154888	CH-53A	Sikorsky	
154889–154902	UH-34D	Sikorsky	FMS
154903–154910	A-4G	Douglas	Australia
154911–154912	TA-4G	Douglas	Australia
154913–154929	A-7A	Vought	Cancelled
154930–154942	EA-6B	Grumman	Cancelled
154943–154969	UH-1E	Bell	
154970–155069	A-4F	Douglas	
155070–155119	TA-4J	Douglas	
155120–155136	C-2A	Grumman	155125–155136 Cancelled
155137–155190	A-6A	Grumman	Cancelled
155191–155238	T-2B	North American	155191–155205 Cancelled
155239–155241	T-2C	North American	
155242–155289	A-4H	Douglas	Israel
155290	H-34G	Sikorsky	FMS
155291–155300	P-3B	Lockheed	Australia
155301–155336	CH-46F	Vertol	155319–155336 Cancelled
155337–155367	UH-1E	Bell	
155368–155389	CH-53A	Sikorsky	Cancelled
155390–155503	OV-1OA	North American	
155504–155580	F-4J	McDonnell	
155581–155721	A-6A	Grumman	
155722–155730	TC-4C	Grumman	
155731–155916	F-4J	McDonnell	155904–155916 Cancelled
155917	LC-13OR	Lockheed	
155918–156169	QT-33A	Lockheed	From Air Force
156170–156177	EC-130Q	Lockheed	
156178–156417	A-7B	Vought	Cancelled
156418–156477	CH-46F	Vertol	
156478–156482	EA-6B	Grumman	
156483–156506	SH-3D	Sikorsky	
156507–156546	P-3C	Lockheed	156531–156546 Cancelled
156547–156591	Unknown	Unknown	Cancelled
156592–156598	UH-34D	Sikorsky	FMS
156599–156603	P-3B	Lockheed	Norway
156604–156607	EA-6B	Grumman	Cancelled
156608–156653	RA-5C	North American	
156654–156677	CH-53D	Sikorsky	
156678–156685	O-1G	Cessna	FMS
156686–156733	T-2C	North American	
156734–156800	A-7C	Vought	
156801–156890	A-7E	Vought	
156891–156950	TA-4J	Douglas	

Bureau Number	Aircraft Type	Manufacturer	Miscellaneous Notes
156951–156970	CH-53D	Sikorsky	
156971–156978	F-111B	Grumman	Cancelled
156979–156993	EA-6A	Grumman	
156994–157029	A-6A	Grumman	
157030–157101	T-2C	North American	157066–157101 Cancelled
157102–157126	OV-12A	Fairchild-Hiller	Cancelled
157127–157176	CH-53D	Sikorsky	
157177–157203	HH-1K	Bell	
157204–157241	AH-1G	Bell	
157242–157309	F-4J	McDonnell	
157310–157341	P-3C	Lockheed	157333–157341 Cancelled
157342–157351	RF-4B	McDonnell	
157352–157354	CT-39E	North American	
157355–157394	TH-57A	Bell	
157395–157428	A-4H	Douglas	Israel
157429–157434	TA-4H	Douglas	Israel
157435–157648	A-7E	Vought	157595–157648 Cancelled
157649–157726	CH-46F	Vertol	
157727–157756	CH-53D	Sikorsky	
157757–157805	AH-1J	Bell	
157806–157850	TH-1L	Bell	
157851–157858	UH-1L	Bell	
157859–157903	TH-1L	Bell	Cancelled
157904–157913	A-4K	Douglas	New Zealand
157914–157917	TA-4K	Douglas	New Zealand
157918–157925	A-4H	Douglas	Israel
157926–157929	TA-4H	Douglas	Israel
157930–157931	CH-53D	Sikorsky	
157932–157933	X-26A	Schweizer	
157934	P-3C	Lockheed	Cancelled
157935–157976	UH-1E	Bell	Cancelled
157977–157979	EA-6B	Grumman	Cancelled
157980–157985	F-14A	Grumman	
157986	F-14B	Grumman	
157987–157991	F-14A	Grumman	
157992–157999	S-3A	Lockheed	
158000–158001	C-130	Lockheed	Cancelled
158002–158028	A-7E	Vought	
158029–158040	EA-6B	Grumman	
158041–158052	A-6E	Grumman	
158053–158072	KA-6D	Grumman	Cancelled
158073–158147	TA-4J	Douglas	
158148–158196	A-4M	Douglas	
158197–158201	T-38A	Northrop	
158202–158203	VC-3A	Martin	
158204–158226	P-3C	Lockheed	

Bureau Number	Aircraft Type	Manufacturer	Miscellaneous Notes
158227	RP-3D	Lockheed	
158228–158229	DC-130A	Lockheed	From Air Force
158230–158291	UH-1N	Bell	
158292–158309	OV-10B	North American	Germany
158310–158333	T-2C	North American	
158334–158345	CH-46F	Vertol	
158346–158379	F-4J	McDonnell	
158380–158383	CT-39G	North American	
158384–158395	AV-8A	Hawker-Siddeley	
158396–158411	OV-10C	North American	Thailand
158412–158435	A-4M	Douglas	
158436–158437	F-86H	North American	
158438–158452	UH-1N	Bell	Cancelled
158453–158527	TA-4J	Douglas	
158528–158539	A-6E	Grumman	
158540–158547	EA-6B	Grumman	
158548–158550	UH-1N	Bell	
158551–158554	VH-1N	Bell	
158555	UH-1N	Bell	
158556–158557	VH-1N	Bell	
158558–158562	UH-1N	Bell	
158563–158574	P-3C	Lockheed	
158575–158610	T-2C	North American	
158611	X-25A	Bensen	
158612–158637	F-14A	Grumman	
158638–158648	E-2C	Grumman	
158649–158651	EA-6B	Grumman	
158652–158681	A-7E	Vought	
158682–158693	RH-53D	Sikorsky	
158694–158711	AV-8A	Hawker-Siddeley	
158712–158723	TA-4J	Douglas	
158724–158725	SH-3D	Sikorsky	Spain
158726–158743	A-4N	Douglas	Israel
158744–158761	RH-53D	Sikorsky	
158762–158785	UH-1N	Bell	
158786	X-28A	Osprey	
158787–158798	A-6E	Grumman	
158799–158817	EA-6B	Grumman	
158818	X-26A	Schweizer	
158819–158842	A-7E	Vought	
158843–158844	CT-39G	North American	
158845–158846	E-2C	Grumman	
158847–158858	HH-3F	Sikorsky	USCG
158859–158873	S-3A	Lockheed	158859–158860 Cancelled
158874–158875	SH-3D	Sikorsky	Spain
158876–158911	T-2C	North American	

Bureau Number	Aircraft Type	Manufacturer	Miscellaneous Notes
158912–158947	P-3C	Lockheed	158936–158947 Cancelled
158948–158977	AV-8A	Hawker-Siddeley	
158978–159025	F-14A	Grumman	
159026–159029	SH-3D	Sikorsky	
159030–159034	C-9B	Douglas	Cancelled
159035–159052	A-4N	Douglas	Israel
159053–159056	SH-3D	Sikorsky	
159057–159072	OV-10E	North American	Venezuela
159073–159074	U-3A	Cessna	
159075–159098	A-4N	Douglas	Israel
159099–159104	TA-4J	Douglas	
159105–159112	E-2C	Grumman	
159113–159120	C-9B	Douglas	
159121–159122	YCH-53E	Sikorsky	
159123–159128	VH-53F	Sikorsky	Cancelled
159129–159133	LC-130R	Lockheed	159132–159133 Cancelled
159134–159149	OV-10C	North American	Thailand
159150–159173	T-2C	North American	
159174–159185	A-6E	Grumman	
159186–159209	UH-1N	Bell	
159210–159229	AH-1J	Bell	
159230–159259	AV-8A	Hawker-Siddeley	
159260	X-26A	Schweizer	
159261–159308	A-7E	Vought	
159309–159317	A-6E	Grumman	
159318–159329	P-3C	Lockheed	
159330–159341	T-2D	North American	Venezuela
159342–159347	P-3F	Lockheed	Iran
159348	EC-130Q	Lockheed	
159349	Unassigned	Unassigned	
159350–159360	VH-3A	Sikorsky	
159361–159365	CT-39G	North American	
159366–159377	AV-8A	Hawker-Siddeley	
159378–159385	TAV-8A	Hawker-Siddeley	
159386–159420	S-3A	Lockheed	
159421–159468	F-14A	Grumman	
159469	EC-130Q	Lockheed	
159470–159493	A-4M	Douglas	
159494–159502	E-2C	Grumman	
159503–159514	P-3C	Lockheed	
159515–159545	A-4N	Douglas	Israel
159546–159556	TA-4J	Douglas	
159557–159562	AV-8A	Hawker-Siddeley	Spain
159563–159564	TAV-8A	Hawker-Siddeley	Spain
159565	UH-1N	Bell	
159566	Unassigned	Unassigned	

Bureau Number	Aircraft Type	Manufacturer	Miscellaneous Notes
159567–159581	A-6E	Grumman	
159582–159587	EA-6B	Grumman	
159588–159637	F-14A	Grumman	
159638–159661	A-7E	Vought	
159662–159667	A-7H	Vought	Greece
159668–159679	A-7E	Vought	
159680–159703	UH-1N	Bell	
159704–159727	T-2C	North American	
159728–159772	S-3A	Lockheed	
159773	WP-3D	Lockheed	
159774–159777	UH-1N	Bell	
159778–159794	A-4M	Douglas	
159795–159798	TA-4J	Douglas	
159799–159824	A-4N	Douglas	Israel
159825–159874	F-14A	Grumman	
159875	WP-3D	Lockheed	
159876–159877	CH-53E	Sikorsky	
159878–159882	F-5E	Northrop	
159883–159894	P-3C	Lockheed	
159895–159906	A-6E	Grumman	
159907–159912	EA-6B	Grumman	
159913–159966	A-7H	Vought	Greece
159967–160006	A-7E	Vought	
160007–160012	E-2C	Grumman	
160013–160021	KC-130R	Lockheed	
160022–160045	A-4M	Douglas	
160046–160052	C-9B	Douglas	160052 Cancelled
160053–160058	CT-39G	North American	
160059–160098	T-2E	North American	Greece
160099–160104	RH-53D	Sikorsky	
160105–160119	AH-1J	Bell	
160120–160164	S-3A	Lockheed	
160165–160179	UH-1N	Bell	
160180–160209	A-4KU	Douglas	Kuwait
160210–160215	TA-4KU	Douglas	Kuwait
160216–160227	OV-10F	North American	Indonesia
160228–160239	T-2D	North American	Morocco
160240	KC-130R	Lockheed	
160241–160264	A-4M	Douglas	
160265–160282	T-34C	Beech	
160283–160294	P-3C	Lockheed	
160295–160298	OV-10F	North American	Indonesia
160299–160378	F-14A	Grumman	Iran
160379–160414	F-14A	Grumman	
160415–160420	E-2C	Grumman	
160421–160431	A-6E	Grumman	

Bureau Number	Aircraft Type	Manufacturer	Miscellaneous Notes
160432–160437	EA-6B	Grumman	
160438–160461	UH-1N	Bell	
160462–160536	T-34C	Beech	
160537–160566	A-7E	Vought	
160567–160607	S-3A	Lockheed	
160608	EC-130Q	Lockheed	
160609	EA-6B	Grumman	
160610–160612	P-3C	Lockheed	
160613–160618	A-7E	Vought	
160619–160624	UH-1N	Bell	
160625–160628	KC-130R	Lockheed	
160629–160651	T-34C	Beech	
160652–160696	F-14A	Grumman	
160697–160703	E-2C	Grumman	
160704–160709	EA-6B	Grumman	
160710–160739	A-7E	Vought	
160740–160741	LC-130R	Lockheed	
160742–160748	AH-1T	Bell	
160749–160750	C-9K	Douglas	Kuwait
160751–160770	P-3C	Lockheed	
160771–160774	E-2C	Grumman	Israel
160775–160785	F/A-18A	McDonnell Douglas	
160786–160791	EA-6B	Grumman	
160792–160796	F-5E	Northrop	From Air Force
160797–160826	AH-1T	Bell	
160827–160838	UH-1N	Bell	
160839–160856	T-44A	Beech	
160857–160886	A-7E	Vought	160881–160886 Cancelled
160887–160930	F-14A	Grumman	
160931–160963	T-34C	Beech	
160964–160966	F-5F	Northrop	
160967–160986	T-44A	Beech	
160987–160992	E-2C	Grumman	
160993–160998	A-6E	Grumman	
160999–161014	P-3C	Lockheed	
161015–161022	AH-1T	Bell	
161023–161056	T-34C	Beech	
161057–161079	T-44A	Beech	
161080–161081	XFV-12A	Rockwell	
161082–161093	A-6E	Grumman	
161094–161099	E-2C	Grumman	
161100–161114	A-6E	Grumman	161112–161114 Cancelled
161115–161120	EA-6B	Grumman	
161121–161132	P-3C	Lockheed	
161133–161168	F-14A	Grumman	
161169–161173	YSH-60B	Sikorsky	

Bureau Number	Aircraft Type	Manufacturer	Miscellaneous Notes
161174–161178	EAV-8A	Hawker-Siddeley	Spain
161179–161184	CH-53E	Sikorsky	
161185–161206	UC-12B	Beech	
161207–161212	SH-3D	Sikorsky	Spain
161213–161217	F/A-18A	McDonnell Douglas	
161218–161222	TA-7H	Vought	Greece
161223	EC-130Q	Lockheed	
161224–161229	E-2C	Grumman	
161230–161241	A-6E	Grumman	161236–161241 Cancelled
161242–161247	EA-6B	Grumman	
161248–161251	F/A-18A	McDonnell Douglas	
161252–161265	CH-53E	Sikorsky	
161266	C-9B	McDonnell Douglas	
161267–161269	P-3C	Lockheed	Japan
161270–161305	F-14A	Grumman	161300–161305 Cancelled
161306–161327	UC-12B	Beech	
161328	EC-130Q	Lockheed	Cancelled
161329–161340	P-3C	Lockheed	
161341–161346	E-2C	Grumman	
161347–161352	EA-6B	Grumman	
161353–161367	F/A-18A	McDonnell Douglas	
161368–161380	P-3C	Lockheed	
161381–161395	CH-53E	Sikorsky	
161396–161399	AV-8B	McDonnell Douglas	
161400–161403	E-2C	Grumman	Cancelled
161404–161415	P-3C	Lockheed	161410 Cancelled
161416–161445	F-14A	Grumman	161420, 161423, 161431, 161436, 161439 Cancelled
161446–161493	F/A-18A	McDonnell Douglas	Cancelled
161494–161496	EC-130Q	Lockheed	
161497–161518	UC-12B	Beech	
161519–161528	F/A-18A	McDonnell Douglas	161522 Cancelled
161529–161530	C-9B	McDonnell Douglas	DC-9
161531	EC-130Q	Lockheed	
161532–161545	CH-53E	Sikorsky	161544–161545 Cancelled
161546	UC-8A	DeHavilland	DHC-5
161547–161552	E-2C	Grumman	
161553–161570	SH-60B	Sikorsky	
161571	X-26A	Schweizer	Cancelled
161572	UC-880	Convair	
161573–161584	AV-8B	McDonnell Douglas	161582 Cancelled
161585–161596	P-3C	Lockheed	
161597–161626	F-14A	Grumman	161602, 161613–161614, 161625 Cancelled
161627	U-8F	Beech	
161628	UC-27A	Fairchild	
161629–161640	F/A-18A	McDonnell Douglas	Cancelled

Bureau Number	Aircraft Type	Manufacturer	Miscellaneous Notes
161641–161652	SH-2F	Kaman	161646, 161648, 161649, 161651 Cancelled
161653	YSH-2G	Kaman	
161654–161658	SH-2F	Kaman	161654, 161655 Cancelled
161659–161694	A-6E	Grumman	161673, 161684, 161685, 161691–161694 Cancelled
161695–161701	TH-57B	Bell	
161702–161703	F/A-18A	McDonnell Douglas	
161704	F/A-18B	McDonnell Douglas	
161705–161706	F/A-18A	McDonnell Douglas	
161707	F/A-18B	McDonnell Douglas	
161708–161710	F/A-18A	McDonnell Douglas	
161711	F/A-18B	McDonnell Douglas	
161712–161713	F/A-18A	McDonnell Douglas	
161714	F/A-18B	McDonnell Douglas	
161715–161718	F/A-18A	McDonnell Douglas	
161719	F/A-18B	McDonnell Douglas	
161720–161722	F/A-18A	McDonnell Douglas	
161723	F/A-18B	McDonnell Douglas	
161724–161739	F/A-18A	McDonnell Douglas	161733 appears as F/A-18A and F/A-18B, 161727 Cancelled
161740	F/A-18B	McDonnell Douglas	
161741–161745	F/A-18A	McDonnell Douglas	161741 Cancelled
161746	F/A-18B	McDonnell Douglas	
161747–161761	F/A-18A	McDonnell Douglas	161754 Cancelled
161762–161773	P-3C	Lockheed	161768–161773 Cancelled
161774–161779	EA-6B	Grumman	161777–161778 Cancelled
161780–161785	E-2C	Grumman	
161786–161789	E-2C	Grumman	Japan
161790–161849	T-34C	Beech	
161850–161879	F-14A	Grumman	161854, 161972, 161874–161879 Cancelled
161880–161885	EA-6B	Grumman	
161886–161897	A-6E	Grumman	Cancelled
161898–161915	SH-2F	Kaman	161902, 161903, 161910, 161915 Cancelled
161916–161923	HXM		Cancelled
161924	F/A-18B	McDonnell Douglas	
161925–161931	F/A-18A	McDonnell Douglas	
161932	F/A-18B	McDonnell Douglas	
161933–161937	F/A-18A	McDonnell Douglas	161933 Cancelled
161938	F/A-18B	McDonnell Douglas	
161939–161942	F/A-18A	McDonnell Douglas	
161943	F/A-18B	McDonnell Douglas	
161944–161946	F/A-18A	McDonnell Douglas	
161947	F/A-18B	McDonnell Douglas	
161948–161987	F/A-18A	McDonnell Douglas	161966, 161971, 161980, 161987 Cancelled
161988–162012	CH-53E	Sikorsky	161999–162000, 162008 Cancelled
162013–162067	TH-57C	Bell	

Bureau Number	Aircraft Type	Manufacturer	Miscellaneous Notes
162068–162091	AV-8B	McDonnell Douglas	161071, 161073, 161079, 162089–162091 Cancelled
162092–162139	SH-60B	Sikorsky	162092, 162097, 162110, 162113 Cancelled
162140–162178	C-2A	Grumman	
162179–162222	A-6E	Grumman	162181, 162203–162222 Cancelled
162223–162246	EA-6B	Grumman	162223, 162226, 162231–162246 Cancelled
162247–162306	T-34C	Beech	
162307	F-5E	Northrop	
162308–162311	KC-130T	Lockheed	
162312–162313	EC-130Q	Lockheed	
162314–162325	P-3C	Lockheed	162319–162325 Cancelled
162326–162389	SH-60B	Sikorsky	162350–162389 Cancelled
162390–162393	C-9B	McDonnell Douglas	DC-9
162394–162401	F/A-18A	McDonnell Douglas	162397, 162399 Cancelled
162402	F/A-18B	McDonnell Douglas	
162403–162407	F/A-18A	McDonnell Douglas	162404, 162405 Cancelled
162408	F/A-18B	McDonnell Douglas	
162409–162418	F/A-18A	McDonnell Douglas	162413 Cancelled
162419	F/A-18B	McDonnell Douglas	
162420–162426	F/A-18A	McDonnell Douglas	
162427	F/A-18B	McDonnell Douglas	
162428–162477	F/A-18A	McDonnell Douglas	162447, 162450, 162476, 162477 Cancelled
162478–162602	CH-53E	Sikorsky	162497, 162498 Cancelled
162503–162526	MH-53E	Sikorsky	
162527–162531	CH-53E	Sikorsky	Cancelled
162532–162575	AH-1W	Bell	162540 Cancelled
162576–162587	SH-2F	Kaman	162579 Cancelled
162588–162611	F-14A	Grumman	162593, 162596, 162605, 162609 Cancelled
162612–162613	YT-45A	McDonnell Douglas	
162614–162619	E-2C	Grumman	
162620–162649	T-34C	Beech	
162650–162655	SH-2F	Kaman	Cancelled
162656–162665	P-3	Lockheed	FMS
162666–162686	TH-57C	Bell	
162687	CH-53E	Sikorsky	Cancelled
162688–162717	F-14A	Grumman	162706, 162712–162717 Cancelled
162718–162720	CH-53E	Sikorsky	Cancelled
162721–162746	AV-8B	McDonnell Douglas	162724, 162745, 162746 Cancelled
162747	TAV-8B	McDonnell Douglas	
162748–162752	AV-8B	McDonnell Douglas	Cancelled
162753–162754	C-9	McDonnell Douglas	DC-9
162755	U-8F	Beech	Cancelled
162755–162769	T-47A	Cessna	Cancelled
162770–162781	P-3C	Lockheed	162779–162781 Cancelled
162782–162784	E-6A	Boeing	
162785–162786	KC-130T	Lockheed	

Bureau Number	Aircraft Type	Manufacturer	Miscellaneous Notes
162787–162790	T-45A	McDonnell Douglas	162789, 162790 Cancelled
162791–162792	E-2C	Grumman	Egypt
162793–162796	E-2C	Grumman	Singapore
162797–162802	E-2C	Grumman	
162803–162810	TH-57B	Bell	
162811–162823	TH-57C	Bell	162824, 162825 Cancelled
162824–162825	E-2C	Grumman	Cancelled
162826–162835	F/A-18A	McDonnell Douglas	
162836	F/A-18B	McDonnell Douglas	
162837–162841	F/A-18A	McDonnell Douglas	
162842	F/A-18B	McDonnell Douglas	
162843–162849	F/A-18A	McDonnell Douglas	162847 Cancelled
162850	F/A-18B	McDonnell Douglas	
162851–162856	F/A-18A	McDonnell Douglas	162855 Cancelled
162857	F/A-18B	McDonnell Douglas	
162858–162863	F/A-18A	McDonnell Douglas	
162864	F/A-18B	McDonnell Douglas	
162865–162869	F/A-18A	McDonnell Douglas	
162870	F/A-18B	McDonnell Douglas	
162871–162875	F/A-18A	McDonnell Douglas	
162976	F/A-18B	McDonnell Douglas	
162977–162884	F/A-18A	McDonnell Douglas	
162885	F/A-18B	McDonnell Douglas	
162886–162909	F/A-18A	McDonnell Douglas	162908 Cancelled
162910–162933	F-14A+	Grumman	162928–162933 Cancelled
162934–162941	EA-6B	Grumman	162940, 162941 Cancelled
162942–162973	AV-8B	McDonnell Douglas	162952, 162961, 162971 Cancelled
162974–162997	SH-60B	Sikorsky	162978, 162992–162997 Cancelled
162998–163009	P-3C	Lockheed	163007–163009 Cancelled
163010–163021	EAV-8B	McDonnell Douglas	Spain
163022–163023	KC-130T	Lockheed	
163024–163029	E-2C	Grumman	
163030–163035	EA-6B	Grumman	
163036–163037	C-9B	McDonnell Douglas	DC-9
163038–163043	SH-60B	Sikorsky	Cancelled
163044–163049	EA-6B	Grumman	163044 Cancelled
163050	EC-24A	Douglas	DC-8
163051–163089	CH-53E	Sikorsky	163051, 163053–163058, 163065–163071, 163088, 163089 Cancelled
163090–163091	XKB-2	Northrop	Cancelled
163092–163103	F/A-18A/B	McDonnell Douglas	
163104	F/A-18B	McDonnell Douglas	
163105–163109	F/A-18A	McDonnell Douglas	163109 Cancelled
163110	F/A-18B	McDonnell Douglas	
163111–163114	F/A-18A	McDonnell Douglas	163112 Cancelled
163115	F/A-18B	McDonnell Douglas	

Bureau Number	Aircraft Type	Manufacturer	Miscellaneous Notes
163116–163122	F/A-18A	McDonnell Douglas	
163123	F/A-18B	McDonnell Douglas	
163124–163175	F/A-18A	McDonnell Douglas	163136 Cancelled
163176–163207	AV-8B	McDonnell Douglas	163180, 163182, 163185, 163186, 163191, 163196, 163202, 163207 Cancelled
163208	C-9B	McDonnell Douglas	DC-9
163209–163214	SH-2F	Kaman	
163215–163232	F-14A+	Grumman	163230–163232 Cancelled
163233–163256	SH-60B	Sikorsky	163236, 163250–163256 Cancelled
163257–163258	UH-60A	Sikorsky	Cancelled
163259–163267	VH-60A	Sikorsky	
163268–163277	F-16N	General Dynamics	
163278–163281	TF-16N	General Dynamics	
163282–163288	SH-60F	Sikorsky	
163289–163297	P-3C	Lockheed	163296, 163297 Cancelled
163298–163309	F-21A	IAI	Cancelled
163310–163311	KC-130T	Lockheed	
163312–163347	TH-57B	Bell	
163348–163394	AV-8B	McDonnell Douglas	Cancelled
163395–163406	EA-6B	Grumman	
163407–163411	F-14A+	Grumman	
163412–163418	F-14D	Grumman	
163419–163426	AV-8B	McDonnell Douglas	
163427–163510	F/A-18D	McDonnell Douglas	163427–163433, 163435, 163437–163440, 163442–163444, 163446, 163448–163451, 163453, 163455, 163456, 163458, 163459, 163461–163463, 163465–163467, 163469–163471, 163473, 163475–163478, 163480, 163481, 163483–163485, 163487, 163489–163491, 163493–163496, 163498, 163499, 163502–163406, 163508, 163509 Cancelled
163511–163513	C-9	McDonnell Douglas	DC-9
163514–163519	AV-8B	McDonnell Douglas	
163520–163531	EA-6B	Grumman	
163532–163534	E-6A	Boeing	Cancelled
163535–163540	E-2C	Grumman	
163541–163546	SH-2G	Kaman	
163547–163552	SH-2F	Kaman	Cancelled
163553–163564	UC-12F	Beech	163563, 163564 Cancelled
163565	E-2C	Grumman	Cancelled
163566–163577	F-16N	General Dynamics	
163578–163590	P-3C	Lockheed	163578–163590 Cancelled
163591–163592	KC-130T	Lockheed	
163593–163598	SH-60B	Sikorsky	
163599–163658	T-45A	McDonnell Douglas	
163659–163690	AV-8B	McDonnell Douglas	
163691–163692	C-20D	Gulfstream	
163693–163698	E-2C	Grumman	

Bureau Number	Aircraft Type	Manufacturer	Miscellaneous Notes
163699–163782	F/A-18D	McDonnell Douglas	163699, 163701–163706, 163708–163719, 163721–163733, 163735–163748, 163750–163762, 163764–163770, 163772–163777, 163779–163782 Cancelled
163783–163800	HH-60H	Sikorsky	
163801–163835	HH-60J	Sikorsky	USCG, 163833–163835 Cancelled
163836–163847	UC-12M	Beech	163846, 163847 Cancelled
163848–163851	E-2C	Grumman	
163852–163855	AV-8B	McDonnell Douglas	
163856–163861	TAV-8B	McDonnell Douglas	
163862–163883	AV-8B	McDonnell Douglas	
163884–163892	EA-6B	Grumman	
163893–163904	F-14D	Grumman	
163905–163919	SH-60B	Sikorsky	163911–163919 Cancelled
163911–163916	YV-22A	Bell	
163917	C-28A	Cessna	
163918–163920	E-6A	Boeing	
163921–163954	AH-1W	Bell	163921–163923, 163925, 163928 Cancelled
163955–163984	A-6F	Grumman	Cancelled
163985–164068	F/A-18D	McDonnell Douglas	163985, 163987, 163988, 163990, 163992, 163993, 163995, 163996, 163998–164000, 164002–164004, 164006–164008, 164010, 164012, 164013, 164015, 164016, 164018, 164020, 164021, 164023, 164025, 164027, 164029–164031, 164033, 164034, 164036, 164037, 164039, 164041, 164042, 164044, 164045, 164047, 164048, 164050, 164052, 164054, 164055, 164057, 164059, 164060, 164062, 164063, 164065–164067 Cancelled
164069–164104	SH-60F	Sikorsky	
164105–164106	KC-130T	Lockheed	
164107–164112	E-2C	Grumman	
164113–164114	TAV-8B	McDonnell Douglas	
164115–164121	AV-8B	McDonnell Douglas	
164122	TAV-8B	McDonnell Douglas	
164123–164154	AV-8B	McDonnell Douglas	164136–164138 Cancelled
164155–164173	T-34C	Beech	
164174–164179	SH-60B	Sikorsky	
164180–164181	KC-130T	Lockheed	
164182–164193	EA-6B	Grumman	Cancelled
164194–164195	KC-130T	Lockheed	Cancelled
164196–164339	F/A-18D	McDonnell Douglas	164197, 164199–164202, 164204–164206, 164208–164210, 164212–164215, 164217, 164218, 164220–164223, 164225–164227, 164229–164232, 164234–164236, 164238–164240, 164242–164244, 164247, 164248, 164250–164253, 164255–164258, 164260, 164261, 164264–164266, 164269–164271, 164273–164278, 164280–164339 Cancelled
164340–164351	F-14D	Grumman	
164352–164357	E-2C	Grumman	164356, 164357 Cancelled
164358–164367	CH-53E	Sikorsky	

Bureau Number	Aircraft Type	Manufacturer	Miscellaneous Notes
164368–164375	MH-53E	Sikorsky	164368–164375 Cancelled
164376–164385	A-6E	Grumman	
164386–164388	E-6A	Boeing	
164389–164400	V-22	Bell	Cancelled
164401–164403	EA-6B	Grumman	
164404–164410	E-6A	Boeing	
164411–164422	F/A-18C	McDonnell Douglas	Cancelled
164423–164440	SH-60F	Sikorsky	Cancelled
164441–164442	KC-130T	Lockheed	
164443–164460	SH-60F	Sikorsky	
164461–164466	SH-60B	Sikorsky	
164467–164469	P-3C	Lockheed	
164470–164482	CH-53E	Sikorsky	Cancelled
164483–164518	E-2C	Grumman	164489–164491, 164498–164518 Cancelled
164519–164523	A-12	McDonnell Douglas and General Dynamics	Cancelled
164524–164525	U-6A	DeHavilland	L-20A, from USDA
164526–164535	A-12	McDonnell Douglas and General Dynamics	Cancelled
164536–164539	CH-53E	Sikorsky	
164540–164542	TAV-8B	McDonnell Douglas	
164543–164571	AV-8B	McDonnell Douglas	164563 Cancelled
164572–164578	AH-1W	Bell	
164579–164583	T-44B	Beech	
164584–164585	X-31A	Grumman	
164586–164596	AH-1W	Bell	
164597–164598	KC-130T	Lockheed	
164599–164604	F-14D	Grumman	
164605–164608	C-9	McDonnell Douglas	DC-9
164609–164620	SH-60F	Sikorsky	164616 Cancelled
164621–164626	E-2C	Grumman	Cancelled
164627–164648	F/A-18C	McDonnell Douglas	164627, 164629–164648 Cancelled
164649–164746	F/A-18D	McDonnell Douglas	164654, 164655, 164657, 164658, 165660, 164661, 164663, 164664, 164666, 164668, 164669, 164671, 164673, 164675, 164676, 164678, 164680–164682, 164684, 164686, 164687, 164689, 164691, 164693, 164695–164698, 164700, 164701, 164703, 164704, 164706–164710, 164712, 164713, 164715, 164716, 164718–164722, 164724, 164725, 164727, 164728, 164730–164734, 164736, 164737, 164739–164746 Cancelled
164747–164758	F/A-18D	McDonnell Douglas	Cancelled
164759–164760	KC-130T	Lockheed	Cancelled
164761	C-28A	Cessna	
164762–164763	C-130T	Lockheed	
164764–164775	MH-53E	Sikorsky	164774, 164775 Cancelled
164776–164791	CH-53E	Sikorsky	
164792–164795	MH-53E	Sikorsky	164794, 164795 Cancelled
164796–164807	SH-60F	Sikorsky	164805–164807 Cancelled

Bureau Number	Aircraft Type	Manufacturer	Miscellaneous Notes
164808–164819	SH-60B	Sikorsky	
164820–164830	HH-60J	Sikorsky	
164831–164846	HH-60H	Sikorsky	164831–164839 Cancelled
164847–164858	SH-60B	Sikorsky	
164859–164860	CH-53E	Sikorsky	
164861–164864	MH-53E	Sikorsky	
164865–164875	F/A-18C	McDonnell Douglas	164868, 164870, 164872, 164974 Cancelled
164876	F/A-18D	McDonnell Douglas	
164877–164883	F/A-18C	McDonnell Douglas	164878, 164880 Cancelled
164884	F/A-18D	McDonnell Douglas	
164885	F/A-18C	McDonnell Douglas	
164886	F/A-18D	McDonnell Douglas	
164887	F/A-18C	McDonnell Douglas	
164888	F/A-18D	McDonnell Douglas	
164889–164897	F/A-18C	McDonnell Douglas	
164898	F/A-18D	McDonnell Douglas	
164899–164900	F/A-18C	McDonnell Douglas	
164901	F/A-18D	McDonnell Douglas	
164902–164912	F/A-18C	McDonnell Douglas	
164913–164938	AH-1W	Bell	Cancelled
164939–164944	MV-22B	Bell-Boeing	164943, 164944 Cancelled
164945	F/A-18D	McDonnell Douglas	
164946	F/A-18C	McDonnell Douglas	
164947	F/A-18D	McDonnell Douglas	
164948	F/A-18C	McDonnell Douglas	
164949	F/A-18D	McDonnell Douglas	
164950	F/A-18C	McDonnell Douglas	
164951	F/A-18D	McDonnell Douglas	
164952	F/A-18C	McDonnell Douglas	
164953	F/A-18D	McDonnell Douglas	
164954	F/A-18C	McDonnell Douglas	
164955	F/A-18D	McDonnell Douglas	
164956	F/A-18C	McDonnell Douglas	
164957	F/A-18D	McDonnell Douglas	
164958	F/A-18C	McDonnell Douglas	
164959	F/A-18D	McDonnell Douglas	
164960	F/A-18C	McDonnell Douglas	
164961	F/A-18D	McDonnell Douglas	
164962	F/A-18C	McDonnell Douglas	
164963	F/A-18D	McDonnell Douglas	
164964	F/A-18C	McDonnell Douglas	
164965	F/A-18D	McDonnell Douglas	
164966	F/A-18C	McDonnell Douglas	
164967	F/A-18D	McDonnell Douglas	
164968–164980	F/A-18C	McDonnell Douglas	
164981–164992	F/A-18D	McDonnell Douglas	Cancelled

Bureau Number	Aircraft Type	Manufacturer	Miscellaneous Notes
164993–164998	C-130T	Lockheed	
164999–165000	KC-130T	Lockheed	
165001–165006	AV-8B	McDonnell Douglas	
165007–165027	AV-8B	McDonnell Douglas	For Italy
165028–165035	AV-8B	McDonnell Douglas	For Spain
165036	TAV-8B	McDonnell Douglas	For Spain
165037–165056	AH-1W	Bell	165037–165041 Cancelled
165057–165079	T-45A	McDonnell Douglas	
165080–165092	T-45C	Boeing	
165093–165094	C-20G	Gulfstream	
165095	SH-60B	Sikorsky	
165096	HH-60J	Sikorsky	
165097	AH-1W	Bell	
165098–165105	P-3C	Lockheed	165098–165105 Cancelled
165106–165112	SH-60B	Sikorsky	
165113–165123	HH-60H	Sikorsky	
165124–165127	HH-60J	Sikorsky	
165128–165134	SH-60B	Sikorsky	Cancelled
165135–165141	SH-60F	Sikorsky	Cancelled
165142–165145	HH-60H	Sikorsky	Cancelled
165146–165150	HH-60J	Sikorsky	
165151–165153	C-20G	Gulfstream	
165154	HH-60H	Sikorsky	
165155–165157	SH-60F	Sikorsky	Cancelled
165158–165161	C-130T	Lockheed	
165162–165163	KC-130T	Lockheed	
165164–165165	F/A-18E	McDonnell Douglas	
165166	F/A-18F	McDonnell Douglas	
165167–165169	F/A-18E	McDonnell Douglas	
165170	F/A-18F	McDonnell Douglas	
165171–165230	F/A-18C	McDonnell Douglas	
165231–165242	F/A-18D	McDonnell Douglas	Cancelled
165243–165254	CH-53E	Sikorsky	
165255–165267	HH-60H	Sikorsky	165260–165267 Cancelled
165268–165270	SH-60F	Sikorsky	Cancelled
165271–165292	AH-1W	Bell	
165293–165304	E-2C	Grumman	
165305–165312	AV-8B	McDonnell Douglas	
165313–165314	C-130T	Lockheed	
165315–165316	KC-130T	Lockheed	
165317–165341	AH-1W	Bell	165334–165341 Cancelled
165342–165343	E-6A	Boeing	Cancelled
165344–165347	CH-53E	Sikorsky	
165348–165351	C-130T	Lockheed	
165352–165353	KC-130T	Lockheed	
165354–165357	AV-8B	McDonnell Douglas	Remanufactured

Bureau Number	Aircraft Type	Manufacturer	Miscellaneous Notes
165358–165377	AH-1W	Bell	165370–165377 Cancelled
165378–165379	C-130T	Lockheed	
165380–165391	AV-8B	McDonnell Douglas	Remanufactured
165392–165396	AH-1W	Bell	
165397–165398	AV-8B	McDonnell Douglas	Remanufactured
165399–165408	F/A-18C	McDonnell Douglas	
165409–165416	F/A-18D	McDonnell Douglas	
165417–165432	AV-8B	McDonnell Douglas/ Boeing	165431, 165432 Cancelled, not accepted
165433–165444	MV-22B	Bell/Boeing	
165445–165450	AH-1W	Bell	
165451–165454	AV-8B	McDonnell Douglas	Cancelled
165455–165456	E-2C	Northrop Grumman	
165457–165498	T-45C	Boeing	
165499–165502	T-45C	Boeing	Cancelled
165503–165504	CH-53E	Sikorsky	
165505–165506	T-45A	McDonnell Douglas/ British Aerospace	Cancelled
165507–165508	E-2C	Grumman	
165509–165525	T-39N	Boeing North American	
165526	F/A-18C	McDonnell Douglas/ Boeing	
165527–165532	F/A-18D	Boeing	
165533–165540	F/A-18E	Boeing	
165541–165544	F/A-18F	Boeing	
165545–165565	AH-1W	Bell	Cancelled
165566–165597	AV-8B	McDonnell Douglas/ Boeing	165568–165579 Remanufactured
165598–165646	T-45C	Boeing	
165647–165650	E-2C	Northrop Grumman	
165651	CH-53E	Sikorsky	
165652–165659	AV-8B	Boeing	Cancelled
165660–165667	F/A-18E	Boeing	
165668–165679	F/A-18F	Boeing	
165680–165687	F/A-18D	Boeing	
165688–165734	RQ-2A	AAI/IAI	Operated by the Marines and never treated like an aircraft and not entered into AIRRS database
165735–165739	KC-130J	Lockheed Martin	
165740–165741	UC-35C	Cessna	
165742–165751	CH-60S	Sikorsky	
165752–165778	MH-60S	Sikorsky	
165779–165792	F/A-18E	Boeing	
165793–165808	F/A-18F	Boeing	
165809–165810	KC-130J	Lockheed Martin	
165811–165828	E-2C	Northrop Grumman	
165829–165836	C-40A	Boeing	
165837–165853	MV-22B	Bell/Boeing	

Bureau Number	Aircraft Type	Manufacturer	Miscellaneous Notes
165854–165859	SH-60B	Sikorsky	Spain
165860–165874	F/A-18E	Boeing	
165875–165895	F/A-18F	Boeing	
165896–165909	F/A-18E	Boeing	
165910–165937	F/A-18F	Boeing	165935–165937 not used or issued to aircraft
165938–165939	UC-35D	Cessna	
165940–165948	MV-22B	Bell/Boeing	
165949–165955	MV-22B	Bell/Boeing	Cancelled
165956	MV-22B	Bell/Boeing	
165957	KC-130J	Lockheed	
165958–166009	T-6A	Raytheon/Beech	165958, 166007–166009 not used or issued to aircraft
166010–166285	T-6B	Raytheon/Beech	166071–166285 not used or issued to aircraft or still to be delivered
166286	TC-18F	Boeing	To be used as trainer for E-6 but struck and never used
166287–166288	AV-8B	Boeing	
166289–166373	MH-60S	Sikorsky	166371–166373 Cancelled
166374	UC-35D	Cessna	
166375	C-37A	Gulfstream	
166376–166379	C-37B	Gulfstream	Issued in a block of 4 but 166379 never used
166380–166382	KC-130J	Lockheed Martin	
166383–166399	MV-22B	Bell/Boeing	Issued in a block of 17 but 166392–166399 never used
166400–166401	RQ-8A	Northrop Grumman	Most likely the pattern for the RQ-2As and not treated like an aircraft or entered into AIRRS database
166402–166408	MH-60R	Sikorsky	166402, 166403 Remanufactured
166409–166410	SH-60R	Sikorsky	Issued in a block of 7 for SH-60R (166404–166410) but 166409 and 166410 never used
166411–166413	AV-8B	Boeing	Issued in a block of 3, possibly for Spain
166414–166416	RQ-8A	Northrop Grumman	Issued in a block of 3 but never used or transferred to Navy
166417–166419	E-2C	Northrop Grumman	166418–166419 Cancelled
166420–166448	F/A-18E	Boeing	
166449–166467	F/A-18F	Boeing	
166468–166471	MH-60S	Sikorsky	166468–166471 Cancelled
166472–166473	KC-130J	Lockheed Martin	
166474	UC-35D	Cessna	
166475–166476	UH-1Y	Bell	
166477–166479	AH-1Z	Bell	
166480–166499	MV-22B	Bell/Boeing	
166500	UC-35D	Cessna	
166501–166503	TE-2C	Northrop Grumman	
166504	E-2C	Northrop Grumman	
166505–166507	TE-2C	Northrop Grumman	
166508	E-2C	Northrop Grumman	

Bureau Number	Aircraft Type	Manufacturer	Miscellaneous Notes
166509–166510	RQ-4A	Northrop Grumman	Global Hawk UA was GHMD RDT&E, now in inventory and deployed but most likely never assigned bureau numbers because they are not listed in AIRRS database
166511–166514	KC-130J	Lockheed Martin	
166515–166597	MH-60R	Sikorsky	
166598–166609	F/A-18E	Boeing	
166610–166642	F/A-18F	Boeing	
166643–166657	F/A-18E	Boeing	
166658–166684	F/A-18F	Boeing	
166685–166692	MV-22B	Bell/Boeing	
166693–166711	C-40A	Boeing	166695–166711 not yet delivered, delivery sometime in 2011 or 2012
166712–166715	UC-35D	Cessna	
166716–166717	C-40A	Boeing	For future procurement
166718–166730	MV-22B	Bell/Boeing	166727–166730 not used or issued to aircraft
166731–166752	MV-22B	Bell/Boeing	166748–166752 not used for issued to aircraft
166753–166758	UH-1Y	Bell	
166759–166761	AH-1Z	Bell	
166762–166765	KC-130J	Lockheed Martin	
166766–166767	UC-35D	Cessna	
166768–166771	UH-1Y	Bell	
166772–166774	AH-1Z	Bell	
166775–166789	F/A-18E	Boeing	
166790–166816	F/A-18F	Boeing	
166817–166841	F/A-18E	Boeing	
166842–166854	F/A-18F	Boeing	
166855–166858	EA-18G	Boeing	
166859–166872	F/A-18E	Boeing	
166873–166892	F/A-18F	Boeing	
166893–166900	EA-18G	Boeing	
166901–166914	F/A-18E	Boeing	
166915–166927	F/A-18F	Boeing	
166928–166946	EA-18G	Boeing	
166947–166960	F/A-18E	Boeing	166953–166960 not yet delivered
166961–166984	F/A-18F	Boeing	166966–166984 not yet delivered
166985–166992	VH-71	Lockheed Martin/Bell	Program cancelled
166993–167011	MH-60R	Sikorsky	167000–167011 not yet delivered
167012–167072	MH-60R	Sikorsky	167012–167072 not yet delivered
167073–167106	T-45C	Boeing	
167107	Not Assigned		Not used
167108–167112	KC-130J	Lockheed Martin	
167113–167778	Not Assigned		Not used
167779–167781	MH-60R	Sikorsky	Not yet delivered
167782–167783	O-2A	Cessna	

Bureau Number	Aircraft Type	Manufacturer	Miscellaneous Notes
167784–167792	MQ-8B	Northrop Grumman/ Schweizer Aircraft	Not delivered or not used
167793–167808	UH-1Y	Bell	
167809–167810	AH-1Z	Bell	
167811	MZ-3A	American Blimp	
167812–167879	MH-60S	Sikorsky	
167880–167901	MH-60S	Sikorsky	Not yet delivered
167902–167922	MV-22B	Bell/Boeing	
167923–167927	KC-130J	Lockheed Martin	
167928	VH-71	Lockheed Martin/Bell	Program cancelled
167929–167931	E-2D	Northrop Grumman	
167932–167950	F/A-18F/EA-18G	Boeing	Cancelled
167951–167956	P-8A	Boeing	167952, 167955, 167956 not yet accepted
167957–167980	F/A-18F	Boeing	Not yet delivered
167981–167985	KC-130J	Lockheed Martin	
167986–167988	MQ-8B	Northrop Grumman/ Schweizer Aircraft	167987, 167988 not yet delivered
167989–167999	UH-1Y	Bell	
168000–168003	AH-1Z	Bell	
168004–168033	MV-22B	Bell/Boeing	Not yet all delivered
168034–168035	MH-60S	Sikorsky	Not yet delivered
168036–168048	UH-1Y	Bell	Not yet delivered
168049–168055	AH-1Z	Bell	168050–168064 not yet delivered
168056	A-29B	Embraer Defense	Was on loan for tests but returned
168057–168062	F-35B	Lockheed Martin	Not yet delivered
168063–168064	X-47B	Northrop Grumman	NUCAS-D, not yet delivered
168065–168075	KC-130J	Lockheed Martin	168069–168073 not yet delivered
168076–168077	E-2D	Northrop Grumman	Not yet delivered
168078–168203	MH-60R	Sikorsky	Not yet delivered
168204–168209	UC-12W	Hawker Beechcraft	168208, 168209 not yet delivered
168210–168213	MQ-8B	Northrop Grumman/ Schweizer Aircraft	Not yet delivered
168214–168244	MV-22B	Bell/Boeing	Not yet delivered
168245–168249	UH-72A	EADS North America	
168250–168259	EA-18G	Boeing	
198003	QF-86F	North American	
201569–201570	YF-17	Northrop	From Air Force
201970	UH-1B	Bell	From Army
210904	C-45H	Beech	
212515	UH-1B	Bell	From Army
212518	UH-1B	Bell	From Army
212522	UH-1B	Bell	From Army
212541–212543	UH-1B	Bell	From Army
212546	UH-1B	Bell	From Army
212549	UH-1B	Bell	From Army
212574–212575	CH-3B/SH-3H	Sikorsky	From Air Force

Bureau Number	Aircraft Type	Manufacturer	Miscellaneous Notes
221252–221253	OH-58A	Bell	
302801	U-6A/L-20A	DeHavilland	
312908	UH-1B	Bell	From Army
312922–312923	UH-1B	Bell	From Army
312929–312931	UH-1B	Bell	From Army
312944	UH-1B	Bell	From Army
313119	OV-1A	Grumman	From Army
313128	OV-1A	Grumman	From Army
313134	OV-1A	Grumman	From Army
313988	UH-1B	Bell	From Army
349218	JC-47D	Douglas	From Army
364651	US-2E	Grumman	
413540	UH-1H	Bell	From Army
413584	UH-1D	Bell	From Army
413632	UH-1D	Bell	From Army
413646	UH-1D	Bell	From Army
413675	UH-1D	Bell	From Army
413691	UH-1H	Bell	From Army
413758	UH-1H	Bell	From Army
413765	UH-1D	Bell	From Army
413827	UH-1D	Bell	From Army
413869	UH-1D	Bell	From Army
413872	UH-1D	Bell	From Army
413901	UH-1H	Bell	
413903	UH-1B	Bell	From Army
413911	UH-1B	Bell	From Army
413919	UH-1B	Bell	From Army
413924	UH-1B	Bell	From Army
413939	UH-1B	Bell	From Army
413940	UH-1B	Bell	From Army
413942	UH-1B	Bell	From Army
413943	UH-1B	Bell	From Army
413948–413949	UH-1B	Bell	From Army
413952	UH-1B	Bell	From Army
413956	UH-1B	Bell	From Army
413958	UH-1B	Bell	From Army
413969	UH-1B	Bell	From Army
413975	UH-1B	Bell	From Army
413980	UH-1B	Bell	From Army
413982	UH-1B	Bell	From Army
413985	UH-1B	Bell	From Army
413989–413990	UH-1B	Bell	From Army
414001	UH-1B	Bell	From Army
414003	UH-1B	Bell	From Army
414007	UH-1B	Bell	From Army
414013	UH-1B	Bell	From Army

Bureau Number	Aircraft Type	Manufacturer	Miscellaneous Notes
414020	UH-1B	Bell	From Army
414022	UH-1B	Bell	From Army
414031	UH-1B	Bell	From Army
414033	UH-1B	Bell	From Army
414036	UH-1B	Bell	From Army
414040	UH-1B	Bell	From Army
414070	UH-1B	Bell	From Army
414076	UH-1B	Bell	From Army
414081	UH-1B	Bell	From Army
414083–414084	UH-1B	Bell	From Army
414087	UH-1B	Bell	From Army
414090–414091	UH-1B	Bell	From Army
414117	UH-1M	Bell	From Army
414145	UH-1C	Bell	From Army
414235	CH-3E	Sikorsky	From Army
414243	OV-1B	Grumman	From Army
414262	OV-1B	Grumman	From Army
459186	NUH-57A	Bell	
510052	UH-1H	Bell	From Army
510054	UH-1D	Bell	From Army
510072	UH-1D	Bell	From Army
510077	UH-1D	Bell	From Army
510085	UH-1D	Bell	From Army
510104	UH-1H	Bell	From Army
510129	UH-1H	Bell	From Army
510327	T-38A	Northrop	From Army
511230	O-1A	Cessna	From Army
511696	O-1A	Cessna	From Army
512686	T-42A	Beech	
512694	T-42A	Beech	
512776	UH-1D	Bell	From Army
512868	UH-1D	Bell	From Army
512873	UH-1H	Bell	From Army
512876	UH-1D	Bell	From Army
512887	UH-1D	Bell	From Army
513278	QF-86F	North American	
513786	YAT-28E	North American	From Army
513788	YAT-28E	North American	From Army
513802	T-29B	Convair	From Army
514651	O-1A	Cessna	Not accepted
515117	T-29B	Convair	From Army
515124	T-29B	Convair	From Army
515129	T-29B	Convair	From Army
515145	T-29B	Convair	From Army
515165–515166	T-29B	Convair	From Army
517895	T-29B	Convair	From Army

Bureau Number	Aircraft Type	Manufacturer	Miscellaneous Notes
517906	T-29B	Convair	From Army
517908	T-29B	Convair	From Army
521118–521119	T-29C	Convair	From Air Force
521160	T-29C	Convair	From Air Force
521162	T-29C	Convair	From Air Force
521167	T-29C	Convair	From Air Force
521175	T-29C	Convair	From Air Force
522090–522091	F-86H/QF-86H	North American	
522094	QF-86H	North American	
522097–522099	F-86H/QF-86H	North American	From Air Force
522116	QF-86H	North American	
522122	QF-86H	North American	
523732	F-86H	North American	
523744	F-86H	North American	
524100	EB-47E	Boeing	
524120	EB-47E	Boeing	
524450	QF-86F	North American	
524647	QF-86F	North American	
525123	U-6A (L-20A)	DeHavilland	
525732	QF-86H	North American	
525736	QF-86H	North American	
525744	QF-86H	North American	
525746	QF-86H	North American	
525747	F-86H	North American	From Air Force
526123	U-6A (L-20A)	DeHavilland	
528176	U-3A	Cessna	
531279	F-86H	North American	
531294	QF-86H	North American	From Air Force
531314	QF-86H	North American	From Air Force
531322	F-86H	North American	From Air Force
531328	QF-86H/F-86H	North American	
531331	F-86H	North American	
531335	QF-86H	North American	
531351	QQF-86H	North American	
531373	F-86H	North American	From Air Force
531381	QF-86H	North American	
531383	QF-86H	North American	
531402	F-86H	North American	
531403	QF-86H	North American	
531406	F-86H	North American	
531408–531409	QF-86H	North American	
531413	QF-86H	North American	
531514	QF-86H	North American	
531521	QF-86H	North American	
531527	F-86H	North American	
532104	NB-47E	Boeing	From Air Force

Bureau Number	Aircraft Type	Manufacturer	Miscellaneous Notes
532104	YOV-1	Grumman	Duplicate number, from Air Force
533227–533228	C-118B	Douglas	
533257	C-118B	Douglas	
533279	C-118B	Douglas	
533291	C-118B	Douglas	
533461	T-29C	Convair	From Air Force
533477	T-29C	Convair	From Air Force
540172	U-6A (L-20A)	DeHavilland	From Army
541720	U-6A (L-20A)	DeHavilland	
542815	C-131H	Convair	From Air Force
542817	C-131H	Convair	From Air Force
550229	C-131H	Convair	From Air Force
552112	QF-86F	North American	
552792	QF-86F	North American	
553134	NKC-135A	Boeing	
553465	U-8G	Beech	From Army
553822–553823	QF-86F	North American	
553829	QF-86F	North American	
553838	QF-86F	North American	
553846	QF-86F	North American	From Air Force
553863–553865	QF-86F	North American	
553868	QF-86F	North American	
553875	QF-86F	North American	
553878	QF-86F	North American	
553881–553883	QF-86F	North American	
553895	QF-86F	North American	
553898	QF-86F	North American	
553900	QF-86F	North American	
553902–553903	QF-86F	North American	
553905–553906	QF-86F	North American	
553912–553913	QF-86F	North American	
553915	QF-86F	North American	
553919	QF-86F	North American	
553926	QF-86F	North American	
553932	QF-86F	North American	
553935–553936	QF-86F	North American	
553939	QF-86F	North American	From Air Force
553942	QF-86F	North American	
553945	QF-86F	North American	
553948	QF-86F	North American	
555017	QF-86F	North American	
555048	QF-86F	North American	
555052–555053	QF-86F	North American	
555057	QF-86F	North American	
555069	QF-86F	North American	
555072–555073	QF-86F	North American	

Bureau Number	Aircraft Type	Manufacturer	Miscellaneous Notes
555078	QF-86F	North American	
555082	QF-86F	North American	
555087	QF-86F	North American	
555091	QF-86F	North American	
555095	QF-86F	North American	
555097–555099	QF-86F	North American	
555101–555102	QF-86F	North American	
555105	QF-86F	North American	
555110	QF-86F	North American	
555111–555112	QF-86F	North American	From Air Force
555114	QF-86F	North American	
555890	QF-86F	North American	
556412	QF-86F	North American	
559118	C-9B	McDonnell Douglas	
560514	DC-130A	Lockheed	
560527	DC-130A	Lockheed	
562782–562784	QF-86F	North American	
562786–562787	QF-86F	North American	
562795	QF-86F	North American	
562797	QF-86F	North American	
562801	QF-86F	North American	
562804	QF-86F	North American	
562807	QF-86F	North American	
562811	QF-86F	North American	
562813–562815	QF-86F	North American	
562818–562819	QF-86F	North American	
562823	QF-86F	North American	
562825–562827	QF-86F	North American	
562829–562831	QF-86F	North American	
562836–562838	QF-86F	North American	562836 from Air Force
562840	QF-86F	North American	
562842	QF-86F	North American	
562845–562846	QF-86F	North American	
562848–562849	QF-86F	North American	
562852	QF-86F	North American	
562855	QF-86F	North American	
562858	QF-86F	North American	
562865	QF-86F	North American	
562874–562875	QF-86F	North American	
562884	QF-86F	North American	
562896	QF-86F	North American	
563596	NKC-135A	Boeing	
564039	U-8G	Beech	From Army
564044	U-8G	Beech	From Army
565103	QF-86F	North American	
566781	QF-86F	North American	

Bureau Number	Aircraft Type	Manufacturer	Miscellaneous Notes
570461	DC-130A	Lockheed	
570496–570497	DC-130A	Lockheed	
570564	QT-33A	Lockheed	
570738	T-33	Lockheed	Cancelled
570758	T-33	Lockheed	Cancelled
573092	U-8G	Beech	From Army
575736	F-86H	North American	
575849	U-3A	Cessna	From Army
575891	U-3A	Cessna	From Air Force
575916	U-3A	Cessna	
576085	U-8G	Beech	From Army
576089	U-8G	Beech	From Army
576183–576184	U-9D	Aero Commander	From Army
576346	QF-86F	North American	
576352	QF-86F	North American	From Army
576363	QF-86F	North American	
576384	QF-86F	North American	
576388	QF-86F	North American	
576404	QF-86F	North American	
576414	QF-86F	North American	
576420	QF-86F	North American	
576422	QF-86F	North American	
576424–576425	QF-86F	North American	
576435–576436	QF-86F	North American	
576438	QF-86F	North American	
576440	QF-86F	North American	
576442	QF-86F	North American	
576444–576445	QF-86F	North American	
576447	QF-86F	North American	
576449–576450	QF-86F	North American	
576459	QF-86F	North American	
576538	OV-1A	Grumman	From Army
576539	YOV-1A	Grumman	From Army
577380	QT-33A	Lockheed	From Air Force
577580	QT-33A	Lockheed	From Air Force
580659	T-33	Lockheed	Cancelled
581194–581195	QT-38A	Lockheed	From Air Force
581339	U-8G	Beech	
581357	U-8G	Beech	From Army
581360	U-8G	Beech	From Army
581363	U-8G	Beech	From Army
582111	U-3A	Cessna	From Air Force
582123	U-3A	Cessna	From Air Force
582131	U-3A	Cessna	From Army
582176	U-3A	Cessna	From Air Force
583055	U-8G	Beech	From Army

Bureau Number	Aircraft Type	Manufacturer	Miscellaneous Notes
583057	U-8G	Beech	From Army
583062	U-8G	Beech	From Army
583091	U-8D	Beech	From Army
586580	QT-33A	Lockheed	From Air Force
586750	QT-33A	Lockheed	From Air Force
591594–591597	QT-38A	Lockheed	
591598	QF-86F	North American	
591600	QT-38A	Lockheed	
591603–591604	T-38A	Lockheed	
592536–592538	U-8G	Beech	From Army
592625	OV-1B	Grumman	
592637	OV-1B	Grumman	
594971	NOH-13K	Bell	From Army
594990	U-8G	Beech	From Army
600540	UH-1C	Bell	From Army
600546	UH-1M	Bell	From Army
600582	T-38A	Lockheed	From Air Force
600610	UH-1C	Bell	From Army
603560	UH-1B	Bell	From Army
603594	UH-1B	Bell	From Army
603741	OV-1A	Grumman	From Army
603747	OV-1C	Grumman	From Army
606047	U-3B	Cessna	From Army
606068	U-3B	Cessna	From Army
610541	CT-39A	N. A. Rockwell	
610654	CT-39A	N. A. Rockwell	From Air Force
610760	UH-1B	Bell	From Army
610851	T-38A	Lockheed	From Air Force
610855	T-38A	Lockheed	From Air Force
610882	T-38A	Lockheed	From Air Force
610889	T-38A	Lockheed	
610904	T-38B	Lockheed	
610913	T-38A	Lockheed	From Air Force
610918	T-38A	Lockheed	From Air Force
610929	T-38A	Lockheed	From Air Force
613291	CH-3E	Sikorsky	From Air Force
613296	CH-3E	Sikorsky	From Air Force
613552	OV-10A	North American	From Army
615017	UH-1M	Bell	From Army
615076–615077	UH-1M	Bell	From Army
615111	UH-1M	Bell	From Army
615200	UH-1M	Bell	From Army
615217	UH-1M	Bell	From Army
615236	UH-1M	Bell	From Army
616912	UH-1H	Bell	
621881–621882	UH-1B	Bell	From Army

Bureau Number	Aircraft Type	Manufacturer	Miscellaneous Notes
621912	UH-1B	Bell	From Army
621918	UH-1B	Bell	From Army
621935–621936	UH-1B	Bell	From Army
621957	UH-1B	Bell	From Army
621970	UH-1B	Bell	From Army
621984–621985	UH-1B	Bell	From Army
622007	UH-1B	Bell	From Army
622025	UH-1B	Bell	From Army
622029	UH-1B	Bell	From Army
622031	UH-1B	Bell	From Army
622034	UH-1B	Bell	From Army
622038	UH-1B	Bell	From Army
622040	UH-1B	Bell	From Army
622043	UH-1B	Bell	From Army
622048	UH-1B	Bell	From Army
622057–622058	UH-1B	Bell	From Army
622060	UH-1B	Bell	From Army
622075	UH-1B	Bell	From Army
622590	UH-1B	Bell	From Army
622602	UH-1B	Bell	From Army
624216	YOH-6A	Hughes	From Army
624567	UH-1B	Bell	From Army
624571–624572	UH-1B	Bell	From Army
624578–624579	UH-1B	Bell	From Army
624581–624584	UH-1B	Bell	From Army
624590	UH-1B	Bell	From Army
624594	UH-1B	Bell	From Army
624597	UH-1B	Bell	From Army
624602	UH-1B	Bell	From Army
624604	UH-1B	Bell	From Army
624897	UH-1B	Bell	From Army
625866	OV-1B	Grumman	From Air Force
625896	OV-1B	Grumman	
627469–627470	QF-86F	North American	From Air Force
627479	QF-86F	North American	
628712	UH-1B	Bell	From Army
628738	UH-1B	Bell	From Army
631034	UH-1B	Bell	From Army
638200	T-38A	Lockheed	
638501	UH-1B	Bell	From Army
638507	UH-1B	Bell	From Army
638521	UH-1B	Bell	From Army
638524	UH-1B	Bell	From Army
638540	UH-1B	Bell	From Army
638544–638545	UH-1B	Bell	From Army
638547	UH-1B	Bell	From Army

Bureau Number	Aircraft Type	Manufacturer	Miscellaneous Notes
638553–638554	UH-1B	Bell	From Army
638561–638562	UH-1B	Bell	From Army
638568	UH-1B	Bell	From Army
638572	UH-1B	Bell	From Army
638587	UH-1B	Bell	From Army
638589	UN-1B	Bell	From Army
638602–638603	UH-1B	Bell	From Army
638607	UH-1B	Bell	From Army
638610	UH-1B	Bell	From Army
638614	UH-1B	Bell	From Army
638643	UH-1B	Bell	From Army
638646	UH-1B	Bell	From Army
638650	UH-1B	Bell	From Army
638664	UH-1B	Bell	From Army
638666	UH-1B	Bell	From Army
638672	UH-1B	Bell	From Army
638678–638680	UH-1B	Bell	From Army
638682–638683	UH-1B	Bell	From Army
638685	UH-1B	Bell	From Army
638687	UH-1B	Bell	From Army
638694	UH-1B	Bell	From Army
638711	UH-1B	Bell	From Army
638715	UH-1B	Bell	From Army
638727	UH-1B	Bell	From Army
638738	UH-1B	Bell	From Army
643816	UH-1D	Bell	From Army
650644	F-4D	McDonnell Douglas	From Army
650979	NC-130H	Lockheed Martin	
652000	HH-65A	Aerospatiale	
652500	HH-65A	Aerospatiale	
652707	T-42A	Beech	
652728	T-42A	Beech	
652800	HH-65A	Aerospatiale	
652967	OH-6B	Hughes	
653300	HH-65A	Aerospatiale	
654500	HH-65A	Aerospatiale	
655698	CH-3E	Sikorsky	
659423	UH-1M	Bell	From Army
659476	UH-1C	Bell	From Army
659548	UH-1M	Bell	From Army
659572	UH-1D	Bell	
659598	UH-1D	Bell	From Army
659609	UH-1H	Bell	
659613–659614	UH-1D	Bell	From Army
659621	UH-1D	Bell	From Army
659632	UH-1D	Bell	From Army

Bureau Number	Aircraft Type	Manufacturer	Miscellaneous Notes
659644	UH-1D	Bell	From Army
659646	UH-1H	Bell	
659662	UH-1D	Bell	From Army
659671	UH-1D	Bell	From Army
659685	UH-1D	Bell	From Army
659715	UH-1D	Bell	From Army
659735–659736	UH-1D	Bell	From Army
659739–659740	UH-1D	Bell	From Army
659777	UH-1D	Bell	From Army
659820	UH-1D	Bell	From Army
659823	UH-1D	Bell	From Army
659834	UH-1D	Bell	From Army
659853	UH-1D	Bell	From Army
659856	UH-1D	Bell	From Army
659859	UH-1D	Bell	From Army
659902	UH-1H	Bell	From Army
659945	UH-1D	Bell	From Army
659947	UH-1D	Bell	From Army
659977	UH-1D	Bell	From Army
660000	U-21A	Beech	
661012	UH-1D	Bell	From Army
661250	TH-1F	Bell	From Air Force
661534	AH-1S	Bell	From Army
664307	T-42A	Beech	
666535	UH-1M	Bell	From Army
666599	UH-1M	Bell	From Army
666655	UH-1M	Bell	From Army
666691	UH-1M	Bell	
668004	U-21A	Beech	
674623	OV-10A	North American	
674626	OV-10A	North American	
674652	OV-10A	North American	
676427	OH-6A	Hughes	
676649	OH-6A	Hughes	
678096	U-21A	Beech	
683796	OV-10A	North American	
683799	OV-10A	North American	
683809	OV-10A	North American	
686958	OH-58C	Bell	From other military service
687333	OH-6B	Hughes	
691643	AH-1S	Bell	From Army
696040–696041	OH-6B	Hughes	From Army
696044	OH-6B	Hughes	
696061	OH-6B	Hughes	From Army
696160	OH-58C	Bell	From other military service
696189	OH-58C	Bell	From other military service

Bureau Number	Aircraft Type	Manufacturer	Miscellaneous Notes
701523	OH-58A	Bell	From Army
701553	OH-58A	Bell	From Army
710376	OH-58C	Bell	From other military service
710388	OH-58A	Bell	
710554	OH-58A	Bell	
710799	OH-58A	Bell	
712098	AH-1S	Bell	From Army
712103	AH-1S	Bell	From Army
714584	YA-7D	LTV	From Air Force
714704	CH-3E	Sikorsky	
714707	CH-3E	Sikorsky	
715106	T-41B	Grumman	From Army
715123	T-41B	Grumman	From Army
715132	T-41B	Grumman	From Army
715184	T-41B	Grumman	From Army
715218–715219	T-41B	Grumman	
715225	T-41B	Grumman	From Army
715345–715346	X-26B	Schweizer	Modified by Lockheed, from Army
715850	AH-1G	Bell	From Army
721193	OH-58A	Bell	
721300	O-2A	Cessna	From Air Force
721310	O-2A	Cessna	
721318	O-2A	Cessna	From Air Force
721349	O-2A	Cessna	From Air Force
721365	O-2A	Cessna	From Air Force
721387	F-5E	Northrop	
721404	O-2A	Cessna	From Air Force
721414	O-2A	Cessna	From Air Force
722716	UH-60A	Sikorsky	
722725	UH-60A	Sikorsky	
722791–722792	AH-1S	Bell	From Army
727709	QF-86F	North American	
727711	QF-86F	North American	
730855	F-5E	Northrop	
730865	F-5E	Northrop	
730879	F-5E	Northrop	
730881	F-5E	Northrop	
730885	F-5E	Northrop	
731635	F-5E	Northrop	
741519	F-5E	Northrop	
741528–741531	F-5E	Northrop	
741536–741537	F-5E	Northrop	
741539–741541	F-5E	Northrop	
741544–741545	F-5E	Northrop	
741547	F-5E	Northrop	
741554	F-5E	Northrop	

Bureau Number	Aircraft Type	Manufacturer	Miscellaneous Notes
741556	F-5E	Northrop	
741558	F-5E	Northrop	
741563–741564	F-5E	Northrop	
741568	F-5E	Northrop	
741570	F-5E	Northrop	
741572	F-5E	Northrop	
741635	F-5E	Northrop	
760086	X-26A	Schweizer	
761551	F-5N	Northrop	
761589	F-5N	Northrop	
762256	UV-18A	De Havilland	From Air National Guard
815037–815039	AH-1G	Bell	From Army
815045–815046	AH-1G	Bell	From Army
815072–815073	AH-1G	Bell	From Army
815074–815078	AH-1G	Bell	Not accepted
815079–815080	AH-1G	Bell	From Army
815081–815084	AH-1G	Bell	Not accepted
815085	AH-1G	Bell	From Army
815086–815103	AH-1G	Bell	Not accepted
815104–815105	AH-1G	Bell	From Army
815106–815111	AH-1G	Bell	Not accepted
815112–815113	AH-1G	Bell	From Army
815134	AH-1G	Bell	From Army
815140	AH-1G	Bell	From Army
815165	AH-1G	Bell	From Army
815170	AH-1G	Bell	From Army
815176	AH-1G	Bell	From Army
815190	AH-1G	Bell	From Army
815194	AH-1G	Bell	From Army
815198	AH-1G	Bell	From Army
815213	AH-1G	Bell	From Army
816695	OH-58A	Bell	From Army
816797	OH-58A	Bell	From Army
817023	AH-1G	Bell	From Army
817027	AH-1G	Bell	From Army
817041	AH-1G	Bell	From Army
817045	AH-1G	Bell	From Army
817049	AH-1G	Bell	From Army
817062	AH-1G	Bell	From Army
817066	AH-1G	Bell	From Army
817070	AH-1G	Bell	From Army
817082	AH-1G	Bell	From Army
817086	AH-1G	Bell	From Army
817090	AH-1G	Bell	From Army
817101	AH-1G	Bell	From Army
817105	AH-1G	Bell	From Army

Bureau Number	Aircraft Type	Manufacturer	Miscellaneous Notes
817108	AH-1G	Bell	From Army
823507	UH-60A	Sikorsky	From Army
827806	QF-86F	North American	
827837	QF-86F	North American	From Air Force
827852	QF-86F	North American	
840456	F-5F	Northrop	
842402	UH-60L	Sikorsky	
870157	NC-130H	Lockheed	
872466–872467	UH-60L	Sikorsky	
891038	TH-57C	Bell	
900528	C-26B	Fairchild	From other military service
900530–900531	C-26B	Fairchild	From other military service
900942–900943	F-16A	General Dynamics	
910502	C-26B	Fairchild	From other military service
910512	C-26B	Fairchild	From other military service
910514	C-26B	Fairchild	From other military service
920378	C-26B	Fairchild	From other military service
966673	UH-60L/YCH-60	Sikorsky	From Army
999703	F-21A	IAI	From Israel
999705	F-21A	IAI	From Israel
999708–999710	F-21A	IAI	From Israel
999716	F-21A	IAI	From Israel
999724–999728	F-21A	IAI	From Israel
999731–999732	F-21A	IAI	From Israel
999734–999735	F-21A	IAI	From Israel
999739	F-21A	IAI	From Israel
999742	F-21A	IAI	From Israel
999747	F-21A	IAI	From Israel
999749–999750	F-21A	IAI	From Israel
999764	F-21A	IAI	From Israel
999786–999787	F-21A	IAI	From Israel
999791	F-21A	IAI	From Israel
999794	F-21A	IAI	From Israel

* Originally XF12C-1, was redesignated XS4C-1 and then XSBC-1. XSBC-1 crashed during contractor's trials and was replaced by XSBC-2, which was converted to XSBC-3.

† Serial 9222 was replaced by new air frame as XSBU-1, 9222. Old 9222 was acquired as 9746.

‡ Variously modified to PBM-3C, -3R and -3S; 6456 reported as XPBM-3 or PBM-3R; 6656 as PBM-3D modified from PBM-3C; and 6693 as experimental PBM-3S although designated PBM-3C.

CHAPTER 8

History of the Naval Aviator and Designations and Numbers

The evolution of the programs and policies regarding the designation of naval aviators and naval aviation pilots is one of confusion, ambiguities, inadequate centralized administration of recordkeeping, and inconsistencies in the implementation of a new and young aviation organization into the Navy. During the early period, divergent views on aviation within the Navy and the onset of WWI brought a great influx of new people, programs, policies, aircraft, and air stations into the fledgling naval aviation community. When the United States entered WWI, naval aviation consisted of one operating air station, 48 aviators and student aviators, and 54 aircraft on hand. It was ill-equipped to handle the huge growth precipitated by the United States' entry into the war.

Background on the Evolution of Naval Aviators

The Navy's aviation program had an aviator before it acquired its first aircraft. Lt. Theodore G. Ellyson was ordered to training in December 1910 at the Glenn Curtiss aviation camp in San Diego, Calif. The Navy received its first aircraft from the Curtiss Company the following July. Flight instruction at that time was informal and remained so during the next couple of years.

Ellyson, a student pilot, became a pilot when Glenn H. Curtiss agreed he could fly airplanes. Subsequently, Ellyson taught John H. Towers, another student pilot, to fly. In addition to flying, however, students also had to become totally familiar with the mechanics of their machines and to be able to repair and rebuild aircraft. Formality arrived when Capt. Washington I. Chambers, the Navy's first Director of Naval Aeronautics, declared that the requirements for becoming a Navy pilot were to follow the same rules employed by the Aero Club of America (the American chapter of the Fédération Aéronautique Internationale). Prior to the Navy establishing these standards, some Navy flyers held pilot certificates from the Aero Club.

The Naval Appropriations Act for fiscal year 1914 formally recognized officers assigned to the "aviation element" of the Navy and who qualified as pilots for their duty as flyers on 4 March 1913. The act provided an increase of 35 percent in pay and allowances for officers detailed to duty as flyers of heavier-than-air craft. On 10 April 1913 Secretary of the Navy Josephus Daniels approved performance standards for qualification and the issuance of a certificate as a "Navy Air Pilot" to qualified officers.

Capt. Chambers had requested the certificate in a letter to the Chief of Bureau of Navigation (BuNav) on 4 April 1913, which stated, "The requirements for a Navy Air Pilot are different from those of the land pilot and are purposely made more exacting than those of the 'license' issued by the International Aeronautical Federation." To receive a Navy Air Pilot certificate officers had to pass an advanced training course and become highly skilled as flyers or pass an examination by a board of qualified officers. The Bureau of Navigation was responsible for issuing the certificates, however, because of administrative problems the issuance was subject to a delay of almost two years from the date that Secretary Daniels approved issuing a Navy Air Pilot certificate.

Although performance standards for qualification as Navy Air Pilots were established in April 1913, it was not until a year later (22 April 1914) that the Bureau of Navigation, which was responsible for all Navy training, approved a course of instruction for student flyers and aviation mechanics, because of delays by the bureau in establishing aviation programs and policies. On 9 January 1915 Rear Adm. Bradley A. Fiske, Aide for Operations and a member of the Joint Board, pointed out to the Bureau of Navigation that unless they recognized some officers as qualified and awarded them certificates, no board of experts could be appointed to examine the qualifications of new applicants. He recommended that Navy Air Pilot certificates be issued to Theodore G. Ellyson, John H. Towers, Henry C. Mustin, Patrick N. L. Bellinger, Victor D. Herbster, Bernard L. Smith, and Godfrey de C. Chevalier, and that they be numbered 1 through 7 and dated sequentially, one per month, from 1 January 1914 for Ellyson to 1 July 1914 for Chevalier.

The Bureau of Navigation followed up on Rear Adm. Fiske's recommendation and, in accordance with what the Secretary of the Navy had approved almost two years before, sent out letters on 21 January 1915 forwarding Navy Air Pilot Certificates to these seven officers, numbering and dating them as the admiral had recommended. The Bureau of Navigation and NAS Pensacola, Fla., however, continued to follow the procedure of identifying those students completing the elementary flight course at Pensacola as "Naval Aviators" to differentiate them from pilots who had completed the advanced course of requirements and qualified as Navy Air Pilots.

Before the Bureau of Navigation could continue its follow up work and issue more Navy Air Pilot Certificates, Congress revised the law on flight pay, and, in a new bill approved 3 March 1915, used the term "Naval Aviator" in specifying those eligible for flight pay. This bill, the Naval Appropriations Act of fiscal year 1916, added enlisted men and student aviators to those eligible for increased pay and allowances while on duty involving flying. It also increased the amount previously provided for qualified aviators. The language of the act provided "flight pay" only for "Naval Aviators," those fliers completing the elementary flight course at Pensacola. It did not cover those who had qualified as the best pilots and received a Navy Air Pilot certificate. Hence, on 22 March 1915, in order to include those pilots designated Navy Air Pilots, a change was made to the Secretary of the Navy's performance standards certificate whereby the designation "Navy Air Pilot" was changed to "Naval Aviator." This was the beginning of the primary emphasis being placed on the designation of Naval Aviator. However, the Navy continued to make references to Navy Air Pilots. In March and April 1915, qualified aviation boards, appointed to give exams at Pensacola, recommended designation of five men as follows: Richard C. Saufley for a Naval Aviator Certificate dated 6 March, William M. McIlvain for a Navy Air Pilot Certificate dated 10 March, Clarence K. Bronson for orders dated 6 April with the designation Navy Air Pilot, Kenneth Whiting and Holden C. Richardson for Naval Aviator Certificates dated 10 and 12 April. The reason for the different use of Naval Aviator and Navy Air Pilot terminology is not known, but the recommendations were approved with a modification as reported by the Bureau of Navigation on 25 May 1915, that all five men had been issued Navy Air Pilot Certificates, numbers 8 through 12. The use of the Navy Air Pilot Certificate and designation continued even after the Secretary of the Navy issued his order to change the designation to Naval Aviator.

Confusion over the issue of Naval Aviator or Navy Air Pilot designations continued within Navy organizations. On 5 May 1915 the Secretary of the Navy informed Whiting: "You are hereby designated as a Naval Aviator for duty involving flying in aircraft, including balloons, dirigibles and airplanes, in accordance with an Act of Congress approved March 3, 1915." The conflict or confusion seems to be in terminology. It was the opinion at that time that an official statement from the Bureau of Navigation was legally necessary for an individual on flying duty (necessary only in the sense of receiving extra pay while assigned to a job involving actual flying in an aircraft) and that the "Certificates" were only evidence of qualification as an aviator. Thus, on 21 May 1915, the Secretary of the Navy signed a circular letter directing that commanding officers "issue orders detailing officers of the Navy and Marine Corps to Duty as Naval Aviators or Student Naval Aviators when they are required to actually fly or operate these machines." Therefore, regardless of the title on the "Certificates," these orders used the title associated with the Naval Appropriations Act, fiscal year 1916.

In January 1916 the Bureau of Navigation issued its "Course of Instructions and Required Qualifications of Personnel for the Air Service of the Navy." This syllabus mentions 11 classifications for personnel assigned to aeronautic duty. For officers they include: Student Naval Aviator; Naval Aviator; Navy Air Pilot, aeroplane; Navy Air Pilot, dirigible; and Military Aviator. The remaining groups were for enlisted personnel classifications. One of the major reasons for the confusion regarding designations was the existence of several different organizations within the Navy that were making policy decisions on naval aviation without adequately coordinating terminology or standardizing applications. Terminology was used for different purposes, such as identifying an individual qualified to pilot an aircraft and, for pay purposes, identifying an individual involved in flight but not necessarily as the pilot.

On 1 May 1917 a new course of instruction was presented as a revision without specifying what it revised, although it must have taken the place of the course dated January 1916. The new course stated that officers detailed to aeronautic duty would be classed as Student Naval Aviator, Naval Aviator, and Navy Air Pilot, either for seaplanes or dirigibles. Completion of the course of instruction for Student Naval Aviator (seaplane) qualified the student for advancement to elementary and solo flying. Upon completion of that stage the student took the exam for Naval Aviator (seaplane) and was then eligible for what appears to be the advanced course. For this course the instruction stated: "Upon successful completion of the examination the Naval Aviator (seaplane) will be designated Navy Air Pilot (seaplane) and issued a certificate numbered according to his standing in the class with which he qualified as a Navy Air Pilot (seaplane)." A revision to the May 1917 course of instruction was issued 1 January 1918, and the term Navy Air Pilot was not mentioned. In this revision, officers and men detailed for pilot duty were classed as student Naval Aviators and Naval Aviators, seaplane or dirigible. By this time the United States was fully engaged in WWI, the naval aviation training program had expanded, and the question of title finally seemed to be settled. It took almost three years, from 22 March 1915, when the SecNav order was issued to change Navy Air Pilot to Naval Aviator, to January 1918, before the terminology Navy Air Pilot was dropped from instructions issued by the Navy.

Designation List of Naval Aviators

Confusion in the designation list of naval aviators seems to have been tied with the precedence for the designation date of a naval aviator and its connection with the adoption of the gold wings insignia (naval aviator wings). A 13 November 1917 Bureau of Navigation letter states, "The Bureau is now compiling a list of all officers and men who are qualified as Naval Aviators, in order that new pins may be delivered as shortly after they are received from the manufacturers as possible." This is followed by a Bureau of Navigation report to Pensacola, Fla., stating, "The new Naval Aviator's pins have been delivered to the Bureau of Navigation and they will be sent out as soon as they can be engraved to show the Aviator's number, his name and branch of service." (See Chapter 9 for an explanation of the design and evolution of Naval Aviator Wings.)

There is some question as to whether BUNAV produced a list of naval aviators at this time. However, the CNO's Aviation Office had a listing of 282 numbers that was forwarded to BUNAV under a letter dated 19 January 1918 with the following:

1. Enclosure (a) is a list of qualified Naval Aviators given in numerical sequence.

2. This list was compiled after careful examination of all the records of this office and numbers assigned according to the date of qualification as Naval Aviator in all cases where such date is shown by the records; but due to the fact that those officers of the regular service who were the first to enter aviation were not required to take a Naval Aviator's test but were merely designated 'Naval Aviator' or 'Navy Air Pilot' because of their recognized qualification as such, the numbers assigned in such cases were determined by the date upon which they were ordered to aviation duty and the length of such duty, full consideration being given each and every individual case so affected.

3. Additions to the attached list will be forwarded to the Bureau from time to time and as rapidly as the students now under instruction pass the necessary test for qualification as Naval Aviators.

The following list, except for the omission of fractional numbers and the differences in two names, is accepted as the precedence list of early naval aviators.

Naval Aviator Number (Navy Air Pilot Number)	Name	Service
1 (1)	Ellyson, Theodore G.	USN
2	Rodgers, John	USN
3 (2)	Towers, John H.	USN
4 (5)	Herbster, Victor D.	USN
5 (14)	Cunningham, Alfred A.	USMC
6 (6)	Smith, Bernard L.	USMC
7 (7)	Chevalier, Godfrey de C.	USN
8 (4)	Bellinger, Patrick N. L.	USN
9	Billingsley, William D.	USN
10	Murray, James M.	USN
11 (3)	Mustin, Henry C.	USN
12 (9)	McIlvain, William M.	USMC
13 (12)	Richardson, Holden C.	USN
14 (8)	Saufley, Richard C.	USN
15 (10)	Bronson, Clarence K.	USN
16 (11)	Whiting, Kenneth	USN
17 (13)	Maxfield, Louis H.	USN
18	McDonnell, Edward O.	USN
19	Capehart, Wadleigh	USN
20	Spencer, Earl W., Jr.	USN
21	Bartlett, Harold T.	USN

Naval Aviator Number	Name	Service
22	Murray, George D.	USN
23	Corry, William M.	USN
24	Read, Albert C.	USN
25	Johnson, Earle F.	USN
26	Evans, Francis T.	USMC
27	Paunack, Robert R.	USN
28	Scofield, Harold W.	USN
29	Child, Warren G.	USN
30	Dichman, Grattan C.	USN
31	Young, Robert T.	USN
32	Gillespie, George S.	USN
33	Mitscher, Marc A.	USN
34	Strickland, Glenn B.	USN
35	Monfort, James C.	USN
36	Cabaniss, Robert W.	USN
37	Chase, Nathan B.	USN
38	Stone, Elmer F.	USCG
39	McKitterick, Edward H.	USN
40	Leighton, Bruce G.	USN
41	Griffin, Virgil C.	USN
42	Cecil, Henry B.	USN
43	Sugden, Charles E.	USCG
44	Bressman, Augustus A.	USN
45	Ramsey, DeWitt C.	USN
46	Hull, Carl T.	USN
47	Peyton, Paul J.	USN
48	Kirkpatrick, Robert D.	USN
49	Geiger, Roy S.	USMC
50	Bonner, Walter D.	USN
51	Murphy, Thomas H.	USN
52	Mason, Charles P.	USN
52 ½	Salsman, James	USN
53	Simpson, Frank, Jr.	National Naval Volunteer (NNV)
54	Donahue, Robert	USCG
55	Brewster, David L. S.	USMC
55 ½	Sunderman, John T.	USN
56	Barin, Louis T.	NNV
57	Parker, Stanley V.	USCG
58	Masek, William	USN
59	Coffin, Eugene A.	USCG
60	Eaton, Phillip B.	USCG
61	Enos, George	USN
62	Varini, Giochino	USN
63	Hawkins, Clarence A.	USN
64	Ruttan, Charles E.	USN
65	Gates, Artemus L.	U.S. Naval Reserve Force (USNRF)

Naval Aviator Number	Name	Service
65 ½	Laud-Brown, Wellesley	USNRF
66	Lovett, Robert A.	USNRF
67	Ames, Allan W.	USNRF
68	Gould, Erl C. B.	USNRF
69	Walker, Guy A.	USN
70	Kilmer, Oliver P.	USN
71	Talbot, Peter	USN
72	Davison, Henry P.	USNRF
73	Vorys, John M.	USNRF
74	MacLeish, Kenneth A.	USNRF
75	Beach, Charles F.	USNRF
76	Farwell, John D.	USNRF
77	Sturtevant, Albert D.	USNRF
78	Read, Russell B.	USNRF
79	Brush, Graham M.	USNRF
80	James, Oliver B.	USNRF
81	Rockefeller, William	USNRF
82	McIlwaine, Archibald G.	USNRF
83	Read, Curtis S.	USNRF
83 ½	Gartz, Richard C.	USNRF
84	Ireland, Robert L.	USNRF
85	Ingalls, David S.	USNRF
86	Walker, Samuel S.	USNRF
87	Smith, Kenneth R.	USNRF
88	Lynch, Francis R. V.	USNRF
89	Lawrence, George F.	USNRF
89 ½	Merrill, Norman E.	NNV
90	McLaughlin, Guy	USN
91	McCrary, Frank R.	USN
92	Coombe, Reginald G.	USNRF
93	Landon, Henry H., Jr.	USNRF
94	Culbert, Frederic P.	USN
95	Feher, Anthony	USN
95a	Fitzsimon, Ricardo	Argentine Navy
95b	Pouchan, Ceferino M.	Argentine Navy
95c	Zar, Marcos A.	Argentine Navy
96	Coil, Emory W.	USN
96 ½	Chamberlain, Edmund G.	USMC
97	Strader, Ralph M.	USNRF
98	Talbot, Andrew B.	USNRF
99	Whitehouse, William P.	USNRF
100	Crompton, George	USNRF
100 ½	Pennoyer, Ralph G.	USN
100 ¾	Presley, Russell A.	USMC
101	Hamlen, Warner	USNRF
102	Little, Charles G.	USNRF

Naval Aviator Number	Name	Service
103	Brewer, Arthur D.	USNRF
104	Delano, Merrill P.	USNRF
104 ½	Kiely, Ralph	USN
105	Lansdowne, Zachary	USN
105 ½	Douglas, Gilbert W.	USNRF
106	Bell, Colley W.	USNRF
107	Chadwick, Noel	USNRF
108	Ditman, Albert J.	USNRF
109	Donnelly, Thorne	NNV
110	Carter, R. C.	USNRF
110 ½	Allen, Charles L.	USN
111	Stone, George W.	USN
111 ½	Bradford, Doyle	USNRF
112	Atwater, William B.	USNRF
112 ½	Webster, Clifford L.	USNRF
113	Fallon, Nugent	USNRF
114	Williams, Arthur S.	USNRF
115	Dietrich, Arthur F.	USN
116	Palmer, Carlton D.	USN
117	Murray, Cecil D.	USNRF
118	Taylor, Moseley	USNRF
119	Townsend, Richard S.	USNRF
120	Walton, Mark W.	USNRF
121	Depew, Ganson G.	USNRF
122	Goodyear, Frank	USNRF
123	McCormick, Alexander A.	USNRF
124	Schieffelin, John J.	USNRF
125	Rodman, Thomas C.	USNRF
126	Smith, Edward T.	USNRF
127	Otis, James S.	USNRF
128	Hawkins, Ashton W.	USNRF
129	Lufkin, Chauncey F.	USNRF
130	Potter, Stephen	USNRF
131	Fuller, Percival S.	USNRF
132	Decernea, Edward	USNRF
133	Ott, George A.	USN
134	Geary, John W.	USNRF
134 ½	Wetherald, Royal W.	USNRF
135	Hinton, Walter	USN
136	Willcox, Westmore	USNRF
137	Lee, Benjamin, II	USNRF
138	Stone, Emory A.	USNRF
139	Fuller, Charles F.	USNRF
140	Hutchins, Hurd	USNRF
141	Stocker, Robert M.	USNRF
142	Foster, John C.	USNRF

Naval Aviator Number	Name	Service
143	Allen, Frederic S.	USNRF
144	Amory, Francis I.	USNRF
145	Read, Duncan H.	USNRF
146	Goldthwaite, Duval R.	USNRF
147	McCann, Richard H.	USNRF
148	Wright, Arthur H.	USNRF
149	Swift, Henry	USNRF
150	Butler, Stuart M.	USNRF
151	Gordon, Harry B.	USNRF
152	Zunino, Frank A.	USNRF
153	Shea, Edward L.	USNRF
154	Forrestal, James V.	USNRF
155	Brackenridge, Gavin	USNRF
156	Gibson, Harold F.	USNRF
157	Mudge, William F.	USNRF
158	Clarkson, William F.	USNRF
159	McCoid, Paul H.	USNRF
160	Halstead, Jacob S.	USNRF
161	Randolph, Robert D.	USNRF
162	Matter, Robert	USNRF
163	Warburton, William J.	USNRF
163 ½	Peterson, Herman A.	NNV
164	Rutherford, John	NNV
165	Laughlin, George M., III	NNV
166	Evans, George B.	NNV
167	Johnson, Albert R.	NNV
168	McCulloch, David H.	USNRF
169	Peirce, Thomas J. H.	NNV
170	Page, Phillips W.	USNRF
171	Shaw, George W.	USNRF
172	Peck, Lyman S.	USNRF
173	Humphreys, William Y., Jr.	NNV
174	Berger, Frederick, G. B.	NNV
175	Boyd, Theodore P.	NNV
175 ½	Alexander, William H.	USN
176	White, Lawrence G.	NNV
177	Coddington, Dave H.	NNV
178	Kerr, Robert H.	USN
179	Whitted, James A.	USN
180	Haskell, Armory L.	USNRF
181	Hyde, Russell N.	USNRF
182	Keyes, Kenneth B.	USNRF
183	Warren, Alfred K.	USNRF
184	Eaton, Joseph A.	USNRF
185	Peterson, William L.	USNRF
186	Stanley, Henry T.	USNRF

Naval Aviator Number	Name	Service
187	Remey, John T.	USNRF
188	Palmedo, Roland	USNRF
189	Forbes, Duncan P.	USNRF
190	Allen, Francis G.	USNRF
191	Baker, Charles S.	USNRF
192	Greenough, Charles W.	USNRF
193	Ames, Charles B.	USNRF
194	Hofer, Myron A.	USNRF
195	Ives, Paul F.	USNRF
196	Clark, Robert F.	USNRF
197	Brewer, Edward S.	USNRF
198	Dumas, Gardner D.	USNRF
199	McNamara, John F.	USNRF
200	Rowen, Harold J.	USNRF
201	Compo, George L.	USNRF
202	Perrin, John	USNRF
203	Hutchinson, Lester B.	USNRF
204	MacCaulay, Donald M.	USNRF
205	Lochman, Dean E.	USNRF
206	Moore, Lloyd Ray	USN
207	Thomas, Reginald de Noyes	USNRF
208	Clements, James R.	USNRF
209	Schermerhorn, Horace	USNRF
210	Murphy, Dudley B.	USNRF
210 ½	Grosvenor, Theodore P.	USNRF
211	Roe, George T.	USNRF
212	Teulon, Arthur P.	USNRF
213	Marriner, Walter T.	USN
214	Pumpelly, Harold A.	USNRF
215	Biggers, Robert L.	USNRF
216	Farmer, Charles R.	USNRF
217	Rumill, George E.	USNRF
218	Greenfield, Edwin R.	USNRF
219	Weld, Lothrop M.	USNRF
220	Phelan, James	USNRF
220 ½	West, Winfield M.	USNRF
221	Lancto, Joseph W.	USNRF
222	Wilcox, Harold M.	USNRF
223	Hawkins, Rees	USNRF
224	Wenz, Edward A.	USNRF
225	Alvord, Donald B.	USNRF
226	Baum, James E., Jr.	USNRF
227	Smith, Frank S.	USNRF
228	Hawkins, Samuel S.	USNRF
229	Clapp, Kenneth H.	USNRF
230	Dowell, Benjamin B.	USNRF

Naval Aviator Number	Name	Service
231	Ostridge, Charles L.	USNRF
232	Bergin, Thomas M.	USNRF
233	Gadsden, Philip H.	USNRF
234	Graves, Justin D.	USNRF
235	Connolly, Leo W.	USNRF
236	McAdoo, William G., Jr.	USNRF
237	Wheeler, Oscar G.	USNRF
238	Benjamin, Henry R.	USNRF
239	Souther, Arthur F.	USNRF
240	Roberts, Charles H.	USNRF
241	Harris, Frederick M.	USNRF
242	Naylor, Henry R.	USNRF
243	Voorhees, Dudley A.	USNRF
244	Maxwell, Howard W., Jr.	USNRF
245	King, Frederick E.	USNRF
246	Lamar, Lamartine E.	USNRF
247	Bancroft, Frederick W., Jr.	USNRF
248	Griswold, Rettig A.	USNRF
249	Chapman, Thomas H.	USNRF
250	Frothingham, Philip B.	USNRF

The confusion regarding precedence and the assignment of numbers resulted in some qualified individuals being left off the list of naval aviator numbers. During WWI qualified civilian aviators joined the naval service and served as naval aviators. They were qualified pilots who flew as a Navy pilot or naval aviator but did not receive a naval aviator number or were overlooked in the assignment of a number because of administrative problems during the huge war build-up.

The Bureau of Navigation (redesignated Bureau of Naval Personnel in 1942) continued to issue naval aviator numbers and was the sole source until 31 July 1942. In a SECNAV letter dated 31 July 1942, the old method of designating naval aviators through the assignment of numbers was discontinued. The following system was put in place:

- Commandant, Naval Air Station, Pensacola, Fla., is directed to commence a series of numbers for the foregoing designations as Naval Aviator (HTA) Number P1, P2, P3, etc.

- Commandant, Naval Air Station, Jacksonville, Fla., is directed to commence a similar series as Naval Aviator (HTA) Number J1, J2, J3, etc.

- Commandant, Naval Air Station Corpus Christi, Tex., is directed to commence a similar series as Naval Aviator (HTA) Number C1, C2, C3, etc.

- Commanding Officer, Naval Air Station, Miami, Fla., is directed to commence a similar series, as Naval Aviator (HTA) Number M1, M2, M3, etc.

- Commanding Officer, Naval Air Station, Norfolk, Va., is directed to commence a similar series, as Naval Aviator (HTA) Number N1, N2, N3, etc.

- Commanding Officer, Naval Air Station, Alameda, Calif., is directed to commence a similar series as Naval Aviator (HTA) Number A1, A2, A3, etc.

- Commanding Officer, Naval Air Station, Lakehurst, N.J., is directed to commence a similar series as Naval Aviator Number L1, L2, L3, etc.

- Commanding Officer, Naval Air Station, Moffett Field, Calif., is directed to commence a similar series as Naval Aviator (LTA) Number S1, S2, S3, etc.

This letter also stated: "The original letter of designation will be delivered directly to the individual without prior reference to the Navy Department for approval." Copies of the letter of designation were to be forwarded to the Bureau of Personnel; Bureau of Aeronautics; Commandant, U.S. Marine Corps; and Bureau of Medicine and Surgery (in the case of flight surgeons). Because of the decentralization of this numbering system, a complete listing of naval aviators and their designation numbers has not been found for the WWII period even though the Bureau of Personnel was to receive a copy of all the letters of designation.

On 28 November 1942, a Secretary of Navy letter issued a modification to the commands designating Naval Aviators. Changes in this letter were as follows:

- The Commandant, Naval Air Training Center, Pensacola, Fla., assumed the duties of designating Naval Aviators vice the Commandant, Naval Air Station, Pensacola. There is no indication the use of the numbering series P1, P2, P3, etc., was changed.

- The Commandant, Naval Air Training Center, Corpus Christi, Tex., assumed the duties of designating Naval Aviators vice the Commandant, Naval Air Station, Corpus Christi. There is no indication the use of the numbering series C1, C2, C3, etc., was changed.

- The Commandant, Naval Air Center, Hampton Roads, Va., was directed to assume the duties of designating Naval Aviators vice the Commanding Officer, Naval Air Station, Norfolk, Va. There is no indication the use of the numbering series N1, N2, N3, etc., was changed.

This system remained in effect until 1949. A Secretary of the Navy letter of 29 March 1949 cancelled its previous letters regarding designation of Naval Aviators (letters of 31 July 1942, 28 November 1942, and 9 January 1943) and authorized the Commander, Naval Air Training; Commander, Naval Air Advanced Training; and the Chief of Naval Airship Training and Experimentation to designate Naval Aviators (and assign numbers). By the time this letter was issued the other training commands had already been disestablished or consolidated under the control of these three commands. In step with the previous decentralized system, the following system was established:

- Chief of Naval Air Training was directed to commence a series of numbers for the foregoing designations as Naval Aviators, (HTA), Number T-1, T-2, T-3, etc.

- Chief of Naval Air Advanced Training is directed to commence a series of numbers for the foregoing designations of Naval Aviators (HTA), Number V-1, V-2, V-3, etc.

- Chief of Naval Airship Training and Experimentation is directed to commence a similar series as Naval Aviators (LTA) using the L series, carrying on from the last number used in this series by the Commanding Officer, Naval Air Station, Lakehurst, N.J.

The Chief of Naval Air Training quit issuing Naval Aviator Numbers sometime in the 1970s. Documentation has not been located that gives the date or provides reasons why the assignment of Naval Aviator numbers was discontinued. To date, no complete listing of all Naval Aviator numbers, including the letter-number designations, has been found. Moreover, it is highly unlikely a complete list exists because of the decentralization of the system during WWII. Bits and pieces of the listing for Naval Aviator numbers is held by the Naval Aviation History Office. However, the WWII and post-war period list is not organized in any alphabetical or chronological order, consequently, it is extremely difficult to find any individual's number.

Background on the Evolution of Naval Aviation Pilots

The evolution of the Naval Aviation Pilot designation for enlisted men is more complicated because of the lack of a clear Navy policy regarding enlisted pilots during naval aviation's first decade and the misconceptions surrounding the terminology regarding designations used for enlisted pilots. By setting the standards for qualification and certification of officers as Naval Aviators in the early phase of naval aviation, a stable policy was put into effect. The failure to establish a clear-cut policy regarding programs for training enlisted pilots caused considerable confusion that affected the enlisted pilot program during its entire existence.

The confusion begins with terminology and how it was applied to those people "involved in actual flight." Enlisted men had been undergoing aeronautic training from the time the aeronautic station was established at Pensacola, Fla., in January 1914. Training for enlisted men can even be traced back to the first aeronautic station at Greenbury Point, Md. However, more publicity for enlisted aeronautic training and its resultant positions developed in March 1915, when a law was passed by Congress that extended increased pay and allowances to enlisted men and student aviators, as well as qualified pilots, while on duty involving flight. Prior to the passage of this law, Congress had authorized special pay only for officers detailed to duty as flyers. The allure of flight, more pay and the continued development of the small aviation section of the Navy brought about a greater interest by enlisted personnel in the naval aeronautic field. It was only natural that some enlisted men, aside from their regular duties of maintaining the craft and flying as crewmembers, developed an interest in piloting aircraft.

There is some confusion surrounding the first training of enlisted men as pilots. References are made to the beginning of pilot training at NAS Pensacola, Fla., for the first group of enlisted men on 6 January 1916.

In a letter to Lt. Cmdr. Henry C. Mustin, Commandant, NAS Pensacola, Fla., dated 4 January 1916, Capt. Mark L. Bristol, Director of Naval Aeronautics, states,

> In an order issued the other day, we organized a class of men for training as aviators, specifying men of the seamen's branch. It may happen that the machinists at the present time are best fitted for this training, but we can not establish such a precedent. It would lead to all kinds of future complications, so start square on this subject.

In his 10 January 1916 response to Bristol's letter, Mustin wrote,

> As regards the distinction between Naval Aviator and Navy Air Pilot, I think that the term Naval Aviator, in view of the term Military Aviator used in the Army, is not altogether suitable for our enlisted men; also in view of the present wording of the law there may be some complications. However, I think we have the sense of what you desire in this line of work regardless of titles and that is a matter that can be straightened out later. In the meantime, we are going ahead with the first class of enlisted men and they are taking hold of the flying part of it very well.

From these two letters we can be fairly certain the first pilot training class for enlisted men began in January 1916 at NAS Pensacola, Fla. The question regarding the designation of an enlisted pilot appears to have been left up in the air. Mustin does make a reference to using the old title "Navy Air Pilot" that had been used for officers prior to March 1913. However, Bristol left his position as Director of Naval Aeronautics in March 1916 before a decision was made on the subject.

The Bureau of Navigation's January 1916 "Course of Instruction ..." mentioned above, identifies enlisted categories of Student Airman; Airman; Quartermaster, aeroplane; Quartermaster, dirigible; and Machinist, aeronautic. Just like the designations involving Naval Aviator, the Navy had two organizations (the Bureau of Navigation and the CNO's Director of Naval Aeronautics) that were dealing with aviation training and issuing directives that sometimes had conflicting uses for designations. The Bureau of Navigation's January 1916 "Course of Instructions and Required Qualifications of Personnel for the Air Service of the Navy" also set up a "Certificate of Qualification for Airman."

Thus, in 1916, NAS Pensacola, Fla., began issuing "Certificates of Qualification as Airman" to enlisted personnel meeting the requirements set up by the Bureau of Navigation. From a handwritten logbook maintained at Pensacola, the certificates were numbered, beginning with 1 and ending at 358. The Number 1 Certificate of Qualification as Airman was issued to CMM Harry E. Adams on 15 December 1916, with a course completion date of 27 November 1916. This airman certificate should not be confused with the enlisted qualifications for a pilot; there is no connection between the two designations. A note in the logbook indicates the issuance of a Certificate of Qualification from the Aeronautic School at Pensacola for Airman was discontinued on 1 October 1917. It is believed Pensacola discontinued the enlisted certificate program because of the changes in the "Course of Instructions," the addition of other training stations, and the influx of a large number of enlisted men during WWI. However, the name Airman continued to be applied to enlisted personnel in the aviation field. Needless to say, there were other qualified enlisted men in naval aeronautics who preceded the establishment of this list of designated "Airman."

The forgoing discussion about "Airman" is provided here to clarify the fact that "Airmen" were not being defined as enlisted pilots. However, some enlisted men who received "Certificates" as Airman did become qualified pilots, and this is where the confusion begins. The first official class of enlisted men to undergo pilot training in January 1916 included:

P. J. Dunleavy, CBM	F. Grompe, CMAA	A. A. Bressman, CTC
L. A. Welty, CTC	A. Hayes, CTC	A. P. Bauer, GM1c
J. Makolin, 1stSgt, USMC	W. E. McCaughtry, GunSgt, USMC	A. F. Dietrich, BM2c.

The last man to join this class was Walter D. Bonner, BM2c, and he appears on the 1 March 1916 Flying School's list of Enlisted Personnel undergoing Flying Instruction.

Capt. Mark Bristol, Director of Naval Aeronautics, sent a memo to the Secretary of the Navy on 4 March 1916, which stated, "On the 1st of January, 1916, a class of 10 enlisted men was formed and placed under instruction in flying. These men were selected from the bluejackets and marines already on duty at the station or on board *North Carolina*. These men are making excellent progress. There will be a class of them ordered every three months hereafter." Records do not indicate any succeeding classes of enlisted pilot training groups every three months as indicated by Bristol's letter. The next reference to a class of enlisted men undergoing flight training at NAS Pensacola is 15 May 1916, in a "Semi-Monthly Report of Aviators (Enlisted Personnel)." This lists the following personnel undergoing training as aviators:

A. A. Bressman	L. A. Welty	A. Hayes
A. F. Dietrich	W. D. Bonner	J. Makolin
W. E. McCaughtry	C. L. Allen	J. Sunderman
W. Diercks	J. Salsman	A. Ward
T. H. Murphy	G. Verini	

In the fall of 1917 several changes were implemented in the pilot training program that affected enlisted personnel. In a CNO letter to the Commandant, Pensacola Aeronautic Station, Fla., dated 8 August 1917, paragraph 2 states "It is desired to train no more enlisted personnel as pilots. Excellent Officer material in enlisted personnel will be treated in accordance with reference (c)." Reference (c) was the Bureau of Navigation's circular letter #9879-495, of 2 August 1917. In a letter from the Commandant, NAS Pensacola, Fla., dated 30 November 1917, to the Bureau of Navigation, clarification was requested regarding aviation designations for 10 enlisted personnel who had qualified and were given orders as Quartermaster Seaplane. This designation identified these personnel as qualified enlisted pilots.

The letter goes on to ask whether new orders should be issued to these men designating them as Naval Aviators. The ten men were:

CBM A. F. Dietrick	CQM J. T. Sunderman	CGM G. Enos
QM2c(A) John H. Bunt	QM2c(A) James A. Whitted	CTC A. Feher
CE Carlton D. Palmer	QM2c George W. Stone	CBM Robert H. Kerr
QM2c(A) C. A. Suber		

The Bureau of Navigation's response, dated 8 December 1917, states, "Men mentioned in this enclosure (the enclosure was a copy of NAS Pensacola's 30 November 1917 letter listing the 10 men) will have their designations changed to Naval Aviators, but no new orders are necessary." The second paragraph of this letter indicated a new policy was being issued with regard to enlisted pilots, it stated, "In separate correspondence, instructions are being issued concerning future designations as Naval Aviators for enlisted men who qualify for pilot duty, and new blanks (Navigation Form N. Nav. 442, October 1917) are being sent out on which reports should be made in the future."

It appears the Bureau of Navigation, in its Aviation Circular dated 1 January 1913, set up the policy that identified the course of flight training instruction and the passing of flight tests for officers, and later on applied it to enlisted men who could qualify for pilot duty. However, it also appears that the Bureau of Navigation did not make any modifications in its circulars to reflect the changes that occurred in pilot designations between 1913 and 1915, such as Navy Air Pilot and Naval Aviator and the appropriate references to enlisted men who became pilots. All ten enlisted men referenced in NAS Pensacola's 30 November 1917 letter were eventually commissioned. However, several of them maintained their enlisted pilot status for more than a year before receiving their commission.

In the latter part of 1917, as a result of the great need to increase the number of aviation personnel, the Navy instituted a policy of taking enlisted men for pilot training and then qualifying them for a commission and designation as a Naval Aviator. Many of the regular enlisted men who could qualify for the pilot training program would be discharged from the regular Navy and enrolled in the Naval Reserve for training and commission in the Naval Reserve Flying Corps. The majority of the personnel entering naval aviation service during the war came from the civilian community and joined the Naval Reserve for duty with the Naval Reserve Flying Corps. Needless to say, there were exceptions to these policies during WWI. This was particularly true for enlisted personnel who received pilot training in Europe.

On 5 June 1917, the Navy's First Aeronautic Detachment, and the first U.S. military unit sent to Europe in WWI, arrived at Pauillac, France. The second section of the detachment arrived on 8 June at St. Nazaire, France. The First Aeronautic Detachment was commanded by Lt. Kenneth Whiting and consisted of 7 officers and 122 enlisted men. Only four of the officers were pilots, two were supply officers, and one a doctor. The majority of the enlisted personnel were students in the aviation field. After a meeting between American and French officers, the French agreed to train the detachment's personnel. Approximately 50 enlisted men were to be trained as seaplane pilots at Tours while another 50 would be trained as "mechanicians" at St. Raphael.

On 22 June 1917, preliminary flight training for the enlisted men began in Caudron aircraft under French instructors at the École d'Aviation Militaire at Tours. One of the French procedures for flight training was to teach their pilots land flying first, hence, Lt. Whiting had to deal with the French Army, as well as with the Navy. Changes were made to the flight training plans and 14 of the enlisted men were redirected to fill the requirement for observer training. Under French training, an observer was a prototype of aircrewmen whose duties involved observing, acting as bombardier, and handling such armament as existed on the plane. On 7 July 1917, Lt. Whiting reported that 50 persons were undergoing pilot instruction at Tours, with 38 taking machinist and 14 observer training at St. Raphael.

The French required a ratio of 10 enlisted men for each pilot under its aviation program. Consequently, the American Navy representative in France, along with Lt. Whiting, requested an increase in personnel for aviation training in France. The Navy Department again found itself divided, some wanted to continue sending men to France for aviation training, while others wanted to conduct the training in the United States and have some final, on-site training conducted in France. By the early summer months of 1918 many of the problems of training, organization, and movement of aviation personnel abroad had begun to be solved. However, all aviation training matters were not smoothed out prior to the signing of the Armistice.

The policy regarding the enlisted pilots that were trained in Europe, either in France, Britain, or Italy, generally followed the same procedures adhered to in the United States at the end of 1917. Many of the enlisted pilots would receive commissions once they had completed flight training and been certified as pilots. They did not, however, always receive their commissions immediately after pilot qualification. Some flew many patrol missions before the administrative system authorized their commissioning in the Naval Reserve Flying Corps. When the Armistice was signed, the total strength of the U.S. Naval Aviation Force, Foreign Service (those serving overseas) was 1,147 officers and 18,308 enlisted men. The majority of them were assigned to air stations in France, followed by those in England, Ireland, and Italy.

With the end of WWI, naval aviation, along with other elements of the Navy, underwent a major demobilization that drastically reduced its size. Some of the officers and enlisted men on active duty in the Naval Reserve were offered a chance to convert to a regular status in the Navy. In some cases, enlisted men who had received their commissions following their completion of pilot training reverted to an enlisted status. This, of course, presented a problem for the Navy since they no longer had a program for enlisted personnel with pilot designations.

Following the massive demobilization, naval aviation again experienced the problems of maintaining an adequate supply of qualified aviation personnel, both enlisted men and officers. In 1919, various aviation issues were discussed by the Navy's General Board; the Commander in Chief Atlantic Fleet, Admiral H. T. Mayo; and various offices of the Chief of Naval Operations and the bureaus. On 23 June 1919, the General Board forwarded its final recommendations on aviation policy to the Secretary of the Navy, via the Chief of Naval Operations. One of those recommendations was "as many enlisted men as possible should be trained and used as pilots." Capt. Thomas T. Craven, the Director of Naval Aviation, submitted his comments on the General Board's recommendations on 17 July 1919. He stated, "It is believed that a limited number of enlisted men should be trained as pilots." On 24 July 1919, the Secretary of the Navy added his endorsement on the board's recommendations. However, his comments on personnel were very brief, stating, "Study will be made with regard to Aviation personnel." While these developments were important, they were eventually superseded by other events that occurred in 1919 between NAS Pensacola, Fla., other naval aviation organizations in the fleet, the CNO, and the Bureau of Navigation. These events set in motion the eventual establishment of the designation Naval Aviation Pilot (enlisted pilots).

During 1919, significant correspondence took place between the Commandant, NAS Pensacola, Fla., and various upper echelon commands regarding flight training and designations for aviation personnel. In a 12 February 1919 letter from the Commandant to the Supervisor Naval Reserve Flying Corps (a CNO office), a request was made to continue flight training and give Naval Aviator designations to four enlisted men. These four—CBM(A) Edwin Nirmaier, CQM(A) George R. Groh, CMM(GE) Lamont C. Fisher, and CQM(A) Percy M. Fuller—all had had foreign duty and had either qualified as pilots on active service or were undergoing pilot training when the war ended. None wanted to be discharged from the regular Navy and reenrolled with a commission in the Reserves.

The Bureau of Navigation returned the request on 31 March 1919 recommending reconsideration and further recommendation for the four enlisted men.

A 17 April 1919 letter from CNO (Aviation) to a wide range of commands, reconsidered the position on training of enlisted personnel and stated,

> 1. It has been decided to consider the flight training, or continuance of the interrupted flight training, of enlisted ratings of the regular service who, in addition to being unquestionable officer material, can successfully meet the following requirements: (a) That had been regularly enlisted in the Navy, and obtained the rating of second class petty officer prior to April 6, 1917, or that enlisted for Aviation duty only, in accordance with Enclosure (a).

However, the letter also indicated that these men would be commissioned in the Naval Reserve Force and retained on active duty until the issue of transferring Naval Reserve officers to the regular Navy had been definitely decided.

A Bureau of Navigation letter of 18 June 1919 modified BuNav's Circular Letter No. 57-19 and authorized the enlisted pilot training policy as stated in the CNO's letter of 17 April 1919. This BuNav circular letter was instrumental in setting in motion the third class of enlisted men authorized for pilot training at NAS Pensacola, Fla. A 20 August 1919 letter from the Bureau of Navigation to the Commandants of All Naval Districts, All Naval Air Stations and Aviation Detachments, set forth the requirements for training of enlisted pilots. The letter indicated that enlisted men would be designated Naval Aviators upon successfully completing the course. However, it made no references to a requirement for commissioning in the Naval Reserves.

This omission resulted in a letter from the Commanding Officer of NAS Pensacola, Fla., dated 15 September 1919, requesting Naval Aviator Appointments for warrant officers. The letter made a reference to Bureau of Navigation's 20 August letter, stating, "1. Reference (b) specifies that enlisted men are to be trained as Naval Aviators and, without commissioning, are to be given Naval Aviator Appointments and Insignia." In the Bureau's letter of 22 September 1919, it disapproved designating warrant officers as Naval Aviators, instead they were to be commissioned and then designated. However, this letter made no mention of commissioning enlisted pilots as officers. It did not take long for NAS Pensacola to send another letter, dated 3 October 1919, questioning the Bureau of Navigation's policy on Naval Aviator Appointments for Warrant Officers. In a 14 October 1919 letter from the Bureau of Navigation, the policy for training of enlisted and warrant officer Aviation Pilots was set forth. This letter cancelled the Bureau of Navigation letter dated 20 August 1919. It stated,

> 1. In the future it will be the policy of the Bureau to select a certain number of warrant officers and enlisted men for flight training and duty as pilots of large heavier-than-air craft and directional pilots of dirigibles. . . . 3. Warrant officers and men who are selected in accordance with this letter will be given the complete course of instruction for qualification as pilot. Upon successfully completing the course, they will be issued certificates of qualification as 'Naval Aviation Pilots' by the Navy Department. Such certificates will entitle the pilots to wear the aviation insignia authorized for Naval Aviators. Warrant Officers and men who hold certificates as Naval Aviation Pilots will, while detailed for duty involving actual flying be entitled to fifty percent additional pay.

This is the first official reference to the designation "Naval Aviation Pilot" and it set in motion the beginning of the enlisted pilot program. Thus, the initial program for Naval Aviation Pilots was done without authorization from Congress. The Congressional program involving enlisted pilots was not developed until the mid-1920s.

In the October and November 1919 letters from the Bureau of Navigation, the bureau notified appropriate commands of its intention to detail classes of approximately 25 enlisted men to begin flight training in heavier-than-air and lighter-than-air. The CNO Daily Aviation News Bulletin for 10 December 1919 stated "A class of twenty-five enlisted men has been ordered to Pensacola, Fla., to take the course preliminary to appointment as Naval Aviation Pilots." An NAS Pensacola letter of 9 December 1919 to the Bureau of Navigation stated, "This Station can start the Heavier-than-Air Course of Training for a class of twenty-five (25) enlisted men on February 1st, 1920." This was the third class of enlisted men to undergo flight training at Pensacola, Fla., but the first class whereby the graduates were identified as Naval Aviation Pilots and retained their enlisted status.

A 5 February 1920 NAS Pensacola memorandum listed classes undergoing instruction in aviation. Enlisted Class No. 1 (Heavier-than-Air) has the following personnel listed:

CMM(A) Floyd Bennett	CMM(A) Chas P. Brenner	CMM(A) Kenneth D. Franklin
CMM(A) Anthony Iannucci	CMM(A) Leo C. Sullivan	CMM George N. Tibbetts
CMM(A) Jacob W. Utley	CMM(A) Thomas P. Wilkinson	CMM(A) Francis C. Barb
CMM(G) John W. Green	CMM(A) Clarence I. Kessler	CMM(A) R. B. Lawrence
CMM(A) Francis E. Ormsbee	CMM(A) Eugene T. Rhoads	CMM(A) Bert Strand
CMM(A) Harry A. Rossier	CMM(A) N. Wayne L. Carleto	CCM(A) Chas. I. Elliott
CGM(A) Ralph A. Jury	CCM(A) Herbert L. Hoobler	CE(G) William B. Livingston
CQM(A) Owen J. O'Connor	CGM George N. Strode	CEL(A) Clyde O. Switzer
BTSN(A) Lamont C. Fisher	CCM(A) Cecil H. Gurley	CEL(R) Claude G. Alexander
CGM(A) Henry Brenner	CQM(A) William August Clutne	CQM Owen J. Darling
CCM(A) Garrett H. Gibson	BM2c Harvey A. Griesy	CEL(R) Arthur E. LaPorte
CGM(A) Cyrus L. Sylvester	GM1c(A) W. T. Sweeny	CBM Stephen J. Williamson.

The list for students (Lighter-than-Air) included the following enlisted men:

BTSN William L. Buckley	MACH William L. Coleman	Gunner Ralph T. Bundy
Gunner Willfred H. Smart	CMM(A) L. E. Crowl	CQM(D) Horace M. Finch
CBM S. R. Soulby	CQM(A) G. K. Wilkinson.	

A second class of enlisted men began undergoing heavier-than-air pilot training on 1 August 1920 at NAS Pensacola, Fla., and consisted of 33 enlisted men. A third class of enlisted pilot training was scheduled to begin on 1 March 1921.

Designation List of Early Naval Aviation Pilots (NAPS)

The program for Naval Aviation Pilot designation numbers produced the same type of situation and confusion that surrounded the numbering of Naval Aviators. The Navy Department, once a policy was decided upon in late 1919 to designate enlisted men as Naval Aviation Pilots, started issuing certificates of qualification as Naval Aviation Pilots to some enlisted personnel who had qualified as pilots during WWI. Hence, the precedence list for Naval Aviation Pilots includes personnel not part of the enlisted class that began training in February 1920. It appears a number of these enlisted personnel were instructors at NAS Pensacola, Fla., in late 1919 and early 1920. CQM(A) Harold H. Karr received a letter, dated 9 March 1920, from the Bureau of Navigation that certified him as a qualified pilot and designated a Naval Aviation Pilot. Naval Aviation Pilot designation numbers were placed on a handwritten ledger maintained at NAS Pensacola, Fla. Karr is listed with Naval Aviation Pilot number 1 with the date of issue as 22 January 1920. It is believed the difference between the 22 January date and the 9 March 1920 date is the time difference between the reporting from NAS Pensacola, Fla., to the Bureau of Navigation and its response to Karr.

The enlisted men who were part of the first two classes to receive training as aviators in 1916 may be considered the forerunners of the enlisted men who were designated Naval Aviation Pilots. However, because the program and designation for Naval Aviation Pilots was not established at the time of their training or because most of them received commissions and designations as Naval Aviators, they are not included in this list of early Naval Aviation Pilots. Discrepancies in the sources listing Naval Aviation Pilots made it impossible to resolve all the numbering problems. For this reason, only the first 69 Naval Aviation Pilots are listed.

Naval Aviation Pilot Designations			
Pilot No.	Name	Rate	Date Designated
1	Karr, Harold H.	CQM(A)	1/22/20
2	Lee, Robert E.	NM1C(A)	1/22/20
3	Niramaier, Edwin	CBM(A)	4/14/20
4	Lovejoy, Francis E.	CQM(A)	11/22/20
5	Seiler, Walter L.	CQM(A)	1/22/20
6	Woods, Clarence	CQM(A)	1/22/20
7	Alexander, Claud G.	CE(R)	10/7/20
8	Barb, Francis C.	CMM(A)	10/8/20
9	Bennett, Floyd	CMM(A)	10/7/20
10	Byrne, Patrick J.	CMM(A)	10/8/20
11	Carleton, Wayne L.	CBM(A)	10/8/20
12	Cluthe, William A.	CQM(A)	10/8/20
13	Darling, Owen M.	CQM(A)	10/8/20
14	Elliott, Charles I.	CCM(A)	10/7/20
15	Fisher, Lawrence C.	CMM(A)	10/7/20
16	Franklin, Kenneth D.	CMM(A)	10/7/20
17	Graham, Paul E.	CMM(A)	10/8/20
18	Griesy, Harvey A.	BM2C	10/8/20
19	Hoobler, Herbert L.	CCM(A)	10/8/20
20	Insley, Cecil H.	CCM(A)	10/7/20
21	Kesler, C. I.	CMM(A)	10/8/20
22	LaPorte, Arthur E.	CE(R)	10/7/20
23	Lawrence, K. B.	CMM(A)	10/7/20
24	O'Conner, Owen J.	CQM(A)	10/7/20
25	Ormsbee, Frank E.	CMM(A)	10/8/20
26	Peterson, Allen K.	Ch.Ptr.(A)	10/8/20
27	Rhoads, Eugene S.	CMM(A)	10/8/20
28	Rossier, Harry A.	CMM(A)	10/8/20
29	Stinson, John H.	CMM(A)	10/7/20
30	Sullivan, Leo C.	CMM(A)	10/7/20
31	Tibbetts, George N.	CMM(A)	10/7/20
32	Utley, Jacob W.	CMbl(A)	10/7/20
33	Wilkinson, Thomas P.	CMM(A)	10/7/20
34	Williamson, S. J.	CBM(A)	10/8/20
35	Demshock, John J.	CE(G)A	3/8/21
36	Baker, H. T.	CMM(A)	3/8/21
37	Buckley, James W.	CMM	3/8/21
38	Elmore, William L.	CGM	3/8/21
39	Griggs, Herbert B.	CE(G)	3/8/21
40	Grobe, C. H.	MM1C	3/8/21
41	Gustafson, R. F.	MM1C(A)	3/8/21
42	Hill, William F.	CMM(A)	3/8/21
43	Jackson, Willard B.	CMM(A)	3/8/21
44	Kirkeby, C. D.	MM1C(A)	3/8/21
45	Linder, Frank M.	CE	3/8/21

Naval Aviation Pilot Designations			
Pilot No.	Name	Rate	Date Designated
46	McPeak, N. B.	MM1C	3/8/21
47	Markham, E. L.	MM2C	3/8/21
48	Merritt, R. J.	GM1C	3/8/21
49	Miller, Joseph H.	CMM	3/8/21
50	McLean, M. C.	CMM	3/8/21
51	McIntosh, Enoch B.	QM1C	3/8/21
52	O'Brien, John J.	CMM	3/8/2l
53	Preeg, Felix F.	CY	3/8/21
54	Raney, Charles B.	CY	3/8/21
55	Rawlings, John E.	CMM	3/8/21
56	Stultz, W. L.	MM1C	3/8/21
57	Steelman, Charlie	CQM(D)*	3/23/21
58	Tobin, Frederick J.	CMM(A)*	3/23/21
59	Andrews, Walter J.	ACMM	8/15/21
60	Dunn, Stephen	AMM1C	8/15/21
61	Frank, Edwin George	ACMM	8/15/21
62	Flynn, Elliott J.	AMM1C	8/15/21
63	Heinz, Edward A.	AMM1C	8/15/21
64	Holdredge, Herman J.	ACMM	8/15/21
65	Krueger, Charley E.	ACMM	8/15/21
66	Muller, Leo G.	AMM1C	8/15/21
67	Smith, Sidney N.	ACMM	8/15/21
68	Sylvester, Cyrus L.	CGM	8/15/21
69	Harrigan, John J.	ACR	8/15/21

* Airship

Enlisted to Warrant Naval Aviator and NFO Program

The CNO issued NavAdmin 031/06 on 19 January 2006 to establish the Active Duty Flying Chief Warrant Officer Pilot and Naval Flight Officer Program. The Navy designed the program to take highly qualified and "hard-charging" enlisted sailors in paygrades E-5 through E-7 and commission them as chief warrant officers. When they completed training as naval aviators or naval flight officers they would be "winged" and designated naval aviators or naval flight officers.

The targeted communities for Warrant Naval Aviator and Naval Flight Officers included HSC, HSL, VP, and VQ squadrons, from whom the service sought an initial 30 applicants. Vice Admiral John C. Harvey Jr., Chief of Naval Personnel, noted that "The CWO program is intended to create flying specialists unencumbered by the traditional career paths of the unrestricted line community." The first group of Aviator Chief Warrant Officers commissioned on 1 December 2006, and included ten pilots and four naval flight officers, four of whom possessed civilian pilot's licenses, and seven already served as naval aircrew.

The first group that completed flight training and "winged" as naval aviators were:

Adams, Michael S., Jr.

Ditamore, Stephen J.

Jacobson, Brandon R.

Reyes, Robert

Chandler, Matthew P.

Haller, Daniel R.

Kleparek, Anton K.

Clements, Joshua A.

Holland, Kevin R.

Miltner, Keith P.

The first group that completed flight training and "winged" as naval flight officers were:

Courtney, Jerry D., Jr.	Greteman, Bernard G.	Langschied, Jason R.
Rittierodt, Joseph A.		

In addition, the July 2007 board selected the remaining 10 pilots and six naval flight officers. Three enlisted sailors—AW1 Robert Antonucci and AD1 John Fuller assigned to HSL-43, and AW2 John Barile of HSL-45—commissioned on 1 December 2007, at NAS North Island, Calif. On the 20th of that month, CWO2s Dale Courtney and Adam Rittierodt of VP-30 received their wings as naval flight officers as two of the initial applicants, at NAS Jacksonville, Fla. Two German officers, Lts. 2nd Grade Christian Hegemann and Patrick Leisner, also received naval flight officer wings.

General Background on Training

The story of naval aviator training is complex, and involved many changes in the various programs and where students received their training. Training of naval aviators first began with the assignment of Lt. Theodore G. Ellyson to the Glenn Curtiss camp at San Diego, Calif., (North Island) in December 1910. He arrived there in January 1911. This established the Navy policy of using the facilities of private aircraft manufacturers to train its aviators, which was tied to contracts that purchased aircraft for the Navy Department. The first aircraft contracts were with Curtiss Aeroplane Company and the Wright Company. So the early naval aviators were trained at San Diego, Calif., and Hammondsport, N.Y., used by the Curtiss company; Dayton, Ohio, used by the Wrights; and Marblehead, Mass., used by the Burgess Company for training in Wright Company aircraft.

With the acquisition of aircraft and the training of several naval aviators, the Navy was able to terminate its dependence on private manufacturers for training. In August 1911 the Navy set up an Engineering Experiment Station and aviation school at Greenbury Point, Annapolis, Md. During the winter of 1912–1913, the aviation camp moved to Guantánamo Bay, Cuba, for its first exercises with the Fleet. Capt. Washington I. Chambers' report to the Chief of the Bureau of Navigation in 1913 identified the following naval aviators:

Theodore G. Ellyson	John Rodgers	John H. Towers
Victor C. Herbster	Patrick N. L. Bellinger	Bernard L. Smith
Godfrey de C. Chevalier	Alfred A. Cunningham	William D. Billingsley
Laurance N. McNair	Holden C. Richardson	Isaac F. Dortch
Henry C. Mustin	J. D. Burray	

The last seven in this list of naval aviators were Navy-trained.

In accordance with the recommendations from the Board on Naval Aeronautic Service, the aviation school at Greenbury Point, Md., was moved to Pensacola, Fla. On 20 January 1914 the Greenbury Point aviation unit arrived at Pensacola to set up a flying school. It consisted of nine officers, 23 men, seven aircraft, portable hangars, and other equipment.

The training of naval aviators at Pensacola was conducted using the same informal methods that had been used at Greenbury Point. Students were taught how to fly, and instructed in the rudiments of the construction and maintenance of their planes. Every man was given as much time as necessary to master his ground and flight instruction. No one washed out.

The Bureau of Navigation issued a formal training syllabus in June 1914, BUNAV Bulletin No. 532. This syllabus established a one-year course for pilots. Revised in January 1916, the new syllabus, "Courses of Instruction and Required Qualification of Personnel of the Air Service of the Navy," outlined courses for Naval Aviation Pilots, Naval Aviators, Student Airmen, Quartermasters (Aviation), Quartermasters (Deck), and Machinists Mates (Aviation). During summer 1916, a syllabus was also established for the training of lighter-than-air pilots (dirigible and balloon). Flight instruction procedures were altered by a constant stream of suggestions from the pioneers at Pensacola.

In 1916 the Naval Appropriation Act provided for the establishment of a Naval Flying Corps. It also provided for the establishment of a Naval Reserve Force of six classes, including a Naval Reserve Flying Corps. One of the first groups to organize under the corps was the First Yale Group/Unit. Most of the men in this organization received their training independently of the Navy and were later qualified as Naval Aviators. Training for many of the corps personnel fell on the shoulders of Pensacola until a training system evolved and was established during WWI.

With the U.S. entry into WWI, numerous changes occurred in the training of naval pilots. Besides the training in England, France, and Italy, a group of 24 Americans reported at the University of Toronto on 9 July 1917 to begin flight instruction under the Canadian Royal Flying Corps. In the United States, training expanded from the site at NAS Pensacola, Fla., to include preliminary flight training at Squantum, Mass.; Bay Shore (Long Island), N.Y.; Miami, Fla.; Key West, Fla.; and San Diego, Calif. By late January 1918, the following air stations were conducting aviation training: Chatham, Mass.; Montauk, N.Y.; Bay Shore, N.Y.; Rockaway, N.Y.; Cape May, N.J.; Hampton Roads, Va.; Miami, Fla.; Key West, Fla.; Pensacola, Fla.; and San Diego, Calif. There were also naval aviation detachments scattered around the country that were involved in aviation training. These included MIT at Cambridge, Mass.; Great Lakes Training Station, Ill.; Goodyear at Akron, Ohio; Curtiss Aeroplane at Buffalo, N.Y.; Aeromarine Company at Keyport, Mass.; the Naval Aircraft Factory at Philadelphia, Pa.; Packard Motor Car Company in Detroit, Mich.; Delco Ignition Laboratories in Dayton, Ohio; Lincoln Motor Company in Detroit, Mich.; and Savage Arms Corporation in Utica, N.Y. With the end of WWI, most of these stations ended their aviation training programs and NAS Pensacola, Fla., again became the primary training location.

With the beginning of WWII the training of Naval Aviators again became decentralized and expanded across the country, just as it had done during WWI. Following the end of WWII, the different phases of training for Naval Aviators continued to be conducted at several different air stations. That situation continues to exist today.

Number of Naval Aviators Designated (Trained)

Obviously, the variances in the naval aviator training program and its decentralization as described above make it very difficult to provide an infallible number for the output of naval aviators since 1911. Personnel trained by the Navy are designated naval aviators, whether they serve in the U.S. Navy, Marine Corps, or Coast Guard. The list below also includes foreign personnel trained by the U.S. Navy Department as naval aviators, as well as a few U.S. military and civilian personnel from other federal agencies. In some cases these special groups were included in the number count, but in other cases they were not. It is extremely difficult to identify the years in which special groups were included and the years in which they were not. Hence, the following list identifying the number of naval aviators trained (and officially designated as naval aviators) is the best available. The numbers for the more recent years are by fiscal year. In 1976 the government changed its fiscal year from 1 July–30 June to 1 October–30 September. Consequently, there is an additional entry for 1976 covering the 1 July to 30 September time frame.

Year	Number Trained (Designated)	Year	Number Trained (Designated)
1911 to 1919	2,834	1939	450
1920	82	1940	708
1921	72	1941	3,112
1922	106	1942	10,869
1923	25	1943	20,842
1924	32	1944	21,067
1925	35	1945	8,880
1926	35	1946	2,635
1927	123	1947	1,646
1928	140	1948	446
1929	66	1949	688
1930	348	1950	1,691
1931	321	1951	1,288
1932	168	1952	932
1933	138	1953	1,701
1934	35	1954	2,338
1935	100	1955	2,851
1936	212	1956	2,571
1937	527	1957	2,951
1938	543	1958	2,513

Year	Number Trained (Designated)
1959	1,785
1960	1,602
1961	1,478
1962	1,413
1963	1,701
1964	1,701
1965	1,715
1966	1,907
1967	2,046
1968	2,334
1969	2,559
1970	2,450
1971	1,809
1972	1,853
1973	1,650
1974	1,447
1975	1,337
1976	1,375
Jul-Sep 1976	314
1977	1,196
1978	934
1979	871
1980	1,471
1981	1,482
1982	1,515
1983	1,424
1984	1,366

Year	Number Trained (Designated)
1985	1,343
1986	1,439
1987	1,482
1988	1,454
1989	1,528
1990	1,483
1991	1,342
1992	1,216
1993	865
1994	874
1995	1,155
1996	983
1997	978
1998	1,156
1999	1,183
2000	1,218
2001	1,109
2002	1,237
2003	1,243
2004	1,170
2005	1,271
2006	1,251
2007	1,231
2008	1,187
2009	1,209
2010	1,191
Total	170,654

CHAPTER 9

Evolution of Naval Wings (Breast Insignia)

Naval Aviator Wings

The origin of a distinctive device for naval aviators is somewhat obscure, but the idea was undoubtedly influenced by outside forces. It appears that the need for a distinguishing mark was voiced by the aviators themselves, particularly after Army aviators began wearing "badges" in 1913. Other influence outside the naval service also appears to have provided some of the initial impetus.

A review of the records indicates a lack of coordination within the Navy during the process to develop a naval aviation device. The dated correspondence of the Bureau of Navigation (BuNav) and the Chief of Naval Operations (CNO) Aviation Section relating to the "wings" does not coincide with the dated changes to the uniform regulations. The change to the uniform regulations that first identified the new "wings" was issued before the CNO's Aviation Section and BuNav had agreed upon a final design. Several separate evolutions occurred in 1917.

A 29 June 1917 letter from the G. F. Hemsley Co., stating that the sender "takes the liberty" of forwarding a design for an aviation cap and collar ornament, may well have started official action. The first official correspondence on the subject appears to have been a CNO letter to BuNav dated 19 July 1917. This letter, which forwarded the suggestion from the G. F. Hemsley Co., rejected the ornaments but went on to say that since foreign countries and the U.S. Army had adopted an aviation device, naval aviators also should be given "some form of mark or badge to indicate their qualification, in order that they have standing with other aviation services." The letter, prepared in the Aviation Section of CNO, enclosed a representative design for wings. From that date, the subject was kept alive by the exchange of correspondence concerning the design and production of the insignia by interested firms.

Lt. Cmdr. John H. Towers, assigned to the aviation desk under CNO, requested the assistance of Lt. Henry Reuterdahl in designing the naval aviator wings. Reuterdahl played an important part in the design development. He was later assigned as an artist to record the first transatlantic flight in May 1919, which was planned to be made by four NC aircraft. In a 28 September 1917 letter to Bailey, Banks, and Biddle Company, he recommended simplifying the wings by bolder chasing (engraving) and a reduction in the number of feathers, noting that "most naval ornaments are too fine and not broad enough in character." He also recommended changes in the anchor and rope and the introduction of a slight curve to conform to the shape of the body. He summarized his remarks by saying, "My idea has been to reduce all corners so that there will be no points which might catch in the clothing."

Several different designs were proposed and submitted for approval. The sample pins passed through a number of changes. Bronze, the first metal suggested, was quickly rejected in favor of a gold and silver combination. This, in turn, was changed to all silver and finally, in October 1917, all gold was selected. The size changed from more than three inches to the final of 2³/₄ inches. The "U.S." was dropped from the design and stars on the shield were proposed and rejected as violating the laws of heraldry.

By October 1917 the Bailey, Banks, and Biddle Company took the lead over its competitors and on 24 October submitted its first sample pin. In early November it submitted other samples and was ready to make "prompt delivery of such number of devices as you may desire." It is believed these various sample pins added to the confusion regarding the existence of official naval aviator wings. On the final decision to place an order, the record is obscure but it may have been a BuNav letter to the supply officer at NAS Pensacola, Fla., dated 21 November 1917, selecting "the higher priced pin" ($1.15 each). The company was not named, but it seems fairly certain that it was Bailey, Banks, and Biddle. Its letter to BuNav dated 19 December 1917 confirms a telegram stating: "balance aviator insignia shipped tomorrow."

The first wings, made by Bailey, Banks, and Biddle of Philadelphia, Pa., were received by the Navy in December 1917 and issued early in the following year. The fact that the first pins were delivered in this month is also confirmed in a 26 December letter from BuNav to NAS Pensacola reporting that the new pins had been received and "will be sent out as soon as they can be engraved to show the Aviator's number, his name and branch of service." The bureau asked the jeweler not to sell the wings to individuals.

The requirement to engrave the aviator's number posed a problem concerning the precedence list of trained naval aviators. This was solved by the preparation of an aviators' precedence list, covering numbers 1 through 282, by the CNO Aviation Section. Thus, the development of wings was responsible for the first precedence list and, in addition, was a factor in the later assignment of fractional numbers to many aviators omitted from this first compilation.

When forwarded to BuNav on 19 January 1918, distribution of the first wings could begin. After almost eight years of naval aviation and nine months of war, naval aviators had wings—a badge of qualification that would set them apart. It seems likely that Cmdr. Towers, senior naval aviator in Washington at the time, was an early—if not the first—recipient. The engraving of the individual's name, naval aviator number, and branch of service was discontinued sometime during WWI.

The official approval for naval aviator wings was announced before a final design had been agreed upon. On 7 September 1917, the Secretary of the Navy approved Change 12 to the 1913 uniform regulations. The pertinent portion stated: "A Naval Aviator's device, a winged foul anchor with the letters 'U.S.', is hereby adopted to be worn by qualified Naval Aviators. This device will be issued by the Bureau of Navigation (BuNav) to officers and men of the Navy and Marine Corps who qualify as Naval Aviators, and will be worn on the left breast."

However, before any such wings were issued, the design was modified by Change 14, approved 12 October 1917 and issued in BuNav Circular Letter 40-17 of 20 November 1917: "The device for Naval Aviators will be a winged foul anchor, but the letters 'U.S.' given in Change in Uniform Regulations No. 12, have been omitted." Several other changes to the 1913 uniform regulations occurred regarding the wings before the design was finalized. Uniform Regulations, Change Number 18 of 1 April 1918, states "Naval Aviator's Device—Device for naval aviators will be a winged foul anchor, to be worn by qualified naval aviators. This device will be issued . . . and worn on the left breast." Change number 20 (undated) has the following pertinent information:

> Chapter 10 and changes 11, 12, 14, 16, and 18 of Uniform Regulations, 1913, are annulled and in lieu thereof this chapter is substituted: NAVAL AVIATOR'S DEVICE—Device for naval aviators will be a winged foul anchor, to be worn by qualified naval aviators. This device will be issued by the Bureau of Navigation to officers and men of the Navy and Marine Corps who qualify as naval aviators, and will be worn on the left breast.

Another modification to the 1913 uniform regulation was made by Change 29, dated 13 May 1920. In Article 262, under "Naval Aviator's Device" the title of the paragraph was changed to read "Naval Aviation Insignia" and the first sentence read: "Insignia to be worn by qualified naval aviators and by warrant officers and enlisted men holding certificate of qualification as naval aviation pilots, is a winged foul anchor."

The 1922 uniform regulations, approved on 20 September 1922, described the wing design in more detail: "A gold embroidered or bronze gold-plated metal pin, winged, foul anchor surcharged with a shield $1/2$ inch in height, $2^3/4$ inches from tip to tip of wings; length of foul anchor 1 inch." Except for a reduction in the length of the foul anchor from 1 to $7/8$ inch, made by Change 1 to the above regulations, and an elaboration of the description in 1951 which added dimensions for the shield ($7/16$ inch high and at its widest point) and for the width of the anchor ($11/16$ inch at the flukes and $7/16$ at the stock), the original design has changed very little since 1922.

The design pictured below was published by the *Air Service Journal* on 27 September 1917. A short article in the journal identified it as a "Naval Aviator's Device" of gold and silver metal as described by a change in Uniform Regulations No. 10. It is believed the article may have been referring to Change 12 in the uniform regulations, which was issued on 7 September 1917. This published design, most likely an artist's rendition, also failed to take into account the shield.

The following artist's rendition is most likely the design referenced in Change 12 of Uniform Regulations, 1913, and issued on 7 September 1917:

The photograph below is of the original design authorized by Change 14 of the 1913 uniform regulations, approved 12 October 1917, and quoted in BuNav Circular Letter 40-17 of 20 November 1917. This is the officially approved design made by Bailey, Banks, and Biddle and issued to naval aviators in early 1918.

The following photographs trace the evolution of the wings during the 1920s, 30s, and early 40s:

During World War II, the wings began showing a series of dots, or circles in the upper part of the design where the wings break. The original design shows these as small feathers, not dots or circles.

On most Naval Aviator wings there is a small dot or circle on one of the anchor flukes. That design is part of the normal structure of an anchor called a becket, which is an eye with a line attached used for securing the anchor to the side of the ship to keep it from moving when the ship is underway.

This wing design in gold or a gold finish has been the standard design since the 1950s.

Aircrew (Air Crew)/Combat Aircrew Wing Insignia

During WWII a new aviation breast insignia was designed in response to numerous recommendations from the fleet to recognize the job done by enlisted aircrew personnel flying in combat. In a Navy Department press release of 18 May 1943, the new Air Crew insignia was described as follows: "The Air Crew insignia consists of silver wings with a center disk surcharged with fouled anchor. Below the disk is a scroll with the legend 'Air Crew,' and above it is a bar on which gold stars can be placed."

The Bureau of Naval Personnel (BuPers) Circular Letter Number 90-43 of 29 May 1943 announced the approval of an air crew insignia, recognizing the air-fighting ability of flight crews. It was intended primarily for enlisted ratings in the flight crews of naval aircraft. However, any commissioned or warrant officer, other than pilots or designated naval aviation observers, who met the qualification requirements, were eligible to wear the insignia. The initial requirements were:

    a. Having served, subsequent to 7 December 1941, for a total of three months as a regularly assigned member of the Air Crew of a combatant craft.

      1. "Combat aircraft" shall be considered as all operating aircraft of the Fleet or Frontier Forces, and excepts utility aircraft, which are neither designed nor fitted out for offensive (or defensive) operations.

      2. The term "regularly assigned member of the Air Crew" shall be interpreted literally, and shall be substantiated by the battle station bill of the unit, under such instructions that may be approved and promulgated by the Bureau of Naval Personnel.

b. Having suffered injuries or other physical impairment, while engaged in combatant operations since 7 December 1941, as a regularly assigned member of a combatant aircraft, which precludes the possibility of fulfillment of the time requirements, stated in subparagraph (a) above, and is recommended by the Commanding Officer of the Unit in which injury or physical impairment was received.

c. Individual combat stars will be authorized by Unit Commanders, in conformance with instructions issued by Commander-in-Chief, United States Fleet, to those members of Air Crews who:

1. Engage enemy aircraft, singly or in formation.

2. Engage armed enemy combatant vessels with bombs, torpedoes, or machine guns.

3. Engage in bombing offensive operations against enemy fortified positions.

4. A maximum of three combat stars shall be awarded for display on the Air Crew Insignia; combat actions reports in excess of three will be credited only in the record of the individual concerned.

d. Personnel qualified by provisions of subparagraphs (a) and (b) above may wear the Air Crew Insignia permanently.

The qualification requirements to wear the insignia were modified several times. BuPers Circular Letter Numbers 173-43 of 8 September 1943, 22-44 of 29 January 1944, and 174-44 of 16 June 1944 all make modifications to the qualifications but do not give a detailed description of the insignia.

BuPers Circular Letter Number 395-44, dated 30 December 1944, provided a comprehensive description of the wings:

> The Aircrew Insignia is a silver-plated or silver-color, winged, metal, pin, with gold-color circular shield with surcharged foul anchor, superimposed on wing roots, with words "AIRCREW" below circular shield; a silver-color bar over the circular shield with three threaded holes to receive three gold-color combat stars when officially awarded. The insignia will measure two inches from tip to tip of the wings: circle on shield 5/16"; total depth of the shield from the top of the circle to the bottom of the shield 9/16".

The uniform regulations of 2 May 1947 provided a modified description of the wings:

> A silver-plated or silver color, winged, metal pin, with gold circular shield surcharged with foul anchor, superimposed on wing roots, with word "AIRCREW" in raised letters on a silver-color background below the circular shield; above the shield there shall be a silver-color scroll; the insignia to measure 2" from tip to tip of the wings; circle on shield 5/16" in diameter; total height of the shield and silver background beneath the shield 9/16". The scroll shall be 1/8" wide and 3/4" long and shall be centered over the wings. Gold stars to a total of three, as merited, shall be mounted on the scroll, necessary holes being pierced to receive them. A silver star may be worn in lieu of three gold stars.

This drawing of an early Aircrew Insignia without stars was published in the April 1943 issue of *Naval Aviation News*.

In 1958 there was a major change in the insignia. On 10 April 1958 Change 5 to the 1951 uniform regulations was issued. The name Aircrew or Air Crew insignia was redesignated Combat Aircrew insignia. Beside the redesignation, there were a few minor changes to the breast insignia. The new description read:

> A silver color, metal pin; winged, with gold color circular shield surcharged with a foul anchor, superimposed on wing roots; with word "AIRCREW" in raised letters on a silver background

below the shield. Above the shield there shall be a silver color scroll. The insignia shall measure 2" from tip to tip of wings; the circular shield shall be ³/₈" in diameter; height of anchor ¹/₄" with other dimensions proportionate; total height of shield and silver background beneath ⁹/₁₆"; the scroll shall be ³/₄" long and ¹/₄" wide; centered over the shield, each end to rest on top of wings. Gold stars of a size to be inscribed in a circle ¹/₈" in diameter, to a total of three, as merited, shall be mounted on the scroll, necessary holes being pierced to receive them. A silver star may be worn in lieu of three gold stars.

In 1958 the Navy redesignated the Aircrew Wing Insignia—that had been approved in 1943 to recognize and be awarded to personnel who flew in combat on naval aircraft—to the new designation Combat Aircrew Wings and then created a new design for Aircrew Wings Insignia. The new aircrew insignia was worn by naval aviation person who flew as crewmembers on board naval aircraft but had nothing to do with whether they flew in combat or non-combat missions.

Following the 1958 redesignation, the Navy continued to allow the wearing of the redesignated Aircrew insignia for those Navy individuals who had previously been authorized to wear the device.

With the establishment of a new aircrew wing insignia the Navy no longer awarded or issued the combat aircrew wing insignia that had been created in 1943 to Navy personnel. The 1978 U.S. Navy uniform regulations removed the Combat Aircrew insignia from the authorized list of aviation breast insignia. However, the Marine Corps continued to use the 1943 aircrew insignia design, now called Combat Aircrew Wings, and awarded the wings to personnel who met the qualification requirements.

A Bureau of Naval Personnel Memorandum, approved by Chief of Naval Operations on 7 November 1994, authorized Navy personnel, who flew as aircrew with Marine Corps units in combat, to wear the combat aircrew wings. However, they are not authorized for Navy personnel flying in combat on board Navy aircraft. They are only authorized to wear the aircrew wings. The appropriate change was made to the Navy uniform regulations.

Aircrew Insignia Wings

Change 5 to the 1951 Uniform Regulations, dated 10 April 1958, redesignated the 1943 designed Aircrew Insignia to Combat Aircrew insignia and also established a new Aircrew insignia design. The new aircrew insignia was patterned along the basic lines of the Naval Aviation Observer insignia and was described as: "Shall be a gold color metal pin; winged, with a circular center design and anchor upon which the block letters AC are superimposed. Width between tips of wings shall be 2³/₄"; circle diameter shall be ³/₄"; height of anchor shall be ¹/₂" with other dimension proportionate."

On 11 August 1965, BuPers Notice 1020 authorized the wearing of the aircrew breast insignia on a permanent basis. From the establishment of the newly designed Aircrew insignia in 1958 and until 1965, the insignia could only be worn by qualified personnel serving in an aircrew position. If an individual was assigned to a shore billet and not involved in aircrew duties, then they were not authorized to wear the insignia. Under the new guidance, a person who qualified to wear the Aircrew insignia could continue to wear the breast device at anytime during their military service or unless the person was disqualified for aircrew duty.

Naval Aviation Experimental Psychologists and Naval Aviation Physiologists Wings

On 12 April 1967, the Under Secretary of the Navy approved a change to the Navy uniform regulations that authorized a new wing insignia for aviation experimental psychologists and aviation physiologists. In February 1966, both were designated as crew members and ordered to duty involving flying. These individuals were assigned to duties such as in-flight analysis of human performance in fleet and training operations covering a myriad of weapons systems and tactics, providing extensive training for all aircrew personnel in airborne protective equipment and egress systems, and test and evaluation of new and improved aircraft systems.

Their gold wings are similar to those worn by flight surgeons, except the gold oak leaf does not have the acorn. The photo below shows the wings of the naval aviation experimental psychologists and physiologists.

Naval Aviation Supply Wings

Plans began in 1982 for the establishment of a naval aviation supply officer program and the authorization for a breast insignia for qualifying Supply Corps officers. On 8 May 1984, during the 73rd annual Aviation Ball, the first naval aviation supply wings were presented by Vice Adm. Robert F. Schoultz, Deputy Chief of Naval Operations (Air Warfare), to Vice Adm. Eugene A. Grinstead Jr., SC, USN; Rear Adm. Andrew A. Giordano, SC, USN (Ret); and Commo. John H. Ruehlin, SC, USN, Commanding Officer, Aviation Supply Office, Philadelphia, Pa. Officers qualified to wear the naval aviation supply wings must complete a demanding qualification program that requires approximately 350 hours of study and practical experience. They must also pass an oral examination administered by supply and aviation maintenance officers at their operating sites.

The naval aviation supply wings consist of the traditional naval aviator wing style with an oak leaf cluster in the center. The photograph below is a line drawing depicting the wings.

Enlisted Aviation Warfare Specialist Wings

In order to recognize enlisted personnel serving in naval aviation who were not aircrew members, a new program and set of wings was established. The Operational Navy Instruction (OPNAVINST) 1412.5 of 19 March 1980 established the Enlisted Aviation Warfare Qualification Program and the new wing insignia. The enlisted aviation warfare specialist wings are issued to enlisted personnel who acquired the specific professional skills, knowledge, and military experience that resulted in unique qualification for service in the aviation activities of the Navy.

The 1981 uniform regulations described the aviation warfare wings as follows: "A silver embroidered or silver color metal pin (for enlisted); winged, with a central device consisting of a shield with an anchor superimposed thereon and a scroll at the bottom of the insignia."

Balloon Pilot Wing Insignia

The exact date the balloon pilot wing device was approved is not clear. However, the description of the wing first appeared in the uniform regulations of 20 September 1922. In this regulation the following statement appears: "Enlisted men holding certificates of qualification as balloon pilots shall wear the same insignia as in paragraph (a) but with the right wing removed." Paragraph (a) was a description of the naval aviator wings. There were no changes between 1922 and 1947. In the uniform regulations of 2 May 1947, the words "Enlisted men" are replaced by "Persons" in the above statement. The 1978 U.S. Navy uniform regulations removed the Balloon Pilot insignia from the authorized list of aviation breast insignia.

Flight Nurse Wing Insignia

BuPers Circular Letter Number 86-45 of 30 March 1945 announced the Secretary of the Navy had approved an insignia for naval flight nurses on 15 March 1945. The change to the 1941 uniform regulations read:

> Aviation Insignia, Naval Flight Nurses—Nurses who have been designated as Naval Flight Nurses shall wear the following insignia: Gold-plated metal pin, wings, with slightly convex oval crest with appropriate embossed rounded edge and scroll. The central device shall be surcharged with gold anchor, gold spread oak leaf and silver acorn, symbol of the Nurse Corps insignia. The insignia shall measure 2" from tip to tip of the wings; oval crest $9/16$" in vertical dimension and $7/16$" in width; oak leaf $13/32$" in length, $7/32$" in width, to be diagonally mounted surcharged on the anchor; silver acorn $1/8$" in length surmounted on oak leaf.

The insignia was to be worn until the designation "Flight Nurse" was revoked.

These are the 1945 Flight Nurse Wings.

On 11 August 1952, the Secretary of the Navy approved a revision to the insignia. The BuPers Change Memo 1-2 of 6 February 1953 described the new version as: "The insignia shall consist of a gold color metal pin of the same design as that prescribed for Flight Surgeons . . . except that the acorn shall be omitted, and the width between wing tips shall be 2"; oval width $15/32$" vertical and $5/16$" horizontal axis; thickness at leaf center, $1/8$"."

This version of the Flight Nurse Wing Insignia was approved in 1952.

Flight Surgeon Wing Insignia

On 18 May 1942, the Chief of Naval Personnel approved an insignia for naval flight surgeons. BuPers Circular Letter Number 107-42 of 29 July 1942 announced changes to the 1941 uniform regulations. These, as approved by the Secretary of the Navy, included the establishment of the new flight surgeon wings. The change read:

> Officers of the Medical Corps who have qualified as Naval Flight Surgeons shall wear the following insignia on the left breast: A gold plated metal pin, winged, with slightly convex oval crest, with appropriate embossed rounded edge and scroll. The central device to be surcharged with gold

oak leaf and silver acorn, symbol of Medical Corps insignia. The metal pin shall be of dull finish. Dimensions: 2³/₄ inches between wing tips, central device 1 inch in vertical dimension to lower edge of fringe. Lateral width of oval crest, ³/₄ inch. Oak leaf ⁷/₈ inch in length, ⁹/₁₆ inch in width, to be vertically mounted surcharged on oval. Silver acorn ³/₈ inch in length surmounted on oak leaf.

A Navy Press Release issued a few days earlier, on 27 July 1942, noted, "It will consist of wings which are a modification of the Perian Feroher with a central design consisting of convex oval crest with appropriate scroll and rounded edge. The central device is to be surcharged with the gold leaf and silver acorn that serves as the Medical Corps symbol."

These are the Flight Surgeon Wings approved in 1942.

On 11 August 1952, the Secretary of the Navy approved a major revision to the flight surgeon wings. The new design superimposed the Medical Corps device (gold oak leaf and silver acorn) on the style of wings used for the naval aviator wing insignia. BuPers Memo 1-2 of 6 February 1953 and the change to the 1951 uniform regulations describes the new design:

A gold embroidered or gold color metal pin; winged; with an oval center design upon which the Medical Corps device (a gold oak leaf and silver acorn) is superimposed. Width between tips of wings shall be 2³/₄"; oval with ⁵/₈" vertical and ¹³/₃₂" horizontal axis; thickness with acorn ³/₁₆"; acorn and cup ⁷/₃₂" long; acorn width ¹/₈"; cup depth ¹¹/₁₆"; cup width ¹¹/₆₄".

These are the revised Flight Surgeon Wings of 1952.

Naval Astronaut (Naval Flight Officer) Wings

The 1984 uniform regulations, issued on 6 February 1984, authorized the wearing of the new naval astronaut (naval fight officer) wings. The regulations described them as: "Naval Astronaut (NFO) Insignia. A gold embroidered or solid gold metal pin; winged and containing a shooting star with an elliptical ring surrounding the trailing shafts; superimposed diagonally from bottom right to top left, on the shield of the traditional Naval Flight Officer's Wings."

A naval flight officer or an active duty officer qualified as a Naval Astronaut (Specialist), who is not a Navy pilot or NFO, may wear the naval astronaut (NFO) wings if they are designated by the CNO or Commandant of the Marine Corps after meeting the following qualifications:

a. Currently on flying status as a naval flight officer or a payload specialist as a shuttle astronaut (but not qualified as a Navy pilot or NFO) in either the Navy, Marine Corps, or their Reserve components.

b. Trained, qualified, and certified to fly as a mission or payload specialist in powered vehicles designed for flight above 50 miles from the earth's surface.

c. Have completed a minimum of one flight as a mission or payload specialist aboard an extraterrestrial vehicle in a flight above 50 miles from the earth's surface.

Naval Astronaut (Pilot) Wings

The Navy's first naval astronaut (pilot) wings were presented to Cmdr. Alan B. Shepard Jr. on 6 December 1961 by the Chief of Naval Operations, Adm. George W. Anderson. On 18 December 1962, the Secretary of the Navy officially approved the Uniform Board's recommendation to include a description and photograph of the naval astronaut wing insignia in the 1959 uniform regulations. The naval astronaut (pilot) wings are identical to the Navy pilot wings with the addition of a shooting star superimposed over the shield. The shooting star symbolized the astronaut's spatial environment.

The *Naval Military Personnel Manual* states the criteria for designation as a Naval Astronaut (Pilot). A naval pilot may wear the wings upon designation by the CNO or Commandant of the Marine Corps after meeting the following qualifications:

    a. Currently on flying status as a naval pilot in either the Navy, Marine Corps, or their reserve components.

    b. Trained, qualified, and certified to fly a powered vehicle designed for flight above 50 miles from the earth's surface.

    c. Completed a minimum of one flight as a pilot or mission specialist aboard an extraterrestrial vehicle in a flight above 50 miles from the earth's surface.

Naval Aviation Observer Wings

The Naval Aviation Observer (NAO) designation had its origin in an act of Congress on 12 July 1921, which created the Bureau of Aeronautics and provided that its chief qualify within one year of his appointment as an "aircraft pilot or observer." The functions and qualifications for an observer were first defined on 27 March 1922; on 17 June of the same year, Rear Adm. William A. Moffett became the first to qualify for the designation as a Naval Aviation Observer.

The 1922 uniform regulations, approved 20 September, provided that officers designated as Naval Aviation Observer wear the same insignia as that worn by naval aviators, except with the right wing and shield removed and an "O" superimposed on the foul anchor.

This, the first Naval Aviation Observer Wing Insignia, was used from 1922 to January 1927.

A 26 January 1927 change to the 1922 uniform regulations (Change Number 3) modified the design and changed it to the same insignia worn by naval aviators except that it was to be in silver.

Between January 1927 and October 1929 the design of Naval Aviation Observer Wings was identical to the gold Naval Aviator Wings except the observer wings were silver.

Bureau of Navigation Circular Letter 71-29 of 19 October 1929 (Change Number 7 to the 1922 uniform regulations) directed another change. This described the new design as: "an insignia the same as for naval aviators as to gold wings, but that the central device shall be an 'O' circumscribing an erect plain anchor, both in silver.

The 'O' and anchor to be in bold relief, the center of the 'O' being filled in gold." The 1941 uniform regulations, of 31 May 1941, repeated the previous description and added dimensions: ". . . outer diameter of 'O' shall be ³/₄ inch, inner diameter ⁹/₁₆ inch. Height of anchor shall be ¹/₂ inch."

This Naval Aviation Observer Wing
design was used by the Navy between
1929 to 1968.

The wings made the same transition that occurred to the naval aviator wings during WWII. A change to the 1951 uniform regulations, issued on 6 February 1953 as BuPers Change Memorandum 1-2, directed the wing style used by the naval aviator breast insignia be adopted for the Naval Aviation Observer insignia. Hence, the series of dots, or circles were incorporated into the upper-part of the design where the wings break.

This detailed description of the insignia is from the uniform regulations of 6 April 1959:

> A gold embroidered or gold color metal pin, winged, with a central device consisting of an O circumscribing an erect, plain anchor, both in silver; the O and the anchor to be in bold relief, the center of the O being filled with gold. The insignia shall measure 2³/₄" between wing tips; outer diameter of O shall be ³/₄"; inner diameter of O shall be ⁹/₁₆"; height of anchor shall be ¹/₂" with other dimensions proportionate.

This Naval Aviation Observer Insignia
shows the dots in the upperpart of the wing.

In the 1950s and 1960s, the naval aviation observer wings were worn by officers who were radar intercept operators (RIOs), bombardier/navigators (BNs), and airborne electronic countermeasures operators (AECMs). They were also worn by enlisted personnel who were qualified navigators, airborne electronic countermeasures operators, airborne radio operators, VG jet aircraft flight engineers, and qualified observers.

On 18 July 1968, the CNO approved a new qualification breast insignia for Navy and Marine Corps personnel designated as Naval Flight Officers (NFOs). BuPers Notice 1020 of 24 August 1968 issued the change to the uniform regulations (NavPers 15665) for the new naval flight officer wings: "This new insignia will replace the Naval Aviation Observer insignia currently worn by Naval Flight Officers and will be authorized for wear upon source availability.

The Naval Aviation Observer insignia will become obsolete after 31 December 1968." This ended the old naval aviation observer wings for a short period of time. However, they were destined for continued use by naval aviation.

Naval Aviation Observer and Flight Meteorologist Wings

On 21 May 1969, the CNO approved the use of the naval aviation observer wings for wear by flight meteorologists and for those officers formerly entitled but not selected as naval flight officers. This change was incorporated into the 1959 uniform regulations by Bureau of Personnel Notice 1020 of 16 June 1969.

The 1969 uniform regulations, issued on 17 October 1969, did not mention the Flight Meteorologist insignia. However, the 1975 uniform regulations, which replaced the 1969 edition, listed the naval aviation observers and flight meteorologist wings. The 1975 regulations state:

> Naval Aviation Observer and Flight Meteorologist Insignia. A gold embroidered or gold color metal pin; winged, with a central device consisting of an O circumscribing an erect, plan anchor, both in silver; the O and the anchor to be in bold relief, the center of the O being filled with gold. The embroidered device shall be on a background to match the color of the uniform on which worn.

Qualifications to wear the naval aviation observer wings, the second oldest wings in the Navy, are outlined in the *Naval Military Personnel Manual*. Although not aeronautically designated, the following types of officers are authorized to wear NAO wings upon initial qualification: Flight Meteorology and Oceanography Officer; Special Evaluator (officers and warrant officers from the cryptologic community); Aviation Operations Limited Duty Officer (632X); Aviation Operations Technician Warrant Officer (732X); and other officers assigned by the Chief of Naval Personnel to duty involving flying as technical observers and airborne command post crew members.

The Marine Corps authorized the use of the old naval aviation observer wings for personnel completing the Naval Aviation Observer School at Marine Corps Air Station New River. Qualified aerial observers were to provide commanders with information of intelligence value not readily available from normal ground sources regarding enemy forces; procure information concerning terrain, and to supplement operational information of friendly forces; direct supporting fires for ground forces to include artillery, naval gunfire, and close air support; to perform utility and liaison missions as directed from an observation aircraft and to advise commanders of ground units on matters pertaining to aerial observation.

See the section on Naval Aviation Observer Wings for a photograph of the device.

Naval Aviation Observer (Navigation) Wings

BuPers Circular Letter 88-45 of 31 March 1945 announced the Secretary of the Navy had approved an insignia for Naval Aviation Observers (Navigation) on 30 March 1945. It revised the 1941 uniform regulations by adding the following:

> Officers designated as Naval Aviation Observers (Navigation) by the Chief of Naval Personnel shall wear the following insignia: A gold-embroidered or bronze gold-plated metal pin, winged, with silver center device superimposed upon crossed gold-color foul anchors. The centerpiece shall have superimposed upon it, in bold relief and in gold color, one gold disc with eight intercardinal points of the compass; superimposed upon this gold disc will be a second disc, in bold relief and in gold color, with four cardinal points and four intercardinal points of the compass. The insignia shall measure 2³/₄" from tip to tip of wings; silver center device shall be approximately ¹⁵/₃₂" in diameter; crossed foul anchors shall be of a size to be inscribed in a circle ³/₄" in diameter; the inner gold disc shall be approximately ¹/₈" in diameter, and the outer gold disc shall be approximately ¹/₄" in diameter. Naval Aviators and Naval Aviation Observers will not wear the Naval Aviation Observer (Navigation) insignia.

A Bureau of Naval Personnel letter dated 18 March 1947 abolished the Naval Aviation Observer (Navigation) insignia and authorized all officers designated as Naval Aviation Observer (Navigation) to wear the same insignia as that worn by Naval Aviation Observers.

Naval Aviation Observers (Radar) Wings

The Secretary of the Navy approved the Naval Aviation Observer (Radar) insignia on 29 August 1945. BuPers Circular Letter Number 313-45 of 17 October 1945 announced the insignia and a subsequent change was made to the 1941 uniform regulations. The letter described the wings as follows: "Naval Aviation Observers (Radar) shall wear a gold embroidered or bronze gold-platted metal pin, winged, with silver center device superimposed upon crossed gold-color foul anchors. The center piece shall have superimposed upon it, in bold relief and in gold color, a symbolic radar manifestation. The insignia shall measure 2³/₄" from tip to tip of wings; silver center device shall be approximately ¹⁵/₃₂" in diameter; crossed foul anchors shall be of a size to be inscribed in a circle ³/₄" in diameter. Naval Aviation Observers (Radar) shall not wear any other aviation breast insignia."

A Bureau of Naval Personnel letter dated 18 March 1947 abolished the Naval Aviation Observers (Radar) insignia, and authorized all officers designated as Naval Aviation Observers (Radar) to wear the same insignia prescribed for Naval Aviation Observers.

Naval Aviation Observers (Tactical) Wing

On 19 January 1946, the Secretary of the Navy approved the naval aviation observers (tactical) wings for Navy and Marine Corps officers performing duty as gunfire and artillery spotters and general liaison operations. A BuPers Circular Letter Number 28-46 of 5 February 1946 changed the 1941 uniform regulations to reflect that Naval Aviation Observers (Tactical) would wear a device similar to the Naval Aviation Observer (Navigation) insignia except "the centerpiece shall have two crossed guns superimposed upon it, in bold relief and in gold color." The BuPers letter provided the following description:

> Naval Aviation Observers (Tactical) shall wear a gold embroidered or bronze gold-plated metal pin, winged, with silver center device superimposed upon crossed gold-color foul anchors. The center piece shall have two crossed guns superimposed upon it, in bold relief and in gold color. The insignia shall measure $2^3/_4$" from tip to tip of wings; silver center device shall be approximately $^{15}/_{32}$" in diameter; crossed foul anchors shall be of a size to be inscribed in a circle $^3/_4$" in diameter and the crossed guns shall be of a size to be inscribed in a circle $^{13}/_{32}$" in diameter.

A Bureau of Naval Personnel letter dated 18 March 1947 abolished the Naval Aviation Observers (Tactical) insignia and authorized all officers designated as Naval Aviation Observers (Tactical) to wear the same insignia prescribed for Naval Aviation Observers.

Naval Aviation Observer (Aerology)

BuPers Circular Letter Number 87-47 of 15 May 1947 established the designation Naval Aviation Observer (Aerology). Besides establishing the qualifications necessary for the designation, the circular letter also stated that: "Officers designated naval aviation observers (aerology) by the Chief of Naval Personnel will be authorized to wear the insignia already established for naval aviation observers . . ." BuPers letter (Pers-329-MEB A2-3) of 24 February 1948 issued Change 1 to the 1947 uniform regulations and states:

> Naval Aviation Observer Insignia. Officers who have been designated as naval aviation observers, Naval Aviation Observers (Aerology), Naval Aviation Observers (Navigation), Naval Aviation Observers (Radar), or Naval Aviation Observers (Tactical) by the Chief of Naval Personnel shall wear the following insignia: A gold embroidered or bronze gold-plated metal pin, winged, with a central device consisting of an "O" circumscribing an erect, plan anchor, both in silver; the "O" and the anchor to be in bold relief, the center of the "O" being filled with gold. The insignia shall measure 2³/4" between wing tips; the outer diameter of the "O" shall be ³/4", the inner diameter ⁹/16"; height of anchor shall be ¹/2". The embroidered device shall be on a background to match the color of the uniform.

See the Naval Aviation Observer Wing section for a photograph of the Naval Aviation Observer wing.

Naval Flight Officer Wings

On 8 February 1965, a change to Bureau of Personnel Instruction 1210.4C authorized a new designator and name, Naval Flight Officer (NFO). The new designator was appropriate for "an unrestricted line officer, a member of the aeronautical organization . . . who may fill any billet not requiring actual control knowledge of an aircraft." Eight subspecialties were available at the time: bombardier, controller, electronic countermeasures evaluator, navigator, interceptor, photographer-navigator, tactical coordinator, and reconnaissance navigator. The new NFOs continued wearing the naval aviation observer wings.

On 18 July 1968, the CNO approved a new qualification breast insignia for Navy and Marine Corps personnel designated as Naval Flight Officers (NFOs). BuPers Notice 1020 of 24 August 1968 changed the uniform regulations (NAVPers 15665). The notice stated: "This new insignia will replace the Naval Aviation Observer insignia currently worn by Naval Flight Officers and will be authorized for wear upon source availability. The Naval Aviation Observer insignia will become obsolete after 31 December 1968." In this change to the uniform regulations (NAVPERS 15665) all references to Naval Aviation Observers were changed to Naval Flight Officer. Article 0157.2d. of the uniform regulations read: "Naval Flight Officer Insignia. A gold embroidered or gold color metal pin; winged, with a central device consisting of a shield superimposed on a set of small, crossed, fouled anchors. The embroidered device shall be on a background to match the color of the uniform on which worn."

The naval flight officer wings were approved to keep pace with the changes to the designators and new titles for personnel that had been designated Naval Aviation Observers. Flight officers are more closely aligned with pilots as opposed to meteorologists and other scientists. Also, the flying officer/crewmen were line officers who were allowed to compete for and earn any command assignment for which they qualify by demonstrated performance and ability, with the exception of a billet that required actual control knowledge of an aircraft. Hence, naval flight officers were line officers who could qualify for command of a ship or carrier or commanding officer of a squadron just like naval aviators.

Professional Aviation Maintenance Officer Wing Insignia

NAVADMIN 051/09 issued by CNO message of 10 February 2009 (102033Z FEB 09) approved the Professional Aviation Maintenance Officer (PAMO) designation and wing insignia that had been recommended for approval by the Navy Uniform Board in November 2008. Qualification requirements for the PAMO were outlined in OPNAV Instruction 1412.11 of 19 May 2009. The designation and wings are designed to recognize the significant contributions made by aviation ground officers in support of the Navy's aviation mission and warfighting capabilities.

The PAMO wing insignia is $2^3/4$ inches by $1^1/8$ inches. It is a gold and silver metal device showing the silver eagle and shield superimposed over gold aviation wings with a gold banner depicting "AERO MAINTENANCE". It will have either an anodized or oxidized finish.

Navy and Marine Corps Parachutist Wing Insignia

BuPers Notice 1020 of 12 July 1963 issued information on a change to the 1959 uniform regulations concerning the adoption of a new wing insignia for Navy and Marine Corps parachutists. This notice stated: "The old parachutist insignia . . . shall be renamed the 'Basic Parachutist Insignia' in conformance with the Army and Air Force nomenclature. The subject insignia shall be referred to as the 'Navy and Marine Corps Parachutist Insignia'." The insignia was described as:

> A gold embroidered (Navy only) or gold-colored metal pin, same as that provided for Naval Aviator's insignia, except that a gold-colored open parachute shall be centered on the wings vice the shield and foul anchor; width of the wings from tip to tip shall be $2^3/4$"; width of the parachute $1/2$" at the widest part; length of the parachute from top to bottom $13/16$".

General qualifications for wearing the Navy and Marine Corps Parachutist Wings were:

1. Have previously qualified for the Basic Parachutist insignia by completing formal parachutist training at an armed services installation.

2. Have completed a minimum of five additional parachute jumps, under competent orders, with a Navy or Marine Corps organization whose mission includes parachute jumping.

Once a person qualified for the Navy and Marine Corps parachutist insignia it will be worn in lieu of the basic parachutist insignia.

Basic Parachutist Wing Insignia

The first mention of a parachutist designation and qualification badge is found in a change to the 1941 uniform regulations issued by a BuNav Circular Letter Number 51-42 of 31 March 1942. It stated:

> The following Parachute Regulations, having been approved by the Secretary of the Navy on 6 February 1942, are published herewith for the information of all concerned:

> 1. (2) DESIGNATION: The designation (ratings) of "Parachutist" and "Student Parachutist" are hereby established for officers, warrant officers, and enlisted men of the Navy and Marine Corps of the United States, which designations (ratings) shall be in addition to such military or Naval ratings or ranks as are now or may hereafter be authorized by law.
> (5) RETENTION OF DESIGNATION AS PARACHUTIST OR STUDENT PARACHUTIST: An officer, warrant officer or enlisted man of the Navy . . . who has attained a designation (rating) as a parachutist or student parachutist . . . provided, that officers, warrant officers, and enlisted men . . . who have been designated as parachutists pursuant to these regulations are authorized to retain permanently and to wear such qualification badge as parachutists as may be prescribed by competent authority.

However, the Secretary of the Navy did not authorize the parachutist badge, even though the above change to the 1941 uniform regulation references the wearing of such a qualification badge. There is no description of a parachutist insignia until January 1947. A BuPers letter (Pers-329-MEB A2-3) of 17 January 1947 issued changes to the 1941 uniform regulations as approved by the Secretary of the Navy. This letter states:

> (j) A parachutist insignia, enclosure (B), has been authorized for enlisted personnel who have been designated as parachutists in accordance with the Bureau of Naval Personnel Manual. This insignia is the same as the parachutist insignia authorized by the Marine Corps and the Army.
> 2. The wearing of the parachutist insignia, enclosure (B), by officers and warrant officers who have been designated as parachutists in accordance with the Bureau of Naval Personnel Manual has also been authorized. Pending a revision of Chapters II and III, U.S. Navy Uniform Regulations, 1941, officers and warrant officers who are eligible to wear the parachutist insignia may do so under similar regulations contained in Art. 8-8 of enclosure (A).

A 14 February 1947 letter from BuPers issued the new Chapter II to the 1941 uniform regulations and included the parachutist insignia.

The 1951 uniform regulations described the parachutist insignia as: "An open parachute, in silver, flanked on each side by wings, curved upward; the device to be 1 1/2" wide and 3/4" high." A BuPers Notice 1020 of 12 July 1963 issued information on a change to the 1959 uniform regulations concerning the adoption of a new wing insignia for Navy and Marine Corps Parachutists. This notice stated: "The old parachutist insignia . . . shall be renamed the 'Basic Parachutist Insignia' in conformance with the Army and Air Force nomenclature."

Marine Aerial Navigator Wings

In June 1976, the Marine Corps approved the use of the old WWII Naval Aviation Observer (Navigation) wings for use by Marine Corps personnel who qualified as Marine Aerial Navigators. *See* the section on Naval Aviation Observer (Navigation) wings for a description and photograph of the wings.

Marine Aerial Observer Wings

See the section on Naval Aviation Observer and Flight Meteorologist Wings. These are the wings worn by Marine aerial observers.

CHAPTER 10

Aviation Ratings

Enlisted men have served in naval aviation since its inception. The first men reported for duty with Lt. Theodore G. Ellyson and Lt. John Rodgers when they began flight training in 1911. Their numbers increased as the number of aviators and aircraft on hand increased. Despite the specialties involved in aviation, it was a number of years before these men were required to meet special qualifications beyond those of their basic rating. Such special courses as enlisted men received in the 1916–1917 period gave them a certificate to prove satisfactory completion and made them better qualified to carry out aviation duty. However, it had no effect on their basic ratings, the qualifications for which were still based on the requirements of the regular naval service.

Greater emphasis on aviation requirements accompanied the expansion for WW I and with it the basic requirements of the pre-war period were somewhat relaxed but not completely forgotten. One indication of change was a parenthetical addition to the rating to indicate aviation duty, as for example, Machinist's Mate (Aviation) or MM (A). But it was not until 1921 that aviation ratings received recognition as a special branch and the first strictly aviation ratings were established. Since then, adjustments to the rating structure have been frequent. These produced a number of changes and additions to the original basic ratings as well as a great variety of subdivisions within them, some representing a mere change in title, others reflecting changing technology.

The following list covers the aviation basic ratings, shown in alphabetical order.

Aerographer

Rating (**Aerog**) established effective 1 Jul 1924 by CL 99-23 of Dec 1923; distinguishing mark approved by CL 62-26 of 29 Oct 1926˙; *See* Aerographer's Mate.

Aerographer's Mate

Aerographer rating (**Aerog**) redesignated Aerographer's Mate (**AerM**) by CL 113-42 of 8 Aug 1942, abbreviation changed to (**AG**) by CL 106-48 of 9 Jun 1948.

Air Controlman

Rating (**SP**) established effective 2 Apr 1948 by CL 40-47 of 21 Feb 1947; abbreviation changed to (**AC**) by CL 106-48 of 9 Jun 1948; *See* Air Traffic Controller.

Aircraft Maintenanceman

A master chief's rating (**AFCM**) approved by SecNav, 5 Nov 1963. *See* Aviation Machinist's Mate.

Aircrew Survival Equipmentman

Parachute Rigger rating (**PR**) redesignated Aircrew Survival Equipmentman effective 7 Dec 1965 by BuPers Note 1440 of 2 Feb 1966, without change of abbreviation.

Airship Rigger

Rating (**AR**) established by CL 205-43 of 12 Oct 1943; distinguishing mark approved by CL 58-44 of 29 Feb 1944'; abolished effective 2 Apr 1948 by CL 246-47 of 15 Dec 1947.

Air Traffic Controller

Air Controlman rating (**AC**) redesignated Air Traffic Controller by BuPers Note 1220 of 10 December 1977, without change in abbreviation.

Aviation Antisubmarine Warfare Operator

Rating (**AW**) established effective 1 Sep 1968 by BuPers Note 1440 of 29 Feb 1968. The Aviation Antisubmarine Warfare Operator rating was redesignated Aviation Warfare Systems Operator by BuPers Note 1440 of 16 November 1993 without change of abbreviation; *See* Aviation Warfare Systems Operator.

Aviation Antisubmarine Warfare Technician

Rating (**AX**) was established effective 1 Dec 1962 by BuPers Note 1440 of 29 Jun 1962. The AX rating was absorbed into the (**AT**) rating by amendments to NAVOP 075/89 of 23 Aug 1990, effective 1 Jan 1991; *See* Aviation Electronics Technician.

Aviation Boatswain's Mate

Rating (**ABM**) established by CL 268-44 of 14 Sep 1944; distinguishing mark approved CL 363-44 of 30 Nov 1944; abbreviation changed to (**AB**) by CL 106-48 of 9 Jun 1948. Three sub-ratings were created for the Aviation Boatswain's Mate. Responsibilities for the (**ABH**) rating (Aviation Boatswain's Mate–Aircraft Handler) include movement, spotting and securing of aircraft and equipment ashore and afloat; performing crash rescue, fire fighting, crash removal, and damage control duties in connection with launching and recovery of aircraft. The (**ABF**) Aviation Boatswain's Mate–Fuels responsibilities include operating, maintaining, and performing organizational maintenance on aviation fueling and lubricating oil systems on CVs, CVNs, LPHs, and LPDs; observing and enforcing handling safety precautions and maintaining fuel quality surveillance and control in aviation fuel systems; supervising the operation and servicing of fuel farms and equipment associated with the fueling and defueling of aircraft ashore and afloat; and training, directing, and supervising fire fighting crews, fire rescue teams, and damage control parties in assigned fuel and lubricating oil spaces. Aviation Boatswain's Mate–Launch/Recovery (**ABE**) responsibilities include maintaining and performing organization maintenance on hydraulic and steam catapults, barricades, arresting gear, and arresting gear engines; operating catapult launch and arresting consoles, firing panels, water brakes, blast deflectors, and cooling panels; and performing aircraft-handling duties related to the operation of launching and recovery of naval aircraft. The (**AB**) designation is used only for the pay grade E-9 (Master Chief).

Aviation Bombsight Mechanic

Rating (**AOMB**) established as a sub-rating of Aviation Ordnanceman by CL 205-43 of 12 Oct 1943; *See* Aviation Bombsight and Fire Control Mechanic.

Aviation Bombsight And Fire Control Mechanic

Aviation Bombsight Mechanic rating (**AOMB**) renamed Aviation Bombsight and Fire Control Mechanic by CL 355-44 of 27 Nov 1944, without change in abbreviation. The Aviation Bombsight and Fire Control Mechanic (**AOMB**) was redesignated Aviation Fire Controlman (**AFC**) and was designated a basic rate by CL 39-45 of 15 Feb 1945; *See* Aviation Fire Controlman.

Aviation Carpenter's Mate

The Aviation Carpenter's mate rating (**ACM**) was established effective 1 Jul 1921 by CL 9-21 of 24 Mar 1921; distinguishing mark approved by CL 62-26 of 29 Oct 1926ˑ; the (**ACM**) rating was abolished effective 30 Jun 1940 by CL 36-40 of 21 May 1940 and redesignated Aviation Metalsmith (**AM**); *See* Aviation Metalsmith.

Aviation Electrician's Mate

The Aviation Electrician's Mate rating (**AEM**) was established by CL 129-42 of 4 Sep 1942; abbreviation changed to (**AE**) by CL 106-48 of 9 Jun 1948.

Aviation Electronicsman

The Aviation Radioman rating (**ARM**) was redesignated Aviation Electronicsman effective 2 Apr 1948 by CL 40-47 of 21 Feb 1947, without change in abbreviation; abbreviation changed to (**AL**) by CL 106-48 of 9 Jun 1948; abolished by BuPers Instruction 1440.10B of 18 Dec 1959.

Aviation Electronics Technician

Aviation Electronics Technician's Mate rating (**AETM**) was redesignated Aviation Electronics Technician (**AET**) effective 2 Apr 1948 by CL 40-47 of 21 Feb 1947; abbreviation changed to (**AT**) by CL 106-48 of 9 Jun 1948. Ratings (**AQ**), (**AX**), and (**AV**) were scheduled to merge and be redesignated (**AT**) by NAVOP 075/89 of 27 Jun 1989; the (**AV**) rating was removed so only ratings (**AQ**) and (**AX**) were absorbed into the already existing rate of (**AT**) by amendments to NAVOP 075/89 of 23 Aug 1990, effective 1 Jan 1991. The Master Chief rating for Aviation Electronics Technician (Intermediate) and (Organization) remained (**AVCM**). *See* Avionics Technician.

Aviation Electronics Technician's Mate

Aviation Radio Technician rating (**ART**) redesignated Aviation Electronics Technician's Mate (**AETM**) by CL 325-45 of 31 Oct 1945. The Aviation Electronics Technician's Mate rating (**AETM**) was redesignated Aviation Electronics Technician (**AET**) effective 2 Apr 1948 by CL 40-47 of 21 Feb 1947; *See* Aviation Electronics Technician.

Aviation Fire Controlman

Aviation Bombsight and Fire Control Mechanic (**AOMB**) was redesignated Aviation Fire Controlman (**AFC**) and became a basic rate by CL 39-45 of 15 Feb 1945; abolished effective 2 Apr 1948 by CL 40-47 of 21 Feb 1947; *See* Aviation Fire Control Technician.

Aviation Fire Control Technician

The Aviation Fire Control Technician rating (**AQ**) was established in 1954 from sub-ratings of the former Aviation Fire Controlman and in a sense a revival of that rating; under amendments to NAVOP 075/89 of 23 Aug 1990 the (**AQ**) rating was absorbed into the (**AT**) rating; *See* Aviation Electronics Technician.

Aviation Guided Missileman

The Aviation Guided Missileman rating (**GF**) was established and approved by SecNav 23 Jan 1953; abolished by BuPers Instruction 1440.25 of 10 Jun 1960, effective 1 Jul 1960.

Aviation Machinist's Mate

The Aviation Machinist's Mate rating (**AMM**) was established effective 1 July 1921 by CL 9-21 of 24 Mar 1921; distinguishing mark approved by CL 17-41 of 11 Feb 1941; abbreviation changed to (**AD**) by CL 106-48 of 9 Jun 1948.

Aviation Maintenance Administrationman

The Aviation Maintenance Administrationman rating (**AZ**) was established effective 1 Jan 1964 by BuPers Note 1440 of 22 Jan 1963.

Aviation Metalsmith

The Aviation Metalsmith rating (**AM**) was established effective 1 Jul 1921 by CL 9-21 of 24 Mar 1921; the Aviation Carpenter's Mate rating (**ACM**) was abolished and incorporated into the Aviation Metalsmith (**AM**) rating by CL 36-40 of 21 May 1940; the Aviation Metalsmith rating (**AM**) was redesignated Aviation Structural Mechanic effective 2 Apr 1948 by CL 40-47 of 21 Feb 1947, without change in abbreviation. *See* Aviation Structural Mechanic.

Aviation Ordnanceman

The Aviation Ordnanceman rating (**AOM**) was established by CL 14-26 of 2 Mar 1926; abbreviation changed to (**AO**) by CL 106-48 of 9 Jun 1948.

Aviation Photographer's Mate

See Photographer's Mate.

Aviation Pilot

Rating (**AP**) established by CL 18-24 of 13 Mar 1924, changed to Chief Aviation Pilot and Aviation Pilot First Class by CL 66-27 of 21 Sep 1927, and abolished by a change from a rating to a designation by CL 10-33 of 28 Mar 1933; distinguishing mark approved by CL 24-33 of 30 June 1933'; reestablished as a rating by CL 43-42 of 17 Mar 1942, and again abolished by a change to a designation, effective 2 Apr 1948 by CL 40-47 of 21 Feb 1947. *See* Chapter 8 for more information on Naval Aviation Pilots.

Aviation Quartermaster (Quartermaster, Aviation)

The Quartermaster, Aviation rating was established by BuNav Letter N9H/B-5690 of 16 October 1918; the Quartermaster, Aviation rating was redesignated Aviation Rigger (**AR**) effective 1 Jul 1921 by CL 9-21 of 24 Mar 1921; *See* Aviation Rigger.

Aviation Radioman

The Aviation Radioman rating (**ARM**) was established by CL 5-42 of 13 Jan 1942; the distinguishing mark for the Aviation Radioman (**ARM**) and Aviation Radio Technician (**ART**) are identified as the same specialty marking used by both in the 1944 edition of *The Bluejackets Manual*; *See* Aviation Electronicsman.

Aviation Radio Technician

Rating (**ART**) established by CL 169-42 of 11 Dec 1942, according to the 1944 edition of *The Bluejackets Manual* the same specialty marking was used for Aviation Radioman (**ARM**) and Aviation Radio Technician (**ART**); *See* Aviation Electronics Technician's Mate.

Aviation Rigger

Aviation Quartermaster rating was redesignated Aviation Rigger (**AR**) effective 1 Jul 1921 by CL 9-21 of 24 Mar 1921; abolished effective 30 Jun 1927 by CL 13-26 of 25 Feb 1926.

Aviation Storekeeper

The Aviation Storekeeper rating (**SKV**) was established and approved by SecNav on 28 Sep 1943; distinguishing mark approved by CL 65-45 of 15 Mar 1945'; abbreviation changed to (**AK**) by CL 106-48 of 9 Jun 1948. Aviation Storekeeper rate (**AK**) was abolished NAVADMIN 023/00 dated 10 Feb 2000 with final conversion of all AKs to Storekeeper (**SK**) by 1 Jan 2003.

Aviation Structural Mechanic

Aviation Metalsmith rating (**AM**) redesignated Aviation Structural Mechanic effective 2 Apr 1948 by CL 40-47 of 21 Feb 1947, without change in abbreviation. Three sub-ratings for (**AM**) were created: (**AME**) Aviation Structural Mechanic–Safety Equipment, (**AMH**) Aviation Structural Mechanic–Hydraulics, and (**AMS**) Aviation Structural Mechanic–Structures. NAVADMIN dated 21 Jun 2000 announced the merger of the sub-ratings (**AMS**) and (**AMH**) into the general (**AM**) rating using the regular (**AM**) rating badge. The effective date for the completion of this action was 1 Mar 2001.

Aviation Support Equipment Technician

The Aviation Support Equipment Technician rating (**AS**) was established effective 1 Sep 1966 by BuPers Note 1440 of 24 Feb 1966.

Aviation Warfare Systems Operator

Aviation Antisubmarine Warfare Operator rating (**AW**) was established on 1 Sep 1968 by BuPers Note 1440 of 29 Feb 1968 and redesignated Aviation Warfare Systems Operator by BuPers Note 1440 of 16 Nov 1993, without change of abbreviation. NavAdmin 092/05 of 2 May 2005 directed the consolidation of Enlisted Naval Aircrew (NAC) ratings into Naval Aircrewman (**AW**) with five subspecialities and eliminated the Aviation Warfare Systems Operator designation. *See* Naval Aircrewman.

Avionics Technician

A master chief's rating (**AVCM**) established and approved by SecNav, 5 Nov 1963, this rating applies to the functional areas of Aviation Electronics Technician (Intermediate) and (Organizational); *See* Aviation Electronics Technician.

Naval Aircrewman

The Naval Aircrewman (**AW**) rating was established by NavAdmin 092/05 of 2 May 2005 and eliminated the rating Aviation Warfare Systems Operator but maintained the (**AW**) designation. The (**AW**) designation is only for Master Chief Naval Aircrewman effective 1 October 2008. There are five subspecialities of Naval Aircrewman: (**AWF**) for Naval Aircrewman Mechanical, (**AWO**) for Naval Aircrewman Operator, (**AWS**) for Naval Aircrewman Helicopter, (**AWR**) for Naval Aircrewman Tactical Helicopter, and (**AWV**) for Naval Aircrewman Avionics. Naval Aircrewman will continue to use the Aviation Warfare Systems Operator rating badge.

Parachute Rigger

The Parachute Rigger rating (**PR**) was established by CL 33-42 of 24 Feb 1942; the Parachute Rigger rating was redesignated Aircrew Survival Equipmentman effective 7 Dec 1965; *See* Aircrew Survival Equipmentman.

Photographer

Rating (**P**) established in the Aviation Branch effective 1 Jul 1921 by CL 9-21 of 24 Mar 1921, apparently later transferred to Special Branch, but returned to the Aviation Branch by CL 14-26 of 2 Mar 1926; *See* Photographer's Mate.

Photographer's Mate

Photographer's rating (**P**) redesignated Photographer's Mate (**PhoM**) by CL 113-42 of 8 Aug 1942 and removed from the Aviation Branch; rating split into Photographer's Mate and Aviation Photographer's Mate (both **PhoM**) effective 2 Apr 1948 by CL 40-47 of 21 Feb 1947; abbreviation changed to (**AF**) by CL 106-48 of 9 Jun 1948; ratings combined to become Photographer's Mate (**PH**) of the Aviation Group by CL 116-50 of 31 Jul 1950. The (**PH**), (**JO**), (**LI**), and (**DM**) ratings were merged to form a new rating called Mass Communications Specialist (**MC**) as directed by NAVADMIN 339/05 OF 28 Dec 2005.

Photographic Intelligenceman

The Photographic Intelligenceman rating (**PT**) was established by BuPers Note 1223 of 2 Oct 1957. The (**PT**) rate merged with (**YN**) NEC 2505 to form Intelligence Specialist (**IS**) (not an aviation rating) by BuPers Note 1440 of 6 Dec 1974.

Tradevman (Training Devices Repairman and Instructor)

The Tradevman rating (**TD**) was established by CL 106-48 of 9 Jun 1948; rate slated for disestablishment by BuPers Note 1440 of 22 Jul 1982 beginning in Fiscal Year (FY) 1984 with all conversions of personnel in this rate to be completed by the end of FY 1988.

---

* Distinguishing marks are for non-rated qualified as striker in a particular aviation rating (e.g. Aviation Machinist's Mate). The mark is worn midway between the wrist and elbow of the left sleeve. Distinguishing marks were superseded by the introduction of group rates used with striker marks by non-rated men in 1948.

CHAPTER 11

Aviation Personnel on Active Duty

1 July	Navy Officers			Navy Enlisted		Marine Corps Officers			Marine Corps Enlisted	
	Pilots	NFO	Other	Pilots	Aviation Rates	Pilots	NFO	Other	Pilots	Aviation Rates
1920	630		243		4,404					
1921	370		108		3,494					
1922	314		220		2,209					
1923	326		241		1,612					
1924	328		161		1,788					
1925	382		137		1,711					
1926	426		173		1,722					
1927	472		177	108	1,984					
1928	466		196	141	2,644					
1929	520		207	173	2,894					
1930	614		221	244	2,651	82		17	24	1,112
1931	737		427	330	2,806	98		15	33	999
1932	803		396	355	2,958	101		17	32	917
1933	826		450	337	11,949	103		15	30	913
1934	834		496	306	11,667	104		16	34	938
1935	867		559	280	12,129	110		15	28	985
1936	963		502	297	13,055	113		20	29	978
1937	1,002		530	355	15,091	135		20	41	1,093
1938	1,059		580	447	19,463	171		23	46	1,082
1939	1,068		609	533	19,907	180		16	47	1,091
1940	2,203		145	349	5,924	304		17	45	1,677
1941	3,483		963	629	10,640	453		27	52	3,051
1942	9,059		5,716	732	27,286	1,284		345	85	12,583
1943	20,847		20,958	774	105,445	4,898		2,419	132	50,485
1944	37,367		26,596	475	183,886	10,416		4,406	41	91,246
1945	49,380		27,946	439	241,364	10,229		5,080	47	96,354
1946 Data not available										
1947	10,052		3,054	537	44,201					
1948	10,232		2,475	629	56,767	1,955		213	352	11,629
1949	11,509		2,343	622	73,631	1,975		221	269	14,631
1950	9,481		1,906	920	63,505	1,922		214	255	12,017
1951	14,079		3,936	775	114,038	3,127		785	237	25,025
1952	15,774		4,633	715	129,412	4,169		1,472	210	38,359
1953	17,612		4,403	684	137,218	4,484		1,475	131	49,742
1954	16,722		4,078	631	125,102	3,848		1,647	123	39,748
1955	16,448		3,823	622	115,011	4,208		1,976	120	38,173
1956	17,193		4,209	264	135,600	4,399		1,778	109	36,232
1957	17,993		4,662	243	140,283	4,348		1,780	101	39,433
1958	18,236		4,683	210	134,212	4,225		1,697	102	37,027

| | Navy | | | | | Marine Corps | | | | |
| | Officers | | | Enlisted | | Officers | | | Enlisted | |
1 July	Pilots	NFO	Other	Pilots	Aviation Rates	Pilots	NFO	Other	Pilots	Aviation Rates
1959	17,813		4,572	179	127,811	3,937		1,281	105	32,900
1960	17,090		4,977	124	121,985	3,958		1,329	96	30,326
1961	17,354		4,475	87	123,134	4,031		1,349	66	34,253
1962	18,301		6,436	70	135,453	4,087		1,437	51	41,476
1963	17,613		6,567	59	132,538	4,131		1,594	27	41,834
1964	17,074		7,069	51	130,742	4,234		2,132	23	41,791
1965§	16,570		7,932	43	126,988	4,372		2,346	17	41,563
1966	16,469		8,649	37	133,359	4,541		2,963	13	36,232
1967	15,973		8,985	35	139,742	4,401		3,987	12	60,192
1968	15,767		9,633	30	141,713	4,440		3,887	9	63,361
1969	15,274		10,220	27	147,679	4,648		3,973	5	62,858
1970	14,594		8,433	22	135,945	4,892		4,241	4	62,032
1971	14,890		8,215	13	120,301	4,917		3,569	4	54,672
1972	14,245		7,978	5	114,136	4,787		2,124	3	53,605
1973	13,665		7,701	3	111,329	4,384		3,126		48,110
1974	13,236		7,690	1	108,203	4,042		2,927		32,527
1975˙	13,056		7,643	1	105,619	3,921		2,671		32,454
1976‖	12,560	4,128	2,302	1	101,058	3,712		2,744		30,338
1977†	11,608	3,970	2,343	1	102,445	3,644		2,679		30,499
30 Sep										
1978	10,632	4,268	2,271	1	108,180	3,429		2,850		28,176
1979	9,707	4,327	2,123	1	107,669	3,219		2,856		29,369
1980	9,487	4,377	2,012	1	107,996	2,312#	61#			34,059#
1981	9,828	4,666	1,954		109,915	2,532#	66#			33,832#
1982	10,203	4,819	1,891		112,209	2,780#	73#			35,532#
1983	10,483	5,160	2,223		114,722	2,991#	82#			37,972#
1984	10,479	5,280	2,425		115,325	3,086#	85#			41,408#
1985	10,559	5,566	2,685		114,866	3,119#	99#			42,050#
1986	10,516	5,734	2,796		117,886	3,056#	96#			39,846#
1987	10,748	5,966	2,749		122,563	3,357#	120#			38,163#
1988	10,835	6,111	2,723		123,428	3,423#	145#			36,523#
1989	11,022	6,241	2,641		123,651	3,429#	154#			36,136#
1990	11,018	6,340	2,534		118,611	3,492#	193#			37,024#
1991	10,491	6,109	2,487		114,056	3,582#	223#			37,114#
1992	10,338	6,060	2,443		113,943	3,536#	259#			36,644#
1993	9,162	5,222	1,116		72,182#	3,556#	303#			34,365#
1994	8,287	4,537	977		69,725#	3,473#	324#			33,260#
1995	7,751	4,079	939		63,309#	3,579#	353#			32,605#
1996	‡	‡	‡		‡	3,552#	361#			32,680#
1997	7,915	4,050	4,109˙˙		69,085#	3,467#	360#			32,843#
1998	7,431	3,848	4,313˙˙		67,179#	3,401#	371#			33,851#
1999	7,276	3,759	4,195˙˙		67,583#	3,441#	384#			34,942#
2000	7,286	3,741	4,254˙˙		68,654#	3,475#	403#			35,401#

30 Sep	Navy					Marine Corps				
	Officers			Enlisted		Officers			Enlisted	
	Pilots	NFO	Other	Pilots	Aviation Rates	Pilots	NFO	Other	Pilots	Aviation Rates
2001	7,348	3,871	4,030**		79,345#	‡	‡			35,580#
2002	7,469	3,871	4,233**		82,293#	‡	‡			36,327#
2003	7,686	3,838	4,308**		82,725#	‡	‡			36,735#
2004	7,859	3,801	4,016**		80,967#	4,006#	458#			37,675#
2005	7,823	3,738	3,860**		78,871#	3,965#	469#			37,768#
2006	7,779	3,618	3,789**		74,132#	3,924#	461#			36,824#
2007	7,808	3,540	4,020**		70,525#	3,956#	465#			37,531#
2008	7,022	3,273	4,080**		62,684#	3,913#	444#			39,345#
2009	7,014	3,236	4,064**		62,184#	3,978#	429#			40,372#
2010	6,929	3,191	4,208**		62,604#	4,088#	401#			40,378#

* Navy figures are for 31 Mar 1975. USMC figures are for 30 Jun 1975.

† Navy figures are for 30 Jun 1977. USMC figures are for 30 Sep 1977.

‡ Data not available.

§ Naval Aviation Observers (NAO) redesignated Naval Flight Officers (NFO) by BuPers Instruction 1210.4C of 8 Feb 1965, effective 1 May 1965.

ǁ NFO designation separated from other non-pilots.

Annual Report, *Bureau of Naval Personnel Statistics* (Report 15658), discontinued in mid FY 1993. Figures for Navy enlisted personnel in aviation rates provided directly from BuPers. Figures for Marine Corps Pilots, NFO and Aviation Rates from 1980 to 2010 provided by HQMC Aviation.

** These figures include Pilot or NFO rating that has been terminated, training to be a pilot or NFO, Aeronautical Engineering and Maintenance Specialties, LDO for Aviation Deck, Aviation Operations, Aviation Maintenance, Aviation Ordnance, Avionics, and Air Traffic Control.

Note: Does not include men in training. Aviation rates under Navy for years 1933–39 include general service ratings assigned to aviation duty. Enlisted pilots for 1920–26 are included under aviation rates. All Navy figures for WWII period, 1940–45, include Coast Guard. Figures not available for Marine Corps, 1920–29.

CHAPTER 12
Medal of Honor Awards in Naval Aviation

To Naval Aviators and Naval Aviation Pilots in Connection with Aviation

Name	Rank/Service	N.A. Number	Occasion for Award
Bauer, Harold W.*	Lt. Col., USMC	4189	Action in air combat, South Pacific area; 28 Sep–3 Oct 1942
Bennett, Floyd	CWO, USN	NAP-9	Piloted plane on first flight over North Pole; 9 May 1926
Boyington, Gregory	Maj., USMC	5160	Action in air combat, Central Solomons area; 12 Sep 1943–3 Jan 1944
Byrd, Richard E.	Lt. Cmdr., USN	608	Commanded plane on first flight over North Pole; 9 May 1926
Corry, William M.*	Lt. Cmdr., USN	23	Attempted rescue of pilot from burning aircraft; 2 Oct 1920
DeBlanc, Jefferson J.	Capt., USMC	12504	Action as leader of a fighter mission in air combat off Kolombangara Island, South Pacific; 31 Jan 1943
Elrod, Henry T.*	Capt., USMC	4093	Action in air and ground combat in defense of Wake Island; 8–23 Dec 1941
Estocin, Michael J.*	Lt. Cmdr., USN		Action as leader of air attack against enemy targets in North Vietnam; 20 and 26 Apr 1967
Fleming, Richard E.*	Capt., USMC	6889	Action as leader of dive bombing attack, Battle of Midway; 4–6 Jun 1942
Foss, Joseph J.	Capt., USMC	7290	Action in air combat in defense of Guadalcanal; 9 Oct–19 Nov 1942
Galer, Robert E.	Maj., USMC	5197	Action in air combat, South Pacific area; Aug–Sep 1942
Gordon, Nathan G.	Lt., USN	11421	Rescue of 15 officers and men under fire in Kavieng Harbor; 15 Feb 1944
Hall, William E.	Lt. j.g., USN	6072	Determined attacks on enemy carrier, Battle of Coral Sea; 7–8 May 1942
Hammann, Charles H.	Ens., USNRF	1494	Rescue of fellow pilot under fire during raid on Pula, Austria; 21 Aug 1918
Hanson, Robert M.*	1st Lt., USMC		Action in air combat at Bougainville; 1 Nov 1943, and New Britain; 24 Jun 1944
Hudner, Thomas J., Jr.	Lt. j.g., USN		Attempted rescue of squadron mate downed behind enemy lines in Korea; 4 Dec 1950
Hutchins, Carlton B.	Lt., USN	3435	Remained at controls of his aircraft after a mid-air collision to allow his crew to escape; 2 Feb 1938
Koelsch, John K.*	Lt. j.g., USN		Attempted rescue by helicopter during heavy overcast and under fire, Korea; 3 Jul 1951
Lassen, Clyde E.	Lt. j.g., USN		Night helicopter rescue under enemy fire of two downed aviators in North Vietnam; 19 Jun 1968
McCampbell, David	Cmdr., USN	5612	Action in air combat during Battle of Philippine Sea and Leyte Gulf; June and Oct 1944
O'Hare, Edward H.	Lt., USN	6405	Action in air combat in defense of carrier off Rabaul; 20 Feb 1942
Pless, Stephen W.	Capt., USMC		Helicopter rescue under enemy fire of four American soldiers beset by a large group of Viet Cong; 19 Aug 1967
Powers, John J.*	Lt., USN	6880	Determined attacks on enemy ships during Battle of Coral Sea; 4–8 May 1942

Name	Rank/Service	N.A. Number	Occasion for Award
Schilt, Christian F.	1st Lt., USMC	2741	Air evacuation of wounded under fire, Qualili, Nicaragua; 6–8 Jan 1928
Smith, John L.	Maj., USMC	5978	Action in air combat in defense of Guadalcanal; 21 Aug–15 Sep 1942
Swett, James E.	1st Lt., USMC	11893	Action in air combat, Solomon Islands area; 7 Apr 1943
Talbot, Ralph	2d Lt., USMC	802	Action in air combat, Europe; 8 and 14 Oct 1918
Van Voorhis, Bruce*	Lt. Cmdr., USN	3859	Determined low-level heavy bomber attack, Battle of the Solomon Islands; 6 Jul 1943
Walsh, Kenneth A.	1st Lt., USMC		Action in air combat at Vella Lavella; 15 and 30 Aug 1943

To Naval Aviators for Action not Associated with Aviation

Name	Rank/Service	N.A. Number	Occasion for Award
Antrim, Richard N.	Lt., USN	6750	Action on behalf of fellow prisoners while POW; April 1942
Edson, Merritt A.	Col., USMC	3026	Leading ground action in defense of the airfield at Guadalcanal; 13–14 Sep 1942
Stockdale, James B.	Capt., USN		Action on behalf of fellow prisoners while POW; 4 Sep 1969

To Officers and Men later Designated Naval Aviator, NAP, Naval Aviation Observer, and NFO

Name	Rank/Service	N.A. Number	Occasion for Award
Commiskey, Henry A.	2d Lt., USMC		Leading ground attack on strong enemy position near Yongdungpo, Korea; 20 Sep 1950
McDonnell, Edward	Ens., USN	18	Establishing signal station ashore and maintaining communications while under fire at Veracruz; 21–22 Apr 1914
Moffett, William A.	Cmdr., USN	NAO-1	Action in command of a ship at Veracruz; 21–22 Apr 1914
Ormsbee, Francis, Jr.	CMM(A), USN†	NAP-25	Rescuing enlisted men and attempted rescue of pilots downed in seaplane crash in Pensacola Bay; 25 Sep 1918

To Non-Aviators for Action Associated with Aviation

Name	Rank/Service	N.A. Number	Occasion for Award
Clausen, Raymond M.	PFC, USMC		Repeated rescues by helicopter of men trapped by enemy fire and minefield, South Vietnam; 30 Jan 1970
Finn, John W.	AOC, USN‡		Action under fire under the attack NAS Kaneohe; 7 Dec 1941
Gary, Donald A.	Lt. j.g., USN		Repeated rescues of trapped men on board *Franklin* (CV 13), severely damaged by enemy attack; 19 Mar 1945
McGunigal, Patrick	SF1c, USN§		Rescue of a kite balloon pilot entangled underwater in the balloon rigging, *Huntington* (ACR 5); 17 Sep 1917
O'Callahan, Joseph T.	Lt. Cmdr., USN (CHC)		Inspiration, leadership, and repeated rescues on board *Franklin* (CV 13) damaged by air attack; 19 Mar 1945
Ricketts, Milton E.*	Lt., USN		Leading damage control party on board *Yorktown* (CV 5) damaged during Battle of Coral Sea; 8 May 1942
Robinson, Robert G.	Gy. Sgt., USMC		Action during air combat as gunner to Lt. Ralph Talbot, USMC; 8 and 14 Oct 1918

To Aviators for Participating in the Space Program

The Congressional Space Medal of Honor, first awarded to former astronauts by President Jimmy Carter on 1 October 1978, was authorized by Congress on 29 September 1969 to recognize "any astronaut who in the performance of his duties has distinguished himself by exceptionally meritorious efforts and contributions to the welfare of the Nation and mankind."

Name	Rank/Service	N.A. Number	Occasion for Award
Armstrong, Neil A.			Participated in the Gemini 8 and Apollo 11 space flight missions. On Apollo 11, he became the first person to walk on the moon; 1 Oct 1978
Conrad, Charles, Jr.	Capt., USN		Participated in four space flight missions: Gemini 5, Gemini 11, Apollo 12, and Skylab 2. Commanded the crew of the first manned Skylab mission that conducted repairs on the orbital workshop; 1 Oct 1978
Glenn, John H., Jr.	Col., USMC		One of the original Mercury Astronauts and the first American to orbit the Earth; 1 Oct 1978
Lovell, James A., Jr.	Capt., USN		Participated in four space flight missions: Gemini 7, Gemini 12, Apollo 8, and Apollo 13. Commanded the crew of Apollo 13; 26 July 1995
Shepard, Alan B., Jr.	Rear Adm., USN		One of the original Mercury Astronauts and the first American into space. Commanded the Apollo 14 mission; 1 Oct 1978
Young, John W.	Capt., USN		Participated in five space flight missions: Gemini 3, Gemini 10, Apollo 10, and Apollo 16, and STS-1 (Space Shuttle *Columbia*) benefiting human progress in space; 19 May 1981

´ Received award posthumously
† Chief Machinist's Mate (Aviation)
‡ Aviation Ordnance Chief; later promoted to commissioned status
§ Shipfitter 1st Class

CHAPTER 13
U.S. Navy and Marine Corps Aces

The Navy Department has never officially compiled or issued a list of "Aces". During WWII, the period with the largest number of aerial shoot-downs for naval flyers, the Navy did not keep an overall record of individual scores in aerial combat; hence, there is no official list of confirmed shoot-downs.

The most comprehensive work done on Navy and Marine Corps WWII aces was written and published by Frank Olynyk. His two books are *USN Credits for the Destruction of Enemy Aircraft in Air-to-Air Combat World War II, Victory List No. 2*, published in 1982, and *USMC Credits for the Destruction of Enemy Aircraft in Air-to-Air Combat World War II*, published in 1981. In 1986 *Naval Aviation News* magazine published a list of U.S. Navy and Marine Corps aces that had been compiled by Olynyk. The following list of aces, as published by the magazine in 1986, includes his WWII list and also those from WWI, Korea, and Vietnam.

	Name	Service	Time Frame[§]		Name	Service	Time Frame[§]
*	Aldrich, Donald N.	USMC		†	Blair, Foster J.	USN	
	Alley, Stuart C., Jr.	USMC			Blair, William K.	USN	
	Amsden, Benjamin C.	USN			Blaydes, Richard B.	USN	
	Anderson, Alexander L.	USN			Blyth, Robert L.	USN	
	Anderson, Robert H.	USN			Bolduc, Alfred G.	USN	
‡	Andre, John W.	USMC			Bolt, John F., Jr.	USMC	
	Axtell, George C.	USMC			Bolt, John F., Jr.	USMC	Korea
	Bailey, Oscar C.	USN			Bonneau, William J.	USN	
	Baird, Robert	USMC			Bordelon, Guy P.	USN	Korea
*	Baker, Douglas	USN			Borley, Clarence A.	USN	
	Baker, Robert M.	USMC		*	Boyington, Gregory	USMC	
	Bakutis, Fred E.	USN			Boyle, Gerald F.	USN	
	Balch, Donald L.	USMC			Brassfield, Arthur J.	USN	
	Baldwin, Frank B.	USMC			Braun, Richard L.	USMC	
	Balsiger, Henry W.	USN			Brewer, Charles W.	USN	
	Banks, John L.	USN			Bridges, Johnnie J.	USNR	
	Barackman, Bruce M.	USN			Bright, Mark K.	USN	
	Bardshar, Frederic A.	USN			Brocato, Samuel J.	USN	
	Bare, James D.	USN			Brown, Carl A., Jr.	USN	
	Barnard, Lloyd G.	USN			Brown, William P., Jr.	USMC	
	Barnes, James M.	USN			Bruneau, Paul J.	USN	
	Bartol, John W.	USN			Brunmier, Carland E.	USN	
†	Bassett, Edgar R.	USN			Bryce, James A.	USN	
	Bate, Oscar M., Jr.	USMC			Buchanan, Robert L.	USN	
	Batten, Hugh N.	USN			Buie, Paul D.	USN	
	Bauer, Harold W.	USMC			Burckhalter, William E.	USN	
	Beatley, Redman C.	USN			Burley, Franklin N.	USN	
	Beaudry, Paul H. N.	USN			Burnett, Roy O., Jr.	USN	
	Beebe, Marshall U.	USN			Burriss, Howard M.	USN	
	Berkheimer, Jack S.	USN		†	Bushner, Frances X.	USN	
	Berree, Norman R.	USN		*	Byrnes, Matthew S., Jr.	USN	
	Bertelson, Richard L.	USN			Cain, James B.	USN	
†	Billo, James D.	USN			Carey, Henry A., Jr.	USN	
	Bishop, Walter D.	USN			Carl, Marion E.	USMC	
	Blackburn, John T.	USN			Carlson, Robert B.	USN	

Name	Service	Time Frame[§]
Carlton, William A.	USMC	
Carmichael, Daniel A., Jr.	USN	
Carr, George R.	USN	
Carroll, Charles H.	USN	
Case, William N.	USMC	
Caswell, Dean	USMC	
Chambers, Cyrus J.	USN	
Champion, Henry K.	USN	
Chandler, Creighton	USMC	
Check, Leonard J.	USN	
Chenoweth, Oscar I., Jr.	USN	
Clark, Lawrence A.	USN	
Clark, Robert A.	USN	
Clarke, Walter E.	USN	
Clements, Robert E.	USN	
Clements, Donald C.	USN	
Coats, Robert C.	USN	
Coleman, Thaddeus T., Jr.	USN	
Coleman, William M.	USN	
Collins, William M., Jr.	USN	
Conant, Arthur R.	USMC	
Conant, Edwin S.	USN	
Conger, Jack E.	USMC	
Conroy, Thomas J.	USN	
Copeland, William E.	USN	
Cordray, Paul	USN	
Cormier, Richard L.	USN	
† Cornell, Leland B.	USN	
Cowger, Richard D.	USN	
Cozzens, Melvin	USN	
Craig, Clement M.	USN	
Cronin, Donald F.	USN	
Crosby, John T.	USN	
Crowe, William E.	USMC	
Cunningham, Daniel G.	USN	
Cunningham, Randall H.	USN	Vietnam
Cupp, James N.	USMC	
Dahms, Kenneth J.	USN	
Davenport, Merl W.	USN	
Davidson, George H.	USN	
Davies, Clarence E.	USN	
Davis, Leonard K.	USMC	
Davis, Robert H.	USN	
Dean, William A., Jr.	USN	
Dear, John W., Jr.	USN	
De Blanc, Jefferson J.	USMC	
De Cew, Leslie	USN	
‡ Delong, Philip C.	USMC	
Denman, Anthony J.	USN	

Name	Service	Time Frame[§]
Denoff, Reuben H.	USN	
Devine, Richard O.	USN	
Dewing, Lawrence A.	USN	
Dibb, Robert A. M.	USN	
Dillard, Joseph V.	USMC	
Dillow, Eugene	USMC	
Dobbin, John F.	USMC	
Donahue, Archie G.	USMC	
Doner, Landis E.	USN	
Dorroh, Jefferson D.	USMC	
Doyle, Cecil J.	USMC	
Drake, Charles W.	USMC	
Driscoll, Daniel B. J.	USN	
Driscoll, William P. (NFO)	USN	Vietnam
Drury, Frank C.	USMC	
Drury, Paul E.	USN	
Duffy, James E.	USN	
Duncan, George C.	USN	
Duncan, Robert W.	USN	
Dungan, Fred L.	USN	
Dunn, Bernard	USN	
Durnford, Dewey F.	USMC	
Eastmond, Richard T.	USN	
Eberts, Byron A.	USN	
† Eccles, William G	USN	
Eckard, Bert	USN	
Eder, William E.	USN	
Edwards, William C., Jr.	USN	
Elliott, Ralph E., Jr.	USN	
Elwood, Hugh M.	USMC	
Enman, Anthony J.	USN	
Erickson, Lyle A.	USN	
Evenson, Eric A.	USN	
Everton, Loren D.	USMC	
Fair, John W.	USN	
Farmer, Charles D.	USN	
Farnsworth, Robert A., Jr.	USN	
Farrell, William	USMC	
Fash, Robert P.	USN	
Fecke, Alfred J.	USN	
Feightner, Edward L.	USN	
Ferko, Leo M.	USN	
Finn, Howard J.	USMC	
Fisher, Don H.	USMC	
† Flatley, James H., Jr.	USN	
Fleming, Francis M.	USN	
Fleming, Patrick D.	USN	
Flinn, Kenneth A.	USN	
Foltz, Frank E.	USN	

Name	Service	Time Frame[§]
Foltz, Ralph E.	USN	
Fontana, Paul J.	USMC	
Ford, Kenneth M.	USMC	
Formanek, George, Jr.	USN	
Forrer, Samuel W.	USN	
* Foss, Joseph J.	USMC	
Foster, Carl C.	USN	
Fowler, Richard E., Jr.	USN	
Franger, Marvin J.	USN	
Franks, John M.	USN	
Fraser, Robert B.	USMC	
Frazier, Kenneth D.	USMC	
Freeman, Doris C.	USN	
Freeman, William B.	USMC	
French, James B.	USN	
Frendberg, Alfred L.	USN	
Funk, Harold N.	USN	
Gabriel, Franklin T.	USN	
Galer, Robert E.	USMC	
Galt, Dwight B., Jr.	USN	
Galvin, John R.	USN	
Gayler, Noel A. M.	USN	
Gildea, John T.	USN	
Gile, Clement D.	USN	
Gillespie, Roy F.	USN	
Godson, Lindley W.	USN	
Gordon, Donald	USN	
Graham, Vernon E.	USN	
Gray, James S., Jr.	USN	
Gray, John F.	USN	
Gray, Lester E., Jr.	USN	
Gregory, Hayden A.	USN	
Griffin, Richard J.	USN	
Gustafson, Harlan I.	USN	
Gutt, Fred E.	USMC	
Haas, Walter A.	USN	
Haberman, Roger A.	USMC	
Hacking, Albert E., Jr.	USMC	
Hadden, Mayo A., Jr.	USN	
Hall, Sheldon O.	USMC	
Hamblin, Lewis R.	USN	
Hamilton, Henry B.	USMC	
Hamilton, Robert M.	USN	
Hanks, Eugene R.	USN	
Hansen, Herman, Jr.	USMC	
* Hanson, Robert M.	USMC	
Hardy, Willis E.	USN	
Hargreaves, Everett C.	USN	
Harman, Walter R.	USN	

Name	Service	Time Frame[§]
* Harris, Cecil E.	USN	
Harris, Leroy E.	USN	
Harris, Thomas S.	USN	
Harris, William H., Jr.	USN	
Haverland, Charles H., Jr.	USN	
Hawkins, Arthur R.	USN	
Hayde, Frank R.	USN	
Hearrell, Frank C., Jr.	USN	
Heath, Horace W.	USN	
Hedrick, Roger R.	USN	
Heinzen, Lloyd P.	USN	
Henderson, Paul M., Jr.	USN	
Henry, William E.	USN	
Hernan, Edwin J., Jr.	USMC	
Hibbard, Samuel B.	USN	
Hildebrandt, Carlos K.	USN	
Hill, Harry E.	USN	
Hills, Hollis H.	USN	
Hippe, Kenneth G.	USN	
Hoag, John B.	USN	
Hoel, Ronald W.	USN	
Hollowell, George L.	USMC	
Hood, William L., Jr.	USMC	
Houck, Herbert N.	USN	
Hudson, Howard R.	USN	
Huffman, Charles W., Jr.	USN	
Humphrey, Robert J.	USN	
Hundley, John C.	USMC	
Hurst, Robert	USN	
Ingalls, David S.	USN	WWI
Ireland, Julius W.	USMC	
Jaques, Bruce D.	USN	
Jennings, Robert H., Jr.	USN	
Jensen, Hayden M.	USN	
Jensen, Alvin J.	USMC	
Johannsen, Delmar K.	USN	
Johnson, Byron M.	USN	
Johnson, Wallace R.	USN	
Johnston, John M.	USN	
Jones, Charles D.	USMC	
Jones, James M.	USN	
Kaelin, Joseph	USN	
Kane, William R.	USN	
Keith, Leroy W. J.	USN	
Kendrick, Charles	USMC	
* Kepford, Ira C.	USN	
Kerr, Leslie H., Jr.	USN	
Kidwell, Robert J.	USN	
Kincaid, Robert A.	USN	

Name	Service	Time Frame[§]
Kingston, William J., Jr.	USN	
Kinsella, James J.	USN	
Kirk, George N.	USN	
Kirkpatrick, Floyd C.	USMC	
Kirkwood, Philip L.	USN	
Knight, William M.	USN	
Kostik, William J.	USN	
Kunz, Charles M.	USMC	
Laird, Dean S.	USN	
Laird, Wayne W.	USMC	
Lake, Kenneth B.	USN	
‡ Lamb, William E.	USN	
Lamoreaux, William E.	USN	
Laney, Willis G.	USN	
Langdon, Ned W.	USN	
Leonard, William N.	USN	
Leppla, John A.	USN	
Lerch, Alfred	USN	
Lillie, Hugh D.	USN	
Lindsay, Elvin L.	USN	
Loesch, Gregory K.	USMC	
Long, Herbert H.	USMC	
Lundin, Walter A.	USN	
Lynch, Joseph P.	USMC	
Maas, John B.	USMC	
Maberry, Lewin A.	USN	
Magee, Christopher L.	USMC	
Mahe, Thomas R., Jr.	USMC	
Mallory, Charles M.	USN	
Mankin, Lee P., Jr.	USN	
Mann, Thomas H., Jr.	USMC	
Manson, Armand G.	USN	
March, Harry A., Jr.	USN	
Marontate, William P.	USMC	
Martin, Albert E., Jr.	USN	
Masoner, William J., Jr.	USN	
Maxwell, William R.	USN	
May, Richard H.	USN	
May, Earl, Jr.	USN	
Mazzocco, Michele A.	USN	
* McCampbell, David	USN	
McCartney, Henry A.	USMC	
McClelland, Thomas G.	USN	
McClure, Edgar B.	USN	
McClurg, Robert W.	USMC	
McCormick, William A.	USN	
McCuddin, Leo B.	USN	
McCuskey, Elbert S.	USN	
McGinty, Selva E.	USMC	

Name	Service	Time Frame[§]
McGowan, Edward C.	USN	
McGraw, Joseph D.	USN	
McKinley, Donald J.	USN	
McLachlin, William W.	USN	
McManus, John	USMC	
McPherson, Donald M.	USN	
McWhorter, Hamilton, III	USN	
Mehle, Roger W.	USN	
Menard, Louis A., Jr.	USN	
Mencin, Adolph	USN	
† Merritt, Robert S.	USN	
Michaelis, Frederick H.	USN	
Miller, Johnnie G.	USN	
Milton, Charles B.	USN	
Mims, Robert	USN	
Mitchell, Harris E.	USN	
Mitchell, Henry E., Jr.	USN	
Mollard, Norman W., Jr.	USN	
Mollenhauer, Arthur P.	USN	
Montapert, John R.	USN	
Moranville, Horace B.	USN	
Morgan, John L., Jr.	USMC	
Morris, Bert D., Jr.	USN	
Moseley, William C.	USN	
Mulcahy, Douglas W.	USN	
Mullen, Paul A.	USMC	
Munsen, Arthur H.	USN	
Murray, Robert E.	USN	
Narr, Joseph L.	USMC	
Nelson, Robert J.	USN	
Nelson, Robert K.	USN	
Noble, Myrvin E.	USN	
* Nooy, Cornelius N.	USN	
Novak, Marvin R.	USN	
Null, Cleveland L.	USN	
O'Hare, Edward H.	USN	
O'Keefe, Jeremiah J.	USMC	
O'Mara, Paul, Jr.	USN	
Olander, Edwin L.	USMC	
Olsen, Austin L.	USN	
Orth, John	USN	
Ostrom, Charles H.	USN	
Outlaw, Edward C.	USN	
Overend, Edmund F.	USMC	
Overton, Edward W., Jr.	USN	
Owen, Donald C.	USMC	
Owen, Edward M.	USN	
Owens, Robert G., Jr.	USMC	
Parrish, Elbert W.	USN	

Name	Service	Time Frame[§]
Paskoski, Joseph J.	USN	
Payne, Frederick R., Jr.	USMC	
Pearce, James L.	USN	
Percy, James G.	USMC	
Philips, David P., III	USN	
Phillips, Edward A.	USN	
Phillips, Hyde	USMC	
Picken, Harvey P.	USN	
Pierce, Francis E., Jr.	USMC	
Pigman, George W., Jr.	USN	
Pittman, Jack, Jr.	USMC	
Plant, Claude W., Jr.	USN	
Pond, Zenneth A.	USMC	
Pool, Tilman E.	USN	
Pope, Albert J.	USN	
Porter, Robert B.	USMC	
Poske, George H.	USMC	
Post, Nathan T., Jr.	USMC	
Pound, Ralston M., Jr.	USN	
Powell, Ernest A.	USMC	
Prater, Luther D., Jr.	USN	
Presley, Frank H.	USMC	
Prichard, Melvin M.	USN	
Quiel, Norwald R.	USN	
† Ramlo, Orvin H.	USMC	
Reber, James V., Jr.	USN	
Redmond, Eugene D.	USN	
Register, Francis R.	USN	
Rehm, Dan R., Jr.	USN	
Reidy, Thomas H.	USN	
Reinburg, Joseph H.	USMC	
Reiserer, Russell L.	USN	
Rennemo, Thomas J.	USN	
Reulet, Joseph E.	USN	
Revel, Glenn M.	USN	
Rhodes, Thomas W.	USN	
Rieger, Vincent A.	USN	
Rigg, James F.	USN	
Roach, Thomas D.	USN	
Robbins, Joe D.	USN	
Robinson, Leroy W.	USN	
Robinson, Ross F.	USN	
Rosen, Ralph J.	USN	
Ross, Robert P.	USN	
Rossi, Herman J., Jr.	USN	
Ruhsam, John W.	USMC	
Runyon, Donald E.	USN	
Rushing, Roy W.	USN	
Sapp, Donald H.	USMC	

Name	Service	Time Frame[§]
Sargent, John J., Jr.	USN	
Savage, Jimmie E.	USN	
Scales, Harrell H.	USN	
Scarborough, Hartwell V., Jr.	USMC	
Schecter, Gordon E.	USN	
Schell, John L.	USN	
Scherer, Raymond F.	USMC	
Schiller, James E.	USN	
Schneider, Frank E.	USN	
Seckel, Albert, Jr.	USN	
See, Robert B.	USMC	
Segal, Harold E.	USMC	
Self, Larry R.	USN	
Shackford, Robert W.	USN	
Shands, Courtney	USN	
Shaw, Edward O.	USMC	
Sherrill, Hugh V.	USN	
Shields, Charles A.	USN	
Shirley, James A.	USN	
Shuman, Perry L.	USMC	
Sigler, Wallace E.	USMC	
Silber, Sam L.	USN	
Singer, Arthur, Jr.	USN	
Sipes, Lester H.	USN	
Sistrunk, Frank	USN	
Skon, Warren A.	USN	
Slack, Albert C.	USN	
Smith, Armistead B., Jr.	USN	
Smith, Carl E.	USN	
Smith, Clinton L.	USN	
Smith, Daniel F., Jr.	USN	
* Smith, John L.	USMC	
Smith, John M.	USN	
Smith, Kenneth D.	USN	
Smith, Nicholas J., III	USN	
Snider, William N.	USMC	
Sonner, Irl V., Jr.	USN	
Southerland, James J., III	USN	
* Spears, Harold L.	USMC	
Spitler, Clyde P.	USN	
Stanbook, Richard E.	USN	
Stanley, Gordon A.	USN	
Starkes, Carlton B.	USN	
Stebbins, Edgar E.	USN	
Stewart, James S.	USN	
* Stimpson, Charles R.	USN	
Stokes, John D.	USN	
Stone, Carl V.	USN	
Stout, Robert F.	USMC	

	Name	Service	Time Frame§
	Strane, John R.	USN	
	Strange, Johnnie C.	USN	
	Streig, Frederick J.	USN	
	Sturdevant, Harvey W.	USN	
	Sutherland, John F.	USN	
*	Swett, James E.	USMC	
	Swinburne, Harry W., Jr.	USN	
	Swope, James S.	USN	
	Symmes, John C. C.	USN	
	Synar, Stanley T.	USMC	
	Taylor, Ray A., Jr.	USN	
	Taylor, Will W.	USN	
	Terrill, Francis A.	USMC	
	Thach, John S.	USN	
	Thelen, Robert H.	USN	
	Thomas, Franklin C., Jr.	USMC	
	Thomas, Robert F.	USN	
*	Thomas, Wilbur J.	USMC	
	Toaspern, Edward W.	USN	
	Topliff, John W.	USN	
	Torkelson, Ross E.	USN	
	Townsend, Eugene P.	USN	
	Tracey, Fredrick W.	USN	
	Troup, Franklin W.	USN	
	Trowbridge, Eugene A.	USMC	
	Traux, Myron M.	USN	
	Turner, Charles H.	USN	
	Turner, Edward B.	USN	
	Twelves, Wendell V.	USN	
	Ude, Vernon R.	USN	
	Umphfres, Donald E.	USN	
*	Valencia, Eugene A.	USN	
	Valentine, Herbert J.	USMC	
	Van Der Linden, Peter J., Jr.	USN	
	Van Dyke, Rudolph D., Jr.	USN	
	Van Haren, Arthur, Jr.	USN	
	Vedder, Milton N.	USMC	
	Vejtasa, Stanley W.	USN	
	Vineyard, Merriwell W.	USN	
	Vita, Harold E.	USN	
	Voris, Roy M.	USN	
	Vorse, Albert O., Jr.	USN	
*	Vraciu, Alexander	USN	
	Wade, Robert	USMC	
*	Walsh, Kenneth A.	USMC	
	Ward, Lyttleton T.	USN	
	Warner, Arthur T.	USMC	
	Watson, Jack O.	USN	
	Watts, Charles E.	USN	

Name	Service	Time Frame§
Webb, Wilbur B.	USN	
Weissenberger, Gregory J.	USMC	
Wells, Albert P.	USMC	
Wesolowski, John M.	USN	
West, Robert G.	USN	
White, Henry S.	USN	
Williams, Bruce W.	USN	
Williams, Gerard M. H.	USMC	
Wilson, Robert C.	USN	
Winfield, Murray	USN	
Winston, Robert A.	USN	
Winters, Theodore H., Jr.	USN	
Wirth, John L.	USN	
Wolf, John T.	USN	
Wood, Walter A.	USN	
Wooley, Millard J.	USN	
Woolverton, Robert C.	USN	
Wordell, Malcolm T.	USN	
Wrenn, George L.	USN	
Yeremain, Harold	USN	
Yost, Donald K.	USMC	
Yunck, Michael R.	USMC	
Zaeske, Earling W.	USN	
Zink, John A.	USN	

* Ace with 15 kills or more.

† Unconfirmed as ace in WWII.

‡ Ace status acquired from combined kills of WWII and Korea.

§ Timeframe is WWII unless indicated otherwise.

CHAPTER 14
Early Naval Jet Pilots

The first flight in a turbojet aircraft in the United States was made at Muroc, Calif., on 1 October 1942, by Robert M. Stanley, chief test pilot of the Bell Aircraft Corporation. The next day Col. Lawrence C. Craigie of the U.S. Army Air Forces, took up the same plane for its first flight by a military pilot. The first jet flight by a naval aviator was made in the same plane at the same location on 21 April 1943 by Capt. Frederick M. Trapnell of Flight Test, NAS Anacostia, D.C. In each instance, the plane was a Bell XP-59A powered by two General Electric 1A turbojet engines. It was the first jet aircraft built in the United States and a prototype of the first jet aircraft acquired by the United States Navy.

Before the end of the war, the Navy had acquired three of the Bell Airacomets and in the first year after the war acquired two more. All were obtained from the Army Air Forces and assigned to NAS Patuxent River, Md. Their purpose was to provide a means of testing the adaptability of jet aircraft to naval requirements and a means of training pilots to fly the new aircraft type. They served through 1947.

Even before their acquisition, the Navy's interest in jet propulsion had been evident as it not only monitored the progress of jet programs in the Army Air Forces and took part in certain joint studies, but also initiated a study contract, which led to the development of the first Westinghouse jet engines. As early as 1943, two carrier fighter designs employing jet engines were initiated. The first with Ryan Aeronautical Company had the immediate objective of developing a fighter capable of operating from escort carriers as a replacement for the FM Wildcat. It resulted in the XFR-1 Fireball, which was powered by a Wright Cyclone engine in the nose, and a General Electric I-16 in the after section of the fuselage. Its development and production were handled on a crash basis and the first model flew in June 1944. Within a year it was assigned to a fleet squadron. Limited operations from escort carriers for short periods in the immediate post-war period uncovered numerous bugs and by July 1947 the decision to withdraw them from service had been made and carried out. A similar concept of composite power, carried out with the XF15C was abandoned after experimental models had been evaluated at Patuxent, Md.

The second contract of 1943 authorized the McDonnell Aircraft Corporation to design a twin-jet carrier fighter. To avoid disrupting wartime production and to meet the not-so-urgent objective of using the plane to explore the feasibility of jet operations on carriers, progress was intentionally slow. Even so, the airplane—the XFD-1 Phantom, powered by two Westinghouse 19B jets—took to the air for the first time on 26 January 1945. After another year and a half of flight testing, a production FD-1 was taken on board *Franklin D. Roosevelt* (CVB 42) and on 21 July 1946 the first jet operations from a U.S. carrier were conducted. A year later, the Phantom became the first jet aircraft assigned to a fleet squadron when two FDs were delivered to VF-17A at NAS Quonset Point, R.I.

In the meantime, studies and contracts had been let for other jet aircraft, which were to become operational. One of these, made in January 1945 with North American Aviation, produced the FJ-1 Fury equipped with a single Allison/GE jet. Claimed by some to be the hottest, straight-wing jet ever built, this airplane made its first flight in September 1946 and, in November of the next year, was delivered to VF-5A at NAS San Diego, Calif. On 10 March 1948, the squadron commanding officer and executive officer took the Fury on board *Boxer* (CV 21) for carrier suitability tests, conducting a number of takeoffs and landings. Shortly after, VF-17A completed carrier qualifications in the Phantom, by then redesignated FH, on board *Saipan* (CVL 48). The Navy's transition to jet aircraft had definitely begun.

By 1948, the number of naval aviators qualified to fly jets had assumed fairly generous proportions. Because it appeared desirable to have a list of the men who pioneered the Navy's effort in this field in the historical record, a project to obtain their names was initiated in October 1961 by Adrian O. Van Weyn, head of the Naval Aviation History Office.

It soon became apparent that there was no ready-made list and, further, that no official records had been kept from which one could be compiled. Even the flight logs from Patuxent, where the first jet aircraft had been assigned, seemed to have disappeared. It was then that a general appeal for help was made through a letter in the March 1962 issue of *Naval Aviation News*.

Help came from many sources. Twenty men in all answered this call giving not only the particulars of their first flights but also the names of others who had flown in the early period. One pilot sent a list of 73 men awarded Phantom Jockey Certificates by McDonnell Aircraft Corporation commemorating their flights in the Phantom jet. Perhaps the most unexpected, but no less useful, was a report from an officer assigned to the Aviation Safety Center listing all men involved in accidents in jet aircraft through 1948. From these replies and from other sources, a list was made up of another 80 men who had probably qualified in the period 1943–48. Each was sent a letter asking for the particulars of his qualification as well as for the names of others who should be questioned. The project developed quickly into a letter writing campaign as almost every third answer added more names, which in turn spawned yet other possibilities.

When these leads had been exhausted, the project seemed about complete and preparations were made to put the list in order for publication. It was then that the earlier search for the Patuxent flight logs produced results. They were found at the Federal Records Center in Alexandria. With some interest but only a little expectancy of finding any more than confirmation of what was already known, a few were called over for leisurely perusal. The first one dispelled all dreams of the project being finished.

About two months and 31 logs later, another 200 names had been added to the probables list. But what names! Almost without fail, the log entries identified the pilot by last name only, giving no initials, no rank, and no indication of service affiliation. This should have presented no difficulty with the more unusual names but experience proved quickly that no names are unusual. Reference to unit rosters and Navy Registers helped some, and the Bureau of Personnel contributed its share, but when all available sources had been used, there were still about 100 names lacking identity.

Some of these were cleared up by a day spent at NATC Patuxent, Md., and the follow-up assistance of RAdm. Paul H. Ramsey's staff. Some remain only names, some of those identified could not be found, and many were not heard from. Several were no longer living. Others were separated from their logs by vacation or change of duty and could not give exact information. Still others reported their logs as lost or destroyed by fire and had no means of confirming their recollections. In spite of these difficulties, the list was compiled and because publication might resolve some still unanswered questions, it was printed in the March 1963 issue of *Naval Aviation News* as a tentative list.

Tabulation of the replies revealed interesting elements of history. The early date at which many qualified was perhaps most surprising, but under the circumstances should not have been. All aspects of early jet aircraft were highly classified. During the war years, the interests of security dictated that early jet engines be called superchargers. Even the XP-59A designation for the first jet airplane had a security angle. The original XP-59 was a conventional experimental fighter, and it was thought that use of the same designation with a suffix letter would hide the true identity of the new model. Its early operations at Muroc were also conducted under the veil of secrecy—if jet flight can be kept a secret. Admiral Frederick M. Trapnell wrote: "When flown, this aircraft was towed well out onto the lake bed, with tarpaulins covering most of the fuselage and with a fake wooden propeller on the nose. This, of course, was removed prior to run-up."

This airplane, relatively unknown even today as the Navy's first jet, was for obvious reason the one in which most Navy pilots made their first jet flights. In the period of its use through 1947, by which time 262 flights are listed, 196 were in the P-59. Because Patuxent was the center of flight testing and the first station to which jet aircraft were assigned, it topped all other locations as the scene of first flights through 1948. A number of pilots received their first indoctrination from the Army Air Forces and made their first flights at AAF bases in the southwest. Others attended RAF schools at Hullavington and Cranfield, England, and made their first flights there. When delivery of the FD Phantoms and FJ Furies began in 1947, the location of first flights extended to St. Louis, Mo.; Quonset Point, R.I.; Cherry Point, N.C.; and San Diego, Calif.

The first Navy pilot to qualify in jets was also the first Navy pilot to fly seven post-war jets, which he listed as the XFJ, XF2H, XF9F, XF3D, XF6U, XF-86, and the XF7U. Only five men with flag rank qualified and, prior to 1948, only three qualified while holding the rank of ensign. The majority qualified as lieutenant commanders (major for the Marines) and lieutenants (captain for the Marines), with the former leading the pack. The pilots of VF-5A and VF-17A, on board at the time the squadrons were being equipped with jets, are all members of this early group although some that were not heard from do not appear on the list.

The replies included many interesting comments supplementing the basic information. The somewhat naive attitude of the historian was rudely jolted very early in the project. Under the assumption that some training was necessary to fly a radically different airplane, he provided a place on the questionnaire to report the extent of training received. The answers, when they were given at all, were unanimously in the vein of one report, which stated: "In contrast to present practice, training consisted of looking at handbook, cockpit checkout, then go." Its elaboration by another qualifier was: "Your request for information on training is amusing. Training was very informal, to put it politely. It consisted of: 'This is the low pressure fuel cock; this is the high pressure fuel cock; it flies real easy.'" Even in the later period when the first squadrons were being equipped with jets, the training does not appear to have been extensive. One pilot reported, "VF-17A trained itself. Checkout consisted of reading the handbook and watching a movie on compressibility."

One pilot told of winning third place in the 1948 Bendix Trophy Race from Long Beach, Calif., to Cleveland, Ohio, in which he "landed at Cleveland dead stick, out of fuel the last 50 miles." Another reported ferrying an FH-1 from Patuxent, Md., to Pensacola, Fla., in 1948 with the comment: "I daresay the only jet ever to use Station Field." In a similar vein, one told of his work with another pilot on chase flights out of Point Mugu, Calif., in which they, "operated P-80s off a 5,000-foot Marston mat with full ammo and fuel, for two years without incident. The P-80 was not supposed to be landed in this configuration (we later found out)."

The men who qualified in flag rank had some toppers. The first of these, Adm. Alfred M. Pride, gave the following account of events leading to his qualification: "I had been ordered to relieve [Harold B.] Sallada as Chief and to report a month before the turnover date of 1 May. That gave me considerable time to look around. It then dawned on me that I would be up to my neck in jet procurement and that I had better find out a little about them at first hand. Furthermore, since no flag officer seemed to have soloed the things, it seemed appropriate that the Chief of the Bureau set the pace. So I went down and asked for a McDonnell but the Patuxent boys were not taking any chances with their new pet, I guess, and were 'so sorry, but it was out of commission.' I looked around and saw the P-59 sitting there and asked how about that one. They admitted it was 'up' and so I said that I would take it. It worked fair enough except that one engine gave out after I got out over the Bay and I had to yell for a clear runway and come on home. Never did find out what the trouble really was."

Adm. Daniel V. Gallery reported: "Rear Admirals Apollo Soucek, Edgar A. 'Bat' Cruise and I checked out in Phantoms and flew a section formation at the opening of Idlewild and also at the Cleveland Air Races. Called ourselves the Gray Angels." To that somewhat noncommittal statement, Adm. Edgar A. Cruise provided a footnote quoted here in full. He wrote:

> For your information Admirals Soucek and Gallery flew with me, with Gallery leading, as the Gray Angels in both the Idlewild, N.Y., dedication and later at the National Air Races in Cleveland, Ohio, in September 1948. In Idlewild on one flight I ran out of fuel on one tank resulting in a flame-out. Inasmuch as our formation was only at 2600 feet and directly over the field, I elected to land dead stick on Idlewild. I never made a more precise approach and landing in my whole life.
>
> At Cleveland the Gray Angels caused some consternation by passing the reviewing stand simultaneously with, but in the opposite direction from, a 90-plane Air Group. The Air Group leader was flying low (about 4–500 feet) which forced us down to 75–100 feet. Needless to say flying wing, I was somewhat perturbed.

Adm. Cruise, who was Head of the Air Warfare Division in DCNO (Air) when he was making the above flights, also reported that his forced landing at Idlewild was directly involved in the subsequent installation of a positive cross connection which would prevent future flame-outs from the same cause.

As might be expected, this list of early jet pilots includes several men who later achieved other prominence in flight. Turner Caldwell set a world speed record in the D-558-1 in August 1947, the first held by the Navy since Al Williams' record in 1923. Marion Carl broke that record one week later in the same plane and later soared to a new altitude record for research aircraft in the D-558-2. Carl and Caldwell were also the first of their respective services to fly faster than sound in level flight. Larry Flint took the Phantom II to a new world altitude record in 1959 and F. Taylor Brown set a time-to-climb record to 20,000 meters in 1962, also in the Phantom II. Thomas H. Miller set a new speed record for 500 kilometers in the Phantom II in September 1960. The first U.S. Navy jet operations on a carrier were flown by James J. Davidson; Marion Carl flew tests of the P-80 on the same ship later in the year. Najeeb Halaby, former head of the FAA, was the first to fly a jet on continuous flight across the United States from Muroc, Calif., to Patuxent, Md., which he did in a P-80A on 28 June 1945. On the other side of the ledger, the list also includes the first pilot to bail out of a jet and the first to crash-land a jet in the water, both of whom shall be nameless.

In regard to the following list itself, words of explanation and caution are necessary. In explanation of the order, flights made on the same day are in the order of time of day when known, and alphabetical when not known. When only the month and year could be given for date, the flight appears after all others made during the month. Rank is that held at the time of first flight, and all are naval aviators on active duty at the time. Designations for the McDonnell Phantom appear as FD initially and as FH after the change made 21 August 1947.

The cautions are particularly important. First, qualification as a jet pilot was defined loosely. For this purpose, it was considered simply as the first flight on which complete command of the aircraft was held. Whether the first flight was also the last made in a jet by a particular pilot or the beginning of a whole career of jet flying, it was accepted as meeting the requirement. Second, only flights in pure jet aircraft were considered. The question of what to do about the Ryan FR-1 Fireball came up early in the project. Several facts of its early existence give weight to its importance in the Navy's transition to jet aircraft. Yet the fact that it was equipped with a reciprocating engine for use in normal operations and with a turbojet engine for use as a booster during takeoff and maximum performance flights, removes it from the jet aircraft class. For this reason, justified or not, flights in the FR are not included.

Thirdly, only those men with whom we could make contact or about whom we could gain specific knowledge appear in the list. Those found in log books or otherwise reported as having flown jets in the early period who could neither be identified nor located had to be omitted. Those who died after their first jet flight (indicated by ˙) could be included only if the necessary information was available from another source. Their flight dates are generally the earliest found in Patuxent flight logs and may not be the actual first flight. Others deceased, reported as having flown in the period but for whom no specific information was found, had to be omitted from the order of precedence. They are: John E. Darden Jr., Ralph Fuoss, Bud B. Gear, John Magda, Alfred E. Nauman Jr., Albert D. Pollock Jr., Horatio G. Sickel, Warren P. Smith, and Conrad J. Wigge.

For the above reasons, the list is the best that could be updated and compiled. On the basis of evidence available, it is concluded that the completeness and accuracy of the list is best at the beginning and decreases as the precedence numbers increase.

The following is a list of the Early Jet Pilots in Order of First Jet Flight:

No.	Name	Rank	Date	Plane	Place
1	Trapnell, Frederick M.	Capt.	21 Apr 43	XP-59A	Muroc
2	Pearson, John B., Jr.	Cmdr.	27 May 43	XP-59	Muroc
3	Ramsey, Paul H.	Cmdr.	29 Jul 43	XP-59A	Muroc
4	Gayler, Noel A. M.	Lt. Cmdr.	13 Jan 44	YP-59A	Patuxent
5	Booth, Charles T.	Cmdr.	14 Jan 44	YP-59A	Patuxent
6	Halaby, Najeeb E.	Lt. j.g.	21 Jan 44	YP-59A	Patuxent
7	Ferguson, John A.	Lt.	14 Feb 44	YP-59A	Patuxent
8	Drewelow, Robert W.	Lt.	21 Apr 44	YP-59A	Patuxent
9	Owen, Edward M.	Lt. Cmdr.	15 May 44	YP-59A	Patuxent
10	Brown, Ira W., Jr.	Lt. Cmdr.	28 Jun 44	YP-59A	Patuxent
11	Burroughs, Sherman E.	Capt.	11 Jul 44	XP-59	Muroc
12	Hayward, John T.	Cmdr.	11 Jul 44	XP-59	Palmdale
13	Storrs, Aaron P.	Capt.	17 Jul 44	YP-59A	Patuxent
14	Canavan, Desmond E.	Lt. Col.	18 Jul 44	YP-59A	Patuxent
15	Rozamus, Michael J.	Lt. Cmdr.	20 Jul 44	YP-59A	Patuxent
16	Davenport, M. W.	Lt.	21 Jul 44	XP-59A	Patuxent
17	Runyon, Donald E.	Lt.	21 Jul 44	YP-59A	Patuxent
18	Gerberding, Jas. H.˙	Lt. Cmdr.	30 Aug 44	YP-59A	Patuxent
19	Elder, Robert M.	Lt.	28 Sep 44	XP-80	Dayton
20	Milner, Robert M.	Lt. Cmdr.	24 Oct 44	YP-59A	Patuxent
21	Soule, Ernest D.	Lt.	24 Oct 44	YP-59A	Patuxent
22	Kelly, William W.	Lt.	30 Oct 44	YP-59A	Patuxent
23	Flint, Lawrence E.	Lt.	30 Oct 44	YP-59A	Patuxent
24	Guerrieri, Mario A.	Lt. Cmdr.	31 Oct 44	YP-59A	Patuxent
25	Harrington, Daniel J.	Lt. Cmdr.	01 Nov 44	YP-59A	Patuxent
26	Davidson, James J.	Lt.	02 Nov 44	YP-59A	Patuxent
27	Christofferson, F. E.	Lt.	02 Nov 44	YP-59A	Patuxent
28	Caffey, Kenneth W.	Lt. Cmdr.	07 Nov 44	YP-59A	Patuxent
29	Miller, Kenneth W., Jr.	Lt.	08 Nov 44	YP-59A	Patuxent
30	McNeely, Henry E.	Lt. Cmdr.	08 Nov 44	YP-59A	Patuxent
31	Wood, Charles R., Jr.	Lt. Cmdr.	08 Nov 44	YP-59A	Patuxent

No.	Name	Rank	Date	Plane	Place
32	Tuttle, Magruder H.	Cmdr.	08 Nov 44	YP-59A	Patuxent
33	Palmer, Fitzhugh L., Jr.	Cmdr.	09 Nov 44	YP-59A	Patuxent
34	Andrews, Clyde C.	Lt.	09 Nov 44	YP-59A	Patuxent
35	Gough, William V., Jr.	Lt. Cmdr.	09 Nov 44	YP-59A	Patuxent
36	Hollar, Frank E.	Maj.	09 Nov 44	YP-59A	Patuxent
37	Bauer, Louis H.	Cmdr.	11 Nov 44	YP-59A	Patuxent
38	Sutherland, John F.	Lt. Cmdr.	24 Nov 44	XP-80	Palmdale
39	Carl, Marion E.	Maj.	14 Feb 45	YP-59A	Patuxent
40	Wheatley, John P.	Lt.	15 Feb 45	YP-59A	Patuxent
41	Kenna, William E.	Cmdr.	15 Feb 45	YP-59A	Patuxent
42	Connolly, Thomas F.	Cmdr.	24 Feb 45	YP-59A	Patuxent
43	Neefus, James L.	Lt. Col.	10 Mar 45	YP-59A	Patuxent
44	Sallenger, Asbury H.	Lt.	14 Mar 45	YP-59A	Patuxent
45	Cleland, Cook	Lt.	– Mar 45	YP-59A	Patuxent
46	Schickel, Norbert H.	Lt.	25 Apr 45	YP-59A	Patuxent
47	Brown, Robert M.	Lt.	05 May 45	YP-59A	Patuxent
48	Schrefer, John F.	Lt. Cmdr.	09 May 45	YP-59A	Patuxent
49	Ellenburg, George W.	Lt. Cmdr.	23 May 45	YP-59A	Patuxent
50	Bakutis, Fred E.	Cmdr.	11 Jun 45	YP-59A	Patuxent
51	Schroeder, F. J.	Lt. Cmdr.	12 Jun 45	YP-59A	Patuxent
52	Larsen, Leif W.	Lt.	12 Jun 45	YP-59A	Patuxent
53	McClelland, T. G.	Lt.	27 Jun 45	YP-59A	Patuxent
54	Schiller, James E.	Lt.	27 Jun 45	YP-59A	Patuxent
55	Beveridge, Richard A.	Lt. Cmdr.	18 Jul 45	YP-59A	Patuxent
56	Thomas, John M.	Lt.	19 Jul 45	YP-59A	Patuxent
57	Hannegan, Edward A.	Capt.	21 Jul 45	YP-59A	Patuxent
58	Billett, Dudley S., Jr.	Lt. Cmdr.	23 Jul 45	YP-59A	Patuxent
59	Thawley, Charles B.	Lt. j.g.	08 Aug 45	YP-59A	Patuxent
60	May, Richard H.	Lt.	20 Aug 45	YP-59A	Patuxent
61	Houck, Herbert N.	Cmdr.	27 Oct 45	P-59B	Patuxent
62	Rees, Joseph R.	Lt.	27 Oct 45	P-59B	Patuxent
63	Tavernetti, Thomas F.	Lt. Cmdr.	29 Oct 45	P-59B	Patuxent
64	Mooty, Alfred F.	Lt.	30 Oct 45	P-59B	Patuxent
65	Franks, John M.	Lt.	30 Oct 45	P-59B	Patuxent
66	Earnest, Albert K.	Lt. Cmdr.	31 Oct 45	P-59B	Patuxent
67	Standring, Frank E.	Lt.	– Oct 45	Meteor	England
68	MacGregor, Robert A.	Lt. Cmdr.	03 Nov 45	P-59B	Patuxent
69	Hackett, Hugh J.	Lt.	29 Nov 45	P-59B	Patuxent
70	Callan, Allie W., Jr.	Lt.	02 Jan 46	P-59B	Patuxent
71	Myers, Raymond F.	Lt. Cmdr.	05 Jan 46	P-59B	Patuxent
72	Friesz, Robert P.	Lt. Cmdr.	11 Jan 46	P-59B	Patuxent
73	Leonard, William N.	Cmdr.	23 Jan 46	P-59B	Patuxent
74	Martin, William I.	Cmdr.	28 Jan 46	P-59B	Patuxent
75	Bolt, William H., Jr.	Lt. Cmdr.	07 Feb 46	P-59B	Patuxent
76	Morrison, Jack W.	Maj.	08 Feb 46	P-59B	Patuxent
77	Umphres, Donald E.	Lt.	09 Feb 46	P-59B	Patuxent

No.	Name	Rank	Date	Plane	Place
78	Holley, Edward B.	Lt. Cmdr.	11 Feb 46	P-59B	Patuxent
79	Quilter, Charles J.	Lt. Col.	13 Feb 46	P-59B	Patuxent
80	Davis, Leslie D.	Lt. Cmdr.	19 Feb 46	P-59B	Patuxent
81	Jorgensen, John B.	Lt. Cmdr.	19 Feb 46	P-59B	Patuxent
82	Reedy, James R.	Cmdr.	20 Feb 46	P-59B	Patuxent
83	Sim, Vincent M.*	Lt. Cmdr.	21 Feb 46	P-59B	Patuxent
84	Sollenberger, Robert L.	Lt. Cmdr.	21 Feb 46	P-59B	Patuxent
85	Burnett, Robert G.	Lt. Cmdr.	26 Feb 46	P-59B	Patuxent
86	Somerville, Henry B.	Lt. Cmdr.	27 Feb 46	P-59B	Patuxent
87	Pugh, Paul E.	Lt. Cmdr.	01 Mar 46	P-59B	Patuxent
88	Smith, James W.	Lt. Cmdr.	01 Mar 46	Meteor	England
89	Fleming, Francis M.	Lt.	09 Mar 46	P-59B	Patuxent
90	Hey, Richard J.	Capt.	20 Mar 46	P-59B	Patuxent
91	Clarke, Robert A.	Lt.	21 Mar 46	YP-59A	Patuxent
92	Murray, Thomas O.	Cmdr.	22 Mar 46	YP-59A	Patuxent
93	Hanks, E. Ralph	Lt.	23 Mar 46	YP-59A	Patuxent
94	Smith, Francis A.	Lt.	26 Mar 46	YP-59A	Patuxent
95	Jackson, Mercer L.	Lt. j.g.	27 Mar 46	YP-59A	Patuxent
96	Guillory, Troy T.	Lt. Cmdr.	27 Mar 46	YP-59A	Patuxent
97	Kunz, Melvin M.	Lt.	27 Mar 46	P-59B	Patuxent
98	Kanze, Robert F.	Lt.	27 Mar 46	YP-59A	Patuxent
99	Mehle, Roger W.	Lt. Cmdr.	27 Mar 46	YP-59A	Patuxent
100	Tracy, Lloyd W.	Lt.	28 Mar 46	P-59B	Patuxent
101	Rodenburg, Eugene E.	Lt.	28 Mar 46	P-59B	Patuxent
102	Thoms, Joseph I.	Lt. j.g.	28 Mar 46	P-59B	Patuxent
103	Weaver, Victor H.	Lt.	01 Apr 46	P-59B	Patuxent
104	McHenry, Robert E.	Lt. Cmdr.	01 Apr 46	P-59B	Patuxent
105	Hoerner, Helmuth E.	Lt. Cmdr.	01 Apr 46	P-59B	Patuxent
106	Alford, William L.*	Lt.	02 Apr 46	P-59B	Patuxent
107	Hine, Thomas L.	Lt.	03 Apr 46	P-59B	Patuxent
108	Cain, Mahlon E.	Lt. Cmdr.	03 Apr 46	P-59B	Patuxent
109	Deitchman, Richard P.	Lt. j.g.	05 Apr 46	YP-59A	Patuxent
110	Ness, Dwight O.	Lt. Cmdr.	05 Apr 46	YP-59A	Patuxent
111	Colvin, Louis E.	Lt. j.g.	09 Apr 46	P-59B	Patuxent
112	Westover, Roland W.	Lt.	09 Apr 46	P-59B	Patuxent
113	Daniel, Walter E.	1st Lt.	09 Apr 46	YP-59A	Patuxent
114	Fitzgerald, Joseph W.	Lt. j.g.	09 Apr 46	YP-59A	Patuxent
115	Valencia, Eugene A.	Lt.	19 Apr 46	P-59B	Patuxent
116	Adair, Robert F.	Lt.	23 Apr 46	P-59B	Patuxent
117	Alley, C. John	Lt. Cmdr.	23 Apr 46	P-59B	Patuxent
118	David, Edmonds	Lt. Cmdr.	23 Apr 46	P-59B	Patuxent
119	Junk, Winfield H.	Lt. Cmdr.	24 Apr 46	P-80A	March Field
120	Blackburn, John T.	Cmdr.	13 May 46	YP-59A	Patuxent
121	Miller, Thomas H.	Capt.	17 May 46	YP-59A	Patuxent
122	Foley, Walter A.	Lt. j.g.	17 May 46	YP-59A	Patuxent
123	Candler, William R.	Lt.	17 May 46	YP-59A	Patuxent

No.	Name	Rank	Date	Plane	Place
124	Mechling, Wallace B.	Capt.	21 May 46	P-59B	Patuxent
125	Sanders, Roger M.	1st Lt.	21 May 46	P-59	Patuxent
126	Matthews, Herbert S.	Lt. j.g.	22 May 46	YP-59A	Patuxent
127	Johnson, D. H.	Capt.	22 May 46	YP-59A	Patuxent
128	Aurand, Evan P.	Cmdr.	07 Jun 46	P-59B	Patuxent
129	Empey, Robert E.	Lt.	12 Jun 46	P-59B	Patuxent
130	Shryock, William A.	Lt. Cmdr.	13 Jun 46	P-59B	Patuxent
131	Giblin, Robert B.	Lt.	20 Jun 46	Meteor	England
132	Giese, Carl E.	Capt.	28 Jun 46	P-59B	Patuxent
133	Metsger, Alfred B.	Cmdr.	10 Jul 46	P-59B	Patuxent
134	Griffin, Edwin C.	Lt.	11 Jul 46	P-80A	Inyokern
135	Hyland, John J.	Cmdr.	15 Aug 46	P-59B	Patuxent
136	Pearce, James L.	Lt.	15 Aug 46	P-59B	Patuxent
137	Cram, Jack E.	Lt. Col.	19 Aug 46	P-59B	Patuxent
138	Ruefle, William J.	Lt. Cmdr.	– Aug 46	YP-59	Patuxent
139	Rembert, John P., Jr.	Capt.	04 Sep 46	P-59B	Patuxent
140	Larson, Vernon H.	Lt. Cmdr.	25 Sep 46	P-59B	Patuxent
141	Vatcher, Walter W.	1st Lt.	26 Sep 46	YP-59A	Patuxent
142	Rand, Herbert C.	Lt. Cmdr.	27 Sep 46	P-59B	Patuxent
143	Harris, Floyd L.	Lt.	03 Oct 46	P-59B	Patuxent
144	Byng, John W.	Cmdr.	07 Oct 46	P-59B	Patuxent
145	Arnold, James T.	Lt.	22 Oct 46	P-59B	Patuxent
146	Deasy, Charles J.	Lt. j.g.	22 Oct 46	YP-59A	Patuxent
147	Puckett, Ronald G.	Lt.	19 Nov 46	P-59B	Patuxent
148	Lee, Earl C.	Lt. j.g.	21 Nov 46	P-59B	Patuxent
149	Chapman, Melvin L.	Lt.	29 Jan 47	FD-1	St. Louis
150	Garton, Norman F.	Capt.	29 Jan 47	FD-1	St. Louis
151	Kneeland, Kenneth P.	Lt. j.g.	31 Jan 47	FD-1	St. Louis
152	Turner, Frank	Capt.	06 Feb 47	P-59B	Patuxent
153	Caldwell, Turner F.	Cmdr.	15 Feb 47	P-80	Muroc
154	Weems, George T.	Lt. Cmdr.	04 Mar 47	P-59B	Patuxent
155	Mulvihill, Francis	Lt. Cmdr.	17 Mar 47	P-59B	Patuxent
156	Pahl, Herschel A.	Lt.	21 Mar 47	P-80A	Chandler
157	Baumall, John F.	Lt.	27 Mar 47	P-59B	Patuxent
158	Nelson, Robert J.	Lt.	29 Mar 47	P-59B	Patuxent
159	Doerflinger, Carl	Cmdr.	31 Mar 47	P-59B	Patuxent
160	Crocker, John A.	Lt.	31 Mar 47	P-59B	Patuxent
161	Provost, Thomas C.	Lt. Cmdr.	31 Mar 47	P-59B	Patuxent
162	Danbury, William T.	Lt. Cmdr.	01 Apr 47	FD-1	St. Louis
163	O'Connor, Harry N.	Lt. j.g.	01 Apr 47	P-59B	Patuxent
164	Thompson, Harley F.	Lt. Cmdr.	03 Apr 47	P-59A	Patuxent
165	Whillans, Jack E.	Lt.	04 Apr 47	P-59A	Patuxent
166	Wood, Robert B.	Lt. Cmdr.	07 Apr 47	P-59A	Patuxent
167	Krantz, William F.	Lt. Cmdr.	10 Apr 47	Vampire	England
168	Reeves, Roy S.	Lt. Cmdr.	10 Apr 47	P-59B	Patuxent
169	McKinley, Charles E.	Lt.	10 Apr 47	P-59B	Patuxent

No.	Name	Rank	Date	Plane	Place
170	Coats, Robert C.	Lt. Cmdr.	15 Apr 47	P-59B	Patuxent
171	Hamilton, Chas. B., Jr.	Lt. j.g.	17 Apr 47	P-59B	Patuxent
172	Pride, Alfred M.	Rear Adm.	24 Apr 47	YP-59A	Patuxent
173	Clifton, Joseph C.	Capt.	01 May 47	P-59B	Patuxent
174	Ballinger, Richard R.	Capt.	01 May 47	P-59A	Patuxent
175	Bott, Alan R.	Lt. j.g.	08 May 47	P-59B	Patuxent
176	Franger, Marvin J.	Lt. Cmdr.	09 May 47	FD-1	Patuxent
177	McGinty, William G.	Lt.	19 May 47	P-80	Williams AFB
178	Cousins, Ralph W.	Cmdr.	20 May 47	P-59B	Patuxent
179	Simpler, Leroy C.	Capt.	21 May 47	FD-1	St. Louis
180	Billo, James D.	Lt. Cmdr.	04 Jun 47	P-59	Patuxent
181	Timmes, Francis X.	Lt. Cmdr.	12 Jun 47	P-59B	Patuxent
182	Neddo, Donald N.	Lt. Cmdr.	13 Jun 47	P-59B	Patuxent
183	Stapler, Charles R.	Lt. Cmdr.	16 Jun 47	YP-59A	Patuxent
184	Bates, Richard S.	Lt.	18 Jun 47	YP-59A	Patuxent
185	Smith, Joseph G.	Lt. Cmdr.	24 Jun 47	YP-59B	Patuxent
186	Weatherup, Robert A.	Lt. Cmdr.	25 Jun 47	P-59	Patuxent
187	Nester, Robert G.	Lt. Cmdr.	30 Jun 47	YP-59A	Patuxent
188	Dibble, Edgar J.	Lt.	30 Jun 47	YP-59A	Patuxent
189	Minter, Chas. S., Jr.	Cmdr.	02 Jul 47	YP-59B	Patuxent
190	Campbell, Robert K.	Lt. Cmdr.	03 Jul 47	YP-59A	Patuxent
191	Gates, Clark H.	Lt. Cmdr.	09 Jul 47	P-59B	Patuxent
192	Weymouth, Ralph	Lt. Cmdr.	11 Jul 47	P-59B	Patuxent
193	Collins, Francis L.	Lt. j.g.	12 Jul 47	FD-1	St. Louis
194	Russell, Hawley	Cmdr.	15 Jul 47	FD-1	Patuxent
195	Brehm, William W.	Lt. Cmdr.	17 Jul 47	FD-1	Patuxent
196	Miller, Charles G.	Lt.	17 Jul 47	P-59B	Patuxent
197	Dace, Carl C.	Lt. j.g.	17 Jul 47	P-59B	Patuxent
198	Perry, Adrian H.	Cmdr.	18 Jul 47	FD-1	Patuxent
199	Phillips, Thomas A.	Capt.	23 Jul 47	P-59	Patuxent
200	Clasen, William E.	Maj.	25 Jul 47	P-59B	Patuxent
201	Glover, John W.	Lt. j.g.	26 Jul 47	FD-1	Patuxent
202	Greenslade, John F.	Capt.	05 Aug 47	P-59B	Patuxent
203	Raposa, William C.	Lt. j.g.	06 Aug 47	FD-1	St. Louis
204	Mryo, Robert A.	Lt. Cmdr.	07 Aug 47	FD-1	Patuxent
205	Bicknell, John R.	Lt. j.g.	07 Aug 47	P-59B	Patuxent
206	Payne, Paul E.	Lt.	07 Aug 47	FD-1	Patuxent
207	Buxton, Elliott A.	Lt.	08 Aug 47	FD-1	Patuxent
208	Sullivan, John	Lt.	08 Aug 47	FD-1	Patuxent
209	Long, John O., Jr.	Ens.	08 Aug 47	FD-1	Patuxent
210	Cauble, Lawrence M.	Lt.	08 Aug 47	P-59B	Patuxent
211	Biggers, William D.	Lt. Cmdr.	09 Aug 47	FD-1	Patuxent
212	Davis, William V.	Capt.	10 Aug 47	P-59B	Patuxent
213	Taylor, Donald C.	Lt.	12 Aug 47	P-59B	Patuxent
214	Genta, John L.	Lt. Cmdr.	12 Aug 47	P-59B	Patuxent
215	McGowan, Edward C.	Lt.	12 Aug 47	XFD-1	NAS Mustin

No.	Name	Rank	Date	Plane	Place
216	Jensen, Alvin J.	Capt.	19 Aug 47	P-59B	Patuxent
217	Heath, Thomas W.	Lt. Cmdr.	23 Aug 47	FH-1	Patuxent
218	Ellis, Paul B.	Lt. Cmdr.	23 Aug 47	FH-1	Patuxent
219	Kimak, Charles	Maj.	26 Aug 47	P-59B	Patuxent
220	Newell, James H.	Cmdr.	29 Aug 47	FH-1	Patuxent
221	Fox, Frank A.	Lt.	10 Sep 47	FH-1	Quonset
222	Laird, Dean S.	Lt.	10 Sep 47	FH-1	Quonset
223	Wiktorski, Peter A.	Capt.	16 Sep 47	FH-1	Patuxent
224	Turner, Frederick G.	Lt. j.g.	18 Sep 47	FH-1	Quonset
225	Roberts, Carson A.	Col.	01 Oct 47	P-59B	Patuxent
226	McElroy, Richard S.	Lt. Cmdr.	02 Oct 47	P-59B	Patuxent
227	Werner, Ralph L.	Lt. Cmdr.	10 Oct 47	P-59B	Patuxent
228	James, George S., Jr.	Cmdr.	14 Oct 47	FH-1	St. Louis
229	Torry, John A., Jr.	Lt. Cmdr.	14 Oct 47	P-59B	Patuxent
230	Parker, Chester A.	Lt.	16 Oct 47	FH-1	Quonset
231	Helms, Jonee L.	1st Lt.	16 Oct 47	P-80	Williams AFB
232	Blackmun, Arvid W.	Maj.	23 Oct 47	P-59B	Patuxent
233	Barnett, Marvin E.	Lt. Cmdr.	04 Nov 47	FH-1	Quonset
234	Sedaker, Thomas S.	Lt.	04 Nov 47	FH-1	Quonset
235	Sells, Warren H.	Ens.	04 Nov 47	FH-1	Quonset
236	Couch, Eugene	Ens.	07 Nov 47	FH-1	Quonset
237	Oelrich, Martin E. W.	Maj.	12 Nov 47	FH-1	Cherry Point
238	Domina, Walter E.	1st Lt.	17 Nov 47	FH-1	Cherry Point
239	Panchision, Walter	1st Lt.	17 Nov 47	FH-1	Cherry Point
240	Connelly, Frederick G.	1st Lt.	18 Nov 47	FH-1	Cherry Point
241	Jeter, Manning T., Jr.	1st Lt.	18 Nov 47	FH-1	Cherry Point
242	Conner, Andrew B.	Lt. Cmdr.	19 Nov 47	P-59B	Patuxent
243	Gordon, Donald	Lt. Cmdr.	19 Nov 47	P-59B	Patuxent
244	Lindley, Johnny D.	Capt.	25 Nov 47	FH-1	Cherry Point
245	Green, Robert D.	1st Lt.	26 Nov 47	FH-1	Cherry Point
246	Iglehart, Louis T., Jr.	1st Lt.	26 Nov 47	FH-1	Cherry Point
247	Mars, William G., Jr.	1st Lt.	26 Nov 47	FH-1	Cherry Point
248	Seaman, Milford V.	1st Lt.	28 Nov 47	FH-1	Cherry Point
249	Blass, Lytton F.	MSgt.	05 Dec 47	FH-1	Cherry Point
250	Tate, Hugh J.	Lt. j.g.	07 Dec 47	P-59B	Patuxent
251	Schilt, C. Frank	Brig. Gen.	09 Dec 47	FH-1	St. Louis
252	Kinser, Dick R.	1st Lt.	09 Dec 47	FH-1	Cherry Point
253	Ramsay, Thomas W.	Lt. Cmdr.	16 Dec 47	FH-1	Patuxent
254	Ives, Donald A.	MSgt.	18 Dec 47	FH-1	Cherry Point
255	Bortz, William H.	1st Lt.	19 Dec 47	FH-1	Cherry Point
256	Roark, Walter N., Jr.	1st Lt.	19 Dec 47	FH-1	Cherry Point
257	McDaniel, James	1st Lt.	23 Dec 47	FH-1	Cherry Point
258	Bosee, Roland A.	Cmdr.	29 Dec 47	FH-1	Patuxent
259	Kibbe, Richard L.	Cmdr.	29 Dec 47	FH-1	Patuxent
260	Rockwell, John H.	Lt. Cmdr.	29 Dec 47	FH-1	Patuxent
261	Speirs, Carl L.	Lt. Cmdr.	30 Dec 47	FH-1	Patuxent

No.	Name	Rank	Date	Plane	Place
262	Morton, Wilbur Y.	Lt. Cmdr.	31 Dec 47	FH-1	Patuxent
263	Armstrong, Alan J.	Maj.	08 Jan 48	FH-1	Patuxent
264	Morton, Wilbur Y.	Maj.	08 Jan 48	FH-1	Patuxent
265	Stefan, Karl H.	Lt. Cmdr.	11 Jan 48	FH-1	Patuxent
266	Beatle, Ralph H.	Lt.	15 Jan 48	P-59B	Patuxent
267	Vail, Malcolm E.	Ens.	15 Jan 48	P-80A	Williams AFB
268	Brown, Nelson E.	1st Lt.	15 Jan 48	FH-1	
269	Jones, Charles D.	Capt.	15 Jan 48	FH-1	
270	Brown, F. Taylor	Ens.	16 Jan 48	P-80A	Williams AFB
271	Hansen, Dale W.	1st Lt.	16 Jan 48	FH-1	
272	Pierozzi, C. Nello	Ens.	18 Jan 48	P-80A	Williams AFB
273	Davis, Donald C.	Lt.	19 Jan 48	P-80A	Williams AFB
274	Pickett, Phillip G.	1st Lt.	22 Jan 48	FH-1	
275	Mooney, Thomas G.	MSgt.	26 Jan 48	FH-1	
276	McLean, Carl T.	Capt.	26 Jan 48	FH-1	
277	Schoch, Edwin F.	Lt. Cmdr.	29 Jan 48	FJ-1	Patuxent
278	Firebaugh, Gordon E.	Lt. Cmdr.	30 Jan 48	FH-1	Patuxent
279	Nifong, James M.	Lt.	31 Jan 48	FH-1	Patuxent
280	Bayers, Edward H.	Lt. Cmdr.	02 Feb 48	FH-1	Patuxent
281	Cotariu, Alan R.	Ens.	02 Feb 48	FH-1	Patuxent
282	Stetson, Thomas H.	Lt. Cmdr.	02 Feb 48	FH-1	Patuxent
283	Folsom, Samuel B.	Capt.	03 Feb 48	FH-1	Patuxent
284	Kelly, Vincent F.	Lt.	04 Feb 48	FJ-1	San Diego
285	Thompson, Lewis E.	Lt.	06 Feb 48	FJ-1	N. Island
286	Roach, Walter, Jr.	Lt.	09 Feb 48	FH-1	Patuxent
287	Capriotti, Anthony	Lt.	11 Feb 48	FJ-1	San Diego
288	Ritchie, James	Lt.	11 Feb 48	FJ-1	San Diego
289	Davidson, Paul D.	Lt. j.g.	12 Feb 48	FJ-1	N. Island
290	Smith, Robert R.	MSgt.	16 Feb 48	FH-1	Cherry Point
291	Wehmeyer, Wilbur J.	Cmdr.	17 Feb 48	FH-1	Patuxent
292	Stacy, James M.	Lt.	19 Feb 48	FH-1	
293	Nemoff, Alfred J.	Ens.	20 Feb 48	FJ-1	San Diego
294	Oeschlin, Robert E.	Ens.	24 Feb 48	FJ-1	San Diego
295	Pettiet, Rudolph L.	Lt. Cmdr.	24 Feb 48	FH-1	Patuxent
296	Coppola, Earnest J.	Lt. j.g.	25 Feb 48	FH-1	Patuxent
297	Bell, William R.	Lt. Cmdr.	06 Mar 48	FH-1	Patuxent
298	Meyersburg, R. B.	Maj.	10 Mar 48	Meteor	
299	Yunck, Michael R.	Maj.	11 Mar 48	P-80	Williams AFB
300	Jackson, Dewey H.	1st Lt.	12 Mar 48	P-80A	Williams AFB
301	Martin, Benjamin G.	1st Lt.	12 Mar 48	P-80A	Williams AFB
302	Ellis, James W.	Lt.	13 Mar 48	FH-1	Patuxent
303	Poulson, George W.	1st Lt.	13 Mar 48	P-80A	Williams AFB
304	Condon, John P.	Lt. Col.	16 Mar 48	P-80A	Williams AFB
305	Galer, Robert	Col.	16 Mar 48	FH-1	
306	Starkes, C. B.	Lt. Cmdr.	22 Mar 48	FH-1	
307	Pankurst, Paul L.	Capt.	23 Mar 48	FH-1	

No.	Name	Rank	Date	Plane	Place
308	Whitaker, James L.	Capt.	30 Mar 48	FH-1	
309	Gibson, Charles E.	Cmdr.	05 Apr 48	FH-1	Quonset
310	Durand, Paul H.	Lt. Cmdr.	06 Apr 48	FH-1	Patuxent
311	Ruehlow, Standley E.	Cmdr.	07 Apr 48	FH-1	
312	Severson, Martin A.	Lt. Col.	09 Apr 48	FH-1	
313	Houser, William D.	Lt. Cmdr.	15 Apr 48	FH-1	Patuxent
314	Spiess, Morris K.	Lt. j.g.	16 Apr 48	FH-1	Patuxent
315	McNeil, Wilfred J.*	Lt.	26 Apr 48	FH-1	Patuxent
316	Gray, James S., Jr.	Cmdr.	11 May 48	P-80B	Okinawa
317	Dawson, Marion L.	Col.	12 May 48	FH-1	
318	Manchester, B. B., III	Lt. Col.	26 May 48	FH-1	
319	Roush, Martin B.	Capt.	29 May 48	FH-1	
320	Soucek, Apollo*	Rear Adm.	01 Jun 48	FH-1	Patuxent
321	Millington, W. A.	Lt. Col.	03 Jun 48	FH-1	
322	Gallery, Daniel V.	Rear Adm.	09 Jun 48	FH-1	Patuxent
323	Peterson, Harry W.	Lt.	18 Jun 48	FJ-1	San Diego
324	McManus, John	1st Lt.	23 Jun 48	FH-1	
325	Cruise, Edgar A.	Rear Adm.	02 Jul 48	FH-1	Patuxent
326	Pawka, E. J.	Cmdr.	02 Jul 48	TO-1	San Diego
327	Weissenberger, G. J.	Lt. Col.	07 Jul 48	FH-1	
328	Johnson, Robert J.	Lt. Col.	07 Jul 48	FH-1	
329	Beebe, Marshall U.	Cmdr.	12 Jul 48	FH-1	Patuxent
330	Harris, Thomas S.	Lt.	15 Jul 48	FH-1	Quonset
331	Mueller, Richard C.	Lt. Cmdr.	22 Jul 48	FH-1	Patuxent
332	Spears, Paul H. A.	Lt.	— Jul 48	TO-1	Burbank
333	Billings, Thomas C.	1st Lt.	27 Jul 48	TO-1	
334	Fiegener, Kenneth G.	1st Lt.	03 Aug 48	TO-1	El Toro
335	Rafferty, Edgar L.	1st Lt.	04 Aug 48	TO-1	
336	Harrison, Patrick	Capt.	04 Aug 48	TO-1	
337	Case, William N.	Capt.	04 Aug 48	TO-1	
338	Perry, Jack E.	1st Lt.	04 Aug 48	TO-1	
339	Smith, Stanley E.	Lt. j.g.	05 Aug 48	FH-1	Quonset
340	Guss, William F.	1st Lt.	05 Aug 48	TO-1	
341	Klingman, Robert R.	1st Lt.	05 Aug 48	TO-1	
342	Abbott, Edwin W., II	Lt. j.g.	05 Aug 48	FH-1	
343	Gourley, Norman W.	1st Lt.	05 Aug 48	TO-1	
344	Mitchell, Weldon R.	1st Lt.	06 Aug 48	TO-1	
345	Jarrett, Clyde R.	1st Lt.	06 Aug 48	TO-1	
346	Wolfe, Ted E., Jr.	Lt. Cmdr.	09 Aug 48	FH-1	Atlantic City
347	Brown, John B.	Capt.	09 Aug 48	FH-1	
348	Wilder, James H.	Ens.	09 Aug 48	FH-1	
349	Ganschow, Edward F.	Capt.	11 Aug 48	FH-1	Cherry Point
350	Parker, Elwin A.	Lt. Cmdr.	12 Aug 48	FH-1	Patuxent
351	Moro, Albert J.	Lt. j.g.	16 Aug 48	FH-1	Quonset
352	Furney, Maynard M.	Lt. Cmdr.	17 Aug 48	FH-1	Patuxent
353	Prahar, T. F.	Lt.	17 Aug 48	FH-1	Patuxent

No.	Name	Rank	Date	Plane	Place
354	Macomber, Brainard	Lt. Cmdr.	18 Aug 48	FH-1	Patuxent
355	Widhelm, William J.	Cmdr.	19 Aug 48	FH-1	Patuxent
356	Cloud, Guy M.	1st Lt.	30 Aug 48	TO-1	
357	Carter, Frank B.	Ens.	17 Sep 48	FH-1	Quonset
358	Nye, Robert D.	Lt. Cmdr.	17 Sep 48	FH-1	Quonset
359	Pugh, Edward L.	Col.	17 Sep 48	FH-1	
360	Ingalls, Chas. E., Jr.	Cmdr.	22 Sep 48	FH-1	Patuxent
361	Everton, Loren D.	Maj.	29 Sep 48	FH-1	
362	Brtek, F. C.	Lt. j.g.	06 Oct 48	FH-1	Quonset
363	Trammel, Thomas B.	Capt.	14 Oct 48	TO-1	El Toro
364	Stuckey, Harry B.	1st Lt.	14 Oct 48	TO-1	
365	Haley, Harold L.	1st Lt.	14 Oct 48	TO-1	
366	Robinson, Robert B.	1st Lt.	14 Oct 48	TO-1	
367	Austin, Marshall S.	1st Lt.	14 Oct 48	TO-1	
368	Pottinger, William K.	Lt. Col.	14 Oct 48	TO-1	
369	Grey, Jack R.	1st Lt.	14 Oct 48	TO-1	
370	Read, Robert R.	Maj.	14 Oct 48	TO-1	El Toro
371	Sharp, James, II	1st Lt.	14 Oct 48	TO-1	
372	Houser, Fred C.	Capt.	14 Oct 48	TO-1	
373	Connell, Herschell G.	1st Lt.	14 Oct 48	TO-1	
374	Johnson, Danny W.	1st Lt.	14 Oct 48	TO-1	
375	Schroeder, Charles	1st Lt.	14 Oct 48	TO-1	
376	Rutledge, Rockwell M.	1st Lt.	14 Oct 48	TO-1	
377	Frankovic, Boris J.	1st Lt.	14 Oct 48	TO-1	
378	Hemstad, Robert S.	1st Lt.	14 Oct 48	TO-1	
379	Davis, Leonard K.	Lt. Col.	14 Oct 48	FH-1	
380	Bright, Cruger L.	Maj.	15 Oct 48	FH-1	
381	Jernigan, Curtis	1st Lt.	22 Oct 48	FH-1	
382	McCullough, William F.	Lt. j.g.	26 Oct 48	F-80	
383	Stapp, Donald H.	Maj.	26 Oct 48	TO-1	El Toro
384	Holloway, Harding H.	1st Lt.	28 Oct 48	FH-1	
385	Russell, Allard G.	Lt. Cmdr.	04 Nov 48	TO-1	San Diego
386	Conger, Jack E.	Maj.	04 Nov 48	FH-1	
387	Jackson, Billy	Lt. j.g.	04 Nov 48	TO-1	San Diego
388	Plog, Leonard H.	Lt. j.g.	04 Nov 48	TO-1	San Diego
389	Lizotte, Wesley E.	Lt. j.g.	04 Nov 48	TO-1	San Diego
390	Freeman, Dewitt L.	Lt. j.g.	04 Nov 48	TO-1	San Diego
391	Lloyd, Marshall O.	Lt.	04 Nov 48	TO-1	
392	Sears, Harry E.	Cmdr.	05 Nov 48	FH-1	Patuxent
393	Johnson, James	1st Lt.	14 Nov 48	FH-1	
394	Jensen, Harvey	1st Lt.	15 Nov 48	TO-1	El Toro
395	King, George J.	1st Lt.	15 Nov 48	TO-1	
396	Oster, Eugene M.	1st Lt.	15 Nov 48	TO-1	
397	Meyer, Eugene W.	1st Lt.	15 Nov 48	TO-1	
398	Turcotte, Edward	1st Lt.	15 Nov 48	TO-1	
399	Toups, Thaddeus J.	1st Lt.	15 Nov 48	TO-1	

No.	Name	Rank	Date	Plane	Place
400	Harper, Edwin A.	Capt.	15 Nov 48	TO-1	
401	Hamilton, John	1st Lt.	15 Nov 48	TO-1	
402	Thornbury, Donald S.	Capt.	15 Nov 48	TO-1	
403	Croyle, Fred K.	1st Lt.	16 Nov 48	TO-1	
404	Keller, Harold F.	1st Lt.	19 Nov 48	TO-1	
405	Logan, Thomas B.	Lt.	01 Dec 48	TO-1	Patuxent
406	Wattenburger, Robert	Lt. j.g.	06 Dec 48	TO-1	Patuxent
407	Adams, Allan M., Jr.	Lt. j.g.	06 Dec 48	TO-1	Patuxent
408	Bunger, Samuel J.	Ens.	06 Dec 48	TO-1	
409	Smith, Mercer R.	1st Lt.	10 Dec 48	FH-1	Cherry Point
410	Regan, Robert F.	Lt.	13 Dec 48	FH-1	Quonset
411	Gilman, George L.	2nd Lt.	14 Dec 48	FH-1	
412	Campbell, Donald L.	Lt. j.g.	15 Dec 48	FH-1	Quonset
413	Davis, Judson C.	Lt.	15 Dec 48	FH-1	Quonset
414	Quilty, Joseph F.	Maj.	21 Dec 48	TO-1	
415	Funk, Harold N.	Cmdr.	22 Dec 48	FH-1	Patuxent
416	Hill, John S.	Lt. Cmdr.	23 Dec 48	FH-1	Patuxent
417	Penne, Harold B.	Maj.	28 Dec 48	FH-1	
418	Wenzell, R. M.	Lt.	28 Dec 48	FH-1	

CHAPTER 15

Early Helicopter Pilots

The Bureau of Aeronautics issued a planning directive on 24 July 1942 calling for procurement of four Sikorsky helicopters for study and development by Navy and Coast Guard aviation forces. However, this was not the Navy's first interest in helicopters. That may be traced back to 5 December 1917 when the policy regarding helicopter development was established by the Secretaries of the Navy and War Departments on the basis of recommendations made by the Joint Technical Board on Aircraft. At that time, it was stated there was a need for improvements in power plants and propellers if a successful helicopter was to be obtained. Actual support of development efforts was to be limited to moral encouragement until a vendor had demonstrated a helicopter of military value.

The Navy's first rotary-wing vehicle was the XOP-1 autogiro ordered on 25 February 1931 from Pitcairn Aircraft. This machine was not a true helicopter because it had fixed wings and could not rise vertically. On 12 March 1935, the Navy issued a contract to Pitcairn Autogiro Company to remove the wings from the XOP-1, thereby converting it to the XOP-2, which thus became the Navy's first heavier-than-air aircraft without wings. Tests were conducted with the XOP-1, including landings on *Langley* (CV 1) in September 1931. However, conclusions from the tests, which compared the autogiros with fixed-wing aircraft, indicated the advantages were not great enough to override the disadvantages of payload, range, and the difficulties of flying. Personnel involved in the testing of the XOP-1 included future naval aviation greats such as Alfred Pride, Ralph A. Ofstie, Robert B. Pirie, and Frederick M. Trapnell. Other attempts were made between 1932 and 1937 to improve rotary-wing capabilities, but they were not successful. The Marine Corps used the OP-1 autogiro in Nicaragua in 1932 with the comment that its chief value in expeditionary duty was in inspecting small fields recommended by ground troops as landing areas, evacuating medical "sitting" cases, and ferrying of important personnel. In 1937 the Navy also experimented with the XOZ-1, a modified N2Y-1 with a cyclic controlled rotor, but the tests were not successful.

In the early 1940s, a class desk was established in the Bureau of Aeronautics for the Navy's helicopter program and staffed by a small group of individuals who saw the potential for rotary-wing development. They included Capt. Clayton C. Marcy, Cmdr. James W. Klopp, and Cmdr. Raymond Doll. The impetus for more Navy involvement in helicopters was spearheaded by the Coast Guard, which was very interested in its ASW and rescue capabilities. Their vision for the use of the helicopter, whose development responsibility had been assigned to the Army Air Corps, resulted in a 15 February 1943 directive from the Commander in Chief, U.S. Fleet that assigned responsibility for sea-going development of helicopters and their operation in convoys to the Coast Guard. Tests were to be carried out to determine if helicopters operating from merchant ships would be of value in combating submarines. On 4 May 1943, to expedite the evaluation of the helicopter in antisubmarine operations, the Commander in Chief, U.S. Fleet, directed that a "joint board" be formed with representatives from the Commander in Chief, U.S. Fleet; the Bureau of Aeronautics, the Coast Guard, the British Admiralty, and the Royal Air Force. The resulting Combined Board for the Evaluation of the Ship-Based Helicopter in Antisubmarine Warfare was later expanded to include representatives of the Army Air Forces (AAF), the War Shipping Administration, and the National Advisory Committee for Aeronautics (NACA). A few days later, on 7 May, Navy representatives witnessed landing trials in Long Island Sound of the XR-4 helicopter on board the merchant tanker SS *Bunker Hill* in a demonstration sponsored by the Maritime Commission. The pilot, Col. R. F. Gregory, AAF, made about 15 flights, some of which he landed on the water before returning to the platform on the deck of the ship. On 10 June 1943, Lt. Cdmr. Frank A. Erickson, USCG, proposed that helicopters be developed for antisubmarine warfare, "not as a killer craft but as the eyes and ears of the convoy escorts." To this end he recommended that helicopters be equipped with radar and dunking sonar. With the foregoing proposals and developments, the Navy ordered and received its first helicopter—a Sikorsky YR-4B, Navy designation HNS-1—on 16 October 1943. It was accepted at Bridgeport, Conn., following a 60-minute acceptance test flight by Lt. Cdmr. Erickson. Cmdr. Charles T. Booth, USN, delivered this helicopter to NAS Patuxent River, Md., on 22 October 1943. As stated by a memo from Cmdr. Booth, he had arrived at Bridgeport "to continue instructions and to deliver to NAS Patuxent the first Navy helicopter . . . Six hours additional flight time was obtained by Commander Booth prior to his return to NAS Patuxent, Md., on 22 October."

On the basis of his belief that tests indicated the practicability of ship-based helicopters, the Chief of Naval Operations, on 18 December 1943, separated the pilot training from test and development functions in the helicopter program. He directed that, effective 1 January 1944, a helicopter pilot training program be conducted by the U.S. Coast Guard at Floyd Bennett Field, N.Y., under the direction of the Deputy Chief of Naval Operations

(Air). This planning directive of 18 December 1943, also named Rockaway, N.Y., as an outlying field for training and stated that three Coast Guard and two Navy officers had qualified as helicopter pilots to date. The directive also indicated "It has been determined that after 25 hours of dual and solo flight time, a fixed-wing pilot is qualified as a helicopter pilot." Thus, during WWII, the Coast Guard, at Floyd Bennett Field, N.Y., was responsible for pilot and enlisted mechanic training in helicopter aviation for the Navy. Helicopter pilots trained by the Coast Guard unit also included personnel from the Army Air Forces, the Civil Aeronautics Administration, and NACA.

Following the end of WWII, the Navy established VX-3 on 1 July 1946 at NAS New York (Floyd Bennett Field). This squadron took over the helicopter pilot training duties that had been done by the Coast Guard unit at Floyd Bennett Field, N.Y. VX-3 moved to NAS Lakehurst, N.J., on 10 September 1946 and continued training helicopter pilots until they were disestablished on 1 April 1948.

Helicopter Utility Squadron 2 (HU-2) was established on 1 April 1948 and took over the responsibility for training helicopter pilots at NAS Lakehurst, N.J. Many of the personnel from VX-3 helped form HU-2 when it was established. On 11 June 1948, the Chief of Naval Operations issued standards for training aviators as helicopter pilots and provided that helicopter pilots previously trained by the Coast Guard or VX-3 would retain their qualification. However, not all personnel received their qualification as a helicopter pilot from VX-3 or HU-2, even though they had been assigned the mission of training helicopter pilots. HU-2 would issue helicopter pilot qualifications to an individual that may have received training at NATC Patuxent River, Md., from HU-1, or from Connally Air Force Base in Texas.

HU-2 was not only responsible for training helicopter pilots but was also involved in providing helicopter detachments for utility services and search and rescue missions. Due to an increased demand for these services, as well as a need for more helicopter pilots, the Chief of Naval Operations decided to transfer the helicopter pilot training mission to the Naval Air Training Command at Ellyson Field, Pensacola, Fla. Helicopter Training Unit 1 (HTU-1) was established on 3 December 1950 at Pensacola, Fla. HU-2 shifted its responsibility for training helicopter pilots to HTU-1 in January 1951. HTU-1 was redesignated HTG-1 in March 1957. The HTG-1 designation was changed to HT-8 on 1 July 1960. HT-8 is still training helicopter pilots in the Pensacola area.

When a new program is established, especially one that entails listing personnel who are designated or qualified for a particular job code, the records for the evolution of that new program can be very sketchy. That is precisely what happened in the training program for helicopter pilots. The early helicopter pilots did not have a formal Navy training program to follow or the correct procedures in place to record and preserve their helicopter pilot qualifications. In fact, in 1943 the first group to qualify was sent to East Hartford, Conn., and trained by the Sikorsky Aircraft Company. They included Lt. Cmdr. Frank Erickson, USCG; Lt. A. N. Fisher, USCG; Lt. Stewart R. Graham, USCG; and Cmdr. Charles T. Booth, USN. None of these individuals were placed on the list of early helicopter pilots. In fact, the list, which appears to originate from VX-3 and HU-2 records, does not list any Coast Guard officers. The following list is the best that could be compiled from the available records on helicopter pilot qualification and training. It does not include the Coast Guard aviators.

Helicopter Pilot Number	Name	Rank	Service	Date of Qualification Designation
1	Knapp, William G.	Lt.	USNR	15 Apr 1944
2	Doll, Raymond E.	Cmdr.	USN	26 Sep 1944
3	Wood, Charles R.	Cmdr.	USNR	26 Sep 1944
4	Brown, Percy	Lt.	USNR	6 Feb 1945
5	Kembro, Marerie D.	Capt.	USN	9 Aug 1945
6	Long, Richard J.	Lt.	USN	9 Aug 1945
7	Marcy, Clayton C.	Capt.	USN	10 Oct 1945
8	Runyon, Joseph W.	Cmdr.	USN	31 Oct 1945
9	Houston, Charles E.	Cmdr.	USN	18 Dec 1945
10	Hoover, George	Lt.	USN	27 Dec 1945
11	Lawrence, M.	Lt.	USNR	28 Dec 1945
12	Wilcox, Donald E.	Capt.	USN	3 Jun 1946
13	Kosciusko, Henry M.	Lt. Cmdr.	USN	17 Jul 1946
14	Kubicki, Edward	Lt.	USN	26 Jul 1946
15	Schaufler, William G.	Lt. j.g.	USN	26 Jul 1946

Helicopter Pilot Number	Name	Rank	Service	Date of Qualification Designation
16	Delalio, Armand H.	Maj.	USMC	8 Aug 1946
17	Rullo, Guiseppe J.	Lt.	USN	28 Aug 1946
18	Reeves, George J.	Lt.	USN	28 Aug 1946
19	Lammi, James W.	Lt.	USN	27 Sep 1946
20	Junghans, Robert L.	Lt. Cmdr.	USN	1 Nov 1946
21	Sessums, Walter M.	Lt. Cmdr.	USN	5 Nov 1946
22	Tanner, Charles S.	Lt. Cmdr.	USN	9 Nov 1946
23	Fink, Christian	Lt. Cmdr.	USN	18 Dec 1946
24	Bott, Alan	Lt.	USN	18 Dec 1946
25	Tracy, Lloyd W.	Lt.	USN	23 Jun 1947
26	Glenzer, Hubert	Lt. j.g.	USN	14 Oct 1947
27	Anderson, Roy L.	1st Lt.	USMC	20 Nov 1947
28	Strieby, Robert A.	Capt.	USMC	20 Nov 1947
29	Garber, C. O.	Capt.	USMC	20 Nov 1947
30	Riley, Russell R.	Maj.	USMC	20 Nov 1947
31	Peters, Maurice A.	Cmdr.	USN	21 Nov 1947
32	Shawcross, William H.	Lt.	USN	24 Nov 1947
33	Bagshaw, James R.	Lt. j.g.	USN	24 Nov 1947
34	Montgomery, Marvin D.	Lt. j.g.	USN	24 Nov 1947
35	Morrison, Gene W.	1st Lt.	USMC	1 Dec 1947
36	Carleton, R. D.	Lt. j.g.	USN	20 Dec 1947
37	Arnold, E. A.	Lt. Cmdr.	USN	21 Dec 1947
38	Moseley, R. H.	Ens.	USN	22 Dec 1947
39	Higbee, J.	Capt.	USN	22 Dec 1947
40	Billett, Dudley S.	Lt. Cmdr.	USN	15 Jan 1948
41	Camp, R. W.	ADC(NAP)'	USN	21 Feb 1948
42	McVicars, A. L.	1st Lt.	USMC	11 Mar 1948
43	Meshier, C. W.	Lt.	USN	12 Mar 1948
44	Blatt, W. D.	Capt.	USMC	17 Mar 1948
45	Polen, R. A.	1st Lt.	USMC	17 Mar 1948
46	Ward, C. E.	1st Lt.	USMC	19 Mar 1948
47	Pope, E. J.	1st Lt.	USMC	22 Mar 1948
48	Sebach, H. U.	Lt. Cmdr.	USN	31 Mar 1948
49	Fisher, A. G.	MSgt.	USMC	1 Apr 1948
50	Schmucker, S.	Ens.	USN	7 Apr 1948
51	Mathewson, F. F.	Lt.	USN	16 Apr 1948
52	Hanies, G. D.	Lt.	USN	16 Apr 1948
53	Matthews, J. H.	Capt.	USN	20 Apr 1948
54	Mounts, L. J.	MSgt.	USMC	26 Apr 1948
55	Fox, J. E.	Lt.	USN	29 Apr 1948
56	Leary, W.	Lt. j.g.	USN	29 Apr 1948
57	Grassi, J.	Ens.	USN	29 Apr 1948
58	Longstaff, R.	1st Lt.	USMC	12 May 1948
59	Hamilton, D. E.	ADC(AP)'	USN	12 May 1948
60	Mitchell, G. D.	ADC(NAP)'	USN	18 May 1948
61	Finn, L. A.	ADC(NAP)'	USN	19 May 1948
62	Collins, V. W.	Lt.	USN	21 May 1948
63	Nebergall, M.	1st Lt.	USMC	19 Jun 1948

Helicopter Pilot Number	Name	Rank	Service	Date of Qualification Designation
64	Griffin, M. C.	Lt. j.g.	USN	7 Jul 1948
65	Brender, B. W.	Lt. j.g.	USN	8 Jul 1948
66	Hutto, C. H.	AC1(NAP)*	USN	8 Jul 1948
67	Lynch, R. E.	Ens.	USN	9 Jul 1948
68	Milner, F. D.	Lt.	USN	13 Jul 1948
69	Matthews, W. R.	Ens.	USN	22 Jul 1948
70	Torry, J. A. H.	Lt. Cmdr.	USN	6 Aug 1948
71	Nickerson, R. L.	Maj.	USMC	6 Aug 1948
72	Dyer, E. C.	Col.	USMC	6 Aug 1948
73	Ellis, W. Y.	Lt. Cmdr.	USNR	6 Aug 1948
74	Leonard, W. R.	Lt. Cmdr.	USN	16 Aug 1948
75	Cunha, G. D. M.	Cmdr.	USN	19 Aug 1948
76	Cox, W. J.	Ens.	USN	24 Aug 1948
77	Fridley, D. C.	Ens.	USN	24 Aug 1948
78	Dixon, W. C.	Lt.	USN	24 Aug 1948
79	Granger, R. P.	ADC(NAP)*	USN	26 Aug 1948
80	Crofoot, A. E.	Lt. j.g.	USN	27 Aug 1948
81	Johnson, F. E.	Ens.	USN	2 Sep 1948
82	Carey, J. F.	Lt. Col.	USMC	2 Sep 1948
83	Kilcore, W. H.	Lt. Cmdr.	USN	3 Sep 1948
84	Miller, R. A.	Lt. j.g.	USN	8 Sep 1948
85	Wrenn, E.	Lt. j.g.	USN	13 Sep 1948
86	Wheat, N. L.	Ens.	USN	14 Sep 1948
87	Garrison, R. G.	Ens.	USN	24 Sep 1948
88	Wiskirchen, R. L.	Lt.	USN	24 Sep 1948
89	Cabell, J. B.	Lt.	USN	24 Sep 1948
90	Zoecklein, W. O.	Lt. Cmdr.	USN	19 Oct 1948
91	Connolly, T. F.	Cmdr.	USN	15 Sep 1948
92	Sherby, S. S.	Cmdr.	USN	15 Sep 1948
93	Hyland, J. J.	Cmdr.	USN	15 Sep 1948
94	Rand, N. C.	Lt. Cmdr.	USN	15 Sep 1948
95	Davis, W. V., Jr.	Capt.	USN	15 Sep 1948
96	Timmins‡	Lt. Cmdr.	USNR	8 Oct 1948
97	Reilly, J. L.	Lt. j.g.	USN	20 Oct 1948
98	Denk, H. J.	Ens.	USN	20 Oct 1948
99	Little, J. C.	Lt.	USN	9 Nov 1948
100	Nash, D. E.	Lt. j.g.	USN	9 Nov 1948
101	Blades, J. L.	Lt. j.g.	USN	12 Nov 1948
102	Gauthier, A. C.	Lt.	USNR	12 Nov 1948
103	McMullen, B. E.	Lt. j.g.	USN	12 Nov 1948
104	Peterson, M. C.	ADC(NAP)*	USN	12 Nov 1948
105	Rust, D. T.	Lt. j.g.	USN	19 Nov 1948
106	Hamilton, R. C.	Ens.	USNR	23 Nov 1948
107	McCarthy, J. R.		CAA⁺	1 Dec 1948
108	Fisher, F. J.	Ens.	USNR	24 Nov 1948
109	Johnson, C. R.	Lt.	USN	6 Dec 1948
110	Berree, N. R.	Lt.	USN	7 Dec 1948
111	Schmeltzer, L. B.	Lt. j.g.	USN	7 Dec 1948

Helicopter Pilot Number	Name	Rank	Service	Date of Qualification Designation
112	Moore, B., Jr.	Cmdr.	USN	10 Dec 1948
113	Lieske, J. M.	ALC(NAP)*	USN	13 Dec 1948
114	Staples, C.		CAA†	14 Jan 1949
115	Olmsted, P. S.	Ens.	USNR	20 Jan 1949
116	Miller, H. M.	Lt. j.g.	USNR	21 Jan 1949
117	Hilton, J. J., Jr.	Cmdr.	USN	1 Feb 1949
118	Montgomery, W. G.	Lt.	USN	9 Feb 1949
119	Brown, H. F.	Lt.	USN	10 Feb 1949
120	Armstrong, J. G.	Lt.	USN	23 Feb 1949
121	Starr, M. R.	Ens.	USN	24 Feb 1949
122	Reed, M.	Lt.	USN	24 Feb 1949
123	Case, R. C.	1st Lt.	USMC	9 Mar 1949
124	Blackwood, R. R.	Ens.	USNR	11 Mar 1949
125	Cole, J. S.	Lt.	USN	14 Mar 1949
126	Mitchell, W. P.	Maj.	USMC	17 Mar 1949
127	Gill, R. J.	Lt. j.g.	USNR	15 Mar 1949
128	Pledger, W. G.	Lt. j.g.	USN	30 Mar 1949
129	Lueddeke, G. F.	Lt. j.g.	USN	5 Apr 1949
130	Marshall, A. R.	Lt.	USN	13 Apr 1949
131	Farwell, J. M.	Lt. j.g.	USN	13 Apr 1949
132	Tucci, F. A.	Lt.	USN	20 Apr 1949
133	Logan, I. C.	Lt. j.g.	USNR	21 Apr 1949
134	McClanan, F. H.	Lt. Cmdr.	USN	21 Apr 1949
135	Mayfield, A.	Lt. j.g.	USN	21 Apr 1949
136	Raddatz, R. W.	Lt.	USN	29 Apr 1949
137	Braun, J. F.	Lt. j.g.	USN	29 Apr 1949
138	Wrigley, G. R.	Lt. j.g.	USN	29 Apr 1949
139	Kaylor, J. O.	1st Lt.	USMC	29 Apr 1949
140	Sullivan, R. J.	1st Lt.	USMC	4 May 1949
141	Bolt, G. W.	Lt. Cmdr.	USN	6 May 1949
142	Duffey, H. J.		CAA†	9 May 1949
143	Kelley, F. E., Jr.	Ens.	USN	9 May 1949
144	Rohrich, W. H.	Lt. j.g.	USN	9 May 1949
145	Griffin‡		CAA†	15 Mar 1949
146	Titterud, S. V.	Capt.	USMC	11 May 1949
147	Lammi, W. S.	Lt.	USN	19 May 1949
148	Holmgren, A. F.	Ens.	USN	15 Apr 1944
149	Crowe, G. T.	AD1(AP)*	USN	19 May 1949
150	Taylor, C. B.	ADC(AP)*	USN	20 May 1949
151	Mullen, J., Jr.	Lt. j.g.	USN	23 May 1949
152	Larkin, H. J.	Lt.	USN	26 May 1949
153	Close, R. A.	Lt. j.g.	USN†	31 May 1949
154	Drinkwater, H. T.	Lt. j.g.	USN	31 May 1949
155	Williams, D. L.	Ens.	USNR	31 May 1949
156	Mundy, E. M.	Lt. Cmdr.	USNR	10 Jun 1949
157	Pennington, B. D.	Lt. j.g.	USN	15 Jun 1949
158	Highsmith, F. L.	Ens.	USNR	15 Jun 1949
159	Crowell, L. T.	Ens.	USNR	15 Jun 1949

Helicopter Pilot Number	Name	Rank	Service	Date of Qualification Designation
160	Buerckholtz, H. M.	Ens.	USNR	15 Jun 1949
161	Banks, W. F.	Lt. j.g.	USN	15 Jun 1949
162	Price, W. J.	Lt. j.g.	USNR	23 Jun 1949
163	Marchand, J. L.	Lt. Cmdr.	USNR	23 Jun 1949
164	Heibr, W. D.	Capt.	USMC	1 Jul 1949
165	Bancroft, A. R.	1st Lt.	USMC	8 Jul 1949
166	Moran, F. P.	1st Lt.	USMC	8 Jul 1949
167	Ford, A.	Lt.	USN	28 Jun 1949
168	Deitrich, V. S.	Cmdr.	USN	14 Jul 1949
169	Neuman, A. E.	Lt.	USNR	15 Jul 1949
170	Bromka, A. C.	Lt. j.g.	USNR	19 Jul 1949
171	Leedom, H. E.	Lt. Cmdr.	USN	20 Jul 1949
172	Seay, G. W.	Lt. j.g.	USN	20 Jul 1949
173	Chagnon, W. G.	PRC(AP)*	USN	26 Jul 1949
174	Butler, W. C.	Lt.	USN	26 Jul 1949
175	Dally, F. E.	Cmdr.	USN	4 Aug 1949
176	Clabaugh, C. L.	Lt. Cmdr.	USNR	4 Aug 1949
177	Farish, G. B.	1st Lt.	USMC	8 Aug 1949
178	Armstrong, V. A.	Capt.	USMC	9 Aug 1949
179	Noble, E. V.	Cmdr.	USN	25 Aug 1949
180	Horn, F. H.	1st Lt.	USMC	7 Sep 1949
181	Vest, J. P. W.	Capt.	USN	16 Sep 1949
182	Tuffanelle, G. T.	Lt. j.g.	USN	17 Sep 1949
183	Marr, R.	AO1(AP)*	USN	23 Sep 1949
184	Woolley, S. R.	MSgt	USMC	26 Sep 1949
185	Barnes, R. O.	Lt. j.g.	USN	27 Sep 1949
186	Anderson, W. A.	AD1(AP)*	USN	27 Sep 1949
187	Dennison, G. E.	Lt. j.g.	USN	30 Sep 1949
188	Fisher, C. E.	Lt. j.g.	USN	5 Oct 1949
189	Treon, H. J.	Lt.	USN	6 Oct 1949
190	Foley, F. D.	Cmdr.	USN	7 Oct 1949
191	Asbury, D. A.	Lt.	USN	14 Oct 1949
192	Percy, G.	Maj.	USMC	17 Oct 1949
193	Rozier, W. R.	Capt.	USMC	17 Oct 1949
194	Cozine, M. E.	ADC(AP)*	USN	20 Oct 1949
195	Holman, E. D.	ADC(AP)*	USN	25 Oct 1949
196	Connant, E. S.	Lt. Cmdr.	USN	30 Sep 1949
197	Hudson, W. N.	Cmdr.	USNR	2 Oct 1949
198	Moody, J. T.	AO1(AP)*	USN	2 Nov 1949
199	Voss, C. M.	Lt. j.g.	USNRV	4 Nov 1949
200	Scott, E. A.	Lt. j.g.	USN	4 Nov 1949
201	Stokes, W. E.	Ens.	USN	8 Nov 1949
202	Russell, J. B.	Lt.	USN	9 Nov 1949
203	Milburn, K. F.	AD1(AP)*	USN	19 Nov 1949
204	Romer, R. D.	Lt. j.g.	USN	14 Nov 1949
205	Collup, W. D.	Capt.	USMC	30 Nov 1949
206	Koelsch, J. H.	Lt. j.g.	USN	9 Dec 1949
207	Proper, W. F.	Lt. j.g.	USN	14 Oct 1949

Helicopter Pilot Number	Name	Rank	Service	Date of Qualification Designation
208	Harrigan, D. W.	Capt.	USN	10 Dec 1949
209	Jenks, R. F.	AMC(AP)*	USN	14 Oct 1949
210	Hamilton, C. B.	Lt. j.g.	USN	20 Jan 1950
211	Brown, S. H.	Lt. Cmdr.	USN	23 Nov 1949
212	Bayers, E. H.	Lt. Cmdr.	USN	23 Nov 1949
213	Bach, H. A.	Lt. Cmdr.	USN	23 Nov 1949
214	Kurtz, L. A.	Lt.	USN	23 Nov 1949
215	Brownfield, R. H.	ADC(AP)*	USN	16 Jan 1950
216	Thorin, D. W.	AMC(AP)*	USN	16 Jan 1950
217	Scroggs, F. W., Jr.	TSgt	USMC	8 Feb 1950
218	Mullkoff, E.	Lt.	USNR	8 Feb 1950
219	Herring, G. W.	Lt. Col.	USMC	10 Feb 1950
220	Davis, R. O.	Lt. j.g.	USN	17 Feb 1950
221	Swinburne, H. W.	Lt.	USN	20 Mar 1950
222	Sundberg, H. J.	Lt.	USN	20 Mar 1950
223	Young, R. E.	Lt. j.g.	USN	20 Mar 1950
224	Cardoza, H.	AD1(AP)*	USN	9 Mar 1950
225	Marsh, E. D.	AD1(AP)*	USN	9 Mar 1950
226	Harbour, C. C.	Lt.	USN	31 Mar 1950
227	Omara, P.	Lt. j.g.	USN	31 Mar 1950
228	Huggins, J. C.	Lt.	USN	20 Apr 1950
229	Jones, C. C.	Lt. j.g.	USN	21 Apr 1950
230	Boegel, W. T.	AOC(AP)*	USN	21 Apr 1950
231	Larson, C. S.	Lt. j.g.	USNR	24 Apr 1950
232	Kakol, J. F.	ADC(AP)*	USN	25 Apr 1950
233	Smolen, F. E.	Lt.	USN	24 Apr 1950
234	Maghan, R. I.	Lt.	USN	28 Apr 1950
235	Richards, F. D.	Lt.	USN	4 May 1950
236	Felten, R. E.	Lt.	USN	4 May 1950
237	Jansen, T. E.	Lt.	USNR	4 May 1950
238	Bowen, J. B.	Capt.	USN	27 Apr 1950
239	Brock, M. A.	Lt.	USN	16 May 1950
240	Falabella, J. J.	Lt.	USNR	17 May 1950
241	Widmar, J. R.	Lt.	USNR	22 May 1950
242	Jensen, E. O.	Lt.	USNR	25 May 1950
243	Stearns, W. G.	Lt.	USN	2 Jun 1950
244	Hudson, F. W.	ACCA(AP)*	USN	9 Jun 1950
245	McFarlane, H.	Capt.	USAF	9 Jun 1950
246	Erwin, W. L.	Lt. j.g.	USN	13 Jun 1950
247	Englehardt, L. J.	1st Lt.	USMC	13 Jun 1950
248	Scott, J. L.	1st Lt.	USMC	13 Jun 1950
249	Waring, E. S.	Cmdr.	USN	27 Jun 1950
250	Albert, W. H.	Lt. j.g.	USNR	1 Jul 1950

Notes:
* NAP and AP: Naval Aviation Pilot, an enlisted pilot.
† Civil Aeronautics Administration
‡ Initials unknown

CHAPTER 16

Naval Astronauts

Sailors have long studied the sky and have used the movements of celestial bodies to guide them across the trackless seas. Realizing the need to observe the movements of the stars and planets, the U.S. Navy established the Depot of Charts and Instruments on 6 December 1830. This is the Navy's oldest scientific institution. The Depot later became the U.S. Naval Observatory. Today it continues to provide the astronomical data necessary for navigation at sea, on land as well as in space.

In 1923 the Naval Research Laboratory (NRL) began operation. The idea for a U.S. Government–supported research laboratory was suggested by the American inventor Thomas Alva Edison during World War I. Secretary of the Navy Josephus Daniels seized the opportunity and invited Edison to become head of the Naval Consulting Board. The board made plans to create a modern scientific research facility, which became the Naval Research Laboratory. Robert Morris Page who was at NRL from the late 1920s to the mid-1960s invented the technology for pulse radar. During WWII his invention assisted the Allies in detecting enemy planes and ships. Without radar, today's space program would be impossible.

Over the nearly two decades since the Navy bought its first aircraft—the Curtiss A-1 Triad—in 1911, aviation advances had aircraft flying ever higher. On 8 May 1929 Lt. Apollo Soucek set the world altitude record for landplanes by flying a Wright Apache to 39,140 feet. Barely a month later, on 4 June, he set the altitude record for seaplanes, also in an Apache, reaching 38,560 feet.

At nearly 40,000 feet, the thin air and decreased pressure made it difficult for human beings to function and survive, but the airplane was a poor vehicle in which to study the upper reaches of the atmosphere. The balloon proved to be more suitable and, in the end, resulted in the first space race between the United States and the Soviet Union.

On 4 August 1933 Lt. Cmdr. Thomas Settle ascended aloft in the sealed life-support gondola of a balloon, but the attempt failed. A similar attempt in a balloon by Soviet aeronauts the following September, achieved the height of 62,230 feet.

Two months later, on 20 November, Settle and Maj. Chester L. Fordney, USMC, flying a 600,000 cubic-foot free balloon, set the world's altitude record of 61,237 feet. While it was an official world's record, it fell 1,000 feet shy of the actual Soviet achievement.

In December 1941, the United States entered WWII with no rocket weapons, while Germany was putting a great deal of effort into rocket development, basing much of its technology on the research of American scientist Robert H. Goddard.

By the end of the war, the U.S. rocket budget was $1.3 million. Research in the use of rockets in jet-assisted takeoff (JATO) had been carried out by rocket pioneer Goddard, assisted by the Navy's Robert Truax. This program laid the groundwork for the use of rocket power in Navy guided missiles. JATO could reduce a takeoff run by 33 to 60 percent, or permit greater payloads.

After WWII, U.S. interest in high-altitude research experiments resumed. The Office of Naval Research (ONR) made plans for a manned balloon flight into the upper atmosphere through Project Helios, which called for the construction of plastic balloons with a gondola equipped with scientific observation instruments. This ambitious plan was replaced in 1947 by Project Skyhook, which used polyethylene balloons to carry instrument packages to extreme altitudes. Thousands of these balloons were sent into the stratosphere for basic research.

In 1952 a new technique was developed in which Deacon rockets were lifted above 70,000 feet by Skyhook balloons and then launched into space. The experiments proved to be so successful that in 1954 plans were made to entrust the lives of men to the Skyhook balloons.

Project Stratolab, a laboratory in the stratosphere, began in 1955. On 8 November 1956, Stratolab I, manned by Lt. Cmdrs. Malcolm D. Ross and Morton Lee Lewis reached a record altitude of 76,000 feet. Balloons, however, could not put a man in space; that would require rocket power.

Naval Research Laboratory scientists had been conducting experiments on the Aerobee and Viking sounding rockets during the early 1950s. An NRL study in 1954 indicated the feasibility of successfully placing a satellite in orbit, using a vehicle based on the Viking as a first stage and the Aerobee as the second.

In 1955 President Eisenhower announced that the United States would launch "small, unmanned, earth-circling satellites" as a part of the U.S. contributions to the International Geophysical Year, 1957–1958. The Naval Research Laboratory proposed that the Vanguard rocket, based on Viking technology, be used to launch the satellite.

The proposal was accepted with Project Vanguard having three missions: place at least one satellite in orbit during 1957–1958, accomplish a scientific experiment in space, and track the flight to demonstrate that the satellite had actually attained orbit.

Before Vanguard could launch a satellite into space, however, the Soviets announced that they had put *Sputnik* into orbit on 4 October 1957. *Sputnik*, the Russian word for travelling companion, was the earth's first artificial satellite. The perception by the United States that it was the leader in space technology was shattered, and the capability of Soviet rockets to fire weapons from space became apparent.

On 31 January 1958, the Army's Jupiter-C, a development of the Redstone rocket, put the first U.S. satellite, Explorer I, into orbit. On 31 March 1958, a Vanguard rocket launched from Cape Canaveral, Fla., put a second earth satellite into orbit.

In response to the Soviet challenge in space, the United States established the National Aeronautics and Space Administration (NASA) in July 1958, and initiated Project Mercury, which would put a man into orbit. On 15 May 1961, President John F. Kennedy went even further and stated in an address that the United States should commit itself to landing a man on the moon by the end of the decade. This goal was named Project Apollo.

The steps to the moon were incremental. First, NASA lobbed a chimpanzee into space on 31 January 1961. After this experiment proved successful, it was then believed possible to put a man into a similar sub-orbital flight. Cmdr. Alan B. Shepard Jr., was chosen to be the first American sent into space. On 5 May 1961, Shepard left earth's atmosphere in his space capsule, *Freedom 7*. It was a ballistic "cannon shot" atop an Army Redstone rocket. The capsule was recovered at sea by an HUS-1 helicopter from Marine Corps squadron HMR(L)-262, which transported it and the astronaut to the carrier *Lake Champlain* (CVS 39).

Subsequent Mercury missions successfully put other men in space and safely recovered each. On 20 February 1962, Lt. Col. John H. Glenn Jr., USMC, and his spacecraft, *Friendship 7*, made three orbits around the earth. In all, six men flew lone missions into space on board Mercury capsules. This program was followed by two-seat Project Gemini missions in 1965 and 1966. Many of these astronauts were naval aviators.

After having succeeded in demonstrating man's capability for surviving in space for extended periods, the ability to change and modify orbits, and of rendezvousing and docking, the moon was the next step. In December 1968, Lt. Cmdr. James A. Lovell Jr., was on the Apollo 8 flight that first flew to the moon and circled it, becoming among the first three men to view the side that is never seen from earth. Seven months later, on 20 July 1969 Neil A. Armstrong, a naval aviator, became the first man to walk on the moon during the Apollo 11 flight. In all, 11 missions were flown in the Apollo moon program, and of the 29 men who flew them, 14 were naval aviators. And of the 12 who walked on the moon, 7 were Navy.

The next U.S space goal was to work and live in space. *Skylab* was the vehicle, a space laboratory in which the astronauts could live a fairly normal life, work on scientific experiments, eat, sleep, and have regular periods of recreation. Three separate crews of *Skylab* astronauts were launched into space during 1973; two were all-Navy crews.

One last Apollo mission was launched on 15 July 1975. Vance D. Brand, a former Navy pilot, was the command module pilot of this mission to dock with a Soviet Soyuz spacecraft. This was the first meeting between American astronauts and Soviet cosmonauts in space. The two crews then conducted scientific experiments before Apollo splashed down in the Pacific near Hawaii and was recovered by *New Orleans* (LPH 11). This was the last splashdown recovery of a manned space capsule by a Navy amphibious ship. The next American manned space vehicle, the Space Shuttle, would make such recoveries unnecessary.

The Space Shuttle was launched by rocket engines, but could land like an airplane, albeit an unpowered glider, thus it could make multiple trips into space. *Columbia* was the first shuttle and was launched on 12 April 1981 with an all Navy-aviator crew. It was followed by Space Shuttles *Challenger, Discovery, Atlantis*, and *Endeavour*. Subsequent shuttle flights were able to take up to ten astronauts on a single flight into space and stay there for longer periods of time and continued to conduct scientific experiments. Limited cooperation with the Russian Republic, part of the former Soviet Union, also continued. In 1995, *Atlantis* transported two Russian cosmonauts to the Russian space station *Mir* where American astronaut Norman Thagard, a former naval aviator, had been living for three months. *Atlantis* docked with *Mir* and returned the American to earth.

Naval aviation continues to play an important role in space. The following three sections provide statistical data on its contributions or involvement in the manned space program.

Members of Naval Aviation Who Have Become Astronauts

(This list includes naval aviators or naval aviation personnel and does not distinguish whether they were on active duty or separated from the Navy/Marine Corps/Coast Guard when involved in space flights.)

Andrew M. Allen	Scott D. Altman	Dominic A. Antonelli
Neil A. Armstrong	Jeffery Ashby	Michael A. Baker
Alan L. Bean	Charles F. Bolden Jr.	Stephen G. Bowen
Kenneth D. Bowersox	Vance D. Brand	Daniel C. Brandenstein
Randolph J. Bresnik	David M. Brown	James F. Buchli
John S. Bull	Daniel C. Burbank	Daniel W. Bursch
Robert D. Cabana	Kenneth D. Cameron	Malcolm Scott Carpenter
Gerald P. Carr	Manley L. Carter Jr.	Eugene A. Cernan
Roger B. Chaffee	Michael L. Coats	Kenneth D. Cockrell
Charles Conrad Jr.	John O. Creighton	Robert L. Crippen
Frank L. Culbertson	R. Walter Cunningham	Robert Curbeam Jr.
Joe F. Edwards Jr.	Ronald E. Evans	Christopher J. Ferguson
Michael J. Foreman	Stephen N. Frick	Dale A. Gardner
Jake E. Garn	Robert L. Gibson	John H. Glenn Jr.
Richard F. Gordon Jr.	Dominic L. Pudwill Gorie	S. David Griggs
Fred W. Haise Jr.	Ken Ham	Frederick H. Hauck
John Herrington	Kathryn P. Hire	David C. Hilmers
Charles O. Hobaugh	Douglas G. Hurley	Brent W. Jett Jr.
Gregory C. Johnson	Mark E. Kelly	Scott J. Kelley
Joseph P. Kerwin	Wendy B. Lawrence	David C. Leestma
Don L. Lind	Michael E. Lopez-Alegria	John M. Lounge
John R. Lousma	James A. Lovell Jr.	Jon A. McBride
Bruce McCandless II	William McCool	Michael J. McCulley
Thomas K. Mattingly II	Bruce E. Melnick	Edgar D. Mitchell
Franklin S. Musgrave	Carlos I. Noriega	Lisa M. Nowak
Bryan D. O'Connor	William Oefelein	Stephen S. Oswald
Robert F. Overmyer	John L. Phillips	Alan G. Poindexter
William F. Readdy	Kenneth S. Reightler Jr.	Richard N. Richards
Kent V. Rominger	Walter M. Schirra Jr.	Winston E. Scott
Elliot M. See	Alan B. Shepard Jr.	Michael John Smith
Robert C. Springer	Susan L. Still	Frederick W. Sturckow
Joseph R. Tanner	Norman E. Thagard	Stephen D. Thorne
Pierre J. Thuot	Richard H. Truly	James D. van Hoften
David M. Walker	Paul J. Weitz	James D. Wetherbee
Terrence W. Wilcutt	Clifton C. Williams	Donald E. Williams
Sunita Williams	Barry E. Wilmore	John W. Young
George D. Zamka		

Members of Naval Aviation Who Have Made Trips Into Space as of March 2011
(This list includes naval aviators or naval aviation personnel and does not distinguish whether they were on active duty or separated from the Navy/Marine Corps/Coast Guard when involved in space flights.)

One Flight

Randolph J. Bresnik	David M. Brown	Malcolm Scott Carpenter
Gerald P. Carr	Manley L. Carter Jr.	R. Walter Cunningham
Joe F. Edwards Jr.	Ronald E. Evans	Michael J. Foreman
Stephen N. Frick	Jake E. Garn	S. David Griggs
Fred W. Haise Jr.	Ken Ham	John Herrington
Douglas G. Hurley	Gregory C. Johnson	Scott J. Kelley
Joseph P. Kerwin	Don L. Lind	Jon A. McBride
William McCool	Michael J. McCulley	Edgar D. Mitchell
Lisa M. Nowak	William Oefelein	Alan G. Poindexter
Michael John Smith	Sunita Williams	Barry E. Wilmore

Two Flights

Dominic A. Antonelli	Neil A. Armstrong	Alan L. Bean
Stephen G. Bowen	Daniel C. Burbank	Frank L. Culbertson
Christopher J. Ferguson	Dale A. Gardner	John H. Glenn Jr.
Richard F. Gordon Jr.	Kathryn P. Hire	John R. Lousma
Bruce McCandless II	Bruce E. Melnick	Carlos I. Noriega
Bryan D. O'Connor	Robert F. Overmyer	John L. Phillips
Kenneth S. Reightler Jr.	Winston E. Scott	Alan B. Shepard Jr.
Robert C. Springer	Susan L. Still	Joseph R. Tanner
Richard H. Truly	James D. van Hoften	Paul J. Weitz
Donald E. Williams	George D. Zamka	

Three Flights

Andrew M. Allen	Jeffery Ashby	Daniel W. Bursch
Kenneth D. Cameron	Eugene A. Cernan	Michael L. Coats
John O. Creighton	Robert Curbeam Jr.	Dominic L. Pudwill Gorie
Frederick H. Hauck	Charles O. Hobaugh	Mark E. Kelly
David C. Leestma	Michael E. Lopez-Alegria	John M. Lounge
Thomas K. Mattingly II	William F. Readdy	Stephen S. Oswald
Walter M. Schirra Jr.	Pierre J. Thuot	Terrence W. Wilcutt

Four Flights

Scott D. Altman	Michael A. Baker	Charles F. Bolden Jr.
Kenneth D. Bowersox	Vance D. Brand	Daniel C. Brandenstein
James F. Buchli	Robert D. Cabana	Kenneth Cockrell
Charles Conrad Jr.	Robert L. Crippen	David C. Hilmers
Brent W. Jett Jr.	Wendy B. Lawrence	James A. Lovell Jr.
Richard N. Richards	Frederick W. Sturckow	David M. Walker

Five Flights

Robert L. Gibson   Kent V. Rominger   Norman E. Thagard

Six Flights

Franklin S. Musgrave   James D. Wetherbee   John W. Young

Order*	Date	Designation	Crew†	Duration
\multicolumn{5}{l}{**U.S. Space Flights with Navy/Marine Corps/Coast Guard Pilots/Astronauts Aboard (As of March 2011)**}
1	5 May 61	Mercury Redstone 3 (*Freedom 7*)	Alan B. Shepard Jr.	15 min 22 sec; 1st American into space, sub-orbital
3	20 Feb 62	Mercury Atlas 6 (*Friendship 7*)	John H. Glenn Jr., USMC	4 hrs 55 min; 1st American to orbit the earth
4	24 May 62	Mercury Atlas 7 (*Aurora 7*)	Malcolm Scott Carpenter	4 hr 56 min 5 sec
5	3 Oct 62	Mercury Atlas 8 (*Sigma 7*)	Walter M. Schirra Jr.	9 hrs 13 min 11 sec
7	23 Mar 65	Gemini 3	John W. Young	4 hrs 53 min
9	21–29 Aug 65	Gemini 5	Charles Conrad Jr.	190 hrs 56 min 1 sec
10	4–18 Dec 65	Gemini 7	James A. Lovell Jr.	330 hrs 35 min 13 sec
11	15–16 Dec 65	Gemini 6	Walter M. Schirra Jr.	25 hrs 51 min 24 sec
12	16 Mar 66	Gemini 8	Neil A. Armstrong	10 hrs 42 min 6 sec
13	3–6 Jun 66	Gemini 9	Eugene A. Cernan	72 hrs 20 min 56 sec
14	18–21 Jul 66	Gemini 10	John W. Young	70 hrs 46 min 45 sec
15	12–15 Sep 66	Gemini 11	Richard F. Gordon Jr., Charles Conrad Jr.	71 hrs 17 min 8 sec
16	11–15 Nov 66	Gemini 12	James A. Lovell Jr.	94 hrs 34 min 31 sec
17	11–22 Oct 68	Apollo 7	Walter M. Schirra Jr., R. Walter Cunningham	206 hrs 9 min
18	21–27 Dec 68	Apollo 8	James A. Lovell Jr.	147 hrs 0 min 42 sec; 1st flight to the moon
20	18–26 May 69	Apollo 10	John W. Young, Eugene A. Cernan	192 hrs 3 min 23 sec
21	16–24 Jul 69	Apollo 11	Neil A. Armstrong	195 hrs 18 min 35 sec; 1st moon landing
22	14–24 Nov 69	Apollo 12	Charles Conrad Jr., Richard F. Gordon Jr., Alan L. Bean	244 hrs 36 min 25 sec
23	11–17 Apr 70	Apollo 13	James A. Lovell Jr., Fred W. Haise Jr.	142 hrs 54 min 41 sec
24	31 Jan–9 Feb 71	Apollo 14	Alan B. Shepard Jr., Edgar D. Mitchell	216 hrs 1 min 57 sec
26	16–27 Apr 72	Apollo 16	John W. Young, Thomas K. Mattingly II	265 hrs 1 min 5 sec
27	7–19 Dec 72	Apollo 17	Eugene A. Cernan, Ronald E. Evans	301 hrs 51 min 59 sec
28	25 May–22 Jun 73	Skylab 2	Charles Conrad Jr., Joseph P. Kerwin, Paul J. Weitz	672 hrs 49 min 49 sec; 1st U.S. manned orbiting space station; all-Navy crew
29	28 Jul–25 Sep 73	Skylab 3	Alan L. Bean; John R. Lousma, USMC	1,427 hrs 9 min 4 sec
30	16 Nov 73–8 Feb 74	Skylab 4	Gerald P. Carr, USMC	2,017 hrs 15 min 32 sec
31	15–24 Jul 75	Apollo-Soyuz Test Project	Vance D. Brand	217 hrs 28 min 24 sec

Flight*	Date	Orbiter	Crew†	Notes
\multicolumn{5}{l}{**Space Shuttle Missions**}
STS-1	12–14 Apr 1981	*Columbia*	John W. Young, Robert L. Crippen	1st flight, all-Navy crew
STS-2	12–14 Nov 1981	*Columbia*	Richard H. Truly	
STS-3	22–30 Mar 1982	*Columbia*	John R. Lousma, USMC	
STS-4	27 Jun–4 Jul 1982	*Columbia*	Thomas K. Mattingly II	
STS-5	11–16 Nov 1982	*Columbia*	Vance D. Brand; Robert F. Overmyer, USMC	
STS-6	4–9 Apr 1983	*Challenger*	Paul J. Weitz; Franklin S. Musgrave, USMC	

Space Shuttle Missions				
Flight*	Date	Orbiter	Crew†	Notes
STS-7	18–24 Jun 1983	*Challenger*	Robert L. Crippen, Frederick H. Hauck, Norman E. Thagard	
STS-8	30 Aug–5 Sep 1983	*Challenger*	Richard H. Truly, Daniel C. Brandenstein, Dale A. Gardner	
STS-9	28 Nov–8 Dec 1983	*Columbia*	John W. Young	
STS-41-B	3–11 Feb 1984	*Challenger*	Vance D. Brand, Robert L. Gibson, Bruce McCandless II	1st untethered walk in space
STS-41-C	6–13 Apr 1984	*Challenger*	Robert L. Crippen, James D. van Hoften	
STS-41-D	30 Aug–5 Sep 1984	*Discovery*	Michael L. Coats	
STS-41-G	5–13 Oct 1984	*Challenger*	Robert L. Crippen, Jon A. McBride, David C. Leestma	
STS-51-A	8–15 Nov 1984	*Discovery*	Frederick H. Hauck, David M. Walker, Dale A. Gardner	
STS-51-C	24–27 Jan 1985	*Discovery*	Thomas K. Mattingly II; James F. Buchli, USMC	
STA-51-D	12–19 Apr 1985	*Discovery*	Donald E. Williams, S. David Griggs, Jake E. Garn	
STS-51-B	29 Apr–6 May 1985	*Challenger*	Robert F. Overmyer, USMC; Don L. Lind; Norman E. Thagard	
STS-51-G	17–24 Jun 1985	*Discovery*	Daniel C. Brandenstein, John O. Creighton	
STS-51-F	29 Jul 85–6 Aug 1985	*Challenger*	Franklin S. Musgrave, USMC	
STS-51-I	27 Aug 85–3 Sep 1985	*Discovery*	James D. van Hoften, John M. Lounge	
STS-51-J	3–7 Oct 1985	*Atlantis*	David C. Hilmers, USMC	
STS-61-A	30 Oct–6 Nov 1985	*Challenger*	James F. Buchli, USMC	
STS-61-B	26 Nov–3 Dec 1985	*Atlantis*	Bryan D. O'Connor, USMC	
STS-61-C	12–18 Jan 1986	*Columbia*	Robert L. Gibson; Charles F. Bolden Jr., USMC	
STS-51-L	28 Jan 1986	*Challenger*	Michael J. Smith	Shuttle destroyed, all on board killed
STS-26	29 Sep–3 Oct 1988	*Discovery*	Frederick H. Hauck; John M. Lounge; David C. Hilmers, USMC	
STS-27	2–6 Dec 1988	*Atlantis*	Robert L. Gibson, William M. Shepherd‡	
STS-29	13–18 Mar 1989	*Discovery*	Michael L. Coats, James Buchli, Robert Springer	
STS-30	4–8 May 1989	*Atlantis*	David M. Walker, Norman E. Thagard	
STS-28	8–13 Aug 1989	*Columbia*	Richard N. Richards, David C. Leestma	
STS-34	18–23 Oct 1989	*Atlantis*	Donald E. Williams, Michael J. McCulley	
STS-33	22–27 Nov 1989	*Discovery*	Manley L. Carter Jr.; Franklin S. Musgrave, USMC	
STS-32	9–20 Jan 1990	*Columbia*	Daniel C. Brandenstein, James D. Wetherbee	
STS-36	28 Feb–4 Mar 1990	*Atlantis*	John O. Creighton; David C. Hilmers, USMC; Pierre J. Thuot	
STS-31	24–29 Apr 1990	*Discovery*	Charles F. Bolden Jr., USMC; Bruce McCandless II	
STS-41	6–10 Oct 1990	*Discovery*	Richard N. Richards; Robert D. Cabana, USMC; Bruce E. Melnick, USCG; William M. Shepherd‡	
STS-38	15–20 Nov 1990	*Atlantis*	Frank L. Culbertson; Robert C. Springer, USMC	
STS-35	2–6 Dec 1990	*Columbia*	Vance D. Brand, John M. Lounge	
STS-37	5–11 Apr 1991	*Atlantis*	Kenneth D. Cameron, USMC	
STS-39	28 Apr–6 May 1991	*Discovery*	Michael L. Coats	
STS-40	5–14 Jun 1991	*Columbia*	Bryan D. O'Connor, USMC	
STS-43	2–11 Aug 1991	*Atlantis*	Michael A. Baker	
STS-48	12–18 Sep 1991	*Discovery*	John O. Creighton; Kenneth S. Reightler Jr.; James F. Buchli, USMC	
STS-44	24 Nov–1 Dec 1991	*Atlantis*	Franklin S. Musgrave, USMC; Mario Runco Jr.‡	
STS-42	22–30 Jan 1992	*Discovery*	Stephen S. Oswald; Norman E. Thagard; William F. Readdy; David C. Hilmers, USMC	
STS-45	24 Mar–2 Apr 1992	*Atlantis*	Charles F. Bolden Jr., USMC; David C. Leestma	

Space Shuttle Missions				
Flight*	Date	Orbiter	Crew†	Notes
STS-49	7–16 May 1992	*Endeavour*	Daniel C. Brandenstein; Bruce E. Melnick, USCG; Pierre J. Thuot	
STS-50	25 Jun–9 Jul 1992	*Columbia*	Richard N. Richards, Kenneth D. Bowersox	
STS-46	31 Jul–8 Aug 1992	*Atlantis*	Andrew M. Allen, USMC	
STS-47	12–20 Sep 1992	*Endeavour*	Robert Gibson	
STS-52	22 Oct–1 Nov 1992	*Columbia*	James D. Wetherbee, Michael A. Baker, William M. Shepherd‡	
STS-53	2–9 Dec 1992	*Discovery*	David M. Walker; Robert D. Cabana, USMC	
STS-54	13–19 Jan 1993	*Endeavour*	Mario Runco Jr.‡	
STS-56	8–17 Apr 1993	*Discovery*	Kenneth D. Cameron, USMC; Stephen S. Oswald; Kenneth D. Cockrell	
STS-51	12–22 Sep 1993	*Discovery*	Frank L. Culbertson Jr., William F. Readdy, Daniel W. Bursch	
STS-61	2–13 Dec 1993	*Endeavour*	Kenneth D. Bowersox; Franklin S. Musgrave, USMC	
STS-60	3–11 Feb 1994	*Discovery*	Charles F. Bolden Jr., USMC; Kenneth S. Reightler Jr.	
STS-62	4–18 Mar 1994	*Columbia*	Andrew M. Allen, USMC; Pierre J. Thuot	
STS-65	8–23 Jul 1994	*Columbia*	Robert D. Cabana, USMC	
STS-64	9–20 Sep 1994	*Discovery*	Richard N. Richards, Jerry M. Linenger‡	
STS-68	30 Sep–11 Oct 1994	*Endeavour*	Michael A. Baker; Terrence W. Wilcutt, USMC; Daniel W. Bursch	
STS-66	3–14 Nov 1994	*Atlantis*	Joseph R. Tanner	
STS-63	2–11 Feb 1995	*Discovery*	James D. Wetherbee	
STS-67	2–18 Mar 1995	*Endeavour*	Stephen S. Oswald, Wendy B. Lawrence	
STS-71	27 Jun–7 Jul 1995	*Atlantis*	Robert L. Gibson	
STS-69	7–18 Sep 1995	*Endeavour*	David M. Walker, Kenneth Cockrell	
STS-73	20 Oct–5 Nov 1995	*Columbia*	Kenneth D. Bowersox, Kent V. Rominger, Michael E. Lopez-Alegria	
STS-74	12–20 Nov 1995	*Atlantis*	Kenneth D. Cameron, USMC	
STS-72	11–20 Jan 1996	*Endeavour*	Brent W. Jett Jr., Winston E. Scott	
STS-75	22 Feb–9 Mar 1996	*Columbia*	Andrew M. Allen, USMC	
STS-77	19–29 May 1996	*Endeavour*	Daniel W. Bursch, Mario Runco Jr.‡	
STS-78	20 Jun–7 Jul 1996	*Columbia*	Charles E. Brady Jr.‡	
STS-79	16–26 Sep 1996	*Atlantis*	William F. Readdy; Terrence W. Wilcutt, USMC	
STS-80	19 Nov–7 Dec 1996	*Columbia*	Kenneth D. Cockrell; Kent V. Rominger; Franklin S. Musgrave, USMC	
STS-81	12–22 Jan 1997	*Atlantis*	Michael A. Baker, Brent W. Jett Jr., Jerry M. Linenger‡	
STS-82	11–21 Feb 1997	*Discovery*	Kenneth D. Bowersox, Joseph R. Tanner	
STS-83	4–8 Apr 1997	*Columbia*	Susan L. Still	
STS-84	15–24 May 1997	*Atlantis*	Carlos I. Noriega, USMC	
STS-94	1–17 Jul 1997	*Columbia*	Susan L. Still	
STS-85	7–19 Aug 1997	*Discovery*	Kent V. Rominger, Robert L. Curbeam Jr.	
STS-86	25 Sep–6 Oct 1997	*Atlantis*	James D. Wetherbee, Wendy B. Lawrence	
STS-87	19 Nov–5 Dec 1997	*Columbia*	Winston E. Scott	
STS-89	22–31 Jan 1998	*Endeavour*	Terrence W. Wilcutt, USMC; Joe F. Edwards Jr.; James F. Reilly‡	
STS-90	17 Apr–3 May 1998	*Columbia*	Scott D. Altman, Kathryn P. Hire	
STS-91	2–12 Jun 1998	*Discovery*	Dominic L. Pudwill Gorie, Wendy B. Lawrence	
STS-95	29 Oct–7 Nov 98	*Discovery*	John H. Glenn Jr., USMC§	
STS-88	4–15 Dec 1998	*Endeavour*	Robert D. Cabana, USMC; Frederick W. Sturckow, USMC	
STS-96	27 May–6 Jun 1999	*Discovery*	Kent V. Rominger	
STS-93	23–27 Jul 1999	*Columbia*	Jeffrey S. Ashby	

Space Shuttle Missions				
Flight[*]	Date	Orbiter	Crew[†]	Notes
STS-103	19–27 Dec 1999	*Discovery*	Scott J. Kelly	
STS-99	11–22 Feb 2000	*Endeavour*	Dominic L. Pudwill Gorie	
STS-106	8–20 Sep 2000	*Atlantis*	Terrence W. Wilcutt, USMC; Scott D. Altman; Daniel C. Burbank, USCG	
STS-92	11–24 Oct 2000	*Discovery*	Michael Lopez-Alegria	
STS-97	30 Nov–11 Dec 2000	*Endeavour*	Brent W. Jett Jr.; Joseph Tanner; Carlos Noriega, USMC	
STS-98	7–20 Feb 2001	*Atlantis*	Kenneth Cockrell, Robert Curbeam Jr.	
STS-102	8–21 Mar 2001	*Discovery*	James Wetherbee	
STS-100	19 Apr–1 May 2001	*Endeavour*	Kent Rominger, Jeffrey Ashby, John L. Phillips	
STS-104	12–24 Jul 2001	*Atlantis*	Charles O. Hobaugh, USMC	
STS-105	10–22 Aug 2001	*Discovery*	Frederick W. Sturckow, USMC	
STS-108	5–17 Dec 2001	*Endeavour*	Dominic L. Gorie, Mark E. Kelly	
STS-109	1–12 Mar 2002	*Columbia*	Scott D. Altman	
STS-110	8–19 Apr 2002	*Atlantis*	Stephen N. Frick, Lee M. E. Morin[‡]	
STS-111	5–19 Jun 2002	*Endeavour*	Kenneth Cockrell	
STS-112	7–18 Oct 2002	*Atlantis*	Jeffrey Ashby	
STS-113	23 Nov–7 Dec 2002	*Endeavour*	Jim Wetherbee, Michael Lopez-Alegria, John Herrington	
STS-107	16 Jan–1 Feb 2003	*Columbia*	William C. McCool, David M. Brown, Laurel B. S. Clark[‡]	Shuttle destroyed, all on board killed
STS-114	26 Jul–9 Aug 2005	*Discovery*	Wendy Lawrence	
STS-121	4–17 Jul 2006	*Discovery*	Mark E. Kelly, Lisa M. Nowak	
STS-115	9–21 Sep 2006	*Atlantis*	Brent W. Jett Jr.; Christopher J. Ferguson; Daniel C. Burbank, USCG; Heidemarie M. Stefanyshyn-Piper[‡]; Joseph R. Tanner	
STS-116	9–22 Dec 2006	*Discovery*	William Oefelein, Robert Curbeam Jr., Sunita Williams	
STS-117	8–22 Jun 2007	*Atlantis*	Frederick W. Sturckow, USMC; James F. Reilly[†]	
STS-118	8–21 Aug 2007	*Endeavor*	Scott J. Kelley; Charles O. Hobaugh, USMC	
STS-120	23 Oct–Nov 2007	*Discovery*	George D. Zamka, USMC	
STS-126	14–30 Nov 2008	*Endeavour*	Christopher J. Ferguson	
STS-119	15–28 Mar 2009	*Discovery*	John L. Phillips, Dominic A. Antonelli	
STS-125	11–24 May 2009	*Atlantis*	Scott D. Altman, Gregory C. Johnson	
STS-127	15–31 Jul 2009	*Endeavour*	Douglas G. Hurley, USMC	
STS-128	28 Aug–11 Sep 2009	*Discovery*	Frederick W. Sturckow, USMC	
STS-129	16–27 Nov 2009	*Atlantis*	Charles O. Hobaugh, USMC; Randolph J. Bresnik, USMC; Michael J. Foreman; Barry E. Wilmore	
STS-130	8–21 Feb 2010	*Endeavour*	George D. Zamka, USMC; Kathryn P. Hire	
STS-131	5–20 Apr 2010	*Discovery*	Alan G. Poindexter	
STS-132	14–26 May 2010	*Atlantis*	Ken Ham, Dominic A. Antonelli, Stephen G. Bowen	
STS-133	24 Feb–9 Mar 2011	*Discovery*	Stephen G. Bowen	
STS-134	16 May–1 June 2011	*Endeavour*	Mark E. Kelly, Roberto Vittori[‖]	
STS-135	8–21 July 2011	*Atlantis*	Christopher J. Ferguson, Douglas G. Hurley	

[*] Flight is by mission date, not mission number. Only flights with naval aviation personnel, active and former, on board are listed.

[†] Only naval aviation personnel on board the flight are listed.

[‡] Navy but not connected with naval aviation.

[§] Passenger.

[‖] Italian Air Force, USN Test Pilot School graduate.

Chapter 17

Naval Aviation Hall of Honor

The Naval Aviation Hall of Honor was established in 1980 to recognize those individuals who by their actions or achievements made outstanding contributions to naval aviation. A bronze plaque of the individual and their contributions is cast and placed in Naval Aviation Hall of Honor located in the National Museum of Naval Aviation at Pensacola, Fla. The first group to be inducted was in 1981. After 1984, enshrinement in the Naval Aviation Hall of Honor was placed on a two-year cycle with no more than a maximum of eight inductees. The selection committee, consisting of seven to 11 members appointed by the Chief of Naval Operations, Director Air Warfare, is responsible for making the final nominee recommendations. Final approval is done by the Chief of Naval Operations.

Personnel eligible for nomination to the Naval Aviation Hall of Honor include civilian or uniformed individuals no longer employed by the federal government or on active duty. Criteria for nomination include:

- Sustained superior performance in or for naval aviation.
- Superior contributions in the technical or tactical development of naval aviation.
- Unique and superior flight achievement in combat or non-combat flight operations.

The following are enshrined in the Naval Aviation Hall of Honor:

Enshrinee	Year
Vice Adm. Patrick N. L. Bellinger, USN	1981
CWO Floyd Bennett, USN	1981
Rear Adm. Richard E. Byrd Jr., USN	1981
Lt. Cmdr. Godfrey de C. Chevalier, USN	1981
Lt. Col. Alfred A. Cunningham, USMC	1981
Mr. Glenn H. Curtiss, Civilian	1981
Cmdr. Theodore G. Ellyson, USN	1981
Mr. Eugene Ely, Civilian	1981
Rear Adm. William A. Moffett, USN	1981
Rear Adm. Albert C. Read, USN	1981
Capt. Holden C. Richardson, USN	1981
Adm. John H. Towers, USN	1981
Gen. Roy S. Geiger, USMC	1983
Mr. Glenn Martin, Civilian	1983
Adm. Marc A. Mitscher, USN	1983
Adm. Arthur W. Radford, USN	1983
Vice Adm. Charles E. Rosendahl, USN	1983
Cmdr. Elmer F. Stone, USCG	1983
Vice Adm. James H. Flatley Jr., USN	1984
Mr. Leroy R. Grumman, Civilian	1984
Adm. John S. Thach, USN	1984
Capt. Kenneth Whiting, USN	1984
Maj. Gen. Marion E. Carl, USMC	1986
Fleet Adm. William F. Halsey, USN	1986
Mr. Edward H. Heinemann, Civilian	1986

Enshrinee	Year
Rear Adm. David S. Ingalls, USNR	1986
Capt. Donald Bantram MacDiarmid, USCG (Ret)	1986
Vice Adm. Robert B. Pirie, USN (Ret)	1986
Gy. Sgt. Robert G. Robinson, USMCR	1986
Vice Adm. Frederick M. Trapnell, USN (Ret)	1986
Capt. Washington I. Chambers, USN	1988
Dr. Jerome C. Hunsaker, Civilian	1988
Capt. David McCampbell, USN (Ret)	1988
Gen. Keith B. McCutcheon, USMC (Ret)	1988
Adm. Thomas H. Moorer, USN (Ret)	1988
Adm. Alfred M. Pride, USN	1988
Capt. Frank A. Erickson, USCG	1990
Capt. Henry C. Mustin, USN	1990
Adm. James S. Russell, USN (Ret)	1990
Rear Adm. Alan B. Shepard Jr., USN (Ret)	1990
Mr. Igor I. Sikorsky, Civilian	1990
Mr. George A. Spangenberg, Civilian	1990
Vice Adm. Gerald F. Bogan, USN	1992
Adm. Austin Kelvin Doyle, USN (Ret)	1992
Lt. Edward H. O'Hare, USN	1992
Vice Adm. William A. Schoech, USN (Ret)	1992
Mr. Lawrence Sperry, Civilian	1992
Col. Gregory Boyington, USMC	1994
Brig. Gen. Joseph Jacob Foss, ANG (Ret)	1994
Capt. Ashton Graybiel, Medical Corp, USN (Ret)	1994
Adm. Frederick H. Michaelis, USN	1994
Vice Adm. Apollo Soucek, USN (Ret)	1994
Rear Adm. Joseph C. Clifton, USN	1996
Mr. Charles H. Kaman, Civilian	1996
Gen. Christian F. Schilt, USMC	1996
Adm. Forrest P. Sherman, USN	1996
Vice Adm. James B. Stockdale, USN (Ret)	1996
Adm. Maurice F. Weisner, USN (Ret)	1996
Adm. Arleigh A. Burke, USN	1998
Sen. John H. Glenn Jr.	1998
Vice Adm. Thomas F. Connolly, USN	1998
Vice Adm. John T. Hayward, USN	1998
Vice Adm. Thomas G. W. Settle, USN	1998
Mr. Rex Beisel, Civilian	2000
Gen. William O. Brice, USMC	2000
Vice Adm. William I. Martin, USN	2000
Capt. Walter M. Schirra Jr., USN	2000
Fleet Adm. Ernest J. King, USN	2002

Enshrinee	Year
Adm. Joseph M. Reeves, USN	2002
Capt. Roy M. Voris, USN	2002
Lt. Col. Kenneth A. Walsh, USMC	2002
Adm. James L. Holloway, USN	2004
Brig. Gen. Robert E. Galer, USMC	2004
Capt. James A. Lovell, USN	2004
Cmdr. Stewart R. Graham, USCG	2004
Capt. Eugene A. Cernan, USN	2006
Capt. Arthur Ray Hawkins, USN	2006
Capt. Robert E. Mitchell, MC, USN	2006
Vice Adm. Donald D. Engen, USN	2006
Adm. Stanley R. Arthur, USN	2008
Lt. Col. Harold W. Bauer, USMC	2008
Rear Adm. Clarence Wade McClusky Jr., USN	2008
Rear Adm. James D. Ramage, USN	2008
Capt. Robert L. Rasmussen, USN	2008
Mr. Neal A. Armstrong, Civilian	2010
Lt. Gen. Thomas H. Miller, USMC	2010
Vice Adm. William P. Lawrence, USN	2010
Capt. Richard P. Bordone, USN	2010

CHAPTER 18

Gray Eagle Award

The Gray Eagle trophy made its first appearance in 1961 during the celebration of the Fiftieth Anniversary of Naval Aviation.

In 1959, while serving as Commander in Chief, Allied Forces, Southern Europe, Adm. Charles R. Brown, wrote to the Deputy Chief of Naval Operations (Air), Vice Adm. Robert B. Pirie, telling of certain discussions he had with Vice Adm. George W. Anderson, then serving as Commander, Sixth Fleet. "We suggest that it be determined from official records who, at all times, is the senior aviator in point of service in flying; that a baton or similar token be awarded him, and that, with due ceremony, this symbol be handed on down to the next man with the passing years."

Adm. Pirie took the matter from there. For a time the title "Bull Naval Aviator" was a leading contender for the choice of names for the senior aviator's title. Various cups, statuettes, plaques, and medals were proposed. Finally, a competition was conducted among aircraft companies desiring to sponsor the award. The Chance Vought Aircraft Company's (later LTV Corporation, Ling Temco Vought) design was selected and the Gray Eagle Award became a reality.

On 5 January 1961, at naval aviation's Fiftieth Anniversary Ball, Sheraton Park Hotel, Washington, D.C., Adm. Charles R. Brown received the Gray Eagle trophy from Adm. James S. Russell, then serving as Vice Chief of Naval Operations.

While Adm. Brown was the first "active" aviator to receive the trophy, replicas of the award were presented to all previous holders of the distinction, or their representative, during the ceremony. The recipients included Mrs. T. G. Ellyson, widow of Naval Aviator Number One, Cmdr. Theodore G. Ellyson. Cmdr. Ellyson would have held the Gray Eagle title from 1911 to 1928, if the award had been in existence.

The trophy, donated by Chance Vought Aircraft (now Ling Temco Vought) depicts a silver eagle landing into the arresting gear of the Navy's first aircraft carrier, *Langley* (CV 1). The inscription reads: "The Venerable Order of the Gray Eagle. The Most Ancient Naval Aviator on Active Duty. In recognition of a clear eye, a stout heart, a steady hand, and a daring defiance of gravity and the law of averages." Names of those who have held the title, either actively or prior to the 1961 ceremony, are inscribed on the trophy's plaque.

Eligibility for the Gray Eagle Award is determined by the official active duty precedence list for naval aviators, on continuous service, not recalled, who has held that designation for the longest period of time. The date of designation as a Naval Aviator is the governing factor for determining who will receive the award from the list of active duty officers. In the event that two or more aviators on active duty have been designated on the same date, the senior one qualified as the Gray Eagle. The award is passed down from the previous holder of the award on his or her retirement, or in case of death. A miniature replica is presented to each incumbent as a personal memento. The Gray Eagle trophy may be kept in possession of and displayed by the command to which the Gray Eagle is assigned. Otherwise, it may be placed in the custody of the National Museum of Naval Aviation on a temporary basis until required for presentation to the successor. It should be noted that the ceremony date for the presentation of the Gray Eagle Award and the retirement date are not always the same.

Gray Eagle Award Recipients				
Name	**Rank Upon Retirement or Death**	**Naval Aviator Number**	**Date Designated Naval Aviator†**	**Dates as Gray Eagle**
Theodore G. Ellyson	Cmdr.	1	2 Jun 1911*	2 Jun 1911–27 Feb 1928
John H. Towers	Adm.	3	14 Sep 1911*	27 Feb 1928–1 Dec 1947
George D. Murray	Vice Adm.	22	20 Sep 1915	1 Dec 1947–1 Aug 1951
William W. Townsley	Capt.	320	13 Feb 1918	1 Aug 1951–1 Jul 1955
Alvin O. Preil	Capt.	538	11 Mar 1918	1 Jul 1955–1 Jan 1959
Irving M. McQuiston	Rear Adm.	905	12 Jun 1918	1 Jan 1959–1 Jul 1959
Alfred M. Pride	Vice Adm.	1119	17 Sep 1918	1 Jul 1959–1 Oct 1959
Thomas S. Combs	Vice Adm.	3064	21 Dec 1922	1 Oct 1959–1 Apr 1960
[The above list of naval aviators was designated retroactively following the establishment of the award in 1961.]				
Charles R. Brown	Adm.	3159	15 Aug 1924	1 Apr 1960–2 Jan 1962

Gray Eagle Award Recipients				
Name	Rank Upon Retirement or Death	Naval Aviator Number	Date Designated Naval Aviator[†]	Dates as Gray Eagle
Frank Akers	Rear Adm.	3228	11 Sep 1925	2 Jan 1962–1 Apr 1963
Wallace M. Beakley	Rear Adm.	3312	24 Nov 1926	1 Apr 1963–31 Dec 1963
Robert Goldthwaite	Rear Adm.	3364	20 May 1927	31 Dec 1963–1 Oct 1965
Richard C. Mangrum	Lt. Gen. (USMC)	4447	20 May 1929	1 Oct 1965–30 Jun 1967
Fitzhugh Lee	Vice Adm.	3512	16 Sep 1929	30 Jun 1967–31 July 1967
Charles D. Griffin	Adm.	3647	6 Jun 1930	31 Jul 1967–1 Feb 1968
Alexander S. Heyward Jr.	Vice Adm.	3867	23 Nov 1931	1 Feb 1968–1 Aug 1968
Robert J. Stroh	Rear Adm.	3888	25 Jan 1932	1 Aug 1968–28 Nov 1969
George P. Koch	Rear Adm.	4085	2 Jan 1935	28 Nov 1969–31 Jul 1971
Alfred R. Matter	Rear Adm.	4164	30 Oct 1935	31 Jul 1971–29 Feb 1972
Francis D. Foley	Rear Adm.	4178	1 Feb 1936	29 Feb 1972–29 Jun 1972
Thomas H. Moorer	Adm.	4255	12 Jun 1936	29 Jun 1972–30 Jun 1974
Leroy V. Swanson	Rear Adm.	5921	9 Dec 1938	30 Jun 1974–29 Aug 1975
Noel A. M. Gayler	Adm.	6879	14 Nov 1940	29 Aug 1975–31 Aug 1976
Martin D. Carmody	Rear Adm.	10911	22 Jan 1942	31 Aug 1976–27 May 1977
George L. Cassel	Rear Adm.	11262	3 Feb 1942	27 May 1977–31 Aug 1977
Henry Wildfang	CWO4 (USMC)	12766	16 Apr 1942	31 Aug 1977–31 May 1978
Frank C. Lang	Maj. Gen. (USMC)		12 Mar 1943	31 May 1978–30 Jun 1978
Thomas H. Miller Jr.	Lt. Gen. (USMC)		24 Apr 1943	30 Jun 1978–28 Jun 1979
Maurice F. Weisner	Adm.		May 1943	28 Jun 1979–31 Oct 1979
Andrew W. O'Donnell	Lt. Gen. (USMC)		8 Jul 1944	31 Oct 1979–26 Jun 1981
Robert F. Schoultz	Vice Adm.			26 Jun 1981–17 Feb 1987
Cecil J. Kempf	Vice Adm.			25 Feb 1987–6 June 1987
James E. Service	Vice Adm.			6 Jun 1987–21 Aug 1987
Frank E. Peterson Jr.	Lt. Gen. (USMC)			21 Aug 1987–15 Jun 1988
Ronald J. Hays	Adm.			15 Jun 1988–15 Sep 1988
Robert F. Dunn	Vice Adm.			15 Sep 1988–25 May 1989
Huntington Hardisty	Adm.			25 May 1989–1 Mar 1991
Jerome L. Johnson	Adm.			1 Mar 1991–26 Jul 1992
Edwin R. Kohn	Vice Adm.		Jun 1956	26 Jul 1992–1 Jul 1993
Jerry O. Tuttle	Vice Adm.			1 Jul 1993–19 Nov 1993
Stanley R. Arthur	Adm.			19 Nov 1993–21 Mar 1995
David R. Morris	Rear Adm.			21 Mar 1995–28 Feb 1996
Walter Davis	Vice Adm.			28 Feb 1996–1 Jan 1997
Luther Schriefer	Rear Adm.			1 Jan 1997–1 Feb 1997
Andrew Granuzzo	Rear Adm.			1 Feb 1997–24 Mar 2000
James I. Maslowski	Rear Adm.			24 Mar 2000–20 Dec 2000
Arthur K. Cebrowski	Vice Adm.		1 Dec 1965	20 Dec 2000–16 Aug 2001
Robert M. Nutwell	Rear Adm.			16 Aug 2001–26 Sep 2001
Michael D. Haskins	Vice Adm.			26 Sep 2001–21 Nov 2002
Charles W. Moore Jr.	Vice Adm.			21 Nov 2002–1 Oct 2004
Gregory G. Johnson	Adm.			1 Oct 2004–29 Nov 2004
Robert Magnus	Lt. Gen. (USMC)			29 Nov 2004–17 Jul 2008
James F. Amos	Gen. (USMC)		1971	17 Jul 2008–

* Dates qualified for Pilot Certificate under Aero Club of America; Navy Air Pilot numbers were first assigned in January 1915 and Naval Aviator numbers were assigned in January 1918.

† In many cases this date was not provided with the award announcement.

CHAPTER 19

Honorary Naval Aviator Designations

The official Honorary Naval Aviator Program was initiated in 1949 to honor individuals for certain extraordinary contributions and/or outstanding performance for service to naval aviation. In recognition of their service, an Honorary Naval Aviator designation is bestowed on the individual with the right to wear the "Wings of Gold."

The program is managed by the Chief of Naval Operations, Director Air Warfare (previously designated Deputy Chief of Naval Operations, Air Warfare and Assistant Chief of Naval Operations, Air Warfare). Final approval of the nomination is made by the Chief of Naval Operations.

The honor designating an individual an Honorary Naval Aviator has not been bestowed lightly. The following is a list of those individuals who have received the honor:

No	Name	Presented By	Date Received	Reason
1	Capt. Richard (Dick) Schram (Stunt Pilot)	Chief, Naval Air Reserve	Oct 1949	"Flying Professor." Outstanding contribution to aviation since the early 1930s.
2	Sgt. Clifford Iknokinok (Alaskan National Guard)	James H. Smith Jr., Asst. Secy. Navy	21 Nov 1955	Rescued 11 Navy men shot down by Soviet MiGs over international waters, Bering Strait, Alaska.
3	Sgt. Willis Walunga (Alaskan National Guard)	James H. Smith Jr., Asst. Secy. Navy	21 Nov 1955	Rescued 11 Navy men shot down by Soviet MiGs over international waters, Bering Strait, Alaska.
4	Dr. Herman J. Schaefer	Vice Adm. Robert Goldwaite	Jun 1960	Received flight surgeon wings. As a scientist, made outstanding contributions to aerospace research while at the Naval School of Aviation Medicine.
5	Dr. Dietrich E. Beischer	Vice Adm. Robert Goldwaite	Jun 1960	Received flight surgeon wings. As a scientist, made outstanding contributions to aerospace research while at the Naval School of Aviation Medicine.
6	Mr. F. Trubee Davison (Asst. Secy. of War for Air)	Vice Adm. Paul H. Ramsey, DCNO (Air)	Jul 1966	Organized the 1st Yale Unit in 1916. Served as Asst. Secy. of War for Air for 6 years, from late 1920s to 1930s.
7	Mr. Jackie Cooper (Navy Reserve commander)	Vice Adm. Bernard M. Strean, Chief, Naval Air Training	10 Jul 1970	Active in Navy's PAO program, recruiting and promoting since World War II.
8	Vice Adm. Hyman G. Rickover	Vice Adm. Thomas F. Connolly, DCNO (Air Warfare)	21 Jul 1970	Vigorously supported naval aviation and achieved great advancements in nuclear propulsion for aircraft carriers.
9	Lt. Col. Barry R. Butler, USAF	Vice Adm. Bernard M. Strean, Chief, Naval Air Training	19 Aug 1970	Made significant contributions as Advanced Training Officer, Naval Air Training Command. He flew several hundred hours in Navy aircraft and made six landings on board *Lexington* (CVT 16).
10	Mr. John Warner (Secretary of the Navy)	Vice Adm. William D. Houser, DCNO (Air Warfare)	14 Oct 1972	Vigorously supported naval aviation. Presented at establishment of VF-1 and VF-2 (first F-14 squadrons) at NAS Miramar.
11	Mr. Robert G. Smith	Vice Adm. William D. Houser, DCNO (Air Warfare)	8 May 1973	Artist, McDonnell Douglas Corp. National recognition as an outstanding aviation artist.
12	Mr. George Spangeberg (NAVAIRSYSCOM)	Vice Adm. William D. Houser, DCNO (Air Warfare)	Sep 1975	Recognized for his many years of service as a Navy aircraft designer.
13	Mr. Jay R. Beasley	Vice Adm. E. C. Waller III, Director of Weapons Sys. Eva. Grp. for Vice Adm. Houser	25 Jul 1977	Presented in recognition of 23 years of exceptionally dedicated and valuable service to naval aviation as production test pilot with Lockheed and P-2/P-3 instructor.
14	Mr. Robert Osborne	Vice Adm. Frederick C. Turner, DCNO (Air Warfare)	21 Jan 1977	Presented for contributions to naval aviation safety; created Dilbert, Spoiler, and Grampaw Pettibone illustrations.
15	Capt. Virgil J. Lemmon	Vice Adm. Wesley L. McDonald, DCNO (Air Warfare)	23 Feb 1981	"Mr. Naval Aviation Maintenance." Awarded for 40 years of distinguished service to naval aviation and the naval aviation maintenance establishment.
16	Adm. Arleigh A. Burke	Vice Adm. Wesley L. McDonald, DCNO (Air Warfare)	13 Oct 1981	Outspoken supporter of naval aviation; made decisions that shaped the Navy's air arm as it is known today.

No	Name	Presented By	Date Received	Reason
17	Gen. James H. Doolittle	Adm. Thomas B. Hayward, CNO	11 Dec 1981	In recognition of many years of support of military aviation.
18	Mr. Paul E. Garber	Vice Adm. Edward H. Martin, DCNO (Air Warfare)	26 Mar 1985	Made significant contributions to naval aviation spanning the age of manned powered flight. Including service in World Wars I and II and impressive contributions in maintaining the history of naval aviation as the Ramsey Fellow and Historian Emeritus of the National Air and Space Museum.
19	Mr. Bob Hope	Vice Adm. Edward H. Martin, DCNO (Air Warfare) and the Secretary of the Navy, Mr. John Lehman	8 May 1986	Presented in recognition of 45 years of selfless dedication to the well-being of those serving their nation in the Navy, Marine Corps, and Coast Guard and for making remarkable contributions to the morale of those in naval aviation.
20	Mr. Edward H. Heinemann	Vice Adm. Edward H. Martin, DCNO (Air Warfare)	18 Oct 1986	Contributed to major achievements in the technical development of naval aircraft and as one of aviation's most highly regarded aircraft designers. The majority of the aircraft he designed served in naval aviation and he has become known as "Mr. Attack Aviation." A man whose professional life has been dedicated largely to designing a superb series of carrier-based aircraft.
21	Capt. Robert E. Mitchell, MC, USN	Rear Adm. E. D. Conner, Deputy, CNET	25 Jun 1990	Recognized for 43 years of contributions in the field of aerospace medicine. Conducted extensive research in the Thousand Aviator Program; worked with the Navy and Marine Corps Vietnam Prisoners of War (Repatriated); wrote and published numerous medical papers; and his operational work as a naval flight surgeon has helped shape the course of naval aviation.
22	Mr. Harold (Hal) Andrews	Vice Adm. Richard M. Dunleavy, ACNO (Air Warfare)	29 Apr 1991	Outstanding contributions to naval aviation as a civilian engineer with 30 years of service to the Navy; provided technical advice and support for the 50th and 75th naval aviation anniversary celebrations; volunteered support to Naval Aviation News magazine as technical advisor since the 1950s and his vast knowledge of naval aviation events, both technical and operational, have contributed to the advancement of naval aviation since his association with it beginning in World War II.
23	Mr. Corwin H. (Corky) Meyer	Adm. Jay L. Johnson, CNO	9 May 1997	A legendary test pilot with a career at Grumman's "Iron Works" that spanned 55 years. His contributions as a project pilot for Navy aircraft from Hellcats to Super Tigers helped provide the Navy with excellent aircraft. He was also the first civilian pilot to carrier qualify and be inducted into the Carrier Aviation Test Pilot Hall of Honor. Throughout his career as a test pilot and administrator, Corky Meyer's dedication contributed to the continued success of naval aviation.
24	Mr. Harry Gann	Adm. Jay L. Johnson, CNO	24 May 1997	A photographer, historian, writer, and engineer, Mr. Gann was a fixture in the world of naval aviation for more than 40 years. His photographs of the Blue Angels are classics and have been shown around the world. His work in naval aviation, especially his photography, was important in disseminating information about naval aviation to the American public. In 1987 he was recognized for his photography skills by being presented the annual award for Continuing Excellence in Aviation/Space Photography by the Aerofax Publishing Company.
25	Gen. James L. Jones, USMC	Adm. William J. Fallon, USN VCNO	10 Jan 2003	General Jones's extraordinary contributions to Navy and Marine Corps aviation included his efforts ensuring the success of Navy and Marine tactical air integration, supporting the Osprey, Joint Strike Fighter, and KC-130J, and upgrading legacy aircraft to bridge the gap between today's and tomorrow's aviation fleet.
26	Adm. Vern Clark, USN	Vice Adm. Mike Malone, CNAF	12 Jun 2004	For his support of naval aviation during his tenure as CNO.
27	Mr. Henry (Hank) Caruso	Vice Adm. Wally Massenburg, USN COMNAVAIR	9 Sep 2006	In recognition of his years of service as an engineer in support of various naval aviation programs and, even more significantly, for his unique aerocatures artwork. His artistic efforts have been far reaching and have conveyed a positive image of naval aviation.

CHAPTER 20

Navy and Marine Corps Air Stations and Fields Named for Aviators

Including Temporary Advanced Air Bases and Fields

Admiral A. W. Radford Field

At NAS Cubi Point, Philippines. Dedicated 21 December 1972, in honor of former Chairman of the Joint Chiefs of Staff, Adm. Arthur W. Radford. (Field inactive)

Alvin Callender Field

At NAS JRB New Orleans, La. Dedicated 26 Apr 1958, in honor of Capt. Alvin A. Callender, RFC, native of New Orleans, killed in aerial combat during WWI while flying with the Royal Flying Corps of Canada. He was not a U.S. naval aviator. (Active)

Archibald Field

At Managua, Nicaragua. A Marine Corps field named in late 1928 or early 1929 for Capt. Robert J. Archibald, USMC, who directed the location of airfield sites in Nicaragua and was killed in line of duty in November 1928. (Inactive)

Armitage Field

At China Lake, Calif. Name apparently assigned locally; dedicated 30 May 1945, in honor of Lt. John M. Armitage, USNR, killed 21 August 1944, while conducting air firing tests of a Tiny Tim rocket. (Active)

Ault Field

At NAS Whidbey Island, Wash. Named in honor of Commo. William B. Ault, who lost his life in the Battle of Coral Sea. Designated by the Secretary of the Navy on 25 February 1943. (Active)

Barin Field

At Foley, Ala. Name assigned 2 July 1942, prior to establishing as a NAAS, in honor of Lt. Louis T. Barin (Naval Aviator No. 56), test pilot extraordinaire and co-pilot of NC-1 on the 1919 transatlantic attempt. The former NAAS now an ALF to NAS Saufley Field. (Inactive)

Bauer Field

On Vila, New Hebrides Islands. Named in June 1943, for Lt. Col. Harold W. Bauer, commanding officer of VMF-212, who was awarded the Medal of Honor posthumously for action in South Pacific, 28 September–3 October 1942. (Inactive)

Bordelon Field

At NAS Hilo, Hawaii. Named for Sgt. William J. Bordelon, USMC, killed in the invasion of Tarawa. A Medal of Honor recipient, he was not an aviator. (Inactive)

Bourne Field

At MCAS St. Thomas, U.S.V.I. Named in late 1930s for Maj. Louis T. Bourne, first to fly nonstop from the United States to Nicaragua. (Inactive)

Brewer Field

At NAS Agana, Guam, in honor of Cmdr. Charles W. Brewer Jr. Dedicated 15 February 1973. (Inactive)

Bristol Field

At NAS Argentia, Newfoundland. Named 1 June 1943 for Rear Adm. Arthur L. Bristol, who as Commander Support Force, Atlantic, contributed much toward planning and building the station. (Inactive)

Bronson Field

A NAAS at Pensacola, Fla. Name assigned 2 July 1942, prior to establishing of the station, in honor of Lt. j.g. Clarence K. Bronson (Naval Aviator No. 15) killed by premature explosion of a bomb during early bomb dropping tests, 8 November 1916. (Inactive)

Brown Field

A NAAS at Chula Vista, Calif. Named in honor of Cmdr. Melville S. Brown killed in an airplane crash in 1936. Assigned 1 June 1943, to the field at NAAS Otay Mesa and became the station name 11 Jun 1943. (Inactive)

Brown Field

At MCAF Quantico, Va. Name assigned in 1922 in honor of 2d Lt. Walter V. Brown, killed at Quantico in an operational crash. (Inactive)

Byrd Field

A Marine Corps field at Puerto Pabezao, Nicaragua, named in the late 1920s for Capt. William C. Byrd, USMC, killed in airplane crash. (Inactive)

Cabaniss Field

At NAS Corpus Christi, Tex. Dedicated 9 July 1941, in honor of Cmdr. Robert W. Cabaniss (Naval Aviator No. 36) killed in a plane crash in 1927. The former NAAS now an OLF to NAS Corpus Christi. (Active)

Carney Field

On Guadalcanal. Named in the fall of 1942 for Capt. James V. Carney, killed early in World War II. (Inactive)

Cecil Field

A NAS near Jacksonville, Fla. Station established 20 February 1943; named in honor of Cmdr. Henry B. Cecil (Naval Aviator No. 42) lost in the crash of the rigid dirigible *Akron* (ZRS 4) 4 April 1933. (Inactive)

Chambers Field

At NAS Norfolk, Va. Named 1 June 1938, in honor of Capt. Washington I. Chambers, first officer-in-charge of aviation and director of early efforts to find a place for aviation in the fleet although he was not an aviator. (NAS Norfolk no longer active but field still active and under control of NAS Oceana).

Chase Field

A NAS at Beeville, Tex. Named 27 April 1943, in honor of Lt. Cmdr. Nathan B. Chase (Naval Aviator No. 37) killed in 1925 in an air collision while exercising his squadron in fighter tactics. (Inactive)

Chevalier Field

At NAS Pensacola, Fla. Name assigned 30 December 1936, to old Station Field, in honor of Lt. Cmdr. Godfrey de C. Chevalier (Naval Aviator No. 7). (Inactive)

Corry Field

A NAAS at Pensacola, Fla. Name initially assigned 1 November 1922, to a temporary field and reassigned to the new station 8 December 1934, in honor of Lt. Cmdr. William M. Corry (Naval Aviator No. 23) who was awarded the Medal of Honor posthumously. (Inactive)

Cuddihy Field

A NAAS at Corpus Christi, Tex. Station established 3 Sep 1941; named in honor of Lt. George T. Cuddihy, test pilot and speed record holder, killed in a 1929 crash. (Inactive)

Cunningham Field

At MCAS Cherry Point, N.C. Dedicated 4 Sep 1941, in honor of Lt. Col. Alfred A. Cunningham, (Naval Aviator No. 5), the first Marine Corps aviator. (Active)

Dowdell Field

A Marine Corps field at Apali, Nicaragua, named in the late 1920s for Sgt. Frank E. Dowdell, USMC, a non-aviator missing in action after a forced landing with Lt. Earl A. Thomas on Sapotilla Ridge, Nicaragua. (Inactive)

Dyess Field

On Roi Island, Kwajalein Atoll. Named 16 April 1944, for Lt. Col. Aquilla J. Dyess, USMCR, killed leading the assault on Roi-Namur. A non-aviator, Dyess was awarded the Medal of Honor posthumously. (Inactive)

Ellyson Field

A NAS at Pensacola, Fla. Station established 20 January 1943; named in honor of Cmdr. Theodore G. Ellyson, the first naval aviator. (Inactive)

Finucane Field

On Efate, New Hebrides. Named for 2d Lt. Arthur E. Finucane, a pilot with VMF-212 who was killed in a 1942 training accident off New Caledonia. (Inactive)

Flatley Field

At NAS Olathe, Kans. Dedicated 20 May 1962, in honor of Vice Adm. James H. Flatley, fighter pilot, carrier commander, Director of Air Warfare Division, and former commanding officer of the station. (Inactive)

Fleming Field

An auxiliary field to NAS Minneapolis, Minn. Named 20 July 1943, in honor of Capt. Richard E. Fleming, USMC, killed leading an attack on an enemy cruiser in the Battle of Midway; Medal of Honor awarded posthumously. (Inactive)

Floyd Bennett Field

At NAS New York, N.Y. Originally assigned to New York Municipal Airport, dedicated 23 May 1931, and retained as station name upon its establishing 2 June 1941. For Floyd Bennett (Naval Aviation Pilot No. 9) who with Rear Adm. Richard E. Byrd was first to fly over the North Pole. (Inactive Navy field.)

Forrest Sherman Field

At NAS Pensacola, Fla., formerly Fort Barrancas Airfield. Dedicated 2 November 1951, in honor of Adm. Forrest P. Sherman, Chief of Naval Operations, 1949–1951. (Active)

Frederick C. Sherman Field

At San Clemente Island, Calif. Dedicated 11 January 1961, in honor of Vice Adm. Frederick C. Sherman, three-time recipient of the Navy Cross and renowned leader of carrier task groups during WWII. (The former NAAS now an active NALF).

Frederick M. Trapnell Field

At NAS Patuxent River, Md. Dedicated 1 April 1976 in honor of naval aviator Vice Adm. Frederick M. Trapnell. (Active)

Frankforter Field

A Marine Corps field at Esteli, Nicaragua. Named in late 1920s for Pvt. Rudolph A. Frankforter, USMC, a non-aviator killed with Capt. William C. Byrd, USMC, in an airplane crash. (Inactive)

Halsey Field

At NAS North Island, Calif. Dedicated 20 August 1961, in honor of Fleet Adm. William F. Halsey, Commander Third Fleet in the advance across the Pacific during World War II. Officially named Admiral Halsey Field. (Active)

Haring Field

On Efate, New Hebrides. Named for 2d Lt. Richard Z. Haring, USMCR. (Inactive)

Harvey Field

At NAF Inyokern, Calif. Name assigned to field formerly known as Inyokern Airfield, 10 May 1944, in honor of Lt. Cmdr. Warren W. Harvey, for his contributions to the development of aviation ordnance and fighter tactics. (Inactive)

Hawkins Field

On Betio Island, Tarawa. Named for Lt. William D. Hawkins, USMCR, killed while landing his platoon during assault on Tarawa; a non-aviator, he was awarded the Medal of Honor posthumously. (Inactive)

Henderson Field

At NS Midway Island. Named 19 August 1942, in honor of Maj. Loften R. Henderson, lost in action during the Battle of Midway. (Active) Field on Guadalcanal, also named in honor of Maj. Henderson in August 1942. (Inactive)

Hensley Field

At NAS Dallas, Tex. Named for Col. William N. Hensley Jr., a non-aviator prominent in the reserve program during the 1920s. (NAS Dallas is inactive.)

Isley Field

A NAS on Saipan, Marianas Island. Named 30 June 1944, prior to its designation as NAS, for Cmdr. Robert H. Isely, who lost his life leading his squadron in an attack on the then enemy installation known as Aslito Airfield. The incorrect spelling of the station name became official through usage. (Inactive)

John Rodgers Field

At NAS Barbers Point, Hawaii. Dedicated on 10 September 1974 in honor of Cmdr. John Rodgers for his exploits in early naval aviation. (Inactive)

Lee Field

At NAS Green Cove Springs, Fla. Named in September 1940 in honor of Ens. Benjamin Lee, who lost his life in a crash at Killingholme, England, during WWI. Originally assigned as the station name, but reassigned to the landing field when station name changed to Green Cove Springs, 8 August 1943. (Inactive)

Maxfield Field

At NAS Lakehurst, N.J. Named 6 January 1944, in honor of Cmdr. Louis H. Maxfield (Naval Aviator No. 17) who lost his life in the crash of the dirigible R-38, 24 August 1921. (Inactive)

Max Kiel Airfield

At Little America, Antarctica. Named in early 1956 in honor of non-aviator Max Kiel, who lost his life while bridging a crevasse in Marie Byrd Land. (Inactive)

McCain Field

At NAS Meridian, Miss. Dedicated with the establishing of the station 14 July 1961, in honor of Adm. John S. McCain, carrier task force commander, Chief of BuAer, and Deputy Chief Naval Operations (Air). (Active)

McCalla Field

At NAS Guantanamo, Cuba. Named for Capt. Bowman H. McCalla, non-aviator skipper of *Marblehead* (Crusier No. 11) participating in the capture of Guantanamo Bay, and commander of a base established there, during the Spanish-American War. (NAS Guantanamo disestablished but NS Guantanamo still active along with the airfield.)

McCutcheon Field

At MCAS New River, N.C. Named in honor of Gen. Keith B. McCutcheon, a pioneer in Marine Corps helicopter assault tactics. Dedicated 1972. (Active)

Merritt Field

At MCAS Beaufort, S.C., in honor of Maj. Gen. Lewis G. Merritt. Dedicated on 19 September 1975. (Active)

Mitchell Field

At NS Adak, Alaska. Named 2 February 1944, in honor of Ens. Albert E. Mitchell, who lost his life in the Aleutians earlier in the war. Officially named Albert Mitchell Field. (Inactive)

Mitscher Field

At NAS Miramar, Calif. Named 14 June 1955, in honor of Adm. Marc A. Mitscher (Naval Aviator No. 33), leader of fast carrier task forces in WWII and Deputy Chief of Naval Operations (Air). NAS Miramar redesignated MCAS Miramar on 1 October 1997. (Active)

Moffett Field

At NAS at Sunnyvale, Calif. Named in honor of Rear Adm. William A. Moffett, naval aviation observer, first Chief of BuAer and leader of naval aviation through the 1920s who lost his life in the crash of the rigid dirigible *Akron* (ZRS 4) 4 April 1933. Name first assigned 17 May 1933, to the landing field at NAS Sunnyvale, Calif., and remained in use after the station was transferred to the U.S. Army in 1935 and after station was returned to the Navy and established as a NAS, 16 April 1942; became station name 20 April 1942. (Inactive)

Moret Field

On Zamboanga, Philippines. Named for Lt. Col. Paul Moret, USMC, killed in a crash in 1943. (Inactive)

Mullinnix Field

On Buota Island, Tarawa. Named in December 1943 in honor of Rear Adm. Henry M. Mullinnix, carrier division commander, lost in sinking of *Liscome Bay* (CVE 56), during the Gilbert Islands campaign, 24 November 1943. (Inactive)

Munn Field

At MCAS Camp Pendleton, Calif. The airfield was designated Munn Field on 12 January 1987 in honor of Lt. Gen. John C. Munn. The general had been Assistant Commandant of the Marine Corps and the first Marine Aviator to command Camp Pendleton. (Active)

Mustin Field

A NAF at Philadelphia, Pa. Dedicated 17 September 1926, in honor of Capt. Henry C. Mustin (Naval Aviator No. 11), an early exponent of aviation as the striking arm of the fleet. (Inactive)

Nimitz Field

At NAS Alameda, Calif. Dedicated 26 January 1967, in honor of non-aviator Fleet Adm. Chester W. Nimitz, Commander-in-Chief of the Pacific during WWII and Chief of Naval Operations. (Inactive)

Ofstie Field

At NS Roosevelt Roads, P.R. Dedicated 21 May 1959, in honor of Vice Adm. Ralph A. Ofstie, test pilot, fleet commander and Deputy Chief of Naval Operations (Air). (Inactive)

O'Hare Field

On Abemama, Gilbert Islands. Named in December 1943 in honor of Lt. Cmdr. Edward H. O'Hare, air group commander, pioneer in night carrier operations, and Medal of Honor recipient, killed in action during the Gilberts Campaign, 26 November 1943. (Inactive)

Page Field

At MCAS Parris Island, S.C. Named 19 September 1938, prior to station establishing, in honor of Capt. Arthur H. Page Jr., USMC, pioneer in instrument flying and racing pilot, who crashed to his death while leading in the 1930 Thompson Trophy Race. (Inactive)

Ramey Field

At NAS Sanford, Fla. Dedicated 6 February 1959, in honor of Lt. Cmdr. Robert W. Ramey, who lost his life by electing to guide his crippled plane away from a residential area. (Inactive)

Ream Field

At NAS Imperial Beach, Calif. Named in 1943 for Maj. William R. Ream, MC, USA, who was a non-aviator medical officer at Rockwell Field on North Island in the WWI period. Initially the station name when the station was renamed Imperial Beach, 1 January 1968. (Inactive)

Reeves Field

At NAS Lemoore, Calif. Dedicated 20 November 1961, in honor of Rear Adm. Joseph M. Reeves, naval aviation observer and farseeing pioneer in the tactical employment of aircraft carriers. Officially, Joseph Mason Reeves Field. (Active) Field at NAB San Pedro (later NAS Terminal Island), Calif., also named in honor of Adm. Reeves in the 1930s. (Inactive)

Rodd Field

A NAAS at Corpus Christi, Tex. Station established 7 June 1941; named in honor of Lt. Herbert C. Rodd, radio officer in NC-4 on the 1919 transatlantic flight. (Inactive)

Sailer Field

On Guadalcanal. Named for Maj. Joseph Sailer, who lost his life leading his squadron in an attack on enemy destroyers. (Inactive)

Saufley Field

A NAS at Pensacola, Fla. Named prior to station establishing 22 August 1940, in honor of Lt. j.g. Richard C. Saufley (Naval Aviator No. 14), killed in a crash while on a record endurance flight. NAS Saufley Field no longer an active air station, however, the field may be used as an auxiliary landing field.

Shea Field

At NAS South Weymouth, Mass. In honor of Lt. Cmdr. John J. Shea, killed in action while serving on board *Wasp* (CV 7) in 1942. Name assigned first to the field at NAS Squantum, Mass., 15 March 1946, and upon closing of that station in 1954 was transferred to the field at South Weymouth. (Inactive)

Smartt Field

An outlying field to NAS St. Louis, Mo. Named in June 1943 in honor of Ens. Joseph G. Smartt, who lost his life 7 December 1941, while serving with VP-11 at Kaneohe, Hawaii. (Inactive)

Soucek Field

At NAS Oceana, Va. Dedicated 4 June 1957, in honor of Vice Adm. Apollo Soucek, world altitude record holder, test pilot, task force commander, and Chief of BuAer. Officially named Apollo Soucek Field. (Active)

Stickell Field

On Eniwetok, Marshall Islands. Named early in 1944 in honor of Lt. John H. Stickell, naval aviator and former RAF pilot, who died from wounds received in action during a low-level attack on Jaluit in the Marshalls. (Inactive)

Taylor Field

On Efate, New Hebrides. Named for Lt. Lawrence C. Taylor, USMCR, killed while intercepting an air attack on Guadalcanal. (Inactive)

Thomas Field

A Marine Corps field at Ocotal, Nicaragua. Named in the late 1920s for Lt. Earl A. Thomas, USMC, missing in action after a forced landing on Sapotilla Ridge, Nicaragua. (Inactive)

Titcomb Field

On Mindanao, Philippines. Named in February 1945 in honor of Capt. John A. Titcomb, USMCR, a non-aviator killed while directing a close air support mission in northern Luzon. (Inactive)

Towers Field

At NAS Jacksonville, Fla. Dedicated 14 October 1960, in honor of Adm. John H. Towers (Naval Aviator No. 3), an outstanding leader in naval aviation from 1911 to his retirement in 1947. Officially named John Towers Field. (Active)

Turner Field

At MCAF Quantico, Va. Named in honor of Col. Thomas C. Turner, USMC, naval aviator and Director of Marine Aviation. Name was first assigned 1 July 1936, to the field at Marine Barracks, Quantico. (Active)

Van Voorhis Field

At NAS Fallon, Nev. Dedicated 1 November 1959, in honor of Cmdr. Bruce A. Van Voorhis, a posthumous Medal of Honor recipient who lost his life on a low-level bombing attack on enemy positions during the Battle of the Solomon Islands. (Active)

Waldron Field

At NAS Corpus Christi, Tex. Named 5 March 1943, prior to establishing of station, in honor of Lt. Cmdr. John C. Waldron, killed in action leading the attack of Torpedo Squadron 8 in the Battle of Midway, 4 June 1942. The former NAAS is now an OLF to NAS Corpus Christi. (Active)

Webster Field

A flight test field at Priest Point, Md., auxiliary to NAS Patuxent River. Named 1 June 1943 for Capt. Walter W. Webster, one-time head of Naval Aircraft Factory and long associated with test and development work. (Active)

Whiting Field

NAS Whiting Field at Milton, Fla. Named 1 June 1943, prior to establishing of station, in honor of Capt. Kenneth Whiting (Naval Aviator No. 16), first to command naval aviation units overseas in WWI, first acting commander of the Navy's first carrier, and leader in the development of carriers. (Active)

Wigley Field

On Engebi Island, Eniwetok Atoll. Named in March 1944 for Lt. Col. Roy C. Wigley, USAAF, a pilot killed in an attack on Jaluit, Marshall Islands. (Inactive)

Williams Field

At McMurdo Sound, Antarctica. Named 16 February 1956, for non-aviator Richard Williams, killed when his vehicle broke through the bay ice. (Inactive)

CHAPTER 21

Aviation Commands

In order of their establishment:

Office in Charge of Aviation
Director of Naval Aeronautics
Director of Naval Aviation

Capt. Washington I. Chambers	26 Sep 1910–17 Dec 1913
Capt. Mark L. Bristol	17 Dec 1913–4 Mar 1916
Capt. Noble E. Irwin	17 May 1917–May 1919
Capt. Thomas T. Craven	May 1919–7 Mar 1921
Capt. William A. Moffett	7 Mar 1921–26 Jul 1921

The person in charge of aviation affairs for the Navy was initially designated as the officer to whom all correspondence on aviation should be referred. This position was a special duty assignment as Officer in Charge of Aviation. The position was identified by the title Director of Naval Aeronautics on 23 November 1914. It was discontinued on 4 March 1916 and reinstituted as Director of Naval Aviation on 7 March 1918. The title Director of Naval Aviation was replaced in July 1921 by the establishment of the Bureau of Aeronautics.

Officer–in–Charge, Aviation, Headquarters Marine Corps
Director of Marine Corps Aviation
Deputy Chief of Staff (Air), Marine Corps
Deputy Chief of Staff for Aviation, Marine Corps
Deputy Commandant for Aviation, Marine Corps

Maj. Alfred A. Cunningham	17 Nov 1919–12 Dec 1920
Lt. Col. Thomas C. Turner	13 Dec 1920–2 Mar 1925
Maj. Edward H. Brainard	3 Mar 1925–9 May 1929
Col. Thomas C. Turner	10 May 1929–28 Oct 1931
Maj. Roy S. Geiger	6 Nov 1931–29 May 1935
Col. Ross E. Rowell	30 May 1935–10 Mar 1939
Brig. Gen. Ralph J. Mitchell	11 Mar 1939–29 Mar 1943
Maj. Gen. Roy S. Geiger	13 May 1943–15 Oct 1943
Brig. Gen. Louis E. Woods	15 Oct 1943–17 Jul 1944
Maj. Gen. Field Harris	18 Jul 1944–24 Feb 1948
Maj. Gen. William J. Wallace	24 Feb 1948–1 Sep 1950
Brig. Gen. Clayton C. Jerome	1 Sep 1950–1 Apr 1952
Lt. Gen. William O. Brice	1 Apr 1952–31 Jul 1955
Lt. Gen. Christian F. Schilt	1 Aug 1955–31 Mar 1957
Lt. Gen. Verne J. McCaul	1 Apr 1957–2 Dec 1957
Maj. Gen. Samuel S. Jack	14 Jan 1958–20 Feb 1958
Maj. Gen. John C. Munn	21 Feb 1958–14 Dec 1959
Maj. Gen. Arthur F. Binney	15 Dec 1959–10 Sep 1961
Col. Keith B. McCutcheon	11 Sep 1961–17 Feb 1962
Col. Marion E. Carl	18 Feb 1962–4 Jul 1962

Brig. Gen. Norman J. Anderson	5 Jul 1962–20 Oct 1963
Maj. Gen. Louis B. Robertshaw	21 Oct 1963–15 Jun 1966
Maj. Gen. Keith B. McCutcheon	15 Jun 1966–18 Feb 1970
Maj. Gen. Homer S. Hill	19 Feb 1970–24 Aug 1972
Maj. Gen. Edward S. Fris	25 Aug 1972–27 Aug 1974
Brig. Gen. Philip D. Shutler	28 Aug 1974–Jan 1975
Maj. Gen. Victor A. Armstrong	Jan 1975–21 Aug 1975
Lt. Gen. Thomas H. Miller Jr.	22 Aug 1975–29 Jun 1979
Lt. Gen. William J. White	1 Jul 1979–30 Jun 1982
Lt. Gen. William H. Fitch	1 Jul 1982–31 Aug 1984
Lt. Gen. Keith A. Smith	1 Sep 1984–29 Apr 1988
Lt. Gen. Charles H. Pitman	30 Apr 1988–1 Aug 1990
Lt. Gen. Duane A. Wills	17 Aug 1990–30 Jun 1993
Lt. Gen. Richard D. Hearney	1 Jul 1993–14 Jul 1994
Lt. Gen. Harold W. Blot	15 Jul 1994–Jul 1996
Lt. Gen. Terrence R. Dake	Jul 1996–28 Jun 1998
Lt. Gen. Fredrick N. McCorkle	28 Jun 1998–2 Aug 2001
Lt. Gen. William L. Nyland	2 Aug 2001–10 Sep 2002
Vacant	11 Sep 2002–2 Oct 2002
Lt. Gen. Michael A. Hough	3 Oct 2002–2 Nov 2006
Lt. Gen. John G. Castellaw	3 Nov 2006–10 Mar 2007
Lt. Gen. George J. Trautman III	10 Mar 2007–

On 1 April 1936 the title of the senior aviator attached to Headquarters, Marine Corps, changed from Officer-in-Charge, Aviation, to Director of Aviation, and on 25 April 1962 became Deputy Chief of Staff (Air). On 16 September 1972 the title changed to Deputy Chief of Staff for Aviation.

Chief of the Bureau of Aeronautics

Rear Adm. William A. Moffett	26 Jul 1921–4 Apr 1933
Rear Adm. Ernest J. King	3 May 1933–12 Jun 1936
Rear Adm. Arthur B. Cook	12 Jun 1936–1 Jun 1939
Rear Adm. John H. Towers	1 Jun 1939–6 Oct 1942
Rear Adm. John S. McCain	9 Oct 1942–7 Aug 1943
Rear Adm. Dewitt C. Ramsey	7 Aug 1943–1 Jun 1945
Rear Adm. Harold B. Sallada	1 Jun 1945–1 May 1947
Rear Adm. Alfred M. Pride	1 May 1947–1 May 1951
Rear Adm. Thomas S. Combs	1 May 1951–30 Jun 1953
Rear Adm. Apollo Soucek	30 Jun 1953–4 Mar 1955
Rear Adm. James S. Russell	4 Mar 1955–15 Jul 1957
Rear Adm. Robert E. Dixon	15 Jul 1957–1 Dec 1959

Established by act of Congress, 12 July 1921, and merged 1 December 1959 with the Bureau of Ordnance to form the Bureau of Naval Weapons.

Assistant Secretary of the Navy for Aeronautics
Assistant Secretary of the Navy for Air

Edward P. Warner	10 Jul 1926–Mar 1929
David S. Ingalls	16 Mar 1929–1 Jun 1932
Vacant	1 Jun 1932–5 Sep 1941
Artemus L. Gates	5 Sep 1941–1 Jul 1945
John L. Sullivan	1 Jul 1945–17 Jun 1946
John N. Brown	12 Nov 1946–8 Mar 1949
Dan A. Kimball	9 Mar 1949–25 May 1949
John F. Floberg	5 Dec 1949–23 Jul 1953
James H. Smith	23 Jul 1953–20 Jun 1956
Garrison R. Norton	28 Jun 1956–5 Feb 1959

Established by act of Congress 24 June 1926 with title Assistant Secretary of the Navy for Aeronautics. On 11 September 1941 it was retitled Assistant Secretary of the Navy for Air and abolished on 5 February 1959.

U.S. Naval Air Forces, Pacific Fleet
Commander, Air Force, Pacific Fleet
Commander, Naval Air Force Pacific Fleet
Commander, Naval Air Forces

Rear Adm. Aubrey W. Fitch	1 Sep 1942–15 Sep 1942
Rear Adm. Leigh Noyes	15 Sep 1942–14 Oct 1942
Vice Adm. John H. Towers	14 Oct 1942–28 Feb 1944
Rear Adm. Charles A. Pownall	28 Feb 1944–17 Aug 1944
Rear Adm. George D. Murray	17 Aug 1944–20 Jul 1945
Rear Adm. Alfred E. Montgomery	20 Jul 1945–31 Aug 1946
Vice Adm. John D. Price	31 Aug 1946–5 Jan 1948
Vice Adm. Harold B. Sallada	5 Jan 1948–1 Oct 1949
Vice Adm. Thomas L. Sprague	1 Oct 1949–1 Apr 1952
Vice Adm. Harold M. Martin	1 Apr 1952–1 Feb 1956
Vice Adm. Alfred M. Pride	1 Feb 1956–30 Sep 1959
Rear Adm. Murr E. Arnold*	30 Sep 1959–12 Oct 1959
Vice Adm. Clarence E. Ekstrom	12 Oct 1959–30 Nov 1962
Vice Adm. Paul D. Stroop	30 Nov 1962–30 Oct 1965
Vice Adm. Thomas F. Connolly	30 Oct 1965–1 Nov 1966
Vice Adm. Allen M. Shinn	1 Nov 1966–31 Mar 1970
Vice Adm. William F. Bringle	31 Mar 1970–28 May 1971
Vice Adm. Thomas J. Walker III	28 May 1971–31 May 1973
Vice Adm. Robert B. Baldwin	31 May 1973–12 Jul 1976
Vice Adm. Robert P. Coogan	12 Jul 1976–31 Jan 1980
Vice Adm. Robert F. Schoultz	31 Jan 1980–4 Aug 1982
Vice Adm. Crawford A. Easterling	4 Aug 1982–16 Aug 1985
Vice Adm. James E. Service	16 Aug 1985–21 Aug 1987
Vice Adm. John H. Fetterman Jr.	21 Aug 1987–14 Dec 1990
Vice Adm. Edwin R. Kohn Jr.	14 Dec 1990–17 Jun 1993

Rear Adm. Steven R. Briggs	17 Jun 1993–26 Oct 1993
Vice Adm. Robert J. Spane	26 Oct 1993–24 Jan 1996
Vice Adm. Brent M. Bennitt	24 Jan 1996–16 Jan 1998
Vice Adm. Michael L. Bowman	16 Jan 1998–23 Aug 2000
Vice Adm. John B. Nathman	23 Aug 2000–2 Aug 2002
Vice Adm. Michael D. Malone	2 Aug 2002–17 Aug 2004
Vice Adm. James M. Zortman	17 Aug 2004–22 Jun 2007
Vice Adm. Thomas J. Kilcline Jr.	22 Jun 2007–1 Jul 2010
Vice Adm. Allen G. Myers	1 Jul 2010–

* Acting Commander Naval Air Force Pacific Fleet

Established 1 September 1942 as an administrative command replacing the commands Carriers, Pacific Fleet and Patrol Wings, Pacific Fleet. The title, U.S. Naval Air Forces, Pacific Fleet was changed 14 October 1942 to Air Force, Pacific Fleet and 30 July 1957 to Naval Air Force Pacific Fleet. In October 2001 the Chief of Naval Operations directed Commander Naval Air Force Pacific Fleet to become the type commander for all air commands and assumed the additional title of Commander, Naval Air Forces.

Commander, Air Force, Atlantic Fleet
Commander, Naval Air Force Atlantic Fleet

Rear Adm. Alva D. Bernhard	1 Jan 1943–8 Mar 1943
Vice Adm. Patrick N. L. Bellinger	20 Mar 1943–2 Feb 1946
Vice Adm. Gerald F. Bogan	2 Feb 1946–Dec 1948
Vice Adm. Felix B. Stump	Dec 1948–11 Apr 1951
Vice Adm. John J. Ballentine	11 Apr 1951–1 May 1954
Vice Adm. Frederick W. McMahon	1 May 1954–29 May 1956
Vice Adm. William L. Rees	29 May 1956–30 Sep 1960
Vice Adm. Frank O'Beirne	30 Sep 1960–30 Sep 1963
Vice Adm. Paul H. Ramsey	30 Sep 1963–31 Mar 1965
Vice Adm. Charles T. Booth	31 Mar 1965–28 Feb 1969
Vice Adm. Robert L. Townsend	1 Mar 1969–29 Feb 1972
Vice Adm. Fredrick H. Michaelis	29 Feb 1972–14 Feb 1975
Vice Adm. Howard E. Greer	14 Feb 1975–31 Mar 1978
Vice Adm. George E. R. Kinnear	31 Mar 1978–31 Jul 1981
Vice Adm. Thomas J. Kilcline Jr.	31 Jul 1981–1 Aug 1983
Vice Adm. Carol C. Smith Jr.	1 Aug 1983–14 Oct 1983
Vice Adm. Robert F. Dunn	8 Dec 1983–23 Dec 1986
Vice Adm. Richard M. Dunleavy	23 Dec 1986–25 May 1989
Vice Adm. John K. Ready	25 May 1989–6 Aug 1991
Vice Adm. Anthony A. Less	6 Aug 1991–18 Mar 1994
Vice Adm. Richard C. Allen	18 Mar 1994–Mar 1996
Vice Adm. John J. Mazach	Mar 1996–Nov 1998
Vice Adm. Joseph S. Mobley	Nov 1998–12 Apr 2001
Rear Adm. Michael D. Malone	12 Apr 2001–10 Jul 2002
Rear Adm. James M. Zortman	10 Jul 2002–17 May 2004
Rear Adm. H. Denby Starling II	17 May 2004–20 Mar 2007

Rear Adm. John W. Goodwin	20 Mar 2007–13 Jan 2009
Rear Adm. Richard J. O'Hanlon	13 Jan 2009–

Established 1 January 1943 as an administrative command replacing the commands Carriers, Atlantic Fleet and Fleet Air Wing, Atlantic Fleet. The original title, Air Force, Atlantic Fleet, was changed 30 July 1957 to Naval Air Force Atlantic Fleet.

Deputy Chief of Naval Operations (Air)
Deputy Chief of Naval Operations (Air Warfare)
Assistant Chief of Naval Operations (Air Warfare)
Director, Air Warfare

Vice Adm. John S. McCain	18 Aug 1943–1 Aug 1944
Vice Adm. Aubrey W. Fitch	1 Aug 1944–14 Aug 1945
Vice Adm. Marc A. Mitscher	14 Aug 1945–15 Jan 1946
Vice Adm. Arthur W. Radford	15 Jan 1946–22 Feb 1947
Vice Adm. Donald B. Duncan	6 Mar 1947–20 Jan 1948
Vice Adm. John D. Price	20 Jan 1948–6 May 1949
Vice Adm. Calvin T. Durgin	16 May 1949–25 Jan 1950
Vice Adm. John H. Cassady	25 Jan 1950–31 May 1952
Vice Adm. Matthias B. Gardner	31 May 1952–16 Mar 1953
Vice Adm. Ralph A. Ofstie	16 Mar 1953–3 Mar 1955
Vice Adm. Thomas S. Combs	11 Apr 1955–1 Aug 1956
Vice Adm. William V. Davis Jr.	1 Aug 1956–22 May 1958
Vice Adm. Robert B. Pirie	26 May 1958–1 Nov 1962
Vice Adm. William A. Schoech	14 Nov 1962–1 Jul 1963
Vice Adm. John S. Thach	8 Jul 1963–25 Feb 1965
Vice Adm. Paul H. Ramsey	31 Mar 1965–1 Oct 1966
Vice Adm. Thomas F. Connolly	1 Nov 1966–31 Aug 1971
Vice Adm. Maurice F. Weisner	1 Sep 1971–4 Aug 1972
Vice Adm. William D. Houser	5 Aug 1972–30 Apr 1976
Vice Adm. Forrest S. Petersen	1 May 1976–5 Oct 1976
Vice Adm. Frederick C. Turner	6 Oct 1976–30 Jun 1979
Vice Adm. Wesley L. McDonald	1 Jul 1979–1 Sep 1982
Vice Adm. Robert F. Schoultz	2 Sep 1982–27 Jan 1985
Vice Adm. Edward H. Martin	25 Feb 1985–14 Jan 1987
Vice Adm. Robert F. Dunn	15 Jan 1987–25 May 1989
Vice Adm. Richard M. Dunleavy	25 May 1989–12 Jun 1992
Rear Adm. Riley D. Mixson	12 Jun 1992–22 Nov 1993
Rear Adm. Brent M. Bennitt	22 Nov 1993–15 Jan 1996
Rear Adm. Dennis V. McGinn	15 Jan 1996–19 Jul 1998
Rear Adm. John B. Nathman	19 Jul 1998–17 Jul 2000
Rear Adm. Michael J. McCabe	17 Jul 2000–9 Sep 2002
Rear Adm. Mark P. Fitzgerald	9 Sep 2002–14 Aug 2004
Rear Adm. Thomas J. Kilcline Jr.	14 Aug 2004–7 Jul 2006
Rear Adm. Bruce W. Clingan	7 Jul 2006–Aug 2007

Rear Adm. Allen G. Myers	Aug 2007–Aug 2008
Rear Adm. Kenneth E. Floyd*	Aug 2008–Feb 2009
Rear Adm. David L. Philman	Feb 2009–May 2010
Rear Adm. Kenneth E. Floyd	May 2010–

*Acting Director

Established by the Secretary of the Navy, 18 August 1943, as Deputy Chief of Naval Operations (Air). Changed to Deputy Chief of Naval Operations (Air Warfare) on 15 July 1971. On 1 October 1987 the Chief of Naval Operations (OPNAV) was reorganized and Deputy Chief of Naval Operations (Air Warfare) was redesignated Assistant Chief of Naval Operations (Air Warfare). On 10 August 1992 the Assistant Chief of Naval Operations (Air Warfare) was changed to Director, Air Warfare Division (N88).

Chief of the Bureau of Naval Weapons

Rear Adm. Paul D. Stroop	10 Sep 1959–29 Oct 1962
Rear Adm. Kleber S. Masterson	27 Nov 1962–24 Mar 1964
Rear Adm. Allen M. Shinn	28 May 1964–1 May 1966

Established as the Bureau of Naval Weapons on 18 August 1959, merging the Bureaus of Ordnance and Aeronautics. It was abolished on 1 May 1966 during the reorganization of the bureaus. The reorganization assigned elements of the Bureau of Naval Weapons to three new commands: Naval Air Systems Command, Naval Ordnance Systems Command, and Naval Electronic Systems Command.

Commander Naval Air Systems Command

Rear Adm. Allen M. Shinn	1 May–1 Sep 1966
Rear Adm. Robert L. Townsend	1 Sep 1966–20 Feb 1969
Rear Adm. Thomas J. Walker III	20 Feb 1969–1 Apr 1971
Rear Adm. Thomas R. McClellan	1 Apr 1971–31 Aug 1973
Vice Adm. Kent L. Lee	31 Aug 1973–29 Aug 1976
Vice Adm. Forrest S. Petersen	29 Oct 1976–30 Apr 1980
Vice Adm. Ernest R. Seymour	30 Apr 1980–22 Jul 1983
Vice Adm. James B. Busey IV	22 Jul 1983–23 Aug 1985
Vice Adm. Joseph B. Wilkinson	23 Aug 1985–19 Sep 1989
Vice Adm. Richard C. Gentz	19 Sep 1989–22 Jan 1991
Vice Adm. William C. Bowes	22 Mar 1991–10 Mar 1995
Vice Adm. John A. Lockard	10 Mar 1995–4 Jun 2000
Vice Adm. Joseph W. Dyer	2 Jun 2000–Jun 2003
Rear Adm. Charles H. Johnston*	Jun–26 Nov 2003
Vice Adm. Walter B. Massenburg	26 Nov 2003–16 Feb 2007
Vice Adm. David J. Venlet	16 Feb 2007–18 May 2010
Vice Adm. David Architzel	18 May 2010–

*Acting

Established by a reorganization of the Navy Department effective 1 May 1966.

CHAPTER 22

Evolution of Carrier Air Groups and Wings

The term Air Group, modified by the name of a carrier, as Saratoga Air Group, came into use during the early days of carrier aviation as a collective title for the squadrons operating on board a particular carrier. It remained a mere title until 1 July 1938, when authorization for Air Group Commander billets became effective. With this action, the squadrons on board acquired the unity of a formal command and the carrier air group as such first took form.

Numerical designation of air groups began in 1942, the first being Carrier Air Group NINE (CVG-9), established 1 March 1942. The carrier air group was sometimes referred to as CAG. However, the official designation was CVG. Existing air groups continued to be known by their carrier names until they were reformed or disbanded, only two of the early groups escaping the latter fate.

On 29 June 1944, new letter designations were set up to bring them in line with standardized complements of different carrier types. The new designations, some of which had been in use for more than a year, showed carrier type affiliation as follows: CVBG for large carrier air group, CVG for medium carrier air group, CVLG for light carrier air group, and CVEG for escort carrier air group. The CVEG designation was assigned to carriers of the *Sangamon* class. The other CVE carrier classes were assigned Composite Squadrons (VC) and listed as air groups. They remained in that category throughout the war period. The CVBG designation was for assignment to the *Midway* class, sometimes referred to as the large carriers.

On 15 November 1946, to correct the results of demobilization, which had left squadron numbers all out of sequence and a system of no apparent order, sweeping changes were made in air unit designations. Carrier Air Groups of four types were designated according to their assigned ship, as CVBG for Battle Carrier, CVG for Attack Carrier, CVLG for Light Carrier, and CVEG for Escort Carrier. Two years later, on 1 September 1948, all carrier air groups became CVG regardless of their carrier affiliation.

Carrier Air Groups were retitled Wings on 20 December 1963, and CVG became CVW. Replacement Air Groups, which were set up in 1958, became Combat Readiness Air Groups on 1 April 1963. Popularly known by the short titles RAG and CRAG in the respective periods, their designation throughout was RCVG. When Groups became Wings, CRAG became CRAW and RCVG became RCVW.

Antisubmarine Carrier Air Groups, CVSG, were established on 1 April 1960. They were slowly phased out during the 1960s, and the last were disestablished on 30 June 1973.

On 1 July 1968, the Naval Air Reserve was reorganized into wings and squadrons similar to the active fleet air organizations to ensure a more rapid and efficient transition to combat status in the event of mobilization. Two Reserve Carrier Air Wings were established and all carrier-type squadrons in the reserves were placed in these two wings. CVWR was the acronym assigned for the Reserve Carrier Air Wings. A similar organization was established for the Reserve Antisubmarine Carrier Air Groups and assigned the acronym CVSGR. The implementation of these two reserve wings and groups did not take place until 1970.

Tabulations below have two deviations from the above: use of CVG instead of the original CAG for the period to 20 June 1944, and use of the unofficial CVAG in the period 1946–48 to identify the Attack Carrier Air Groups.

Carrier Air Wings—CVW		
CVW-1	*Ranger* Air Group Formed	1 Jul 1938
	Reformed as CVG-4	3 Aug 1943
	Became CVAG-1	15 Nov 1946
	Became CVG-1	1 Sep 1948
	Became CVW-1	20 Dec 1963
CVW-2	CVBG-74 Established	1 May 1945
	Became CVBG-1	15 Nov 1946
	Became CVG-2	1 Sep 1948
	Became CVW-2	20 Dec 1963

Evolution of Carrier Air Groups and Wings | 299

CVW-3		*Saratoga* Air Group Formed	1 Jul 1938
		Reformed as CVG-3	25 Sep 1943
		Became CVAG-3	15 Nov 1946
		Became CVG-3	1 Sep 1948
		Became CVW-3	20 Dec 1963
CVW-4		CVG-4 Established	1 Sep 1950
		Became RCVG-4	Apr 1958
		Became RCVW-4	20 Dec 1963
		Disestablished	1 Jul 1970
CVW-5		CVG-5 Established	15 Feb 1943
		Became CVAG-5	15 Nov 1946
		Became CVG-5	1 Sep 1948
		Became CVW-5	20 Dec 1963
CVW-6		CVG-17 Established	1 Jan 1943
		Became CVBG-17	22 Jan 1946
		Became CVBG-5	15 Nov 1946
		Became CVG-6	27 Jul 1948
		Became CVW-6	20 Dec 1963
		Disestablished	1 Apr 1992
CVW-7		CVG-18 Established	20 Jul 1943
		Became CVAG-7	15 Nov 1946
		Became CVG-7	1 Sep 1948
		Became CVW-7	20 Dec 1963
CVW-8		CVG-8 Established	9 Apr 1951
		Became CVW-8	20 Dec 1963
CVW-9		CVG-9 Established	26 Mar 1952
		Became CVW-9	20 Dec 1963
CVW-10	A	CVG-10 Established	1 May 1952
		Became CVW-10	20 Dec 1963
		Disestablished	20 Nov 1969
	B	Established	1 Nov 1986
		Disestablished	1 Jun 1988
CVW-11		CVG-11 Established	10 Oct 1942
		Became CVAG-11	15 Nov 1946
		Became CVG-11	1 Sep 1948
		Became CVW-11	20 Dec 1963
CVW-12		CVG-102 Established for reserve squadrons called to active duty for Korea	1 Aug 1950
		Became CVG-12	4 Feb 1953
		Became RCVG-12	Apr 1958
		Became RCVW-12	20 Dec 1963
		Disestablished	1 Jun 1970
CVW-13		Established	1 Mar 1984
		Disestablished	1 Jan 1991
CVW-14		CVG-101 Established for reserve squadrons called to active duty for Korea	1 Aug 1950
		Became CVG-14	4 Feb 1953
		Became CVW- 14	20 Dec 1963

CVW-15		CVG-15 Established	5 Apr 1951
		Became CVW-15	20 Dec 1963
		Disestablished	31 Mar 1995
CVW-16		CVG-16 Established	1 Sep 1960
		Became CVW-16	20 Dec 1963
		Disestablished	30 Jun 1971
CVW-17		Established	1 Nov 1966
CVW-19		CVG-19 Established	15 Aug 1943
		Became CVAG-19	15 Nov 1946
		Became CVG-19	1 Sep 1948
		Became CVW-19	20 Dec 1963
		Disestablished	30 Jun 1977
CVW-21		CVG-21 Established	1 Jul 1955
		Became CVW-21	20 Dec 1963
		Disestablished	12 Dec 1975

Reserve Carrier Air Wings—CVWR

CVWR-20		Established	1 Apr 1970
		Became Tactical Support Wing (TSW)	1 Apr 2007
CVWR-30		Established	1 Apr 1970
		Disestablished	31 Dec 1994

Carrier Air Groups—CVG

CVG-1	A	Established	1 May 1943
		Disestablished	25 Oct 1945
	B	See CVW-1	
CVG-2	A	Established	1 Jun 1943
		Disestablished	9 Nov 1945
	B	See CVW-2	
CVG-3		See CVW-3	
CVG-4	A	CVBG-75	1 Jun 1945
		Became CVBG-3	15 Nov 1946
		Became CVG-4	1 Sep 1948
		Disestablished	8 Jun 1950
	B	See CVW-1	
	C	See CVW-4	
CVG-5		See CVW-5	
CVG-6	A	Established	15 Mar 1943
		Disestablished	29 Oct 1945
	B	See CVW-6	
CVG-7	A	Established	3 Jan 1944
		Disestablished	8 Jul 1946
	B	See CVW-7	
CVG-8	A	Established	1 Jun 1943
		Disestablished	23 Nov 1945
	B	Established	15 Sep 1948
		Disestablished	29 Nov 1949
	C	See CVW-8	

CVG-9	A	Established	1 Mar 1942
		Disestablished	15 Oct 1945
	B	CVG-20	15 Oct 1943
		Became CVAG-9	15 Nov 1946
		Became CVG-9	1 Sep 1948
		Disestablished	1 Dec 1949
	C	See CVW-9	
CVG-10	A	Established	16 Apr 1942
		Disestablished	16 Nov 1945
	B	See CVW-10	
CVG-11		See CVW-11	
CVG-12	A	Established	9 Jan 1943
		Disestablished	17 Sep 1945
	B	See CVW-12	
CVG-13	A	Established	2 Nov 1942
		Disestablished	20 Oct 1945
	B	CVG-81 Established	1 Mar 1944
		Became CVAG-13	15 Nov 1946
		Became CVG-13	1 Sep 1948
		Disestablished	30 Nov 1949
	C	Established	21 Aug 1961
		Disestablished	1 Oct 1962
CVG-14	A	Established	1 Sep 1943
		Disestablished	14 Jun 1946
	B	See CVW-14	
CVG-15	A	Established	1 Sep 1943
		Disestablished	30 Oct 1945
	B	CVG-153 Established	26 Mar 1945
		Became CVAG-15	15 Nov 1946
		Became CVG-15	1 Sep 1948
		Disestablished	1 Dec 1949
	C	See CVW-15	
CVG-16	A	Established	16 Nov 1943
		Disestablished	6 Nov 1945
	B	See CVW-16	
CVG-17	A	CVG-82 Established	1 Apr 1944
		Became CVAG-17	15 Nov 1946
		Became CVG-17	1 Sep 1948
		Disestablished	15 Sep 1958
	B	See CVW-6	
CVG-18		See CVW-7	
CVG-19		See CVW-19	
CVG-20		See CVG-9	
CVG-21	A	Established	15 Sep 1948
		Disestablished	15 Mar 1949
	B	CVG-98 Established	28 Aug 1944
		Became CVAG-21	15 Nov 1946
		Disestablished	5 Aug 1947
	C	See CVW-21	

CVG-74	See CVW-2	
CVG-75	See CVG-4	
CVG-80	Established	1 Feb 1944
	Disestablished	16 Sep 1946
CVG-81	See CVG-13	
CVG-82	See CVG-17	
CVG-83	Established	1 May 1944
	Disestablished	24 Sep 1945
CVG-84	Established	1 May 1944
	Disestablished	8 Oct 1945
CVG-85	Established	15 May 1944
	Disestablished	27 Sep 1945
CVG-86	Established	15 Jun 1944
	Disestablished	21 Nov 1945
CVG-87	Established	1 Jul 1944
	Disestablished	2 Nov 1945
CVG-88	Established	18 Aug 1944
	Disestablished	29 Oct 1945
CVG-89	Established	2 Oct 1944
	Disestablished	27 Apr 1946
CVG-92	Established	2 Dec 1944
	Disestablished	18 Dec 1945
CVG-93	Established	21 Dec 1944
	Disestablished	30 Apr 1946
CVG-94	Established	15 Nov 1944
	Disestablished	7 Nov 1945
CVG-95	Established	2 Jan 1945
	Disestablished	31 Oct 1945
CVG-97	Established	1 Nov 1944
	Disestablished	31 Mar 1946
CVG-98	See CVG-21	
CVG-99	Established	15 Jul 1944
	Disestablished	6 Sep 1945
CVG-100	Established	1 Apr 1944
	Disestablished	20 Feb 1946
CVG-101	See CVW-14	
CVG-102	See CVW-12	
CVG-150	Established	22 Jan 1945
	Disestablished	2 Nov 1945
CVG-151	Established	12 Feb 1945
	Disestablished	6 Oct 1945
CVG-152	Established	5 Mar 1945
	Disestablished	21 Sep 1945
CVG-153	See CVG-15	
Attack Carrier Air Groups—CVAG		
CVAG 1	See CVW-1	
CVAG 3	See CVW-3	
CVAG 5	See CVW-5	
CVAG 7	See CVW-7	
CVAG 9	See CVG-9	

CVAG 11	See CVW-11	
CVAG 13	See CVW-13	
CVAG 15	See CVG-15	
CVAG 17	See CVG-17	
CVAG 19	See CVW-19	
CVAG 21	See CVG-21	

Battle Carrier Air Groups—CVBG

CVBG 1	See CVW-2	
CVBG 3	See CVG-4	
CVBG 5	See CVW-6	
CVBG 17	See CVW-6	
CVBG 74	See CVW-2	
CVBG 75	See CVG-4	

Light Carrier Air Groups—CVLG

CVLG-1	CVLG-58 Established	15 Mar 1946
	Redesignated CVLG-1	14 Nov 1946
	Disestablished	20 Nov 1948
CVLG-21	Established	16 May 1943
	Disestablished	5 Nov 1945
CVLG-22	Established	30 Sep 1942
	Disestablished	19 Sep 1945
CVLG-23	Established	16 Nov 1942
	Disestablished	19 Sep 1945
CVLG-24	See CVEG-24	
CVLG-25	See CVEG-25	
CVLG-27	Established	1 Mar 1943
	Disestablished	26 Oct 1945
CVLG-28	CVEG-28 Established	6 May 1942
	Became CVLG-28	20 Jan 1944
	Disestablished	6 Nov 1945
CVLG-29	CVEG-29 Established	18 Jul 1942
	Became CVLG-29	1 Mar 1944
	Disestablished	10 Sep 1945
CVLG-30	Established	1 Apr 1943
	Disestablished	12 Sep 1945
CVLG-31	Established	1 May 1943
	Disestablished	28 Oct 1945
CVLG-32	Established	1 Jun 1943
	Disestablished	13 Nov 1945
CVLG-34	Established	1 Apr 1945
	Disestablished	5 Dec 1945
CVLG-38	See CVEG-38	
CVLG-39	CVEG-39 Established	15 Mar 1945
	Became CVLG-39	27 Jul 1945
	Disestablished	10 Sep 1945
CVLG-40	See CVEG-40	
CVLG-43	Established	1 Aug 1943
	Disestablished	8 Nov 1943

CVLG-44	Established	1 Feb 1944
	Disestablished	18 Sep 1945
CVLG-45	Established	1 Apr 1944
	Disestablished	10 Sep 1945
CVLG-46	Established	15 Apr 1944
	Disestablished	14 Sep 1945
CVLG-47	Established	15 May 1944
	Disestablished	21 Sep 1945
CVLG-48	Established	15 Jun 1944
	Disestablished	2 Jan 1945
CVLG-49	CVEG-49 Established	10 Aug 1944
	Became CVLG-49	2 Jan 1945
	Disestablished	27 Nov 1945
CVLG-50	See CVEG-50	
CVLG-51	Established	22 Sep 1943
	Disestablished	13 Nov 1945
CVLG-52	Established	1 Sep 1943
	Disestablished	8 Nov 1943
CVLG-58	See CVLG-1	
Escort Carrier Air Groups—CVEG		
CVEG-1	CVEG-41 Established	26 Mar 1945
	Became CVEG-1	15 Nov 1946
	Became VC-21	1 Sep 1948
	Became VS-21	23 Apr 1950
CVEG-2	CVEG-42 Established	19 Jul 1945
	Became CVEG-2	15 Nov 1946
	Disestablished	1 Sep 1948
CVEG-3	Established	21 Apr 1947
	Disestablished	1 Sep 1948
CVEG-24	CVLG-24 Established	31 Dec 1942
	Became CVEG-24	15 Aug 1944
	Disestablished	25 Sep 1945
CVEG-25	CVLG-25 Established	15 Feb 1943
	Became CVEG-25	28 Aug 1944
	Disestablished	20 Sep 1945
CVEG-26	Established	4 May 1942
	Disestablished	13 Nov 1945
CVEG-28	See CVLG-28	
CVEG-29	See CVLG-29	
CVEG-33	Established	15 May 1944
	Disestablished	19 Nov 1945
CVEG-35	Established	15 Jul 1943
	Disestablished	19 Nov 1945
CVEG-36	Established	15 May 1944
	Disestablished	28 Jan 1946
CVEG-37	Established	15 Jul 1943
	Disestablished	20 Dec 1945

CVEG-38	CVLG-38 Established	16 Jun 1943
	Became CVEG-38	15 Aug 1944
	Disestablished	31 Jan 1946
CVEG-39	*See* CVLG-39	
CVEG-40	CVLG-40 Established	15 Jun 1943
	Became CVEG-40	15 Aug 1944
	Disestablished	19 Nov 1945
CVEG-41	*See* CVEG-1	
CVEG-42	*See* CVEG-2	
CVEG-43	Established	9 Aug 1945
	Disestablished	17 Jun 1946
CVEG-49	*See* CVLG-49	
CVEG-50	CVLG-50 Established	10 Aug 1943
	Became CVEG-50	1 Oct 1944
	Disestablished	29 Oct 1945
CVEG-60	Established	15 Jul 1943
	Disestablished	19 Nov 1945
CVEG-66	Established	1 Jan 1945
	Disestablished	6 Jun 1945

Night Carrier Air Groups—CVG(N)

CVG(N)-52	CVLG(N)-52 Established	20 Oct 1944
	Became CVG(N)-52	6 Jan 1945
	Disestablished	15 Dec 1945
CVG(N)-53	Established	2 Jan 1945
	Disestablished	11 Jun 1946
CVG(N)-55	Established	1 Mar 1945
	Disestablished	11 Dec 1945
CVG(N)-90	Established	25 Aug 1944
	Disestablished	21 Jun 1946
CVG(N)-91	Established	5 Oct 1944
	Disestablished	21 Jun 1946

CVLG(N)

CVLG(N)-41	Established	28 Aug 1944
	Disestablished	25 Feb 1945
CVLG(N)-42	Established	25 Aug 1944
	Disestablished	2 Jan 1945
CVLG(N)-43	Established	24 Aug 1944
	Disestablished	2 Jan 1945
CVLG(N)-52	*See* CVG(N)-52	

CVEG(N)

CVEG(N)-63	Established	20 Jun 1945
	Disestablished	11 Dec 1945

Ship-Named Air Groups

Langley Air Group	Ship commissioned	20 Mar 1922
	Squadrons first assigned	1925
	Air group had not formally organized when ship was reclassified AV	15 Sep 1936

Lexington Air Group	Ship commissioned	14 Dec 1927
	Ships squadrons established individually. Air group organized	1 Jul 1938
	Disbanded after ship was sunk	8 May 1942
Saratoga Air Group	Ship commissioned	16 Nov 1927
	Ship squadrons established individually. Air group organized	1 Jul 1938
	Reformed as CVG-3	25 Sep 1943
	See CVW-3	
Ranger Air Group	Ship commissioned	4 Jun 1934
	Ship squadrons established individually. Air group organized	1 Jul 1938
	Reformed as CVG-4	3 Aug 1943
	See CVW-1	
Yorktown Air Group	Ship commissioned	30 Sep 1937
	Ship squadrons established	1 Apr 1937
	Air group organized	1 Jul 1938
	Disbanded after ship was sunk	7 Jun 1942
Enterprise Air Group	Ship commissioned	12 May 1938
	Ship squadrons established	1 Jun 1937
	Air group organized	1 Jul 1938
	Disbanded	Sep 1942
Wasp Air Group	Ship commissioned	25 Apr 1940
	Air group established	1 Jul 1939
	Disbanded after ship was sunk	15 Sep 1942
Hornet Air Group	Ship commissioned	20 Oct 1941
	Air group established	6 Oct 1941
	Disbanded after ship was sunk	26 Oct 1942
Antisubmarine Carrier Air Groups—CVSG		
CVSG-50	Established as RCVSG	30 Jun 1960
	Disestablished	17 Feb 1971
CVSG-51	Established as RCVSG	30 Jun 1960
	Disestablished	30 Jun 1970
CVSG-52	Established	1 Jun 1960
	Disestablished	15 Dec 1969
CVSG-53	Established	1 Apr 1960
	Disestablished	1 Jun 1973
CVSG-54	Established	18 May 1960
	Disestablished	1 Jul 1972
CVSG-55	Established	1 Sep 1960
	Disestablished	27 Sep 1968
CVSG-56	Established	25 May 1960
	Disestablished	30 Jun 1973
CVSG-57	Established	3 Jan 1961
	Disestablished	30 Sep 1969
CVSG-58	Established	6 Jun 1960
	Disestablished	31 May 1966
CVSG-59	Established	1 Apr 1960
	Disestablished	30 Jun 1973
CVSG-60	Established	2 May 1960
	Disestablished	1 Oct 1968

CVSG-62		Established	25 Sep 1961
		Disestablished	1 Oct 1962
Reserve Antisubmarine Carrier Air Groups—CVSGR			
CVSGR-70		Established	1 Apr 1970
		Disestablished	30 Jun 1976
CVSGR-80		Established	1 Apr 1970
		Redesignated COMHELWINGRES	1 Jan 1976
Composite Squadrons—VC (World War II)			
VC-1	A	VS-201 Established	5 Apr 1941
		Became VGS-1	1 Apr 1942
		Became VC-1	1 Mar 1943
		Disestablished	1 Apr 1944
	B	VOF-1 Established	15 Dec 1943
		Became VOC-1	18 Dec 1944
		Became VC-1	1 Aug 1945
		Disestablished	17 Sep 1945
VC-2	A	See VC-25	
	B	VOF-2 Established	1 Mar 1944
		Became VOC-2	13 Dec 1944
		Became VC-2	20 Aug 1945
		Disestablished	13 Sep 1945
VC-3		Established	26 Aug 1943
		Disestablished	28 Oct 1945
VC-4		Established	2 Sep 1943
		Disestablished	16 Oct 1945
VC-5		Established	16 Sep 1943
		Disestablished	1 Oct 1945
VC-6		VGS-25 Established	1 Jan 1943
		Became VC-25	1 Mar 1943
		Became VC-6	1 Sep 1943
		Disestablished	5 Oct 1945
VC-7		VGS-31 Established	24 Feb 1943
		Became VC-31	1 Mar 1943
		Became VC-7	1 Sep 1943
		Disestablished	1 Oct 1945
VC-8		Established	9 Sep 1943
		Disestablished	9 Oct 1945
VC-9		VGS-9 Established	6 Aug 1942
		Became VC-9	1 Mar 1943
		Disestablished	19 Sep 1945
VC-10		Established	23 Sep 1943
		Disestablished	25 Oct 1945

VC-11	A	VGS-11 Established	5 Aug 1942
		Became VC-11	1 Mar 1943
		Became VF-21	16 May 1943
		Disestablished	5 Nov 1945
	B	Established	30 Sep 1943
		Disestablished	10 Oct 1945
VC-12	A	VGS-12 Established	28 May 1942
		Became VC-12	1 Mar 1943
		Became VT-21	16 May 1943
		Disestablished	7 Aug 1945
	B	Established	6 Oct 1943
		Disestablished	7 Jun 1945
VC-13		VGS-13 Established	5 Aug 1942
		Became VC-13	1 Mar 1943
		Disestablished	24 Sep 1945
VC-14		Established	12 Oct 1943
		Disestablished	1 Oct 1945
VC-15		Established	18 Oct 1943
		Disestablished	14 Jun 1945
VC-16		VGS-16 Established	8 Aug 1942
		Became VC-16	1 Mar 1943
		Became VF-33	15 Nov 1945
		Disestablished	19 Nov 1945
VC-17		*See* VC-31	
VC-18		VGS-18 Established	15 Oct 1942
		Became VC-18	1 Mar 1943
		Became VF-36	15 Aug 1943
		Became VF-18	5 Mar 1944
		Became VF-7A	15 Nov 1946
		Became VF-71	28 Jul 1948
		Disestablished	31 Mar 1959
VC-19		VGS-23 Established	1 Jan 1943
		Became VC-19	1 Mar 1943
		Disestablished	14 Jun 1945
VC-20	A	VGS-20 Established	6 Aug 1942
		Became VC-20	1 Mar 1943
		Disestablished	15 Jun 1943
	B	Established	24 Oct 1943
		Disestablished	1 Oct 1945
VC-21	A	VGS-21 Established	15 Oct 1942
		Became VC-21	1 Mar 1943
		Disestablished	16 Jun 1943
	B	Established	30 Oct 1943
		Disestablished	15 Sep 1945

VC-22		VS-22 Established	16 Nov 1942
		Became VC-22	1 Mar 1943
		Became VT-22	15 Dec 1943
		Disestablished	22 Aug 1945
VC-23		VS-23 Established	16 Nov 1942
		Became VC-23	1 Mar 1943
		Became VT-23	15 Nov 1943
		Disestablished	19 Sep 1945
VC-24		VS-24 Established	31 Dec 1942
		Became VC-24	1 Mar 1943
		Became VB-98	15 Dec 1943
		Disestablished	25 Jun 1944
VC-25	A	VS-25 Established	15 Feb 1943
		Became VC-2	1 Mar 1943
		Became VC-25	15 Sep 1943
		Became VT-25	15 Dec 1943
		Disestablished	20 Sep 1945
	B	*See* VC-6	
VC-26		VGS-26 Established	5 May 1942
		Became VC-26	1 Mar 1943
		Became VT-26	15 Nov 1943
		Disestablished	13 Nov 1945
VC-27		Established	5 Nov 1943
		Disestablished	11 Sep 1945
VC-28		VGS-28 Established	4 May 1942
		Became VC-28	1 Mar 1943
		Became VT-28	20 Jan 1944
		Disestablished	8 Aug 1945
VC-29		VGS-29 Established	20 Jul 1942
		Became VC-29	1 Mar 1943
		Became VT-29	15 Dec 1943
		Disestablished	1 Aug 1945
VC-30		Established	1 Apr 1943
		Became VT-30	15 Dec 1943
		Disestablished	18 Aug 1945
VC-31	A	*See* VC-7	
	B	VC-17 Established	1 May 1943
		Became VC-31	15 Sep 1943
		Became VT-31	1 Nov 1943
		Disestablished	20 Oct 1945
VC-32		Established	1 Jun 1943
		Became VT-32	1 Nov 1943
		Disestablished	20 Aug 1945
VC-33		VGS-33 Established	22 Jan 1943
		Became VC-33	1 Mar 1943
		Disestablished	16 Nov 1945

VC-34	VGS-34 Established	24 Feb 1943
	Became VC-34	1 Mar 1943
	Became VF-34	15 Aug 1943
	Disestablished	8 Jul 1944
VC-35	VGS-35 Established	28 Jan 1943
	Became VC-35	1 Mar 1943
	Became VT-35	10 Mar 1944
	Disestablished	19 Nov 1945
VC-36	VGS-36 Established	21 Feb 1943
	Became VC-36	1 Mar 1943
	Disestablished	30 Jul 1945
VC-37	VGS-37 Established	22 Jan 1943
	Became VC-37	1 Mar 1943
	Became VT-37	10 Mar 1944
	Disestablished	20 Dec 1945
VC-38	Established	16 Jun 1943
	Became VT-38	11 May 1944
	Disestablished	31 Jan 1946
VC-39	Established	1 Apr 1943
	Disestablished	15 Dec 1943
VC-40	Established	15 Jun 1943
	Became VT-40	1 Jun 1944
	Disestablished	19 Nov 1945
VC-41	Established	5 May 1943
	Disestablished	16 Nov 1945
VC-42	Established	15 Apr 1943
	Disestablished	5 Jul 1945
VC-43	Established	1 Aug 1943
	Disestablished	8 Nov 1943
VC-50	Established	10 Aug 1943
	Became VT-50	8 Nov 1943
	Disestablished	29 Oct 1945
VC-51	Established	22 Sep 1943
	Became VT-51	8 Nov 1943
	Disestablished	7 Aug 1945
VC-52	Established	1 Sep 1943
	Disestablished	8 Nov 1943
VC-55	VGS-55 Established	16 Jan 1943
	Became VC-55	1 Mar 1943
	Disestablished	21 Jun 1945
VC-58	VGS-58 Established	24 Feb 1943
	Became VC-58	1 Mar 1943
	Disestablished	8 Jun 1945
VC-60	VGS-60 Established	24 Feb 1943
	Became VC-60	1 Mar 1943
	Became VT-60	10 Mar 1944
	Disestablished	19 Nov 1945
VC-63	Established	20 May 1943
	Disestablished	23 Oct 1945

VC-64	Established	1 Jun 1943
	Became VF-39	15 Aug 1943
	Disestablished	15 Mar 1944
VC-65	Established	10 Jun 1943
	Disestablished	8 Oct 1945
VC-66	Established	21 Jun 1943
	Disestablished	12 Oct 1945
VC-68	Established	1 Jul 1943
	Disestablished	1 Oct 1945
VC-69	Established	1 Jul 1943
	Disestablished	22 Jun 1945
VC-70	Established	5 Aug 1944
	Disestablished	6 Oct 1945
VC-71	Established	20 Aug 1944
	Disestablished	6 Oct 1945
VC-72	Established	1 Sep 1944
	Disestablished	1 Oct 1945
VC-75	Established	11 Nov 1943
	Disestablished	21 Sep 1945
VC-76	Established	17 Nov 1943
	Disestablished	11 Sep 1945
VC-77	Established	23 Nov 1943
	Disestablished	17 Sep 1945
VC-78	Established	29 Nov 1943
	Disestablished	21 Sep 1945
VC-79	Established	6 Dec 1943
	Disestablished	11 Sep 1945
VC-80	Established	16 Dec 1943
	Disestablished	11 Sep 1945
VC-81	Established	22 Dec 1943
	Disestablished	20 Sep 1945
VC-82	Established	28 Dec 1943
	Disestablished	18 Sep 1945
VC-83	Established	3 Jan 1944
	Disestablished	17 Sep 1945
VC-84	Established	6 Jan 1944
	Disestablished	17 Sep 1945
VC-85	Established	12 Jan 1944
	Disestablished	15 Sep 1945
VC-86	Established	18 Jan 1944
	Disestablished	7 Jun 1945
VC-87	Established	24 Jan 1944
	Disestablished	12 Jun 1945
VC-88	Established	29 Jan 1944
	Disestablished	3 Jul 1945
VC-89	Established	Jan 1944
	Disestablished	Apr 1944
VC-90	Established	3 Feb 1944
	Disestablished	19 Sep 1945

VC-91	Established	11 Feb 1944
	Disestablished	22 Sep 1945
VC-92	Established	17 Feb 1944
	Disestablished	18 Sep 1945
VC-93	Established	23 Feb 1944
	Disestablished	11 Aug 1945
VC-94	Established	29 Feb 1944
	Disestablished	27 Jul 1945
VC-95	Established	1 Feb 1944
	Disestablished	28 Jun 1945
VC-96	Established	1 Mar 1944
	Disestablished	28 Jul 1945
VC-97	Established	8 Mar 1944
	Disestablished	24 Jul 1945
VC-98	Established	15 Mar 1944
	Disestablished	11 Oct 1945
VC-99	Established	22 Mar 1944
	Disestablished	30 Oct 1945

CHAPTER 23

Squadron Designations and Abbreviations

The system of squadron designations was established to help define part of naval aviation's organizational structure and help identify the operational and administrative functions of aviation within the fleet. Just as the designations for ships, such as DD, CA, BB, etc., were used to define the duties of the specific units and their alignment within the fleet organization, so also were the squadron designations established to formulate the responsibilities and alignment within naval aviation and the fleet structure.

During naval aviation's early years, due to the limited capabilities of the aircraft, there were big question marks concerning its ability to succeed as a functional component of the fleet and whether it even would survive. In official publications and references, such as the *Daily Aviation News Bulletin* of 1 October 1919, casual terms were used to describe or identify various aircraft squadrons and units. The casual terms were used because no specific fleet aviation organizational structure for squadrons had been officially established. Prior to 1919, naval aircraft, excluding Marine Corps planes, were assigned primarily to shore stations. Therefore, in order to integrate aviation into the fleet, it was necessary to develop a fleet organization that included aviation units.

On 17 July 1920, the Secretary of the Navy prescribed a standard nomenclature for types and classes of naval vessels, including aircraft, in which lighter-than-air craft were identified by the type "Z" and heavier-than-air craft by the letter "V". Class letters assigned within the Z type were R, N, and K for rigid dirigibles, non-rigid dirigibles, and kite balloons respectively, while F, O, S, P, T, and G were established for fighter, observation, scouting, patrol, torpedo and bombing, and fleet planes as classes within the V type.

The use of the "V" designation with fixed-wing heavier-than-air squadron designations has been a question of debate since the 1920s. However, no conclusive evidence has been found to identify why the letter "V" was chosen. It is generally believed it was in reference to the French word *volplane*. As a verb, the word means to glide or soar. As a noun, it described an aeronautical device sustained in the air by lifting surfaces (wings), as opposed to the bag of gas that the airships (denoted by "Z") used. The same case may be made regarding the use of "Z". It is generally believed it was used in deference to Count Ferdinand von Zeppelin, the German general and developer of the airship in 1900. However, documentation has not been located to verify this assumption.

In general terms, the Navy's system for designating naval aircraft squadrons has usually conformed to the following loose classification structure:

1. Squadron designations were based on specific letters used for indicating the missions for each particular type of squadron and its assigned aircraft. As an example, a WWII squadron operating the F4U Corsair aircraft would have been designated a fighting squadron (VF). The letter F, for fighting or fighter, was the key in identifying the type of squadron and was also used in the aircraft's designation.

2. Identification numbers were assigned to each squadron, such as VF-1. The number 1 separates Fighter Squadron 1 (VF-1) from Fighter Squadron 10 (VF-10).

There have been many variations to this basic system throughout naval aviation's history. Changes were also made to the designation system when new plane types were developed and new squadrons were formed to carry out new missions. There is no logical sequence for the numerical designation assigned the various squadrons throughout most of naval aviation's history. The Marine Corps did establish a logical sequence for their squadron designations, however, there are variations to this system, as well.

As Navy squadrons were established, disestablished, or redesignated, many of the same letters and numbers were reused and assigned at a later date for newly established or redesignated units, hence, the lineage of a squadron cannot always be traced or linked by using the same designation. As an example, VF-1 from WWII has no direct relationship to VF-1 established in the 1970s. The rich tradition and heritage of the various squadrons in the Navy has not always been carried over because of the break in continuity between units. Once a squadron is disestablished, that ends its history. If a new squadron is established using the same designation of a previous squadron, it does not have any direct relationship with that unit. The reuse of many of the same letters and numerical designations adds considerable confusion to the squadron designation system. A new squadron may carry on the traditions of a previous squadron, just as a ship that has been assigned the name used by a previous ship, carries on the traditions of the past ships with the same name. However, a squadron, just like a ship, cannot claim a heritage or historical link to the old unit with the same designation.

Consistency has been the major ingredient lacking in the Navy's squadron designation system. As an example, the use of "Plane" in squadron designations was not consistent during the 1920s. Sometimes the full designation would be written differently, depending on the squadron's assignment to the Battle Fleet, Scouting Fleet, or Asiatic Fleet. A designation such as Scouting Squadron and Scouting Plane Squadron, which used the same abbreviation, VS, was listed in the *Navy Directory* as Scouting Squadron under the Battle Fleet and Scouting Plane Squadron under the Scouting Fleet. The use of "Plane" in squadron designations was most likely designed to identify the squadron as an aviation unit, vice a destroyer squadron. This seems to be especially true during the 1920s when aviation was first being integrated into the fleet organization and operations. The *Navy Directory; Monthly Report, Status of Naval Aircraft;* and the *Bureau of Aeronautics Weekly Newsletter* all list squadron designations using "Plane." The Chief of Naval Operations' "Naval Aeronautical Organization," published for each fiscal year, lists the squadron designations without using "Plane" in the designation. It is obvious there is no difference between the squadrons with or without the use of "Plane" in the squadron designation. The acronym remained the same, with or without the use of "Plane" in the full squadron designation. In the 1930s the squadron designations listed in all four sources identified above usually refer to the squadron using its abbreviated designation, such as VF Squadron 1 (VF-1) instead of Fighting Plane Squadron 1. In the 1940s, the use of "Plane" in the full squadron designation is dropped.

In the late 1940s and early 1950s the VC squadron designation was used to identify a group of squadrons with several different missions but all assigned the VC designation. Missions for specific Composite Squadrons (VC) included all-weather night, attack, and defense; air early warning; antisubmarine warfare; and photographic. The only identifying factor to separate the different types of Composite Squadrons was the numerical designation. In the late 1940s, the single-digit numbers were for the Composite Night or Attack and Defense units, those numbers in the teens were for Composite Air Warning squadrons, numbers in the 20s and 30s were for Composite Anti-Submarine units, and the numbers in the 60s were for Composite Photographic squadrons.

Besides the composite squadrons (VC), several patrol squadrons (VP) had specific mission requirements that were different from their normal patrol and reconnaissance duties. However, these squadrons still maintained the normal VP designation. In the late 1940s there were two VP squadrons with a primary photographic mission and one with an air early warning mission. VP-61 and VP-62 were the photographic squadrons and VP-51 was the air early warning squadron.

The special VC and VP designated units were on the cutting edge of technology, which eventually led to the development of specialized squadron designations in the 1950s and 1960s. Squadrons such as VAW (Carrier Airborne Early Warning), VAQ (Tactical Electronic Warfare), and VQ (Electronic Countermeasures or Air Reconnaissance) were the result of technical developments in the late 1940s and early 1950s.

The use of an abbreviated squadron designation with different missions occurred in the early 1950s when the VJ designation was used for both photographic squadrons and weather squadrons. VJ-1 and -2 were designated Weather Squadrons or Weather Reconnaissance Squadrons. VJ-61 and -62 were designated Photographic Squadrons. The missions were totally different for these two types of squadrons but they used a common abbreviated squadron designation.

There are four factors that play a role in developing or changing squadron designations. They have been around since the introduction of aviation in the Navy and will continue to be the primary factors affecting squadron designations. The factors are:

1. the duties or mission of a squadron

2. technical advances in aircraft or equipment

3. changes in tactics or development of new tactics

4. changes in naval aviation or fleet organization

The following is a list of various squadron designations used by the Navy since the early 1920s. The list is in alphabetical order rather than in the chronological order of squadron development. The general time frame for when the designation was in use is listed with most of the squadron designations. Further elaboration on the assignment of squadrons to other organizations and their designations such as: a battle group, carrier air wing, cruiser group, fleet air force, scouting fleet, Asiatic Fleet, naval district, reserves, etc., has not been included in this list to prevent it from becoming too confusing or extensive. The only exception to this is for the reserves. Reserve squadron designations, beginning in 1970, are included in this list. In 1970 the naval air reserve was reorganized and the squadron structure and arrangement was aligned to mirror the squadron designation system in existence for active fleet units.

U.S. Navy Squadron Designations and Abbreviations		
Acronym	Full Squadron Designation	Time Frame in Use
BLIMPHEDRON	LTA Headquarters Squadron	1943–1946
BLIMPRON	LTA Squadron	1942–1961
BLPHEDRON	Blimp Headquarters Squadron	1943–1946
BLPRON	Blimp Squadron	1942–1961
FASRON	Fleet Aircraft Service Squadron	1946–1960
HAL or HA(L)	Helicopter Attack Squadron Light	1967–1972 1976–1988
HC	Helicopter Combat Support Squadron	1965–2007
HCS	Helicopter Combat Support Special Squadron	1988–2006
HCT	Helicopter Combat Support Training Squadron	1974–1977
HM	Helicopter Mine Countermeasures Squadron	1971–present
HS	Helicopter Antisubmarine Squadron [Note: All HS squadrons slowly undergoing redesignation to HSC; HS designation will eventually be eliminated.]	1951–present
HSC	Helicopter Sea Combat Squadron	2005–present
HSL	Helicopter Antisubmarine Squadron (Light) [Note: All HSL squadrons slowly undergoing redesignation to HSM; HSL designation will eventually be eliminated.]	1972–present
HSM	Helicopter Maritime Strike Squadron	2005–present
HT	Helicopter Training Squadron	1960–present
HTU	Helicopter Training Unit	1950–1957
HU	Helicopter Utility Squadron	1948–1965
HX	Rotary Wing Air Test and Evaluation Squadron	2002–present
RVAH	Reconnaissance Attack Squadron	1964–1979
RVAW	Carrier Airborne Early Warning Training Squadron	1967–1983
STAGRON	Special Air Task Force Squadron (VK)	1943–1944
TACRON	Tactical Squadron or Tactical Air Control Squadron or Tactical Control Squadron [Note: The designation VTC is used by the SNDL office but is not a correct designation.]	1946–present
VA	Attack Squadron	1946–1994
VA(AW)	All-Weather Attack Squadron	1956–1959
VAH or VA(H)	Heavy Attack Squadron	1955–1971
VA(HM)	Attack Mining Squadron	1956–1959
VAK	Tactical Aerial Refueling Squadron	1979–1989
VAL or VA(L)	Light Attack Squadron	1969–1972
VAP or VA(P)	Heavy Photographic Reconnaissance Squadron or Photographic Reconnaissance Squadron (Heavy) or Heavy Photographic Squadron	1956–1971
VAQ	Carrier Tactical Electronics Warfare Squadron or Tactical Electronics Warfare Squadron	1968–1998
VAQ	Electronic Attack Squadron	1998–present
VAW	Carrier Airborne Early Warning Squadron	1948 1956–present
VAW	Carrier Tactical Electronics Warfare Squadron	1968
VB	Bombing Squadron or Light Bombing Plane Squadron	1928–1946
VBF	Bombing Fighting Squadron	1945–1946
VC	Composite Squadron	1943–1945 1948–1956
VC	Fleet Composite Squadron	1965–2008
VCN	Night Composite Squadron	1946–1948
VCP	Photographic Composite Squadron	1959–1961
VCS	Cruiser Scouting Squadron	1937–1945
VD	Photographic Squadron	1943–1946

U.S. Navy Squadron Designations and Abbreviations		
Acronym	**Full Squadron Designation**	**Time Frame in Use**
VE	Evacuation Squadron	1944–1945
VF	Combat Squadron	1922
VF	Fighting Plane Squadron or Fighting Squadron	1922–1948
VF	Fighter Squadron	1948–2006
VFA	Fighter Attack Squadron	1980–1983
VFA	Strike Fighter Squadron	1983–present
VF(AW)	All-Weather Fighter Squadron or Fighter (All-Weather) Squadron	1956–1963
VFC	Fighter Squadron Composite	1988–present
VFN or VF(N)	Night Fighting Squadron	1944–1946
VFP or VF(P)	Light Photographic Reconnaissance Squadron or Photographic Reconnaissance Squadron or Photographic Reconnaissance Squadron (Light) or Light Photographic Squadron	1956–1987
VGF	Escort-Fighter Squadron	1942–1943
VGS	Escort-Scouting Squadron	1942–1943
VH	Rescue Squadron	1944–1946
VJ	Utility Squadron or General Utility Squadron	1925–1946
VJ	Weather Squadron or Weather Reconnaissance Squadron	1952–1953
VJ	Photographic Squadron	1952–1956
VK	Special Air Task Force Squadron (STAGRON)	1943–1944
VN	Training Squadron	1927–1947
VO	Spotting Squadron	1922
VO	Observation Plane Squadron or Observation Squadron	1923–1945 1947–1949 1967–1968
VOC	Composite Spotting Squadron	1944–1945
VOF	Observation Fighter Squadron	1942–1945
VOS	Air Spotting Squadron or Observation Spotter Squadron	1944
VP	Seaplane Patrol Squadron	1922
VP	Patrol Squadron	1924–1944 1946 1948–present
VP-AM	Amphibian Patrol Squadron	1946–1948
VPB	Patrol Bombing Squadron	1944–1946
VP-HL	Heavy Patrol Squadron (landplane)	1946–1948
VP-HS	Heavy Seaplane Patrol Squadron	1946–1948
VPM	Meteorological Squadron	1946–1947
VP-ML	Medium Patrol Squadron (landplane)	1946–1948
VP-MS	Medium Patrol Squadron (seaplane)	1946–1948
VPP or VP(P)	Photographic Squadron or Patrol Squadron (photographic)	1946–1948
VPU	Patrol Squadron Special Unit	1982–1998
VPU	Special Projects Patrol Squadron	1998–present
VPW	Weather Reconnaissance Squadron	1945–1948
VPW	Air Early Warning Squadron	1948
VQ	Electronic Countermeasures Squadron	1955–1960
VQ	Fleet Air Reconnaissance Squadron	1961–present
VR	Transport Squadron or Air Transport Squadron or Fleet Logistic Air Squadron	1942–1958
VR	Fleet Tactical Support Squadron	1958–1976
VR	Fleet Logistics Support Squadron	1976–present
VRC or VR(C)	Fleet Tactical Support Squadron	1960–1976
VRC	Fleet Logistics Support Squadron	1976–present

U.S. Navy Squadron Designations and Abbreviations		
Acronym	**Full Squadron Designation**	**Time Frame in Use**
VRE	Air Transport Evacuation Squadron	1945
VRF	Transport Ferry and Service Squadron	1943–1946
VRF	Air Ferry Transport Squadron or Air Ferry Squadron	1943–1948
VRF or VR(F)	Aircraft Ferry Squadron	1957–1986
VRJ	Utility Transport Squadron	1945–1946
VRS	Air Ferry Service Squadron or Ferry Command Service Squadron	1943–1946
VRU	Transport Utility Squadron	1946–1948
VS	Scouting Plane Squadron or Scouting Squadron	1922–1946
VS	Antisubmarine Squadron or Air Antisubmarine Squadron or Carrier Air Antisubmarine Squadron	1950–1993
VS	Sea Control Squadron	1993–2009
VSF	Antisubmarine Fighter Squadron	1965–1973
VT	Torpedo & Bombing Plane Squadron or Torpedo & Bombing Squadron	1922–1930
VT	Torpedo Plane Squadron	1921
VT	Torpedo Squadron	1930–1946
VT	Training Squadron	1960–present
VTN	Night Torpedo Squadron	1944–1946
VU	Utility Squadron	1946–1965
VW	Air Early Warning Squadron or Airborne Early Warning Squadron or Fleet Early Warning Squadron	1952–1971
VW	Weather Reconnaissance Squadron or Fleet Weather Reconnaissance Squadron	1967–1975
VX	Experimental Squadron	1927–circa 1943
VX	Experimental and Development Squadron or Operational Development Squadron or Air Operational Development Squadron or Air Development Squadron	1946–1968
VX	Air Test and Evaluation Squadron	1969–present
VXE	Antarctic Development Squadron	1969–1999
VXN	Oceanographic Development Squadron	1969–1993
VXS	Scientific Development Squadron	2004–present
XVF	Experimental Development Squadron	1945–1946
XVJ	Experimental Utility Squadron	1945–1946
ZJ	Blimp Utility Squadron	1944–1945
ZK	Kite Balloon Squadron	1922–1924
ZKN	Kite Balloon Training Squadron	*
ZKO	Kite Balloon Observation Squadron	*
ZNN	Non-rigid Airship Training Squadron	*
ZNO	Non-rigid Airship Observation Squadron	*
ZNP	Non-rigid Airship Patrol Squadron	*
ZNS	Non-rigid Airship Scouting Squadron	*
ZP	Airship Patrol Squadron	1942–1961
ZP	Blimp Squadron	1942–1961
ZP	Airship Patrol Squadron (All-Weather Antisubmarine) or Airship Squadron or LTA Patrol Squadron	1942–1961
ZRN	Rigid Airship Training Squadron	*
ZRP	Rigid Airship Patrol Squadron	*
ZRS	Rigid Airship Scouting Squadron	*
ZS	Airship Antisubmarine Squadron	*
ZW	Airship Early Warning Squadron	1956–1961
ZX	Airship Operational Development Squadron or Airship Development Squadron	1950–1957

* These squadron designations were developed, however, the Navy never established any squadrons using the designations.

Marine Corps Squadron Designations/Abbreviations		
Acronym	**Full Squadron Designation**	**Time Frame in Use**
AES	Marine Aircraft Engineering Squadron	1941–present
ARS	Marine Air Regulating Squadron	1942–1943
AWRS	Marine Aviation Women's Reserve Squadron	1944–1945
AWS	Marine Air Warning Squadron	1943–1954
AWS(AT)	Marine Air Warning Squadron (Air Transportable)	1944
H&HS	Marine Headquarters & Headquarters Squadron	1954–circa 1977
HMA	Marine Helicopter Attack Squadron	1971–1983
HMH	Marine Heavy Helicopter Squadron	1962–present
HMHT	Marine Heavy Helicopter Training Squadron	1968–1972
HML	Marine Light Helicopter Squadron	1968–1987
HMLA	Marine Light Attack Helicopter Squadron	1987–present
HMM	Marine Medium Helicopter Squadron	1962–present
HMMT	Marine Medium Helicopter Training Squadron	1966–1972
HMR	Marine Helicopter Transport Squadron	1951–1956
HMR(C)	Marine Helicopter Reconnaissance Squadron	1958–1960
HMR(L)	Marine Helicopter Transport Squadron (light)	1956–1962
HMR(M)	Marine Helicopter Transport Squadron (medium)	1957–1962
H&MS	Marine Headquarters & Maintenance Squadron	1954–1988
HMT	Marine Helicopter Training Squadron	1972–present
HMX	Marine Helicopter Squadron	1947–present
MAAWS	Marine Assault Air Warning Squadron	1944–1945
MABS	Marine Air Base Squadron	1943–1946, 1951–1986
MACS	Marine Air Casual Squadron	1945–1946
MACS	Marine Air Control Squadron	1954–present
MADS	Marine Air Depot Squadron	1942–1945
MALS	Marine Aviation Logistics Squadron	1988–present
MAR&S	Marine Aircraft Repair and Salvage Squadron	1942–1944
MASS	Marine Air Support Squadron	1954–present
MATCS	Marine Air Traffic Control Squadron	1978–1994
MATTS	Marine Aviation Training Support Squadron	1974–1979, 2000–present
MAWTS	Marine Aviation Weapons and Tactics Squadron	1978–present
MGCIS	Marine Ground Control Intercept Squadron	1946–1954
MOTS	Marine Operational Training Squadron	1943–1944
MTACS	Marine Tactical Air Command Squadron	1993–present
MWCS	Marine Wing Communications Squadron	1967–present
MWFS	Marine Wing Facilities Squadron	1967–1971
MWHS	Marine Wing Headquarters Squadron	1971–present
MWSS	Marine Wing Service Squadron	1943–1947
MWSS	Marine Wing Support Squadron	1986–present
SOES	Marine Station Operations and Engineering Squadron	1961–1977
SOMS	Marine Station Operation and Maintenance Squadron	1982–1997
VMA	Marine Attack Squadron	1951–present
VMA(AW)	Marine All-Weather Attack Squadron	1965–1992
VMAQ	Marine Tactical Electronic Warfare Squadron	1975–present
VMAT	Marine Attack Training Squadron	1951–1958
VMAT(AW)	Marine All-Weather Attack Training Squadron	1968–1986
VMB	Marine Bombing Squadron	1937–1946
VMBF	Marine Fighter/Bomber Squadron	1944–1946

Marine Corps Squadron Designations/Abbreviations		
Acronym	**Full Squadron Designation**	**Time Frame in Use**
VMC	Marine Composite Squadron	1952–1955
VMCJ	Marine Composite Reconnaissance Squadron	1955–1975
VMD	Marine Photographic Squadron	1942–1946
VMF	Marine Fighting Squadron	1937–1949
VMF	Marine Fighter Squadron	1948–1965
VMFA	Marine Fighter Attack Squadron	1963–present
VMFA(AW)	Marine All-Weather Fighter Attack Squadron	1947–1951, 1958–1972, 1989–present
VMFAT	Marine Fighter Attack Training Squadron	1968–present
VMF(AW)	Marine All-Weather Fighter Squadron	1948–1967
VMF(N)	Marine Night Fighter Squadron	1942–1958
VMFP	Marine Tactical Reconnaissance Squadron	1975–1990
VMFT	Marine Fighter Training Squadron	1951–present
VMFT(AW)	Marine All-Weather Fighter Training Squadron	1955–1958
VMFT(N)	Marine Night Fighter Training Squadron	1951–1958
VMGR	Marine Aerial Refueler Transport Squadron	1962–present
VMGRT	Marine Aerial Refueler Transport Training Squadron	1986–present
VMIT	Marine Instrument Training Squadron	1951–1958
VMJ	Marine Utility Squadron	1945–1952
VMJ	Marine Photographic Squadron	1952–1955
VML	Marine Glider Squadron	1942–1943
VMM	Marine Medium Tiltrotor Squadron	2006–present
VMMT	Marine Medium Tiltrotor Training Squadron	1999–present
VMO	Marine Observation Squadron	1941–1993
VMP	Marine Photographic Squadron	1946–1949
VMR	Marine Transport Squadron	1944–1962
VMS	Marine Scouting Squadron	1937–1944
VMSB	Marine Scout Bombing Squadron	1941–1946
VMT	Marine Training Squadron	1947–present
VMTB	Marine Torpedo Bomber Squadron	1943–1946
VMU	Marine Unmanned Aerial Vehicle Squadron	1996–present
VMX	Marine Tiltrotor Test and Evaluation Squadron	2003–present
WERS	Marine Wing Equipment and Repair Squadron	1966–1976
WES	Marine Wing Engineer Squadron	1974–1986
WTS	Marine Wing Transportation Squadron	1974–1986
ZMQ	Marine Barrage Balloon Squadron	1941–1943

Note: In 1924 the letter "M" was adopted to differentiate Marine Corps squadrons from Navy squadrons.

CHAPTER 24
Current Squadron Lineage

The lineage and history of U.S. naval aviation squadrons has been a source of confusion since the birth of naval aviation in 1911. Much of this confusion arose from the terminology used by the Navy, the lack of a consistent policy in selecting the alphanumeric designations for squadrons, constantly reusing the same letter and numeric designations, and the many establishments, redesignations, and deactivations of aviation squadrons.

When dealing with a squadron's lineage, the only correct terms to use are establishment, deactivation, and redesignation. The terms commissioning and establishment have been used interchangeably for years and that is incorrect. Only ships are commissioned, decommissioned, and receive commissioning pennants. Squadrons have establishment and deactivation ceremonies.

A unit's history and lineage begins when it is established and ends at the time it is deactivated. Determining a squadron's "family tree" may seem cut and dried, but that is not the case. A squadron may undergo numerous redesignations during the period between its establishment and deactivation. A newly established squadron bearing the same designation of a unit that had previously existed may carry on the traditions of the old organization, but it cannot claim the history or lineage of the previous unit. The same is true of U. S. Navy ships and, thus, the rationale for such a policy becomes apparent. For example, *Ranger* (CV 61) is the seventh ship to bear the name *Ranger* and may carry on the traditions of the previous six ships. *Ranger* (CV 61) is obviously not the same Continental Navy Ship *Ranger* commanded by Capt. John Paul Jones during the War of Independence. The history of *Ranger* (CV 61) begins with its commissioning date, not with the commissioning date of the first *Ranger*.

The most recent squadron with the designation Fighter Squadron One (VF-1) was established 1 October 1972 and disestablished 1 October 1993. It was the seventh squadron in the Navy to be designated VF-1. This squadron is not the same VF-1 that used the designation for the first time in 1922. Designations, like ship's names, are reused again and again. If there is a break in the active status of a unit designation as a result of disestablishment, then there is no connection between the units bearing the same designation.

Another common problem area involves squadron insignia. The lineage or history of a squadron cannot be traced using only its insignia, because the same insignia may have been adopted and approved for official use by more than one squadron during different time frames. The insignia of a disestablished squadron may be officially approved for use by another squadron, but this does not confer upon the new squadron the right to the previous unit's history and lineage. The following outline of the Jolly Roger insignia is an example of the confusion that results if one attempts to trace the lineage and history of a squadron insignia without considering other factors.

VF-17 was established on 1 January 1943, and during WWII—when it produced an outstanding record as a fighter squadron—it adopted the Jolly Roger insignia. On 15 November 1946, all Navy squadrons were redesignated and VF-17 became VF-5B. Subsequently, it was redesignated VF-61 on 28 April 1948, and then disestablished on 15 April 1959 with Cmdr. Robert T. Hoppe as commanding officer. The Jolly Roger insignia had been used by VF-17/VF-5B/VF-61 from 1943 until 15 April 1959.

On 2 July 1955, VA-86 was established and on the same day was redesignated VF-84. This squadron was equipped with the FJ Fury and adopted the nickname Vagabonds. An insignia consisting of a lightning bolt striking the globe in the area of Norfolk, Va., with a sword behind the bolt, was approved on 27 September 1955. The squadron operated under this name and insignia until it replaced the FJs with F8U Crusaders in 1959. Cmdr. Hoppe assumed command of VF-84 two days after the disestablishment of VF-61, the Jolly Roger squadron. He initiated the request to have VF-84 adopt the old Jolly Roger insignia, which had been used by VF-61 and was no longer active. This request was approved by CNO on 1 April 1960. There is no direct connection between the former Jolly Roger squadron (VF-17/VF-5B/VF-61) and VF-84, which adopted the insignia.

To further complicate a review of the records, there have been other squadrons with the designation VF-84. During World War II, a VF-84 was established on 1 May 1944 and disestablished 8 October 1945. Naval Air Reserve squadron VF-921 was called to active duty 1 February 1951 and was redesignated VF-84 on 4 February 1954. This squadron then became VA-86 on 2 July 1955. This occurred on the same day Cmdr. Hoppe's Jolly Roger squadron was established as VA-86 and immediately redesignated VF-84. Neither of these two VF-84 squadrons had any connection with the original Jolly Rogers. Thus, Cmdr. Hoppe's VF-84 operating with the insignia and title of Jolly Roger could lay claim to the traditions of VF-17, VF-5B, and VF-61, if it wished to do so, but could only claim a history that commenced on 2 July 1955, and it was not a direct descendant of the original Jolly Roger squadron. The current Jolly Rogers are VFA-103.

A squadron's history and lineage covers only the period during which a unit is officially declared active (established by CNO), has personnel assigned to it, and is listed in the Naval Aeronautical Organization. When a squadron is disestablished, its history and lineage ends. If a squadron is redesignated while it is active, the lineage and history of the unit is carried on by the newly redesignated squadron. The following is an example of what occurs when a squadron is redesignated and its lineage and history remain unbroken.

The current VFA-25 was originally established as Torpedo Squadron 17 (VT-17) on 1 January 1943. On 15 November 1946, VT-17 was redesignated VA-6B and carried this designation until 27 April 1948, when it was redesignated VA-65. On 1 July 1959, VA-65 was redesignated VA-25 and the unit remained VA-25 until it was redesignated VFA-25 on 1 July 1983. The history and lineage of the present VFA-25 may be traced to 1 January 1943, because there was no break in active duty status of the squadron, even though its designation changed four times.

The current VFA-106 provides an example of what happens when a squadron is disestablished and then, years later, the same number is used again. This squadron was established at NAS Cecil Field on 27 April 1984. VFA-106 adopted the old insignia of VA-106 and had it officially approved. The squadron may carry on the traditions of the old VA-106, but it cannot trace its lineage and history back to VA-106. The list of commanding officers for VA-106 is not part of the list of commanding officers for VFA-106. The history of VA-106 came to an end on 7 November 1969, when it was disestablished and its personnel were transferred to other duty stations. At this time, VA-106 was removed from the active list in the Naval Aeronautical Organization.

These are the Navy squadrons as of January 2011:

Squadron Designation	Changes in Squadron Designations	Date of Change
Helicopter Combat Support Squadron (Designation no longer in use)		
HC-2	(See HSC-2)	
HC-3	(See HSC-3)	
HC-4	HC-4 Established HC-4 Deactivated	6 May 1983 30 Sep 2007
HC-5	(See HSC-25)	
HC-6	(See HSC-26)	
HC-8	(See HSC-28)	
HC-11	(See HSC-21)	
HC-85	(See HSC-85)	
Helicopter Combat Support Special Squadron (Designation no longer in use)		
HCS-4	(See HSC-84)	
HCS-5	HAL-5 Established HAL-5 Redesignated HCS-5 HCS-5 Deactivated	1 Mar 1977 1 Oct 1988 31 Dec 2006
Helicopter Mine Countermeasures Squadron		
HM-14	HM-14 Established	12 May 1978
HM-15	HM-15 Established	2 Jan 1987
Helicopter Anti-Submarine Squadron (HS designation slowly changing to HSC)		
HS-2	(See HSC-12)	
HS-3	(See HSC-9)	
HS-4	HS-4 Established	30 Jun 1952
HS-5	(See HSC-5)	
HS-6	HS-6 Established	1 Jun 1956
HS-7	HS-7 Established	15 Dec 1969
HS-8	(See HSC-8)	
HS-10	HS-10 Established	1 Jul 1960
HS-11	HS-11 Established	27 Jun 1957
HS-14	HS-14 Established	10 Jul 1984
HS-15	HS-15 Established	29 Oct 1971
HS-75	HS-75 Established HS-75 Deactivated	1 Jun 1970 1 Apr 2007

Squadron Designation	Changes in Squadron Designations	Date of Change
Helicopter Sea Combat Squadron		
HSC-2	HC-2 Established HC-2 Redesignated HSC-2	1 Apr 1987 24 Aug 2005
HSC-3	HC-3 Established HC-3 Redesignated HSC-3	1 Sep 1967 31 Oct 2005
HSC-5	HS-5 Established HS-5 Redesignated HSC-5	3 Jan 1956 28 Feb 2009
HSC-8	HS-8 Established HS-8 Redesignated HSC-8	1 Nov 1969 1 Apr 2007
HSC-9	HS-3 Established HS-3 Redesignated HSC-9	18 Jun 1952 1 Jun 2009
HSC-12	HS-2 Established HS-2 Redesignated HSC-12	7 Mar 1952 1 Jan 2009
HSC-21	HC-11 Established HC-11 Redesignated HSC-21	1 Oct 1977 7 Nov 2005
HSC-22	HSC-22 Established	1 Oct 2006
HSC-23	HSC-23 Established	1 Oct 2006
HSC-25	HC-5 Established HC-5 Redesignated HSC-25	3 Feb 1984 24 Oct 2005
HSC-26	HC-6 Established HC-6 Redesignated HSC-26	1 Sep 1967 24 Aug 2005
HSC-28	HC-8 Established HC-8 Redesignated HSC-28	3 Dec 1984 13 May 2005
HSC-84	HAL-4 Established HAL-4 Redesignated HCS-4 HCS-4 Redesignated HSC-84	1 Jul 1976 1 Oct 1989 1 Oct 2006
HSC-85	HS-85 Established HS-85 Redesignated HC-85 HC-85 Redesignated HSC-85	1 Jul 1970 1 Oct 1994 8 Feb 2006
Helicopter Maritime Strike Squadron		
HSM-40	Established as HSL-40 HSL-40 Redesignated HSM-40	4 Oct 1985 1 Nov 2009
HSM-41	Established as HSL-41 HSL-41 Redesignated HSM-41	21 Jan 1983 8 Dec 2005
HSM-70	Established as HSM-70	1 Mar 2008
HSM-71	Established as HSM-71	1 Jan 2007
HSM-77	Established as HSL-47 HSL-47 Redesignated HSM-77	25 Sep 1987 1 Feb 2009
Helicopter Anti-Submarine Squadron Light (HSL designation slowly changing to HSM)		
HSL-37	HSL-37 Established	3 Jul 1975
HSL-40	(See HSM-40)	
HSL-41	(See HSM-41)	
HSL-42	HSL-42 Established	5 Oct 1984
HSL-43	HSL-43 Established	5 Oct 1984
HSL-44	HSL-44 Established	21 Aug 1986
HSL-45	HSL-45 Established	3 Oct 1986
HSL-46	HSL-46 Established	7 Apr 1988
HSL-47	(See HSM-77)	
HSL-48	HSL-48 Established	7 Sep 1989
HSL-49	HSL-49 Established	23 Mar 1990
HSL-51	HSL-51 Established	1 Oct 1991
HSL-60	HSL-60 Established	1 Apr 2001
HSL-84	HS-84 Established HS-84 Redesignated HSL-84 HSL-84 Deactivated	1 Jul 1970 1 Mar 1984 30 Jun 2001

Squadron Designation	Changes in Squadron Designations	Date of Change
HSL-94	HSL-94 Established HSL-94 Deactivated	1 Oct 1985 1 Apr 2001
Helicopter Training Squadron		
HT-8	HTU-1 Established HTU-1 Redesignated HTG-1 HTG-1 Redesignated HT-8	3 Dec 1950 Mar 1957 1 Jul 1960
HT-18	HT-18 Established	1 Mar 1972
HT-28	HT-28 Established	1 Nov 2006
Tactical Electronic Warfare Squadron Redesignated Electronic Attack Squadron on 30 March 1998 (the VAQ designation remained the same)		
VAQ-128	VAQ-128 Established VAQ-128 Deactivated	1 Oct 1997 30 Sep 2004
VAQ-129	VAH-10 Established VAH-10 Redesignated VAQ-129	1 May 1961 1 Sep 1970
VAQ-130	VAW-13 Established VAW-13 Redesignated VAQ-130	1 Sep 1959 1 Oct 1968
VAQ-131	VP-931 Reserve squadron to active duty VP-931 Redesignated VP-57 VP-57 Redesignated VAH-4 VAH-4 Redesignated VAQ-131	2 Sep 1950 4 Feb 1953 3 Jul 1956 1 Nov 1968
VAQ-132	VAH-2 Established VAH-2 Redesignated VAQ-132	1 Nov 1955 1 Nov 1968
VAQ-133	VAQ-133 Established	1 Apr 1996
VAQ-134	VAQ-134 Established	17 Jun 1969
VAQ-135	VAQ-135 Established	15 May 1969
VAQ-136	VAQ-136 Established	6 Apr 1973
VAQ-137	VAQ-137 Established	1 Oct 1996
VAQ-138	VAQ-138 Established	27 Feb 1976
VAQ-139	VAQ-139 Established	1 Jul 1983
VAQ-140	VAQ-140 Established	1 Oct 1985
VAQ-141	VAQ-141 Established	1 Jul 1987
VAQ-142	VAQ-142 Established	1 Apr 1997
VAQ-143	VAQ-143 Established	1 Aug 2002
	VAQ-143 was on the books as being established on 1 August 2002 but funding for the squadron was never provided and shortage of aircraft made it impossible to effectively activate the command. The squadron was removed from the books (SNDL) and the file closed on 12 Nov 2009.	
VAQ-209	VAQ-209 Established	1 Oct 1977
Carrier Airborne Early Warning Squadron		
VAW-77	VAW-77 Established	1 Oct 1995
VAW-78	VAW-78 Established VAW-78 Deactivated	1 Jul 1970 31 Mar 2005
VAW-112	VAW-112 Established	20 Apr 1967
VAW-113	VAW-113 Established	20 Apr 1967
VAW-115	VAW-115 Established	20 Apr 1967
VAW-116	VAW-116 Established	20 Apr 1967
VAW-117	VAW-117 Established	1 Jul 1974
VAW-120	RVAW-120 Established RVAW-120 Redesignated VAW-120	1 Jul 1967 1 May 1983
VAW-121	VAW-121 Established	1 Apr 1967
VAW-123	VAW-123 Established	1 Apr 1967
VAW-124	VAW-124 Established	1 Sep 1967
VAW-125	VAW-125 Established	1 Oct 1968
VAW-126	VAW-126 Established	1 Apr 1969

Squadron Designation	Changes in Squadron Designations	Date of Change
Composite Squadron (Designation no longer in use)		
VC-6	VU-6 Established VU-6 Redesignated VC-6 VC-6 Deactivated	1 Mar 1952 1 Jul 1965 30 Jun 2008
VC-8	GMSRON-2 (Guided Missile Service Squadron 2) Established GMSRON-2 Redesignated VU-8 VU-8 Redesignated VC-8 VC-8 Deactivated	1 Jul 1958 1 Jul 1960 1 Jul 1965 1 Oct 2003
Fighter Squadron (Designation no longer in use)		
VF-2	(See VFA-2)	
VF-11	(See VFA-11)	
VF-14	(See VFA-14)	
VF-31	(See VFA-31)	
VF-32	(See VFA-32)	
VF-41	(See VFA-41)	
VF-101	VF-101 Established VF-101 Deactivated	1 May 1952 30 Sep 2005
VF-102	(See VFA-102)	
VF-103	(See VFA-103)	
VF-143	(See VFA-143)	
VF-154	(See VFA-154)	
VF-201	(See VFA-201)	
VF-211	(See VFA-211)	
VF-213	(See VFA-213)	
Strike-Fighter Squadron		
VFA-2	VF-2 Established VF-2 Redesignated VFA-2	14 Oct 1972 1 Jul 2003
VFA-11	VF-43 Established VF-43 Redesignated VF-11	1 Sep 1950 16 Feb 1959
	VF-11 adopted the insignia used by the previous VF-11, which had been disestablished on 15 Feb 1959. The newly designated VF-11 (16 Feb 1959) carried on the insignia and traditions of the Red Ripper squadron dating back to 1 Feb 1927, but not the lineage.	
	VF-11 Redesignated VFA-11	18 Oct 2005
VFA-14	Air Detachment, Pacific Fleet Established Became VT-5, an element of AirDet, PACFLT VT-5 Redesignated VP-4-1 VP-4-1 Redesignated VF-4 VF-4 Redesignated VF-1 VF-1 Redesignated VF-IB VF-IB Redesignated VB-2B VB-2B Redesignated VB-3 VB-3 Redesignated VB-4 VB-4 Redesignated VS-41 VS-41 Redesignated VB-41 VB-41 Redesignated VB-4 VB-4 Redesignated VA-1A VA-1A Redesignated VA-14 VA-14 Redesignated VF-14 VF-14 Redesignated VFA-14	Sep 1919 15 Jun 1920 7 Sep 1921 23 Sep 1921 1 Jul 1922 1 Jul 1927 1 Jul 1934 1 Jul 1937 1 Jul 1939 15 Mar 1941 1 Mar 1943 4 Aug 1943 15 Nov 1946 2 Aug 1948 15 Dec 1949 1 Dec 2001
VFA-15	VA-67 Established VA-67 Redesignated VA-15 VA-15 Redesignated VFA-15	1 Aug 1968 2 Jun 1969 1 Oct 1986
VFA-22	VF-63 Established VF-63 Redesignated VA-63 VA-63 Redesignated VA-22 VA-22 Redesignated VFA-22	28 Jul 1948 Mar 1956 1 Jul 1959 4 May 1990
VFA-25	VT-17 Established VT-17 Redesignated VA-6B VA-6B Redesignated VA-65 VA-65 Redesignated VA-25 VA-25 Redesignated VFA-25	1 Jan 1943 15 Nov 1946 27 Jul 1948 1 Jul 1959 1 Jul 1983

Squadron Designation	Changes in Squadron Designations	Date of Change
VFA-27	VA-27 Established VA-27 Redesignated VFA-27	1 Sep 1967 24 Jan 1991
VFA-31	VF-1B Established VF-1B Redesignated VF-6 VF-6 Redesignated VF-3 VF-3 Redesignated VF-3A VF-3A Redesignated VF-31 VF-31 Redesignated VFA-31	1 Jul 1935 1 Jul 1937 15 Jul 1943 15 Nov 1946 7 Aug 1948 1 Aug 2006
VFA-32	VBF-3 Established VBF-3 Redesignated VF-4A VF-4A Redesignated VF-32 VF-32 Redesignated VFA-32	1 Feb 1945 15 Nov 1946 7 Aug 1948 1 Aug 2006
VFA-34	VA-34 Established VA-34 Redesignated VFA-34	1 Jan 1970 30 Aug 1996
VFA-37	VA-37 Established VA-37 Redesignated VFA-37	1 Jul 1967 28 Nov 1990
VFA-41	VF-41 Established VF-41 Redesignated VFA-41	1 Sep 1950 1 Dec 2001
VFA-81	VA-66 Established VA-66 Redesignated VF-81 (same day) VF-81 Redesignated VA-81 VA-81 Redesignated VFA-81	1 Jul 1955 1 Jul 1955 1 Jul 1959 4 Feb 1988
VFA-82	VA-82 Established VA-82 Redesignated VFA-82 VFA-82 Deactivated	1 May 1967 15 Jul 1987 30 Jun 2005
VFA-83	VF-916 Reserve squadron called to active duty VF-916 Redesignated VF-83 VF-83 Redesignated VA-83 VA-83 Redesignated VFA-83	1 Feb 1951 4 Feb 1953 1 Jul 1955 1 Mar 1988
VFA-86	VF-921 Reserve squadron called to active duty VF-921 Redesignated VF-84 VF-84 Redesignated VA-86 VA-86 Redesignated VFA-86	1 Feb 1951 4 Feb 1953 1 Jul 1955 15 Jul 1987
VFA-87	VA-87 Established VA-87 Redesignated VFA-87	1 Feb 1968 1 May 1986
VFA-94	VF-94 Established VF-94 Redesignated VA-94 VA-94 Redesignated VFA-94	26 Mar 1952 1 Aug 1958 24 Jan 1991
VFA-97	VA-97 Established VA-97 Redesignated VFA-97	1 Jun 1967 24 Jan 1991
VFA-102	VA-36 Established VA-36 Redesignated VF-102	1 Jul 1955 1 Jul 1955
	On the same day, 1 Jul 1955, the old VF-102 was redesignated VA-36. This unit is separate from the VA-36 that was established on 1 Jul 1955 and then immediately redesignated VF-102.	
	VF-102 Redesignated VFA-102	1 May 2002
VFA-103	VF-103 Established VF-103 Redesignated VFA-103	1 May 1952 27 Apr 2006
VFA-105	VA-105 Established VA-105 Redesignated VFA-105	4 Mar 1968 17 Dec 1990
VFA-106	VFA-106 Established	27 Apr 1984
VFA-113	VF-113 Established VF-113 Redesignated VA-113 VA-113 Redesignated VFA-113	15 Jul 1948 Mar 1956 25 Mar 1983
VFA-115	VT-11 Established VT-11 Redesignated VA-12A VA-12A Redesignated VA-115	10 Oct 1942 15 Nov 1946 15 Jul 1948
	VA-115 was in an inactive status from Aug 1967 to 1 Jan 1970. It was not disestablished during this time frame and had a very limited number of personnel assigned to the squadron, which was located at NAS Lemoore during the period.	
	VA-115 Reactivated VA-115 Redesignated VFA-115	1 Jan 1970 30 Sep 1996
VFA-122	VFA-122 Established	1 Oct 1998

Squadron Designation	Changes in Squadron Designations	Date of Change
VFA-125	VFA-125 Established VFA-125 Deactivated	13 Nov 1980 1 Oct 2010
VFA-131	VFA-131 Established	3 Oct 1983
VFA 136	VFA-136 Established	1 Jul 1985
VFA-137	VFA-137 Established	1 Jul 1985
VFA-143	VF-871 Reserve squadron called to active duty VF-871 Redesignated VF-123 VF-123 Redesignated VF-53 VF-53 Redesignated VF-143 VF-143 Redesignated VFA-143	20 Jul 1950 4 Feb 1953 12 Apr 1958 20 Jun 1962 27 Apr 2006
VFA-146	VA-146 Established VA-146 Redesignated VFA-146	1 Feb 1956 21 Jul 1989
VFA-147	VA-147 Established VA-147 Redesignated VFA-147	1 Feb 1967 20 Jul 1989
VFA-151	VF-23 Established VF-23 Redesignated VF-151 VF-151 Redesignated VFA-151	6 Aug 1948 23 Feb 1959 1 Jun 1986
VFA-154	VF-837 Reserve squadron called to active duty VF-837 Redesignated VF-154 VF-154 Redesignated VFA-154	1 Feb 1951 4 Feb 1953 1 Oct 2003
VFA-192	VF-153 Established VF-153 Redesignated VF-15A VF-15A Redesignated VF-151 VF-151 Redesignated VF-192 VF-192 Redesignated VA-192 VA-192 Redesignated VFA-192	26 Mar 1945 15 Nov 1946 15 Jul 1948 15 Feb 1950 15 Mar 1956 10 Jan 1985
VFA-195	VT-19 Established VT-19 Redesignated VA-20A VA-20A Redesignated VA-195 VA-195 Redesignated VFA-195	15 Aug 1943 15 Nov 1946 24 Aug 1948 1 Apr 1985
VFA-201	VF-201 Established VF-201 Redesignated VFA-201 VFA-201 Deactivated	25 Jul 1970 1 Jan 1999 30 Jun 2007
VFA-203	VA-203 Established VA-203 Redesignated VFA-203 VFA-203 Deactivated	1 Jul 1970 1 Oct 1989 30 Jun 2004
VFA-204	VA-204 Established VA-204 Redesignated VFA-204	1 Jul 1970 1 May 1991
VFA-211	VB-74 Established VB-74 Redesignated VA-1B VA-1B Redesignated VA-24 VA-24 Redesignated VF-24 VF-24 Redesignated VF-211 VF-211 Redesignated VFA-211	1 May 1945 15 Nov 1946 1 Sep 1948 1 Dec 1949 9 Mar 1959 1 Aug 2006
VFA-213	VF-213 Established VF-213 Redesignated VFA-213*	22 Jun 1955 1 Aug 2006*

* No official paperwork (OPNAV NOTICE 3111) has been promulgated stating the official date for VF-213's redesignation to VFA-213.

Fighter Squadron Composite		
VFC-12†	VC-12 Established VC-12 Redesignated VFC-12	1 Sep 1973 22 Apr 1988
VFC-13†	VC-13 Established VC-13 Redesignated VFC-13	1 Sep 1973 22 Apr 1988
VFC-111	VFC-111 Established	1 Nov 2006

Patrol Squadron		
VP-1†	VB-128 Established VB-128 Redesignated VPB-128 VPB-128 Redesignated VP-128 VP-128 Redesignated VP-ML-1 VP-ML-1 Redesignated VP-1	15 Feb 1943 1 Oct 1944 15 May 1946 15 Nov 1946 1 Sep 1948
VP-4†	VB-144 Established VB-144 Redesignated VPB-144 VPB-144 Redesignated VP-144 VP-144 Redesignated VP-ML-4 VP-ML-4 Redesignated VP-4	1 Jul 1943 1 Oct 1944 15 May 1946 15 Nov 1946 1 Sep 1948

Squadron Designation	Changes in Squadron Designations	Date of Change
VP-5†	VP-17F (VP-17) Established VP-17 Redesignated VP-42 VP-42 Redesignated VB-135 VB-135 Redesignated VPB-135 VPB-135 Redesignated VP-135 VP-135 Redesignated VP-ML-5 VP-ML-5 Redesignated VP-5	2 Jan 1937 1 Jul 1939 15 Feb 1943 1 Oct 1944 15 May 1946 15 Nov 1946 1 Sep 1948
VP-8†	VP-201 Established VP-201 Redesignated VPB-201 VPB-201 Redesignated VP-201 VP-201 Redesignated VP-MS-1 VP-MS-1 Redesignated VP-ML-8 VP-ML-8 Redesignated VP-8	1 Sep 1942 1 Oct 1944 15 May 1946 15 Nov 1946 5 Jun 1947 1 Sep 1948
VP-9†	VP-9 Established	15 Mar 1951
VP-10†	VP-10 Established	19 Mar 1951
VP-16†	VP-741 Reserve squadron called to active duty VP-741 Redesignated VP-16	1 May 1951 4 Feb 1953
VP-26†	VB-114 Established VB-114 Redesignated VPB-114 VPB-114 Redesignated VP-114 VP-114 Redesignated VP-HL-6 VP-HL-6 Redesignated VP-26	26 Aug 1943 1 Oct 1944 15 May 1946 15 Nov 1946 1 Sep 1948
VP-30	VP-30 Established	30 Jun 1960
VP-40†	VP-40 Established	20 Jan 1951
VP-45†	VP-205 Established VP-205 Redesignated VPB-205 VPB-205 Redesignated VP-205 VP-205 Redesignated VP-MS-5 VP-MS-5 Redesignated VP-45	1 Nov 1942 1 Oct 1944 15 May 1946 15 Nov 1946 1 Sep 1948
VP-46	VP-5S Established VP-5S Redesignated VP-5F VP-5F Redesignated VP-5 VP-5 Redesignated VP-33 VP-33 Redesignated VP-32 VP-32 Redesignated VPB-32 VPB-32 Redesignated VP-32 VP-32 Redesignated VP-MS-6 VP-MS-6 Redesignated VP-46	1 Sep 1931 1 Apr 1933 1937 1 Jul 1939 1 Jul 1941 1 Oct 1944 15 May 1946 15 Nov 1946 1 Sep 1948
VP-47	VP-27 Established VP-27 Redesignated VPB-27 VPB-27 Redesignated VP-27 VP-27 Redesignated VP-MS-7 VP-MS-7 Redesignated VP-47	1 Jun 1944 1 Oct 1944 15 May 1946 15 Nov 1946 1 Sep 1948
VP-62	VP-62 Established	1 Nov 1970
VP-64	(See VR-64)	
VP-65	VP-65 Established VP-65 Deactivated	16 Nov 1970 31 Mar 2006
VP-66	VP-66 Established VP-66 Deactivated	1 Nov 1970 31 Mar 2006
VP-69	VP-69 Established	1 Nov 1970
VP-91†	VP-91 Established VP-91 Deactivated	1 Nov 1970 31 Mar 1999
VP-92†	VP-92 Established VP-92 Deactivated	1 Nov 1970 30 Nov 2007
VP-94†	VP-94 Established VP-94 Deactivated	1 Nov 1970 31 Mar 2006
Patrol Squadron Special Project Unit Redesignated Special Projects Patrol Squadron on 8 Apr 1998 for VPU-1 and on 14 Apr 1998 for VPU-2 (the designation VPU remained the same)		
VPU-1	VPU-1 Established	1 Jul 1982
VPU-2	VPU-2 Established	1 Jul 1982
Fleet Air Reconnaissance Squadron		
VQ-1	VQ-1 Established	1 Jun 1955
VQ-2	VQ-2 Established	1 Sep 1955

Squadron Designation	Changes in Squadron Designations	Date of Change
VQ-3	VQ-3 Established	1 Jul 1968
VQ-4	VQ-4 Established	1 Jul 1968
VQ-5	VQ-5 Established VQ-5 Deactivated	15 Apr 1991 30 Jul 1999
VQ-6	VQ-6 Established VQ-6 Deactivated	5 Aug 1991 30 Sep 1999
VQ-7	Naval Training Support Unit Redesignated VQ-7	1 Nov 1999
VQ-11	VQ-11 Established VQ-11 Deactivated	1 Jul 1997 31 Mar 2000
Fleet Logistic Support Squadron		
VR-1†	VR-1 Established	1 May 1997
VR-46	VR-46 Established	1 Mar 1981
VR-48	VR-48 Established	1 Oct 1980
VR-51	VR-51 Established	1 Jun 1997
VR-52†	VR-52 Established	24 Jun 1972
VR-53	VR-53 Established	1 Oct 1992
VR-54	VR-54 Established	1 Jun 1991
VR-55	VR-55 Established	1 Apr 1976
VR-56	VR-56 Established	1 Jul 1976
VR-57	VR-57 Established	1 Nov 1977
VR-58	VR-58 Established	1 Nov 1977
VR-59	VR-59 Established	1 Oct 1982
VR-61	VR-61 Established	1 Oct 1982
VR-62	VR-62 Established	1 Jul 1985
VR-64	Established as VP-64 Redesignated VR-64	1 Nov 1970 18 Sep 2004
Fleet Logistics Support Squadron		
VRC-30	VR-30 Established VR-30 Redesignated VRC-30	1 Oct 1966 1 Oct 1978
VRC-40	VRC-40 Established	1 Jul 1960
Sea Control Squadron		
VS-21†	CVEG-41 Established CVEG-41 Redesignated CVEG-1 CVEG-1 Redesignated VC-21 VC-21 Redesignated VS-21 VS-21 Deactivated	26 Mar 1945 15 Nov 1946 1 Sep 1948 23 Apr 1950 28 Feb 2005
VS-22†	VS-22 Established VS-22 Deactivated	18 May 1960 31 Mar 2009
VS-24†	VS-24 Established VS-24 Deactivated	25 May 1960 31 Mar 2007
VS-29	VS-29 Established VS-29 Deactivated	1 Apr 1960 30 Apr 2004
VS-30†	VS-801 Reserve squadron called to active duty VS-801 Redesignated VS-30 VS-30 Deactivation Ceremony Official Deactivation	9 Apr 1951 4 Feb 1953 9 Dec 2005 20 Apr 2007
VS-31†	VC-31 Established VC-31 Redesignated VS-31 VS-31 Deactivated	28 Sep 1948 20 Apr 1950 31 Mar 2008
VS-32	VC-32 Established VC-32 Redesignated VS-32 VS-32 Deactivated	31 May 1949 20 Apr 1950 30 Sep 2008
VS-33	VS-33 Established VS-33 Deactivated	1 Apr 1960 31 Jul 2006
VS-35†	VS-35 Established VS-35 Deactivated	4 Apr 1991 31 Mar 2005

Squadron Designation	Changes in Squadron Designations	Date of Change
VS-38†	VC-892 Reserve squadron Activated VC-892 Redesignated VS-892 VS-892 Reserve squadron called to active duty VS-892 Redesignated VS-38 VS-38 Deactivated	20 Jul 1950 4 Aug 1950 4 Aug 1950 4 Feb 1953 30 Apr 2004
VS-41†	VS-41 Established VS-41 Deactivated	30 Jun 1960 30 Sep 2006
Training Squadron		
VT-2	BTG-2 Redesignated VT-2 (Basic Training Group 2)	1 May 1960
VT-3	BTG-3 Redesignated VT-3	1 May 1960
VT-4	BTG-9 Redesignated VT-4	1 May 1960
VT-6	Multi-Engine Training Group, Whiting Field Redesignated VT-6	1 May 1960
VT-7	BTG-7 Activated BTG-7 Redesignated VT-7	1 Jun 1958 1 Jul 1960
VT-9	VT-19 Established VT-19 Redesignated VT-9	2 Aug 1971 1 Oct 1998
VT-10	BNAO School Redesignated VT-10	15 Jan 1968
	Basic Naval Aviation Officers School was established within the training department of NAS Pensacola in June 1960. BNAO School became a separate command under the Chief of Naval Air Training 15 Jan 1968.	
VT-19	(See VT-9)	
VT-21	ATU-202 (Advanced Training Unit 202) Redesignated VT-21	1 May 1960
VT-22	ATU-212 Redesignated VT-22	1 May 1960
VT-23	ATU-222 Established ATU-222 Redesignated VT-23 VT-23 Deactivated	Nov 1958 1 May 1960 30 Sep 1999
VT-27	ATU-402 Redesignated VT-27	1 Jul 1960
VT-28	ATU-611 Redesignated VT-28	1 May 1960
VT-31	ATU-601 Redesignated VT-31	1 May 1960
VT-35	VT-35 Established	29 Oct 1999
VT-86	VT-86 Established	5 Jun 1972
Air Test and Evaluation Squadron (VX/HX), Antarctic Development Squadron (VXE), Scientific Development Squadron (VXS)		
HX-21	Established as Naval Rotary Wing Aircraft Test Squadron Redesignated HX-21	21 Jul 1995 1 May 2002
VX-1	Established as Aircraft Antisubmarine Development Detachment, Atlantic Fleet	1 Apr 1943
	Aircraft Antisubmarine Development Detachment became part of a new unit called Antisubmarine Development Det, Atlantic Fleet	17 Sep 1943
	Antisubmarine Development Det, Atlantic Fleet redesignated VX-1	15 Mar 1946
VXE-6	VX-6 Established VX-6 Redesignated VXE-6 VXE-6 Deactivated	17 Jan 1955 1 Jan 1969 27 Mar 1999
VX-9	VX-9 Established	30 Apr 1994
VX-20	Established Naval Force Aircraft Test Squadron Redesignated VX-20	21 Jul 1995 1 May 2002
VX-23	Established Naval Strike Aircraft Test Squadron Redesignated VX-23	21 Jul 1995 1 May 2002
VX-30	Established Naval Weapons Test Squadron, Point Mugu Redesignated VX-30	8 May 1995 1 May 2002
VX-31	Established Naval Weapons Test Squadron, China Lake Redesignated VX-31	8 May 1995 1 May 2002
VXS-1	VXS-1 Established	13 Dec 2004

† Previous squadrons have been assigned this designation.

CHAPTER 25

Visual Identification System (Tail Codes)

The rapid and accurate identification of aircraft has always been of prime importance within naval aviation and its explosive expansion during WWII compounded the problem.

A three-part identification system had been in use in the fleet from 1923 until WWII. Under this system, the aircraft identification number 5-F-1, which was placed on the fuselage of the plane, meant this was the first airplane in Fighting Squadron 5. After July 1937, the squadron number for carrier-based squadrons was the same as the hull number of the carrier. Thus *Yorktown* (CV 5) would have had VB-5, VS-5, and VF-5 assigned as part of her complement of squadrons.

This system was modified by Commander Carriers, Pacific Fleet, on 29 April 1942. To help conceal the identity of carriers engaged in operations in enemy waters, the squadron number was eliminated, leaving just the letter designating the type of squadron and the aircraft number within the squadron. Thus, the marking on the fuselage of the plane would have been F-1 to identify it as the first plane in a fighting squadron without identifying the squadron's number. This was further modified on 22 December 1943, by the deletion of the squadron type letter. All identification as to a specific unit was now removed which allowed aircraft to be drawn from a pool as necessary without the requirement of painting identification information on them.

During WWII, with the increase in the number of fleet aircraft operating in the same area as training planes, the necessity grew even more acute to quickly differentiate the large number of training planes from the operational fleet aircraft. To alleviate this problem, Naval Air Operational Training Command, on 12 January 1943, directed that all aircraft within the command be identified by an alpha/numeric system consisting of three groups of characters. The first letter(s) designated the base assignment for the aircraft. The second letter identified the aircraft mission, while the third group was the number of the aircraft within the squadron. For example, V-T-29 would indicate the aircraft was from Vero Beach, Fla., it was a torpedo plane, and the 29th aircraft in that training unit.

During the last two years of the war, many of the aircraft assigned to the carriers in the Pacific carried symbols denoting the ship or air group to which they were assigned. No directives specifying these markings are known to exist, if there ever were any. From a review of photos of the period, it appears that the symbols were assigned to the CV designated aircraft carriers while the escort carriers, designated CVE, had the symbol assigned to the squadrons that operated on board the ships. Squadrons operating on board the CVs only had that specific symbol while assigned to that particular carrier while this was a step in the right direction, the lack of a uniform system was soon apparent when a large number of aircraft were trying to rendezvous after takeoff, before landing, or over target areas.

The United States Navy Air Force, Pacific Fleet, issued on 27 January 1945 a standard set of 28 geometrical designs for the CV and CVL class carriers, which constituted Task Force 58. These designs were assigned to the vessel and were applied to all aircraft of the attached air group as long as it was on board. They were applied to both sides of the fin and rudder. While the drawings in the directive only showed the design on the top surface of the right wing, subsequent directives indicate that it was also to be applied on the under surface of the left wing tip.

The Commander, Air Force, Pacific Fleet, on 11 February 1945, issued an instruction for the aircraft in the Hawaiian Sea Frontier. All carrier and training type aircraft were to be identified with a letter followed by the individual aircraft number running from 1 to 99. These markings were not for the purpose of security, but rather to identify U.S. Navy aircraft after numerous reports of violations of air discipline involving flying too close to transport aircraft and ground installations.

Air Force, Pacific Fleet, on 2 June 1945, prescribed a series of recognition symbols for CVEs. These markings were to be painted on both sides of the vertical tail surfaces, as well as the upper right and lower left wing tips. All CVEGs, MCVGs, and VCs assigned to ships of the Escort Carrier Force, Pacific, were to carry these designs. Each carrier division was assigned a basic design. The position of the individual vessel within the division was indicated by a series of narrow stripes.

The system of geometrical symbols carried by Task Force 58 aircraft was difficult to describe over the radio and was not always readily identifiable in the air. To eliminate this problem, Commander Task Force 38, in July 1945, specified a system of 24-inch block capital letters to be used to identify CV and CVB aircraft. These were to be applied to both sides of the fin and rudder as well as the top right and lower left wing tips. In its original form some ships used a single letter, while others were assigned double letters. This was the beginning of the two-letter Visual Identification System in use today.

Naval Air Stations in Hawaii were assigned letter designations on 10 September 1945, by the Commander, Air Force, Pacific Fleet. These were to be followed by a number from 1 to 99 inclusive. In the event all available numbers in the 1 to 99 series were used, and no additional letters were available, the use of numbers over 100 was authorized.

On 8 January 1946, Air Force, Pacific Fleet, issued instructions for the application of markings on the fast carrier aircraft. This directive also assigned new alphabetical designations for the CVs, CVBs, and CVLs in place of those specified by Commander Task Force 38. This assignment of the same letter to a different carrier than previously designated may well have caused the erroneous identification of some photographs as to what ship the aircraft were actually assigned.

All of the previous directives or instructions were a search for an easy system to rapidly identify aircraft. Finally, on 7 November 1946, the Chief of Naval Operations (CNO) established the Visual Identification System for all Navy and Marine Corps aircraft. To be effective, such a system had to be simple, readable, and possess enough different combinations to cover the number of aircraft carriers and all types of squadrons to which naval aviation might expand in case of war. A system using letters satisfies these requirements as long as distinctive characters are used. The elimination of the ambiguous letters G, J, N, O, Q and Y left ample combinations to cover such expansion. Since each letter has a phonetic equivalent in communication procedures, the problem of describing geometric markings was replaced by the simple process of enunciating the names of the letters of the alphabet. Under this system each aircraft carrier had either a single or double letter symbol, some of which were a holdover from the previous system. On 12 December 1946, the Visual Identification System of Naval Aircraft was modified by CNO. Under this change the tail codes assigned to the carriers were now reassigned to individual air groups. This permitted greater flexibility since an air group was not permanently assigned to a specific carrier.

Under the CNO system, non-carrier based squadrons, such as VP, VPP, VPW, VPM, VU, VRU, VX, and VCN, also used a letter system. In these squadrons the first of the two letters designated the wing or class while the second letter designated the squadron within the wing. Marine Corps carrier-based squadrons used the letters assigned to the parent carrier while shore-based Marine squadrons used the first letter to designate the wing or other command, and the second letter identified the squadron within the wing or command. The letters in all cases were underscored to denote Marine. It was possible under this system to have the same code letters assigned to a Navy squadron and a Marine Corps squadron concurrently. This requirement to underscore the letters on Marine Corps aircraft was rescinded on 4 August 1948.

The Training Command continued to use the letter number designation system in which the first of one or two letters designated the base or station, while the second identified the squadron and/or class designation. The aircraft within the squadron were identified by a one-, two-, or three-digit number. The Chief, Naval Air Training, controlled the assignment of the letter symbols within the command.

Naval Air Reserve aircraft were also identified by two letters. The first denoted the air station to which the aircraft was assigned, while the second identified the type of squadron. From this it can be seen that it was possible to have a fleet squadron and a reserve squadron identified with the same two letters. This was resolved by the use of an orange band around the fuselage to denote a Reserve aircraft. Reorganization of the Naval Air Reserve in 1970 arranged the reserve squadron system along the same lines as the active fleet structure. The tail code assignments for these squadrons were redone to follow the procedures used for the fleet squadrons.

Naval Air Advanced Training Command on 6 January 1947 issued a directive for identifying aircraft within the command. This alpha/numeric system used a letter to identify the naval air station, followed by a second letter designating the squadron at that activity and then a three-digit aircraft number. On 31 August 1950, the Chief Naval Air Basic Training issued a directive that involved single letters to denote aircraft assigned to the various bases. This was modified on 27 September 1950 to a two-letter system whereby the first designated the base and the second the squadron. These letters were followed by a three-digit number to denote the individual aircraft within the squadron. On 6 September 1956, Chief of Naval Air Training established a new tail code identification system for the training commands. This system included two character alpha/numeric codes whereby the number 2 designated Chief Naval Air Basic Training Command aircraft, 3 designated Chief Naval Air Advanced Training Command, and 4 designated Chief Naval Technical Training Command aircraft.

One major change to occur was the move from a single letter to two letters to identify an air group's tail code. The effective date for this change was most likely the beginning of Fiscal Year 1958 (1 July 1957). Specific documentation has not been discovered to verify this date. However, the tail code (Visual Identification System) listing in the Naval Aeronautical Organization for 1957 shows the changes for the air group tail codes to two letters.

Even though numerous changes have been made since 7 November 1946 to the Visual Identification System, the basic tenet of the system has remained intact. The following is a listing of Tail Codes (Visual Identification System for Naval Aircraft) for Naval Aviation as of 31 December 2010:

Command	Tail Code
Blue Angels	BA
Carrier Air Wings (former designation Carrier Air Groups)	
CVW-1	AB
CVW-2	NE
CVW-3	AC
CVW-5	NF
CVW-7	AG
CVW-8	AJ
CVW-9	NG
CVW-11	NH
CVW-14	NK
CVW-17	AA
RCVW-4*	AD
RCVW-12†	NJ
Tactical Support Wing	AF
ASW Air Commands	
CVSG-51‡	RA
HS-10	RA
HELWINGRES§	NW
HSC-84	NW
HSC-85	NW
Fleet Logistic Support	
VRC-30	RW
VRC-40	Does not use tail code
Fleet Logistics Support Reserve	
VR-1	Does not use tail code
VR-46	JS
VR-48	JR
VR-51	RV
VR-52	JT
VR-53	AX
VR-54	CW
VR-55	RU
VR-56	JU
VR-57	RX
VR-58	JV
VR-59	RY
VR-61	RS
VR-62	JW
VR-64	BD
Helicopter Sea Combat	
HSC-2	HU
HSC-3	SA
HSC-5	AG
HSC-8	NG
HSC-9	AJ
HSC-12	NE
HSC-21	VR
HSC-22	AM

Command	Tail Code
HSC-23	WC
HSC-25	RB
HSC-26	HW
HSC-28	BR
HSC-84	NW§
HSC-85	NW§

Note: Many HSC squadrons are assigned to carrier air wings and use the tail code of the assigned air wing.

Command	Tail Code
Helicopter Maritime Strike	
HSM-40	HK
HSM-41	TS
HSM-70	Tail code to be assigned
HSM-71	Tail code to be assigned
HSM-77	Tail code to be assigned
Helicopter Antisubmarine Light‖	
HSL-37	TH
HSL-42	HN
HSL-43	TT
HSL-44	HP
HSL-45	TZ
HSL-46	HQ
HSL-48	HR
HSL-49	TX
HSL-51	TA
HSL-60	NW§
Helicopter Mine Countermeasure Squadron	
HM-14	BJ
HM-15	TB
Patrol	
VP-1	YB
VP-4	YD
VP-5	LA
VP-8	LC
VP-9	PD
VP-10	LD
VP-16	LF
VP-26	LK
VP-30	LL
VP-40	QE
VP-45	LN
VP-46	RC
VP-47	RD
Special Projects Patrol	
VPU-1	OB
VPU-2	SP
Patrol Reserve	
VP-62	LT
VP-69	PJ

Command	Tail Code
Fleet Air Reconnaissance	
VQ-1	PR
VQ-2	LQ
VQ-3	TC
VQ-4	HL
VQ-7	TL
Electronic Attack Expeditionary*	
VAQ-133	NL
VAQ-134	NL
VAQ-142	NL
VAQ-143	NL
Air Test and Evaluation	
HX-21	JH
VX-1	JA
VX-9	XE
VX-20	WB
VX-23	SD
VX-30	VX
VX-31	DD
VXS-1	RL
Chief of Naval Air Training	
TRAWING ONE	
Meridian	A
VT-7	A
VT-9	A
TRAWING TWO	
Kingsville	B
VT-21	B
VT-22	B
TRAWING FOUR	
Corpus Christi	G
VT-27	G
VT-28	G
VT-31	G
VT-35	G
TRAWING FIVE	
Whiting Field	E
VT-2	E
VT-3	E
VT-6	E
HT-8	E
HT-18	E
HT-28	E
TRAWING SIX	
Pensacola	F
VT-4	F
VT-10	F
VT-86	F
Naval Air Systems Command	

Command	Tail Code
Test Pilot School	TPS
Fleet Marine and Marine Support Units	
Headquarters	
MWHS-1	SZ
MALS-11	TM
MALS-12	WA
MALS-13	YU
MALS-14	CN
HAMS-16	WW
MALS-24	EW
MALS-26	EL
MALS-31	EX
MALS-36	WK
MALS 41	Tail code to be assigned
MALS 49	Tail code to be assigned
HQSSDN-37	QF
Marine Attack	
VMA-211	CF
VMA-214	WA
VMA-223	WP
VMA-231	CG
VMA-311	WL
VMA-513	WF
VMA-542	CR
Marine Strike Fighter (Fighter Attack)	
VMFA-115	VE
VMFA-121 (AW)	VK
VMFA-122	DC
VMFA-134	MF
VMFA-142	MB
VMFA-212	WD
VMFA-224 (AW)	WK
VMFA-225 (AW)	CE
VMFA-232	WT
VMFA-242 (AW)	DT
VMFA-251	DW
VMFA-312	DR
VMFA-314	VW
VMFA-323	WS
VMFA-533 (AW)	ED
Marine Electronic Attack	
VMAQ-1	CB
VMAQ-2	CY
VMAQ-3	MD
VMAQ-4	RM
Marine Aerial Refueler/Transport	
VMGR-152	QD
VMGR-234	QH
VMGR-252	BH

Command	Tail Code
VMGR-352	QB
VMGR-452	NY
Marine Fleet Training/Readiness	
VMAT-203	KD
VMFAT-101	SH
VMFAT-501	Tail code to be assigned
VMFT-401	LS
VMGRT-253	GR
VMMT-204	GX
Marine Helicopter Heavy	
HMH-361	YN
HMH-362	YL
HMH-363	YZ
HMH-461	CJ
HMH-462	YF
HMH-463	YH
HMH-464	EN
HMH-465	YJ
HMH-466	YK
HMH-769	MS
HMH-772	MT
Marine Helicopter Medium	
HMM-161	YR
HMM-163	YP
HMM-165	YW
HMM-166	YX
HMM-261	EM
HMM-262	ET
HMM-264	EH
HMM-265	EP
HMM-268	YQ
HMM-364	PF
HMM-365	YM
HMM-764	ML
HMM-774	MQ
Marine Helicopter Light Attack	
HMLA-167	TV
HMLA-169	SN
HMLA-267	UV
HMLA-269	HF
HMLA-367	VT
HMLA-369	SM
HMLA-773	MP
HMLA-775	MM
Marine Medium Tiltrotor	
VMM-162	YS
VMM-263	EG
VMM-266	ES
Marine Helicopter Training	

Command	Tail Code
HMMT-164	YT
HMT-302	MR
HMT-303	QT
Marine Helicopter Experimental	
HMX-1	MK
Marine Fixed-Wing Experimental	
VMX-22	MV
Unmanned Aerial Vehicle Operations	
VMU-1	WG
VMU-2	EZ

*RCVW-4	AD
VAW-120	AD
VFA-106	AD

RCVW-4 was disestablished on 1 June 1970. Its tail code was retained by VAW-120 and VFA-106.

†RCVW-12	NJ
VAQ-129	NJ
VFA-122	NJ

RCVW-12 was disestablished on 1 June 1970. Its tail code was retained by VAQ-129 and VFA-122.

‡CVSG-51 was disestablished on 30 June 1971. Its tail code was retained by HS-10.

§All helicopter squadrons assigned to Commander Helicopter Wing Reserve use the same NW tail code.

∥The tail code TY has been set aside effective 4 April 2004. On this date HSL-47 was assigned to CVW-2 and will be using the air wing's tail code until it is transferred to another command.

¶The VAQ expeditionary squadrons all fall under COMVAQMIGPAC and have been assigned the same NL tail code.

Tail Code Alphabetical Listing	
Tail Code	**Command**
A	Meridian (TRAWING ONE)
A	VT-7 (TRAWING ONE)
A	VT-9 (TRAWING ONE)
B	Kingsville (TRAWING TWO)
B	VT-21 (TRAWING TWO)
B	VT-22 (TRAWING TWO)
E	Whiting Field (TRAWING FIVE)
E	HT-8 (TRAWING FIVE)
E	HT-18 (TRAWING FIVE)
E	HT-28 (TRAWING FIVE)
E	VT-2 (TRAWING FIVE)
E	VT-3 (TRAWING FIVE)
E	VT-6 (TRAWING FIVE)
F	Pensacola (TRAWING SIX)
F	VT-4 (TRAWING SIX)
F	VT-10 (TRAWING SIX)
F	VT-86 (TRAWING SIX)
G	Corpus Christi (TRAWING FOUR)
G	VT-27 (TRAWING FOUR)
G	VT-28 (TRAWING FOUR)
G	VT-31 (TRAWING FOUR)
G	VT-35 (TRAWING FOUR)

Tail Code Alphabetical Listing	
Tail Code	**Command**
AA	CVW-17
AB	CVW-1
AC	CVW-3
AD	RCVW-4*
AD	VAW-120
AD	VFA-106
AF	Tactical Support Wing
AG	CVW-7
AG	HSC-5
AJ	CVW-8
AJ	HSC-9
AM	HSC-22
AX	VR-53
BA	Blue Angels
BD	VR-64
BH	VMGR-252
BJ	HM-14
BR	HSC-28
CB	VMAQ-1
CE	VMFA-225 (AW)
CF	VMA-211
CG	VMA-231
CJ	HMH-461
CN	MALS-14
CR	VMA-542
CW	VR-54
CY	VMAQ-2
DC	VMFA-122
DD	VX-31
DR	VMFA-312
DT	VMFA-242 (AW)
DW	VMFA-251
ED	VMFA-533 (AW)
EG	VMM-263
EH	HMM-264
EL	MALS-26
EM	HMM-261
EN	HMH-464
EP	HMM-265
ES	VMM-266
ET	HMM-262
EW	MALS-24
EX	MALS-31
EZ	VMU-2
GR	VMGRT-253
GX	VMMT-204
HF	HMLA-269
HK	HSM-40

Tail Code Alphabetical Listing	
Tail Code	**Command**
HL	VQ-4
HN	HSL-42
HP	HSL-44
HQ	HSL-46
HR	HSL-48
HU	HSC-2
HW	HSC-26
JA	VX-1
JH	HX-21
JR	VR-48
JS	VR-46
JT	VR-52
JU	VR-56
JV	VR-58
JW	VR-62
KD	VMAT-203
LA	VP-5
LC	VP-8
LD	VP-10
LF	VP-16
LK	VP-26
LL	VP-30
LN	VP-45
LQ	VQ-2
LS	VMFT-401
LT	VP-62
MB	VMFA-142
MD	VMAQ-3
MF	VMFA-134
MK	HMX-1
ML	HMM-764
MM	HMLA-775
MP	HMLA-773
MQ	HMM-774
MR	HMT-302
MS	HMH-769
MT	HMH-772
MV	VMX-22
NE	CVW-2
NE	HSC-12
NF	CVW-5
NG	CVW-9
NG	HSC-8
NH	CVW-11
NJ	RCVW-12†
NJ	VAQ-129
NJ	VFA-122
NK	CVW-14

Tail Code Alphabetical Listing	
Tail Code	**Command**
NL	VAQ-133*
NL	VAQ-134*
NL	VAQ-142*
NL	VAQ-143*
NW	HELWINGRES§
NW§	HSC-84
NW§	HSC-85
NW§	HSL-60
NY	VMGR-452
OB	VPU-1
PD	VP-9
PF	HMM-364
PJ	VP-69
PR	VQ-1
QB	VMGR-352
QD	VMGR-152
QE	VP-40
QF	HQSSDN-37
QH	VMGR-234
QT	HMT-303
RA	CVSG-51‡
RA	HS-10
RB	HSC-25
RC	VP-46
RD	VP-47
RL	VXS-1
RM	VMAQ-4
RS	VR-61
RU	VR-55
RV	VR-51
RW	VRC-30
RX	VR-57
RY	VR-59
SA	HSC-3
SD	VX-23
SH	VMFAT-101
SM	HMLA-369
SN	HMLA-169
SP	VPU-2
SZ	MWHS-1
TA	HSL-51
TB	HM-15
TC	VQ-3
TH	HSL-37
TL	VQ-7
TM	MALS-11
TPS	Test Pilot School
TS	HSM-41

Tail Code Alphabetical Listing	
Tail Code	**Command**
TT	HSL-43
TV	HMLA-167
TX	HSL-49
TY	I
TZ	HSL-45
UV	HMLA-267
VE	VMFA-115
VK	VMFA-121 (AW)
VR	HSC-21
VT	HMLA-367
VW	VMFA-314
VX	VX-30
WA	MALS-12
WA	VMA-214
WB	VX-20
WC	HSC-23
WD	VMFA-212
WF	VMA-513
WG	VMU-1
WK	MALS-36
WK	VMFA-224 (AW)
WL	VMA-311
WP	VMA-223
WS	VMFA-323
WT	VMFA-232
WW	HAMS-16
XE	VX-9
YB	VP-1
YD	VP-4
YF	HMH-462
YH	HMH-463
YJ	HMH-465
YK	HMH-466
YL	HMH-362
YM	HMM-365
YN	HMH-361
YP	HMM-163
YQ	HMM-268
YR	HMM-161
YS	VMM-162
YT	HMMT-164
YU	MALS-13
YW	HMM-165
YX	HMM-166
YZ	HMH-363
To be assigned	HSM-70
To be assigned	HSM-71
To be assigned	HSM-77

Tail Code Alphabetical Listing	
Tail Code	**Command**
To be assigned	MALS 41
To be assigned	MALS 49
To be assigned	VMFAT-501
None	VR-1
None	VRC-40

* RCVW-4 was disestablished on 1 June 1970. Its tail code was retained by VAW-120 and VFA-106.

† RCVW-12 was disestablished on 1 June 1970. Its tail code was retained by VAQ-129 and VFA-122.

‡ CVSG-51 was disestablished on 30 June 1971. Its tail code was retained by HS-10.

§ All helicopter squadrons assigned to Commander Helicopter Wing Reserve use the same NW tail code.

‖ The tail code TY has been set aside effective 4 April 2004. On this date HSL-47 was assigned to CVW-2 and will be using the air wing's tail code until it is transferred to another command.

¶ The VAQ expeditionary squadrons all fall under COMVAQMIGPAC and have been assigned the same NL tail code.

CHAPTER 26
Aviation Ships

Attack Carriers (CV, CVA, CVB, CVL, CVAN, CVN)

The Navy established the CVB and CVL designations within the original CV designation on 15 July 1943. CVA replaced CV and CVB on 1 October 1952; CVL went out of use on 15 May 1959. CV and CVN replaced CVA and CVAN, respectively, on 30 June 1975 to designate the multi-mission character of aircraft carriers after the last CVS decommissioned in 1974.

During U.S. involvement in WWII (7 December 1941 to 2 September 1945) the Navy operated 110 carriers (including those designated CV, CVE, and CVL) of which 102 were commissioned in that period. The Navy also operated two training carriers during the war with the designation IX; *Sable* (IX 81) and *Wolverine* (IX 64).

Original Classes	*Langley*	1 ship, CV 1
	Lexington	2 ships, CV 2 and 3
	Ranger	1 ship, CV 4
	Yorktown	2 ships, CV 5 and 6
	Wasp	1 ship, CV 7
	Hornet	1 ship, CV 8
Subequent Classes	*Essex* Class	24 ships; CV 9–21, 31–34, 36–40, 45, and 47.
		(Of these numbers, 14, 15, 19, 21, 32–34, 36–40, 45, and 47 are sometimes referred to as "Long-Hull" *Essex* class or *Ticonderoga* class.)
	Independence	9 ships, CVL 22–30
	Midway	3 ships, CVB 41–43
	Saipan	2 ships, CVL 48 and 49
	Forrestal	4 ships, CVA 59–62
	Kitty Hawk	4 ships, CVA 63, 64, 66, and 67
	Enterprise	1 ship, CVAN 65
	Nimitz	10 ships, CVN 68–77
	Gerald R. Ford	1 ship, CVN 78

Carrier Listing for CV, CVA, CVB, CVAN, CVN, and CVL

Hull No.	Name	Commission and Decommission or Loss	New Designation or Change of Designation	Designation Change	Conversion Project*	Conversion Completed	Comments
1	*Langley*	20 Mar 1922 27 Feb 1942	CV 1 AV 3	21 Apr 1937			Lost, enemy action
2	*Lexington*	14 Dec 1927 8 May 1942	CV 2				Lost, enemy action
3	*Saratoga*	16 Nov 1927	CV 3				Expended, Operation Crossroads, 26 Jul 1946
4	*Ranger*	4 Jun 1934 18 Oct 1946	CV 4				Sold for scrap 31 Jan 1947
5	*Yorktown*	30 Sep 1937 7 Jun 1942	CV 5				Lost, enemy action
6	*Enterprise*	12 May 1938 17 Feb 1947	CV 6 CVA 6 CVS 6	1 Oct 1952 8 Aug 1953			Sold, 1 Jul 1958

Hull No.	Name	Commission and Decommission or Loss	New Designation or Change of Designation	Designation Change	Conversion Project*	Conversion Completed	Comments
7	*Wasp*	25 Apr 1940 15 Sep 1942	CV 7				Lost, enemy action
8	*Hornet*	20 Oct 1941 26 Oct 1942	CV 8				Lost, enemy action
9	*Essex*	31 Dec 1942 30 Jun 1969	CV 9 CVA 9 CVS 9	1 Oct 1952 8 Mar 1960	27A 125	Feb 1951 Mar 1956	Stricken 1 Jun 1973
10	*Yorktown*	15 Apr 1943 27 Jun 1970	CV 10 CVA 10 CVS 10	1 Oct 1952 1 Sep 1957	27A 125	Jan 1953 Oct 1955	Stricken 1 Jun 1973 Floating museum, Charleston, S.C., 1975
11	*Intrepid*	16 Aug 1943 15 Mar 1974	CV 11 CVA 11 CVS 11	1 Oct 1952 31 Mar 1962	27C 27C	Jun 1954 Apr 1957	Stricken 23 Mar 1982 Floating museum, New York City, N.Y., 1982
12	*Hornet*	29 Nov 1943 26 May 1970	CV 12 CVA 12 CVS 12	1 Oct 1952 27 Jun 1958	27A 125	Oct 1953 Aug 1956	Stricken 19 Aug 1989 Floating museum, Alameda, Calif., 1998
13	*Franklin*	31 Jan 1944 17 Feb 1947	CV 13 CVA 13 CVS 13	1 Oct 1952 8 Aug 1953			Stricken 10 Oct 1964
14	*Ticonderoga*	8 May 1944 1 Sep 1973	CV 14 CVA 14 CVS 14	1 Oct 1952 21 Oct 1969	27C 27C	Dec 1954 Mar 1957	Stricken 16 Nov 1973
15	*Randolph*	9 Oct 1944 13 Feb 1969	CV 15 CVA 15 CVS 15	1 Oct 1952 31 Mar 1959	27A 125	Jul 1953 Feb 1956	Stricken 1 Jun 1973
16	*Lexington*	17 Feb 1943 8 Nov 1991	CV 16 CVA 16 CVS 16 CVT 16 AVT 16	1 Oct 1952 1 Oct 1962 1 Jan 1969 1 Jul 1978	27C	Sep 1955	Stricken 8 Nov 1991 Floating museum, Corpus Christi, Texas, 1992
17	*Bunker Hill*	25 May 1943 9 Jul 1947	CV 17 CVA 17 CVS 17	1 Oct 1952 8 Aug 1953			Stricken 1 Nov 1966, retained as moored electronic test ship San Diego, Calif., until Nov 1972. Scrapped 1973.
18	*Wasp*	24 Nov 1943 1 Jul 1972	CV 18 CVA 18 CVS 18	1 Oct 1952 1 Nov 1956	27A 125	Sep 1951 Dec 1955	Stricken 1 Jul 1972 Sold for scrap 21 May 1973
19	*Hancock*	15 Apr 1944 30 Jan 1976	CV 19 CVA 19 CV 19	1 Oct 1952 30 Jun 1975	27C 17C	Mar 1954 Nov 1956	Stricken 31 Jan 1976. Sold for scrap 1 Sep 1976
20	*Bennington*	6 Aug 1944 15 Jan 1970	CV 20 CVA 20 CVS 20	1 Oct 1952 30 Jun 1959	27A 125	Nov 1952 Apr 1955	Stricken 1989
21	*Boxer*	16 Apr 1945 1 Dec 1969	CV 21 CVA 21 CVS 21 LPH 4	1 Oct 1952 1 Feb 1956 30 Jan 1959			Stricken 1 Dec 1969
22	*Independence*	14 Jan 1943 28 Aug 1946	CVL 22				Sunk in weapons test 29 Jan 1951
23	*Princeton*	25 Feb 1943 24 Oct 1944	CVL 23				Lost, enemy action
24	*Belleau Wood*	31 Mar 1943 13 Jan 1947	CVL 24				Transferred to France 5 Sep 1953 – Sep 1960, renamed *Bois Belleau* (R 97). Stricken 1 Oct 1960.
25	*Cowpens*	28 May 1943 13 Jan 1947	CVL 25 AVT 1	15 May 1959			Stricken 1 Nov 1959
26	*Monterey*	17 Jun 1943 16 Jan 1956	CVL 26 AVT 2	15 May 1959			Stricken 1 Jun 1970
27	*Langley*	31 Aug 1943 11 Feb 1947	CVL 27				Transferred to France 6 Jun 1951–1963, renamed *La Fayette* (R 96). Sold 19 Feb 1964.

Carrier Listing for CV, CVA, CVB, CVAN, CVN, and CVL

Hull No.	Name	Commission and Decommission or Loss	New Designation or Change of Designation	Designation Change	Conversion Project*	Conversion Completed	Comments
28	*Cabot*	24 Jul 1943 21 Jan 1955	CVL 28 AVT 3	15 May 1959			Transferred to Spain on 30 Aug 1967, renamed *Dedalo* (R 01), returned to private U.S. organization in 1989, and then scrapped.
29	*Bataan*	17 Nov 1943 9 Apr 1954	CVL 29 AVT 4	15 May 1959			Stricken 1 Sep 1959
30	*San Jacinto*	15 Dec 1943 1 Mar 1947	CVL 30 AVT 5	15 May 1959			Stricken 1 Jun 1970
31	*Bon Homme Richard*	26 Nov 1944 2 Jul 1971	CV 31 CVA 31	1 Oct 1952			Stricken 1989
32	*Leyte*	11 Apr 1946 15 May 1959	CV 32 CVA 32 CVS 32 AVT 10	1 Oct 1952 8 Aug 1953 15 May 1959			Stricken 1 Jun 1969
33	*Kearsarge*	2 Mar 1946 15 Jan 1970	CV 33 CVA 33 CVS 33	1 Oct 1952 1 Oct 1958	27A 125	Mar 1952 Jan 1957	Stricken 1 May 1973
34	*Oriskany*	25 Sep 1950 20 Sep 1976	CV 34 CVA 34 CV 34	1 Oct 1952 30 Jun 1975	27A 125	Oct 1950 May 1959	Stricken 1989. Sunk as artificial reef 17 May 2006.
36	*Antietam*	28 Jan 1945 8 May 1963	CV 36 CVA 36 CVS 36	1 Oct 1952 8 Aug 1953	†		Stricken 1 May 1973
37	*Princeton*	18 Nov 1945 30 Jan 1970	CV 37 CVA 37 CVS 37 LPH 5	1 Oct 1952 1 Jan 1954 2 Mar 1959			Stricken 30 Jan 1970
38	*Shangri-La*	15 Sep 1944 30 Jul 1971	CV 38 CVA 38 CVS 38	1 Oct 1952 30 Jun 1969	27C	Feb 1955	Stricken 15 Jul 1982
39	*Lake Champlain*	3 Jun 1945 2 May 1966	CV 39 CVA 39 CVS 39	1 Oct 1952 1 Aug 1957	27A	Sep 1952	Stricken 1 Dec 1969
40	*Tarawa*	8 Dec 1945 13 May 1960	CV 40 CVA 40 CVS 40 AVT 12	1 Oct 1952 10 Jan 1955 17 Apr 1961	27A	Sep 1952	Stricken 1 Jun 1967
41	*Midway*	10 Sep 1945 11 Apr 1992	CVB 41 CVA 41 CV 41	1 Oct 1952 30 Jun 1975	110	Nov 1957	Stricken 17 Mar 1997 Floating museum, San Diego, Calif., 2003
42	*Franklin D. Roosevelt*	27 Oct 1945 1 Oct 1977	CVB 42 CVA 42 CV 42	1 Oct 1952 30 Jun 1975	110	Jun 1956	Stricken 30 Sep 1977. Sold for scrap 1 Apr 1978.
43	*Coral Sea*	1 Oct 1947 26 Apr 1990	CVB 43 CVA 43 CV 43	1 Oct 1952 30 Jun 1975	110A	Jan 1960	Stricken 30 Apr 1990 Sold for scrap 8 Sep 2000
45	*Valley Forge*	3 Nov 1946 15 Jan 1970	CV 45 CVA 45 CVS 45 LPH 8	1 Oct 1952 1 Jan 1954 1 Jul 1961			Stricken 15 Jan 1970
47	*Philippine Sea*	11 May 1946 28 Dec 1958	CV 47 CVA 47 CVS 47 AVT 11	1 Oct 1952 15 Nov 1955 15 May 1959			Stricken 1 Dec 1969
48	*Saipan*	14 Jul 1946 14 Jan 1970	CVL 48 AVT 6 AGMR 2	15 May 1959 1 Sep 1964			Following redesignation as AGMR-2, *Saipan* was renamed *Arlington* and operated under this name from 1965 to her decommissioning on 14 Jan 1970. Stricken 15 Aug 1975 and sold for scrapping.
49	*Wright*	9 Feb 1947 22 May 1970	CVL 49 AVT 7 CC 2	15 May 1959 11 May 1963			Sold for scrapping 1 Aug 1980

Carrier Listing for CV, CVA, CVB, CVAN, CVN, and CVL							
Hull No.	Name	Commission and Decommission or Loss	New Designation or Change of Designation	Designation Change	Conversion Project*	Conversion Completed	Comments
59	*Forrestal*	1 Oct 1955 11 Sep 1993	CVA 59 CV 59 AVT 59	30 Jun 1975 4 Feb 1992			Stricken 11 Sep 1993
60	*Saratoga*	14 Apr 1956 20 Aug 1994	CVA 60 CV 60	30 Jun 1972			Stricken 20 Aug 1994
61	*Ranger*	10 Aug 1957 10 Jul 1993	CVA 61 CV 61	30 Jun 1975			Stricken 8 Apr 2004
62	*Independence*	10 Jan 1959 30 Sep 1998	CVA 62 CV 62	28 Feb 1973			Stricken 8 Mar 2004
63	*Kitty Hawk*	29 Apr 1961 12 May 2009	CVA 63 CV 63	29 Apr 1973			In Reserve
64	*Constellation*	27 Oct 1961 7 Aug 2003	CVA 64 CV 64	30 Jun 1975			Stricken 2 Dec 2003
65	*Enterprise*	25 Nov 1961	CVAN 65 CVN 65	30 Jun 1975			Active
66	*America*	23 Jan 1965 9 Aug 1996	CVA 66 CV 66	30 Jun 1975			Sunk in fleet training exercise 14 May 2005
67	*John F. Kennedy*	7 Sep 1968 23 Mar 2007	CVA 67 CV 67	29 Apr 1973			Stricken 16 Oct 2009
68	*Nimitz*	3 May 1975	CVAN 68 CVN 68	30 Jun 1975			Active
69	*Dwight D. Eisenhower*	18 Oct 1977	CVN 69				Active
70	*Carl Vinson*	13 Mar 1982	CVN 70				Active
71	*Theodore Roosevelt*	25 Oct 1986	CVN 71				Active
72	*Abraham Lincoln*	11 Nov 1989	CVN 72				Active
73	*George Washington*	4 Jul 1992	CVN 73				Active
74	*John C. Stennis*	9 Dec 1995	CVN 74				Active
75	*Harry S. Truman*	25 Jul 1998	CVN 75				Active
76	*Ronald Reagan*	12 Jul 2003	CVN 76				Active
77	*George H. W. Bush*	10 Jan 2009	CVN 77				Active
78	*Gerald R. Ford*		CVN 78				Keel laid 14 Nov 2009

* Projects 27A and the first 27Cs are axial deck modernizations; all others are angled deck conversions. For more detail, see chronology entries for 4 Jun 1947, 1 Feb 1952, 2 Sep 1953, and 27 May 1954.

† Experimental angled deck installation completed Dec 1952.

Note on Decommissioning Dates: The Navy decommissioned and then recommissioned a number of carriers for further service. Only the final decommissioning date is listed for these ships. Several carriers were also placed out of commission during major renovations or yard periods. In some cases the records regarding decommissioning dates were incomplete; consequently, the decommissioning date is blank if unknown.

• Construction of hull numbers omitted above were either terminated or cancelled. Numbers 35, 46, and 50–55 were scheduled for *Essex* class; 44, 56, and 57 for *Midway* class; and No. 58 for *United States*.

• The contracts originally let for CV 59 and 60 (*Forrestal* and *Saratoga*) did not include an angled deck in their designs. In 1953 the Navy redesigned the flight deck plans for *Forrestal* to incorporate an angled landing deck, and made similar changes to the designs for *Saratoga*. The contract for *Forrestal* was awarded in 1951 and for *Saratoga* in 1952. The contract for *Ranger* and *Independence* (CV 61 and 62) were not awarded until 1954. Therefore, the original contract designs for *Ranger* and *Independence* would have included an angled deck, and *Ranger* (CVA 61) thus became the first carrier designed and built as an angled deck carrier.

Escort Carriers (AVG, ACV and CVE)

The Navy assigned the original escort carrier designation AVG (Aircraft Escort Vessel) on 31 March 1941. The classification was changed to ACV (Auxiliary Aircraft Carrier) on 20 August 1942 and to CVE (Escort Carrier) on 15 July 1943. The CVE designation went out of use when the remaining escort carriers were reclassified AKV (Aircraft Ferry) on 7 May 1959.

Classes:

Long Island	1 ship, hull number 1
Charger	1 ship, hull number 30 (originally built for Royal Navy)
Bogue	11 ships, hull numbers 9, 11–13, 16, 18, 20, 21, 23, 25, and 31
Sangamon	4 ships, hull numbers 26–29
Casablanca	50 ships, hull numbers 55–104
Commencement Bay	19 ships, hull numbers 105–123

Hull numbers not listed below are accounted for as follows:

2–5 not assigned

6, 7, 8, 10, 14, 15, 17, 19, 22, 24, and 32–54 transferred to the Royal Navy

124–139 cancelled

Carrier Listing for CVE Designations

Hull No.	Name	Commission and Decommission or Loss	New Designation or Change of Designation	Designation Change	Comments
1	*Long Island*	2 Jun 1941 20 Mar 1946			Stricken 12 Apr 1946
9	*Bogue*	26 Sep 1942 30 Nov 1946	CVHE 9	12 Jun 1955	Stricken 1 Mar 1959
11	*Card*	8 Nov 1942 13 May 1946	CVHE 11 CVU 11 AKV 40	12 Jun 1955 1 Jun 1958 7 May 1959	Stricken 15 Sep 1970
12	*Copahee*	15 Jun 1942 5 Jul 1946	CVHE 12	12 Jun 1955	Stricken 1 Mar 1959
13	*Core*	10 Dec 1942 4 Oct 1946	CVHE 13 CVU 13 AKV 41	12 Jun 1955 1 Jul 1958 7 May 1959	Stricken 15 Sep 1970
16	*Nassau*	20 Aug 1942 28 Oct 1946	CVHE 16	12 Jun 1955	Stricken 1 Mar 1959
18	*Altamaha*	15 Sep 1942 27 Sep 1946	CVHE 18	12 Jun 1955	Stricken 1 Mar 1959
20	*Barnes*	20 Feb 1943 29 Aug 1946	CVHE 20	12 Jun 1955	Stricken 1 Mar 1959
21	*Block Island*	8 Mar 1943 29 May 1944			Lost to enemy action
23	*Breton*	12 Apr 1943 30 Aug 1946	CVHE 23 CVU 23 AKV 42	12 Jun 1955 1 Jul 1958 7 May 1959	Stricken 6 Aug 1971
25	*Croatan*	28 Apr 1943 20 May 1946	CVHE 25 CVU 25 AKV 43	12 Jun 1955 1 Jul 1958 7 May 1959	Stricken 15 Sep 1970
26	*Sangamon*	25 Aug 1942 24 Oct 1945	AO 28 AVG 26	23 Oct 1940 14 Feb 1942	Stricken 1 Nov 1945. *Sangamon* (AO 28) commissioned as a fleet oiler 23 Oct 1940, before conversion to an escort carrier.
27	*Suwannee*	24 Sep 1942 8 Jan 1947	AO 33 AVG 27 CVHE 27	16 Jul 1941 14 Feb 1942 12 Jun 1955	Stricken 1 Mar 1959. *Suwannee* (AO 33) commissioned as a fleet oiler 16 Jul 1941, before conversion to an escort carrier.

Hull No.	Name	Commission and Decommission or Loss	New Designation or Change of Designation	Designation Change	Comments
Carrier Listing for CVE Designations					
28	Chenango	19 Sep 1942 14 Aug 1946	AO 31 ACV 28 CVHE 28	20 Jun 1941 19 Sep 1942 12 Jun 1955	Stricken 1 Mar 1959. Chenango (AO 31) commissioned as a fleet oiler 20 Jun 1941, before conversion to an escort carrier.
29	Santee	24 Aug 1942 21 Oct 1946	AO 29 ACV 29 CVHE 29	30 Oct 1940 24 Aug 1942 12 Jun 1955	Stricken 1 Mar 1959. Santee (AO 29) commissioned as a fleet oiler 30 Oct 1941, before conversion to an escort carrier.
30	Charger	3 Mar 1942 15 Mar 1946			Stricken 29 Mar 1946
31	Prince William	9 Apr 1943 29 Aug 1946	CVHE 31	12 Jun 1955	Stricken 1 Mar 1959
55	Casablanca	8 Jul 1943 10 Jun 1946			Sold 23 Apr 1947
56	Liscome Bay	7 Aug 1943 24 Nov 1943			Lost to enemy action
57	Anzio (ex-Coral Sea)	27 Aug 1943 5 Aug 1946	CVHE 57	12 Jun 1955	Stricken 1 Mar 1959
58	Corregidor	31 Aug 1943 4 Sep 1958	CVU 58	12 Jun 1955	Stricken 1 Oct 1958
59	Mission Bay	13 Sep 1943 21 Feb 1947	CVU 59	12 Jun 1955	Stricken 1 Sep 1958
60	Guadalcanal	25 Sep 1943 15 Jul 1946	CVU 60	12 Jun 1955	Stricken 27 May 1958
61	Manila Bay	5 Oct 1943 31 Jul 1946	CVU 61	12 Jun 1955	Stricken 27 May 1958
62	Natoma Bay	14 Oct 1943 20 May 1946	CVU 62	12 Jun 1955	Stricken 27 May 1958
63	St. Lo (ex-Midway)	23 Oct 1943 25 Oct 1944			Commissioned 23 Oct 1943 as Midway (CVE 63), and renamed St. Lo (CVE 63) 10 Oct 1944. Lost to enemy action.
64	Tripoli	31 Oct 1943 25 Nov 1958	CVU 64	12 Jun 1955	Stricken 1 Feb 1959
65	Wake Island	7 Nov 1943 5 Apr 1946			Stricken 17 Apr 1946
66	White Plains	15 Nov 1943 10 Jul 1946	CVU 66	12 Jun 1955	Stricken 1 Jul 1958
67	Solomons	21 Nov 1943 15 May 1946			Stricken 5 Jun 1946. Launched as Nassuk Bay (CVE 67) 6 Oct 1943 and renamed Solomons (CVE 67) Nov 1943.
68	Kalinin Bay	27 Nov 1943 15 May 1946			Stricken 5 Jun 1946
69	Kasaan Bay	4 Dec 1943 6 Jul 1946	CVHE 69	12 Jun 1955	Stricken 1 Mar 1959
70	Fanshaw Bay	9 Dec 1943 14 Aug 1946	CVHE 70	12 Jun 1955	Stricken 1 Mar 1959
71	Kitkun Bay	15 Dec 1943 19 Apr 1946			Sold 18 Nov 1946
72	Tulagi	21 Dec 1943 30 Apr 1946			Stricken 8 May 1946
73	Gambier Bay	28 Dec 1943 25 Oct 1944			Lost to enemy action
74	Nehenta Bay	3 Jan 1944 15 May 1946	CVU 74 AKV 24	12 Jun 1955 7 May 1959	Stricken 1 Aug 1959
75	Hoggatt Bay	11 Jan 1944 20 Jul 1946	CVHE 75 AKV 25	12 Jun 1955 7 May 1959	Stricken 1 Aug 1959
76	Kadashan Bay	18 Jan 1944 14 Jun 1946	CVU 76 AKV 26	12 Jun 1955 7 May 1959	Stricken 1 Aug 1959

Hull No.	Name	Commission and Decommission or Loss	New Designation or Change of Designation	Designation Change	Comments
			Carrier Listing for CVE Designations		
77	*Marcus Island*	26 Jan 1944 12 Dec 1946	CVHE 77 AKV 27	12 Jun 1955 7 May 1959	Stricken 1 Aug 1959
78	*Savo Island*	3 Feb 1944 12 Dec 1946	CHVE 78 AKV 28	12 Jun 1955 7 May 1959	Stricken 1 Sep 1959
79	*Ommaney Bay*	11 Feb 1944 4 Jan 1945			Lost to enemy action
80	*Petrof Bay*	18 Feb 1944 30 Jul 1946	CVU 80	12 Jun 1955	Stricken 27 Jun 1958
81	*Rudyerd Bay*	25 Feb 1944 11 Jun 1946	CVU 81 AKV 29	12 Jun 1955 7 May 1959	Stricken 1 Aug 1959
82	*Saginaw Bay*	2 Mar 1944 19 Jun 1946	CVHE 82	12 Jun 1955	Stricken 1 Mar 1959
83	*Sargent Bay*	9 Mar 1944 23 Jul 1946	CVU 83	12 Jun 1955	Stricken 27 Jun 1958
84	*Shamrock Bay*	15 Mar 1944 6 Jul 1946	CVU 84	12 Jun 1955	Stricken 27 Jun 1958
85	*Shipley Bay*	21 Mar 1944 28 Jun 1946	CVHE 85	12 Jun 1955	Stricken 1 Mar 1959
86	*Sitkoh* Bay	28 Mar 1944 27 Jul 1954	CVU 86 AKV 30	12 Jun 1955 7 May 1959	Stricken 1 Apr 1960
87	*Steamer Bay*	4 Apr 1944 8 Aug 1946	CVHE 87	12 Jun 1955	Stricken 1 Mar 1959
88	*Cape Esperance*	9 Apr 1944 15 Jan 1959	CVU 88	12 Jun 1955	Stricken 1 Mar 1959
89	*Takanis Bay*	15 Apr 1944 1 May 1946	CVU 89 AKV 31	12 Jun 1955 7 May 1959	Stricken 1 Aug 1959
90	*Thetis Bay*	21 Apr 1944 1 Mar 1964	CVHA 1 LPH 6	1 Jul 1955 28 May 1959	Stricken 1 Mar 1964
91	*Makassar Strait*	27 Apr 1944 9 Aug 1946	CVU 91	12 Jun 1955	Stricken 1 Sep 1958
92	*Windham Bay*	3 May 1944 Jan 1959	CVU 92	12 Jun 1955	Stricken 1 Feb 1959
93	*Makin Island*	9 May 1944 19 Apr 1946			Stricken 5 Jun 1946
94	*Lunga Point*	14 May 1944 24 Oct 1946	CVU 94 AKV 32	12 Jun 1955 7 May 1959	Stricken 1 Apr 1960
95	*Bismarck Sea*	20 May 1944 21 Feb 1945			Lost to enemy action
96	*Salamaua*	26 May 1944 9 May 1946			Stricken 21 May 1946
97	*Hollandia*	1 Jun 1944 17 Jan 1947	CVU 97 AKV 33	12 Jun 1955 7 May 1959	Stricken 1 Apr 1960
98	*Kwajalein*	7 Jun 1944 16 Aug 1946	CVU 98 AKV 34	12 Jun 1955 7 May 1959	Stricken 1 Apr 1960
99	*Admiralty Islands*	13 Jun 1944 24 Apr 1946			Stricken 8 May 1946
100	*Bougainville*	18 Jun 1944 3 Nov 1946	CVU 100 AKV 35	12 Jun 1955 7 May 1959	Stricken 1 Apr 1960
101	*Matanikau*	24 Jun 1944 11 Oct 1946	CVU 101 AKV 36	12 Jun 1955 7 May 1959	Stricken 1 Apr 1960
102	*Attu*	30 Jun 1944 8 Jun 1946			Stricken 3 Jul 1946
103	*Roi*	6 Jul 1944 9 May 1946			Stricken 21 May 1946
104	*Munda*	8 Jul 1944 13 Sep 1946	CVU 104	12 Jun 1955	Stricken 1 Sep 1958
105	*Commencement Bay*	27 Nov 1944 30 Nov 1946	CVHE 105 AKV 37	12 Jun 1955 7 May 1959	Stricken 1 Apr 1971

Hull No.	Name	Commission and Decommission or Loss	New Designation or Change of Designation	Designation Change	Comments
			Carrier Listing for CVE Designations		
106	*Block Island*	30 Dec 1944 27 Aug 1954	LPH 1 CVE 106 AKV 38	22 Dec 1957 17 Feb 1959 7 May 1959	Stricken 1 Jul 1959
107	*Gilbert Islands*	5 Feb 1945 15 Jan 1955	AKV 39	7 May 1959	Stricken 1 Jun 1961
108	*Kula Gulf*	12 May 1945 15 Dec 1955	AKV 8	7 May 1959	Stricken 15 Sep 1970
109	*Cape Gloucester*	5 Mar 1945 5 Nov 1946	CVHE 109 AKV 9	12 Jun 1955 7 May 1959	Stricken 1 Apr 1971
110	*Salerno Bay*	19 May 1945 16 Feb 1954	AKV 10	7 May 1959	Stricken 1 Jun 1960
111	*Vella Gulf*	9 Apr 1945 9 Aug 1946	CVHE 111 AKV 11	12 Jun 1955 7 May 1959	Stricken 1 Jun 1960
112	*Siboney*	14 May 1945 31 Jul 1956	AKV 12	7 May 1959	Stricken 1 Jun 1970
113	*Puget Sound*	18 Jun 1945 18 Oct 1946	CVHE 113 AKV 13	12 Jun 1955 7 May 1959	Stricken 1 Jun 1960
114	*Rendova*	22 Oct 1945 30 Jun 1955	AKV 14	7 May 1959	Stricken 1 Apr 1971
115	*Bairoko*	16 Jul 1945 18 Feb 1955	AKV 15	7 May 1959	Stricken 1 Apr 1960
116	*Badoeng Strait*	14 Nov 1945 17 May 1957	AKV 16	7 May 1959	Stricken 1 Dec 1970
117	*Saidor*	4 Sep 1945 12 Sep 1947	CVHE 117 AKV 17	12 Jun 1955 7 May 1959	Stricken 1 Dec 1970
118	*Sicily*	27 Feb 1946 4 Oct 1954	AKV 18	7 May 1959	Stricken 1 Jul 1960
119	*Point Cruz*	16 Oct 1945 31 Aug 1956	AKV 19	7 May 1959	Stricken 15 Sep 1970
120	*Mindoro*	4 Dec 1945 4 Aug 1955	AKV 20	7 May 1959	Stricken 1 Dec 1959
121	*Rabaul*		CVHE 121 AKV 21	12 Jun 1955 7 May 1959	Stricken 1 Sep 1971. Inactivated after trials 30 Aug 1946; never commissioned.
122	*Palau*	15 Jan 1946 15 Jun 1954	AKV 22	7 May 1959	Stricken 1 Apr 1960
123	*Tinian*		CVHE 123 AKV 23	12 Jun 1955 7 May 1959	Stricken 1 Jun 1970. The Navy accepted the ship 30 Jul 1946; but she never commissioned.

World War II Training Carriers

During WWII the Navy's requirements for pilots provided an increased demand on the training command for carrier flight decks for carrier qualification training. To alleviate the need to take a front line carrier out of action for qualification training, the Navy acquired two vessels that had operated on the Great Lakes and converted them to training carriers with the designation IX, miscellaneous auxiliary.

Hull Number	Name	Commission and Decommission	Disposition and Status
64	*Wolverine*	12 Aug 1942 7 Nov 1945	American Shipbuilding Co., of Wyandotte, Mich., built side-wheel steamer *Seeandbee* in 1913. The Navy acquired her 12 Mar 1942 and the ship began conversion to a training carrier 6 May 1942. Stricken 28 Nov 1945.
81	*Sable*	8 May 1943 7 Nov 1945	American Shipbuilding Co., of Lorain, Ohio, built side-wheel steamer *Greater Buffalo* in 1924. The Navy acquired her 7 Aug 1942; renamed *Sable* 19 Sep 1942 and converted to a training carrier. Stricken 28 Nov 1945.

Antisubmarine Support Aircraft Carriers (CVS)

Classification and designation for CVS (Antisubmarine Support Aircraft Carrier) established 8 August 1953. The service used *Essex*-class carriers modified to serve in the ASW role. *Enterprise* (CV 6) was designated CVS-6 but was never used as such. This listing is for quick reference, with the reclassification dates and other data found in the Carrier Listing for CV, CVA, CVB, CVAN, CVN, and CVL.

Hull Number	Name
6	*Enterprise*
9	*Essex*
10	*Yorktown*
11	*Intrepid*
12	*Hornet*
13	*Franklin*
14	*Ticonderoga*
15	*Randolph*
16	*Lexington*
17	*Bunker Hill*
18	*Wasp*
20	*Bennington*
21	*Boxer*
32	*Leyte*
33	*Kearsarge*
36	*Antietam*
37	*Princeton*
38	*Shangri-La*
39	*Lake Champlain*
40	*Tarawa*
45	*Valley Forge*
47	*Philippine Sea*

Amphibious Assault Ships (LPH)				
Hull No.	Name	Commission and Decommission	New Designation or Change of Designation	Designation Change	Disposition and Status

Hull No.	Name	Commission and Decommission	New Designation or Change of Designation	Designation Change	Disposition and Status
1	*Block Island*	30 Dec 1944 27 Aug 1954	CVE 106 LPH 1ˑ CVE 106 AKV 38	 22 Dec 1957 17 Feb 1959 7 May 1959	Stricken 1 Jul 1959
2	*Iwo Jima*	26 Aug 1961 14 Jul 1993			Stricken 10 Jul 1993
3	*Okinawa*	14 Apr 1962 17 Dec 1992			Stricken 17 Dec 1992
4	*Boxer*	16 Apr 1945 1 Dec 1969	CV 21 CVA 21 CVS 21 LPH 4†	16 Apr 1945 1 Oct 1952 1 Feb 1956 30 Jan 1959	Stricken 1 Dec 1969
5	*Princeton*	18 Nov 1945 30 Jan 1970	CV 37 CVA 37 CVS 37 LPH 5‡	18 Nov 1945 1 Oct 1952 1 Jan 1954 2 Mar 1959	Stricken 30 Jan 1970
6	*Thetis Bay*	21 Apr 1944 1 Mar 1964	CVHA 1 LPH 6§	1 Jul 1955 28 May 1959	Stricken 1 Mar 1964
7	*Guadalcanal*	20 Jul 1963 31 Aug 1994			Stricken 31 Aug 1994
8	*Valley Forge*	3 Nov 1946 15 Jan 1970	CV 45 CVA 45 CVS 45 LPH 8‖	3 Nov 1946 1 Oct 1952 1 Jan 1954 1 Jul 1961	Stricken 15 Jan 1970
9	*Guam*	16 Jan 1965 25 Aug 1998			Stricken 25 Aug 1998. Sunk in fleet training exercise 16 Oct 2001.
10	*Tripoli*	6 Aug 1966 15 Sep 1995			Stricken 15 Sep 1995. On loan U.S. Army.
11	*New Orleans*	16 Nov 1968 1 Oct 1997			Stricken 23 Oct 1998
12	*Inchon*	20 Jun 1970 20 Jun 2002	MCS 12	1 Mar 1995	Stricken 24 May 2004. Sunk in fleet training exercise 5 Dec 2004.

ˑ *Block Island* was reclassified LPH 1 on 22 Dec 1957, but the service cancelled the conversion and did not reassign the LPH 1 designation, so the ship never operated with the LPH 1 designation.

† *Boxer* operated with the designation LPH 4 from 30 Jan 1959 until decommissioned 1 December 1969.

‡ *Princeton* operated with the designation LPH 5 from 2 Mar 1959 until decommissioned 30 Jan 1970.

§ *Thetis Bay* operated with the designation LPH 6 from 28 May 1959 until decommissioned 1 Mar 1964.

‖ *Valley Forge* operated with the designation LPH 8 from 1 Jul 1961 until decommissioned 15 Jan 1970.

Note on Decommissioning Dates: The Navy decommissioned and then recommissioned a number of ships for further service. Only the final decommissioning date is listed for these ships. Many ships were also placed out of commission during major renovations or yard periods.

Amphibious Assault Ships (General Purpose) (LHA)
Class: *Tarawa* 5 ships; *America* 1 ship

Hull No.	Name	Commission and Decommission	Disposition and Status
1	*Tarawa*	29 May 1976 31 Mar 2009	In Reserve
2	*Saipan*	15 Oct 1977 25 Apr 2007	Stricken 25 Apr 2007
3	*Belleau Wood*	23 Sep 1978 28 Oct 2005	Stricken 28 Oct 2005. Sunk in fleet exercise 12 Jul 2006.
4	*Nassau*	28 Jul 1979	Active
5	*Peleliu*	3 May 1980	Active
6	*America*		Keel laid 17 Jul 2009

Amphibious Assault Ships (Multi-Purpose) (LHD)
Class: *Wasp* 8 ships

Hull No.	Name	Commissioned	Disposition and Status
1	*Wasp*	29 Jul 1989	Active
2	*Essex*	17 Oct 1992*	Active
3	*Kearsarge*	16 Oct 1993	Active
4	*Boxer*	11 Feb 1995	Active
5	*Bataan*	20 Sep 1997	Active
6	*Bonhomme Richard*	15 Aug 1998	Active
7	*Iwo Jima*	30 Jun 2001	Active
8	*Makin Island*	24 Oct 2009	Active

* The ship commissioned without ceremony on 24 Aug 1992 to permit her to go to sea to avoid a hurricane that threatened Pascagoula, Miss. The official commissioning ceremony convened 17 Oct 1992.

Seaplane Tenders (AV)
Classes: Five single ships AV 1, 2, 3, 6, and 8; *Curtiss* Class 2 ships, AV 4 and 5; *Currituck* Class 4 ships, AV 7, 11–13; *Pocomoke* Class 2 ships, AV 9 and 10; *Kenneth Whiting* Class 4 ships, AV 14–17

Hull No.	Name	Commission and Decommission	New Designation or Change of Designation	Designation Change	Disposition and Status
1	*Wright* *San Clemente**	16 Dec 1921 21 Jun 1946	AZ 1 AV 1 AG 79 AG 79	17 Jul 1920 1 Nov 1923 1 Oct 1944 1 Feb 1945	Stricken 1 Jul 1946
2	*Jason*	23 Jun 1913 30 Jun 1932	AC 12 AV 2	21 Jan 1930	Stricken 19 May 1936
3	*Langley*†	7 Apr 1913	AC 3 CV 1 AV 3	7 Apr 1913 20 Mar 1922 21 Apr 1937	Lost to enemy action 27 Feb 1942
4	*Curtiss*	15 Nov 1940 24 Sep 1957			Stricken 1 Jul 1963
5	*Albemarle*‡	20 Dec 1940 21 Oct 1960	T-ARVH 1	11 Jan 1966	Stricken 31 Dec 1974
6	*Patoka*	13 Oct 1919 1 Jul 1946	AO 9 AV 6§ AO 9 AG 125	13 Oct 1919 11 Oct 1939 19 Jun 1940 15 Aug 1945	Stricken 31 Jul 1946
7	*Currituck*	26 Jun 1944 31 Oct 1967			Stricken 1 Apr 1971
8	*Tangier*	8 Jul 1940			Decommissioned sometime between May 1946 and Jan 1947. Stricken 1 Jun 1961.
9	*Pocomoke*	18 Jul 1941 10 Jul 1946			Stricken 1 Jun 1961

Seaplane Tenders (AV)
Classes: Five single ships AV 1, 2, 3, 6, and 8; *Curtiss* Class 2 ships, AV 4 and 5; *Currituck* Class 4 ships, AV 7, 11–13; *Pocomoke* Class 2 ships, AV 9 and 10; *Kenneth Whiting* Class 4 ships, AV 14–17 (continued)

Hull No.	Name	Commission and Decommission	New Designation or Change of Designation	Designation Change	Disposition and Status
10	*Chandeleur*	19 Nov 1942			Placed in reserve 12 Feb 1947. Stricken 1 Apr 1971.
11	*Norton Sound*	8 Jan 1945 11 Dec 1986	AVM 1	8 Aug 1951	Stricken 26 Jan 1987
12	*Pine Island*	26 Apr 1945 16 Jun 1967			Stricken 1 Feb 1971
13	*Salisbury Sound*	26 Nov 1945 31 Mar 1967			Stricken 1 Feb 1971
14	*Kenneth Whiting*	8 May 1944 30 Sep 1958			Stricken 1 Jul 1961
15	*Hamlin*	26 Jun 1944 15 Jan 1947			Stricken 1 Jul 1963
16	*St. George*	24 Jul 1944 1 Aug 1946			Stricken 1 Jul 1963
17	*Cumberland Sound*	21 Aug 1944 27 May 1947			Stricken 1 Jul 1961

* *Wright* was renamed *San Clemente* on 1 Feb 1945 to permit the use of the name *Wright* for a carrier under construction.

† *Jupiter* was commissioned as a collier on 7 Apr 1913 and decommissioned on 24 Mar 1920 for conversion to an aircraft carrier. She was renamed *Langley* on 21 Apr 1920 and recommissioned as *Langley* (CV 1) on 20 Mar 1922.

‡ *Albemarle* was decommissioned on 21 Oct 1960 and stricken from the Naval Vessel Register on 1 Sep 1962 and placed in the custody of the Maritime Administration James River Fleet. However, she was transferred back to the Navy on 7 Aug 1964 for conversion to a floating aeronautical maintenance facility for helicopters. On 27 March 1965 *Albemarle* was renamed *Corpus Christi Bay* and redesignated T-ARVH 1. On 11 Jan 1966 she was transferred to the Military Sealift Command (MSC). She was eventually taken out of service by MSC and stricken.

§ *Patoka* was authorized for conversion to AV on 25 Feb 1924 and operated as such, but was not reclassified an AV until 11 Oct 1939.

Note on Decommissioning Dates: There were a number of ships that were decommissioned and then recommissioned for further service. Only the final decommissioning date is listed for these ships. Many ships were also placed out of commission during major renovations or yard periods. In some cases the records regarding decommissioning dates were not complete. Consequently, the decommissioning date was left blank if it was unknown.

Small Seaplane Tenders (AVP)
Classes: *Lapwing* Class Converted minesweepers assigned to aviation duty in the 1920s first given aviation designation 22 Jan 1936, 9 ships, AVP 1–9; *Barnegat* Class 32 ships, AVP 10–13, 21–26, 28–41, and 48–55; *Childs* Class 7 ships, AVP 14–20. Hull numbers omitted may be accounted for as follows: 27, 56, and 57 were commissioned as AGPs, 42–47 and 58–67 were cancelled.

Hull No.	Name	Commission and Decommission	New Designation or Change of Designation	Designation Change	Disposition
1	*Lapwing*	12 Jun 1918 29 Nov 1945	AM 1 AVP 1	22 Jan 1936	Transferred to Maritime Commission 19 Aug 1946
2	*Heron*	30 Oct 1918 12 Feb 1946	AM 10 AVP 2	22 Jan 1936	Transferred to Force Logistics Command 25 Jul 1947
3	*Thrush*	25 Apr 1919 13 Dec 1945	AM 18 AVP 3	17 Jul 1920 22 Jan 1936	Stricken 8 Jan 1946. Transferred to Maritime Commission 19 Aug 1946.
4	*Avocet*	17 Sep 1918 10 Dec 1945	AM 19 AVP 4	22 Jan 1936	Stricken 3 Jan 1946
5	*Teal*	20 Aug 1918 23 Nov 1945	AM 23 AVP 5	30 Apr 1931 22 Jan 1936	Stricken 5 Dec 1945. Transferred to Maritime Commission 19 Jan 1948.
6	*Pelican*	10 Oct 1918 30 Nov 1945	AM 27 AVP 6	22 Jan 1936	Stricken 19 Dec 1945. Transferred to Maritime Commission 22 Nov 1946.
7	*Swan*	31 Jan 1919 13 Dec 1945	AM 34 AVP 7	30 Apr 1931 22 Jan 1936	Stricken 8 Jan 1946. Transferred to Maritime Commission 12 Oct 1946.
8	*Gannet*	10 Jul 1919 7 Jun 1942	AM 41 AVP 8	22 Jan 1936	Lost to enemy action 7 Jun 1942
9	*Sandpiper*	9 Oct 1919 10 Dec 1945	AM 51 AVP 9	Jul 1920 22 Jan 1936	Stricken 17 Apr 1946. Transferred to Maritime Commission 12 Oct 1946.
10	*Barnegat*	3 Jul 1941 17 May 1946			Stricken 23 May 1958
11	*Biscayne*	3 Jul 1941 29 Jun 1946	AGC 18	10 Oct 1944	Transferred to USCG 19 Jul 1946; returned to USN as target, 9 Jul 1968.

Small Seaplane Tenders (AVP)

Classes: *Lapwing* Class Converted minesweepers assigned to aviation duty in the 1920s first given aviation designation 22 Jan 1936, 9 ships, AVP 1–9; *Barnegat* Class 32 ships, AVP 10–13, 21–26, 28–41, and 48–55; *Childs* Class 7 ships, AVP 14–20. Hull numbers omitted may be accounted for as follows: 27, 56, and 57 were commissioned as AGPs, 42–47 and 58–67 were cancelled.

Hull No.	Name	Commission and Decommission	New Designation or Change of Designation	Designation Change	Disposition
12	*Casco*	27 Dec 1941 10 Apr 1947			Transferred to USCG 19 Apr 1949
13	*Mackinac*	24 Jan 1942 Jan 1947			Transferred to USCG 19 Apr 1949; returned 15 Apr 1968, expended as target.
14	*Childs*	22 Oct 1920 10 Dec 1945	DD 241 AVP 14 AVD 1	1 Jul 1938 1 Oct 1940	Stricken 8 Jan 1946
15	*Williamson*	29 Oct 1920 8 Nov 1945	DD 244 AVP 15 AVD 2 DD 244	1 Jul 1938 2 Aug 1940 1 Dec 1943	Stricken 19 Dec 1945
16	*George E. Badger*	28 Jul 1920 3 Oct 1945	DD 196 AVP 16 AVD 3 APD 33 DD 196	1 Oct 1939 2 Aug 1940 19 May 1944 20 Jul 1945	Transferred to Treasury Dept. in 1930 and returned 1934. Stricken 25 Oct 1945.
17	*Clemson*	29 Dec 1919 12 Oct 1945	DD 186 AVP 17 AVD 4 DD 186 APD 31 DD 186	15 Nov 1939 6 Aug 1940 1 Dec 1943 7 Mar 1944 17 Jul 1945	Stricken 24 Oct 1945
18	*Goldsborough*	26 Jan 1920 11 Oct 1945	DD 188 AVP 18 AVD 5 DD 188 APD 32 DD 188	15 Nov 1939 2 Aug 1940 1 Dec 1943 7 Mar 1944 10 Jul 1945	Stricken 24 Oct 1945
19	*Hulbert*	27 Oct 1920 2 Nov 1945	DD 342 AVP 6 DD 342	2 Aug 1940 1 Dec 1943	Stricken 28 Nov 1945
20	*William B. Preston*	23 Aug 1920 6 Dec 1945	DD 344 AVP 20 AVD 7	18 Nov 1939 2 Aug 1940	Stricken 3 Jan 1946
21	*Humboldt*	7 Oct 1941 19 Mar 1947	AG 121 AVP 21	30 Jul 1945 10 Sep 1945	Transferred to USCG 24 Jan 1949
22	*Matagorda*	16 Dec 1941 20 Feb 1946	AG 122 AVP 22	30 Jul 1945 10 Sep 1945	Transferred to USCG 7 Mar 1949; returned to USN in 1968 used as target in 1969.
23	*Absecon*	28 Jan 1943 19 Mar 1947			Transferred to USCG 5 Jan 1949 and then to South Vietnamese Navy on 15 Jul 1972.
24	*Chincoteague*	12 Apr 1943 12 Dec 1946			Transferred to USCG 7 Mar 1949
25	*Coos Bay*	15 May 1943 30 Apr 1946			Transferred to USCG 5 Jan 1949; returned 16 Aug 1967 expended as target.
26	*Half Moon*	15 Jun 1943 4 Sep 1946			Transferred to USCG 14 Sep 1948
28	*Oyster Bay*	17 Nov 1943 26 Mar 1946	AVP 28 AGP 6 AVP 28	1 May 1943 16 Mar 1949	The ship never operated as an AVP for the U.S. Navy. Transferred to Italy 23 Oct 1957.
29	*Rockaway*	6 Jan 1943 21 Mar 1946	AG 123 AVP 29	30 Jul 1945 26 Oct 1945	Transferred to USCG 24 Dec 1948. Stricken Sep 1966.
30	*San Pablo*	15 Mar 1943 29 May 1969	AGS 30	25 Aug 1949	Decommissioned as AVP 30 on 13 Jan 1947. Stricken 1 Jun 1969.
31	*Unimak*	31 Dec 1943 26 Jul 1946			Transferred to USCG 14 Sep 1948

Classes: *Lapwing* Class Converted minesweepers assigned to aviation duty in the 1920s first given aviation designation 22 Jan 1936, 9 ships, AVP 1–9; *Barnegat* Class 32 ships, AVP 10–13, 21–26, 28–41, and 48–55; *Childs* Class 7 ships, AVP 14–20. Hull numbers omitted may be accounted for as follows: 27, 56, and 57 were commissioned as AGPs, 42–47 and 58–67 were cancelled.

Hull No.	Name	Commission and Decommission	New Designation or Change of Designation	Designation Change	Disposition
32	*Yakutat*	31 Mar 1944 29 Jul 1946			Transferred to USCG 31 Aug 1948, returned to USN 1970. Transferred to Navy of South Vietnam on 10 Jan 1971 until its fall in 1975, then transferred to Philippine government on 5 Apr 1976.
33	*Barataria*	13 Aug 1944 24 Jul 1946			Transferred to USCG 17 Sep 1948
34	*Bering Strait*	19 Jul 1944 21 Jun 1946			Transferred to USCG 14 Sep 1948
35	*Castle Rock*	8 Oct 1944 6 Aug 1946			Transferred to USCG 16 Sep 1948
36	*Cook Inlet*	5 Nov 1944 31 Mar 1946			Transferred to USCG 20 Sep 1948. Transferred to South Vietnam as HQ-05, 21 Dec 1971.
37	*Corson*	3 Dec 1944 9 Mar 1956			Stricken 1 Apr 1966
38	*Duxbury Bay*	31 Dec 1944 29 Apr 1966			Stricken 1 May 1966
39	*Gardiners Bay*	11 Feb 1945 1 Feb 1958			Transferred to Norway under Military Assistance Program. Stricken 1 Jul 1966.
40	*Floyds Bay*	25 Mar 1945 26 Feb 1960			Stricken 1 Mar 1960
41	*Greenwich Bay*	20 May 1945			Stricken 1 Jul 1966
48	*Onslow*	22 Dec 1943 22 Apr 1960			Stricken 1 Jun 1960
49	*Orca*	23 Jan 1944 Mar 1960			Transferred to Ethiopia 31 Jan 1962
50	Rehoboth	23 Feb 1944 15 Apr 1970	AGS 50	2 Sep 1948	Decommissioned as AVP 50 on 30 Jun 1947. Recommissioned under AGS-50 designation on 2 Sep 1948 and operated under decommissioned on 15 Apr 1970. Stricken 15 Apr 1970.
51	*San Carlos*	21 Mar 1944 30 Jun 1947	AGOR 1	15 Dec 1958	Transferred to MSTS 11 Jul 1958, renamed *Josiah Willard Gibbs* on 15 Dec 1958. Transferred to Greece 15 Dec 1971.
52	*Shelikof*	17 Sep 1944 30 Jun 1947			Stricken 1 May 1960
53	*Suisun*	13 Sep 1944 5 Aug 1955			Stricken 1 Apr 1966
54	*Timbalier*	24 May 1946 15 Nov 1954			Stricken 1 May 1960
55	*Valcour*	5 Jul 1946	AGF 1	15 Dec 1965	Stricken 15 Jan 1973

Note on Decommissioning Dates: There were a number of ships that were decommissioned and then recommissioned for further service. Only the final decommissioning date is listed for these ships. Many ships were also placed out of commission during major renovations or yard periods. In some cases the records regarding decommissioning dates were not complete. Consequently, the decommissioning date was left blank if it was unknown.

| | | | Destroyer Seaplane Tenders (AVD) | | | |
| | | | Class: *Clemson* Class DD 14 ships, ex–flush deck 1,190-ton DDs converted for seaplane tending duties from 1938 to 1940 | | | |

Hull No.	Name	Commission and Decommission	New Designation or Change of Designation	Designation Change	Disposition
1	*Childs*	22 Oct 1920 10 Dec 1945	DD 241 AVP 14 AVD 1	 1 Jul 1938 1 Oct 1940	Stricken 8 Jan 1946
2	*Williamson*	29 Oct 1920 8 Nov 1945	DD 244 AVP 15 AVD 2 DD 244	 1 Jul 1938 2 Aug 1940 1 Dec 1943	Stricken 19 Dec 1945
3	*George E. Badger*	28 Jul 1920 3 Oct 1945	DD 196 AVP 16 AVD 3 APD 33 DD 196	 1 Oct 1939 2 Aug 1940 19 May 1944 20 Jul 1945	Transferred to Treasury Dept. in 1930 and returned 1934. Stricken 25 Oct. 1945.
4	*Clemson*	29 Dec 1919 12 Oct 1945	DD 186 AVP 17 AVD 4 DD 186 APD 31 DD 186	 15 Nov 1939 6 Aug 1940 1 Dec 1943 7 Mar 1944 17 Jul 1945	Stricken 24 Oct 1945
5	*Goldsborough*	26 Jan 1920 11 Oct 1945	DD 188 AVP 18 AVD 3 DD 188 APD 32 DD 188	 15 Nov 1939 2 Aug 1940 1 Dec 1943 7 Mar 1944 10 Jul 1945	Stricken 24 Oct 1945
6	*Hulbert*	27 Oct 1920 2 Nov 1945	DD 342 AVP 6 DD 342	 2 Aug 1940 1 Dec 1943	Stricken 28 Nov 1945
7	*William B. Preston*	23 Aug 1920 6 Dec 1945	DD 344 AVP 20 AVD 7	 18 Nov 1939 2 Aug 1940	Stricken 3 Jan 1946
8	*Belknap*	28 Apr 1919 4 Aug 1945	DD 251 AVD 8 DD 251 APD 38	 2 Aug 1940 14 Nov 1943 22 Jun 1944	Sold for scrap 30 Nov 1945
9	*Osmond Ingram*	28 Jun 1919 8 Jan 1946	DD 255 AVD 9 DD 255 APD 35	 2 Aug 1940 4 Nov 1943 22 Jun 1944	Stricken 21 Jan 1946
10	*Ballard*	5 Jun 1919 5 Dec 1945	DD 267 AVD 10	 2 Aug 1940	Stricken 3 Jan 1946
11	*Thornton*	15 Jul 1919 2 May 1945	DD 270 AVD 11	 2 Aug 1940	Stricken 13 Aug 1945
12	*Gillis*	3 Sep 1919 15 Oct 1945	DD 260 AVD 12	 2 Aug 1940	Stricken 1 Nov 1945
13	*Greene*	9 May 1919 23 Nov 1945	DD 266 AVD 13 APD 36	 6 Apr 1941 1 Feb 1944	Stricken 5 Dec 1945
14	*McFarland*	30 Sep 1920 8 Nov 1945	DD 237 AVD 14 DD 237	 2 Aug 1940 1 Dec 1943	Stricken 19 Dec 1945

Aviation Logistic Support Ships
Various types of ships fitted out to support operations, logistics and repair activities of Naval aircraft.
Aircraft Ferry (AKV)

Hull No.	Name	Commission and Decommission	New Designation or Change of Designation	Designation Change	Disposition and Status
1	Kitty Hawk	26 Nov 1941 24 Jan 1946	AVP 1 AKV 1	15 Sep 1943	Returned to owner, Seatrain Lines, 24 Jan 1946
2	Hammondsport	11 Dec 1941 7 Mar 1946	AVP 2 AKV 2	15 Sep 1943	Returned to Maritime Commission 7 Mar 1946

Note: Other ships classified AKV appear on Escort Carrier List.

Transport and Aircraft Ferry (APV)

Hull No.	Name	Commission and Decommission	New Designation or Change of Designation	Designation Change	Disposition and Status
4	Lafayette		AP 53 AVP 4	24 Dec 1941 15 Sep 1943	Caught fire and capsized during AP conversion from French liner Normandie, never repaired or commissioned. Stricken 11 Oct 1945.

Aircraft Repair Ships (ARV)

Hull No.	Name	Commission and Decommission	New Designation or Change of Designation	Designation Change	Disposition and Status
1	Chourre	7 Dec 1944 13 Sep 1955	ARV 1		Stricken 1 Sep 1962
2	Webster	17 Mar 1945 28 Jun 1946	ARV 2		Stricken 1 Sep 1962

Aircraft Repair Ships (Aircraft) (ARVA)

Hull No.	Name	Commission and Decommission	New Designation or Change of Designation	Designation Change	Disposition and Status
5	Fabius	7 Jun 1945 4 Apr 1952	ARVA 5		Stricken 1 Jun 1973
6	Megara	27 Jun 1945 16 Jan 1956	ARVA 6		Placed in commission status 19 Jun 1945 for ferry purposes. Stricken 1 Jun 1973.

Aircraft Repair Ships (Engines) (ARVE)

Hull No.	Name	Commission and Decommission	New Designation or Change of Designation	Designation Change	Disposition and Status
3	Aventinus	30 May 1945 4 Apr 1952	ARVE 3		Transferred to Chile in Aug 1963
4	Chloris	19 Jun 1945 9 Dec 1955	ARVE 4		Scrapped 1 Jun 1973

Advanced Aviation Base Ships (AVB)

Hull No.	Name	Commission and Decommission	New Designation or Change of Designation	Designation Change	Disposition and Status
1	Alameda County	12 Jul 1943 25 Jun 1962	LST 32 AVB 1	28 Sep 1957	Stricken 30 Jun 1962
2	Tallahatchie County	24 May 1949 15 Jan 1970	LST 1154 AVB 2	3 Feb 1962	Stricken 15 Jan 1970

1	*Supply*	8 Feb 1944 4 Feb 1946	IX 147 AVS 1	25 May 1945	Stricken 25 Feb 1946
2	*Fortune*	19 Feb 1944 18 Oct 1945	IX 146 AVS 2	25 May 1945	Returned to War Shipping Administration 18 Oct 1945
3	*Grumium*	20 Oct 1943 20 Dec 1945	AK 112 IX 174 AVS 3	20 Jun 1944 25 May 1945	Returned to Maritime Commission 28 Dec 1945
4	*Alioth*	25 Oct 1943 18 May 1946	AK 109 IX 204 AVS 4	31 Dec 1944 25 May 1945	Transferred to Maritime Commission 13 May 1947
5	*Gwinnett*	10 Apr 1945 11 Feb 1946	AG 92 AVS 5	25 May 1945	Returned to Maritime Commission 11 Feb 1946
6	*Nicollet*	27 Apr 1945 17 Jun 1946	AG 93 AVS 6	25 May 1945	Stricken 3 Jul 1946
7	*Pontotoc*	22 Mar 1945 26 Apr 1946	AG 94 AVS 7	25 May 1945	Stricken and returned to owner 26 Apr 1946
8	*Jupiter*	22 Aug 1942	AK 43 AVS 8	31 Jul 1945	Stricken 1 Aug 1965

Patrol Craft Tenders (AGP).
These ships were fitted to service PBRs and UH-1 helicopters and worked with the Navy's Riverine Task Force in South Vietnam beginning in 1967.

Hull No.	Name	Commission and Decommission	New Designation or Change of Designation	Designation Change	Disposition and Status
786	*Garrett County*	28 Aug 1944	LST 786 AGP 786	25 Sep 1970	Transferred to South Vietnam 23 Apr 1971
821	*Harnett County*	22 Nov 1944	LST 821 AGP 821	25 Sep 1970	Transferred to South Vietnam 12 Oct 1970
838	*Hunterdon County*	4 Dec 1944	LST 838 AGP 838	25 Sep 1970	Transferred to Malaysia 1 Jul 1971
846	*Jennings County*	9 Jan 1945	LST 846		Stricken 25 Sep 1970

* *Jennings County* was never redesignated AGP although she served in that capacity in Vietnam.

Ship Designations	
AC	Collier
AG	Miscellaneous Auxiliary
AGC	Amphibious Force Flagship
AGMR	Major Communications Relay Ship
AGOR	Oceanographic Research Ship
AGP	Patrol Craft Tender (Motor Torpedo Boat Tender, Old Design)
AGS	Surveying Ship
AKV	Aircraft Ferry; later, Cargo Ship and Aircraft Ferry
AM	Minesweeper
AO	Fleet Oiler
AP	Transport
APV	Transport and Aircraft Ferry
ARG	Repair Ship, Engines
ARV	Aircraft Repair Ship
ARVA	Aircraft Repair Ship (Aircraft)
ARVE	Aircraft Repair Ship (Engines)
ARVH	Aircraft Repair Ship (Helicopter)
AV	Seaplane Tender
AVB	Advanced Aviation Base Ship
AVD	Seaplane Tender (Destroyer)
AVM	Guided Missiles Ship
AVP	Seaplane Tender (Small)
AVS	Aviation Supply Ship
AVT	Auxiliary Aircraft Transport
AZ	Lighter-than-air Tender
CV	Aircraft Carrier
CVA	Attack Aircraft Carrier
CVAN	Nuclear-Powered Attack Aircraft Carrier
CVB	Aircraft Carrier, Large (Old)
CVE	Escort Aircraft Carrier
CVHA	Assault Helicopter Aircraft Carrier until 1963 — later LPH
CVHE	Escort Helicopter Aircraft Carrier (Old)
CVL	Small Aircraft Carrier
CVN	Nuclear-Powered Aircraft Carrier
CVS	Antisubmarine Warfare Support Aircraft Carrier
CVU	Utility Aircraft Carrier
DD	Destroyer
IX	Miscellaneous auxiliary
LHA	Amphibious Assault Ship (General Purpose)
LHD	Amphibious Assault Ship (Multi-Purpose)
LPH	Amphibious Assault Ship (Helicopter)
LPD	Amphibious Assault Ship
LST	Landing Ship, Tank
MSC	Mine Countermeasure Support
T-ARVH	Associated with ARVH, indicates operated by Military Sealift Command, formerly Military Sea Transportation Service

Aviation Ships in Active Status															
YEAR	CV†	CVS	CVL	CVE	LHA/ LPH/ LHD‡	AV	AVD	AVP	AVM	ARV	AVS	AKV	AGP	AVB	CVT/ AVT
1922	1	—	—	—	—	1	—	2	—	—	—	—	—	—	—
1923	1	—	—	—	—	1	—	2	—	—	—	—	—	—	—
1924	1	—	—	—	—	1	—	3	—	—	—	—	—	—	—
1925	1	—	—	—	—	1	—	6	—	—	—	—	—	—	—
1926	1	—	—	—	—	1	—	6	—	—	—	—	—	—	—
1927	3	—	—	—	—	1	—	8	—	—	—	—	—	—	—
1928	3	—	—	—	—	1	—	10	—	—	—	—	—	—	—
1929	3	—	—	—	—	1	—	10	—	—	—	—	—	—	—
1930	3	—	—	—	—	2	—	10	—	—	—	—	—	—	—
1931	3	—	—	—	—	2	—	11	—	—	—	—	—	—	—
1932	3	—	—	—	—	2	—	10	—	—	—	—	—	—	—
1933	3	—	—	—	—	2	—	10	—	—	—	—	—	—	—
1934	4	—	—	—	—	2	—	9	—	—	—	—	—	—	—
1935	4	—	—	—	—	2	—	8	—	—	—	—	—	—	—
1936	4	—	—	—	—	1	—	9	—	—	—	—	—	—	—
1937	3	—	—	—	—	2	—	9	—	—	—	—	—	—	—
1938	5	—	—	—	—	2	—	9	—	—	—	—	—	—	—
1939	5	—	—	—	—	2	—	11	—	—	—	—	—	—	—
1940	6	—	—	—	—	2	—	16	—	—	—	—	—	—	—
1941	6	—	—	1	—	5	14	9	—	—	—	—	—	—	—
1942	5	—	—	3	—	5	14	14	—	—	—	2	—	—	—
1943	7	—	5	17	—	6	14	20	—	—	—	2	—	—	—
1944	13	—	9	63	—	10	5	27	—	—	—	2	—	—	—
1945	20	—	8	70	—	11	5	36	—	6	7	2	—	—	—
1946	14	—	1	10	—	8	—	11	—	4	1	—	—	—	—
1947	12	—	2	8	—	5	—	9	—	1	—	—	—	—	—
1948	11	—	2	7	—	5	—	7	—	1	—	—	—	—	—
1949	8	—	3	7	—	5	—	9	—	—	—	—	—	—	—
1950	7	—	4	4	—	3	—	7	—	—	—	—	—	—	—
1951	14	—	4	10	—	4	—	9	1	4	1	—	—	—	—
1952	16	—	5	12	—	5	—	11	1	3	1	—	—	—	—
1953	17	—	5	12	—	5	—	11	1	3	1	—	—	—	—
1954	16	4	3	7	—	5	—	11	1	2	1	—	—	—	—
1955	17	5	2	3	—	5	—	8	1	2	1	—	—	—	—
1956	19	7	1	3	—	5	—	7	1	—	1	—	—	—	—
1957	16	8	1	—	1	4	—	7	1	—	1	—	—	1	—
1958	15	11	—	—	1	4	—	6	1	—	1	—	—	1	—
1959	14	10	—	—	3	3	—	6	1	—	1	—	—	1	—
1960	14	10	—	—	3	3	—	3	1	—	1	—	—	1	—
1961	15	10	—	—	4	3	—	3	1	—	1	—	—	1	—
1962	16	10	—	—	6	3	—	3	1	—	1	—	—	1	—
1963	15	10	—	—	6	3	—	3	1	—	1	—	—	1	—
1964	15	10	—	—	6	3	—	3	1	—	1	—	—	1	—
1965	15	10	—	—	7	3	—	3	1	—	1	—	—	1	—
1966	17	10	—	—	8	4	—	4	1	—	1	—	4	1	—
1967	16	9	—	—	8	4	—	—	1	—	1	—	4	1	—

YEAR	CV†	CVS	CVL	CVE	LHA/LPH/LHD‡	AV	AVD	AVP	AVM	ARV	AVS	AKV	AGP	AVB	CVT/AVT
1968	15	9	—	—	9	3	—	—	1	—	1	—	4	1	—
1969	15	8	—	—	8	3	—	—	1	—	—	—	4	1	1
1970	15	4	—	—	7	3	—	—	1	—	—	—	4	1	1
1971	14	4	—	—	7	3	—	—	1	—	—	—	2	—	1
1972	14	2	—	—	7	—	—	—	1	—	—	—	—	—	1
1973	14	2	—	—	7	—	—	—	1	—	—	—	—	—	1
1974	14	—	—	—	7	—	—	—	1	—	—	—	—	—	1
1975	15	—	—	—	7	—	—	—	1	—	—	—	—	—	1
1976	13	—	—	—	8	—	—	—	1	—	—	—	—	—	1
1977	13	—	—	—	9	—	—	—	1	—	—	—	—	—	1
1978	13	—	—	—	9	—	—	—	1	—	—	—	—	—	1
1979	13	—	—	—	11	—	—	—	1	—	—	—	—	—	1
1980	13	—	—	—	12	—	—	—	1	—	—	—	—	—	1
1981*	12	—	—	—	12	—	—	—	1	—	—	—	—	—	1
1982*	13	—	—	—	12	—	—	—	1	—	—	—	—	—	1
1983*	13	—	—	—	12	—	—	—	1	—	—	—	—	—	1
1984*	13	—	—	—	12	—	—	—	1	—	—	—	—	—	1
1985*	13	—	—	—	12	—	—	—	1	—	—	—	—	—	1
1986*	13	—	—	—	12	—	—	—	1	—	—	—	—	—	1
1987*	14	—	—	—	12	—	—	—	—	—	—	—	—	—	1
1988*	14	—	—	—	12	—	—	—	—	—	—	—	—	—	1
1989*	14	—	—	—	12	—	—	—	—	—	—	—	—	—	1
1990*	14	—	—	—	13	—	—	—	—	—	—	—	—	—	1
1991*	14	—	—	—	13	—	—	—	—	—	—	—	—	—	1
1992*	13	—	—	—	13	—	—	—	—	—	—	—	—	—	1
1993*	13	—	—	—	12	—	—	—	—	—	—	—	—	—	1
1994*	12	—	—	—	13	—	—	—	—	—	—	—	—	—	—
1995*	12	—	—	—	13	—	—	—	—	—	—	—	—	—	—
1996*	13	—	—	—	13	—	—	—	—	—	—	—	—	—	—
1997	12	—	—	—	12	—	—	—	—	—	—	—	—	—	—
1998	12	—	—	—	12	—	—	—	—	—	—	—	—	—	—
1999	12	—	—	—	12	—	—	—	—	—	—	—	—	—	—
2000	12	—	—	—	12	—	—	—	—	—	—	—	—	—	—
2001	12	—	—	—	13	—	—	—	—	—	—	—	—	—	—
2002	12	—	—	—	12	—	—	—	—	—	—	—	—	—	—
2003	12	—	—	—	12	—	—	—	—	—	—	—	—	—	—
2004	12	—	—	—	12	—	—	—	—	—	—	—	—	—	—
2005	12	—	—	—	11	—	—	—	—	—	—	—	—	—	—
2006	12	—	—	—	11	—	—	—	—	—	—	—	—	—	—
2007	11	—	—	—	10	—	—	—	—	—	—	—	—	—	—
2008	11	—	—	—	10	—	—	—	—	—	—	—	—	—	—
2009	11	—	—	—	10	—	—	—	—	—	—	—	—	—	—
2010	11	—	—	—	10	—	—	—	—	—	—	—	—	—	—

Aviation Ships in Active Status (continued)

* During this reporting period, 1981–1996, the total carriers listed under CV does not include the carrier undergoing a major Service Life Extension Program.

† Includes all designations—CV, CVA, CVB, CVAN, and CVN—that have been used for the fleet carriers; missions the same.

‡ These LHA/LPH/LHDs are counted the same since mission is very similar.

CHAPTER 27

Ships Named for Naval Aviators

This listing covers only ships that were commissioned and designated as United States Ships (USS).

Ship	Hull No.	Named for	Commissioned
Abercrombie	DE-343	Ens. William W. Abercrombie, USN	1 May 1944
Adams	DM-27 [ex-DD-739]*	Lt. Samuel Adams, USN	10 Oct 1944
Allen, Edward H.	DE-531	Lt. Edward H. Allen, USN	16 Dec 1943
Antrim	FFG-20	Rear Adm. Richard N. Antrim, USN	26 Sep 1981
Ault	DD-698	Cmdr. William B. Ault, USN	31 May 1944
Baker	DE-190	Ens. John D. Baker, USNR	23 Dec 1943
Baker, Paul G.	DE-642	Lt. j.g. Paul G. Baker, USN	25 May 1944
Barnes, Doyle C.	DE-353	Ens. Doyle C. Barnes, USN	13 Jul 1944
Bass, Brinkley	DD-887	Lt. Cmdr. Harry B. Bass, USN	1 Oct 1945
Bass, Horace A.	APD-124 [ex-DE-691]*	Ens. Horace A. Bass, USNR	21 Dec 1944
Bassett	APD 73 [ex-DE-672]*	Ens. Edgar R. Bassett, USNR	23 Feb 1945
Bauer	DE-1025	Lt. Col. Harold W. Bauer, USMC	21 Nov 1957
Bebas	DE-10	Ens. Gus G. Bebas, USNR	15 May 1943
Berry, Fred T.	DD-858	Cmdr. Fred T. Berry, USN	12 May 1945
Billingsley	Destroyer No. 293	Ens. William D. Billingsley, USN	1 Mar 1920
Blakely	DE-1072	Capt. Johnston Blakely, USN, and great-grandnephew Vice Adm. Adam Blakely, USN aviator	18 Jul 1970
Blessman	APD-49 [ex-DE-69]†	Lt. Edward M. Blessman, USN	19 Sep 1943
Bowers	APD-40 [ex-DE-367]†	Ens. Robert K. Bowers, USNR	27 Jan 1944
Brackett	DE-41	Lt. Bruce G. Brackett, USNR	18 Oct 1943
Brannon, Charles E.	DE-446	Ens. Charles E. Brannon, USNR	1 Nov 1944
Bridget	DE-1024	Capt. Francis J. Bridget, USN	24 Oct 1957
Bristol, Arthur L.	APD-97 [ex-DE-281]*	Vice Adm. Arthur L. Bristol, USN	25 Jun 1945
Brock	APD-93 [ex-DE-234]*	Ens. John W. Brock, USN	9 Feb 1945
Bronson, Clarence K.	DD-668	Lt. j.g. Clarence K. Bronson, USN	11 Jun 1943
Brough	DE-148	Lt. j.g. David A. Brough, USNR	18 Sep 1943
Brown, Jesse L.	DE-1089	Ens. Jesse L. Brown, USN	17 Feb 1973
Bull	APD-78 [ex-DE-693]†	Lt. j.g. Richard Bull, USNR	12 Aug 1943
Bull, Richard S.	DE-402	Lt. Richard S. Bull, USN	26 Feb 1944
Bush, George H. W.	CVN-77	Pres. George H. W. Bush	10 Jan 2009
Butler, John C.	DE-339	Ens. John C. Butler, USNR	31 Mar 1944
Byrd, Richard E.	DDG-23	Rear Adm. Richard E. Byrd Jr., USN	7 Mar 1964
Camp	DE-251	Ens. Jack H. Camp, USNR	16 Sep 1943
Campbell, Joseph E.	APD-49 [ex-DE-70]†	Ens. Joseph E. Campbell, USNR	23 Sep 1943
Campbell, Kendall C.	DE-443	Ens. Kendall C. Campbell, USNR	31 Jul 1944
Carpenter	DDK-825 [ex-DD-825]†	Lt. Cmdr. Donald M. Carpenter, USN	15 Dec 1949
Chaffee	DE-230	Ens. Davis E. Chaffee, USNR	9 May 1944
Chevalier	DD-451 DD-805	Lt. Cmdr. Godfrey de C. Chevalier, USN	20 Jul 1942 9 Jan 1945
Chourre	ARV-1 [ex-ARG-14]§	Lt. Cmdr. Emile Chourre, USN	7 Dec 1944
Clark	FFG-11	Adm. Joseph J. Clark, USN	9 May 1980
Clark, Howard F.	DE-533	Lt. j.g. Howard F. Clark, USN	25 May 1944
Collett	DD-730	Lt. Cmdr. John A. Collett, USN	16 May 1944

Ship	Hull No.	Named for	Commissioned
Cook	DE-1083	Lt. Cmdr. Wilmer P. Cook, USN	18 Dec 1971
Coolbaugh	DE-217	Lt. j.g. Walter W. Coolbaugh, USNR	15 Oct 1943
Cooner	DE-172	Ens. Bunyan R. Cooner, USNR	21 Aug 1943
Cooper	DD-695	Lt. Elmer G. Cooper, USN	27 Mar 1944
Corl, Harry L.	APD-108 [ex-DE-598][†]	Ens. Harry L. Corl, USN	5 Jun 1945
Corry	DD-334 DD-463 DD-817	Lt. Cmdr. William M. Corry, USN	25 May 1921 18 Dec 1941 27 Feb 1946
Craig, James E.	DE-201	Lt. Cmdr. James E. Craig, USN	1 Nov 1943
Crommelin	FFG-37	Cmdr. Charles L. Crommelin, USN Lt. Cmdr. Richard G. Crommelin, USN Vice Adm. Henry Crommelin, USN	18 Jun 1983
Cross	DE-448	Lt. j.g. Frederick C. Cross, USNR	8 Jan 1945
Cunningham, Alfred A.	DD-752	Lt. Col. Alfred A. Cunningham, USMC	23 Nov 1944
Davis, Frederick C.	DE-136	Ens. Frederick C. Davis, USNR	14 Jul 1943
Deede	DE-263	Lt. j.g. Leroy C. Deede, USNR	29 Jul 1943
Dickson, Harlan R.	DD-708	Lt. Cmdr. Harlan R. Dickson, USN	17 Feb 1945
Dobler	DE-48 [ex-BDE-48][‡]	Lt. Joseph J. Dobler, USNR	17 May 1943
Doherty	DE-14 [ex-BDE-14][‡]	Ens. John J. Doherty, USNR	6 Feb 1943
Donnell	DE-56	Ens. Earl R. Donnell, USNR	26 Jun 1943
Doyle, Cecil J.	DE-368	2d Lt. Cecil J. Doyle, USMC	16 Oct 1944
Duffy	DE-27 [ex-BDE-27][†]	Ens. Charles J. Duffy, USNR	5 Aug 1943
Dufilho	DE-423	Lt. Marion W. Dufilho, USN	21 Jul 1944
Duncan	FFG-10	Adm. Donald B. Duncan, USN	15 May 1980
Edson	DD-946	Maj. Gen. Merritt A. Edson, USMC	7 Nov 1958
Eichenberger	DE-202	Ens. Charles E. Eichenberger, USNR	17 Nov 1943
Eldridge	DE-173	Lt. Cmdr. John Eldridge Jr., USN	27 Aug 1943
Ellison, Harold J.	DD-864	Ens. Harold J. Ellison, USNR	23 Jun 1945
Ellyson	DMS-19 [ex-DD-454][†]	Cmdr. Theodore G. Ellyson, USN	28 Nov 1941
Elrod	FFG-55	Maj. Henry T. Elrod, USMC	18 May 1985
Estocin	FFG-15	Capt. Michael J. Estocin, USN	10 Jan 1981
Eversole	DE-404 DD-789	Lt. j.g. John T. Eversole, USN	21 Mar 1944 10 May 1946
Fechteler	DE-157 DD-870	Lt. Frank C. Fechteler, USN	1 Jul 1943 2 Mar 1946
Fieberling	DE-640	Lt. Langdon K. Fieberling, USN	11 Apr 1944
Fitch, Aubrey	FFG-34	Adm. Aubrey W. Fitch, USN	9 Oct 1982
Flatley	FFG-21	Vice Adm. James H. Flatley Jr., USN	20 Jun 1981
Fleming	DE-32	Capt. Richard E. Fleming, USMC	18 Sep 1943
Fletcher	DD-445	Adm. Frank Friday Fletcher, USN	30 Jun 1942
	DD-992	Adm. Frank Jack Fletcher, USN	12 Jul 1980
Fogg	DE-57	Lt. j.g. Carleton T. Fogg, USN	7 Jul 1943
Forrestal	CVA-59 CV-59	James Vincent Forrestal	1 Oct 1955
Fox, Lee	APD-45 [ex-DE-65][†]	Ens. Lee Fox Jr., USNR	30 Aug 1943
Gallery	FFG-26	Rear Adm. Daniel V. Gallery, USN Rear Adm. Philip Daly Gallery, USN Rear Adm. William G. Gallery, USN	5 Dec 1981
Geiger	AP-197	Gen. Roy Stanley Geiger, USMC	13 Sep 1952
Gentry	DE-349	2d Lt. Wayne R. Gentry, USMC	14 Jun 1944
Gillette	DE-270 DE-681	Lt. j.g. Douglas W. Gillette, USNR	8 Sep 1943 27 Oct 1943
Gray, John P.	APD-74 [ex-DE-673][†]	Lt. j.g. John P. Gray, USNR	15 Mar 1944

Ship	Hull No.	Named for	Commissioned
Greene, Eugene A.	DD-711	Ens. Eugene A. Greene, USNR	8 Jun 1945
Griswold	DE-7	Ens. Don T. Griswold, USNR	28 Apr 1943
Groves, Stephen W.	FFG-29	Ens. Stephen W. Groves, USNR	17 Apr 1982
Hale, Roy O.	DE-336	Lt. j.g. Roy O. Hale Jr., USN	3 Feb 1944
Halsey	DLG-23 DDG-97	Fleet Adm. William F. Halsey Jr., USN	20 Jul 1963 30 Jul 2005
Hammann	DD-412 DE-131	Ens. Charles H. Hammann, USNR	11 Aug 1939 17 May 1943
Hancock, Lewis	DD-675	Lt. Cmdr. Lewis Hancock Jr., USN	29 Sep 1943
Hanson	DD-832	1st Lt. Robert M. Hanson, USMC	11 May 1945
Hart	DD-594	Lt. Patrick H. Hart, USN	4 Nov 1944
Harwood	DD-861	Cmdr. Bruce L. Harwood, USN	28 Sep 1945
Hastings, Burden R.	DE-19 [ex-BDE-19]‡	Lt. Burden R. Hastings, USN	1 May 1943
Henderson	DD-785	Maj. Lofton R. Henderson, USMC	4 Aug 1945
Hissem	DE-400	Ens. Joseph M. Hissem, USNR	13 Jan 1944
Hodges	DE-231	Ens. Flourenoy G. Hodges, USNR	27 May 1944
Holder	DE-401 DD-819	Lt. j.g. Randolph M. Holder, USNR	18 Jan 1944 18 May 1946
Holt	DE-706	Lt. j.g. William M. Holt, USNR	9 Jun 1944
Hopping	APD-51 [ex-DE-155]†	Lt. Cmdr. Halsted L. Hopping, USN	21 May 1943
Hurst	DE-250	Lt. Edwin W. Hurst, USN	30 Aug 1943
Hutchins	DD-476	Lt. Carleton B. Hutchins, USN	17 Nov 1942
Irwin	DD-794	Rear Adm. Noble E. Irwin, USN	14 Feb 1944
Isbell, Arnold J.	DD-869	Capt. Arnold J. Isbell, USN	5 Jan 1946
Jaccard	DE-355	Ens. Richard A. Jaccard, USNR	26 Jul 1944
Johnson, Earl V.	DE-702	Lt. j.g. Earl V. Johnson, USN	18 Mar 1944
Keller, Robert F.	DE-419	Ens. Robert F. Keller, USNR	17 Jun 1944
Kennedy, Jr., Joseph P.	DD-850	Lt. Joseph P. Kennedy Jr., USNR	15 Dec 1945
Kenyon, Henry R.	DE-683	Ens. Henry R. Kenyon, USNR	30 Nov 1943
King	DLG-10	Fleet Adm. Ernest J. King, USN	17 Nov 1960
Kinzer	APD-91 [ex-DE-232]*	Ens. Edward B. Kinzer, USNR	1 Nov 1944
Koelsch	DE-1049	Lt. j.g. John K. Koelsch, USN	10 Jun 1967
Knox, Leslie L. B.	DE-580	Lt. j.g. Leslie L. B. Knox, USNR	22 Mar 1944
Lansdowne	DD-486	Lt. Cmdr. Zachary Lansdowne, USN	29 Apr 1942
Lassen	DDG-82	Cmdr. Clyde E. Lassen, USN	21 Apr 2001
Lawrence, William P.	DDG-110	Vice Adm. William P. Lawrence, USN	4 June 2011
Lewis	DE-535	Ens. Victor A. Lewis, USNR	5 Sep 1944
Lindsey	DM-32 [ex-DD-771]*	Lt. Eugene E. Lindsey, USN	20 Aug 1944
Lough	DE-586	Ens. John C. Lough, USNR	2 May 1944
Lovelace	DE-198	Lt. Cmdr. Donald A. Lovelace, USN	7 Nov 1943
Macleish	DD-220	Lt. Kenneth MacLeish, USNR	2 Aug 1920
Mason	DE-529	Ens. Newton H. Mason, USNR	20 Mar 1944
Massey	DD-778	Lt. Cmdr. Lance E. Massey, USN	24 Nov 1944
McCain, John S.	DL-3 [ex-DD-928]* DDG-56	Adm. John S. McCain, USN	12 Oct 1953 2 Jul 1994
McCampbell	DDG-85	Capt. David McCampbell, USN	17 Aug 2002
McClusky	FFG-41	Rear Adm. Clarence W. McClusky Jr., USN	10 Dec 1983
McCord	DD-534	Cmdr. Frank C. McCord, USN	19 Aug 1943
McDonnell, Edward O.	DE-1043	Vice Adm. Edward O. McDonnell, USNR	15 Feb 1965
McCormick	DD-223	Lt. j.g. Alexander A. McCormick, USNR	30 Aug 1920

Ship	Hull No.	Named for	Commissioned
Menges	DE-320	Ens. Herbert H. Menges, USNR	26 Oct 1943
Milius	DDG-69	Capt. Paul L. Milius, USN	23 Nov 1996
Mills	DE-383	Ens. Lloyd J. Mills, USNR	2 Oct 1943
Mitchell	DE-43 [ex-BDE-43]†	Ens. Albert E . Mitchell, USNR	17 Nov 1943
Mitchell, Oliver	DE-417	2d Lt. Oliver Mitchell, USMCR	14 Jun 1944
Mitscher	DL-2 [ex-DD-927]˙ DDG-57	Adm. Marc A. Mitscher, USN	15 May 1953 10 Dec 1994
Moore, Ulvert M.	DE-442	Ens. Ulvert M. Moore, USNR	18 Jul 1944
Mosley	DE-321	Ens. Walter H. Mosley, USNR	30 Oct 1943
Mullinnix	DD-944	Rear Adm. Henry M. Mullinnix, USN	7 Mar 1958
Mustin	DD-413 DDG-89	Capt. Henry C. Mustin, USN Capt. Henry C. Mustin, USN Vice Adm. Lloyd Mustin, USN Vice Adm. Henry C. Mustin II, USN Lt. Cmdr. Thomas M. Mustin, USN	15 Sep 1939 26 Jul 2003
Nawman, Melvin R.	DE-416	2d Lt. Melvin R. Nawman, USMCR	16 May 1944
O'Flaherty	DE-340	Ens. Frank W. O'Flaherty, USNR	8 Apr 1944
O'Hare	DD-889	Lt. Cmdr. Edward H. O'Hare, USN	29 Nov 1945
Osberg	DE-538	Ens. Carl A. Osberg, USNR	10 Dec 1945
Osmus	DE-701	Ens. Wesley F. Osmus, USNR	23 Feb 1945
Owens, James C.	DD-776	Lt. James C. Owens, USN	17 Feb 1945
Parks, Floyd B.	DD-884	Maj. Floyd B. Parks, USMC	31 Jul 1945
Peiffer	DD-588	Ens. Carl D. Peiffer, USN	15 Jun 1944
Pennewill	DE-175	Lt. Cmdr. William E. Pennewill, USN	15 Sep 1943
Peterson, Dale W.	DE-337	Ens. Dale W. Peterson, USN	17 Feb 1944
Potter, Stephen	DD-538	Ens. Stephen Potter, USN	21 Oct 1943
Powers, John J.	DE-528	Lt. John J. Powers, USN	29 Feb 1944
Raby	DE-698	Rear Adm. James J. Raby, USN	7 Dec 1943
Radford, Arthur W.	DD-968	Adm. Arthur W. Radford, USN	16 Apr 1977
Ramsey	DEG-2	Adm. Dewitt C. Ramsey, USN	3 Jun 1967
Raven, Julius A.	APD-110 [ex-DE-600]˙	Lt. Julius A. Raven, USNR	28 Jun 1945
Reid, Beverly W.	APD-119 [ex-DE-722]˙	Ens. Beverly W. Reid, USN	25 Jun 1945
Rich	DE-695 DD-820	Lt. j.g. Ralph M. Rich, USN	10 Oct 1943 3 Jul 1946
Richey	DE-385	Ens. Joseph L. Richey, USNR	30 Oct 1943
Riddle	DE-185	Ens. Joseph Riddle, USNR	17 Nov 1943
Riley	DE-579	Lt. Paul J. Riley, USN	13 Mar 1944
Rinehart	DE-196	Lt. j.g. Clark F. Rinehart, USN	12 Feb 1944
Roark	DE-1053	Lt. William M. Roark, USN	22 Nov 1969
Roberts, John Q.	APD-94 [ex-DE-235]˙	Ens. John Q. Roberts, USNR	8 Mar 1945
Roche	DE-197	Ens. David J. Roche, USNR	21 Feb 1944
Rodgers, John	DD-574 DD-983	Commo. John Rodgers, USN Rear Adm. John Rodgers, USN Cmdr. John Rodgers, USN naval aviator	9 Feb 1943 14 Jul 1979
Rombach	DE-364	Lt. j.g. Severin L. Rombach, USNR	20 Sep 1944
Rowell, Richard M.	DE-403	Ens. Richard M. Rowell, USNR	9 Mar 1944
Sample	DE-1048	Rear Adm. William D. Sample, USN	23 Mar 1968
Saufley	DD-465	Lt. j.g. Richard C. Saufley, USN	29 Aug 1942
Seaman	DD-791‖	Lt. Cmdr. Allen L. Seaman, USNR	
Seid	DE-256	Ens. Daniel Seid, USNR	11 Jun 1943
Sellstrom	DER-255	Ens. Edward R. Sellstrom, USNR	12 Oct 1943
Shea	DM-30 [ex-DD-750]˙	Cmdr. John J. Shea, USN	30 Sep 1944

Ship	Hull No.	Named for	Commissioned
Shelton	DE-407 DD-790	Ens. James A. Shelton, USNR	4 Apr 1944
Sherman, Forrest P.	DD-931 DDG-98	Adm. Forrest P. Sherman, USN	21 Jun 1946 9 Nov 1955 28 Jan 2006
Smartt	DE-257	Ens. Joseph G. Smartt, USNR	18 Jun 1943
Snyder	DE-745	Ens. Russell Snyder, USNR	5 May 1944
Sprague, Clifton	FFG-16	Vice Adm. Clifton A. F. Sprague, USN	21 Mar 1981
Stickell	DD-888	Lt. John H. Stickell, USNR	31 Oct 1945
Stockdale	DDG-106	Vice Adm. James B. Stockdale, USN	18 Apr 2009
Strickland	DE-333	Ens. Everett C. Strickland, USNR	10 Jan 1944
Stump	DD-978	Adm. Felix B. Stump, USN	19 Aug 1978
Sturtevant	DD-240	Ens. Albert D. Sturtevant, USNR	21 Sep 1920
Suesens, Richard W.	DE-342	Lt. j.g. Richard W. Suesens, USN	29 Apr 1944
Tabberer	DE-418	Lt. j.g. Charles A. Tabberer, USNR	23 May 1944
Talbot, Ralph	DD-390	2d Lt. Ralph Talbot, USMC	14 Oct 1937
Taylor, Jesse Junior	FFG-50	Cmdr. Jesse J. Taylor, USN	1 Dec 1984
Taylor, Lawrence C.	DE-415	2d Lt. Lawrence C. Taylor, USMC	13 May 1944
Thach	FFG-43	Adm. John S. Thach, USN	17 Mar 1984
Thomas, Leland E.	DE-420	2d Lt. Leland E. Thomas, USMCR	19 Jun 1944
Thomas, Lloyd	DE-764	Lt. j.g. Lloyd Thomas, USN	21 Mar 1947
Thomason, John W.	DD-760	Col. John W. Thomason, USMC	11 Oct 1945
Thornhill	DE-195	Lt. j.g. Leonard W. Thornhill, USN	1 Feb 1944
Tills	DE-748	Ens. Robert G. Tills, USN	8 Aug 1944
Towers	DDG-9	Adm. John H. Towers, USN	6 Jun 1961
Trumpeter	DE-180	Lt. j.g. George N. Trumpeter, USNR	16 Oct 1943
Tweedy	DE-532	2d Lt. Albert W. Tweedy Jr., USMC	12 Feb 1944
Turner, Richmond K.	DLG-20	Adm. Richmond K. Turner, USN	13 Jun 1964
Underhill	DE-682	Ens. Samuel J. Underhill, USNR	15 Nov 1943
Vammen	DE-644	Ens. Charles E. Vammen Jr., USNR	27 Jul 1944
Vandivier	DER-540	Lt. j.g. Norman F. Vandivier, USNR	11 Oct 1955
Van Voorhis	DE-1028	Lt. Cmdr. Bruce A. Van Voorhis, USN	22 Apr 1957
Varian	DE-798	Ens. Bertram S. Varian Jr., USNR	29 Feb 1944
Waldron	DD-699	Lt. Cmdr. John C. Waldron, USN	7 Jun 1944
Ware, Charles R.	DD-865	Lt. Charles R. Ware, USN	21 Jul 1945
Weber	APD-75 [ex-DE-675]†	Lt. j.g. Frederick T. Weber, USNR	30 Jun 1943
Whiting, Kenneth	AV-14	Capt. Kenneth Whiting, USN	8 May 1944
Wileman	DE-22 [ex-BDE-22]‡	Ens. William W. Wileman, USNR	11 Jun 1943
Wilhoite	DE-397	Ens. Thomas M. Wilhoite, USNR	16 Dec 1943
Wilke, Jack W.	DE-800	Ens. Jack W. Wilke, USNR	7 Mar 1944
Willis	DE-395	Ens. Walter M. Willis, USNR	10 Dec 1943
Wiltsie	DD-716	Capt. Irving D. Wiltsie, USN	21 Jan 1946
Wingfield	DE-194	Ens. John D. Wingfield, USNR	28 Jan 1944
Wiseman	DE-667	Lt. j.g. Osborne B. Wiseman, USN	4 Apr 1944
Woodson	DE-359	Lt. j.g. Jeff D. Woodson, USN	24 Aug 1944

* Redesignated before commissioning.

† Redesignated after commissioning.

‡ Launched under different names and renamed before being commissioned.

§ Redesignated and renamed from ship already in service.

‖ Never commissioned.

CHAPTER 28

Post–World War II Carrier Deployments by Year

The carrier deployment list covers those for escort carriers (CVE), small carriers (CVL), antisubmarine carriers (CVS), and carriers with the designations CV, CVB, CVA, CVAN, and CVN. However, the list does not include carriers, usually CVEs, that deployed as part of the Military Sea Transportation Service to transport men, aircraft, and aviation cargo or when used as replenishment carriers. The deployment list also does not include carriers that may have been used in "Magic Carpet" operations or other missions involved in transporting men from or to the United States. Departure and return dates are normally from the carrier's homeport or other stateside port.

Major Overseas Deployments for 1946				
Departure	**Return**	**Air Group**	**Carrier**	**Area of Operations**[ı]
08 Jan 1946	19 Mar 1946	CVBG-75	CVB-42	Carib/SoLant
15 Feb 1946	07 May 1946	†	CVE-112	WestPac
20 Apr 1946	09 Aug 1946	CVG-19	CV-36	WestPac
06 May 1946	Aug 1946	‡	CVE-117	‡
03 Jul 1946	15 Apr 1947	CVG-81˙	CV-37	WestPac
01 Aug 1946	29 Apr 1947	CVG-4§	CV-40	WestPac
08 Aug 1946	04 Oct 1946	CVBG-75	CVB-42	Med
16 Sep 1946	12 Dec 1946	CVG-18	CV-32	Carib/East Coast of South America
22 Oct 1946	21 Dec 1946	CVG-82ı	CV-15	Med

˙ CVG-81 redesignated CVAG-13
† No Air Group assigned.
‡ *Saidor* (CVE 117) deployed to Bikini to take part in Operation Crossroads, atomic bomb testing. She did not have an air group or squadrons embarked during the testing.
§ CVG-4 redesignated CVAG-1
ı CVG-82 redesignated CVAG-17

Major Overseas Deployments for 1947				
Departure	**Return**	**Air Group**	**Carrier**	**Area of Operations**
02 Jan 1947	27 Feb 1947	˙	CV-47	Antarctica
02 Feb 1947	19 Mar 1947	CVAG-17	CV-15	EastLant/Carib
31 Mar 1947	16 Jun 1947	CVG-5	CV-38	WestPac
31 Mar 1947	08 Oct 1947	CVAG-15	CV-36	WestPac
03 Apr 1947	09 Jun 1947	CVAG-7	CV-32	Med
20 May 1947	11 Aug 1947	CVAG-17	CV-15	NorLant/Carib
07 Jun 1947	11 Aug 1947	CVAG-3	CV-33	NorLant/Carib
05 Jul 1947	16 Aug 1947	VMF-461	CVE-122	SoLant
30 Jul 1947	19 Nov 1947	CVAG-7	CV-32	Med
09 Oct 1947	11 Jun 1948	CVAG-11	CV-45	World Cruise
29 Oct 1947	11 Mar 1948	CVBG-1	CVB-41	Med

˙ *Philippine Sea* (CV 47) deployed to Antarctica to participate in Operation Highjump and carried R4D transports for the operation.

Major Overseas Deployments for 1948

Departure	Return	Air Group	Carrier	Area of Operations
07 Feb 1948	24 Feb 1948	CVLG-1	CVL-48	Carib
09 Feb 1948	26 Jun 1948	CVAG-9	CV-47	Carib/Med
29 Feb 1948	Jun 1948	˙	CVE-115	˙
01 Jun 1948	02 Oct 1948	CVG-3	CV-33	Med
07 Jun 1948	06 Aug 1948	CVG-17	CVB-43	Med/Carib
Jun 1948	Oct 1948	VMF-225	CVE-112	Med/Persian Gulf
13 Sep 1948	23 Jan 1949	CVG-4	CVB-42	Med
01 Oct 1948	23 Dec 1948	CVG-13	CV-37	WestPac
01 Oct 1948	21 Feb 1949	CVG-1	CV-40	World Cruise

˙ *Bairoko* (CVE 115) deployed to Eniwetok Island to participate in Operation Sandstone, atmospheric nuclear tests. The carrier did not have any assigned squadrons aboard during the deployment.

Major Overseas Deployments for 1949

Departure	Return	Air Group	Carrier	Area of Operations
04 Jan 1949	05 Mar 1949	CVG-6	CVB-41	Med
04 Jan 1949	22 May 1949	CVG-7	CV-47	Med
03 May 1949	26 Sep 1949	CVG-2	CVB-43	Med
06 Sep 1949	26 Jan 1950	CVG-7	CV-32	Med
27 Oct 1949	23 Nov 1949	CVG-6	CVB-42	NorLant

Major Overseas Deployments for 1950

Departure	Return	Air Group	Carrier	Area of Operations
06 Jan 1950	23 May 1950	CVG-4	CVB-41	Med
11 Jan 1950	13 Jun 1950	CVG-19	CV-21	WestPac
27 Jan 1950	23 Feb 1950	#	CV-33	East to West Coast
01 May 1950	01 Dec 1950	CVG-5	CV-45	WestPac/Korea
02 May 1950	24 Aug 1950	CVG-3	CV-32	Med
04 Jul 1950	05 Feb 1951	ı	CVE-118	WestPac/Korea
05 Jul 1950	09 Jun 1951	CVG-11*	CV-47	WestPac/Korea
10 Jul 1950	10 Nov 1950	CVG-7	CVB-41	Med
14 Jul 1950	07 Feb 1951	§	CVE-116	WestPac/Korea
24 Aug 1950	11 Nov 1950	CVG-2	CV-21	WestPac/Korea
02 Sep 1950	14 Nov 1950	††	CVE-120	Med
09 Sep 1950	01 Feb 1951	CVG-17	CVB-43	Med
19 Sep 1950	03 Feb 1951	CVG-3	CV-32	WestPac/Korea
09 Nov 1950	09 Jun 1951	CVG-19	CV-37	WestPac/Korea
14 Nov 1950	15 Aug 1951	‡	CVE-115	WestPac/Korea
16 Nov 1950	25 Jun 1951	†	CVL-29	WestPac/Korea
06 Dec 1950	07 Apr 1951	CVG-2**	CV-45	WestPac/Korea

* CVG-11 deployed to Korea embarked in *Philippine Sea* (CV 47) and on 29 March 1951 transferred to *Valley Forge* (CV 45) and CVG-2 transferred from *Valley Forge* to *Philippine Sea*. CVG-11 returned to the States embarked in *Valley Forge*.

† While deployed to Korea for combat operations, *Bataan* (CVL 29) operated with VMF-211 on board from 11 December 1950 to 4 March 1951 and with VMF-312 from 5 March to 6 June 1951. The carrier also had HU-1 Det on board.

‡ While deployed to Korea, *Bairoko* (CVE 115) operated with VS-21 (3 Dec–16 Feb), VS-23 (17 Feb–15 Aug) and HU-1 Det on board.

§ While deployed to Korea, *Badoeng Strait* (CVE 116) operated with VMF-323 and HU-1 Det on board.

ı While deployed to Korea, *Sicily* (CVE 118) operated with VMF-214 (1 Aug–13 Nov), VS-21 (to 3 Dec) and HU-1 Det on board.

During the cruise from East to West Coast, *Kearsarge* (CV 33) did not have any aircraft, air group, or squadrons embarked.

** CVG-2 deployed to Korea embarked in *Valley Forge* (CV 45). On 29 March 1951 CVG-2 transferred to *Philippine Sea* (CV 47) and CVG-11 transferred to *Valley Forge*.

†† *Mindoro* (CVE 120) deployed with VS-22 and VC-33 Det 12.

Major Overseas Deployments for 1951				
Departure	**Return**	**Air Group**	**Carrier**	**Area of Operations**
10 Jan 1951	18 May 1951	CVG-6	CVB-42	Med
11 Jan 1951	31 Mar 1951	VF-14	CVL-49	Med
02 Mar 1951	24 Oct 1951	CVG-101	CV-21	WestPac/Korea
06 Mar 1951	08 Jun 1951	AirDet	CVL-48	Med
20 Mar 1951	06 Oct 1951	CVG-1	CVB-43	Med
10 May 1951	17 Dec 1951	CVG-102	CV-31	Korea
12 May 1951	12 Oct 1951	§	CVE-118	WestPac/Korea
15 May 1951	04 Oct 1951	CVG-4	CV-34	Med
16 May 1951	29 Aug 1951	CVG-19	CV-37	WestPac/Korea
26 Jun 1951	25 Mar 1952	CVG-5	CV-9	WestPac/Korea
08 Jul 1951	22 Dec 1951	*	CVE-114	WestPac/Korea
03 Sep 1951	21 Dec 1951	CVG-3	CV-32	Med
03 Sep 1951	04 Feb 1952	CVG-17	CVB-42	Med
08 Sep 1951	02 May 1952	CVG-15	CV-36	Korea
Sep 1951	14 Nov 1951	ǀ	CVE-112	NorLand/Med
15 Sep 1951	01 Mar 1952	‡	CVE-116	WestPac/Korea
15 Oct 1951	03 Jul 1952	ATG-1	CV-45	WestPac/Korea
28 Nov 1951	11 Jun 1952	CVG-8	CV-40	Med
01 Dec 1951	09 Jun 1952	†	CVE-115	WestPac/Korea
31 Dec 1951	08 Aug 1952	CVG-11	CV-47	WestPac/Korea

* While deployed to Korea, *Rendova* (CVE 114) operated with VMF-212 (22 Sep–6 Dec), VS-892 (16 Jul–19 Sep and 11–22 Dec) and HU-1 Det on board.

† While deployed to Korea, *Bairoko* (CVE 115) operated with VS-25 (on board to 21 Jan and returned in May) and HU-1 Det on board.

‡ While deployed to Korea, *Badoeng Strait* (CVE 116) operated with VMF-212, VS-892 (on board 5 Oct–8 Dec), and HU-1 Det on board.

§ While deployed to Korea, *Sicily* (CVE 118) operated with VMF-323 (5 Jun–30 Sep), VS-892 (to 13 Jul), and HU-1 Det on board.

ǀ *Siboney* (CVE 112) deployed with VS-22, VC-4 Det, and HU-2 Det on board.

Major Overseas Deployments for 1952				
Departure	**Return**	**Air Group**	**Carrier**	**Area of Operations**
09 Jan 1952	05 May 1952	CVG-6	CVB-41	Med
09 Jan 1952	26 Mar 1952	*	CVL-28	Med
27 Jan 1952	26 Aug 1952	†	CVL-29	WestPac/Korea
08 Feb 1952	26 Sep 1952	CVG-2	CV-21	WestPac/Korea
21 Mar 1952	03 Nov 1952	CVG-19	CV-37	WestPac/Korea
19 Apr 1952	12 Oct 1952	CVG-4	CVB-43	Med
19 Apr 1952	28 Jun 1952	ǁ	CVE-122	Med
08 May 1952	04 Dec 1952	**	CVE-118	WestPac/Korea
20 May 1952	08 Jan 1953	CVG-7	CV-31	WestPac/Korea
24 May 1952	11 Oct 1952	CVG-1	CV-18	Med/NorLant
16 Jun 1952	06 Feb 1953	ATG-2	CVA-9	WestPac/Korea
19 Jul 1952	27 Feb 1953	#	CVE-116	WestPac/Korea
11 Aug 1952	17 Mar 1953	CVG-101	CVA-33	WestPac/Korea
26 Aug 1952	09 Oct 1952	ǀ	CVL-49	NorLant
26 Aug 1952	07 Dec 1952	††	CVE-110	NorLant/Med
26 Aug 1952	08 Oct 1952	CVG-6	CVB-41	NorLant
26 Aug 1952	19 Dec 1952	CVG-17	CVB-42	NorLant/Med
27 Aug 1952	11 Oct 1952	§§	CVE-120	NorLant
28 Aug 1952	04 Feb 1953	CVG-3	CVA-32	Med
15 Sep 1952	18 May 1953	CVG-102	CVA-34	WestPac/Korea

Major Overseas Deployments for 1952				
Departure	Return	Air Group	Carrier	Area of Operations
15 Sep 1952	05 Dec 1952	‡‡	CVE-114	‡‡
28 Oct 1952	26 May 1953	‡	CVL-29	WestPac/Korea
20 Nov 1952	25 Jun 1953	CVG-5	CVA-45	WestPac/Korea
01 Dec 1952	19 May 1953	CVG-6	CVA-41	Med
15 Dec 1952	14 Aug 1953	CVG-9	CVA-47	WestPac/Korea

* *Cabot* (CVL 28) deployed to the Mediterranean Sea with one squadron aboard, VS-24.

† While deployed to Korea, *Bataan* (CVL 29) operated with VS-25 and HU-1 Det on board as well as VMA-312 for the period 21 April–21 July 1952.

‡ While deployed to Korea, *Bataan* (CVL 29) operated with VS-871, VS-21, and HU-1 Det on board as well as VMA-312 for the period 9 February–8 May 1953.

ˡ *Wright* (CVL 49) deployed to the North Atlantic and operated with detachments from VC-4 and VF-42.

ⁿ While deployed to Korea, *Badoeng Strait* (CVE 116) operated with VMA-312 (19 Oct–9 Feb), VS-931 (10 Aug–19 Oct), and HU-1 Det on board.

** While deployed to Korea, *Sicily* (CVE 118) operated with VMA-312 (4 Sep–19 Oct), VS-931 (to 9 Aug and 19 Oct–4 Dec), and HU-1 Det on board.

†† While deployed, *Salerno Bay* (CVE 110) operated with VS-26 and HU-2 Det 4 on board.

‡‡ *Rendova* (CVE 114) deployed to the Marshall Islands to participate in atomic tests Operation Ivy. Units on board during the deployment included FASRON-7 Det, HS-2, VC-3 Det, and HMR-362 Det.

ˢ *Mindoro* (CVE 120) deployed to the North Atlantic with VS-22, VC-4 Det 12, and HU-2 Det 12.

ʳ *Palau* (CVE 122) deployed with VS-27 and HU-2 Det 9.

Major Overseas Deployments for 1953				
Departure	Return	Air Group	Carrier	Area of Operations
07 Jan 1953	03 Jul 1953	CVG-10	CVA-40	Med
21 Jan 1953	24 Aug 1953	§	CVE-115	WestPac/Korea
24 Jan 1953	21 Sep 1953	CVG-15	CVA-37	Korea/WestPac
Feb 1953	Apr 1953	†	CVL-49	Med
30 Mar 1953	28 Nov 1953	ATG-1	CVA-21	WestPac/Korea
11 Apr 1953	18 Dec 1953	ˡ	CVE-119	WestPac/Korea
17 Apr 1953	Jun 1953	‡	CVE-106	NorLant/Med
26 Apr 1953	04 Dec 1953	CVG-4	CVA-39	Med/IO/WestPac/Korea
26 Apr 1953	21 Oct 1953	CVG-8	CVA-43	Med
11 Jun 1953	03 Dec 1953	CVG-1	CVA-42	Med
11 Jun 1953	21 Jul 1953	*	CV-36	NorLant
01 Jul 1953	18 Jan 1954	CVG-11	CVA-33	Korea/WestPac
14 Jul 1953	25 Feb 1954	**	CVE-118	WestPac
31 Jul 1953	Aug 1953	††	CVL-29	WestPac
03 Aug 1953	03 Mar 1954	CVG-2	CVA-10	WestPac
14 Sep 1953	22 Apr 1954	CVG-19	CVA-34	WestPac
16 Sep 1953	01 May 1954	CVG-17	CVA-18	World Cruise
16 Sep 1953	21 Feb 1954	CVG-7	CVA-20	NorLant/Med
16 Sep 1953	01 Dec 1953	#	CVE-112	NorLant/Med
Oct 1953	20 Jul 1954	VMA-324	CVL-48	World Cruise
12 Nov 1953	19 Aug 1954	CVG-3	CVA-40	World Cruise
01 Dec 1953	12 Jul 1954	ATG-2	CVA-9	WestPac

* The carrier deployed with VF-84, VC-4, and VS-27 but did not have an assigned air group.

† The carrier deployed with VS-27 and VS-24 Det but did not have an assigned air group.

‡ The carrier deployed with VS-22 and HU-2 Det 37 but did not have an assigned air group.

§ While deployed to Korea, *Bairoko* (CVE 115) operated with VS-21 (3 Feb–8 May), VS-23 (ashore at Guam Feb–Apr), VMA-312 (9 May–8 Jun), and HU-1 Det on board.

ˡ While deployed to Korea, *Point Cruz* (CVE 119) operated with VMA-332, VS-38 (put ashore at Agana 28 Apr), VS-23 (on board 28 Apr, Japan), HS-2, and HU-1 Det on board.

ⁿ *Siboney* (CVE 112) deployed with VS-31 and HU-2 Det 14 on board.

** *Sicily* (CVE 118) deployed with VS-38 and HS-2 Det A on board.

†† *Bataan* (CVL 29) deployed as a transport carrying planes and equipment for delivery to Japan.

Major Overseas Deployments for 1954				
Departure	**Return**	**Air Group**	**Carrier**	**Area of Operations**
Jan 1954	Jun 1954	VS-20	CVE-114	WestPac
04 Jan 1954	04 Aug 1954	CVG-6	CVA-41	Med
05 Jan 1954	12 Mar 1954	‡	CVE-107	Med
09 Jan 1954	28 May 1954	ı	CVE-115	ı
03 Feb 1954	06 Aug 1954	CVG-14	CVA-15	Med
03 Mar 1954	11 Oct 1954	CVG-12	CVA-21	WestPac
12 Mar 1954	19 Nov 1954	CVG-5	CVA-47	WestPac
05 Apr 1954	31 Oct 1954	VMA-211	CVL-49	WestPac
04 May 1954	22 Jun 1954	*	CVE-120	Med
11 May 1954	12 Dec 1954	CVG-9	CVA-12	World Cruise
07 Jun 1954	03 Aug 1954	§	CVE-112	NorLant
07 Jul 1954	20 Dec 1954	CVG-10	CVA-43	Med
01 Jul 1954	28 Feb 1955	CVG-15	CVA-10	WestPac
01 Sep 1954	11 Apr 1955	ATG-1	CVA-18	WestPac
28 Sep 1954	22 Apr 1955	CVG-8	CVA-39	Med
Sep 1954	Oct 1954	*	CVS-47	NorLant
Oct 1954	May 1955	†	CVS-37	WestPac
07 Oct 1954	12 May 1955	CVG-11	CVA-33	WestPac
03 Nov 1954	21 Jun 1955	CVG-2	CVA-9	WestPac
30 Nov 1954	18 Jun 1955	ATG-181	CVA-15	Med
27 Dec 1954	14 Jul 1955	CVG-1	CVA-41	World Cruise

* *Valley Forge* (CVS 47) deployed with VS-39, VC-4 Det 52, and HU-2 Det 52 on board. CVSGs (Antisubmarine Carrier Air Groups) were not established until various times in 1960.

† *Princeton* (CVS 37) deployed with VS-23, VS-37, VC-3 Det N, and HS-4 Det N on board. CVSGs were not established until various times in 1960.

‡ *Gilbert Islands* (CVE 107) deployed with VS-36 and HU-2 Det 40 on board.

§ *Siboney* (CVE 112) deployed with VC-4 Det 58 and HU-2 Det 58 on board.

ı *Bairoko* (CVE 115) deployed to the Marshal Islands to participate in Operation Castle, atmospheric thermonuclear tests. Squadrons deployed during this operation were VC-3 and HMR-362.

* *Mindoro* (CVE 120) deployed with VS-30, HS-1 Det 57, and HU-2 Det 57.

Major Overseas Deployments for 1955				
Departure	Return	Air Group	Carrier	Area of Operations
05 Jan 1955	15 Mar 1955	*	CVS-36	Med
02 Mar 1955	21 Sep 1955	CVG-19	CVA-34	WestPac
01 Apr 1955	23 Nov 1955	ATG-2	CVA-47	WestPac
05 Apr 1955	29 Sep 1955	CVG-17	CVA-43	Med
Apr 1955	01 Oct 1955	‡	CVE-116	WestPac
04 May 1955	10 Dec 1955	CVG-7	CVA-12	WestPac
28 May 1955	22 Nov 1955	CVG-4	CVA-11	Med
03 Jun 1955	03 Feb 1956	CVG-14	CVA-21	WestPac
06 Jun 1955	02 Aug 1955	†	CVE-112	Med/NorLant
10 Aug 1955	15 Mar 1956	CVG-12	CVA-19	WestPac
24 Aug 1955	Feb 1956	§	CVE-119	WestPac
09 Oct 1955	30 Apr 1956	CVG-6	CVA-39	Med
29 Oct 1955	17 May 1956	CVG-5	CVA-33	WestPac
31 Oct 1955	16 Apr 1956	ATG-201	CVA-20	WestPac
04 Nov 1955	02 Aug 1956	CVG-3	CVA-14	Med

* *Antietam* (CVS 36) deployed with VS-26, VC-4 Det 50, HS-1 Det 50, and HU-2 Det 50 aboard. CVSGs (Antisubmarine Carrier Air Groups) were not established until various times in 1960.

† *Siboney* (CVE 112) deployed with VS-22 Det, VS-30 Det, VC-33 Det and HU-2 Det aboard.

‡ *Badoeng Strait* (CVE 116) deployed with VS-38 and HS-2 Det aboard.

§ *Point Cruz* (CVE 119) deployed with VS-25 and HS-4 Det R aboard.

Major Overseas Deployments for 1956				
Departure	Return	Air Group	Carrier	Area of Operations
Jan 1956	May 1956	*	CVS-37	WestPac
05 Jan 1956	23 Jun 1956	ATG-3	CVA-38	WestPac
11 Feb 1956	13 Jun 1956	CVG-9	CVA-34	WestPac
Feb 1956	08 Aug 1956	‡	CVE-116	‡
12 Mar 1956	05 Sep 1956	CVG-8	CVA-11	Med
19 Mar 1956	13 Sep 1956	ATG-4	CVA-10	WestPac
23 Apr 1956	15 Oct 1956	CVG-15	CVA-18	WestPac
26 May 1956	06 Jul 1956	HMR-262	CVE-112	Med
28 May 1956	20 Dec 1956	ATG-1	CVA-16	WestPac
14 Jul 1956	19 Feb 1957	ATG-202	CVA-15	Med
16 Jul 1956	26 Jan 1957	CVG-11	CVA-9	WestPac
13 Aug 1956	11 Feb 1957	CVG-10	CVA-43	Med
16 Aug 1956	28 Feb 1957	CVG-21	CVA-31	WestPac
29 Sep 1956	21 Dec 1956	†	CVS-36	Med
15 Oct 1956	22 May 1957	ATG-181	CVA-20	WestPac
07 Nov 1956	12 Dec 1956	CVG-1	CVA-59	Azores
13 Nov 1956	20 May 1957	CVG-2	CVA-38	WestPac

* *Princeton* (CVS 37) deployed with VS-20 and VS-21 on board. CVSGs (Antisubmarine Carrier Air Groups) were not established until various times in 1960.

† *Antietam* (CVS 36) deployed with VS-36, VFAW-4 Det 50, HS-3 Det 50, and HU-2 Det 50 on board. CVSGs were not established until various times in 1960.

‡ *Badoeng Strait* (CVE 116) deployed to the Marshal Islands to participate in Operation Redwing, atmospheric thermonuclear tests. She deployed with HMR-363 on board.

Major Overseas Deployments for 1957				
Departure	Return	Air Group	Carrier	Area of Operations
Jan 1957	06 Aug 1957	׀	CVS-47	WestPac
15 Jan 1957	22 Jul 1957	CVG-1	CVA-59	Med
21 Jan 1957	25 Jul 1957	CVG-14	CVA-12	WestPac
21 Jan 1957	27 Jul 1957	ATG-182	CVA-39	Med
09 Mar 1957	15 Aug 1957	CVG-19	CVA-10	WestPac
06 Apr 1957	18 Sep 1957	ATG-2	CVA-19	WestPac
19 Apr 1957	17 Oct 1957	CVG-12	CVA-16	WestPac
01 Jul 1957	24 Feb 1958	CVG-4	CVA-15	Med
12 Jul 1957	13 Feb 1958	‡	CVS-37	WestPac/IO
12 Jul 1957	09 Dec 1957	CVG-5	CVA-31	WestPac
12 Jul 1957	05 Mar 1958	CVG-17	CVA-42	Med
09 Aug 1957	02 Apr 1958	ATG-3	CVA-33	WestPac
16 Aug 1957	21 Oct 1957	CVG-1	CVA-59	NorLant
30 Aug 1957	22 Oct 1957	*	CVS-18	NorLant
03 Sep 1957	11 Oct 1957	§	CVS-40	NorLant
03 Sep 1957	22 Oct 1957	CVG-6	CVA-11	NorLant
03 Sep 1957	22 Oct 1957	CVG-7	CVA-60	NorLant
05 Sep 1957	31 Oct 1957	MAG-26†	CVS-39	Med
16 Sep 1957	25 Apr 1958	CVG-9	CVA-14	WestPac

Wasp deployed with VS-27, VS-30, and HS-5 on board. CVSGs (Antisubmarine Carrier Air Groups) were not established until various times in 1960.

† MAG-26 consisted of VMA-533, VMA-324, and VMF-312.

‡ *Princeton* (CVS 37) deployed with VS-38 and HS-8 on board. CVSGs were not established until various times in 1960.

§ *Tarawa* (CVS 40) deployed with VS-32, VA-172, VF(AW)-4 Det 38, HU-2 Det 38, and HS-1 on board. CVSGs were not established until various times in 1960.

׀ *Philippine Sea* (CVS 47) deployed with VS-37 and HS-2 on board. CVSGs were not established until various times in 1960.

Major Overseas Deployments for 1958				
Departure	Return	Air Group	Carrier	Area of Operations
06 Jan 1958	30 Jun 1958	ATG-4	CVA-12	WestPac
13 Jan 1958	15 Jul 1958	#	CVS-47	WestPac
01 Feb 1958	01 Oct 1958	CVG-3	CVA-60	Med
02 Feb 1958	17 Nov 1958	ATG-201	CVA-9	Med/IO/WestPac
15 Feb 1958	02 Oct 1958	CVG-15	CVA-19	WestPac
08 Mar 1958	21 Nov 1958	CVG-11	CVA-38	WestPac
*1958	23 Sep 1958	*	CVS-21	Eniwetok-Bikini
10 May 1958	12 Oct 1958	†	CVS-18	Med
09 Jun 1958	08 Aug 1958	ATG-181	CVA-11	NorLant
09 Jun 1958	07 Aug 1958	‡	CVS-39	NorLant
20 Jun 1958	02 Dec 1958	ı	CVS-37	WestPac
20 Jun 1958	20 Aug 1958	CVG-14	CVA-61	SoLant/SoPac
14 Jul 1958	19 Dec 1958	CVG-21	CVA-16	WestPac
16 Aug 1958	12 Mar 1959	CVG-2	CVA-41	WestPac
21 Aug 1958	12 Jan 1959	ATG-4	CVA-20	WestPac
02 Sep 1958	12 Mar 1959	CVG-10	CVA-59	Med
02 Sep 1958	12 Mar 1959	CVG-7	CVA-15	Med
01 Oct 1958	01 Nov 1958	None	CVS-21	West to East Coast via Panama Canal
04 Oct 1958	16 Feb 1959	ATG-1	CVA-14	WestPac
01 Nov 1958	18 Jun 1959	CVG-19	CVA-31	WestPac
02 Nov 1958	22 May 1959	§	CVS-10	WestPac

* Records not available to determine exact departure date, estimated to be Feb or Mar 1958. *Boxer* (CVS 21) deployed to the Eniwetok-Bikini-Johnston Island operating area as the flagship for CTG 7.3 involved in balloon launching and various atomic tests. She deployed with only HRM(L)-361 Det on board.

† Squadrons deployed on board *Wasp* (CVS 18) included VS-31, HS-11, VAW-12 Det 48, HU-2 Det 48, and HMR-262 Det. Antisubmarine Carrier Air Groups (CVSG) were not established until various periods in 1960.

‡ Squadrons deployed on board *Lake Champlain* (CVS 39) included VS-27 and HS-3. CVSGs were not established until various periods in 1960.

§ Squadrons deployed on board *Yorktown* (CVS 10) included VS-37, HS-2, and VF-92 Det N. CVSGs were not established until various periods in 1960.

ı *Princeton (CVS 37) deployed with VS-23 and HS-4. CVSGs were not established until various times in 1960.*

Philippine Sea (CVS 47) deployed with VS-21 and HS-6. CVSGs were not established until various times in 1960. Upon arrival in WestPac, the carrier also operated with VMA-332, HMR-163, and VMO-2 on board from 11–31 March 1958.

Major Overseas Deployments for 1959				
Departure	Return	Air Group	Carrier	Area of Operations
03 Jan 1959	27 Jul 1959	CVG-14	CVA-61	WestPac
13 Feb 1959	01 Sep 1959	CVG-1	CVA-42	Med
13 Feb 1959	30 Aug 1959	CVG-6	CVA-11	Med
09 Mar 1959	03 Oct 1959	CVG-11	CVA-38	WestPac
04 Apr 1959	10 Oct 1959	*	CVS-12	WestPac
26 Apr 1959	02 Dec 1959	CVG-21	CVA-16	WestPac
05 Jun 1959	03 Sep 1959	†	CVS-39	Med
01 Aug 1959	18 Jan 1960	CVG-15	CVA-19	WestPac
07 Aug 1959	26 Feb 1960	CVG-10	CVA-9	Med
15 Aug 1959	25 Mar 1960	CVG-2	CVA-41	WestPac
15 Aug 1959	26 Feb 1960	CVG-3	CVA-60	Med
05 Sep 1959	15 Mar 1960	‡	CVS-33	WestPac
21 Nov 1959	14 May 1960	CVG-19	CVA-31	WestPac

* Squadrons deployed on board *Hornet* (CVS 12) included VS-38, HS-8, and VAW-11 Det P. Antisubmarine Carrier Air Groups (CVSG) were not established until various periods in 1960.

† Squadrons deployed on board *Lake Champlain* (CVS 39) included VS-30, HS-1, HU-2 Det 34, and VAW-12 Det 34. CVSGs were not established until various periods in 1960.

‡ Squadrons deployed on board *Kearsarge* (CVS 33) included VS-21, HS-6, and VAW-13 Det A. CVSGs were not established until various periods in 1960.

Major Overseas Deployments for 1960				
Departure	**Return**	**Air Group**	**Carrier**	**Area of Operations**
04 Jan 1960	28 Jul 1960	*	CVS-10	WestPac
28 Jan 1960	24 Aug 1960	CVG-1	CVA-42	Med
28 Jan 1960	31 Aug 1960	CVG-8	CVA-59	Med
06 Feb 1960	30 Aug 1960	CVG-9	CVA-61	WestPac
05 Mar 1960	11 Oct 1960	CVG-5	CVA-14	WestPac
14 May 1960	15 Dec 1960	CVG-14	CVA-34	WestPac
17 May 1960	18 Dec 1960	†	CVS-12	WestPac
09 Jun 1960	31 Aug 1960	CVSG-56	CVS-47	Med
17 Jun 1960	20 Aug 1960	‡	CVS-18	Carib/SoLant
16 Jul 1960	18 Mar 1961	CVG-11	CVA-19	WestPac
04 Aug 1960	17 Feb 1961	CVG-6	CVA-11	Med
04 Aug 1960	03 Mar 1961	CVG-7	CVA-62	Med
22 Aug 1960	26 Feb 1961	CVG-3	CVA-60	Med/NorLant
06 Sep 1960	20 Oct 1960	CVG-10	CVA-38	NorLant
06 Sep 1960	15 Dec 1960	CVSG-60	CVS-9	NorLant/Med/IO
19 Sep 1960	27 May 1961	CVG-15	CVA-43	WestPac
01 Oct 1960	02 May 1961	CVSG-59	CVS-20	WestPac
29 Oct 1960	06 Jun 1961	CVG-21	CVA-16	WestPac
14 Nov 1960	27 Nov 1960	CVG-10	CVA-38	Carib

* Squadrons deployed on board *Yorktown* (CVS 10) included VS-23, HS-4, and VAW-11 Det T. Antisubmarine Carrier Air Groups (CVSG) were not established until various periods in 1960.

† Squadrons deployed on board *Hornet* (CVS 12) included VS-37, HS-2, and VAW-13 Det N. At different times during the deployment *Hornet* also had HMR-162, HMX-1, and VU-1 Det KD-21 on board. CVSGs were not established until various periods in 1960.

‡ Elements of CVSG-52 remained on board *Wasp* (CVS 18) during her emergency cruise to the Belgian Congo to evacuate American nationals.

Major Overseas Deployments for 1961				
Departure	**Return**	**Air Group**	**Carrier**	**Area of Operations**
02 Feb 1961	15 May 1961	CVG-10	CVA-38	Med
09 Feb 1961	25 Aug 1961	CVG-8	CVA-59	Med
15 Feb 1961	28 Aug 1961	CVG-1	CVA-42	Med
16 Feb 1961	28 Sep 1961	CVG-2	CVA-41	WestPac
03 Mar 1961	18 Sep 1961	CVSG-53	CVS-33	WestPac
26 Apr 1961	13 Dec 1961	CVG-19	CVA-31	WestPac
10 May 1961	15 Jan 1962	CVG-5	CVA-14	WestPac
06 Jun 1961	01 Sep 1961	CVSG-55	CVS-18	Med
05 Jul 1961	22 Aug 1961	CVG-3	CVA-60	Carib
29 Jul 1961	02 Mar 1962	CVSG-55	CVS-10	WestPac
03 Aug 1961	01 Mar 1962	CVG-6	CVA-11	Med
04 Aug 1961	19 Dec 1961	CVG-7	CVA-62	Med
11 Aug 1961	08 Mar 1962	CVG-9	CVA-61	WestPac
11 Aug 1961	01 Nov 1961	CVG-11	CVA-63	*
24 Oct 1961	22 Feb 1962	CVSG-56	CVS-9	NorLant
09 Nov 1961	12 May 1962	CVG-14	CVA-16	WestPac
19 Nov 1961	30 Nov 1961	CVG-1	CVA-42	Carib
28 Nov 1961	12 May 1962	CVG-3	CVA-60	Med
12 Dec 1961	17 Jul 1962	CVG-15	CVA-43	WestPac

* *Kitty Hawk* (CVA 63) changed homeports from the Atlantic to the Pacific. During the transit to the Pacific, via Cape Horn, the carrier and its embarked squadrons participated in operations in the Caribbean, South Atlantic, and eastern Pacific.

Major Overseas Deployments for 1962				
Departure	**Return**	**Air Group**	**Carrier**	**Area of Operations**
06 Jan 1962	25 Jul 1962	CVSG-59	CVS-20	WestPac
02 Feb 1962	24 Aug 1962	CVG-21	CVA-19	WestPac
07 Feb 1962	28 Aug 1962	CVG-10	CVA-38	Med
17 Feb 1962	17 Jun 1962	CVSG-52	CVS-18	NorLant
06 Apr 1962	20 Oct 1962	CVG-2	CVA-41	WestPac
19 Apr 1962	27 Aug 1962	CVG-7	CVA-62	Med
07 Jun 1962	17 Dec 1962	CVG-16	CVA-34	WestPac
07 Jun 1962	21 Dec 1962	CVSG-57	CVS-12	WestPac
07 Jun 1962	30 Aug 1962	CVSG-58	CVS-15	Med
12 Jul 1962	11 Feb 1963	CVG-19	CVA-31	WestPac
21 Jul 1962	11 Sep 1962	CVG-5*	CVA-16	SoPac/SoLant
25 Jul 1962	17 Sep 1962	CVG-5	CVA-64	SoLant/West Coast
03 Aug 1962	11 Oct 1962	CVG-6	CVAN-65	Med
03 Aug 1962	02 Mar 1963	CVG-8	CVA-59	Med
13 Sep 1962	02 Apr 1963	CVG-11	CVA-63	WestPac
14 Sep 1962	22 Apr 1963	CVG-1	CVA-42	Med
15 Oct 1962	15 Nov 1962	CVSG-60	CVS-9	Carib/Cuban Missile Crisis
19 Oct 1962	06 Dec 1962	CVG-6	CVAN-65	Carib
24 Oct 1962	22 Nov 1962	CVSG-52	CVS-18	Carib/Cuban Missile Crisis
26 Oct 1962	18 Jun 1963	CVSG-55	CVS-10	WestPac
09 Nov 1962	14 Jun 1963	CVG-9	CVA-61	WestPac
03 Dec 1962	21 Dec 1962	CVG-3	CVA-60	Carib

* Only two squadrons from CVG-5 were on board *Lexington* (CVA 16) during her homeport change and transit from the Pacific Fleet to the Atlantic Fleet.

Major Overseas Deployments for 1963				
Departure	**Return**	**Air Group**	**Carrier**	**Area of Operations**
03 Jan 1963	15 Jul 1963	CVG-5	CVA-14	WestPac/NorPac
06 Feb 1963	04 Sep 1963	CVG-6	CVAN-65	Med
21 Feb 1963	10 Sep 1963	CVG-14	CVA-64	WestPac
29 Mar 1963	25 Oct 1963	CVG-3	CVA-60	Med
03 Apr 1963	25 Nov 1963	CVG-15	CVA-43	WestPac
19 Apr 1963	03 Dec 1963	CVSG-53	CVS-33	WestPac
07 Jun 1963	16 Dec 1963	CVG-21	CVA-19	WestPac
01 Aug 1963	10 Mar 1964	CVW-16	CVA-34	WestPac
06 Aug 1963	04 Mar 1964	CVG-7	CVA-62	Med
12 Aug 1963	31 Aug 1963	CVSG-59	CVS-20	NorPac
01 Oct 1963	24 Dec 1963	CVSG-60	CVS-9	Med/IO
01 Oct 1963	23 May 1964	CVG-10	CVA-38	Med
09 Oct 1963	15 Apr 1964	CVSG-57	CVS-12	WestPac
17 Oct 1963	20 Jul 1964	CVW-11	CVA-63	WestPac
08 Nov 1963	26 May 1964	CVW-2	CVA-41	WestPac

Major Overseas Deployments for 1964				
Departure	Return	Air Group	Carrier	Area of Operations
28 Jan 1964	21 Nov 1964	CVW-19	CVA-31	WestPac/IO/Vietnam
08 Feb 1964	03 Oct 1964	CVW-6	CVAN-65	Med/World Cruise
19 Feb 1964	11 Aug 1964	CVSG-59	CVS-20	WestPac
14 Apr 1964	15 Dec 1964	CVW-5	CVA-14	WestPac/Vietnam
28 Apr 1964	22 Dec 1964	CVW-1	CVA-42	Med
05 May 1964	01 Feb 1965	CVW-14	CVA-64	WestPac/Vietnam
09 Jun 1964	25 Jul 1964	CVSG-60	CVS-9	NorLant
11 Jun 1964	04 Sep 1964	CVSG-56	CVS-11	Med
19 Jun 1964	17 Dec 1964	CVSG-53	CVS-33	WestPac
10 Jul 1964	13 Mar 1965	CVW-8	CVA-59	Med
05 Aug 1964	06 May 1965	CVW-9	CVA-61	WestPac/Vietnam
08 Sep 1964	05 Nov 1964	CVW-7	CVA-62	NorLant/Med
08 Sep 1964	18 Dec 1964	CVSG-52	CVS-18	NorLant/Med
10 Oct 1964	24 Nov 1964	CVSG-54	CVS-39	Med
21 Oct 1964	29 May 1965	CVW-21	CVA-19	WestPac/Vietnam
23 Oct 1964	17 May 1965	CVSG-55	CVS-10	WestPac
28 Nov 1964	12 Jul 1965	CVW-3	CVA-60	Med
07 Dec 1964	01 Nov 1965	CVW-15	CVA-43	WestPac/Vietnam

Major Overseas Deployments for 1965				
Departure	Return	Air Group	Carrier	Area of Operations
10 Feb 1965	20 Sep 1965	CVW-10	CVA-38	Med
06 Mar 1965	23 Nov 1965	CVW-2	CVA-41	WestPac/Vietnam
22 Mar 1965	07 Oct 1965	CVSG-59	CVS-20	WestPac
05 Apr 1965	16 Dec 1965	CVW-16	CVA-34	WestPac/Vietnam
21 Apr 1965	13 Jan 1966	CVW-19	CVA-31	WestPac/Vietnam
10 May 1965	13 Dec 1965	CVW-7	CVA-62	WestPac/Vietnam
11 Jun 1965	02 Sep 1965	CVSG-58	CVS-15	Med
28 Jun 1965	17 Dec 1965	CVW-1	CVA-42	Med
12 Aug 1965	23 Mar 1966	CVSG-57	CVS-12	WestPac
24 Aug 1965	07 Apr 1966	CVW-8	CVA-59	Med
28 Sep 1965	13 May 1966	CVW-5	CVA-14	WestPac/Vietnam
19 Oct 1965	13 Jun 1966	CVW-11	CVA-63	WestPac/Vietnam
26 Oct 1965	21 Jun 1966	CVW-9	CVAN-65	SoLant/IO/WestPac/Vietnam
10 Nov 1965	01 Aug 1966	CVW-21	CVA-19	WestPac/Vietnam
30 Nov 1965	10 Jul 1966	CVW-6	CVA-66	Med
10 Dec 1965	25 Aug 1966	CVW-14	CVA-61	WestPac/Vietnam

Major Overseas Deployments for 1966				
Departure	Return	Air Group	Carrier	Area of Operations
06 Jan 1966	28 Jul 1966	CVSG-55	CVS-10	WestPac
11 Mar 1966	26 Oct 1966	CVW-3	CVA-60	Med
04 Apr 1966	21 Nov 1966	CVW-10	CVS-11	Med/IO/WestPac/Vietnam
12 May 1966	03 Dec 1966	CVW-15	CVA-64	WestPac/Vietnam
26 May 1966	16 Nov 1966	CVW-16	CVA-34	WestPac/Vietnam
09 Jun 1966	21 Dec 1966	CVSG-53	CVS-33	WestPac/Vietnam
13 Jun 1966	01 Feb 1967	CVW-7	CVA-62	Med

Major Overseas Deployments for 1966

Departure	Return	Air Group	Carrier	Area of Operations
21 Jun 1966	21 Feb 1967	CVW-1	CVA-42	SoLant/IO/WestPac/Vietnam
29 Jul 1966	23 Feb 1967	CVW-2	CVA-43	WestPac/Vietnam
29 Sep 1966	20 May 1967	CVW-8	CVA-38	Med
15 Oct 1966	29 May 1967	CVW-19	CVA-14	WestPac/Vietnam
04 Nov 1966	23 May 1967	CVSG-59	CVS-20	WestPac/Vietnam
05 Nov 1966	19 Jun 1967	CVW-11	CVA-63	WestPac/Vietnam
19 Nov 1966	06 Jul 1967	CVW-9	CVAN-65	WestPac/Vietnam

Major Overseas Deployments for 1967

Departure	Return	Air Group	Carrier	Area of Operations
05 Jan 1967	22 Jul 1967	CVW-5	CVA-19	WestPac/Vietnam
10 Jan 1967	20 Sep 1967	CVW-6	CVA-66	Med
26 Jan 1967	25 Aug 1967	CVW-21	CVA-31	WestPac/Vietnam
27 Mar 1967	28 Oct 1967	CVSG-57	CVS-12	WestPac/Vietnam
29 Apr 1967	04 Dec 1967	CVW-14	CVA-64	WestPac/Vietnam
02 May 1967	06 Dec 1967	CVW-3	CVA-60	Med
11 May 1967	30 Dec 1967	CVW-10	CVS-11	Med/IO/WestPac/Vietnam
29 May 1967	23 Sep 1967	CVSG-54	CVS-9	NorLant/Med
06 Jun 1967	15 Sep 1967	CVW-17	CVA-59	WestPac/Vietnam
16 Jun 1967	31 Jan 1968	CVW-16	CVA-34	WestPac/Vietnam
26 Jul 1967	06 Apr 1968	CVW-15	CVA-43	WestPac/Vietnam
17 Aug 1967	06 Apr 1968	CVSG-53	CVS-33	WestPac/Vietnam
24 Aug 1967	19 May 1968	CVW-1	CVA-42	Med
22 Sep 1967	16 Dec 1967	CVSG-56	CVS-15	Med
04 Nov 1967	25 May 1968	CVW-2	CVA-61	WestPac/Vietnam
15 Nov 1967	04 Aug 1968	CVW-8	CVA-38	Med
18 Nov 1967	28 Jun 1968	CVW-11	CVA-63	WestPac/Vietnam
28 Dec 1967	17 Aug 1968	CVW-19	CVA-14	WestPac/Vietnam
28 Dec 1967	05 Jul 1968	CVSG-55	CVS-10	WestPac/Vietnam

Major Overseas Deployments for 1968

Departure	Return	Air Group	Carrier	Area of Operations
03 Jan 1968	18 Jul 1968	CVW-9	CVAN-65	WestPac/Vietnam
27 Jan 1968	10 Oct 1968	CVW-5	CVA-31	WestPac/Vietnam
15 Feb 1968	13 Jun 1968	CVSG-60	CVS-9	NorLant/Med
10 Apr 1968	16 Dec 1968	CVW-6	CVA-66	World Cruise/Vietnam
30 Apr 1968	27 Jan 1969	CVW-7	CVA-62	Med
30 Apr 1968	09 Nov 1968	CVSG-59	CVS-20	WestPac/Vietnam
29 May 1968	31 Jan 1969	CVW-14	CVA-64	WestPac/Vietnam
04 Jun 1968	08 Feb 1969	CVW-10	CVS-11	SoLant/IO/Pacific/Vietnam
18 Jul 1968	03 Mar 1969	CVW-21	CVA-19	WestPac/Vietnam
22 Jul 1968	29 Apr 1969	CVW-17	CVA-59	Med
22 Jul 1968	03 Sep 1968	CVSG-56	CVS-16	SoLant/UNITAS IX
20 Aug 1968	20 Dec 1968	CVSG-52	CVS-18	NorLant/Med
07 Sep 1968	18 Apr 1969	CVW-15	CVA-43	WestPac/Vietnam
30 Sep 1968	13 May 1969	CVSG-57	CVS-12	WestPac/Vietnam
26 Oct 1968	17 May 1969	CVW-2	CVA-61	WestPac/Vietnam
30 Dec 1968	04 Sep 1969	CVW-11	CVA-63	WestPac/Vietnam

Major Overseas Deployments for 1969				
Departure	**Return**	**Air Group**	**Carrier**	**Area of Operations**
06 Jan 1969	02 Jul 1969	CVW-9	CVAN-65	WestPac/Vietnam
07 Jan 1969	29 Jul 1969	CVW-8	CVA-38	Med
21 Jan 1969	28 Feb 1969	CVSG-56	CVS-10	West to East Coast via Cape Horn
01 Feb 1969	18 Sep 1969	CVW-16	CVA-14	WestPac/Vietnam
18 Mar 1969	29 Oct 1969	CVW-5	CVA-31	WestPac/Vietnam
29 Mar 1969	04 Sep 1969	CVSG-53	CVS-33	WestPac/Vietnam
01 Apr 1969	11 Jul 1969	CVSG-54	CVS-18	NorLant
05 Apr 1969	21 Dec 1969	CVW-1	CVA-67	Med
14 Apr 1969	17 Nov 1969	CVW-19	CVA-34	WestPac/Vietnam
09 Jul 1969	22 Jan 1970	CVW-3	CVA-60	Med
02 Aug 1969	15 Apr 1970	CVW-21	CVA-19	WestPac/Vietnam
11 Aug 1969	08 May 1970	CVW-14	CVA-64	WestPac/Vietnam
02 Sep 1969	11 Dec 1969	CVSG-56	CVS-10	NorLant
03 Sep 1969	09 Oct 1969	CVW-7	CVA-62	NorLant
23 Sep 1969	01 Jul 1970	CVW-15	CVA-43	WestPac/Vietnam
14 Oct 1969	01 Jun 1970	CVW-2	CVA-61	WestPac/Vietnam
02 Dec 1969	08 Jul 1970	CVW-17	CVA-59	Med

Major Overseas Deployments for 1970				
Departure	**Return**	**Air Group**	**Carrier**	**Area of Operations**
02 Jan 1970	27 Jul 1970	CVW-6	CVA-42	Med
05 Mar 1970	17 Dec 1970	CVW-8	CVS-38	SoLant/IO/WestPac/Vietnam
02 Apr 1970	12 Nov 1970	CVW-5	CVA-31	WestPac/Vietnam
10 Apr 1970	21 Dec 1970	CVW-9	CVA-66	WestPac/Vietnam
05 May 1970	08 Sep 1970	CVSG-54	CVS-18	NorLant
14 May 1970	10 Dec 1970	CVW-19	CVA-34	WestPac/Vietnam
17 Jun 1970	09 Nov 1970	CVW-3	CVA-60	Med
23 Jun 1970	31 Jan 1971	CVW-7	CVA-62	Med
14 Sep 1970	01 Mar 1971	CVW-1	CVA-67	Carib/Med/NorLant
22 Oct 1970	03 Jun 1971	CVW-21	CVA-19	WestPac/Vietnam
27 Oct 1970	17 Jun 1971	CVW-2	CVA-61	WestPac/Vietnam
06 Nov 1970	17 Jul 1971	CVW-11	CVA-63	WestPac/Vietnam

Major Overseas Deployments for 1971				
Departure	**Return**	**Air Group**	**Carrier**	**Area of Operations**
05 Jan 1971	02 Jul 1971	CVW-17	CVA-59	Med
14 Jan 1971	03 Mar 1971	CVSG-54	CVS-18	Med
29 Jan 1971	23 Jul 1971	CVW-6	CVA-42	Med
11 Mar 1971	06 Jul 1971	CVSG-59	CVS-14	WestPac/IO/NorPac
16 Apr 1971	06 Nov 1971	CVW-5	CVA-41	WestPac/Vietnam
16 Apr 1971	15 Oct 1971	CVSG-56	CVS-11	NorLant/Med
14 May 1971	18 Dec 1971	CVW-19	CVA-34	WestPac/Vietnam
07 Jun 1971	28 Oct 1971	CVW-3	CVA-60	NorLant/Med
11 Jun 1971	12 Feb 1972	CVW-14	CVAN-65	WestPac/Vietnam/IO
06 Jul 1971	16 Dec 1971	CVW-8	CVA-66	Med
16 Sep 1971	16 Mar 1972	CVW-7	CVA-62	NorLant/Med
01 Oct 1971	30 Jun 1972	CVW-9	CVA-64	WestPac/Vietnam
12 Nov 1971	17 Jul 1972	CVW-15	CVA-43	WestPac/Vietnam
01 Dec 1971	06 Oct 1972	CVW-1	CVA-67	Med/NorLant

Major Overseas Deployments for 1972

Departure	Return	Air Group	Carrier	Area of Operations
07 Jan 1972	03 Oct 1972	CVW-21	CVA-19	WestPac/Vietnam
15 Feb 1972	08 Dec 1972	CVW-6	CVA-42	Med
17 Feb 1972	28 Nov 1972	CVW-11	CVA-63	WestPac/Vietnam
10 Mar 1972	23 Apr 1972	CVSG-56	CVS-11	EastLant
10 Apr 1972	03 Mar 1973	CVW-5	CVA-41	WestPac/Vietnam
11 Apr 1972	13 Feb 1973	CVW-3	CV-60	SoLant/IO/WestPac/Vietnam
17 May 1972	30 Jul 1972	CVSG-53	CVS-14	WestPac/Vietnam
05 Jun 1972	24 Mar 1973	CVW-8	CVA-66	WestPac/Vietnam
05 Jun 1972	30 Mar 1973	CVW-19	CVA-34	WestPac/Vietnam
11 Jul 1972	20 Oct 1972	CVSG-56	CVS-11	NorLant
12 Sep 1972	12 Jun 1973	CVW-14	CVAN-65	WestPac/Vietnam
22 Sep 1972	06 Jul 1973	CVW-17	CVA-59	Med
16 Nov 1972	23 Jun 1973	CVW-2	CVA-61	WestPac/Vietnam
24 Nov 1972	04 May 1974	CVSG-56	CVS-11	Med

Major Overseas Deployments for 1973

Departure	Return	Air Group	Carrier	Area of Operations
05 Jan 1973	11 Oct 1973	CVW-9	CVA-64	WestPac/Vietnam
09 Mar 1973	08 Nov 1973	CVW-15	CVA-43	WestPac
16 Apr 1973	01 Dec 1973	CVW-1	CVA-67	Med/NorLant/Med
08 May 1973	08 Jan 1974	CVW-21	CVA-19	WestPac/IO
21 Jun 1973	19 Jan 1974	CVW-7	CV-62	Med
11 Sep 1973	05 Oct 1973	CVW-5	CVA-41*	WestPac
14 Sep 1973	17 Mar 1974	CVW-6	CVA-42	Med
18 Oct 1973	05 Jun 1974	CVW-19	CVA-34	WestPac/IO
23 Nov 1973	09 Jul 1974	CVW-11	CV-63	WestPac/IO
26 Nov 1973	22 Dec 1973	CVW-5	CVA-41*	WestPac

* *Midway* (CVA 41) with CVW-5 and its assigned squadrons were forward deployed and homeported overseas at Naval Station Yokosuka, Japan. Only operations outside the home waters of Japan are listed as deployments.

Major Overseas Deployments for 1974

Departure	Return	Air Group	Carrier	Area of Operations
03 Jan 1974	03 Aug 1974	CVW-8	CVA-66	Med
29 Jan 1974	06 Mar 1974	CVW-5	CVA-41*	WestPac
11 Mar 1974	11 Sep 1974	CVW-17	CVA-59	Med
07 May 1974	18 Oct 1974	CVW-2	CVA-61	WestPac
21 Jun 1974	22 Dec 1974	CVW-9	CVA-64	WestPac/IO
19 Jul 1974	21 Jan 1975	CVW-7	CV-62	Med
06 Sep 1974	12 Oct 1974	CVW-8	CVA-66	NorLant
17 Sep 1974	20 May 1975	CVW-14	CVAN-65	WestPac/IO
27 Sep 1974	19 Mar 1975	CVW-3	CV-60	Med
18 Oct 1974	20 Dec 1974	CVW-5	CVA-41*	WestPac
05 Dec 1974	02 Jul 1975	CVW-15	CVA-43	WestPac

* *Midway* (CVA 41) with CVW-5 and its assigned squadrons were forward deployed and homeported overseas at Naval Station Yokosuka, Japan. Only operations outside the home waters of Japan are listed as deployments.

Major Overseas Deployments for 1975				
Departure	Return	Air Group	Carrier	Area of Operations
03 Jan 1975	16 Jul 1975	CVW-6	CV-42	Med
13 Jan 1975	18 Feb 1975	CVW-5	CVA-41*	WestPac
05 Mar 1975	22 Sep 1975	CVW-17	CV-59	Med
18 Mar 1975	20 Oct 1975	CVW-21	CV-19	WestPac
31 Mar 1975	29 May 1975	CVW-5	CVA-41*	WestPac
21 May 1975	15 Dec 1975	CVW-11	CV-63	WestPac
28 Jun 1975	27 Jan 1976	CVW-1	CV-67	Med
16 Jul 1975	24 Sep 1975	CVW-8	CVN-68	Carib/NorLant
16 Sep 1975	03 Mar 1976	CVW-19	CV-34	WestPac
04 Oct 1975	19 Dec 1975	CVW-5	CV-41*	WestPac/IO
15 Oct 1975	05 May 1976	CVW-7	CV-62	NorLant/Med

* *Midway* (CVA 41) with CVW-5 and its assigned squadrons were forward deployed and homeported overseas at Naval Station Yokosuka, Japan. Only operations outside the home waters of Japan are listed as deployments.

Major Overseas Deployments for 1976				
Departure	Return	Air Group	Carrier	Area of Operations
06 Jan 1976	28 Jul 1976	CVW-3	CV-60	Med
30 Jan 1976	07 Sep 1976	CVW-2	CV-61	WestPac/IO
13 Mar 1976	26 Apr 1976	CVW-5	CV-41*	WestPac
15 Apr 1976	25 Oct 1976	CVW-6	CV-66	Med
19 May 1976	22 Jun 1976	CVW-5	CV-41*	WestPac
07 Jul 1976	07 Feb 1977	CVW-8	CVN-68	Med
09 Jul 1976	04 Aug 1976	CVW-5	CV-41*	WestPac
30 Jul 1976	28 Mar 1977	CVW-14	CVN-65	WestPac/IO
02 Sep 1976	09 Nov 1976	CVW-1	CV-67	NorLant
04 Oct 1976	21 Apr 1977	CVW-19	CV-42	Med
01 Nov 1976	17 Dec 1976	CVW-5	CV-41*	WestPac

* *Midway* (CV 41) with CVW-5 and its assigned squadrons were forward deployed and homeported overseas at Naval Station Yokosuka, Japan. Only operations outside the home waters of Japan are listed as deployments.

Major Overseas Deployments for 1977				
Departure	Return	Air Group	Carrier	Area of Operations
11 Jan 1977	01 Mar 1977	CVW-5	CV-41*	WestPac
15 Jan 1977	01 Aug 1977	CVW-1	CV-67	Med
15 Feb 1977	05 Oct 1977	CVW-15	CV-43	WestPac
31 Mar 1977	21 Oct 1977	CVW-7	CV-62	Med
12 Apr 1977	21 Nov 1977	CVW-9	CV-64	WestPac
19 Apr 1977	05 Sep 1977	CVW-5	CV-41*	WestPac
10 Jun 1977	19 Jul 1977	CVW-6	CV-66	SoLant
11 Jul 1977	23 Dec 1977	CVW-3	CV-60	Med
27 Sep 1977	21 Dec 1977	CVW-5	CV-41*	WestPac/IO
29 Sep 1977	25 Apr 1978	CVW-6	CV-66	Med
25 Oct 1977	15 May 1978	CVW-11	CV-63	WestPac
01 Dec 1977	20 Jul 1978	CVW-8	CVN-68	Med/NorLant

* *Midway* (CV 41) with CVW-5 and its assigned squadrons were forward deployed and homeported overseas at Naval Station Yokosuka, Japan. Only operations outside the home waters of Japan are listed as deployments.

Major Overseas Deployments for 1978

Departure	Return	Air Group	Carrier	Area of Operations
04 Apr 1978	26 Oct 1978	CVW-17	CV-59	Med/NorLant
04 Apr 1978	30 Oct 1978	CVW-14	CVN-65	WestPac/IO
11 Apr 1978	23 May 1978	CVW-5	CV-41*	WestPac
29 Jun 1978	08 Feb 1979	CVW-1	CV-67	Med
26 Sep 1978	17 May 1979	CVW-9	CV-64	WestPac/IO
03 Oct 1978	05 Apr 1979	CVW-3	CV-60	Med
09 Nov 1978	23 Dec 1978	CVW-5	CV-41*	WestPac

* *Midway* (CV 41) with CVW-5 and its assigned squadrons were forward deployed and homeported overseas at Naval Station Yokosuka, Japan. Only operations outside the home waters of Japan are listed as deployments.

Major Overseas Deployments for 1979

Departure	Return	Air Group	Carrier	Area of Operations
11 Jan 1979	20 Feb 1979	CVW-5	CV-41*	WestPac
16 Jan 1979	13 Jul 1979	CVW-7	CVN-69	Med
21 Feb 1979	22 Sep 1979	CVW-2	CV-61	WestPac
13 Mar 1979	22 Sep 1979	CVW-11	CV-66	Med
07 Apr 1979	18 Jun 1979	CVW-5	CV-41*	IO
30 May 1979	25 Feb 1980	CVW-15	CV-63	WestPac/IO
28 Jun 1979	14 Dec 1979	CVW-6	CV-62	Med
20 Aug 1979	14 Sep 1979	CVW-5	CV-41*	WestPac
10 Sep 1979	26 May 1980	CVW-8	CVN-68	Med/SoLant/IO
30 Sep 1979	20 Feb 1980	CVW-5	CV-41*	IO
13 Nov 1979	11 Jun 1980	CVW-14	CV-43	WestPac/IO
27 Nov 1979	07 May 1980	CVW-17	CV-59	Med

* *Midway* (CV 41) with CVW-5 and its assigned squadrons were forward deployed and homeported overseas at Naval Station Yokosuka, Japan. Only operations outside the home waters of Japan are listed as deployments.

Major Overseas Deployments for 1980

Departure	Return	Air Group	Carrier	Area of Operations
26 Feb 1980	15 Oct 1980	CVW-9	CV-64	WestPac/IO
10 Mar 1980	27 Aug 1980	CVW-3	CV-60	Med
15 Apr 1980	22 Dec 1980	CVW-7	CVN-69	IO
14 Jul 1980	26 Nov 1980	CVW-5	CV-41*	WestPac/IO
04 Aug 1980	28 Mar 1981	CVW-1	CV-67	Med
29 Aug 1980	17 Oct 1980	CVW-8	CVN-68	NorLant
10 Sep 1980	05 May 1981	CVW-2	CV-61	WestPac/IO
19 Nov 1980	10 Jun 1981	CVW-6	CV-62	SoLant/IO/Med

* *Midway* (CV 41) with CVW-5 and its assigned squadrons were forward deployed and homeported overseas at Naval Station Yokosuka, Japan. Only operations outside the home waters of Japan are listed as deployments.

Major Overseas Deployments for 1981

Departure	Return	Air Group	Carrier	Area of Operations
23 Feb 1981	05 Jun 1981	CVW-5	CV-41*	WestPac/IO
02 Mar 1981	15 Sep 1981	CVW-17	CV-59	Med/NorLant
01 Apr 1981	23 Nov 1981	CVW-15	CV-63	WestPac/IO
14 Apr 1981	12 Nov 1981	CVW-11	CV-66	Med/IO
26 Jun 1981	16 Jul 1981	CVW-5	CV-41*	WestPac

Major Overseas Deployments for 1981

Departure	Return	Air Group	Carrier	Area of Operations
03 Aug 1981	12 Feb 1982	CVW-8	CVN-68	Med
20 Aug 1981	07 Oct 1981	CVW-7	CVN-69	NorLant
20 Aug 1981	23 Mar 1982	CVW-14	CV-43	WestPac/IO
03 Sep 1981	06 Oct 1981	CVW-5	CV-41*	WestPac
20 Oct 1981	23 May 1982	CVW-9	CV-64	WestPac/IO

* *Midway* (CV 41) with CVW-5 and its assigned squadrons were forward deployed and homeported overseas at Naval Station Yokosuka, Japan. Only operations outside the home waters of Japan are listed as deployments.

Major Overseas Deployments for 1982

Departure	Return	Air Group	Carrier	Area of Operations
04 Jan 1982	14 Jul 1982	CVW-3	CV-67	Med/IO
05 Jan 1982	13 Jul 1982	CVW-7	CVN-69	Med
07 Apr 1982	19 Oct 1982	CVW-2	CV-61	WestPac/IO
26 Apr 1982	18 Jun 1982	CVW-5	CV-41*	WestPac
07 Jun 1982	22 Dec 1982	CVW-6	CV-62	Med
08 Jun 1982	16 Nov 1982	CVW-17	CV-59	Med/IO
23 Aug 1982	30 Oct 1982	CVW-1	CV-66	NorLant/Med/Carib
01 Sep 1982	28 Apr 1983	CVW-11	CVN-65	NorPac/WestPac
14 Sep 1982	11 Dec 1982	CVW-5	CV-41*	NorPac/WestPac
10 Nov 1982	20 May 1983	CVW-8	CVN-68	Carib/Med
08 Dec 1982	02 Jun 1983	CVW-1	CV-66	Med/IO

* *Midway* (CV 41) with CVW-5 and its assigned squadrons were forward deployed and homeported overseas at Naval Station Yokosuka, Japan. Only operations outside the home waters of Japan are listed as deployments.

Major Overseas Deployments for 1983

Departure	Return	Air Group	Carrier	Area of Operations
01 Mar 1983	29 Oct 1983	CVW-15	CVN-70	World Cruise
21 Mar 1983	12 Sep 1983	CVW-14	CV-43	World Cruise
27 Apr 1983	02 Dec 1983	CVW-7	CVN-69	Med
25 May 1983	01 Jul 1983	CVW-3	CV-67	NorLant
02 Jun 1983	08 Aug 1983	CVW-5	CV-41*	WestPac
15 Jul 1983	29 Feb 1984	CVW-9	CV-61	Central America/WestPac/IO
27 Sep 1983	02 May 1984	CVW-3	CV-67	SoLant/Med
25 Oct 1983	11 Dec 1983	CVW-5	CV-41*	WestPac
18 Oct 1983	11 Apr 1984	CVW-6	CV-62	Carib/Med/NorLant
28 Dec 1983	23 May 1984	CVW-5	CV-41*	IO

* *Midway* (CV 41) with CVW-5 and its assigned squadrons were forward deployed and homeported overseas at Naval Station Yokosuka, Japan. Only operations outside the home waters of Japan are listed as deployments.

Major Overseas Deployments for 1984				
Departure	**Return**	**Air Group**	**Carrier**	**Area of Operations**
13 Jan 1984	01 Aug 1984	CVW-2	CV-63	WestPac/IO
02 Apr 1984	20 Oct 1984	CVW-17	CV-60	Med
24 Apr 1984	14 Nov 1984	CVW-1	CV-66	Carib/Med/IO
08 May 1984	20 Jun 1984	CVW-7	CVN-69	Carib/NorLant
30 May 1984	20 Dec 1984	CVW-11	CVN-65	WestPac/IO/NorPac
10 Oct 1984	08 May 1985	CVW-7	CVN-69	Med
15 Oct 1984	12 Dec 1984	CVW-5	CV-41*	WestPac
16 Oct 1984	19 Feb 1985	CVW-6	CV-62	Med/IO
18 Oct 1984	24 May 1985	CVW-15	CVN-70	NorPac/WestPac/IO

* *Midway* (CV 41) with CVW-5 and its assigned squadrons were forward deployed and homeported overseas at Naval Station Yokosuka, Japan. Only operations outside the home waters of Japan are listed as deployments.

Major Overseas Deployments for 1985				
Departure	**Return**	**Air Group**	**Carrier**	**Area of Operations**
01 Feb 1985	28 Mar 1985	CVW-5	CV-41*	WestPac
21 Feb 1985	24 Aug 1985	CVW-14	CV-64	WestPac/IO
08 Mar 1985	04 Oct 1985	CVW-8	CVN-68	Carib/Med
10 Jun 1985	14 Oct 1985	CVW-5	CV-41*	IO/WestPac
08 Jul 1985	22 Aug 1985	CVW-7	CVN-69	Carib
24 Jul 1985	21 Dec 1985	CVW-9	CV-63	WestPac/IO
24 Aug 1985	09 Oct 1985	CVW-1	CV-66	NorLant
25 Aug 1985	16 Apr 1986	CVW-17	CV-60	Med/IO
01 Oct 1985	19 May 1986	CVW-13	CV-43	Med
15 Nov 1985	12 Dec 1985	CVW-5	CV-41*	WestPac

* *Midway* (CV 41) with CVW-5 and its assigned squadrons were forward deployed and homeported overseas at Naval Station Yokosuka, Japan. Only operations outside the home waters of Japan are listed as deployments.

Major Overseas Deployments for 1986				
Departure	**Return**	**Air Group**	**Carrier**	**Area of Operations**
15 Jan 1986	12 Aug 1986	CVW-11	CVN-65	World Cruise
17 Jan 1986	30 Mar 1986	CVW-5	CV-41*	WestPac
10 Mar 1986	10 Sep 1986	CVW-1	CV-66	Med
02 Jun 1986	10 Nov 1986	CVW-6	CV-59	Med
12 Aug 1986	05 Feb 1987	CVW-15	CVN-70	NorPac/WestPac/IO
15 Aug 1986	16 Oct 1986	CVW-8	CVN-68	NorLant
18 Aug 1986	03 Mar 1987	CVW-3	CV-67	Med
18 Aug 1986	20 Oct 1986	CVW-2	CV-61	NorPac/WestPac
04 Sep 1986	20 Oct 1986	CVW-14	CV-64	NorPac
30 Dec 1986	26 Jul 1987	CVW-8	CVN-68	Med/SoLant/West Coast

* *Midway* (CV 41) with CVW-5 and its assigned squadrons were forward deployed and homeported overseas at Naval Station Yokosuka, Japan. Only operations outside the home waters of Japan are listed as deployments.

Major Overseas Deployments for 1987				
Departure	**Return**	**Air Group**	**Carrier**	**Area of Operations**
03 Jan 1987	29 Jun 1987	CVW-9	CV-63	World Cruise
09 Jan 1987	20 Mar 1987	CVW-5	CV-41*	WestPac
02 Mar 1987	29 Apr 1987	CVW-2	CV-61	NorPac

Major Overseas Deployments for 1987

Departure	Return	Air Group	Carrier	Area of Operations
11 Apr 1987	13 Oct 1987	CVW-14	CV-64	WestPac/IO
23 Apr 1987	13 Jul 1987	CVW-5	CV-41*	WestPac
05 Jun 1987	17 Nov 1987	CVW-17	CV-60	Med
14 Jul 1987	29 Dec 1987	CVW-2	CV-61	WestPac/IO
28 Aug 1987	09 Oct 1987	CVW-6	CV-59	NorLant
29 Sep 1987	28 Mar 1988	CVW-13	CV-43	Med
15 Oct 1987	12 Apr 1988	CVW-5	CV-41*	WestPac/IO
25 Oct 1987	24 Nov 1987	CVW-11	CVN-65	NorPac

* *Midway* (CV 41) with CVW-5 and its assigned squadrons were forward deployed and homeported overseas at Naval Station Yokosuka, Japan. Only operations outside the home waters of Japan are listed as deployments.

Major Overseas Deployments for 1988

Departure	Return	Air Group	Carrier	Area of Operations
05 Jan 1988	03 Jul 1988	CVW-11	CVN-65	WestPac/IO/NorPac
29 Feb 1988	29 Aug 1988	CVW-7	CVN-69	Med
25 Apr 1988	07 Oct 1988	CVW-6	CV-59	Med/IO/NorLant
15 Jun 1988	14 Dec 1988	CVW-15	CVN-70	NorPac/WestPac/IO
02 Aug 1988	01 Feb 1989	CVW-3	CV-67	Med
25 Aug 1988	11 Oct 1988	CVW-8	CVN-71	NorLant
02 Sep 1988	02 Mar 1989	CVW-9	CVN-68	WestPac/IO
18 Oct 1988	09 Nov 1988	CVW-5	CV-41*	WestPac
01 Dec 1988	01 Jun 1989	CVW-14	CV-64	WestPac/IO
30 Dec 1988	30 Jun 1989	CVW-8	CVN-71	Med

* *Midway* (CV 41) with CVW-5 and its assigned squadrons were forward deployed and homeported overseas at Naval Station Yokosuka, Japan. Only operations outside the home waters of Japan are listed as deployments.

Major Overseas Deployments for 1989

Departure	Return	Air Group	Carrier	Area of Operations
21 Jan 1989	24 Feb 1989	CVW-5	CV-41*	WestPac
08 Feb 1989	03 Apr 1989	CVW-1	CV-66	Carib/NorLant
24 Feb 1989	24 Aug 1989	CVW-2	CV-61	WestPac/IO
27 Feb 1989	09 Apr 1989	CVW-5	CV-41*	WestPac
11 May 1989	10 Nov 1989	CVW-1	CV-66	Med/IO
31 May 1989	25 Jul 1989	CVW-5	CV-41*	WestPac
31 May 1989	30 Sep 1989	CVW-13	CV-43	Med
15 Jun 1989	09 Jul 1989	CVW-9	CVN-68	NorPac
15 Aug 1989	11 Dec 1989	CVW-5	CV-41*	WestPac/IO
05 Sep 1989	09 Nov 1989	CVW-15	CVN-70	NorPac/WestPac
16 Sep 1989	19 Oct 1989	CVW-14	CV-64	NorPac
17 Sep 1989	16 Mar 1990	CVW-11	CVN-65	World Cruise
04 Nov 1989	12 Apr 1990	CVW-6	CV-59	Med

* *Midway* (CV 41) with CVW-5 and its assigned squadrons were forward deployed and homeported overseas at Naval Station Yokosuka, Japan. Only operations outside the home waters of Japan are listed as deployments.

Major Overseas Deployments for 1990				
Departure	Return	Air Group	Carrier	Area of Operations
25 Jan 1990	06 Apr 1990	CVW-5	CV-41*	WestPac
01 Feb 1990	31 Jul 1990	CVW-15	CVN-70	WestPac/IO
08 Mar 1990	12 Sep 1990	CVW-7	CVN-69	Med/Red Sea
23 Jun 1990	20 Dec 1990	CVW-14	CV-62	WestPac/IO/Persian Gulf
07 Aug 1990	28 Mar 1991	CVW-17	CV-60	Med/Red Sea
15 Aug 1990	28 Mar 1991	CVW-3	CV-67	Med/Red Sea
02 Oct 1990	17 Apr 1991	CVW-5	CV-41*	WestPac/IO/Persian Gulf
08 Dec 1990	08 Jun 1991	CVW-2	CV-61	WestPac/IO/Persian Gulf
28 Dec 1990	18 Apr 1991	CVW-1	CV-66	Med/Red Sea/Persian Gulf
28 Dec 1990	28 Jun 1991	CVW-8	CVN-71	Med/Red Sea/Persian Gulf

* *Midway* (CV 41) with CVW-5 and its assigned squadrons were forward deployed and homeported overseas at Naval Station Yokosuka, Japan. Only operations outside the home waters of Japan are listed as deployments.

Major Overseas Deployments for 1991				
Departure	Return	Air Group	Carrier	Area of Operations
25 Feb 1991	24 Aug 1991	CVW-9	CVN-68	WestPac/IO/Persian Gulf
28 May 1991	28 Nov 1991	CVW-11	CVN-72	WestPac/IO/Persian Gulf
30 May 1991	21 Dec 1991	CVW-6	CV-59	Med
05 Aug 1991	11 Sep 1991	*	CV-62*	WestPac
10 Aug 1991	14 Sep 1991	*	CV-41*	WestPac
26 Sep 1991	02 Apr 1992	CVW-7	CVN-69	Med/Red Sea/Persian Gulf/NorLant
18 Oct 1991	11 Dec 1991	CVW-15	CV-63†	Around Cape Horn (east to west)
02 Dec 1991	06 Jun 1992	CVW-1	CV-66	NorLant/Med/Red Sea/Persian Gulf

* Change of homeports for *Midway* (CV 41) and *Independence* (CV 62) as well as a swap of air wings between the two in Hawaii. *Midway*'s CVW-5 returned to Yokosuka, Japan, on board *Independence* and *Independence*'s CVW-14 returned to San Diego on board *Midway*.

† *Kitty Hawk* (CV 63) conducted a homeport change from East to West Coasts with a transit around Cape Horn.

Major Overseas Deployments for 1992				
Departure	Return	Air Group	Carrier	Area of Operations
15 Apr 1992	13 Oct 1992	CVW-5	CV-62*	Australia/IO/Persian Gulf
06 May 1992	06 Nov 1992	CVW-17	CV-60	Med
01 Aug 1992	31 Jan 1993	CVW-2	CV-61	IO/Persian Gulf
07 Oct 1992	07 Apr 1993	CVW-3	CV-67	Med
03 Nov 1992	03 May 1993	CVW-15	CV-63	IO/Persian Gulf

* *Independence* (CV 62) with CVW-5 and its assigned squadrons were forward deployed and homeported overseas at Naval Station Yokosuka, Japan. Only operations outside the home waters of Japan are listed as deployments.

Major Overseas Deployments for 1993				
Departure	Return	Air Group	Carrier	Area of Operations
02 Feb 1993	29 Jul 1993	CVW-9	CVN-68	IO/Persian Gulf
11 Mar 1993	08 Sep 1993	CVW-8*	CVN-71	Med
27 May 1993	22 Jul 1993	CVW-2	CV-64†	Around Cape Horn (east to west)
15 Jun 1993	15 Dec 1993	CVW-11	CVN-72	WestPac/IO
11 Aug 1993	05 Feb 1994	CVW-1	CV-66	Med
17 Nov 1993	17 Mar 1993	CVW-5	CV-62‡	WestPac/IO

* *Theodore Roosevelt* (CVN 71) and CVW-8 deployed to the Mediterranean Sea augmented with a special Marine Air-Ground Task Force consisting of VMFA-312 and HMH-362.

† *Constellation* (CV 64) conducted a homeport change from East to West Coasts with a transit around Cape Horn.

‡ *Independence* (CV 62) with CVW-5 and its assigned squadrons were forward deployed and homeported overseas at Naval Station Yokosuka, Japan. Only operations outside the home waters of Japan are listed as deployments.

Major Overseas Deployments for 1994

Departure	Return	Air Group	Carrier	Area of Operations
11 Jan 1994	24 Jun 1994	CVW-17	CV-60	Med
18 Feb 1994	15 Aug 1994	CVW-14	CVN-70	WestPac/IO
20 May 1994	17 Nov 1994	CVW-7	CVN-73	Med
24 Jun 1994	22 Dec 1994	CVW-15	CV-63	WestPac/IO
12 Sep 1994	22 Oct 1994	*	CV-66	Haiti/Carib
13 Sep 1994	23 Sep 1994	†	CVN-69	Haiti/Carib
20 Oct 1994	14 Apr 1994	CVW-3	CVN-69	Med
10 Nov 1994	10 May 1995	CVW-2	CV-64	WestPac/IO

* *America* (CV 66) deployed to Haiti for Operation Uphold Democracy with 160th Army Special Operations Aviation Regiment (Airborne) and 64 helicopters on board. The carrier did not have a Navy air wing or squadron embarked.

† *Dwight D. Eisenhower* (CVN 69) deployed to Haiti for Operational Uphold Democracy with the 10th Army Mountain Division, 51 helicopters, and 1,800 troops embarked.

Major Overseas Deployments for 1995

Departure	Return	Air Group	Carrier	Area of Operations
22 Mar 1995	22 Sep 1995	CVW-8	CVN-71	Med/Red Sea/Persian Gulf
10 Apr 1995	09 Oct 1995	CVW-11	CVN-72	WestPac/IO/Persian Gulf
19 Aug 1995	18 Nov 1995	CVW-5	CV-62*	WestPac/IO/Persian Gulf
28 Aug 1995	24 Feb 1996	CVW-1	CV-66	Med/Red Sea/Persian Gulf
27 Nov 1995	20 May 1996	CVW-9	CVN-68	WestPac/IO/Persian Gulf

* *Independence* (CV 62) with CVW-5 and its assigned squadrons were forward deployed and homeported overseas at Naval Station Yokosuka, Japan. Only operations outside the home waters of Japan are listed as deployments.

Major Overseas Deployments for 1996

Departure	Return	Air Group	Carrier	Area of Operations
26 Jan 1996	23 Jul 1996	CVW-7	CVN-73	Med/Persian Gulf
05 Mar 1996	24 Mar 1996	CVW-5	CV-62*	China/Taiwan
11 Apr 1996	09 Oct 1996	CVW-11	CV-63	WestPac
14 May 1996	14 Nov 1996	CVW-14	CVN-70	WestPac/IO/Persian Gulf
28 Jun 1996	20 Dec 1996	CVW-17	CVN-65	Med/Persian Gulf
25 Nov 1996	22 May 1997	CVW-3	CVN-71	Med/Persian Gulf

* *Independence* (CV 62) with CVW-5 and its assigned squadrons were forward deployed and homeported overseas at Naval Station Yokosuka, Japan. Only operations outside the home waters of Japan are listed as deployments.

Major Overseas Deployments for 1997

Departure	Return	Air Group	Carrier	Area of Operations
15 Feb 1997	10 Jun 1997	CVW-5	CV-62*	WestPac/IO
01 Apr 1997	01 Oct 1997	CVW-2	CV-64	WestPac/IO
29 Apr 1997	28 Oct 1997	CVW-8	CV-67	Med/Persian Gulf
01 Sep 1997	01 Mar 1998	CVW-9	CVN-68	WestPac/IO
03 Oct 1997	03 Apr 1998	CVW-1	CVN-73	Med/Persian Gulf

* *Independence* (CV 62) with CVW-5 and its assigned squadrons were forward deployed and homeported overseas at Naval Station Yokosuka, Japan. Only operations outside the home waters of Japan are listed as deployments.

Major Overseas Deployments for 1998

Departure	Return	Air Group	Carrier	Area of Operations
23 Jan 1998	06 Jun 1998	CVW-5	CV-62*	IO/Persian Gulf
26 Feb 1998	26 Aug 1998	CVW-7	CVN-74	Med/Persian Gulf/WestPac
10 Jun 1998	10 Dec 1998	CVW-17	CVN-69	Med/Adriatic Sea/Persian Gulf
Jul 1998	15 Aug 1998	CVW-5	CV-63†	WestPac
06 Jul 1998	Jul 1998	†	CV-62†	WestPac
11 Jul 1998	07 Dec 1998	CVW-14	CVN-72	WestPac/IO/Persian Gulf
06 Nov 1998	06 May 1999	CVW-3	CVN-65	Med/Persian Gulf/Adriatic Sea
06 Nov 1998	06 May 1999	CVW-11	CVN-70	WestPac

* *Independence* (CV 62) with CVW-5 and its assigned squadrons were forward deployed and homeported overseas at Naval Station Yokosuka, Japan. Only operations outside the home waters of Japan are listed as deployments.

† Change of homeports for *Kitty Hawk* (CV 63) and *Independence* (CV 62) as well as a transfer of CVW-5 from *Independence* to *Kitty Hawk*. The transfer of Air Wing 5 took place in Hawaii on 18 July 1998. CVW-5 returned to Yokosuka, Japan, on board *Kitty Hawk* and *Independence* returned to the West Coast in July 1998 for decommissioning.

Major Overseas Deployments for 1999

Departure	Return	Air Group	Carrier	Area of Operations
02 Mar 1999	25 Aug 1999	CVW-5	CV-63*	IO/Persian Gulf
26 Mar 1999	22 Sep 1999	CVW-8	CVN-71	Med/Persian Gulf/Adriatic Sea
18 Jun 1999	18 Dec 1999	CVW-2	CV-64	WestPac
17 Sep 1999	17 Mar 2000	CVW-1	CV-67	Med/Persian Gulf

* *Kitty Hawk* (CV 63) with CVW-5 and its assigned squadrons were forward deployed and homeported overseas at Naval Station Yokosuka, Japan. Only operations outside the home waters of Japan are listed as deployments.

Major Overseas Deployments for 2000

Departure	Return	Air Group	Carrier	Area of Operations
07 Jan 2000	03 Jul 2000	CVW-9	CVN-74	IO/Persian Gulf
18 Feb 2000	18 Aug 2000	CVW-7	CVN-69	Med/Persian Gulf
11 Apr 2000	05 Jun 2000	CVW-5	CV-63*	WestPac
21 Jun 2000	19 Dec 2000	CVW-17	CVN-73	Med/Persian Gulf
14 Aug 2000	12 Feb 2001	CVW-14	CVN-72	IO/Persian Gulf
26 Sep 2000	20 Nov 2000	CVW-5	CV-63*	WestPac
28 Nov 2000	23 May 2001	CVW-3	CVN-75	Med/Persian Gulf

* *Kitty Hawk* (CV 63) with CVW-5 and its assigned squadrons were forward deployed and homeported overseas at Naval Station Yokosuka, Japan. Only operations outside the home waters of Japan are listed as deployments.

Major Overseas Deployments for 2001

Departure	Return	Air Group	Carrier	Area of Operations
02 Mar 2001	11 Jun 2001	CVW-5	CV-63*	WestPac
15 Mar 2001	15 Sep 2001	CVW-2	CV-64	WestPac/IO
25 Apr 2001	10 Nov 2001	CVW-8	CVN-65	Med/IO
23 Jul 2001	23 Jan 2002	CVW-11	CVN-70	IO
19 Sep 2001	27 Mar 2002	CVW-1	CVN-71	Med/IO
01 Oct 2001	23 Dec 2001	CVW-5	CV-63*	IO
12 Nov 2001	12 May 2002	CVW-9	CVN-74	IO

* *Kitty Hawk* (CV 63) with CVW-5 and its assigned squadrons were forward deployed and homeported overseas at Naval Station Yokosuka, Japan. Only operations outside the home waters of Japan are listed as deployments.

Major Overseas Deployments for 2002

Departure	Return	Air Group	Carrier	Area of Operations
07 Feb 2002	17 Aug 2002	CVW-7	CV-67	Med/IO
20 Jun 2002	20 Dec 2002	CVW-17	CVN-73	Med/IO
24 Jul 2002	20 May 2003	CVW-14	CVN-72	WestPac/IO
02 Nov 2002	02 May 2003	CVW-2	CV-64	WestPac/IO
05 Dec 2002	04 Jun 2003	CVW-3	CVN-75	Med/IO

Major Overseas Deployments for 2003

Departure	Return	Air Group	Carrier	Area of Operations
23 Jan 2003	06 May 2003	CVW-5	CV-63*	IO/Persian Gulf
04 Feb 2003	29 May 2003	CVW-8	CVN-71	Med
07 Feb 2003	19 Sep 2003	CVW-9	CVN-70	WestPac
03 Mar 2003	05 Nov 2003	CVW-11	CVN-68	WestPac/IO/Persian Gulf
01 Oct 2003	29 Feb 2004	CVW-1	CVN-65	IO/Persian Gulf

* *Kitty Hawk* (CV 63) with CVW-5 and its assigned squadrons were forward deployed and homeported overseas at Naval Station Yokosuka, Japan. Only operations outside the home waters of Japan are listed as deployments.

Major Overseas Deployments for 2004

Departure	Return	Air Group	Carrier	Area of Operations
20 Jan 2004	26 Jul 2004	CVW-7	CVN-73	Med/Persian Gulf
24 May 2004	01 Nov 2004	CVW-14	CVN-74	WestPac
07 Jun 2004	13 Dec 2004	CVW-17	CV-67	Med/Persian Gulf
13 Oct 2004	18 Apr 2005	CVW-3	CVN-75	Med/Persian Gulf
19 Oct 2004	01 Mar 2005	CVW-2	CVN-72	WestPac

Major Overseas Deployments for 2005

Departure	Return	Air Group	Carrier	Area of Operations
01 Feb 2005	31 Jul 2005	CVW-9	CVN-70	WestPac/Persian Gulf/Atlantic
07 May 2005	08 Nov 2005	CVW-11	CVN-68	WestPac/Persian Gulf
23 May 2005	20 Aug 2005	CVW-5	CV-63*	WestPac
01 Sep 2005	11 Mar 2006	CVW-8	CVN-71	Med/Persian Gulf

* *Kitty Hawk* (CV 63) with CVW-5 and its assigned squadrons were forward deployed and homeported overseas at Naval Station Yokosuka, Japan. Only operations outside the home waters of Japan are listed as deployments.

Major Overseas Deployments for 2006

Departure	Return	Air Group	Carrier	Area of Operations
04 Jan 2006	06 Jul 2006	CVW-14	CVN-76	WestPac/IO/Persian Gulf
02 Feb 2006	08 Aug 2006	CVW-2	CVN-72	WestPac
02 May 2006	18 Nov 2006	CVW-1	CVN-65	Med/IO/Persian Gulf/WestPac
08 Jun 2006	15 Sep 2006	CVW-5	CV-63*	WestPac/IO
03 Oct 2006	23 May 2007	CVW-7	CVN-69	Med/IO/Persian Gulf

* *Kitty Hawk* (CV 63) with CVW-5 and its assigned squadrons were forward deployed and homeported overseas at Naval Station Yokosuka, Japan. Only operations outside the home waters of Japan are listed as deployments.

Major Overseas Deployments for 2007

Departure	Return	Air Group	Carrier	Area of Operations
20 Jan 2007	27 Aug 2007	CVW-9	CVN-74	IO/WestPac
27 Jan 2007	20 Apr 2007	CVW-14	CVN-76	WestPac
02 Apr 2007	30 Sep 2007	CVW-11	CVN-68	WestPac/IO/Persian Gulf
23 May 2007	21 Sep 2007	CVW-5	CV-63*	WestPac/IO
07 Jul 2007	19 Dec 2007	CVW-1	CVN-65	Med/IO/Persian Gulf
05 Nov 2007	04 Jun 2008	CVW-3	CVN-75	Med/IO/Persian Gulf

* *Kitty Hawk* (CV 63) with CVW-5 and its assigned squadrons were forward deployed and homeported overseas at Naval Station Yokosuka, Japan. Only operations outside the home waters of Japan are listed as deployments.

Major Overseas Deployments for 2008

Departure	Return	Air Group	Carrier	Area of Operations
24 Jan 2008	03 Jun 2008	CVW-11	CVN-68	WestPac
13 Mar 2008	12 Oct 2008	CVW-2	CVN-72	IO/Persian Gulf/North Arabian Sea
19 May 2008	25 Nov 2008	CVW-14	CVN-76	WestPac/North Arabian Sea
28 May 2008	07 Aug 2008	CVW-5	CV-63*	Yokosuka/Central Pacific/San Diego
08 Sep 2008	18 Apr 2009	CVW-8	CVN-71	NorLant
01 Oct 2008	21 Nov 2008	CVW-5	CVN-73†	WestPac

* *Kitty Hawk*'s (CV 63) final deployment concluded in San Diego, Calif., where the Navy's last conventionally powered carrier turned over duties as the forward-deployed carrier in the Pacific to *George Washington* (CVN 73). Originally scheduled to take place in Pearl Harbor, Hawaii, in June 2008, the turnover was rescheduled to August as *George Washington* underwent repairs following a shipboard fire in May.

† While not a major deployment, *George Washington*'s first underway period as the forward-deployed carrier is included in this listing.

Major Overseas Deployments for 2009

Departure	Return	Air Group	Carrier	Area of Operations
13 Jan 2009	10 Jul 2009	CVW-9	CVN-74	WestPac/NorPac
21 Feb 2009	30 Jul 2009	CVW-7	CVN-69	Med/North Arabian Sea
29 May 2009	10 Oct 2009	CVW-14	CVN-76	WestPac
10 Jun 2009	03 Sep 2009	CVW-5	CVN-73*	WestPac
31 Jul 2009	26 Mar 2010	CVW-11	CVN-68	WestPac
08 Sep 2008	18 Apr 2009	CVW-8	CVN-71	IO/Med/North Arabian Sea

* *George Washington* (CVN 73) forward deployed to WestPac.

Major Overseas Deployments for 2010

Departure	Return	Air Group	Carrier	Area of Operations
01 Jan 2010	31 Dec 2010	CVW-5	CVN-73*	WestPac
02 Jan 2010	28 Jul 2010	CVW-7	CVN-69	Med/IO
10 Feb 2010	08 Apr 2010	CVW-17	CVN-70	Carib/Central and South American waters (Com4thFlt)
21 May 2010	20 Dec 2010	CVW-3	CVN-75	Med/IO
07 Sep 2010	circa Mar 2011	CVW-2	CVN-72	WestPac/IO
14 Dec 2010	circa Jul 2011	CVW-1	CVN-65	Med/IO
21 Dec 2010	circa Jun 2011	CVW-17	CVN-70	WestPac/IO

' *George Washington* (CVN 73) forward deployed to WestPac.

Acronyms/Designations	
CV-9, CVA-9, CVS-9	Essex
CV-10, CVA-10, CVS-10	Yorktown
CV-11, CVA-11, CVS-11	Intrepid
CV-12, CVA-12 , CVS-12	Hornet
CV-14, CVA-14, CVS-14	Ticonderoga
CV-15, CVA-15, CVS-15	Randolph
CV-16, CVA-16, CVS-16	Lexington
CV-18, CVA-18, CVS-18	Wasp
CV-19, CVA-19	Hancock
CV-20, CVA-20, CVS-20	Bennington
CV-21, CVA-21, CVS-21	Boxer
CVL-26	Monterey
CVL-28	Cabot
CVL-29	Bataan
CV-31, CVA-31	Bon Homme Richard
CV-32, CVA-32, CVS-32	Leyte
CV-33, CVA-33, CVS-33	Kearsarge
CV-34, CVA-34	Oriskany
CV-36, CVA-36, CVS-36	Antietam
CV-37, CVA-37, CVS-37	Princeton
CV-38, CVA-38, CVS-38	Shangri-La
CV-39, CVA-39, CVS-39	Lake Champlain
CV-40, CVA-40, CVS-40	Tarawa
CVB-41, CVA-41, CV-41	Midway
CVB-42, CVA-42, CV-42	Franklin D. Roosevelt
CVB-43, CVA-43, CV-43	Coral Sea
CV-45, CVA-45, CVS-45	Valley Forge
CV-47, CVA-47, CVS-47	Philippine Sea
CVL-48	Saipan
CVL-49	Wright
CVA-59, CV-59	Forrestal
CVA-60, CV-60	Saratoga
CVA-61, CV-61	Ranger
CVA-62, CV-62	Independence
CVA-63, CV-63	Kitty Hawk
CVA-64, CV-64	Constellation
CVAN-65, CVN-65	Enterprise
CVA-66, CV-66	America
CVA-67, CV-67	John F. Kennedy
CVAN-68, CVN-68	Nimitz
CVN-69	Dwight D. Eisenhower
CVN-70	Carl Vinson
CVN-71	Theodore Roosevelt
CVN-72	Abraham Lincoln
CVN-73	George Washington
CVN-74	John C. Stennis
CVN-75	Harry S. Truman
CVN-76	Ronald Reagan
CVN-77	George H. W. Bush

Acronyms/Designations	
AirDet	Air Detachment
ATG	Air Task Group
CVAG	Attack Carrier Air Group
CVBG	Battle Carrier Air Group
CVG	Carrier Air Group
CVLG	Light Carrier Air Group
CVSG	Antisubmarine Carrier Air Group
CVW	Carrier Air Wing
HMR	Marine Helicopter Transport Squadron
HS	Helicopter Antisubmarine Squadron
HU	Helicopter Utility Squadron
MAG	Marine Air Group
VA	Attack Squadron
VAW	Carrier Airborne Early Warning Squadron
VC	Composite Squadron
VF	Fighter Squadron
VFAW	All-Weather Fighter Squadron
VMA	Marine Corps Attack Squadron
VMF	Marine Corps Fighter Squadron
VMO	Marine Observation Squadron
VS	Antisubmarine Squadron
VU	Utility Squadron

[1] Area of Operations abbreviations:	
Carib	Caribbean Sea
EastLant	Eastern Atlantic Ocean
IO	Indian Ocean
Med	Mediterranean Sea
NorLant	North Atlantic Ocean
SoLant	South Atlantic Ocean
WestPac	Western Pacific Ocean

CHAPTER 29

Post–Korean War Amphibious Assault Ship Deployments by Year

This deployment list covers those by amphibious assault ships with the designations LPH, LHA, LHD, and CVHA. Departure and return dates are normally from the ship's homeport or other stateside port. This listing is only for major overseas deployments or operations. It does not include normal deployments to the Caribbean or Hawaii for training.

Major Overseas Deployments for 1957			
Departure	Return	Ship	Area of Operations*
10 Jul 1957	11 Dec 1957	CVHA-1	WestPac

Major Overseas Deployments for 1958			
None			

Major Overseas Deployments for 1959			
Departure	Return	Ship	Area of Operations
01 Apr 1959	18 Nov 1959	LPH-6	WestPac

Major Overseas Deployments for 1960			
Departure	Return	Ship	Area of Operations
10 Feb 1960	11 Jul 1960	LPH-5	WestPac

Major Overseas Deployments for 1961			
Departure	Return	Ship	Area of Operations
01 Mar 1961	circa Aug 1961	LPH-6	WestPac
03 Jun 1961	08 Aug 1961	LPH-4	Carib, unrest in Dominican Republic
09 Sep 1961	Jun 1962	LPH-5	WestPac
Oct 1961	Dec 1961	LPH-8	Carib/Dominican Republic
Nov 1961	Dec 1961	LPH-6	West to East Coast via Panama Canal

Major Overseas Deployments for 1962			
Departure	Return	Ship	Area of Operations
06 Jan 1962	23 Jan 1962	LPH-8	East to West Coast via Panama Canal
16 Apr 1962	Dec 1962	LPH-8	WestPac/Indochina
18 Apr 1962	10 Aug 1962	LPH-2	Pacific
Sep 1962	Nov 1962	LPH-5	Pacific nuclear test series
Oct 1962	Dec 1962	LPH-4	Cuban Missile Crisis
14 Oct 1962	04 Dec 1962	LPH-6	Cuban Missile Crisis
21 Oct 1962	03 Dec 1962	LPH-3	Cuban Missile Crisis
27 Oct 1962	13 Dec 1962	LPH-2	Panama Canal/Carib

Major Overseas Deployments for 1963

Departure	Return	Ship	Area of Operations
05 Feb 1963	26 Oct 1963	LPH-5	WestPac
05 Jun 1963	13 Jul 1963	LPH-6	NorLant
30 Aug 1963	28 Apr 1964	LPH-2	WestPac/Vietnam

Major Overseas Deployments for 1964

Departure	Return	Ship	Area of Operations
11 Feb 1964	May 1964	LPH-7	Carib/Panama
20 Mar 1964	05 Nov 1964	LPH-8	WestPac/Vietnam
16 Sep 1964	29 May 1965	LPH-5	WestPac/Vietnam
07 Oct 1964	29 Nov 1964	LPH-3	EastLant/NorLant
07 Oct 1964	circa Nov 1964	LPH-7	EastLant/NorLant
12 Oct 1964	28 Nov 1964	LPH-4	EastLant/NorLant

Major Overseas Deployments for 1965

Departure	Return	Ship	Area of Operations
08 Mar 1965	17 Apr 1965	LPH-8	Transport Marines to Okinawa
01 Apr 1965	29 Jun 1965	LPH-4	Carib/Dominican Republic Crisis
12 Apr 1965	17 Nov 1965	LPH-2	WestPac/Vietnam
24 May 1965	01 Jul 1965	LPH-8	Transport Marines to Okinawa
10 Aug 1965	28 Oct 1965	LPH-4	Med/IO/WestPac, transported Army 1st Cavalry Div. (Air Mobile) to South Vietnam
30 Aug 1965	09 Apr 1966	LPH-8	WestPac/Vietnam
29 Nov 1965	04 Mar 1966	LPH-9	Carib/Central America

Major Overseas Deployments for 1966

Departure	Return	Ship	Area of Operations
08 Feb 1966	06 Mar 1966	LPH-4	SoLant, Project Apollo recovery
16 Feb 1966	02 Sep 1966	LPH-5	WestPac/Vietnam
26 Apr 1966	13 Jul 1966	LPH-4	Med/IO/WestPac, transit of HMM-265 to South Vietnam
Jul 1966	Jul 1966	LPH-7	Gemini 10 recovery
09 Jul 1966	08 Apr 1967	LPH-2	WestPac/Vietnam
06 Sep 1966	18 Sep 1966	LPH-9	Carib/Gemini 11 recovery
07 Sep 1966	01 Dec 1966	LPH-8	WestPac/Vietnam
06 Nov 1966	22 Nov 1966	LPH-10	East to West Coast via Panama Canal
28 Nov 1966	09 Apr 1967	LPH-9	Carib

Major Overseas Deployments for 1967

Departure	Return	Ship	Area of Operations
24 Jan 1967	08 Feb 1967	LPH-3	East to West Coast via Panama Canal
30 Jan 1967	19 Jun 1967	LPH-5	WestPac/Vietnam
10 Mar 1967	05 Dec 1967	LPH-3	WestPac/Vietnam
01 May 1967	23 Dec 1967	LPH-10	WestPac/Vietnam
10 Aug 1967	13 Dec 1967	LPH-7	Carib
02 Oct 1967	28 Jun 1968	LPH-2	WestPac/Vietnam
10 Nov 1967	03 Aug 1968	LPH-8	WestPac/Vietnam
06 Dec 1967	23 Mar 1968	LPH-9	Carib

Major Overseas Deployments for 1968

Departure	Return	Ship	Area of Operations
Mar 1968	Apr 1968	LPH-3	Pacific, Apollo 6 Recovery
01 May 1968	16 Dec 1968	LPH-5	WestPac/Vietnam
10 Jun 1968	06 Nov 1968	LPH-7	Carib/Panama
12 Jun 1968	19 Mar 1969	LPH-10	WestPac/Vietnam
02 Nov 1968	26 Jun 1969	LPH-3	WestPac/Vietnam

Major Overseas Deployments for 1969

Departure	Return	Ship	Area of Operations
30 Jan 1969	23 Sep 1969	LPH-8	WestPac/Vietnam
12 Feb 1969	12 Jul 1969	LPH-9	Carib
18 Feb 1969	03 Mar 1969	LPH-11	East to West Coast via Panama Canal
Mar 1969	Mar 1969	LPH-7	Apollo 9 recovery
28 Apr 1969	09 Jun 1969	LPH-5	Pacific, Apollo 10 recovery
01 May 1969	27 Oct 1969	LPH-2	WestPac/Vietnam
01 Aug 1969	07 May 1970	LPH-11	WestPac/Vietnam
12 Sep 1969	11 Oct 1969	LPH-5	NorPac, nuclear testing
15 Sep 1969	25 Nov 1969	LPH-9	Carib
01 Nov 1969	16 Feb 1970	LPH-10	WestPac/Vietnam

Major Overseas Deployments for 1970

Departure	Return	Ship	Area of Operations
12 Jan 1970	22 May 1970	LPH-7	Carib/Panama
27 Feb 1970	24 Jun 1970	LPH-10	WestPac/Vietnam
21 Mar 1970	01 May 1970	LPH-2	Pacific
Apr 1970	Apr 1970	LPH-2	Apollo 13 recovery
May 1970	Dec 1970	LPH-3	WestPac/Vietnam
12 May 1970	16 Jul 1970	LPH-9	Carib/West coast of South America
24 Jul 1970	07 Sep 1970	LPH-7	NorLant
17 Sep 1970	21 Nov 1970	LPH-9	Med
02 Nov 1970	07 Jun 1971	LPH-2	WestPac/Vietnam

Major Overseas Deployments for 1971

Departure	Return	Ship	Area of Operations
07 Jan 1971	25 Feb 1971	LPH-11	Pacific, Apollo 14 recovery
16 Apr 1971	10 Oct 1971	LPH-9	Med
30 Apr 1971	16 Jun 1971	LPH-3	WestPac
01 May 1971	05 Nov 1971	LPH-11	WestPac
08 Jul 1971	16 Aug 1971	LPH-3	Pacific, Apollo 15 recovery
Sep 1971	Mar 1972	LPH-12	Med
21 Sep 1971	09 Nov 1971	LPH-7	Med
01 Oct 1971	20 Aug 1972	LPH-10	WestPac/Vietnam/IO

Major Overseas Deployments for 1972			
Departure	**Return**	**Ship**	**Area of Operations**
22 Feb 1972	22 Aug 1972	LPH-7	Med
20 May 1972	03 Jun 1972	LPH-2	West to East Coast via Panama Canal
17 Jul 1972	13 May 1973	LPH-11	WestPac/Vietnam
28 Jul 1972	26 Jan 1973	LPH-2	Med
Aug 1972	Oct 1972	LPH-12	NorLant
09 Nov 1972	01 Sep 1973	LPH-12	Panama Canal/WestPac/Vietnam/IO/South Atlantic†

Major Overseas Deployments for 1973			
Departure	**Return**	**Ship**	**Area of Operations**
06 Mar 1973	27 Oct 1973	LPH-10	WestPac/Vietnam (Operation Endsweep)
04 May 1973	20 Dec 1973	LPH-7	Med
18 Aug 1973	26 Sep 1973	LPH-11	Pacific, Skylab 3 recovery
20 Sep 1973	26 Apr 1974	LPH-3	WestPac
15 Oct 1973	May 1974	LPH-2	Med

Major Overseas Deployments for 1974			
Departure	**Return**	**Ship**	**Area of Operations**
27 Jan 1974	09 Feb 1974	LPH-11	Pacific, Skylab 4 recovery
16 Mar 1974	31 Aug 1974	LPH-11	WestPac
29 Apr 1974	31 Oct 1974	LPH-12	Med
27 Jul 1974	11 Feb 1975	LPH-10	WestPac
20 Sep 1974	26 Mar 1975	LPH-9	NorLant/Med

Major Overseas Deployments for 1975			
Departure	**Return**	**Ship**	**Area of Operations**
08 Jan 1975	20 Aug 1975	LPH-3	WestPac
25 Feb 1975	21 Aug 1975	LPH-2	Med
05 Jul 1975	23 Mar 1976	LPH-11	WestPac
29 Jul 1975	04 Feb 1976	LPH-12	Med
25 Sep 1975	10 Nov 1975	LPH-7	Med

Major Overseas Deployments for 1976			
Departure	**Return**	**Ship**	**Area of Operations**
12 Jan 1976	15 Jul 1976	LPH-7	Med
16 Feb 1976	25 Oct 1976	LPH-10	WestPac
07 Jun 1976	11 Dec 1976	LPH-2	Med
07 Jul 1976	06 Aug 1976	LPH-1	East to West Coast via Panama Canal
01 Sep 1976	10 Nov 1976	LPH-7	NorLant
25 Sep 1976	05 May 1977	LPH-3	WestPac
11 Nov 1976	12 May 1977	LPH-9	Med/IO

Major Overseas Deployments for 1977			
Departure	**Return**	**Ship**	**Area of Operations**
08 Sep 1977	13 Mar 1978	LPH-7	Med
03 Nov 1977	22 Jul 1978	LPH-10	WestPac

Major Overseas Deployments for 1978			
Departure	Return	Ship	Area of Operations
16 Jan 1978	19 Apr 1978	LPH-12	SoLant/Africa/South America
27 Feb 1978	25 Aug 1978	LPH-9	Med
21 Jun 1978	05 Oct 1978	LPH-11	WestPac
27 Jul 1978	07 Feb 1979	LPH-2	Med
22 Aug 1978	31 Oct 1978	LPH-7	NorLant
31 Aug 1978	11 Apr 1979	LPH-3	WestPac

Major Overseas Deployments for 1979			
Departure	Return	Ship	Area of Operations
10 Jan 1979	19 Jun 1979	LPH-12	Med
01 Mar 1979	21 Sep 1979	LHA-1	WestPac
23 May 1979	07 Nov 1979	LPH-9	Med
11 Jun 1979	09 Aug 1979	LHA-2	Carib/Nicaragua
23 Jul 1979	14 Feb 1980	LPH-10	WestPac
12 Sep 1979	27 Feb 1980	LPH-2	Med

Major Overseas Deployments for 1980			
Departure	Return	Ship	Area of Operations
04 Jan 1980	03 Jul 1980	LPH-3	WestPac/IO
15 Feb 1980	18 Apr 1980	LHA-2	NorLant
13 May 1980	10 Jun 1980	LHA-5	East to West Coast via Panama Canal
23 May 1980	22 Nov 1980	LPH-11	WestPac/IO
04 Jun 1980	09 Nov 1980	LPH-7	Med/IO
27 Aug 1980	25 Feb 1981	LHA-2	NorLant/Med/IO
14 Oct 1980	16 Apr 1981	LHA-1	WestPac/IO

Major Overseas Deployments for 1981			
Departure	Return	Ship	Area of Operations
20 Jan 1981	02 Jul 1981	LPH-2	Med
22 Jan 1981	04 Aug 1981	LHA-3	WestPac/IO
04 Feb 1981	16 Apr 1981	LPH-9	NorLant
13 Apr 1981	29 Jun 1981	LHA-4	Med
03 Jun 1981	11 Nov 1981	LPH-7	Med
25 Jun 1981	23 Dec 1981	LPH-3	WestPac/IO
03 Sep 1981	24 Feb 1982	LHA-2	Med/IO
12 Nov 1981	15 May 1982	LPH-10	WestPac/IO

Major Overseas Deployments for 1982			
Departure	Return	Ship	Area of Operations
19 Jan 1982	30 Jun 1982	LHA-4	Med/IO
27 Jan 1982	15 Apr 1982	LPH-7	NorLant
31 Jan 1982	19 Apr 1982	LPH-9	NorLant
27 Mar 1982	04 Oct 1982	LHA-5	WestPac
15 Jul 1982	20 Sep 1982	LPH-11	WestPac
20 Aug 1982	18 Oct 1982	LPH-7	NorLant
23 Aug 1982	10 Mar 1983	LPH-12	NorLant/Med
24 Aug 1982	30 Oct 1982	LHA-4	NorLant
24 Aug 1982	24 Feb 1983	LHA-3	WestPac/IO

Major Overseas Deployments for 1983

Departure	Return	Ship	Area of Operations
26 Jan 1983	27 Jun 1983	LPH-7	Med/Carib
30 Jan 1983	14 Jul 1983	LPH-11	WestPac
31 Jan 1983	19 Apr 1983	LPH-9	NorLant
27 Apr 1983	23 Oct 1983	LPH-10	WestPac/IO
27 Apr 1983	22 Nov 1983	LHA-1	WestPac/IO/Med
10 May 1983	08 Dec 1983	LPH-2	Med
11 Aug 1983	21 Oct 1983	LPH-12	NorLant
20 Aug 1983	02 Sep 1983	LHA-4	Central America
02 Sep 1983	11 Nov 1983	LHA-2	Carib/Grenada‡
12 Sep 1983	06 Mar 1984	LHA-5	WestPac/IO
18 Oct 1983	02 May 1984	LPH-9	Carib/Med (Grenada Operation Urgent Fury)
09 Nov 1983	02 Dec 1983	LPH-7	Carib/Central America

Major Overseas Deployments for 1984

Departure	Return	Ship	Area of Operations
17 Jan 1984	27 Jul 1984	LHA-3	WestPac
13 Feb 1984	28 Apr 1984	LHA-2	NorLant
13 Feb 1984	24 Aug 1984	LHA-4	NorLant/Med
14 Feb 1984	10 Apr 1984	LPH-12	NorLant
30 May 1984	19 Sep 1984	LPH-3	WestPac
30 May 1984	06 Dec 1984	LPH-11	WestPac/IO
25 Jul 1984	20 Feb 1985	LPH-12	Med
18 Oct 1984	26 Apr 1985	LHA-1	WestPac

Major Overseas Deployments for 1985

Departure	Return	Ship	Area of Operations
22 Jan 1985	09 Aug 1985	LHA-2	Med
04 Apr 1985	04 Sep 1985	LHA-5	WestPac
02 Jul 1985	20 Dec 1985	LPH-2	Med
09 Aug 1985	16 Dec 1985	LPH-3	WestPac
27 Aug 1985	12 Oct 1985	LHA-4	NorLant
21 Nov 1985	04 Jun 1986	LPH-7	Med

Major Overseas Deployments for 1986

Departure	Return	Ship	Area of Operations
16 Jan 1986	16 Sep 1986	LPH-11	WestPac
07 May 1986	04 Nov 1986	LPH-9	Med
19 Jun 1986	20 Dec 1986	LHA-1	WestPac
17 Aug 1986	21 Oct 1986	LPH-12	NorLant
17 Aug 1986	24 Feb 1987	LHA-2	NorLant/Med

Major Overseas Deployments for 1987

Departure	Return	Ship	Area of Operations
09 Jan 1987	09 Jul 1987	LHA-3	WestPac
15 Jan 1987	17 May 1987	LPH-3	WestPac
21 Jan 1987	17 Jul 1987	LPH-12	Med
18 Jun 1987	17 Dec 1987	LPH-7	Med/IO
18 Jun 1987	18 Dec 1987	LPH-10	WestPac

| 29 Sep 1987 | 29 Mar 1988 | LHA-4 | Med |
| 08 Oct 1987 | 06 Apr 1988 | LPH-3 | WestPac/IO/Med/Carib† |

Major Overseas Deployments for 1988			
Departure	**Return**	**Ship**	**Area of Operations**
14 Jan 1988	14 Jul 1988	LHA-5	WestPac
29 Feb 1988	29 Aug 1988	LPH-2	Med
16 Jun 1988	16 Dec 1988	LPH-11	WestPac
02 Aug 1988	02 Feb 1989	LPH-9	Med
25 Aug 1988	15 Oct 1988	LHA-4	NorLant
25 Aug 1988	15 Oct 1988	LPH-12	NorLant
30 Dec 1988	30 Jun 1989	LPH-7	Med

Major Overseas Deployments for 1989			
Departure	**Return**	**Ship**	**Area of Operations**
12 Jan 1989	19 Jun 1989	LHA-3	WestPac
30 May 1989	10 Nov 1989	LHA-4	Med
08 Jul 1989	20 Dec 1989	LHA-1	WestPac
06 Sep 1989	16 Dec 1989	LPH-10	WestPac
18 Sep 1989	29 Oct 1989	LHA-5	NorPac
11 Oct 1989	11 Apr 1990	LPH-2	Med

Major Overseas Deployments for 1990			
Departure	**Return**	**Ship**	**Area of Operations**
12 Jan 1990	12 Jul 1990	LHA-5	WestPac
07 Mar 1990	07 Sep 1990	LHA-2	Med/West Africa
20 Jun 1990	17 Apr 1991	LPH-3	WestPac/IO/Persian Gulf
06 Aug 1990	04 Mar 1991	LPH-12	Med
18 Aug 1990	20 Apr 1991	LHA-4	Med/IO/Persian Gulf
19 Aug 1990	20 Apr 1991	LPH-9	Med/IO/Persian Gulf
20 Aug 1990	17 Apr 1991	LPH-2	Med/Persian Gulf
01 Dec 1990	08 Aug 1991	LPH-10	WestPac/IO
01 Dec 1990	28 Aug 1991	LPH-11	WestPac/IO/Persian Gulf

Major Overseas Deployments for 1991			
Departure	**Return**	**Ship**	**Area of Operations**
23 Jan 1991	07 Aug 1991	LPH-7	Med
29 May 1991	27 Nov 1991	LHA-5	WestPac/IO
20 Jun 1991	20 Dec 1991	LHD-1	Med
17 Sep 1991	17 Mar 1992	LHA-2	Med/IO
05 Dec 1991	05 Jun 1992	LPH-12	Med

Major Overseas Deployments for 1992

Departure	Return	Ship	Area of Operations
06 Jan 1992	06 Jul 1992	LPH-3	WestPac/IO
26 Feb 1992	17 Apr 1992	LPH-7	NorLant
Mar 1992	Apr 1992	LHA-4	NorLant
27 May 1992	26 Nov 1992	LPH-2	Med
28 May 1992	21 Jul 1992	LHD-1	Carib/Drug law enforcement
28 May 1992	25 Nov 1992	LHA-1	WestPac/IO/Arabian Sea
31 Aug 1992	31 Dec 1992	LHA-3	WestPac§
16 Oct 1992	16 Apr 1993	LPH-10	WestPac/IO
20 Oct 1992	17 Apr 1993	LPH-9	Med

Major Overseas Deployments for 1993

Departure	Return	Ship	Area of Operations
01 Jan 1993	31 Dec 1993	LHA-3	WestPac§
23 Feb 1993	20 Aug 1993	LHD-1	Med/IO
17 Mar 1993	10 Sep 1993	LHA-2	Med
22 Mar 1993	17 Jun 1993	LPH-12	NorLant
11 Aug 1993	05 Feb 1994	LPH-7	Med/IO
03 Sep 1993	18 Mar 1994	LPH-11	WestPac/IO

Major Overseas Deployments for 1994

Departure	Return	Ship	Area of Operations
01 Jan 1994	31 Dec 1994	LHA-3	WestPac§
05 Jan 1994	24 Jun 1994	LPH-12	Med/IO
21 Jan 1994	21 Jul 1994	LHA-5	WestPac/IO
20 May 1994	20 Nov 1994	LPH-9	Med/IO
01 Jun 1994	09 Dec 1994	LPH-10	WestPac/IO
06 Jul 1994	17 Aug 1994	LPH-12	Carib/Haiti
12 Aug 1994	20 Oct 1994	LHD-1	Carib/Haiti
20 Oct 1994	16 Apr 1995	LHA-4	Med
25 Oct 1994	25 Apr 1995	LHD-2	WestPac/IO

Major Overseas Deployments for 1995

Departure	Return	Ship	Area of Operations
01 Jan 1995	31 Dec 1995	LHA-3	WestPac§
20 Feb 1995	15 Mar 1995	LHD-4	East to West Coast via Panama Canal
22 Mar 1995	22 Sep 1995	LHD-3	Med
23 Jun 1995	22 Dec 1995	LPH-11	WestPac/IO
28 Aug 1995	28 Feb 1996	LHD-1	Med
13 Nov 1995	13 May 1996	LHA-5	WestPac/IO

Major Overseas Deployments for 1996

Departure	Return	Ship	Area of Operations
01 Jan 1996	31 Dec 1996	LHA-3	WestPac§
26 Jan 1996	24 Jul 1996	LPH-9	Med
19 Apr 1996	19 Oct 1996	LHA-1	WestPac/IO
28 Jun 1996	21 Dec 1996	LHA-2	Med
10 Oct 1996	10 Apr 1997	LHD-2	WestPac/IO
25 Nov 1996	23 May 1997	LHA-4	Med

Major Overseas Deployments for 1997			
Departure	**Return**	**Ship**	**Area of Operations**
01 Jan 1997	31 Dec 1997	LHA-3	WestPac[§]
31 Jan 1997	02 May 1997	LPH-11	WestPac
24 Mar 1997	24 Sep 1997	LHD-4	WestPac/IO
15 Apr 1997	15 Oct 1997	LHD-3	SouthEastLant/Med
28 Aug 1997	27 Feb 1998	LHA-5	WestPac/IO
03 Oct 1997	Apr 1998	LPH-9	Med

Major Overseas Deployments for 1998			
Departure	**Return**	**Ship**	**Area of Operations**
01 Jan 1998	31 Dec 1998	LHA-3	WestPac[§]
07 Feb 1998	07 Aug 1998	LHA-1	WestPac/IO
22 Jun 1998	22 Dec 1998	LHD-2	WestPac/IO
01 Jul 1998	09 Dec 1998	LHA-2	Med
17 Aug 1998	28 Sep 1998	LHD-6	East to West Coast via Cape Horn
13 Nov 1998	13 May 1999	LHA-4	Med
05 Dec 1998	05 Jun 1999	LHD-4	WestPac/IO

Major Overseas Deployments for 1999			
Departure	**Return**	**Ship**	**Area of Operations**
01 Jan 1999	Mar 1999	LHA-3	IO
14 Apr 1999	14 Oct 1999	LHD-3	Med/IO
21 Jun 1999	21 Dec 1999	LHA-5	WestPac/IO
15 Sep 1999	17 Mar 2000	LHD-5	Med/IO

Major Overseas Deployments for 2000			
Departure	**Return**	**Ship**	**Area of Operations**
01 Jan 2000	13 Oct 2000	LHA-3	WestPac[‖]
24 Jan 2000	14 Jul 2000	LHD-6	WestPac
18 Feb 2000	08 Aug 2000	LHD-1	Med
02 Jun 2000	31 Dec 2000	LHD-2	WestPac[#]
11 Jul 2000	21 Dec 2000	LHA-2	Med
14 Aug 2000	14 Feb 2001	LHA-1	WestPac/IO
28 Nov 2000	24 May 2001	LHA-4	Med

Major Overseas Deployments for 2001			
Departure	**Return**	**Ship**	**Area of Operations**
01 Jan 2001	31 Dec 2001	LHD-2	WestPac[#]
12 Mar 2001	12 Sep 2001	LHD-4	WestPac/IO
25 Apr 2001	15 Oct 2001	LHD-3	Med
13 Aug 2001	04 Mar 2002	LHA-5	WestPac/IO
18 Sep 2001	20 Apr 2002	LHD-5	Med
01 Dec 2001	18 Jun 2002	LHD-6	WestPac/IO

Major Overseas Deployments for 2002

Departure	Return	Ship	Area of Operations
01 Jan 2002	31 Dec 2002	LHD-2	WestPac*
22 Feb 2002	30 Aug 2002	LHD-1	Med/IO
15 Jun 2002	14 Dec 2002	LHA-3	WestPac/IO
26 Aug 2002	29 May 2003	LHA-4	Med/IO

Major Overseas Deployments for 2003

Departure	Return	Ship	Area of Operations
01 Jan 2003	31 Dec 2003	LHD-2	WestPac*
06 Jan 2003	13 Jul 2003	LHA-1	WestPac/IO
16 Jan 2003	25 Jun 2003	LHD-5	Med/IO
16 Jan 2003	26 Jun 2003	LHA-2	Med/IO
16 Jan 2003	30 Jun 2003	LHD-3	Med/IO
17 Jan 2003	26 Jul 2003	LHD-4	WestPac/IO
17 Jan 2003	26 Jul 2003	LHD-6	WestPac/IO
04 Mar 2003	24 Oct 2003	LHD-7	Med/SoLant
22 Aug 2003	09 Mar 2004	LHA-5	WestPac/IO

Major Overseas Deployments for 2004

Departure	Return	Ship	Area of Operations
01 Jan 2004	22 Aug 2004	LHD-2	WestPac*
14 Jan 2004	29 Apr 2004	LHD-4	WestPac/IO
19 Jan 2004	31 Mar 2004	LHD-5	Med/IO
17 Feb 2004	18 Sep 2004	LHD-1	Med/IO
27 May 2004	24 Oct 2004	LHA-3	WestPac/IO
07 Jun 2004	15 Aug 2004	LHD-3	Med/IO
22 Aug 2004	31 Dec 2004	LHD-2	IO
06 Dec 2004	06 Jun 2005	LHD-6	WestPac/IO

Major Overseas Deployments for 2005

Departure	Return	Ship	Area of Operations
01 Jan 2005	05 Apr 2005	LHD-2	IO
25 Mar 2005	27 Sep 2005	LHD-3	Med/IO
05 Apr 2005	31 Dec 2005	LHD-2	WestPac*
29 Apr 2005	14 Sep 2005	LHD-4	WestPac
25 May 2005	25 Aug 2005	LHA-2	Med
16 Jul 2005	20 Feb 2006	LHA-1	WestPac/IO/Med
07 Nov 2005	04 May 2006	LHA-4	Med/IO

Major Overseas Deployments for 2006

Departure	Return	Ship	Area of Operations
01 Jan 2006	31 Dec 2006	LHD-2	WestPac*
15 Feb 2006	16 Aug 2006	LHA-5	WestPac/IO
06 Jun 2006	06 Dec 2006	LHD-7	Med/IO/Persian Gulf
25 Aug 2006	11 Nov 2006	LHD-1	Med/NorLant
13 Sep 2006	31 May 2007	LHD-4	WestPac/IO/Persian Gulf

Major Overseas Deployments for 2007

Departure	Return	Ship	Area of Operations
01 Jan 2007	31 Dec 2007	LHD-2	WestPac*
04 Jan 2007	03 Jul 2007	LHD-5	Med/IO
10 Apr 2007	19 Nov 2007	LHD-6	WestPac/IO/Persian Gulf
30 Jul 2007	01 Feb 2008	LHD-3	IO
05 Nov 2007	03 Jun 2008	LHA-1	WestPac/IO

Major Overseas Deployments for 2008

Departure	Return	Ship	Area of Operations
01 Jan 2008	31 Dec 2008	LHD-2	WestPac*
20 Feb 2008	11 Jul 2008	LHA-4	Med/IO
28 Apr 2008	26 Jun 2008	LHD-4	EastPac
04 May 2008	04 Nov 2008	LHA-5	WestPac/IO
08 Aug 2008	02 Dec 2008	LHD-3	Carib
26 Aug 2008	27 Mar 2009	LHD-7	Med/IO

Major Overseas Deployments for 2009

Departure	Return	Ship	Area of Operations
01 Jan 2009	31 Dec 2009	LHD-2	WestPac*
09 Jan 2009	01 Aug 2009	LHD-4	WestPac/IO
13 May 2009	08 Dec 2009	LHD-5	Med/IO
24 Sep 2009	14 Apr 2010	LHD-6	WestPac/IO
04 Oct 2009	22 Dec 2009	LHD-1	GITMO/Carib

Major Overseas Deployments for 2010

Departure	Return	Ship	Area of Operations
01 Jan 2010	31 Dec 2010	LHD-2	WestPac*
18 Jan 2010	15 Aug 2010	LHA-4	Med/IO
22 May 2010	15 Dec 2010	LHA-5	WestPac/IO
12 Jul 2010	18 Nov 2010	LHD-7	Carib/Central and South American waters (Com4thFlt)
27 Aug 2010	circa May 2011	LHD-3	Med/IO

Amphibious Assault Ship Designations			
CVHA-1	Thetis Bay	Operated with the designation CVHA-1 from 1 Jul 1955 until redesignated LPH-6 on 28 May 1959.	
LPH-1	Block Island	Reclassified LPH-1 on 22 Dec 1957, but the conversion was cancelled and the designation was not reassigned. The ship never operated with the LPH-1 designation.	
LPH-2	Iwo Jima		
LPH-3	Okinawa		
LPH-4	Boxer	Operated with the designation LPH-4 from 30 Jan 1959 until her decommissioning on 1 Dec 1969.	
LPH-5	Princeton	Operated with the designation LPH-5 from 2 Mar 1959 until her decommissioning on 30 Jan 1970.	
LPH-6	Thetis Bay	Operated with the designation LPH-6 from 28 May 1959 until her decommissioning on 1 Mar 1964.	
LPH-7	Guadalcanal		
LPH-8	Valley Forge	Operated with the designation LPH-8 from 1 Jul 1961 until her decommissioning on 15 Jan 1970.	
LPH-9	Guam		
LPH-10	Tripoli		
LPH-11	New Orleans		
LPH-12	Inchon	On 1 March 1995 Inchon (LPH 12) was redesignated Inchon (MCS 12). Tracking of deployments for Inchon came to an end in 1994 following her redesignation as a mine countermeasure command and control support ship.	
LHA-1	Tarawa		
LHA-2	Saipan		
LHA-3	Belleau Wood		
LHA-4	Nassau		
LHA-5	Peleliu		
LHD-1	Wasp		
LHD-2	Essex		
LHD-3	Kearsarge		
LHD-4	Boxer		
LHD-5	Bataan		
LHD-6	Bonhomme Richard		
LHD-7	Iwo Jima		
LHD-8	Makin Island		

˙ Area of Operations abbreviations:

Carib   Caribbean Sea

EastLant   Eastern Atlantic Ocean

GITMO   Guantanamo Bay, Cuba

IO   Indian Ocean

Med   Mediterranean Sea

NorLant   North Atlantic Ocean

SoLant   South Atlantic Ocean

WestPac   Western Pacific Ocean

† World cruise

‡ Saipan deployed on 21 Sep for refresher training at Guantanamo Bay. While there, she was ordered to Grenada on 30 Oct and participated in Urgent Fury operations from 1–7 Nov.

§ On 30 Sep 1992 Belleau Wood's homeport was changed from San Diego to Sasebo, Japan. She became the only forward deployed amphibious assault ship. The time frame reflects her permanent forward deployment.

‖ In July/August 2000 timeframe Belleau Wood's homeport was changed from Sasebo, Japan to San Diego. She was relieved by Essex (LHD 2) as the only forward deployed amphibious assault ship.

In July 2000 Essex's homeport was changed from San Diego to Sasebo, Japan. She relieved Belleau Wood as the only forward deployed amphibious assault ship. The time frame reflects her permanent forward deployment.

CHAPTER 30

Carrier and Squadron Deployments During the Korean War

Carrier, Air Group, and Carrier-Based Squadron Deployments		
Essex (CV 9) with CVG-5 (26 Jun 1951–25 Mar 1952)		
Squadron	**Aircraft**	**Tail Code**
VF-51	F9F-2	S
VF-172	F2H-2	R
VF-53	F4U-4/B	S
VF-54	AD-2/4/L/Q	S
VC-3 Det B	F4U-5NL	NP
VC-11 Det B	AD-4W	ND
VC-35 Det B	AD-4NL	NR
VC-61 Det B	F9F-2P	PP
HU-1 Det	HO3S-1	UP
Essex (CVA 9) with ATG-2 (16 Jun 1952–6 Feb 1953)		
Squadron	**Aircraft**	**Tail Code**
VF-23	F9F-2	M
VF-821	F9F-2	A
VF-871	F4U-4	D
VA-55	AD-4	S
VC-3 Det I	F4U-5N	NP
VC-11 Det I	AD-4W	ND
VC-35 Det I	AD-4N	NR
VC-61 Det I	F2H-2P	PP
HU-1 Det	HO3S-1	UP
Boxer (CV 21) with CVG-2 (24 Aug 1950–11 Nov 1950)		
Squadron	**Aircraft**	**Tail Code**
VF-23	F4U-4	M
VF-63	F4U-4	M
VF-64	F4U-4	M
VF-24	F4U-4	M
VA-65	AD-2	M
VC-3 Det	F4U-5N	NP
VC-11 Det A	AD-3W	ND
VC-33 Det	AD-4N	SS
VC-61 Det	F4U-4P	PP
HU-1 Det	HO3S-1	UP
Boxer (CV 21) with CVG-101 (2 Mar 1951–24 Oct 1951)		
Squadron	**Aircraft**	**Tail Code**
VF-721	F9F-2B	A
VF-791	F4U-4	A
VF-884	F4U-4	A
VA-702	AD-2/4Q	A
VC-3 Det F	F4U-5NL	NP
VC-11 Det F	AD-4W	ND

VC-35 Det F	AD-4N	NR
VC-61 Det F	F9F-2P	PP
HU-1 Det	HO3S-1	UP

Boxer (CVA 21) with CVG-2 (8 Feb 1952–26 Sep 1952)		
Squadron	**Aircraft**	**Tail Code**
VF-64	F4U-4	M
VF-63	F4U-4	M
VF-24	F9F-2	M
VA-65	AD-4	M
VC-3 Det A	F4U-5N	NP
VC-11 Det A	AD-4W	ND
VC-35 Det A	AD-3N/4N/2Q	NR
VC-61 Det A	F9F-2P	PP
HU-1 Det	HO3S-1	UP
GMU-90	AD-2Q/F6F-5K	V

Boxer (CVA 21) with ATG-1 (30 Mar 1953–28 Nov 1953)		
Squadron	**Aircraft**	**Tail Code**
VF-111*	F9F-5	V
VF-52	F9F-2	S
VF-151	F9F-2	H
VF-44*	F4U-4	F
VF-194	AD-4NA/Q	B
VC-3 Det H	F4U-5N	NP
VC-11 Det H	AD-4W	ND
VC-35 Det H	AD-4N	NR
VC-61	F2H-2P	PP
HU-1 Det	HO3S-1	UP

*VF-111 crossdecked (transferred) from CVA-21 to CVA-39 on 30 June 1953 and returned to the United States in October 1953. VF-44 crossdecked from CVA-39 to CVA-21 on 30 June 1953.

Bon Homme Richard (CV 31) with CVG-102 (10 May 1951–17 Dec 1951)		
Squadron	**Aircraft**	**Tail Code**
VF-781	F9F-2B	D
VF-783	F4U-4	D
VF-874	F4U-4	D
VA-923	AD-3/4Q	D
VC-3 Det G	F4U-5NL	NP
VC-11 Det G	AD-4W	ND
VC-35 Det G	AD-4N	NR
VC-61 Det G	F9F-2P	PP
HU-1 Det	HO3S-1	UP

Bon Homme Richard (CVA 31) with CVG-7 (20 May 1952–8 Jan 1953)		
Squadron	**Aircraft**	**Tail Code**
VF-71	F9F-2	L
VF-72	F9F-2	L
VF-74	F4U-4	L
VA-75	AD-4	L
VC-4 Det 41	F4U-5N	NA
VC-33 Det 41	AD-4NL	SS
VC-12 Det 41	AD-4W	NE

| VC-61 Det N | F2H-2P/F9F-2P | PP |
| HU-1 Det | HO3S-1 | UP |

Leyte (CV 32) with CVG-3 (6 Sep 1950–3 Feb 1951)		
Squadron	**Aircraft**	**Tail Code**
VF-31	F9F-2	K
VF-32	F4U-4	K
VF-33	F4U-4	K
VA-35	AD-3	K
VC-4 Det 3	F4U-5N	NA
VC-33 Det 3	AD-4N	SS
VC-12 Det 3	AD-3W	NE
VC-62 Det 3	F4U-5P	PL
HU-2 Det 3	HO3S-1	UR

Kearsarge (CVA 33) with CVG-101* (11 Aug 1952–17 Mar 1953)		
Squadron	**Aircraft**	**Tail Code**
VF-11	F2H-2	T
VF-721	F9F-2	A
VF-884	F4U-4	A
VA-702	AD-4/L	A
VC-3 Det F	F4U-5N	NP
VC-11 Det F	AD-4W	ND
VC-35 Det F	AD-4N	NR
VC-61 Det F	F2H-2P	PP
HU-1 Det 15	HO3-1	UP

*CVG-101 redesignated CVG-14 on 4 February 1953.
VF-721, VF-884, and VA-702 became VF-141, VF-144, and VA-145, respectively.

Oriskany (CVA 34) with CVG-102* (15 Sep 1952–18 May 1953)		
Squadron	**Aircraft**	**Tail Code**
VF-781	F9F-5	D
VF-783	F9F-5	D
VF-874	F4U-4	D
VA-923	AD-3	D
VC-3 Det G	F4U-5N	NP
VC-11 Det G	AD-3W	ND
VC-35 Det G	AD-4N	NR
VC-61 Det G	F2H-2P	PP
HU-1 Det	HO3S-1	UP

*CVG-102 redesignated CVG-12 on 4 February 1953.
VF-781, VF-783, VF-874, and VA-923 became VF-121, VF-122, VF-124, and VA-125, respectively.

Antietam (CV 36) with CVG-15 (8 Sep 1951–2 May 1952)		
Squadron	**Aircraft**	**Tail Code**
VF-713	F4U-4	H
VF-831	F9F-2B	H
VF-837	F9F-2B	H
VA-728	AD-4/L/Q	H
VC-3 Det D	F4U-5N	NP
VC-11 Det D	AD-4W	ND
VC-35 Det D	AD-4NL	NR

| VC-61 Det D | F9F-2P | PP |
| HU-1 Det | HO3S-1 | UP |

Princeton (CV 37) with CVG-19 (9 Nov 1950–29 May 1951*)		
Squadron	**Aircraft**	**Tail Code**
VF-191	F9F-2	B
VF-192	F4U-4	B
VF-193	F4U-4	B
VA-195	AD-4	B
VC-3 Det F	F4U-5N	NP
VC-11 Det	AD-4W	ND
VC-35 Det 3	AD-4N	NR
VC-61 Det	F9F-2P	PP
HU-1 Det	HO3S-1	UP

*Air Group transferred at Yokosuka, Japan; CV-37 remained in WestPac.

Princeton (CV 37) with CVG-19X (31 May 1951–29 Aug 1951)		
Squadron	**Aircraft**	**Tail Code**
VF-23	F9F-2	B
VF-821	F4U-4	B
VF-871	F4U-4	B
VA-55	AD-4	B
VC-3 Det	F4U-5N	NP
VC-11 Det	AD-4W	ND
VC-35 Det 7	AD-4N	NR
VC-61 Det	F9F-2P	PP
HU-1 Det	HO3S-1	UP

Princeton (CVA 37) with CVG-19 (21 Mar 1952–3 Nov 1952)		
Squadron	**Aircraft**	**Tail Code**
VF-191	F9F-2	B
VF-192	F4U-4	B
VF-193	F4U-4	B
VA-195	AD-4	B
VC-3 Det E	F4U-5N	NP
VC-11 Det E	AD-4W	ND
VC-35 Det E	AD-4NL	NR
VC-61 Det E	F9F-2P	PP
HU-1 Det	HO3S-1	UP

Princeton (CVA 37) with CVG-15 (24 Jan 1953–21 Sep 1953)		
Squadron	**Aircraft**	**Tail Code**
VF-152	F4U-4	H
VF-153	F9F-5	H
VF-154	F9F-5	H
VA-155	AD-4	H
VC-3 Det D	F4U-5N	NP
VC-11 Det D	AD-4W	ND
VC-35 Det D	AD-4N	NR
VC-61 Det D	F9F-5P	PP
HU-1 Det	HO3S-1	UP

Lake Champlain (CVA 39) with CVG-4 (26 Apr 1953–4 Dec 1953)		
Squadron	**Aircraft**	**Tail Code**

VF-22	F2H-2	F
VF-62	F2H-2	F
VF-44	F4U-4	F (to 30 Jun)
VF-111	F9F-5	V (from 30 Jun)
VA-45	AD-4B	F
VC-4 Det 44	F2H-2B/F3D-2	NA
VC-12 Det 44	AD-4W	NE
VC-33 Det 44	AD-4N	SS
VC-62 Det 44	F2H-2P	PL
HU-2 Det	HO3S-1	UR

Valley Forge (CV 45) with CVG-5 (1 May 1950–1 Dec 1950)		
Squadron	**Aircraft**	**Tail Code**
VF-51	F9F-3	S
VF-52	F9F-3	S
VF-53	F4U-4B	S
VF-54	F4U-4B	S
VA-55	AD-4/Q	S
VC-3 Det C	F4U-5N/AD-3N	NP
VC-11 Det	AD-3W	ND
HedRon 1 Det	F4U-5P	AZ
HU-1 Det	HO3S-1	UP

Valley Forge (CV 45) with CVG-2 (6 Dec 1950-7 Apr 1951')		
Squadron	**Aircraft**	**Tail Code**
VF-64	F4U-4	M
VF-63	F4U-4	M
VF-24	F4U-4	M
VA-65	AD-2/4Q	M
VC-3 Det	F4U-5N	NP
VC-11 Det	AD-4W	ND
VC-35 Det 4	AD-4N	NR
VC-61 Det F	F4U-4P	PP
HU-1 Det	HO3S-1	UP

'CVG-2 crossdecked with CVG-11 from CV-47 on 28 March 1951 and CV-45 returned to San Diego, Calif., 7 April with CVG-11.

Valley Forge (CV 45) with ATG-1 (15 Oct 1951–3 Jul 1952)		
Squadron	**Aircraft**	**Tail Code**
VF-111	F9F-2/B	V
VF-52	F9F-2/B	S
VF-653	F4U-4/B	H
VF-194	AD-2/3	B
VC-3 Det H	F4U-5N/NL	NP
VC-11 Det H(7)	AD-4W/2Q	ND
VC-35 Det H(10)	AD-4NL	NR
VC-61 Det H	F9F-2P/F2H-2P	PP
HU-1 Det 20	HO3S-1	UP

Valley Forge (CVA 45) with CVG-5 (20 Nov 1952–25 Jun 1953)		
Squadron	**Aircraft**	**Tail Code**
VF-51	F9F-5	S
VF-92	F4U-4	N

VF-53	F9F-5	S
VF-54	AD-4	S
VC-3 Det B	F4U-5N	NP
VC-11 Det B	AD-4W	ND
VC-35 Det B	AD-4N	NR
VC-61 Det B	F9F-5P	PP
HU-1 Det 6	HO3S-1	UP

Philippine Sea (CV 47) with CVG-11 (5 Jul 1950–26 Mar 1951)*		
Squadron	**Aircraft**	**Tail Code**
VF-111	F9F-2	V
VF-112	F9F-2	V
VF-113	F4U-4B	V
VF-114	F4U-4B	V
VA-115	AD-4/Q	V
VC-3 Det 3	F4U-5N/AD-4N	NP
VC-11 Det	AD-4W	ND
VC-61 Det 3	F4U-4P	PP
HU-1 Det 3	HO3S-1	UP

*CVG-11 crossdecked with CVG-2 from CV-45; CV-45 returned to San Diego, Calif., 26 March with CVG-11.

Philippine Sea (CV 47) with CVG-2 (28 Mar 1951–9 Jun 1951)		
Squadron	**Aircraft**	**Tail Code**
VF-64	F4U-4	M
VF-63	F4U-4	M
VF-24	F4U-4	M
VA-65	AD-2/Q	M
VC-3 Det	F4U-5N	NP
VC-11 Det	AD-4W	ND
VC-35 Det 4	AD-4N	NR
VC-61 Det	F4U-4P	PP
HU-1 Det	HO3S-1	UP

Philippine Sea (CV 47) with CVG-11 (31 Dec 1951–8 Aug 1952)		
Squadron	**Aircraft**	**Tail Code**
VF-112	F9F-2	V
VF-113	F4U-4	V
VF-114	F4U-4	V
VA-115	AD-4	V
VC-3 Unit C	F4U-5N/NL	NP
VC-11 Unit C	AD-4W	ND
VC-35 Unit C	AD-4NL/Q/-2Q	NR
VC-61 Unit C	F2H-2P/F9F-2P	PP
HU-1 Unit	HO3S-1	UP

Philippine Sea (CVA 47) with CVG-9 (15 Dec 1952–14 Aug 1953)		
Squadron	**Aircraft**	**Tail Code**
VF-91	F9F-2	N
VF-93	F9F-2	N
VF-94	F4U-4	N
VA-95	AD-4/NA/NL	N
VC-3 Det M	F4U-5N	NP

VC-11 Det M	AD-4W	ND
VC-35 Det M	AD-4N	NR
VC-61 Det M	F9F-5P	PP
HU-1 Det	HO3S-1	UP

Bataan (CVL 29) (16 Nov 1950–25 Jun 1951)		
Squadron	**Aircraft**	**Tail Code**
VMF-212 (on board 11 Dec–5 Mar)	F4U-4	LD
VMF-312 (on board 5 Mar–6 Jun)	F4U-4	WR
HU-1 Det 8	HO3S-1	UP

Bataan (CVL 29) (27 Jan 1952–26 Aug 1952)		
Squadron	**Aircraft**	**Tail Code**
VMA-312 (on board 21 Apr–21 Jul)	F4U-4/B	WR
VS-25	AF-2S/W	SK
HU-1 Det	HO3S-1	UP

Bataan (CVL 29) (28 Oct 1952–26 May 1953)		
Squadron	**Aircraft**	**Tail Code**
VMA-312 (on board 9 Feb–8 May)	F4U-4/B	WR
VS-871	TBM-3S/W	SU
VS-21	AF-2S/W	BS
HU-1 Det	HO3S-1	UP

Rendova (CVE 114) (8 Ju1 1951–22 Dec 1951)		
Squadron	**Aircraft**	**Tail Code**
VMF-212 (on board 22 Sep–6 Dec)	F4U-4	LD
VS-892 (on board 16 Jul–19 Sep, 11–22 Dec)	TBM-3S/W	ST
HU-1 Det	HO3S-1	UP

Bairoko (CVE 115) (14 Nov 1950–15 Aug 1951)		
Squadron	**Aircraft**	**Tail Code**
VS-21 (on board 3 Dec–16 Feb)	TBM-3S/W	BS
VS-23 (on board 17 Feb–15 Aug)	TBM-3E/S/W	MI
HU-1 Det	HO3S-1	UP

Bairoko (CVE 115) (1 Dec 1951–9 Jun 1952)		
Squadron	**Aircraft**	**Tail Code**
VS-25 (on board to 21 Jan, returned in May)	AF-2S/W	SK
HU-1 Det	HO3S-1	UP

Bairoko (CVE 115) (12 Jan 1953–24 Aug 1953)		
Squadron	**Aircraft**	**Tail Code**
VMA-312 (on board 9 May–8 Jun)	F4U-4/B	WR
VS-21 (on board 3 Feb–8 May)	AF-2S/W	BS
VS-23 (ashore at Agana, Guam, Feb–Apr)	TBM-3S/W	MI
HU-1 Det	HO3S-1	UP

Badoeng Strait (CVE 116) (14 Jul 1950–7 Feb 1951)		
Squadron	**Aircraft**	**Tail Code**
VMF-323	F4U-4B	WS

HU-1 Det	HO3S-1	UP

Badoeng Strait (CVE 116) (15 Sep 1951–1 Mar 1952)		
Squadron	**Aircraft**	**Tail Code**
VMF-212	F4U-4	LD
VS-892 (on board 5 Oct–8 Dec)	TBM-3S/W	ST
HU-1 Det 18	HO3S-1	UP

Badoeng Strait (CVE 116) (19 Jul 1952–27 Feb 1953)		
Squadron	**Aircraft**	**Tail Code**
VMA-312 (on board 19 Oct–9 Feb)	F4U-4/B	WR
VS-931 (on board 10 Aug–19 Oct)	AF-2S/W	SV
HU-1 Det	HO3S-1	UP

Sicily (CVE 118) (4 Jul 1950–5 Feb 1951)		
Squadron	**Aircraft**	**Tail Code**
VMF-214 (on board 1 Aug–13 Nov)	F4U-4B	WE
VS-21 (on board to 3 Dec)	TBM-3E/S	BS
HU-1 Det	HO3S-1	UP

Sicily (CVE 118) (12 May 1951–12 Oct 1951)		
Squadron	**Aircraft**	**Tail Code**
VMF-323 (on board c. 5 Jun–20 Sep)	F4U-4	WS
VS-892 (on board to 13 Jul)	TBM-3S/W	ST
HU-1 Det	HO3S-1	UP

Sicily (CVE 118) (8 May 1952–4 Dec 1952)		
Squadron	**Aircraft**	**Tail Code**
VMA-312 (on board 4 Sep–19 Oct)	F4U-4B	WR
VS-931 (on board to 9 Aug and 19 Oct–4 Dec)	AF-2S/W	SV
HU-1 Det	HO3S-1	UP

Point Cruz (CVE 119) (11 Apr 1953–18 Dec 1953)		
Squadron	**Aircraft**	**Tail Code**
VMA-332	F4U-4B	MR
VS-38 (put shore at Agana, Guam, 28 Apr)	TBM-3S/W	ST
VS-23 (on board 28 Apr— Japan)	TBM-3S/W	MI
HS-2	HRS-2	HV
HU-1 Det	HO3S-1	UP

Shore-Based Marine Corps Squadrons Operating in Korea				
Squadron Designation	**Departed U.S.**	**Departed Korean Area**	**Tail Code**	**Aircraft Operated**
VMC-1	15 May 1952		RM	AD-2Q, -3N, -4N, -4NL, -4Q, -4W
VMJ-1	23 Mar 1952		MW	F2H-2P, F9F-2P, F7F-3P, F4U-5P
VMO-6	14 Jul 1950		WB	OY-2, HO3S-1, HTL-4, TBM-3E, OE-1, HO5S-1
VMF-115	17 Feb 1952		AE	F9F-2, -4, -5
VMA-121	2 Oct 1951		AK	AD-2, -3, -4

Shore-Based Marine Corps Squadrons Operating in Korea				
Squadron Designation	Departed U.S.	Departed Korean Area	Tail Code	Aircraft Operated
HMR-161	16 Aug 1951		HR	HRS-1, -2, HO5S-1
VMF/VMA-212	15 Sep 1950		LD	F4U-4, -4B, -5, -5N, AU-1
VMF-214	14 Jun 1950	15 Nov 1951	WE	F4U-4B
VMA-251	9 Jun 1953		AL	AD-3, -4, -4B
VMF-311	14 Nov 1950		WL	F9F-2, -2B, -5, F4U-4B
VMF/VMA-312	24 Aug 1950	16 Jun 1950	WR	F4U-4, -4B
VMF/VMA-323	14 Jul 1950		WS	F4U-4B, AU-1
VMA-332	15 May 1953		MR	F4U-4, -4B
VMF(N)-513	14 Jul 1950		WF	F4U-5N, -5NL, F7F-3N, F3D-2
VMF(N)-542	27 Aug 1950	9 Mar 1951	WH	F7F-3N

Note: Many of the Marine Corps squadrons remained permanently assigned in the Korean operating area during the Korean War.

Navy Patrol Squadrons Deployed to Korean Area				
Squadron Designation	Arrived	Departed	Tail Code	Aircraft Operated
VP-1	7 Aug 1950	27 Jul 1953	CD	P2V-3/5
VP-2	1 Sep 1951	1 Dec 1951	SB	P2V-4
VP-6	28 Jun 1950	15 Jan 1952	BE	P2V-3
VP-7	30 Jun 1953	Jan 1954	HE	P2V-5
VP-9	29 Jun 1952	16 Nov 1952	CB	P4Y-2/2S
VP-22	14 Nov 1950	30 May 1953	CE	P2V-3/4/5
VP-28	14 Jul 1950	30 Nov 1952	CF	P4Y-2/2S
VP-29	27 Sep 1952	5 Apr 1953	BF	P2V-5/6
VP-40	1 Jun 1951	24 Feb 1953	CA	PBM-5/5S
VP-42	21 Aug 1950	2 Jun 1952	SA	PBM-5/5S2
VP-46	15 Jul 1950	15 Mar 1952	BD	PBM-5
VP-47	25 Jun 1950	1 Jun 1953	BA	PBM-5
VP-48	29 May 1952	15 Mar 1953	SF	PBM-5/5S2
VP-50	5 Jul 1953	27 Jul 1953	SE	PBM-5
VP-57	29 Mar 1953	30 Sep 1953	BI	P2V-5
VP-731	29 May 1952	8 Dec 1952	SF	PBM-5
VP-772	1 Jan 1951	3 Aug 1951	BH/ZE*	P4Y-2/2S
VP-871 Det A	Oct 1951	Mar 1952	CH	P4Y-2/2S
VP-892	23 Nov 1950	1 Sep 1953	SE/SG*	PBM-5

*Note: Tail codes for two Reserve patrol squadrons VP-772 and VP-892 changed but the date of change is unknown. Both tail codes used by the squadrons have been listed. PB4Y-2 aircraft designations were changed to P4Y-2 in 1951.

CHAPTER 31

Carrier and Squadron Deployments to Vietnam

Deployments for Carriers and Carrier-Based Squadrons in the Western Pacific (WestPac) and Vietnam (1964–1975)

See Notes Section at the end of this listing for clarification on specific entries and Tail Code List.

1964 WestPac/Vietnam Deployments	
Kitty Hawk (CVA 63) with CVW-11 (17 Oct 1963–20 Jul 1964)	
VA-112	A-4C
VA-113	A-4C
VA-115	A-1H
VF-114	F-4B
VF-111	F-8D
VAH-13	A-3B
VFP-63 Det C	RF-8A
VAW-11 Det C	E-1B
HU-1 D1 Unit C	UH-2A
VQ-1 Det*	EA-3B
VAP-61 Det*	RA-3B
Oriskany (CVA 34) with CVW-16 (1 Aug 1963–10 Mar 1964)†	
VF-161	F-3B
VF-162	F-8A
VA-163	A-4B
VA-164	A-4B
VA-165	A-1H, -1J
VAH-4 Det G	A-3B
VFP-63 Det G	RF-8A
VAW-11 Det G	E-1B
HU-1 D1 Unit G	UH-2A
VQ-1 Det*	EA-3B
Bon Homme Richard (CVA 31) with CVW-19 (28 Jan 1964–21 Nov 1964)	
VF-191	F-8E
VF-194	F-8C
VA-192	A-4C
VA-195	A-4C
VA-196	A-1H, -1J
VAH-4 Det E	A-3B
VAW-11 Det E	E-1B
VFP-63 Det E	RF-8A
HU-1 D1 Unit E	UH-2A
VQ-1 Det*	EA-3B
VAP-61 Det*	RA-3B

Ticonderoga (CVA 14) with CVW-5 (14 Apr 1964–15 Dec 1964)	
VF-51*	F-8E
VF-53	F-8E
VA-52	A-1H, -1J
VA-55	A-4E
VA-56	A-4E
VFP-63 Det B	RF-8A
VAW-11 Det B	E-1B
HU-1 D1 Unit B	UH-2A
VAW-13 Det*	(most likely used EA-1F)
VQ-1 Det*	EA-3B
VAP-61 Det*	RA-3B, KA-3B
VAH-10 Det*	A-3B
VMCJ-1 Det*	RF-8A
VAH-4 Det B	A-3B
Constellation (CVA 64) with CVW-14 (5 May 1964–1 Feb 1965)	
VF-142	F-4B
VF-143	F-4B
VA-144	A-4C
VA-145	A-1H, -1J
VA-146	A-4C
VAH-10	A-3B
VFP-63 Det F	RF-8A
VAW-11 Det F	E-1B
HU-1 D1 Unit F	UH-2A
VAP-61 Det*	RA-3B
VQ-1 Det*	EA-3B
VF-51*	F-8E
VMCJ-1 Det*	RF-8A
Ranger (CVA 61) with CVW-9 (5 Aug 1964–6 May 1965)	
VF-92	F-4B
VF-96	F-4B
VA-93	A-4C
VA-95	A-1H, -1J
VA-94	A-4C
RVAH-5	RA-5C

VFP-63 Det M	RF-8A
VAW-11 Det M	E-1B
VAH-2 Det M	A-3B
HU-1 D1 Unit M	UH-2A
VAP-61 Det*	RA-3B
VQ-1 Det*	EA-3B

Hancock (CVA 19) with CVW-21 (21 Oct 1964–29 May 1965)

VA-212	A-4E
VA-215	A-1H, -1J
VA-216	A-4C
VF-24	F-8C
VF-211	F-8E
VAW-11 Det L	E-1B
VFP-63 Det L	RF-8A
VAH-4 Det L	A-3B
HU-1 Det L	UH-2A
VAP-61 Det*	RA-3B
VQ-1 Det*	EA-3B

Yorktown (CVS 10) with CVSG-55 (23 Oct 1964–16 May 1965)

VS-23	S-2E
VS-25	S-2E
HS-4	SH-3A
VAW-11 Det T	EA-1E
VMA-223 Det T	A-4C

Coral Sea (CVA 43) with CVW-15 (7 Dec 1964–1 Nov 1965)

VA-153	A-4C
VA-155	A-4E
VA-165	A-1H, -1J
VAH-2	A-3B
VF-151	F-4B
VF-154	F-8D
VFP-63 Det D	RF-8A
VAW-11 Det D	E-1B
HU-1 D1 Unit D (redesignated HC-1 Det D on 1 Jul 1965)	UH-2A
VAP 61 Det*	RA-3B
VQ-1 Det*	EA-3B
VAW-13 Det*	EA-1F
VMCJ-1 Det*	RF-8A

Bennington (CVS 20) with CVSG-59 (20 Feb 1964–11 Aug 1964)

HS-8	SH-3A
VS-33	S-2E
VS-38	S-2E
VAW-11 Det Q	EA-1E
VA-93 Det Q	A-4B

Kearsarge (CVS 33) with CVSG-53 (19 Jun 1964–16 Dec 1964)

HS-6	SH-3A
VS-21	S-2F
VS-29	S-2F
VAW-11 Det R	EA-1E
VA-153 Det R	A-4B

1965 WestPac/Vietnam Deployments

Midway (CVA 41) with CVW-2 (6 Mar 1965–23 Nov 1965)

VF-111	F-8D
VA-22	A-4C
VA-23	A-4E
VA-25	A-1H, -1J
VF-21	F-4B
VAH-8	A-3B
VFP-63 Det A	RF-8A
VAW-11 Det A	E-1B
HU-1 Det A (redesignated HC-1 Det A on 1 Jul 1965)	UH-2A
VAW-13 Det*	EA-1F
VAP-61 Det*	RA-3B
VQ-1 Det*	EA-3B

Oriskany (CVA 34) with CVW-16 (5 Apr 1965–16 Dec 1965)

VF-162	F-8E
VA-152	A-1H, -1J
VA-163	A-4E
VA-164	A-4E
VMF(AW)-212	F-8E
VFP-63 Det G	RF-8A
VAW-11 Det G	E-1B
HU-1 Det G (redesignated HC-1 Det G on 1 Jul 1965)	UH-2A, -2B
VMCJ-1 Det*	(most likely used EF-10B)
VAW-13 Det*	EA-1F
VQ-1 Det*	EA-3B
VAH-4 Det G	A-3B

Independence (CVA 62) with CVW-7 (10 May 1965–13 Dec 1965)

VF-41	F-4B
VF-84	F-4B
VA-72	A-4E
VA-75	A-6A
VA-86	A-4E
RVAH-1	RA-5C
VAW 12 Det 62	E-1B
HU-2 Det 62 (redesignated HC-1 Det 62 on 1 Jul 1965)	UH-2A
VAH-4 Det 62	A-3B
VAW-13 Det*	EA-1F
VQ-1 Det*	EA-3B
VAP-61 Det*	RA-3B

Bon Homme Richard (CVA 31) with CVW-19 (21 Apr 1965–13 Jan 1966)	
VF-191	F-8E
VF-194	F-8E
VA-192	A-4C
VA-195	A-4C
VA-196	A-1H, -1J
VFP-63 Det E	RF-8A
VAW-11 Det E	E-1B
HU-1 D1 Unit E (redesignated HC-1 D1 Unit E on 1 Jul 1965)	UH-2A, -2B
VQ-1 Det*	EA-3B
VAW-13 Det*	EA-1F
Hornet (CVS 12) with CVSG-57 (12 Aug 1965–23 Mar 1966)	
HS-2	SH-3A
VS-35	S-2D
VS-37	S-2D
VAW-11 Det N	E-1B
H&MS-15 Det N	A-4C
Ticonderoga (CVA 14) with CVW-5 (28 Sep 1965–13 May 1966)	
VF-51	F-8E
VF-53	F-8E
VA-52	A-1H, -1J
VA-56	A-4E
VA-144	A-4C
VAH-4 Det B	A-3B
VAW-11 Det B	E-1B
VFP-63 Det B	RF-8A
HC-1 D1 Unit B	UH-2A, -2B
VQ-1 Det*	EA-3B
Enterprise (CVAN 65) with CVW-9 (26 Oct 1965–21 Jun 1966)	
VA-36	A-4C
VA-76	A-4C
VA-93	A-4C
VA-94	A-4C
VAH-4 Det M	A-3B
RVAH-7	RA-5C
VAW-11 Det M	E-1B
VF-92	F-4B
VF-96	F-4B
HC-1 Det M	UH-2A, -2B
VQ-1 Det*	EA-3B
VAP-61 Det*	RA-3B
Hancock (CVA 19) with CVW-21 (10 Nov 1965–1 Aug 1966)	
VA-212	A-4E
VA-215	A-1H, -1J
VA-216	A-4C
VAW-11 Det L	E-1B

VFP-63 Det 1	RF-8A
VF-211	F-8E
VF-24	F-8C
HC-1 D1 Unit L	UH-2A, -2B
VQ-1 Det*	EA-3B
VAP-61 Det*	RA-3B
Kitty Hawk (CVA 63) with CVW-11 (19 Oct 1965–13 Jun 1966)	
VA-85	A-6A
VA-113	A-4C
VA-115	A-1H, -1J
VAH-4 Det C	A-3B
VAW-11 Det C	E-2A
VF-114	F-4B
VF-213	F-4B, -4G
RVAH-13	RA-5C
HC-1 D1 Unit C	UH-2A, -2B
VAP-61 Det*	RA-3B
VQ-1 Det*	EA-3B
Ranger (CVA 61) with CVW-14 (10 Dec 1965–25 Aug 1966)	
VF-142	F-4B
VF-143	F-4B
VA-145	A-1H, -1J
VA-146	A-4C
VA-55	A-4E
RVAH-9	RA-5C
VAH-2 Det F	A-3B
VAW-11 Det F	E-2A
HC-1 D1 Unit F	UH-2A, -2B
VQ-1 Det*	EA-3B
VAP-61 Det*	RA-3B
Bennington (CVS 20) with CVSG-59 (22 Mar 1965–7 Oct 1965)	
VS-38	S-2E
VS-33	S-2E
HS-8	SH-3A
VAW-11 Det Q	E-1B
VA-113 Det Q	A-4B
1966 WestPac/Vietnam Deployments[1]	
Yorktown (CVS 10) with CVSG-55 (6 Jan 1966–27 Jul 1966)	
VS-23	S-2E
VS-25	S-2E
HS-4	SH-3A
VAW-11 Det T	E-1B
Intrepid (CVS 11) with CVW-10 (4 Apr 1966–21 Nov 1966)	
VA-95	A-4B
VA-165	A-1H
VA-15	A-4B

VA-176	A-1H
HC-2 Det 11	UH-2A, -2B
Constellation (CVA 64) with CVW-15 (12 May 1966–3 Dec 1966)	
VF-151	F-4B
VF-161	F-4B
VA-153	A-4C
VA-155	A-4E
VA-65	A-6A
RVAH-6	RA-5C
VAH-8	A-3B
VAW-11 Det D	E-2A
HC-1 D1 Unit D	UH-2A, -2B
VQ-1 Det*	EA-3B
VAP-61 Det*	RA-3B
VAW-13 Det*	EA-1F
HS-6 Det*	SH-3A
Oriskany (CVA 34) with CVW-16 (26 May 1966–16 Nov 1966)	
VF-111	F-8E
VF-162	F-8E
VA-163	A-4E
VA-164	A-4E
VA-152	A-1H
VAH-4 Det G	A-3B
VAW-11 Det G	E-1B
VFP-63 Det G	RF-8G
HC-1 D1 Unit G	UH-2A, -2B
VAP-61 Det*	RA-3B
Franklin D. Roosevelt (CVA 42) with CVW-1 (21 Jun 1966–21 Feb 1967)	
VF-14	F-4B
VF-32	F-4B
VA-12	A-4E
VA-72	A-4E
VA-172	A-4C
VAH-10 Det 42	A-3B
VAW-12 Det 42	E-1B
VFP-62 Det 42	RF-8G
HC-2 Det 42	UH-2A, -2B
VQ-1 Det 42*	EA-3B
VAW-13 Det 42*	EA-1F
Coral Sea (CVA 43) with CVW-2 (29 Jul 1966–23 Feb 1967)	
VF-21	F-4B
VF-154	F-4B
VA-22	A-4C
VA-23	A-4E
VA-25	A-1H
VAW-11 Det A	E-2A

VAH-2 Det A	A-3B
VFP-63 Det A	RF-8G
HC-1 D1 Unit A	UH-2A, -2B
VQ-1 Det*	EA-3B
VAP-61 Det*	RA-3B
Ticonderoga (CVA 14) with CVW-19 (15 Oct 1966–29 May 1967)	
VF-191	F-8E
VF-194	F-8E
VA-192	A-4E
VA-195	A-4C
VA-52	A-1H, -1J
VFP-63 Det E	RF-8G
VAH-4 Det E	A-3B
VAW-11 Det E	E-1B
HC-1 D1 Unit E	UH-2A, -2B
VQ-1 Det*	EA-3B
VAP-61 Det*	RA-3B
Kitty Hawk (CVA 63) with CVW-11 (5 Nov 1966–19 Jun 1967)	
VF-213	F-4B
VF-114	F-4B
VA-112	A-4C
VA-144	A-4C
VA-85	A-6A
RVAH-13	RA-5C
VAW-114 (previously a detachment of VAW-11)	E-2A
VAH-4 Det C	KA-3B
HC-1 D1 Unit C	UH-2A, -2B
VQ-1 Det*	EA-3B
VAP-61 Det*	RA-3B
Enterprise (CVAN 65) with CVW-9 (19 Nov 1966–6 Jul 1967)	
VA-56	A-4C
VA-113	A-4C
VA-35	A-6A
VF-92	F-4B
VF-96	F-4B
VAH-2 Det M	A-3B
RVAH-7	RA-5C
VAW-11 Det M	E-2A
HC-1 Det M	UH-2A
VQ-1 Det*	EA-3B
VAP-61 Det*	RA-3B
Kearsarge (CVS 33) with CVSG-53 (9 Jun 1966–20 Dec 1966)	
HS-6	SH-3A
VS-29	S-2E
VS-21	S-2E

Squadron	Aircraft
VAW-11 Det R	E-1B
Bennington (CVS 20) with CVSG-59 (4 Nov 1966–23 May 1967)	
VS-3B	S-2E
VS-33	S-2E
HS-8	SH-3A
VAW-11 Det Q[||]	E-1B
1967 WestPac/Vietnam Deployments[2]	
Hancock (CVA 19) with CVW-5 (5 Jan 1967–22 Jul 1967)	
VF-51	F-8E
VF-53	F-8E
VA-93	A-4E
VA-94	A-4C
VA-115	A-1H
VAH-4 Det B	A-3B
VFP-63 Det B	RF-8G
HC-1 Det B	UH-2A, -2B
VAW-11 Det 31[||]	E-1B
Bon Homme Richard (CVA 31) with CVW-21 (26 Jan 1967–25 Aug 1967)	
VF-211	F-8E
VF-24	F-8C
VA-212	A-4E
VA-76	A-4C
VA-215	A-1H
VAH-4 Det 31	A-3B
VAW-11 Det L[||]	E-1B
VFP-63 Det 31	RF-8G
HC-1 D1 Unit L	UH-2A, -2B
VAW-13 Det 31[*]	EA-1F
Hornet (CVS 12) with CVSG-57 (27 Mar 1967–28 Oct 1967)	
VS-35	S-2E
VS-37	S-2E
HS-2	SH-3A
VAW-11 Det N[||]	E-1B
Constellation (CVA 64) with CVW-14 (29 Apr 1967–4 Dec 1967)	
VF-142	F-4B
VF-143	F-4B
VA-55	A-4C
VA-146	A-4C
VA-196	A-6A
RVAH-12	RA-5C
VAW-113	E-2A
VAH-8	KA-3B
HC-1 D1 Unit F/64	UH-2A, -2B
VAP-61 Det[*]	RA-3B
VQ-1 Det[*]	EA-3B
VAW-13 Det[*]	EA-1F
VA-65[*]	A-6A
Intrepid (CVS 11) with CVW-10 (11 May 1967–30 Dec 1967)	
VSF-3	A-4B
VA-15	A-4C
VA-34	A-4C
VA-145	A-1H
VAW-33 Det 11	EA-1F
VAW-121 Det 11	E-1B
VFP-63 Det 11	RF-8G
VF-111 Det 11	F-8C
HC-2 Det 11	UH-2A, -2B
Forrestal (CVA 59) with CVW-17 (6 Jun 1967–15 Sep 1967)	
VF-11	F-4B
VF-74	F-4B
VA-46	A-4E
VA-65	A-6A
VA-106	A-4E
RVAH-11	RA-5C
VAW-123	E-2A
VAW-13 Det	EA-1F
VAH-10 Det 59	KA-3B
HC-2 Det 59	UH-2A
VAP-61 Det[*]	RA-3B
Oriskany (CVA 34) with CVW-16 (16 Jun 1967–31 Jan 1968)	
VF-111	F-8C
VF-162	F-8E
VA-152	A-1H, -1J
VA-163	A-4E
VA-164	A-4E
VFP-63 Det G/34	RF-8G
VAH-4 Det G/34	KA-3B
VAW-111 Det G/34	E-1B
VAW-13 Det[*]	EA-1F
HC-1 Det 34	UH-2A, -2B
VAP-61 Det[*]	RA-3B
Coral Sea (CVA 43) with CVW-15 (26 Jul 1967–6 Apr 1968)	
VF-151	F-4B
VF-161	F-4B
VA-153	A-4E
VA-155	A-4E
VA-25	A-1H, -1J
VFP-63 Det 43	RF-8G
VAH-2 Det 43	KA-3B
VAW-116	E-2A
HC-1 Det 43	UH-2A
VAW-13 Det[*]	EA-1F
VAP-61 Det[*]	RA-3B

Ranger (CVA 61) with CVW-2 (4 Nov 1967–25 May 1968)	
VF-154	F-4B
VF-21	F-4B
VA-22	A-4C
VA-165	A-6A
VA-147	A-7A
RVAH-6	RA-5C
VAW-115	E-2A
VAH-2 Det 61	KA-3B
HC-1 Det 61	UH-2A, -2C
VAW-13 Det 61	EKA-3B
VAP-61 Det*	RA-3B

Kitty Hawk (CVA 63) with CVW-11 (18 Nov 1967–28 Jun 1968)	
VF-213	F-4B
VF-114	F-4B
VA-75	A-6A, -6B
VA-112	A-4C
VA-144	A-4E
RVAH-11	RA-5C
VAW-114	E-2A
VAH-4 Det 63	KA-3B
VAW-13 Det 63	EA-1F
HC-1 Det 63	UH-2C

Ticonderoga (CVA 14) with CVW-19 (28 Dec 1967–17 Aug 1968)	
VF-191	F-8E
VF-194	F-8E
VA-23	A-4F
VA-192	A-4F
VA-195	A-4C
VAH-4 Det 14	KA-3B
VAW-111 Det 14	E-1B
VFP-63 Det 14	RF-8G
VAQ-33 Det 14	EA-1F
HC-1 Det 14	UH-2A, -2B

Kearsarge (CVS 33) with CVSG-53 (17 Aug 1967–6 Apr 1968)	
HS-6	SH-3A
VS-29	S-2E
VS-21	S-2E
VAW-111 Det 33	E-1B
HC-7 Det 110*	SH-3A

Yorktown (CVS 10) with CVSG-55 (28 Dec 1967–5 Jul 1968)	
VS-23	S-2E
VS-25	S-2E
HS-4	SH-3D
VAW-111 Det 10	E-1B
HC-7 Det 111*	SH-3A

1968 WestPac/Vietnam Deployments[3]	
Enterprise (CVAN 65) with CVW-9 (3 Jan 1968–18 Jul 1968)	
VF-92	F-4B
VF-96	F-4B
VA-35	A-6A, -6B
VA-56	A-4E
VA-113	A-4F
RVAH-1	RA-5C
VAW-112	E-2A
VAH-2 Det 65	KA-3B
HC-1 Det 65	UH-2C
VAW-13 Det 65**	EKA-3B
HC-7 Det 111*	SH-3A

Bon Homme Richard (CVA 31) with CVW-5 (27 Jan 1968–10 Oct 1968)	
VF-51	F-8H
VF-53	F-8E
VA-93	A-4F
VA-94	A-4E
VA-212	A-4F
VFP-63 Det 31	RF-8G
VAW-13 Det 31**	EKA-3B
VAW-111 Det 31	E-1B
HC-1 Det 31	UH-2C

America (CVA 66) with CVW-6 (10 Apr 1968–16 Dec 1968)	
VF-33	F-4J
VF-102	F-4J
VA-82	A-7A
VA-86	A-7A
VA-85	A-6A, -6B
VAW-122	E-2A
RVAH-13	RA-5C
VAH-10 Det 66	KA-3B
VAW-13 Det 66**	EKA-3B
HC-2 Det 66	UH-2A, -2B

Constellation (CVA 64) with CVW-14 (29 May 1968–31 Jan 1969)	
VF-142	F-4B
VF-143	F-4B
VA-27	A-7A
VA-97	A-7A
VA-196	A-6A, -6B
RVAH-5	RA-5C
VAW-113	E-2A
VAH-2 Det 64 (in Nov 1968, when VAH-2 was redesignated VAQ-132, VAH-2 Det 64 became a Det of VAH-10 and operated as VAH-10 Det 64)	KA-3B
VAW-13 Det 64**	EKA-3B

HC-1 Det 64	UH-2C
Intrepid (CVS 11) with CVW-10 **(4 Jun 1968–8 Feb 1969)**	
VA-36	A-4C
VA-66	A-4C
VA-106	A-4E
VF-111 Det 11	F-8C
VFP-63 Det 11	RF-8G
VAW-121 Det 11	E-1B
VAQ-33 Det 11	EA-1F
HC-2 Det 11	UH-2A, -2B
Hancock (CVA 19) with CVW-21 **(18 Jul 1968–3 Mar 1969)**	
VA-55	A-4F
VA-163	A-4E
VA-164	A-4E
VF-24	F-8H
VF-211	F-8H
VFP-63 Det 19	RF-8G
VAW-111 Det 19	E-1B
HC-1 Det 19	UH-2C
VAW-13 Det 19**	EKA-3B
Coral Sea (CVA 43) with CVW-15 **(7 Sep 1968–18 Apr 1969)**	
VF-151	F-4B
VF-161	F-4B
VA-52	A-6A
VA-153	A-4F
VA-216	A-4C
VAH-10 Det 43	KA-3B
VAW-13 Det 43**	EKA-3B
VAW-116	E-2A
VFP-63 Det 43	RF-8G
HC-1 Det 43	UH-2C
Hornet (CVS 12) with CVSG-57 **(30 Sep 1968–13 May 1969)**	
VS-35	S-2E
VS-37	S-2E
HS-2	SH-3A
VAW-111 Det 12	E-1B
Ranger (CVA 61) with CVW-2 **(26 Oct 1968–17 May 1969)**	
VA-165	A-6A
VF-21	F-4J
VAW-115	E-2A
VA-147	A-7A
VA-155	A-4F
VF-154	F-4J
RVAH-9	RA-5C
VAH-10 Det 61	KA-3B
VAQ-130 Det 61	EKA-3B

HC-1 Det 61	UH-2C
HS-2*	SH-3A
HC-7 Det 110*	SH-3A
Kitty Hawk (CVA 63) with CVW-11 **(30 Dec 1968–4 Sep 1969)**	
VF-114	F-4B
VF-213	F-4B
VA-37	A-7A
VA-65	A-6A, -6B
VA-105	A-7A
RVAH-11	RA-5C
VAQ-131	KA-3B, EKA-3B
VAW-114	E-2A
HC-1 Det 63	UH-2C
HC-7 Det 110*	SH-3A
Bennington (CVS 20) with CVSG-59 **(1 May 1968–9 Nov 1968)**	
VS-33	S-2E
VS-38	S-2E
HS-8	SH-3A
VAW-111 Det 20	E-1B
1969 WestPac/Vietnam Deployments[4]	
Enterprise (CVAN 65) with CVW-9 **(6 Jan 1969–2 Jul 1969)**	
VF-92	F-4J
VF-96	F-4J
VA-145	A-6A, -6B
VA-146	A-7B
VA-215	A-7B
VAQ-132	EKA-3B, KA-3B
VAW-112	E-2A
RVAH-6	RA-5C
HC-1 Det 65	UH-2C
Ticonderoga (CVA 14) with CVW-16 **(1 Feb 1969–18 Sep 1969)**	
VA-87	A-7B
VF-111	F-8H
VF-162	F-8J
VA-25	A-7B
VA-112	A-4C
VFP-63 Det 14	RF-8G
VAQ-130 Det 14	EKA-3B
VAW-111 Det 14	E-1B
HC-1 Det 14	UH-2C
HC-7 Det 110*	SH-3A
Bon Homme Richard (CVA 31) with CVW-5 **(18 Mar 1969–29 Oct 1969)**	
VF-51	F-8J
VF-53	F-8J
VA-22	A-4F
VA-94	A-4E

VA-144	A-4E
VFP-63 Det 31	RF-8G
VAQ-130 Det 31	EKA-3B
VAW-111 Det 31	E-1B
HC-1 Det 31	UH-2C
HC-7 Det 110˙	SH-3A

Kearsarge (CVS 33) with CVSG-53 (29 Mar 1969–4 Sep 1969)	
VS-21	S-2E
VS-29	S-2E
HS-6	SH3A
VAW-111 Det 33	E-1B
HC-7 Det 111˙	SH-3A
HC-7 Det 110˙	SH-3A

Oriskany (CVA 34) with CVW-19 (14 Apr 1969–17 Nov 1969)	
VF-191	F-8J
VF-194	F-8J
VA-23	A-4F
VA-192	A-4F
VA-195	A-4E
VAW-111 Det 34	E-1B
VFP-63 Det 34	RF-8G
VAQ-130 Det 34	EKA-3B
HC-1 Det 34	UH-2C

Hancock (CVA 19) with CVW-21 (2 Aug 1969–15 Apr 1970)	
VF-24	F-8H
VF-211	F-8J
VA-55	A-4F
VA-164	A-4F
VA-212	A-4F
VAH-10 Det 19	KA-3B
VAW-111 Det 19	E-1B
VFP-63 Det 19	RF-8G
HC-1 Det 19	SH-3A

Constellation (CVA 64) with CVW-14 (11 Aug 1969–8 May 1970)	
VF-142	F-4J
VF-143	F-4J
VA-27	A-7A
VA-85	A-6A, -6B
VA-97	A-7A
RVAH-7	RA-5C
VAW-113	E-2A
VAQ-133	EKA-3B, KA-3B
HC-1 Det 5	SH-3A
HC-7 Det 110˙	SH-3A

Coral Sea (CVA 43) with CVW-15 (23 Sep 1969–1 Jul 1970)	
VF-151	F-4B
VF-161	F-4B
VA-82	A-7A
VA-86	A-7A
VA-35	A-6A
VAW-116	E-2A
VAQ-135	KA-3B, EKA-3B
VFP-63 Det 43	RF-8G
HC-1 Det 9	UH-2C

Ranger (CVA 61) with CVW-2 (14 Oct 1969–1 Jun 1970)	
VF-21	F-4J
VF-154	F-4J
VA-56	A-7B
VA-93	A-7B
VA-196	A-6A
RVAH-5	RA-5C
VAQ-134	EKA-3B, KA-3B
VAW-115	E-2A
HC-1 Det 8	SH-3A
VC-3 Det	147SK drones

1970 WestPac/Vietnam Deployments

Shangri-La (CVS 38) with CVW-8 (5 Mar 1970–17 Dec 1970)	
VA-12	A-4C
VA-152	A-4E
VA-172	A-4C
VF-111	F-8H
VF-162	F-8H
VAH-10 Det 38˙	KA-3D
VFP-63 Det 38	RF-8G
VAW-121 Det 38	E-1B
HC-2 Det 38	UH-2C

Bon Homme Richard (CVA 31) with CVW-5 (2 Apr 1970–12 Nov 1970)	
VF-51	F-8J
VF-53	F-8J
VA-22	A-4F
VA-94	A-4E
VA-144	A-4F
VFP-63 Det 31	RF-8G
VAQ-130 Det 31	EKA-3B
VAW-111 Det 14	E-1B
HC-1 Det 3	UH-2C

America (CVA 66) with CVW-9 (10 Apr 1970–21 Dec 1970)	
VF-92	F-4J
VF-96	F-4J
VA-146	A-7E
VA-147	A-7E
VA-165	A-6A, -6B, -6C
RVAH-12	RA-5C

VAW-124	E-2A
VAQ-132	EKA-3B, KA-3B
HC-2 Det 66	UH-2C
HC-7 Det 110*	SH-3A

Oriskany (CVA 34) with CVW-19 (14 May 1970–10 Dec 1970)

VF-191	F-8J
VF-194	F-8J
VA-153	A-7A
VA-155	A-7B
VAQ-130 Det 34	EKA-3B
VAW-111 Det 34	E-1B
VFP-63 Det 34	RF-8G
HC-1 Det 6	UH-2C

Hancock (CVA 19) with CVW-21 (22 Oct 1970–3 Jun 1971)

VF-24	F-8J
VF-211	F-8J
VA-55	A-4F
VA-164	A-4F
VAQ-129 Det 62	EKA-3B
VAW-111 Det 19	E-1B
VFP-63 Det 19	RF-8G
VA-212	A-4F
HC-1 Det 7	UH-2C
HC-5 Det 103*	UH-2C

Ranger (CVA 61) with CVW-2 (27 Oct 1970–17 Jun 1971)

VF-21	F-4J
VF-154	F-4J
VA-25	A-7E
VA-113	A-7E
VA-145	A-6A, -6C
RVAH-1	RA-5C
VAQ-134	KA-3B, EKA-3B
VAW-111 Det 7	E-1B
HC-1 Det 1	SH-3G
HC-7 Det 110*	SH-3A

Kitty Hawk (CVA 63) with CVW-11 (6 Nov 1970–17 Jul 1971)

VF-114	F-4J
VF-213	F-4J
VA-192	A-7E
VA-195	A-7E
VA-52	A-6B
RVAH-6	RA-5C
VAQ-133	EKA-3B, KA-3B
VAW-114	E-2B
HC-1 Det 2	UH-2C
HC-7 Det 110*	SH-3A

1971 WestPac/Vietnam Deployments

Midway (CVA 41) with CVW-5 (16 Apr 1971–6 Nov 1971)

VF-151	F-4B
VF-161	F-4B
VA-56	A-7B
VA-93	A-7B
VA-115	A-6A, KA-6D
VAQ-130 Det 2	EKA-3B
VFP-63 Det 3	RF-8G
VAW-115	E-2B
HC-1 Det 8	SH-3G
HC-7 Det 110*	HH-3A

Oriskany (CVA 34) with CVW 19 (14 May 1971–18 Dec 1971)

VF-191	F-8J
VF-194	F-8J
VA-153	A-7A
VA-155	A-7B
VA-215	A-7B
VAQ-130 Det 3	EKA-3B
VFP-63 Det 34	RF-8G
VAW-111 Det 1	E-1B
HC-1 Det 5	UH-2C
HC-7 Det 110*	SH-3A, -3G

Enterprise (CVAN 65) with CVW-14 (11 Jun 1971–12 Feb 1972)

VF-143	F-4J
VF-142	F-4J
VA-97	A-7E
VA-27	A-7E
VA-196	A-6A, -6B, KA-6D
RVAH-5	RA-5C
VAW-113	E-2B
VAQ-130 Det 4	EKA-3B
HC-1 Det 4	SH-3G

Constellation (CVA 64) with CVW-9 (1 Oct 1971–30 Jun 1972)

VF-92	F-4J
VF-96	F-4J
VA-146	A-7E
VA-147	A-7E
VA-165	A-6A, KA-6D
RVAH-11	RA-5C
VAQ-130 Det 1	EKA-3B
VAW-116	E-2B
HC-1 Det 3	SH-3G

Coral Sea (CVA 43) with CVW-15 (12 Nov 1971–17 Jul 1972)

VF-51	F-4B
VF-111	F-4B
VA-22	A-7E

VA-94	A-7E
VMA(AW)-224	A-6A, KA-6D
VFP-63 Det 5	RF-8G
VAW-111 Det 4	E-1B
VAQ-135 Det 3	EKA-3B
HC-1 Det 6	SH-3G
HC-7 Det 110*	HH-3A
Ticonderoga (CVS 14) with CVSG-59 (11 Mar 1971–6 Jul 1971)	
VS-33	S-2E
VS-37	S-2E
VS-38	S-2E
HS-4	SH-3D
HS-8	SH-3D
1972 WestPac/Vietnam Deployments	
Hancock (CVA 19) with CVW-21 (7 Jan 1972–3 Oct 1972)	
VA-55	A-4F
VA-164	A-4F, TA-4F
VA-212	A-4F
VF-24	F-8J
VF-211	F-8J
VFP-63 Det 1	RF-8G
VAQ-135 Det 5	EKA-3B
VAW-111 Det 2	E-1B
HC-1 Det 7	SH-3G
Kitty Hawk (CVA 63) with CVW-11 (17 Feb 1972–28 Nov 1972)	
VA-195	A-7E
VA-192	A-7E
VA-52	A-6A, -6B, KA-6D
VF-114	F-4J
VF-213	F-4J
RVAH-7	RA-5C
VAW-114	E-2B
VAQ-135 Det 1	EKA-3B
HC-1 Det 1	SH-3G
HC-7 Det*	HH-3A
Midway (CVA 41) with CVW-5 (10 Apr 1972–3 Mar 1973)	
VF-151	F-4B
VF-161	F-4B
VA-56	A-7B
VA-93	A-7B
VA-115	A-6A, KA-6D
VAQ-130 Det 2	EKA-3B
VFP-63 Det 3	RF-8G
VAW-115	E-2B
HC-1 Det 2	SH-3G
HC-7 Det 110*	HH-3A

Saratoga (CV 60) with CVW-3 (11 Apr 1972–13 Feb 1973)	
VF-31	F-4J
VF-103	F-4J
VA-75	A-6A, -6B, KA-6D
VA-37	A-7A
VA-105	A-7A
RVAH-1	RA-5C
VAW-123	E-2B
HS-7	SH-3D
HC-7 Det 110*	HH-3A
VMCJ-2 Det*	EA-6A
Ticonderoga (CVS 14) with CVSG-53 (17 May 1972–29 Jul 1972)	
VS-21	S-2E
VS-29	S-2E
VS-35	S-2E
VS-38	S-2E
VAW-111 Det 3	E-1B
HS-4	SH-3D
HS-8	SH-3D
America (CVA 66) with CVW-8 (5 Jun 1972–24 Mar 1973)	
VF-74	F-4J
VA-35	A-6A, -6C, KA-6D
VA-82	A-7C
VA-86	A-7C
RVAH-6	RA-5C
VAW-124	E-2B
VMFA-333	F-4J
VAQ-132	EA-6B
HC-2 Det 66	SH-3G
HC-7 Det 110*	HH-3A
Oriskany (CVA 34) with CVW-19 (5 Jun 1972–30 Mar 1973)	
VF-191	F-8J
VF-194	F-8J
VA-153	A-7A
VA-155	A-7B
VA-215	A-7B
VFP-63 Det 4	RF-8G
VAQ-130 Det 3	EKA-3B
VAW-111 Det 6	E-1B
HC-1 Det 5	SH-3G
Enterprise (CVAN 65) with CVW-14 (12 Sep 1972–12 Jun 1973)	
VF-143	F-4J
VF-142	F-4J
VA-27	A-7E
VA-97	A-7E
VA-196	A-6E, -6B, KA-6D

VAW-113	E-2B
VAQ-131	EA-6B
RVAH-13	RA-5C
HS-2 Det 1	SH-3G
Ranger (CVA 61) with CVW-2 **(16 Nov 1972–23 Jun 1973)**	
VF-21	F-4J
VF-154	F-4J
VA-25	A-7E
VA-113	A-7E
VA-145	A-6A, -6B, KA-6D
RVAH-5	RA-5C
VAW-111 Det 1	E-1B
VAQ-130 Det 4	EKA-3B
HC-1 Det 1	SH-3G
HC-7 Det 110˙	HH-3A
VQ-1 Det˙	EA-3B
1973 WestPac/Vietnam Deployments	
Constellation (CVA 64) with CVW-9 **(5 Jan 1973–11 Oct 1973)**	
VF-92	F-4J
VF-96	F-4J
VA-146	A-7E
VA-147	A-7E
VA-165	A-6A, KA-6D
HS-6 Det 1	SH-3G
VAQ-134	EA-6B
VAW-116	E-2B
RVAH-12	RA-5C
VQ-1 Det˙	EA-3B
Hancock (CVA 19) with CVW-21 **(8 May 1973–8 Jan 1974)**	
VF-24	F-8J
VF-211	F-8J
VA-55	A-4F
VA-164	A-4F, TA-4F
VA-212	A-4F
VFP-63 Det 1	RF-8G
VAQ-135 Det 5‡	EKA-3B
VAW-111 Det 2	E-1B
HC-1 Det 3	SH-3G
HC-7 Det 110˙	HH-3A
Coral Sea (CVA 43) with CVW-15 **(9 Mar 1973–8 Nov 1973)**	
VF-51	F-4B
VF-111	F-4B
VA-22	A-7E
VA-94	A-7E
VA-95	A-6A, -6B, KA-6D
VAQ-135 Det 3‡	EKA-3B
VAW-111 Det 4	E-1B

VFP-63 Det 5	RF-8G
HC-1 Det 6	SH-3G
HC-7 Det 110˙	HH-3A
Midway (CVA 41) with CVW-5 **(11 Sep 1973–31 Dec 1973)§**	
VF-151	F-4N
VF-161	F-4N
VA-56	A-7A
VA-93	A-7A
VA-115	A-6A, -6B, KA-6D
VFP-63 Det 3	RF-8G
VAW-115	E-2B
HC-1 Det 2	SH-3G
VMCJ-1 Det 101	EA-6A
Oriskany (CVA 34) with CVW-19 **(18 Oct 1973–5 Jun 1974)**	
VF-191	F-8J
VF-194	F-8J
VA-153	A-7B
VA-155	A-7B
VA-215	A-7B
VFP-63 Det 4	RF-8G
VAW-111 Det 6§	E-1B
VAQ-130 Det 3	EKA-3B
HC-1 Det 1	SH-3G
Kitty Hawk (CVA 63) with CVW-11 **(23 Nov 1973–9 Jul 1974)**	
VF-114	F-4J
VF-213	F-4J
VA-192	A-7E
VA-195	A-7E
VA-52	A-6A, KA-6D
VAQ-136	EA-6B
RVAH-7	RA-5C
VAW-114	E-2B
VS-37	S-2G
VS-38	S-2G
HS-4	SH-3D
VQ-1 Det 63˙	EA-3B
1974 WestPac/Vietnam Deployments	
Midway (CVA 41) with CVW-5 **(1 Jan–31 Dec 1974)§**	
VF-161	F-4N
VF-151	F-4N
VA-93	A-7A
VA-56	A-7A
VA-115	A-6A, -6B, KA-6D
VAW-115	E-2B
HC-1 Det 2	SH-3G
VMCJ-1 Det 101	EA-6A, RF-4B
VQ-1 Det˙	EA-3B

Ranger (CVA 61) with CVW-2 (7 May 1974–18 Oct 1974)	
VA-25	A-7E
VA-113	A-7E
VA-145	A-6A, KA-6D
VF-21	F-4J
VF-154	F-4J
RVAH-13	RA-5C
VAW-112	E-2B
HC-1 Det 4	SH-3G
VQ-1 Det 61*	EA-3B

Constellation (CVA 64) with CVW-9 (21 Jun 1974–22 Dec 1974)	
VF-92	F-4J
VF-96	F-4J
VA-146	A-7E
VA-147	A-7E
VA-165	A-6A, KA-6D
RVAH-5	RA-5C
VAW-116	E-2B
VAQ-131	EA-6B
HS-6	SH-3A
VQ-1 Det 64*	EA-3B

Enterprise (CVAN 65) with CVW-14 (17 Sep 1974–20 May 1975)	
VF-1	F-14A
VF-2	F-14A
VA-27	A-7E
VA-97	A-7E
VA-196	A-6A, KA-6D
VAQ-137	EA-6B
HS-2	SH-3D
VAW-113	E-2B
RVAH-12	RA-5C
VQ-1 Det 65*	EA-3B

Coral Sea (CVA 43) with CVW-15 (5 Dec 1974–2 Jul 1975)	
VF-51	F-4N
VF-111	F-4N
VFP-63 Det 5	RF-8G
VA-22	A-7E
VA-94	A-7E
VA-95	A-6A, KA-6D
RVAW-110 Det 3	E-1B
HC-1 Det 2	SH-3G

1975 WestPac/Vietnam Deployments[a]	

Midway (CV 41) with CVW-5 (1 Jan–31 Dec 1975)[a]	
VF-161	F-4N
VF-151	F-4N
VA-93	A-7A

VA-56	A-7A
VA-115	A-6A, -6B, KA-6D
VAW-115	E-2B
HC-1 Det 2	SH-3G
VMFP-3 Det*	RF-4B
VMAQ-2 Det*	EA-6B
VMCJ-1 Det 101*	EA-6A, RF-4B

Hancock (CV 19) with CVW-21 (18 Mar 1975–20 Oct 1975)	
VA-55	A-4F
VA-164	A-4F, TA-4F
VA-212	A-4F
VF-24	F-8J
VF-211	F-8J
RVAW-110 Det 6	E-1B
HC-1 Det 1	SH-3G
VFP-63 Det 1	RF-8G

Kitty Hawk (CV 63) with CVW-11 (21 May 1975–15 Dec 1975)[a]	
VF-213	F-4J
VF-114	F-4J
VA-52	A-6E, KA-6D
VA-192	A-7E
VA-195	A-7E
VS-37	S-2G
VS-38	S-2G
VAQ-136	EA-6B
RVAH-6	RA-5C
HS-8	SH-3G
VAW-114	E-2B
VQ-1 Det 63*	EA-3

Oriskany (CV 34) with CVW-19 (16 Sep 1975–3 Mar 1976)	
VF-191	F-8J
VF-194	F-8J
VA-153	A-7B
VA-155	A-7B
VA-215	A-7B
VFP-63 Det 4	RF-8G
RVAW-110 Det 4	E-1B
HC-1 Det 4	SH-3G

Tail Codes	
Carrier Air Wings (CVW) from 1964 to 1975	
CVW-1	AB
CVW-2	NE
CVW-3	AC
CVW-5	NF
CVW-6	AE
CVW-7	AG

CVW-8	AJ		VFP-62	GA
CVW-9	NG		VFP-63	PP
CVW-10	AK		VAW-11	RR
CVW-11	NH		VAW-12	GE
CVW-14	NK		VAW-13	VR
CVW-15	NL		VAW-33	GD
CVW-16	AH		VAW-111	RR
CVW-17	AA		VAH-1/RVAH-1	GH
CVW-19	NM		VAH-3/RVAH-3	GJ
CVW-21	NP		VAH-4	ZB
RCVW-4	AD		VAH-5/RVAH-5	GK
RCVW-12	NJ		RVAH-6	GS
CVSG-50/RCVSG-50	AR		VAH-7/RVAH-7	GL
CVSG-51/RCVSG-51	RA		VAH-9/RVAH-9	GM
CVSG-52	AS		VAH-11	GN
CVSG-53	NS		RVAH-12	GP
CVSG-54	AT		RVAH-13	GR
CVSG-55	NU		RVAH-14	GQ
CVSG-56	AU		VAH-21	SL
CVSG-57	NV		VR-30	RW
CVSG-58	AV		VRC-40	CD
CVSG-59	NT		VRC-50	RG
CVSG-60	AW		VQ-1	PR
Various squadrons not part of the normal air wing composition but deployed on carriers from 1964 to 1975			VQ-2	JQ
			VSF-1	NA
VAP-61	SS		VAQ-130	VR
VAP-62	GB		HM-12	DH

Some of the squadrons, such as VAQ, VAW, and RVAH, lost their individually assigned tail codes in the late 1960s or early 1970s and are authorized to use those of their permanently assigned carrier air wing.

Tail codes for Marine Corps squadrons that deployed on board carriers are not included in the list.

Notes and explanations-specific entries:

* These squadron detachments were not on board the carrier for the entire deployment.

† This carrier returned from deployment prior to the beginning of combat operations in Vietnam during 1964.

‡ VAQ-135 Detachments 3 and 5 were transferred on 25 August 1973 to VAQ-130. VAQ-135 Det 3 became VAQ-130 Det 2 and VAQ-135 Det 5 became VAQ-130 Det 5.

§ VAW-111 Det 6 was transferred in March 1974 to RVAW-110 and became RVAW-110 Det 6.

‖ On 20 April 1967 VAW-111 was established and VAW-11 detachments became part of VAW-111. VAW-11 Det Q became VAW-111 Det 20.

This deployment involved an experiment with the composition of the carrier air wing in a multimission role. Several of the squadrons were shore-based in the Philippines during different periods of this deployment.

" On 1 October 1968 VAQ-13 and its detachments were redesignated VAQ-130.

Numbered Notes

1. VAW-13's records for 1966 do not specify the carriers they operated on board. However, the records indicate VAW-13 Det 1 (located at Cubi Point, P.I.) provided detachments in support of fleet strikes from the carriers on Yankee Station.

2. VAW-13 did not submit a Command History Report for 1967, consequently, it is not possible to verify all the squadron's detachments operating on board carriers on Yankee Station in 1967. VQ-1's Command History Report for 1967 did not identify the detachments or carriers they operated from in support of combat operations against Vietnam.

3. VAP-61's Command History Report for 1968 indicated continued support of 7th Fleet carriers on Yankee Station. However, the squadron's report does not identify the detachments deployed on board carriers in WESTPAC during 1968. HC-7 was established on 1 September 1967. In 1968 an HC-7 detachment was formed and given the mission of maintaining year-round combat configured helicopters on board carriers and other ships operating on Yankee Station for combat search and rescue missions. The 1968 HC-7 Command History Report does not identify all the specific ships that Detachment 110 operated on board. VQ-1 detachments continued to support carrier operations in Vietnam. However, the 1968 VQ-1 Command History Report does not mention any detachments that were on board carriers operating on Yankee Station.

4. VQ-1 and VAP-61 detachments provided support from DaNang Air Base, Republic of South Vietnam, for fleet carriers operating on Yankee Station in 1969.

5. On 30 June 1975, all carriers with the designation CVA or CVAN were changed to CV or CVN to reflect the multimission capability of the carrier.

6. *Midway* permanently home ported in WESTPAC.

Deployments for Patrol Squadrons and other Non-Carrier Based Squadrons in Vietnam (1964–1972)[1]

1964 Deployments				
Squadron	**To**	**In**	**Out**	**Aircraft**
VP-48	NS Sangley Point	May 1964	22 Sep 1964	SP-5B
VAP-61	(See detachments)	17 May 1964	See Note 2	RA-3B
Detachment Location:				
	NAS Cubi Point			
	RTAB Don Muang			
	FASU Da Nang/ RTNB			
	U-Tapao	17 May 1964	1 Jul 1971	
VW-1	(See detachments)	01 Oct 1964	See Note 2	EC-121K, C-121J, WC-121N
Detachment Location:				
	NS Sangley Point			
	NSAD Chu Lai	01 Oct 1964	01 Jul 1971	
VQ-1	(See detachments)	01 Oct 1964	See Note 2	EC-121M, E/RA-3B, C-121J, EP-3B
Detachment Location:				
	RTAB Don Muang			
	NAS Cubi Point			
	NAF Da Nang	01 Oct 1964	17 Feb 1973	
VP-17	NAF Naha	27 Apr 1964	30 Sep 1964	SP-2H
Detachment Location:				
	None			
VP-28	MCAS Iwakuni	16 May 1964	18 Oct 1964	SP-2H
Detachment Location:				
	NS Sangley Point	05 Aug 1964	30 Sep 1964	
VP-42	MCAS Iwakuni	11 Jul 1964	16 Nov 1964	SP-2E
Detachment Location:				
	NS Sangley Point	03 Sep 1964	18 Sep 1964	
	NAF Tan Son Nhut	18 Sep 1964	19 Sep 1964	
	NAS Cubi Point	06 Oct 1964	24 Oct 1964	
Special Det Deployment:				
	NAF Tan Son Nhut	Oct 1964	late Feb 1965	
VP-6	NAF Naha			
	MCAS Iwakuni	12 Aug 1964	25 Jan 1965	SP-2E
Detachment Location:				
	NAS Cubi Point	01 Sep 1964	28 Sep 1964	
VP-47	NS Sangley Point	17 Aug 1964	28 Feb 1965	SP-5B
Detachment Location:				
	AV-13	various	various	
VP-1	MCAS Iwakuni	07 Oct 1964	01 Apr 1965	SP-2H
Detachment Location:				
	NAF Tan Son Nhut			
	Da Nang			
VP-9	NAF Naha	12 Nov 1964	08 Jul 1965	P-3A
Detachment Location:				
	None			

1965 Deployments				
Squadron	**To**	**In**	**Out**	**Aircraft**
VQ-2	(*See* detachments)	01 Dec 1965	*See* Note 2	EA-3B
Detachment Location:				
	NAS Cubi Point			
	FASU Da Nang	01 Dec 1965	30 Sep 1969	
VP-2	MCAS Iwakuni	24 Jan 1965	16 Jul 1965	SP-2H
Detachment Location:				
	NAF Tan Son Nhut	15 Mar 1965	01 May 1965	
	various (Naha, Sangley Point, Iwo Jima, Bangkok, Tainan, Da Nang)			
VP-40	NS Sangley Point	27 Feb 1965	03 Sep 1965	SP-5B
Detachment Location:				
	AV-13	14 May 1965	20 May 1965	
	AV-7	29 May 1965	03 Aug 1965	
VP-4	MCAS Iwakuni	26 Mar 1965	28 Sep 1965	SP-2H
Detachment Location:				
	NAF Tan Son Nhut	19 Apr 1965	19 Apr 1965	
	NS Sangley Point	26 Mar 1965	20 Apr 1965	
	NAS Cubi Point	20 Apr 1965	26 Apr 1965	
VP-22	NS Sangley Point	23 Apr 1965	13 Dec 1965	P-3A
Detachment Location:				
	None			
VP-46	NAF Naha	07 Jun 1965	08 Jan 1966	P-3A
Detachment Location:				
	NS Sangley Point	07 Jun 1965	08 Jan 1966	
VP-17	MCAS Iwakuni	09 Jul 1965	06 Feb 1966	SP-2H
Detachment Location:				
	NAF Tan Son Nhut			
VP-50	NS Sangley Point	01 Sep 1965	14 Mar 1966	SP-5B
Detachment Location:				
	NAF Camh Ranh Bay			
	AV-12	various	various	
VP-42	MCAS Iwakuni	26 Sep 1965	05 Apr 1966	SP-2H
Detachment Location:				
	NAF Tan Son Nhut	08 Oct 1965	13 Feb 1966	
VP-48	(*See* detachment)			SP-5B
Detachment Location:				
	NS Sangley Point	Aug 1965	04 Sep 1966	
VP-28	NS Sangley Point	02 Nov 1965	02 Jun 1966	P-3A
Detachment Location:				
	None			
1966 Deployments				
Squadron	**To**	**In**	**Out**	**Aircraft**
VXN-8	(*See* detachment)			NC-121J
Detachment Location:				
	NAF Tan Son Nhut	Oct 1965	Dec 1965	
	NAF Tan Son Nhut	03 Jan 1966	01 Dec 1970	

HC-1	(See detachment)			UH-1B
Detachment Location:				
	Various in Mekong Delta	01 Jul 1966	01 Apr 1967	
VRC-50	(See detachments)	01 Oct 1966	See Note 2	C-1A, C-2A, CT-39E
Detachment Location:				
	NAS Cubi Point	See Note 2	See Note 2	
	Da Nang	01 Feb 1970	02 Jan 1971	
		15 Dec 1971	19 Feb 1973	
VAP-62	(See detachments)	31 Oct 1966	See Note 2	RA-3B
Detachment Location:				
	NAS Cubi Point			
	FASU Da Nang	31 Oct 1966	01 Feb 1969	
VP-47	NAF Naha	04 Jan 1966	30 Jun 1966	P-3B
Detachment Location:				
	NS Sangley Point (augmented occasionally)			
VP-1	MCAS Iwakuni	03 Feb 1966	01 Aug 1966	SP-2H
Detachment Location:				
	NAF Tan Son Nhut	13 Feb 1966	27 May 1966	
VP-40	NS Sangley Point	15 Mar 1966	03 Sep 1966	SP-5B
Detachment Location:				
	AV-13	10 Mar 1966	26 Mar 1966	
		03 Apr 1966	10 Apr 1966	
		14 May 1966	03 Jun 1966	
		10 Jul 1966	09 Aug 1966	
		15 Jul 1966	21 Jul 1966	
VP-2	MCAS Iwakuni	01 Apr 1966	01 Oct 1966	SP-2H
Detachment Location:				
	NAF Tan Son Nhut	25 May 1966	30 Sep 1966	
VP-8	NS Sangley Point	01 Jul 1966	02 Dec 1966	P-3A
Detachment Location:				
	None			
VP-9	NAF Naha	25 Jul 1966	10 Jan 1967	P-3B
Detachment Location:				
	NAF Sangley Point	25 Jun 1966	12 Dec 1966	
VP-19	MCAS Iwakuni	01 Aug 1966	31 Jan 1967	P-3A
Detachment Location:				
	Unknown			
VP-50	Cam Ranh Bay, AV-7	19 Aug 1966	06 Feb 1967	SP-5B
Detachment Location:				
	None			
VP-17	MCAS Iwakuni			SP-2H
	NS Sangley Point	01 Oct 1966	30 Mar 1967	
Detachment Location:				
	NAF Tan Son Nhut	01 Oct 1966	30 Mar 1967	
VP-16	NS Sangley Point	02 Dec 1966	02 Jun 1967	P-3A
Detachment Location:				
	NAF U-Tapao	18 Jan 1967	18 Feb 1967	

1967 Deployments				
Squadron	**To**	**In**	**Out**	**Aircraft**
VO-67	RTAB Nakhon Phanom	15 Nov 1967	01 Jul 1968	OP-2E
Detachment Location:				
	None			
HAL-3	Vung Tau	01 Apr 1967	01 May 1969	UH-1B/1C/1L/1M, HH-1K
	Binh Thuy	02 May 1969	16 Mar 1972	
Detachment Location:				
	various			
VR-1	(See detachment)	14 Jun 1967	See Note 2	C-130F
Detachment Location:				
	NAS Cubi Point	14 Jun 1967	23 Jun 1967	
VP-46	NAF Naha	14 Jan 1967	30 Jun 1967	P-3B
Detachment Location:				
	NS Sangley Point	05 Feb 1967	18 Feb 1967	
	RTNB U-Tapao	18 Feb 1967	30 Jun 1967	
VP-4	MCAS Iwakuni	31 Jan 1967	31 Jul 1967	P-3A
Detachment Location:				
	NS Sangley Point	See Note 2	See Note 2	
	NAF Naha	15 Jul 1967	20 Jul 1967	
VP-40	NS Sangley Point	24 Feb 1967	10 May 1967	SP-5B
Detachment Location:				
	AV-7	01 Mar 1967	30 Apr 1967	
VP-42	NS Sangley Point	31 Mar 1967	30 Sep 1967	SP-2H
Detachment Location:				
	NAF Cam Ranh Bay	02 Apr 1967	18 May 1967	
	NAF Tan Son Nhut	31 Mar 1967	30 Sep 1967	
VP-1	NS Sangley Point	06 May 1967	12 Nov 1967	SP-2H
Detachment Location:				
	NAF Cam Rahn Bay	15 May 1967	12 Nov 1967	
VP-5	NS Sangley Point	01 Jun 1967	03 Dec 1967	P-3A
Detachment Location:				
	None			
VP-47	NAF Naha	01 Jul 1967	04 Jan 1968	P-3B
Detachment Location:				
	RTNB U-Tapao	01 Jul 1967	04 Jan 1968	
	NS Sangley Point	(dates unknown)		
VP-48	MCAS Iwakuni	31 Jul 1967	31 Jan 1968	P-3A
Detachment Location:				
	NS Sangley Point	28 Dec 1967	08 Jan 1968	
VP-2	NS Sangley Point	01 Oct 1967	01 Apr 1968	SP-2H
Detachment Location:				
	NAF Tan Son Nhut	01 Oct 1967	Unknown	
	NAF Cam Ranh Bay	01 Feb 1968	30 Mar 1968	
VP-17	NS Sangley Point	09 Nov 1967	29 Apr 1968	SP-2H
Detachment Location:				
	NAF Cam Ranh Bay	09 Nov 1967	29 Apr 1968	
VP-26	NS Sangley Point	27 Nov 1967	07 Jun 1968	P-3B
Detachment Location:				
	RTNB U-Tapao	16 Dec 1967	02 Jun 1968	

1968 Deployments				
Squadron	To	In	Out	Aircraft
VAH-21	*(See* detachment)	01 Sep 1968	*See* Note 2	AP-2H
Detachment Location:				
	NAF Cam Ranh Bay	01 Sep 1968	16 Jul 1969	
VP-6	NAF Naha	01 Jan 1968	01 Jul 1968	P-3A
Detachment Location:				
	NS Sangley Point	21 Jan 1968	24 Jan 1968	
	NAF Cam Ranh Bay	13 May 1968	07 Jun 1968	
VP-19	MCAS Iwakuni	01 Feb 1968	31 Jul 1968	P-3B
Detachment Location:				
	NS Sangley Point	01 Apr 1968	14 Apr 1968	
	RTNB U-Tapao	01 Apr 1968	14 Apr 1968	
	NAF Cam Ranh Bay	15 Jun 1968	15 Jul 1968	
VP-42	NS Sangley Point	10 Mar 1968	03 Sep 1968	SP-2H
Detachment Location:				
	NAF Cam Ranh Bay	(dates unknown)		
VP-50	NS Sangley Point	01 May 1968	01 Nov 1968	P-3A
Detachment Location:				
	NAF Cam Ranh Bay	01 May 1968	01 Nov 1968	
VP-49	NS Sangley Point	01 Jun 1968	16 Dec 1968	P-3A
Detachment Location:				
	RTNB U-Tapao	01 Jun 1968	16 Dec 1968	
VP-22	NAF Naha	30 Jun 1968	11 Jan 1969	P-3A
Detachment Location:				
	NAF Cam Ranh Bay	16 Jul 1968	15 Aug 1968	
		20 Sep 1968	30 Sep 1968	
		01 Oct 1968	15 Oct 1968	
		15 Nov 1968	10 Dec 1968	
VP-4	MCAS Iwakuni	01 Aug 1968	29 Jan 1969	P-3A
Detachment Location:				
	NAF Cam Ranh Bay	15 Aug 1968	15 Sep 1968	
		15 Oct 1968	10 Nov 1968	
		16 Dec 1968	10 Jan 1969	
VP-1	NS Sangley Point	15 Aug 1968	25 Feb 1969	SP-2H
Detachment Location:				
	NAF Cam Ranh Bay	15 Aug 1968	25 Feb 1969	
VP-47	NS Sangley Point	01 Nov 1968	31 Mar 1969	P-3B
Detachment Location:				
	NAF Cam Ranh Bay	01 Nov 1968	31 Mar 1969	
VP-45	NS Sangley Point	16 Dec 1968	01 Jun 1969	P-3A
Detachment Location:				
	RTNB U-Tapao	16 Dec 1968	30 May 1969	
	NAF Cam Ranh Bay	18 Apr 1969	28 Apr 1969	

1969 Deployments				
Squadron	**To**	**In**	**Out**	**Aircraft**
VAL-4	Binh Thuy; Vung Tau	09 Apr 1969	31 Mar 1972	OV-10A, YOV-10D
Detachment Location:				
	None			
VC-5	(See detachment)	02 Oct 1969	See Note 2	C-1A, US-2C
Detachment Location:				
	FASU Da Nang	02 Oct 1969	31 Dec 1969	
VRC-30	(See detachment)	11 Oct 1969	See Note 2	C-1A
Detachment Location:				
	FASU Da Nang	11 Jan 1969	01 Feb 1973	
VP-28	NAF Naha	15 Jan 1969	15 Jul 1969	P-3A
Detachment Location:				
	NAF Cam Ranh Bay	17 Jan 1969	11 Feb 1969	
		29 Apr 1969	15 May 1969	
		13 Jun 1969	18 Jul 1969	
VP-40	MCAS Iwakuni	01 Feb 1969	01 Aug 1969	P-3B
Detachment Location:				
	NAF Cam Ranh Bay	(dates unknown)		
VP-2	NS Sangley Point	17 Feb 1969	17 Aug 1969	SP-2H
VP-9	NS Sangley Point	01 Apr 1969	01 Oct 1969	P-3B
Detachment Location:				
	NAF Cam Ranh Bay	01 Apr 1969	01 Oct 1969	
VP-6	NS Sangley Point	01 Jun 1969	15 Nov 1969	P-3A
Detachment Location:				
	RTNB U-Tapao	27 May 1969	15 Nov 1969	
VP-50	NAF Naha	15 Jul 1969	15 Jan 1970	P-3A
Detachment Location:				
	NAF Cam Ranh Bay	01 Aug 1969	15 Jan 1970	
VP-17	MCAS Iwakuni	01 Aug 1969	01 Feb 1970	P-3A
Detachment Location:				
	NAF Cam Ranh Bay	09 Aug 1969	11 Sep 1969	
		03 Nov 1969	15 Nov 1969	
		15 Dec 1969	22 Dec 1969	
VP-46	NS Sangley Point	01 Oct 1969	31 Mar 1970	P-3B
Detachment Location:				
	NAF Cam Ranh Bay	02 Oct 1969	31 Mar 1970	
VP-22	NS Sangley Point	15 Nov 1969	01 May 1970	P-3A
Detachment Location:				
	RTNB U-Tapao	30 Nov 1969	29 Apr 1970	
1970 Deployments				
Squadron	**To**	**In**	**Out**	**Aircraft**
HC-3	(See detachment)	15 May 1970	See Note 2	CH-46D
Detachment Location:				
	NAF Tan Son Nhut	15 May 1970	01 Dec 1970	
VP-47	NAF Naha	16 Jan 1970	13 Jul 1970	P-3B
Detachment Location:				
	RTNB U-Tapao	09 May 1970	13 Jul 1970	
	NAF Cam Ranh Bay	(dates unknown)		

Squadron	To	In	Out	Aircraft
VP-1	MCAS Iwakuni	01 Feb 1970	31 Jul 1970	P-3B
Detachment Location:				
	RTNB U-Tapao	01 Feb 1970	15 Apr 1970	
	NAF Tan Son Nhut	01 May 1970	27 Jul 1970	
	NAF Cam Ranh Bay	(dates unknown)		
VP-48	NS Sangley Point	01 Apr 1970	30 Sep 1970	P-3B
Detachment Location:				
	NAF Cam Ranh Bay	01 Apr 1970	30 Sep 1970	
VP-40	NS Sangley Point	01 May 1970	30 Oct 1970	P-3B
Detachment Location:				
	RTNB U-Tapao	29 Apr 1970	30 Oct 1970	
VP-6	NAF Naha	14 Jul 1970	15 Jan 1971	P-3A
Detachment Location:				
	None			
VP-19	MCAS Iwakuni	31 Jul 1970	30 Jan 1971	P-3B
Detachment Location:				
	NAF Cam Ranh Bay	10 Oct 1970	24 Oct 1970	
	NS Sangley Point	(dates unknown)		
	RTNB U-Tapao	(dates unknown)		
VP-50	NS Sangley Point	30 Sep 1970	31 Mar 1971	P-3A
Detachment Location:				
	NAF Cam Ranh Bay	30 Sep 1970	31 Mar 1971	
VP-17	NS Sangley Point	29 Oct 1970	29 Apr 1971	P-3A
Detachment Location:				
	RTNB U-Tapao	29 Oct 1970	29 Apr 1971	
1971 Deployments				
Squadron	**To**	**In**	**Out**	**Aircraft**
VP-22	NAF Naha	14 Jan 1971	14 Jul 1971	P-3A
Detachment Location:				
	NAF Cam Ranh Bay	25 Jan 1971	02 Feb 1971	
	RTNB U-Tapao	27 Mar 1971	03 Apr 1971	
VP-4	MCAS Iwakuni	01 Feb 1971	31 Jul 1971	P-3B
Detachment Location:				
	NAF Cam Ranh Bay	(dates unknown)		
VP-1	NS Sangley Point	01 Apr 1971	01 Jul 1971	P-3B
	NAS Cubi Point	01 Jul 1971	01 Oct 1971	
Detachment Location:				
	NAF Cam Ranh Bay	01 Apr 1971	01 Oct 1971	
VP-48	NS Sangley Point	01 May 1971	01 Jul 1971	P-3B
	NAS Cubi Point	01 Jul 1971	30 Sep 1971	
Detachment Location:				
	RTNB U-Tapao	01 May 1971	30 Sep 1971	
VP-40	NAF Naha	14 Jul 1971	13 Jan 1972	P-3B
Detachment Location:				
	NAS Guam	(dates unknown)		
VP-9	MCAS Iwakuni	29 Jul 1971	11 Feb 1972	P-3B
Detachment Location:				
	unknown			

Squadron	To	In	Out	Aircraft
VP-6	NAS Cubi Point	21 Sep 1971	12 Jan 1972	P-3A
Detachment Location:				
	NAF Cam Ranh Bay	21 Sep 1971	02 Dec 1971	
	NAS Cubi Point	12 Jan 1972	10 May 1972	
VP-19	NAS Cubi Point	01 Nov 1971	29 Apr 1972	P-3B
Detachment Location:				
	RTNB U-Tapao	01 Nov 1971	29 Apr 1972	

1972 Deployments				
Squadron	To	In	Out	Aircraft
VP-17	NAF Naha	13 Jan 1972	01 Aug 1972	P-3A
Detachment Location:				
	NAS Cubi Point	09 Apr 1972	23 Apr 1972	
VP-46	MCAS Iwakuni	01 Feb 1972	14 Aug 1972	P-3B
Detachment Location:				
	NAS Cubi Point	23 Feb 1972	01 Mar 1972	
		16 Mar 1972	01 Apr 1972	
VP-4	NAS Cubi Point	26 Mar 1972	01 Nov 1972	P-3A
Detachment Location:				
	RTNB U-Tapao	01 May 1972	01 Nov 1972	
VP-22	NAF Naha	21 Apr 1972	30 Nov 1972	P-3A
Detachment Location:				
	NAS Cubi Point	29 Apr 1972	16 May 1972	
VP-9	(See detachment)	05 May 1972	24 Jul 1972	P-3B
Detachment Location:				
	NAS Cubi Point	05 May 1972	24 Jul 1972	
VP-11	NAS Cubi Point	23 Jul 1972	10 Nov 1972	P-3B
Detachment Location:				
	RTNB U-Tapao	(dates unknown)		
VP-40	MCAS Iwakuni	01 Aug 1972	14 Jan 1973	P-3B
Detachment Location:				
	RTNB U-Tapao	16 Nov 1972	20 Dec 1972	
VP-1	NAS Cubi Point	01 Nov 1972	30 Apr 1973	P-3B
Detachment Location:				
	RTNB U-Tapao	01 Nov 1972	30 Apr 1973	
VP-6	NAF Naha	30 Nov 1972	28 May 1973	P-3A
Detachment Location:				
	RTNB U-Tapao	20 Dec 1972	01 Feb 1973	

Tail Codes for the VP and other Non-Carrier Based Squadrons deploying to Vietnam:	
HAL-3	(no assigned tail code)
HC-1	UP
HC-3	SA
VAH-21	SL
VAL-4	UM
VAP-61	SS
VAP-62	GB
VC-5	UE
VO-67	MR
VP-1	YB
VP-16	LF
VP-17	ZE
VP-19	PE
VP-11	LE
VP-2	YC
VP-22	QA
VP-28	QC
VP-4	YD
VP-40	QE
VP-42	RB
VP-45	LN
VP-46	RC
VP-47	RD
VP-48	SF
VP-49	LP
VP-5	LA
VP-50	SG
VP-6	PC
VP-8	LC
VP-9	PD
VQ-1	PR
VQ-2	JQ
VR-1	JK
VRC-30	RW
VRC-50	RG
VW-1	TE
VXN-8	JB

Tail Codes for the VP and other Non-Carrier Based Squadrons deploying to Vietnam:	
HAL-3	(no assigned tail code)
HC-1	UP
HC-3	SA
VAH-21	SL
VAL-4	UM
VAP-61	SS
VAP-62	GB
VC-5	UE
VO-67	MR
VP-1	YB
VP-16	LF
VP-17	ZE
VP-19	PE
VP-11	LE
VP-2	YC
VP-22	QA
VP-28	QC
VP-4	YD
VP-40	QE
VP-42	RB
VP-45	LN
VP-46	RC
VP-47	RD
VP-48	SF
VP-49	LP
VP-5	LA
VP-50	SG
VP-6	PC
VP-8	LC
VP-9	PD
VQ-1	PR
VQ-2	JQ
VR-1	JK
VRC-30	RW
VRC-50	RG
VW-1	TE
VXN-8	JB

Notes for VP and Non-Carrier Based Squadron Deployments to Vietnam (1964–1972):

1. Date In and Date Out are normally the dates the squadron arrived and departed from the air station or base it operated from during its deployment. Squadron detachment numbers or letters are not listed. There were numerous changes and rotation of patrol squadron aircraft and crews from the squadron's main base of operation during its deployment. A squadron's detachment was usually identified by using the name of the base from which the detachment operated. Some of the squadrons that deployed to Vietnam did not have or use detachments.

2. In some cases specific dates for the squadron or its detachments were not known or could not be determined from official sources.

CHAPTER 32

Grenada Combat Operations
25 October–2 November 1983

Operation Urgent Fury

The mission of Operation Urgent Fury, as stated by Adm. Wesley L. McDonald, while testifying before the Senate Committee on Armed Services on 3 November 1983, was to

> protect and/or evacuate American citizens, to provide stability for the area, and at the invitation of the Organization of Eastern Caribbean States, to help establish a government, which would be more democratic in nature than the existing government, which had taken over rather rigorously and had placed the country into complete isolation for a period of four days.

Adm. McDonald was Commander in Chief, U.S. Atlantic Command, during the Grenada operations. The following is a list of naval aviation forces (does not include all Marine Corps aviation) participating in the Grenada operations:

Carriers	
Independence (CV 62) with CVW-6 (Tail Code AE)	
Squadron	**Aircraft**
VA-87	A-7E
VA-15	A-7E
VA-176	A-6E, KA-6D
VF-32	F-14A
VF-14	F-14A
VAW-122	E-2C
VAQ-131	EA-6B
VS-28	S-3A
HS-15	SH-3H
Amphibious Ships	
Guam (LPH 9) (HMM-261 Tail Code EM)	
HMM-261	AH-1T, CH-53D
Saipan (LHA 2) [1–7 November 1983]	

Saipan provided seaborne security, surveillance operations, communications, and medical support during the operation. It did not have a deployed Marine Corps squadron on board.

Non-Carrier Based Squadrons		
Squadron	**Aircraft**	**Tail Code**
VP-10	P-3C	LD
VP-16	P-3C	LF
VP-23	P-3C	LJ
HSL-34 Dets	SH-2F	HX
HSL-32 Dets	SH-2F	HV

HSL-32 Detachments provided support for the Grenada operations from 30 October to 8 December, but were not involved in flying combat missions.

VR-56	C-9B	JU
VR-58	C-9B	JV
VR-59	C-9B	RY
VRC-40	C-1A	JK

Transport squadrons were used to provide support for units operating in Grenada, but were not involved in flying combat missions.

Operations by CVW-6 Aircraft

CVW-6 aircraft embarked on *Independence* flew search and rescue (SAR), medical evacuation (MEDEVAC), combat air patrol (CAP), reconnaissance, close air support, and surface, sub-surface search coordination (SSSC) missions.

Attack squadrons conducted daily surgical bombing missions (close air support) to quell enemy resistance, as well as reconnaissance missions. Their activities during Operation Urgent Fury included:

- VA-15 flew 143 combat sorties.
- VA-176 flew 350 combat flight hours (the number of combat sorties is not listed).
- VA-87 flew close air support combat missions (the specific number of sorties was not identified).
- HS-15 flew combat SAR missions under enemy fire and also dropped leaflets over the central portion of the island. The squadron flew 97 sorties.

Fighter squadrons flew CAP, reconnaissance and photographic missions over the island using the Tactical Air Reconnaissance Pod System (TARPS). VF-32 aircraft participated in the TARPS evolution. Fighter squadron activities included: 256 combat sorties flown by VF-32 in 1983 (includes sorties in Grenada and Lebanon, with no break down on how many for each operation) and 82 combat sorties flown during Operation Urgent Fury by VF-14.

- VAQ-131 flew electronic surveillance missions (the specific number of combat sorties not identified).
- VS-28: Combat sorties unknown.
- VAW-122: Combat sorties unknown.

The Navy did not lose any aircraft or aviation personnel to combat action during Operation Urgent Fury. However, several Marine Corps and Army helicopters were shot down by antiaircraft batteries and personnel were lost to combat action.

Chapter 33

Squadrons Involved in Libyan Operations 24 March–15 April 1986

The time frames for squadron involvement in Operation Prairie Fire during March and Operation Eldorado Canyon during April 1986 are not listed. Some of the squadrons involved in the March operations were not present during the April operations, and vice versa.

Carrier-Based Squadrons	
America (CV 66) with CVW-1 (Tail Code AB)	
VA-34	A-6E, KA-6D
VA-46	A-7E
VA-72	A-7E
VF-33	F-14A
VF-102	F-14A
VS-32	S-3A
VAW-123	E-2C
HS-11	SH-3H
VMAQ-2 Det	EA-6B
VQ-2 Det	EA-3B
Coral Sea (CV 43) with CVW-13 (Tail Code AK)	
VFA-131	F/A-18A
VFA-132	F/A-18A
VA-55	A-6E, KA-6D
VAW-127	E-2C
VAQ-135	EA-6B
VQ-2 Det	EA-3B
VMFA-314	F/A-18A
VMFA-323	F/A-18A
HS-17	SH-3H
Saratoga (CV 60) with CVW-17 (Tail Code AA)	
VA-81	A-7E
VA-83	A-7E
VF-74	F-14A
VF-103	F-14A
VA-85	A-6E, KA-6D
VAQ-137	EA-6B
VAW-125	E-2C
VS-30	S-3A
HS-3	SH-3H
VQ-2 Det	EA-3B
Guadalcanal (LPH 7) (HMM-263 Tail Code EG)	
HMM-263	AH-1T, CH-53E, CH-46E

Note: Detachments (Dets) on board the carriers did not use the same tail code assigned to the air wing (CVW).

Non-Carrier Based Squadrons		
Squadron	**Tail Code**	**Aircraft**
HSL-32 Dets	HV	SH-2F
HSL-34 Dets	HX	SH-2F
HSL-36 Dets	HY	SH-2F
HSL-42 Dets	HN	SH-60B
VP-23	LJ	P-3C
VP-56	LQ	P-3C
HC-4	HC	CH-53E
HC-6 Det	HW	UH-46D, CH-46D
VR-22	JL	C-130F
VAQ-138 Det	*	EA-6B
VR-24	JM	C-2A
HC-8 Dets	BR	UH-46A, CH-46D
HS-1 Det	AR	SH-3
HC-9 Det	NW	HH-3A
VQ-2	JQ	EP-3A

* VAQ-138 was under the control of Commander Medium Attack Tactical Electronic Warfare Wing, U.S. Pacific Fleet and did not have a permanently assigned tail code until it became part of CVW-8 in June 1986.

CHAPTER 34

Operation Desert Shield and Desert Storm

Naval Aviation Units Involved in the Persian Gulf War 16 January–27 February 1991

Carrier and Carrier-Based Squadrons	
Saratoga (CV 60) with CVW-17 (Tail Code AA) 7 Aug 1990–28 Mar 1991	
Squadron	**Aircraft**
VF-74	F-14A+
VF-103	F-14A+
VFA-83	F/A-18C
VFA-81	F/A-18C
VA-35	A-6E KA-6D
VAW-125	E-2C
VAQ-132	EA-6B
HS-3	SH-3H
VS-30	S-3B
John F. Kennedy (CV 67) with CVW-3 (Tail Code AC) 15 Aug 1990–28 Mar 1991	
Squadron	**Aircraft**
VF-14	F-14A
VF-32	F-14A
VA-46	A-7E
VA-72	A-7E
VA-75	A-6E KA-6D
VAW-126	E-2C
HS-7	SH-3H
VAQ-130	EA-6B
VS-22	S-3B
Midway (CV 41) with CVW-5 (Tail Code NF) 2 Oct 1990–17 Apr 1991	
Squadron	**Aircraft**
VFA-195	F/A-18A
VFA-151	F/A-18A
VFA-192	F/A-18A
VA-185	A-6E KA-6D
VA-115	A-6E KA-6D
VAW-115	E-2C
VAQ-136	EA-6B
HS-12	SH-3H
VRC-50 Det	C-2A
Ranger (CV 61) with CVW-2 (Tail Code NE) 8 Dec 1990–8 Jun 1991	
Squadron	**Aircraft**
VF-1	F-14A
VF-2	F-14A
VA-155	A-6E
VA-145	A-6E

VAW-116	E-2C
VAQ-131	EA-6B
HS-14	SH-3H
VS-38	S-3A
VRC-30 Det	C-2A
America (CV 66) with CVW-1 (Tail Code AB) 28 Dec 1990–18 Apr 1991	
Squadron	**Aircraft**
VF-102	F-14A
VF-33	F-14A
VFA-82	F/A-18C
VFA-86	F/A-18C
VA-85	A-6E KA-6D
VAW-123	E-2C
HS-11	SH-3H
VAQ-137	EA-6B
VS-32	S-3B
Theodore Roosevelt (CVN 71) with CVW-8 (Tail Code AJ) 28 Dec 1990–28 Jun 1991	
Squadron	**Aircraft**
VF-41	F-14A
VF-84	F-14A
VFA-15	F/A-18A
VFA-87	F/A-18A
VA-65	A-6E
VA-36	A-6E
VAW-124	E-2C
HS-9	SH-3H
VAQ-141	EA-6B
VS-24	S-3B
VRC-40 Det	C-2A

Non-Carrier Based Navy Squadrons		
Squadron	**Tail Code**	**Aircraft**
HC-1	UP	SH-3G, SH-3H, CH-53E
HC-2	SA	SH-3G, CH-53E
HC-4	HC	CH-53E
HC-5	RB	HH-46D
HC-6	HW	CH-46D, HH-46D, UH-46D
HC-8	BR	CH-46D, HH-46D, UH-46D

Squadron	Tail Code	Aircraft
HC-11	VR	CH-46D, HH-46D, UH-46D
HCS-4*	NW	HH-60H
HCS-5*	NW	HH-60H
HM-14	BJ	MH-53E
HM-15	TB	MH-53E
HS-75*	NW	SH-3H
HSL-32	HV	SH-2F
HSL-33	TF	SH-2F
HSL-34	HX	SH-2F
HSL-35	TG	SH-2F
HSL-36	HY	SH-2F
HSL-37	TH	SH-2F
HSL-42	HN	SH-60B
HSL-43	TT	SH-60B
HSL-44	HP	SH-60B
HSL-45	TZ	SH-60B
HSL-46	HQ	SH-60B
HSL-47	TY	SH-60B
HSL-48	HR	SH-60B
HSL-49	TX	SH-60B
VC-6	JG	Pioneer RPV
VP-1	YB	P-3C
VP-4	YD	P-3C
VP-5	LA	P-3C
VP-8	LC	P-3C
VP-11	LE	P-3C
VP-19	PE	P-3C
VP-23	LJ	P-3C
VP-40	QE	P-3C
VP-45	LN	P-3C
VP-46	RC	P-3C
VP-91*	PM	P-3C
VP-MAU*	LB	P-3C
VPU-1	OB	P-3
VPU-2	SP	P-3
VQ-1	PR	EP-3E, UP-3A, P-3B
VQ-2	JQ	EP-3E, EA-3B, UP-3A
VQ-4	HL	TC-130Q
VR-22	JL	C-130F, KC-130F
VR-24	JM	C-2A, CT-39G
VR-51*	RV	C-9B
VR-52*	JT	DC-9
VR-55*	RU	C-9B
VR-56*	JU	C-9B
VR-57*	RX	C-9B
VR-58*	JV	C-9B

Squadron	Tail Code	Aircraft
VR-59*	RY	C-9B
VR-60*	RT	DC-9
VR-61*	RS	DC-9
VR-62*	JW	DC-9
VRC-30	RW	C-2A
VRC-40	JK	C-2A
VRC-50	RG	C-2A, US-3A, C-130F

* Naval Air Reserve unit.

Marine Corps Squadrons		
Squadron	Tail Code	Aircraft
HMA-773†	MP	AH-1J
HMA-775†	WR	AH-1J
HMH-362	YL	CH-53D
HMH-461	CJ	CH-53E
HMH-462	YF	CH-53E
HMH-465	YJ	CH-53E
HMH-466	YK	CH-53E
HMH-772 Det A†	MT	RH-53D
HML-767†	MM	UH-1N
HMLA-169	TV	UH-1N, AH-1W
HMLA-269	HF	UH-1N, AH-1W, AH-1T
HMLA-367	VT	UH-1N, AH-1W
HMLA-369	SM	UH-1N, AH-1W
HMM-161	YR	CH-46E
HMM-164(C)	YT	CH-46E, CH-53E, UH-1N, AH-1W
HMM-165	YW	CH-46E
HMM-261	TV	CH-46E
HMM-263	EG	CH-46E
HMM-265	EP	CH-46E
HMM-266	ES	CH-46E
HMM-268(C)	YQ	CH-46E, CH-53E, UH-1N, AH-1W
HMM-365	YM	CH-46E
HMM-774†	MQ	CH-46E
VMA-231	CG	AV-8B
VMA-311	WL	AV-8B
VMA-331	VL	AV-8B
VMA-513 Det B	WF	AV-8B
VMA-542	CR	AV-8B
VMA(AW)-224	WK	A-6E
VMA(AW)-533	ED	A-6E
VMFA-212	WD	F/A-18C
VMFA-232	WT	F/A-18C
VMFA-235	DB	F/A-18C
VMFA-314	VW	F/A-18A

Squadron	Tail Code	Aircraft
VMFA-451	VM	F/A-18A
VMFA(AW)-121	VK	F/A-18D
VMGR-252	BH	KC-130F, KC-130R
VMGR-352	QB	KC-130R
VMGR-452[†]	NY	KC-130T
VMO-1	ER	OV-10A, OV-10D+
VMO-2	UU	OV-10A, OV-10D, OV-10D+

[†] Marine Corps Reserve Unit

Brief Chronology Of Operation Desert Shield
(August–December 1990)

2 Aug—Iraq invaded Kuwait. At the time, eight U.S. Navy Middle East Force ships were in the Persian Gulf. The carrier battle group of *Independence* (CV 62), with CVW-14 on board, was in the Indian Ocean and *Dwight D. Eisenhower* (CVN 69), with CVW-7, was in the Mediterranean.

2 Aug—The *Independence* battle group was directed to proceed to the northern Arabian Sea in support of Operation Desert Shield.

5 Aug—*Independence*'s battle group arrived on station in the Gulf of Oman.

7 Aug—*Saratoga* (CV 60) left the United States for a previously scheduled deployment to the eastern Mediterranean with CVW-17 on board.

7 Aug—*Dwight D. Eisenhower* and her battle group transited the Suez Canal and entered the Red Sea on 8 August.

15 Aug—Leading a carrier battle group, *John F. Kennedy* (CV 67) deployed from her homeport, Norfolk, Va., with CVW-3 on board. The battle group would be available for potential relief of the *Dwight D. Eisenhower* battle group or additional tasking to be determined by the situation in the Middle East.

16 Aug—Consistent with UN Security Council Resolution 661, a multinational maritime intercept operation involving naval aviation forces began intercepting ships going to or from Iraq and Kuwait.

22 Aug—*Saratoga* transited the Suez Canal to take up her station in the Red Sea where she would relieve *Dwight D. Eisenhower* who would then proceed home.

30 Aug—*John F. Kennedy*'s battle group transited the Strait of Gibraltar en route to the Mediterranean Sea.

3 Sep—*Dwight D. Eisenhower* transited the Strait of Gibraltar en route to homeport.

6 Sep—Amphibious assault ship *Nassau* (LHA 4) transited the Suez Canal.

7 Sep—Amphibious assault ships *Iwo Jima* (LPH 1) and *Guam* (LPH 9) transited the Suez Canal.

14 Sep—*Nassau* arrived in the Gulf of Oman.

14 Sep—*John F. Kennedy*'s battle group transited the Suez Canal into the Red Sea.

16 Sep—*Iwo Jima* and *Guam* arrived in the Gulf of Oman.

1 Oct—*Independence* transited the Strait of Hormuz en route to the Persian Gulf.

3 Oct—*Independence* conducted flight operations in the Persian Gulf. She was the first carrier to do so since 1974 when *Constellation* (CV 64) operated there.

4 Oct—*Independence* left the gulf after spending three days in its relatively confined and shallow waters. A Pentagon spokesman said the aircraft carrier had successfully completed its mission, which was "to demonstrate to our friends and allies in the region that it is possible to put a carrier in the Gulf and carry out operations."

8 Oct—The two U.S. Marine Corps UH-1N Huey helicopters based on the amphibious assault ship *Okinawa* (LPH 3) in the Gulf of Oman disappeared with eight men on board during "routine night training operations." No survivors were found.

28 Oct—U.S. Marines from the amphibious transport ship *Ogden* (LPD 5) boarded the Iraqi vessel *Amuriyah*, bound for Iraq through the gulf. The vessel refused to halt despite summons from U.S. and Australian ships. The allied ships fired shots across *Amuriyah*'s bow and warplanes from *Independence* buzzed low in warning passes. The Marine boarding party found no banned cargo and the Iraqi craft was allowed to proceed.

1 Nov—*Midway* (CV 41), with CVW-5 on board, replaced *Independence* in the northern Arabian Sea.

8 Nov—President George H. W. Bush announced a decision to double the number of carrier battle groups deployed in support of Operation Desert Shield. *Ranger* (CV 61) with CVW-2, *America* (CV 66) with CVW-1, and *Theodore Roosevelt* (CVN 71) with CVW-8 were scheduled to be on station by 15 January 1991. The three were to join *Saratoga*, *John F. Kennedy*, and *Midway*, which had replaced *Independence*.

15 Nov—U.S. and Saudi forces began Imminent Thunder, an eight-day combined amphibious landing exercise in northeastern Saudi Arabia, which involved about 1,000 U.S. Marines, 16 warships, and more than 1,100 aircraft. Close air support was provided by Marine aircraft as well as planes from the carrier *Midway*, which had entered the gulf from the northern Arabian Sea for the exercise.

29 Nov—The UN Security Council approved a resolution authorizing the use of military force unless Iraq vacated Kuwait by 15 January 1991.

8 Dec—*Ranger*, with CVW-2 on board, departed San Diego, Calif., on an unscheduled deployment in support of Desert Shield.

20 Dec—*Independence* returned to San Diego homeport from her Persian Gulf deployment.

21 Dec—An Israeli-chartered liberty ferry shuttling 102 crewmembers from the Israeli port of Haifa back to *Saratoga* capsized and sank off the coast of Israel. Israeli military and police officers rushed out in boats and helicopters to pull sailors from the water. Helicopters flew injured men to two hospitals in Haifa. Twenty U.S. sailors died. In addition, one crewmember was missing and presumed drowned.

28 Dec—*America*, with CVW-1 on board, and *Theodore Roosevelt*, with CVW-8, departed Norfolk, Va., on deployment in support of Desert Shield.

Brief Chronology Of Operation Desert Storm
(January–August 1991)

1 Jan—HC-4 relocated its detachment from Jeddah, Saudi Arabia, to Hurghada, Egypt, constructed an airhead operating site within 48 hours, and began transporting passengers, cargo, and mail to the Red Sea carrier battle groups.

6 Jan—*Saratoga* (CV 60) transited the Suez Canal en route to the Red Sea.

9 Jan—*America* (CV 66) transited the Strait of Gibraltar and arrived in the Mediterranean Sea.

12 Jan—Congress voted 52-to-47 in the Senate and 250-to-183 in the House on a joint resolution that gave President Bush the authority to go to war against Iraq.

12 Jan—*Ranger* (CV 61) carrier battle group arrived on station in the north Arabian Sea.

12 Jan—Amphibious Group 3 (with 5th Marine Expeditionary Brigade embarked) arrived on station in the Arabian Sea. Eighteen ships, including *Okinawa* (LPH 3), *Tarawa* (LHA 1), *Tripoli* (LPH 10), and *New Orleans* (LPH 11) were to join the 13-ship amphibious group, to comprise the largest amphibious task force since the Korean War.

12 Jan—*Midway* (CV 41) carrier battle group reentered the Persian Gulf.

14 Jan—*Theodore Roosevelt* (CVN 71) carrier battle group passed through the Suez Canal and assumed battle station in the Red Sea.

15 Jan—*America* carrier battle group transited the Suez Canal and arrived on station in the Red Sea.

15 Jan—*Ranger*, with CVW-2 onboard, and her carrier battle group transited to station in the Persian Gulf.

16 Jan—*Theodore Roosevelt* transited the Bab el-Mandeb Strait from the Red Sea to the Gulf of Aden.

16 Jan—At 1650 EST, a squadron of fighter-bombers took off from an air base in central Saudi Arabia. Targets in Iraq and Kuwait began being hit before 1900 EST. (It was the night of January 17 in the Middle East.) At the time, six Navy carrier battle groups, two battleships, and a 31-ship amphibious task force were operating in the Red Sea, Persian Gulf, and Arabian Sea areas. The Navy had more than 100 ships in the area and 75,000 Navy personnel afloat and ashore, while more than 67,000 Marines ashore comprised a Marine Expeditionary Force and nearly 18,000 Marines embarked on board naval vessels brought the Marine Corps presence to nearly 85,000.

16 Jan—President Bush addressed the nation at 2100 EST and announced that the liberation of Kuwait, Operation Desert Storm, had begun.

17 Jan—More than 100 Tomahawk cruise missiles were launched at preprogrammed targets by nine U.S. Navy ships in the Mediterranean, Persian Gulf, and Red Sea. This was the start of Operation Desert Storm and marked the first combat launch of the Tomahawk missile. Next, the Navy launched 228 combat sorties from six aircraft carriers. *John F. Kennedy* (CV 67), *Saratoga*, and *America* were in the Red Sea; *Midway* and *Ranger* were in the Persian Gulf; and *Theodore Roosevelt* was en route to the Persian Gulf.

17 Jan—An F/A-18C from *Saratoga*'s VFA-81 was shot down by an Iraqi surface-to-air missile. Pilot Lt. Cmdr. Michael Speicher became the first American casualty of the Persian Gulf War.

17 Jan—At 1915 EST (0215 local time), an estimated eight Iraqi Scud missiles attacked the Israeli cities of Haifa and Tel Aviv, causing property damage. The Pentagon announced that stationary Scud sites in Iraq had been destroyed and the mobile sites were being sought out. The United States was also preparing to send additional Patriot antimissile missiles to Israel.

17 Jan—F/A-18Cs piloted by Lt. Cmdr. Mark Fox and Lt. Nick Mongillo of VFA-81, assigned to *Saratoga*, each shot down a MiG-21. They were the first-ever aerial victories for the Hornet.

18 Jan—Navy lost two additional aircraft, both A-6s. The crewmen, Lts. Jeffrey Zaun and Robert Wetzel of *Saratoga*'s VA-35 and Lts. Charles Turner and William Costen of *Ranger*'s VA-155 were first reported missing and later as prisoners of war.

18 Jan—A Marine Corps OV-10A observation aircraft was shot down by Iraqi forces. Lt. Col. Clifford M. Acree and CWO4 Guy L. Hunter Jr. of VMO-2 were both captured.

18 Jan—*Nicholas*'s (FFG 47) HSL-44 (Det 8) SH-60Bs provided air targeting while a Kuwaiti patrol boat, two Army helicopter gunships, and *Nicholas* engaged and neutralized Iraqi forces on nine oil platforms in the Durrah oil field. The Iraqi forces were manning antiaircraft artillery sites on the platforms. This was the first combined helicopter, missile, and surface-ship gun engagement of the war and resulted in the destruction of the positions and capture of the first Iraqi prisoners of wars.

19 Jan—*Theodore Roosevelt* and her battle group transited the Strait of Hormuz and entered the Persian Gulf.

19 Jan—The first combat use of the Standoff Land Attack Missile occurred with launches from A-6 Intruders and A-7 Corsair IIs based on *John F. Kennedy* and *Saratoga*.

20 Jan—Iraqi television broadcast what it claimed were interviews with three U.S. and four allied military airmen shot down in the war in the Persian Gulf. The U.S. State Department called the Iraqi charge d'affaires in Washington to protest that the broadcast was contrary to the Third Geneva Convention governing treatment of prisoners of war and to demand that any prisoners be given immediate access to representatives of the International Committee of the Red Cross, the internationally recognized overseer of the convention. The tapes were shown on U.S. television the following day.

20 Jan—Department of Defense announced that an Iraqi artillery battery was destroyed by USN A-6 and USAF A-10 aircraft.

21 Jan—President Bush signed an executive order designating the Arabian Peninsula areas, airspace, and adjacent waters as a combat zone.

21 Jan—An F-14 was downed by a surface-to-air missile over Iraq. Pilot Lt. Devon Jones and radar intercept officer Lt. Lawrence Slade of *Saratoga*'s VF-103 were reported missing. Jones was recovered the next day.

21 Jan—*Theodore Roosevelt* carrier battle group arrived on station in the Persian Gulf.

23 Jan—Navy A-6s disabled an *al-Qaddisiya*-class Iraqi tanker that had been collecting and reporting intelligence data. The A-6s also attacked and sank a *Winchester*-class hovercraft (being refueled by the tanker) and a Zhuk-class patrol boat.

24 Jan—Navy A-6s attacked and destroyed an Iraqi Spasilac minelayer. An A-6 sank an Iraqi Zhuk-class patrol boat and another Iraqi minesweeper hit an Iraqi mine while attempting to evade the attack. A-6s and F/A-18s attacked the Umm Qasr Naval Base.

24 Jan—The first Kuwaiti territory, the island of Jazirat Qurah, was reclaimed.

28 Jan—Navy A-6s attacked Iraqi ships at Bubiyan Channel, at Umm Qasr Naval Base, and in Kuwait harbor.

28 Jan—Capt. Michael Berryman of VMA-311 was captured by Iraqi forces after his AV-8B Harrier was shot down.

30 Jan—Navy A-6s attacked three Iraqi landing craft in the vicinity of Shatt al-Arab Channel.

30 Jan—All 18 F/A-18s on board *Saratoga* delivered 100,000 pounds of MK 83 1,000-pound bombs on Iraqi positions in Kuwait. This was the largest amount by weight carried in a single mission.

1 Feb—VAW-123 coordinated aircraft on the first of 11 Scud missile patrols flown from 1–7 February. On 3 February, *America* confirmed the destruction of two Scud-related vehicles.

2 Feb—A Navy A-6 with crew Lt. Cmdr. Barry Cooke and Lt. Patrick Kelly Connor, from *Theodore Roosevelt*'s VA-36, were shot down by antiaircraft fire. The crewmen were reported missing in what was the carrier's first combat loss of the war.

5 Feb—A Navy F/A-18A crashed while returning from a combat mission. The pilot, Lt. Robert Dwyer of VFA-87 from *Theodore Roosevelt*, was killed.

6 Feb—A VF-1 F-14A off *Ranger*, piloted by Lt. Stuart Broce, with Cmdr. Ron McElraft as radar intercept officer, downed a Mi-8 Hip helicopter with an AIM-9M Sidewinder missile.

7 Feb—A-6s attacked and heavily damaged two Iraqi patrol boats in the northern Persian Gulf near al-Faw Peninsula.

8 Feb—A-6s attacked and neutralized an Iraqi training frigate collocated with a TMC-45–class patrol boat (Exocet-capable craft) at Cor al-Zubayr.

9 Feb—Capt. Russell Sanborn was captured by Iraqi forces after his VMA-231 AV-8B was shot down.

14 Feb—*America* carrier battle group transited Strait of Hormuz en route to operations in the Persian Gulf.

15 Feb—*America* became the first and only carrier to conduct strikes from both sides of the Arabian Peninsula.

18 Feb—An Iraqi mine blasted a 20-by-30 foot hole in the forward section of the 18,000-ton helicopter carrier *Tripoli* during mine clearance operations in the northern Persian Gulf. After continuing her duty for five days, the flagship of the minesweeping operation sailed to a shipyard drydock in Bahrain for a month of repairs.

20 Feb—*America*'s VS-32 became the first S-3 squadron to engage, bomb, and destroy a hostile vessel—an Iraqi gunboat.

20–24 Feb—Using AV-8B Harriers, the VMA-331 Bumblebees flew 243 sorties along the Iraqi border and throughout Kuwait.

23 Feb—*America*, *Midway*, *Theodore Roosevelt*, and *Ranger* were in the Persian Gulf. *John F. Kennedy* and *Saratoga* were operating from the Red Sea.

23 Feb—Aircraft from *America* destroyed a Silkworm antiship missile battery after Iraq unsuccessfully fired a missile at *Missouri* (BB 63).

23 Feb—A VMA-542 AV-8B Harrier was shot down by Iraqi forces. Capt. James Wilbourn was killed in action.

24 Feb—Operation Desert Sabre, the ground offensive against Iraq, began. General Norman Schwarzkopf's plan was based on the classic principles of deception, concentration of force, and speed.

25 Feb—Two Marine Corps aircraft were shot down by Iraqi forces. Capt. Scott Walsh was rescued after his VMA-542 AV-8B was lost and Maj. Joseph Small was captured and Capt. David Spellacy was killed when their OV-10A went down.

26 Feb—A-6Es from *Ranger*'s VA-155 bombed Iraqi troops fleeing Kuwait City to Basra in bumper-to-bumper convoys along two multi-lane highways. Numerous tanks, armored vehicles, jeeps, cars, and tractor-trailers were destroyed.

27 Feb—At 2100 EST, President Bush declared that Kuwait had been liberated and the Persian Gulf War over. At midnight EST, all U.S. and coalition forces would suspend further offensive combat operations.

27 Feb—Forty Iraqi soldiers surrendered to battleship *Wisconsin*'s (BB 64) remotely piloted vehicle when it flew over their position.

27 Feb—Capt. Reginald Underwood was killed when his VMA-331 AV-8B was shot down by Iraqi forces.

3 Mar—CH-46 helicopters with loudspeakers rounded up surrendering Iraqi troops on Faylaka Island. The enemy prisoners of war were ferried by helicopter to *Ogden* (LPD 5) for further transport to Saudi POW facilities.

4 Mar—Iraq released POWs including the Navy's Lts. Jeffrey Zaun, Robert Wetzel, and Lawrence Slade. They were turned over to U.S. officials by the International Committee of the Red Cross near the Jordanian border station of Ruwayshid.

4 Mar—*America* departed the Persian Gulf and returned to the Red Sea after conducting 3,008 combat sorties during the war.

6 Mar—*New Orleans*, with a mine countermeasures squadron on board and four minecountermeasures ships, led minesweeping activities.

6 Mar—President Bush reported to a joint session of Congress, "Aggression is defeated. The war is over."

8 Mar—The first Navy personnel from the Persian Gulf theater arrived in CONUS.

9 Mar—*America* arrived on station in the Red Sea.

11 Mar—*Saratoga* and *Midway* carrier battle groups departed the Persian Gulf area for their respective homeports. *Saratoga* transited the Suez Canal en route to Mayport, Fla.; *Midway* departed the Persian Gulf en route to Yokosuka, Japan.

12 Mar—*John F. Kennedy* transited the Suez Canal en route to the Mediterranean.

13 Mar—President Bush established the Southwest Asia Service Medal by executive order. It was awarded to U.S. military personnel who served in the Persian Gulf area during the operations.

16–22 Mar—*America* conducted a port visit to Hurghada, Egypt, making the first port call of the deployment after 78 consecutive days at sea.

17 Mar—Crew of *Tripoli* awarded Combat Action Ribbon for being endangered by enemy mine attack on February 18.

28 Mar—*John F. Kennedy* and *Saratoga*, leading their carrier battle groups, arrived at their homeports of Norfolk, Va., and Mayport, Fla., respectively. They were the first carrier battle groups involved in the Persian Gulf War to return to CONUS.

1 Apr—*Theodore Roosevelt* transited the Strait of Bab el-Mandeb and began three weeks of Red Sea operations.

3 Apr—America transited the Suez Canal and returned to the Mediterranean.

6 Apr—Iraq accepted United Nations terms for formal ceasefire in the Persian Gulf War.

8 Apr—*America* transited the Strait of Gibraltar and returned to the Atlantic.

8 Apr—Having left from both NAS Sigonella, Sicily, and Hurghada, Egypt, for Diyarbakir, Turkey, on 6 April, HC-4 detachments flew Secretary of State James Baker and his party of 60 along the border between Turkey and civil war–torn Iraq to a remote Kurdish refugee camp. A popular uprising in Kurdistan had taken place in March against Saddam Hussein, but the Iraqi forces quickly recaptured the main towns and cities of Kurdistan. The Iranians had allowed the Kurds to flee into their country, but the Turks had not, and the Kurds were stranded in the mountains in the cold.

9 Apr—HC-4 returned to Incirlik, Turkey, to become the primary and first heavy-lift helicopter combat logistics support asset for Operation Provide Comfort. The squadron delivered massive amounts of relief aid to Kurdish refugees and flew needy people to safe havens.

9 Apr—UN Security Council approved Resolution 689 establishing a United Nations-Iraq-Kuwait Observer Mission to monitor permanent ceasefire.

11 Apr—The Persian Gulf War came to its official conclusion at 1000 EDT as UN Security Council Resolution No. 687, establishing a permanent ceasefire in the Persian Gulf War, went into effect.

17 Apr—*Midway* returned from the Persian Gulf War to her homeport of Yokosuka, Japan.

17 Apr—Secretary of Defense Dick Cheney signed an order directing military commanders to begin implementing the president's plan, announced the previous day at a press conference, which called for the establishment of several encampments in northern Iraq. U.S., British, French, and Turkish military personnel had been delivering relief supplies to the refugees. The U.S. Sixth Fleet's 24th Marine Expeditionary Unit commenced operations 17 hours after arrival at the Humanitarian Service Support Base at Silopi, Iraq. A forward humanitarian service support base was also established at Diyarbakir, Turkey.

18 Apr—*America* returned from the Persian Gulf War to Norfolk, Va.

20 Apr—*Theodore Roosevelt* transited the Suez Canal and began support of Operation Provide Comfort, the allied nations' effort to aid Kurdish refugees in the aftermath of the Persian Gulf War.

20 Apr—*Theodore Roosevelt* joined the U.S. naval forces, including *Guadalcanal* (LPH 7), positioned off Turkey to support an estimated 7,000 American ground troops participating in Operation Provide Comfort.

7–8 May—Two A-6E Intruders on a reconnaissance mission over northern Iraq were attacked by Iraqi artillery units. These were the first confirmed incidents of hostile fire since allied forces began occupying a designated security zone for Kurdish refugees. The planes were unscathed, continued their mission, and returned safely to *Theodore Roosevelt*, positioned off the coast of Turkey to support U.S. military operations in northern Iraq.

23 May—The Commander of the Naval Forces in the Middle East declared the Kuwaiti port of Ash-Shuwaikh free of ordnance and Iraqi mines, making it the fifth and final in a series of port clearing missions by allied forces.

30 May—*Forrestal* (CV 59), leading a carrier battle group, departed from its homeport of Mayport, Fla., for a scheduled deployment to the Mediterranean Sea to relieve the *Theodore Roosevelt* battle group on station in the eastern Mediterranean in support of Operation Provide Comfort.

6 Jun—*America* was among the ten U.S. Navy ships that, returning from the Persian Gulf, sailed into New York Harbor as part of the city's fourth annual Fleet Week celebration.

10 Jun—A traditional New York ticker tape "Parade of Heroes" to salute all the men and women who served during Desert Storm culminated the city's Fleet Week.

18 Jun—*Tripoli* turned over her duties as flagship for Commander, U.S. Mine Countermeasures Group, to *Texas* (CGN 39). The group had located and destroyed nearly 1,200 mines in the Persian Gulf.

23 Jun—*Tripoli* transited the Strait of Hormuz en route to San Diego, Calif., her homeport, completing a tour in the Persian Gulf, which began on 1 December 1990.

28 Jun—*Theodore Roosevelt* battle group returned to Norfolk, Va. She was the last carrier involved in the Persian Gulf War to return to homeport.

13 Jul—*Nimitz* (CVN 68) carrier battle group turned over operations in the Persian Gulf to *Abraham Lincoln* (CVN 72) carrier battle group and transited the Strait of Hormuz.

27 Aug—The last U.S. Navy participants of the Persian Gulf War arrived home, including *New Orleans*, with HMM-268 embarked.

CHAPTER 35

Operation Desert Fox
16–20 December 1998

From 16 to 20 December 1998 the coalition launched Operation Desert Fox—strikes against Iraq in response to Saddam Hussein's failure to comply with UN resolutions to allow international inspections of sites suspected of housing Iraqi weapons of mass destruction programs. The Iraqi air defenses included 310 combat aircraft—operational strength varied—approximately 100 ground radars, and mobile and fixed antiaircraft guns and surface-to-air missiles.

Lts. Lyndsi N. Bates and Carol E. Watts of VFA-37 and Kendra Williams of VFA-105 became the first Navy female fighter/strike pilots to fly into battle from a carrier. Allied aircraft flew more than 650 strike and strike support sorties. Ten vessels fired 330 BGM/UGM-109 Tomahawk Land Attack Missiles, and Air Force Boeing B-52H Stratofortresses launched more than 90 AGM-86C Conventional Air-Launched Cruise Missiles. These attacks eviscerated Iraqi air defense and early warning systems, airfields, command and control, communications, presidential sites (palaces), and facilities housing Special Republican Guard and Republican Guard security details. The campaign continued the ongoing disruption of the weapons of mass destruction program caused by sanctions, inspections, and air and missile strikes; temporarily crippled the Republican Guard infrastructure; and impeded a plan to convert Aero L-29 Delphin trainers into unmanned aerial vehicles capable of carrying biological or nerve agents. The allies did not lose any aircraft.

Carrier Based Squadrons		
Squadron	Aircraft	Tail Code
Enterprise (CVN 65)		AC (CVW-3)
VF-32	F-14B	
VFA-37	F/A-18C	
VFA-105	F/A-18C	
VMFA-312	F/A-18C	
VAW-126	E-2C	
VAQ-130	EA-6B	
VQ-6 Det A	ES-3A	
VRC-40 Det 4	C-2A	
VS-22	S-3B	
HS-7	SH-60F/HH-60H	
Carl Vinson (CVN 70)*		NH (CVW-11)
VF-213	F-14D	
VFA-22	F/A-18C	
VFA-94	F/A-18C	
VFA-97	F/A-18C	
VAW-117	E-2C	
VAQ-135	EA-6B	
VQ-5 Det C	ES-3A	
VRC-30 Det 2	C-2A	
VS-29	S-3B	
HS-6	SH-60F/HH-60H	
Non-Carrier Based Squadrons		
Squadron	Aircraft	Tail Code
HC-2 Det†	UH-3H	HU
HC-4 Det	MH-53E	HC
HC-6 Det	CH-46D/HH-46D	HW

HC-11 Det	CH-46D/HH-46D	VR
HSL-37 Det	SH-60B	TH
HSL-42 Det	SH-60B	HN
HSL-43 Det	SH-60B	TT
HSL-44 Dets	SH-60B	HP
HSL-45 Det	SH-60B	TZ
HSL-46 Det	SH-60B	HQ
HSL-47 Dets	SH-60B	TY
HSL-48 Dets	SH-60B	HR
VAQ-128 Det	EA-6B	8K
VP-4 Det	P-3C	YD
VP-9 Det	P-3C	PD
VQ-1 Det	EP-3E	PR
Belleau Wood Amphibious Ready Group		
Belleau Wood (LHA 3) Staging platform for combat search and rescue		
Dubuque (LPD 8)		
Germantown (LSD 42)		

31st Marine Expeditionary Unit
Predominately landed at Camp Doha, Kuwait, on 18 December

HC-5 Det 6‡	HH-46D	RB
VMA-311 Det	AV-8B	EP
HMLA-169 Det	UH-1N/AH-1W	EP
HMM-265	CH-46E	EP
HMH-465 Det	CH-53E	EP

˙ Launched her first strikes on 19 December.

† Permanently deployed to Manama, Bahrain.

‡ While on deployment, HC squadron detachments served under the command of the amphibious assault carriers rather than their embarked Marine helicopter squadrons, and therefore retained their own squadron tail codes.

CHAPTER 36

Operation Enduring Freedom Phase I
7 October–30 November 2001

On 7 October 2001, aircraft flying from *Carl Vinson* (CVN 70) and *Enterprise* (CVN 65) took part in the first coalition strikes of the Global War on Terrorism against al-Qaeda terrorists and Taliban Islamic extremists within Afghanistan. Waves of about 25 Navy and 15 Air Force jets and approximately 50 BGM-109 Tomahawk Land Attack Missiles struck 40 target areas including aircraft on the ground, airfields, antiaircraft and surface-to-air missile batteries and radar sites, command and control nodes, and terrorist training camps. Critics questioned the raids on the camps because al-Qaeda had largely abandoned the facilities, but the assaults destroyed terrorist infrastructure.

EA-6B Prowlers suppressed Taliban and al-Qaeda air defense electronic emissions and jammed their ground communications. The Taliban refused to give battle in the air, but Navy fighters escorted Air Force bombers until air supremacy was attained. Strike jets flew time-staggered missions supported by S-3B Vikings and Air Force and British tankers, which refueled them. P-3C Orions and EP-3E Aries IIs flew intelligence, surveillance, and reconnaissance patrols. Strike aircraft then flew close air support missions for coalition special operations teams and allied Northern Alliance (the United Islamic Front for the Salvation of Afghanistan) tribesmen, and a confederation of primarily Pashtun tribesmen known as the Eastern Alliance. Enemy antiaircraft fire and surface-to-air missiles failed to shoot down a single aircraft. The attacks devastated al-Qaeda and Taliban command and control, communication, computer, and intelligence capabilities; but terrorist leader Osama bin Laden and professed Taliban head of state Mullah Muhammad A. Umar subsequently escaped.

Carrier Based Squadrons		
Squadron	**Aircraft**	**Tail Code**
Carl Vinson (CVN 70)		NH (CVW-11)
VF-213	F-14D	
VFA-22	F/A-18C	
VFA-94	F/A-18C	
VFA-97	F/A-18C	
VAW-117	E-2C	
VAQ-135	EA-6B	
VRC-30 Det 3	C-2A	
VS-29	S-3B	
HS-6	SH-60F/HH-60H	
Enterprise (CVN 65)		AJ (CVW-8)
VF-14	F-14B	
VF-41	F-14B	
VFA-15	F/A-18C	
VFA-87	F/A-18C	
VAW-124	E-2C	
VAQ-141	EA-6B	
VRC-40 Det 5	C-2A	
VS-24	S-3B	
HS-3	SH-60F/HH-60H	
Kitty Hawk (CV 63)*		NF (CVW-5)
VFA-27	F/A-18C	
VFA-192	F/A-18C	
VFA-195	F/A-18C	
VS-21	S-3B	

Squadron	Aircraft	Tail Code
VRC-30 Det 5	C-2A	
HS-14	SH-60F/HH-60H	
2nd Bn 160th SOAR	MH-60L/MH-47E	
Theodore Roosevelt (CVN 71)		AB (CVW-1)
VF-102	F-14B	
VFA-82	F/A-18C	
VFA-86	F/A-18C	
VMFA-251 (DW)‡	F/A-18C	
VAW-123	E-2C	
VAQ-137	EA-6B	
VS-32	S-3B	
VRC-40 Det 2	C-2A	
HS-11	SH-60F/HH-60H	

Non-Carrier Based Squadrons		
Squadron	**Aircraft**	**Tail Code**
HC-2 Det‡	UH-3H	HU
HC-5 Det	HH-46D	RB
HC-6 Det	HH-46D/UH-46D	HW
HC-8 Dets	CH-46D/HH-46D/UH-46D	BR
HC-11 Dets	CH-46D/HH-46D/UH-46D	VR
HM-14 Det‡	MH-53E	BJ
HSL-42 Dets	SH-60B	HN
HSL-43 Det	SH-60B	TT
HSL-44 Dets	SH-60B	HP
HSL-45 Det	SH-60B	TZ

Squadron	Aircraft	Tail Code
HSL-46 Dets	SH-60B	HQ
HSL-47 Det	SH-60B	TY
HSL-48 Dets	SH-60B	HR
HSL-51 Det	SH-60B	TA
VAQ-133 Det	EA-6B	8K
VAQ-142 Det	EA-6B	8K
VP-4 Det	P-3C	YD
VP-9 Dets	P-3C	PD
VQ-1 Det	EP-3E	PR
VR-48 Det	C-20G	JR
Bataan Amphibious Ready Group		
Bataan (LHD 5)		
Shreveport (LPD 12)		
Whidbey Island (LSD 41)		
26th MEU[§]		
HC-6 Det 1[‖]	HH-46D/UH-46D	HW
VMA-223	AV-8B	WP
HMLA-269[‡]	UH-1N/AH-1W	HF
HMM-365	CH-46D	YM
HMH-464 Det	CH-53E	EN
Peleliu Amphibious Ready Group		
Peleliu (LHA 5)		
Dubuque (LPD 8)		
Comstock (LSD 45)		
15th MEU[§]		
HC-11 Det 6	HH-46D	VR
VMA-311	AV-8B	WL
HMLA-169 Det	UH-1N/AH-1W	SN
HMM-163	CH-46E	YP
HMH-361 Det	CH-53E	YN
20th SOS Det[#]	MH-53M	

[*] Served as an afloat forward staging base for Task Force Sword, USA, including Special Forces Operational Detachment Delta and the 2d Battalion, 160th Special Operations Aviation Regiment.

[†] While on deployment, VMFA-251 used the tail code of the air wing. The squadron's original tail code is noted in parentheses.

[‡] Permanently deployed to Manama, Bahrain.

[§] Marine Expeditionary Unit

[‖] While on deployment, HC squadron detachments served under the command of the amphibious assault carriers rather than their embarked Marine helicopter squadrons, and therefore retained their own squadron tail codes.

[#] USAF Special Operations Squadron, embarked 5–9 October 2001.

Operation Iraqi Freedom Phase I
19 March–1 May 2003

On 19 March 2003 the coalition began Operation Iraqi Freedom, the principal objectives of which included the end of the regime of Saddam Hussein and the elimination of suspected Iraqi weapons of mass destruction. Enemy aerial opposition proved minimal at 325 combat aircraft, but they deployed numerous surface-to-air missiles and more than 6,000 mobile and fixed antiaircraft guns. The allies also contended with a strong *shamal* (sandstorm) that swept across portions of southern Iraq.

On 20 March, two Air Force Lockheed F-117A Nighthawks and other coalition aircraft and 24 BGM-109 Tomahawk Land Attack Missiles (TLAMs) struck the Dora Farms complex near Baghdad. The CIA had uncovered intelligence that indicated a meeting of Hussein and his senior Iraqi leadership, but the dictator survived. Following the raid, an additional 537 strike sorties and 34 TLAM launches shaped the battlespace.

On 21 March the coalition initiated strategic air operations. Aircraft flew more than 1,700 sorties—832 strike—that day, and aircraft, ships, and submarines let loose a staggering barrage of 381 TLAMs and 124 AGM-86C Conventional Air-Launched Cruise Missiles against Iraqi command and control, communications, computers, and intelligence, airfields, and air defense facilities.

EA-6B Prowlers suppressed Iraqi air defenses through the use of electronic warfare and AGM-88 High-speed Anti-Radiation Missiles. A P-3C Orion of VP-46, SH-60F and HH-60H Seahawks of HS-2, and SH-60Bs of HSL-47 and -48 supported special operations forces that secured the Rumaylah oil fields before their Iraqi garrisons set the platforms afire. The enemy set other gas oil separation plants ablaze and the smoke hindered low-flying aircraft.

The allies recorded the largest use of precision guided munitions to date, the first drop of a Joint Direct Attack Munition by an F-14D Tomcat, and the initial operations of F/A-18E Super Hornets for aerial refueling. In addition, the Marines operated RQ-2A/B Pioneer and RQ-14A Dragon Eye unmanned aerial vehicles. Naval aircraft combat losses comprised one F/A-18C of VFA-195 on 2 April and one AH-1W of MAG-39 on 14 April. The operational losses consisted of: one CH-46E of HMM-268 on 21 March; one UH-1N of HMLA-169 on 30 March; one S-3B of VS-38, one AV-8B of VMA-231, and one F-14A of VF-154 on 1 April; one AH-1W of HMLA-267 on 4 April; one SA.330 from combat store ship *Spica* (T-AFS 9) on 7 April; one CH-46E of HMM-264 on 22 April; and one CH-53E of HMH-465 on 30 April.

Carrier Based Squadrons		
Squadron	**Aircraft**	**Tail Code**
Abraham Lincoln **(CVN 72)**		**NK (CVW-14)**
VF-31	F-14D	
VFA-25	F/A-18C	
VFA-113	F/A-18C	
VFA-115	F/A-18E	
VAW-113	E-2C	
VAQ-139	EA-6B	
VRC-30 Det 1	C-2A	
VS-35	S-3B	
HS-4	SH-60F/HH-60H	
Constellation **(CV 64)**		**NE (CVW-2)**
VF-2	F-14D	
VFA-137	F/A-18C	
VFA-151	F/A-18C	
VMFA-323 (WS)*	F/A-18C	
VAW-116	E-2C	
VAQ-131	EA-6B	

Squadron	Aircraft	Tail Code
VRC-30 Det 2	C-2A	
VS-38	S-3B	
HS-2	SH-60F/HH-60H	
HSL-47 Det 4	SH-60B	
Harry S. Truman **(CVN 75)**		**AC (CVW-3)**
VF-32	F-14B	
VFA-37	F/A-18C	
VFA-105	F/A-18C	
VMFA-115 (VE)*	F/A-18A+	
VAW-126	E-2C	
VAQ-130	EA-6B	
VRC-40 Det 1	C-2A	
VS-22	S-3B	
HS-7	SH-60F/HH-60H	
Kitty Hawk **(CV 63)**		**NF (CVW-5)**
VF-154	F-14A	
VFA-14	F/A-18C	
VFA-27	F/A-18C	

Squadron	Aircraft	Tail Code
VFA-195	F/A-18C	
VAW-115	E-2C	
VAQ-135	EA-6B	
VRC-30 Det 5	C-2A	
VS-21	S-3B	
HS-14	SH-60F/HH-60H	
Nimitz (CVN 68)		**NH (CVW-11)**
VFA-14	F/A-18E	
VFA-41	F/A-18F	
VFA-94	F/A-18C	
VFA-97	F/A-18A	
VAW-117	E-2C	
VAQ-135	EA-6B	
VRC-30 Det 3	C-2A	
VS-29	S-3B	
HS-6	SH-60F/HH-60H	
Theodore Roosevelt (CVN 71)		**AJ (CVW-8)**
VF-213	F-14D	
VFA-15	F/A-18C	
VFA-87	F/A-18C	
VFA-201†	F/A-18A	
VAW-124	E-2C	
VAQ-141	EA-6B	
VRC-40 Det 5	C-2A	
VS-24	S-3B	
HS-3	SH-60F/HH-60H	

Non-Carrier Based Squadrons		
Squadron	**Aircraft**	**Tail Code**
HC-2 Det‡	UH-3H	HU
HC-4 Det§	MH-53E	HC
HC-5 Dets	MH-60S	RB
HC-11 Dets	CH-46D/HH-46D/UH-46D	VR
HM-14 Det‡	MH-53E	BJ
HM-15 Det‖	MH-53E	TB
HSL-37 Dets	SH-60B	TH
HSL-42 Dets	SH-60B	HN
HSL-43 Dets	SH-60B	TT
HSL-44 Dets	SH-60B	HP
HSL-45 Dets	SH-60B	TZ
HSL-46 Dets	SH-60B	HQ
HSL-47 Dets	SH-60B	TY
HSL-48 Dets	SH-60B	HR
HSL-49 Dets	SH-60B	TX
HSL-51 Dets	SH-60B	TA
VAQ-134 Det	EA-6B	8K
VP-46 Dets	P-3C	RC
VQ-1 Det	EP-3E	PR
VR-48 Det	C-20G	JR

Squadron	Aircraft	Tail Code
VR-51 Det	C-20G	RV
VR-52	DC-9	JT
VR-54	C-130T	CW
VR-57	C-9B/DC-9	RX
VR-61	DC-9	RS
VR-62	C-130T	JW
Coast Guard Det#	HH-65A	CG 6502
HMLA-169	UH-1N/AH-1W	SN
HMLA-369	UH-1N/AH-1W	SM
HMM-163	CH-46E	YP
HMM-262	CH-46E	ET
HMM-264	CH-46E	EH
HMM-268	CH-46E	YQ
HMM-364	CH-46E	PF
HMH-462	CH-53E	YF
VMA-214	AV-8B	WE
VMFA-232	F/A-18C	WT
VMFA-251	F/A-18C	DW
VMFA(AW)-121	F/A-18D	VK
VMFA(AW)-225	F/A-18D	CE
VMFA(AW)-533	F/A-18D	ED
VMAQ-1 Det	EA-6B	CB
VMAQ-2 Det	EA-6B	CY
VMGR-234 Det	KC-130T	QH
VMGR-352 (-)	KC-130F/R	QB
VMGR-452 Det	KC-130T	NY
VMU-1	RQ-2A/B	FZ
VMU-2	RQ-2A/B	FF
Bataan (LHD 5)		
HC-6 Det 3**	MH-60S	HW
VMA-223 (-)	AV-8B	WP
VMA-542	AV-8B	WH
Bonhomme Richard (LHD 6)		
HC-11 Det 4	CH-46	VR
VMA-211 (-)	AV-8B	CF
VMA-311 (-)	AV-8B	WL
HMH-465 Det	CH-53E	YJ
Boxer (LHD 4)		
HC-11 Det 6	CH-46	VR
HMM-165	CH-46E	YW
HMH-465	CH-53E	YN
Kearsarge (LHD 3)		
HC-8 Det 6	CH-46	BR
HMLA-269 Det	AH-1W	HF
HMM-365 (-)	CH-46E	YM
HMH-464	CH-53E	EN
Nassau (LHA 4)		
HC-6 Det 7	HH-46D	HW
VMA-231 Det	AV-8B	EG

Squadron	Aircraft	Tail Code
HMLA-269 Det	UH-1N/AH-1W	EG
HMM-263	CH-46E	EG
HMH-772 Det	CH-53E	EG
Saipan (LHA 2)		
HC-6 Det 2	MH-60S	HW
HMLA-167 Det††	UH-1N/AH-1W	HF
HMLA-269 (-)	UH-1N/AH-1W	HF
HMM-162	CH-46E	YS
Tarawa (LHA 1)		
HC-11 Det 7	CH-46	VR
VMA-311 Det	AV-8B	YR
HMLA-267 Det	UH-1N/AH-1W	YR
HMM-161	CH-46E	YR
HMH-361 Det	CH-53E	YR

Aviation-capable dock landings ships and amphibious transport docks comprised: *Anchorage* (LSD 36), *Ashland* (LSD 48), *Comstock* (LSD 45), *Duluth* (LPD 6), *Dubuque* (LPD 8), *Gunston Hall* (LSD 44), *Pearl Harbor* (LSD 52), *Ponce* (LPD 15), *Rushmore* (LSD 47), *Tortuga* (LSD 46)

* While on deployment, VMFA squadrons used the tail codes of their air wings. Their original tail codes are noted in parentheses.

† Naval Air Reserve squadron.

‡ Permanently deployed to Manama, Bahrain.

§ Permanently deployed to Fujairah, U.A.E.

‖ HM-15 Det 2 relieved HM-14 Det 1 permanently deployed to Manama, Bahrain.

Deployed from CGAS Barbers Point, Hawaii, on board cutter *Boutwell* (WHEC 719).

** While on deployment, HC squadron detachments served under the command of amphibious assault carriers rather than their embarked Marine helicopter squadrons, and therefore retained their own squadron tail codes.

†† The detachment from HMLA-167 reinforced HMLA-269 to make up for the aircraft assigned to the already deployed HMLA-269 Det attached to HMM-263 on board *Nassau* (LHA 4).

CHAPTER 38

Navy and Marine Corps Shoot Downs Since 1950

The following list of enemy aircraft shot down since 1950 covers only those that are confirmed. There are a number of cases in which adequate information or verification was not available or could not be substantiated. These shoot downs, usually identified as "probables," are not placed on this list. The Navy Department does not have a written policy regarding the requirements for the verification of a shoot down. It is generally accepted or believed that when an aerial engagement occurs, the pilot, NFO (RIO), or other witness must actually see the enemy aircraft crash, explode, or the pilot ejecting from the aircraft. The Navy has used gun camera footage since WWII. However, during the 1980s the Navy began using modern equipment more extensively, such as heads-up displays and gun camera footage, to document and verify shoot downs.

Aircraft Shot Down During the Korean War by USN/USMC Pilots								
Date	Enemy Aircraft	Squadron	Aircraft	Weapon	Carrier	Service	Pilot	RIO/NFO
03 Jul 1950	YAK-9	VF-51	F9F-3	Guns	CV-45	USN	Lt. j.g. Leonard H. Plog	
03 Jul 1950	YAK-9	VF-51	F9F-3	Guns	CV-45	USN	Ens. Eldon W. Brown	
04 Sep 1950	IL-4	VF-53	F4U-4B	Guns	CV-45	USN	Ens. Edward V. Laney Jr.	
09 Nov 1950	MiG-15	VF-111	F9F-2B	Guns	CV-47	USN	Lt. Cmdr. William T. Amen	
18 Nov 1950	MiG-15‡	VF-52	F9F-3	Guns	CV-45	USN	Lt. Cmdr. William E. Lamb (shared with Lt. Parker)	
18 Nov 1950	MiG-15‡	VF-52	F9F-3	Guns	CV-45	USN	Lt. Robert E. Parker (shared with Lt. Cmdr. Lamb)	
18 Nov 1950	MiG-15	VF-31	F9F-2	Guns	CV-32	USN	Ens. Frederick C. Weber	
22 Dec 1950	MiG-15	5th A.F.	F-86	Guns	*	USN	Lt. Cmdr. Paul E. Pugh	
21 Apr 1951	YAK-9	VMF-312	F4U-4	Guns	CVL-29	USMC	Lt. Harold D. Daigh	
21 Apr 1951	2 YAKs	VMF-312	F4U-4	Guns	CVL-29	USMC	Capt. Phillip C. DeLong	
01 Jun 1951	MiG-15	5th A.F.	F-86D	Guns	*	USN	Lt. Simpson Evans Jr.	
01 Jul 1951	PO-2	VMF(N)-513	F7F-3N	Guns	*	USMC	Capt. Edwin B. Long	WO Robert C. Buckingham
12 Jul 1951	PO-2	VMF(N)-513	F4U-5NL	Guns	*	USMC	Capt. Donald L. Fenton	
23 Sep 1951	PO-2	VMF(N)-513	F7F-3N	Guns	*	USMC	Maj. Eugene A. Van Gundy	MSgt. Thomas H. Ullom
23 Oct 1951	MiG	5th A.F.	F-84E	Guns	*	USN	Lt. Walter M. Schirra Jr.	
04 Nov 1951	MiG-15	5th A.F.	F-86	Guns	*	USMC	Maj. William F. Guss	
05 Mar 1952	MiG-15	5th A.F.	F-86	Guns	*	USMC	Capt. Vincent J. Marzello	
16 Mar 1952	MiG-15	5th A.F.	F-86	Guns	*	USMC	Lt. Col. John S. Payne	
07 Jun 1952	YAK-9	VMF(N)-513	F4U-5NL	Guns	*	USMC	Lt. John W. Andre	
10 Sep 1952	MiG	VMA-312	F4U-4B	Guns	CVE-118	USMC	Capt. Jesse G. Folmar	
15 Sep 1952	MiG-15	5th A.F.	F-86	Guns	*	USMC	Maj. Alexander J. Gillis	
28 Sep 1952	2 MiG-15s	5th A.F.	F-86	Guns	*	USMC	Maj. Alexander J. Gillis	
03 Nov 1952	YAK-15	VMF(N)-513	F3D-2	Guns	*	USMC	Maj. William T. Stratton Jr.	MSgt. Hans C. Hoglind

Aircraft Shot Down During the Korean War by USN/USMC Pilots								
Date	Enemy Aircraft	Squadron	Aircraft	Weapon	Carrier	Service	Pilot	RIO/NFO
08 Nov 1952	MiG	VMF(N)-513	F3D-2	Guns	*	USMC	Capt. Oliver R. Davis	WO Dramus F. Fessler
18 Nov 1952	MiG-15	VF-781	F9F-5	Guns	CVA-34	USN	Lt. Elmer Royce Williams	
18 Nov 1952	MiG-15	VF-781	F9F-5	Guns	CVA-34	USN	Lt. j.g. John D. Middleton	
10 Dec 1952	PO-2	VMF(N)-513	F3D-2	Guns	*	USMC	Lt. Joseph A. Corvi	MSgt. Don R. George
12 Jan 1953	MiG	VMF(N)-513	F3D-2	Guns	*	USMC	Maj. Elswin P. Dunn	MSgt. Lawrence J. Fortin
20 Jan 1953	MiG-15	5th A.F.	F-86	Guns	*	USMC	Capt. Robert Wade	
28 Jan 1953	MiG	VMF(N)-513	F3D-2	Guns	*	USMC	Capt. James R. Weaver	MSgt. Robert P. Becker
31 Jan 1953	MiG	VMF(N)-513	F3D-2	Guns	*	USMC	Lt. Col. Robert F. Conley	MSgt. James N. Scott
07 Apr 1953	MiG-15	5th A.F.	F-86	Guns	*	USMC	Maj. Roy L. Reed	
12 Apr 1953	MiG-15	5th A.F.	F-86	Guns	*	USMC	Maj. Roy L. Reed	
16 May 1953	MiG-15	5th A.F.	F-86F	Guns	*	USMC	Maj. John F. Bolt	
17 May 1953	MiG-15‡	5th A.F.	F-86	Guns	*	USMC	Capt. Dewey F. Durnford (credit for half kill)	
18 May 1953	MiG-15	5th A.F.	F-86	Guns	*	USMC	Capt. Harvey L. Jensen	
16 Jun 1953	PO-2	VMC-1	AD-4	Guns	*	USMC	Maj. George H. Linnemeier	CWO Vernon S. Kramer
22 Jun 1953	MiG-15	5th A.F.	F-86F	Guns	*	USMC	Maj. John F. Bolt	
24 Jun 1953	MiG-15	5th A.F.	F-86F	Guns	*	USMC	Maj. John F. Bolt	
30 Jun 1953	MiG-15	5th A.F.	F-86F	Guns	*	USMC	Maj. John F. Bolt	
30 Jun 1953	2 YAK-18s	VC-3 Det D†	F4U-5N	Guns	CV-37†	USN	Lt. Guy P. Bordelon Jr.	
05 Jul 1953	2 PO-2s	VC-3 Det D†	F4U-5N	Guns	CV-37†	USN	Lt. Guy P. Bordelon Jr.	
11 Jul 1953	2 MiG-15s	5th A.F.	F-86F	Guns	*	USMC	Maj. John F. Bolt	
12 Jul 1953	MiG-15	5th A.F.	F-86F	Guns	*	USMC	Maj. John H. Glenn Jr.	
16 Jul 1953	PO-2	VC-3 Det D†	F4U-5N	Guns	CV-37†	USN	Lt. Guy P. Bordelon Jr.	
19 Jul 1953	MiG-15	5th A.F.	F-86F	Guns	*	USMC	Maj. John H. Glenn Jr.	
20 Jul 1953	2 MiG-15s	5th A.F.	F-86	Guns	*	USMC	Maj. Thomas M. Sellers	
22 Jul 1953	MiG-15	5th A.F.	F-86F	Guns	*	USMC	Maj. John H. Glenn Jr.	

* Shore based or exchange duty with the 5th Air Force in Korea.

† Temporary additional duty (TAD) from *Princeton* to U.S. 5th Air Force in Korea (Navy and Marine Corps pilots had exchange duty with the 5th Air Force).

‡ The credit for the shoot down of this aircraft is shared with another pilot so the person is credited for only a half a shoot down.

Aircraft Shot Down During the Post-Korean War Period by USN/USMC Pilots							
Date	Enemy Aircraft	Squadron	Aircraft	Weapon	Carrier	Service	Pilot
26 Jul 1954	LA-7	VF-54*	AD-4	Guns	CV-47	USN	Lt. Roy M. Tatham
26 Jul 1954	LA-7	VF-54*	AD-4	Guns	CV-47	USN	Ens. Richard R. Crooks
26 Jul 1954	LA-7	VF-54†	AD-4	Guns	CV-47	USN	Lt. Cmdr. Paul J. Wahlstrom
26 Jul 1954	LA-7	VF-54†	AD-4	Guns	CV-47	USN	Lt. j.g. Richard S. Ribble
26 Jul 1954	LA-7	VF-54†	AD-4	Guns	CV-47	USN	Lt. j.g. John L. Damian
26 Jul 1954	LA-7	VF-54†	AD-4	Guns	CV-47	USN	Lt. j.g. John M. Rochford
26 Jul 1954	LA-7	VC-3†	F4U-5N	Guns	CV-47	USN	Lt. Cmdr. Edgar B. Salsig

* The credit for the shoot down of this aircraft is shared with another pilot so the person is credited for only a half a shoot down.
† The credit for the shoot down of this aircraft is shared other pilots, so the person is credited for only a fraction of a shoot down.

Date	Enemy Aircraft	Squadron	Aircraft	Weapon	Carrier or Unit	Service	Pilot	RIO/NFO
17 Jun 1965	MiG-17	VF-21	F-4B	AIM-7	CVA-41	USN	Cmdr. Louis Page	Lt. John C. Smith Jr.
17 Jun 1965	MiG-17	VF-21	F-4B	AIM-7	CVA-41	USN	Lt. Jack E. D. Batson Jr.	Lt. Cmdr. Robert B. Doremus
20 Jun 1965	MiG-17	VA-25	A-1H	Guns	CVA-41	USN	Lt. Clinton B. Johnson*	
20 Jun 1965	MiG-17	VA-25	A-1H	Guns	CVA-41	USN	Lt. j.g. Charles W. Hartman III*	
12 Jun 1966	MiG-17	VF-211	F-8E	AIM-9D	CVA-19	USN	Cmdr. Harold L. Marr	
21 Jun 1966	MiG-17	VF-211	F-8E	Guns	CVA-19	USN	Lt. Eugene J. Chancy	
21 Jun 1966	MiG-17	VF-211	F-8E	AIM-9D	CVA-19	USN	Lt. j.g. Phillip V. Vampatella	
13 Jul 1966	MiG-17	VF-161	F-4B	AIM-9D	CVA-64	USN	Lt. William M. McGuigan	Lt. j.g. Robert M. Fowler
09 Oct 1966	MiG-21	VF-162	F-8E	AIM-9	CVA-34	USN	Cmdr. Richard M. Bellinger	
09 Oct 1966	MiG-17	VA-176	A-1H	Guns	CVS-11	USN	Lt. j.g. William T. Patton	
20 Dec 1966	An-2	VF-114	F-4B	AIM-7E	CVA-63	USN	Lt. Hugh D. Wisely	Lt. j.g. David L. Jordan
20 Dec 1966	An-2	VF-213	F-4B	AIM-7E	CVA-63	USN	Lt. David A. McRae	Ens. David N. Nichols
24 Apr 1967	MiG-17	VF-114	F-4B	AIM-9D	CVA-63	USN	Lt. Hugh D. Wisely	Lt. j.g. Gareth L. Anderson
24 Apr 1967	MiG-17	VF-114	F-4B	AIM-9B	CVA-63	USN	Lt. Cmdr. Charles E. Southwick	Ens. James W. Laing
01 May 1967	MiG-17	VF-211	F-8E	AIM-9D	CVA-31	USN	Lt. Cmdr. Marshall O. Wright	
01 May 1967	MiG-17	VA-76	A-4C	Zuni	CVA-31	USN	Lt. Cmdr. Theodore R. Swartz	
19 May 1967	MiG-17	VF-211	F-8E	AIM-9D	CVA-31	USN	Cmdr. Paul H. Speer	
19 May 1967	MiG-17	VF-211	F-8E	AIM-9D	CVA-31	USN	Lt. j.g. Joseph M. Shea	
19 May 1967	MiG-17	VF-24	F-8C	AIM-9D	CVA-31	USN	Lt. Cmdr. Bobby C. Lee	
19 May 1967	MiG-17	VF-24	F-8C	AIM-9D	CVA-31	USN	Lt. Phillip R. Wood	
21 Jul 1967	MiG-17	VF-24	F-8C	AIM-9D	CVA-31	USN	Cmdr. Marion H. Isaacks	
21 Jul 1967	MiG-17	VF-24	F-8C	†	CVA-31	USN	Lt. Cmdr. Robert L. Kirkwood	
21 Jul 1967	MiG-17	VF-211	F-8E	‡	CVA-31	USN	Lt. Cmdr. Ray G. Hubbard Jr.	
10 Aug 1967	MiG-21	VF-142	F-4B	AIM-9	CVA-64	USN	Lt. j.g. Guy H. Freeborn	Ens. Robert J. Elliot
10 Aug 1967	MiG-21	VF-142	F-4B	AIM-9	CVA-64	USN	Lt. Cmdr. Robert C. Davis	Lt. Cmdr. Gayle O. Elie
26 Oct 1967	MiG-21	VF-143	F-4B	AIM-7	CVA-64	USN	Lt. j.g. Robert P. Hickey Jr.	Lt. j.g. Jeremy G. Morris
30 Oct 1967	MiG-17	VF-142	F-4B	AIM-7E	CVA-64	USN	Lt. Cmdr. Eugene P. Lund	Lt. j.g. James R. Borst
14 Dec 1967	MiG-17	VF-162	F-8E	AIM-9D	CVA-34	USN	Lt. Richard E. Wyman	
17 Dec 1967	MiG-17	13 TFS	F-4D	AIM-4	432 TRW	USAF	1st Lt. John D. Ryan Jr.	Capt. Doyle D. Baker, USMC
26 Jun 1968	MiG-21	VF-51	F-8H	AIM-9	CVA-31	USN	Cmdr. Lowell R. Myers	
09 Jul 1968	MiG-17	VF-191	F-8E	†	CVA-14	USN	Lt. Cmdr. John B. Nichols III	
10 Jul 1968	MiG-21	VF-33	F-4J	AIM-9	CVA-66	USN	Lt. Roy Cash Jr.	Lt. Joseph E. Kain Jr.
29 Jul 1968	MiG-17	VF-53	F-8E	AIM-9	CVA-31	USN	Cmdr. Guy Cane	
01 Aug 1968	MiG-21	VF-51	F-8H	AIM-9	CVA-31	USN	Lt. Norman K. McCoy	
19 Sep 1968	MiG-21	VF-111	F-8C	AIM-9	CVS-11	USN	Lt. Anthony J. Nargi	
28 Mar 1970	MiG-21	VF-142	F-4J	AIM-9	CVA-64	USN	Lt. Jerome E. Beaulier	Lt. Steven J. Barkley
19 Jan 1972	MiG-21	VF-96	F-4J	AIM-9	CVA-64	USN	Lt. Randall H. Cunningham	Lt. j.g. William P. Driscoll

Aircraft Shot Down During the Vietnam War by USN/USMC Pilots

Date	Enemy Aircraft	Squadron	Aircraft	Weapon	Carrier or Unit	Service	Pilot	RIO/NFO
06 Mar 1972	MiG-17	VF-111	F-4B	AIM-9	CVA-43	USN	Lt. Gary L. Weigand	Lt. j.g. William Freckleton
06 May 1972	MiG-17	VF-51	F-4B	AIM-9	CVA-43	USN	Lt. Cmdr. Jerry B. Houston	Lt. Kevin T. Moore
06 May 1972	MiG-21	VF-114	F-4J	AIM-9	CVA-63	USN	Lt. Robert G. Hughes	Lt. j.g. Adolph J. Cruz
06 May 1972	MiG-21	VF-114	F-4J	AIM-9	CVA-63	USN	Lt. Cmdr. Kenneth W. Pettigrew	Lt. j.g. Michael J. McCabe
08 May 1972	MiG-17	VF-96	F-4J	AIM-9	CVA-64	USN	Lt. Randall H. Cunningham	Lt. j.g. William P. Driscoll
10 May 1972	MiG-21	VF-92	F-4J	AIM-9	CVA-64	USN	Lt. Curt Dose	Lt. Cmdr. James McDevitt
10 May 1972	2 MiG-17s	VF-96	F-4J	AIM-9	CVA-64	USN	Lt. Matthew J. Connelly III	Lt. Thomas J. J. Blonski
10 May 1972	MiG-17	VF-51	F-4B	AIM-9	CVA-43	USN	Lt. Kenneth L. Cannon	Lt. Roy A. Morris Jr.
10 May 1972	3 MiG-17s	VF-96	F-4J	AIM-9	CVA-64	USN	Lt. Randall H. Cunningham	Lt. j.g. William P. Driscoll
10 May 1972	MiG-17	VF-96	F-4J	AIM-9	CVA-64	USN	Lt. Steven C. Shoemaker	Lt. j.g. Keith V. Crenswhaw
18 May 1972	MiG-19	VF-161	F-4B	AIM-9	CVA-41	USN	Lt. Henry A. Bartholomay	Lt. Oran R. Brown
18 May 1972	MiG-19	VF-161	F-4B	AIM-9	CVA-41	USN	Lt. Patrick E. Arwood	Lt. James M. Bell
23 May 1972	2 MiG-17s	VF-161	F-4B	AIM-9	CVA-41	USN	Lt. Cmdr. Ronald E. McKeown	Lt. John C. Ensch
11 Jun 1972	MiG-17	VF-51	F-4B	AIM-9	CVA-43	USN	Cmdr. Foster S. Teague	Lt. Ralph M. Howell
11 Jun 1972	MiG-17	VF-51	F-4B	AIM-9	CVA-43	USN	Lt. Winston W. Copeland	Lt. Donald R. Bouchoux
21 Jun 1972	MiG-21	VF-31	F-4J	AIM-9	CVA-60	USN	Cmdr. Samuel C. Flynn Jr.	Lt. William H. John
10 Aug 1972	MiG-21	VF-103	F-4J	AIM-7E	CVA-60	USN	Lt. Cmdr. Robert E. Tucker Jr.	Lt. j.g. Stanley B. Edens
12 Aug 1972	MiG-21	58 TFS	F-4E	AIM-7	432 TRW	USMC	Capt. Lawrence G. Richard	Lt. Cmdr. Michael J. Ettel, USN
11 Sep 1972	MiG-21	VMFA-333	F-4J	AIM-9	CVA-66	USMC	Maj. Lee T. Lassiter	Capt. John D. Cummings
28 Dec 1972	MiG-21	VF-142	F-4J	AIM-9	CVAN-65	USN	Lt. j.g. Scott H. Davis	Lt. j.g. Geoffrey H. Ulrich
12 Jan 1973	MiG-17	VF-161	F-4B	AIM-9	CVA-41	USN	Lt. Victor T. Kovaleski	Lt. James A. Wise

* These two pilots shared the credit for the shoot down of the MiG-17 and each was credited for only a half a shoot down.

† Shoot down involved use of AIM-9 missile and guns.

‡ Shoot down involved use of guns and Zuni rockets.

Aircraft Shot Down During the Libyan Incidents of the 1980s

Date	Enemy Aircraft	Squadron	Aircraft	Weapon	Carrier	Service	Pilot	RIO/NFO
19 Aug 1981	Su-22	VF-41	F-14A	AIM-9L	CVN-68	USN	Cmdr. Henry M. Kleeman	Lt. David J. Venlet
19 Aug 1981	Su-22	VF-41	F-14A	AIM-9L	CVN-68	USN	Lt. Lawrence M. Muczynski	Lt. James Anderson
04 Jan 1989	MiG-23	VF-32	F-14A	AIM-7	CV-67	USN	Lt. Herman C. Cook III	Lt. Cmdr. Steven P. Collins
04 Jan 1989	MiG-23	VF-32	F-14A	AIM-9	CV-67	USN	Cmdr. Joseph B. Connelly	Cmdr. Leo F. Enwright Jr.

| Aircraft Shot Down During the Persian Gulf War | | | | | | | | |
Date	Enemy Aircraft	Squadron	Aircraft	Weapon	Carrier	Service	Pilot	RIO/NFO
17 Jan 1991	MiG-21	VFA-81	F/A-18C	AIM-9M and -7	CV-60	USN	Lt. Cmdr. Mark I. Fox	
17 Jan 1991	MiG-21	VFA-81	F/A-18C	AIM-9M and -7	CV-60	USN	Lt. Nicolas Mongillo	
06 Feb 1991	Mi-8	VF-1	F-14A	AIM-9M	CV-61	USN	Lt. Donald S. Broce	Cmdr. Ronald D. McElraft

Aircraft Carrier Names and Designations	
CVS-11	Intrepid
CVA-14	Ticonderoga
CVA-19	Hancock
CVL-29	Bataan
CVA-31	Bon Homme Richard
CV-32	Leyte
CVA-34	Oriskany
CV-37	Princeton
CVA-41	Midway
CVA-43	Coral Sea
CV-45	Valley Forge
CV-47	Philippine Sea
CVA-60	Saratoga
CV-61	Ranger
CVA-63	Kitty Hawk
CVA-64	Constellation
CVAN-65	Enterprise
CVA-66	America
CV-67	John F. Kennedy
CVN-68	Nimitz
CVE-118	Sicily

Acronyms:

TRW—Tactical Reconnaissance Wing
TFS—Tactical Fighter Squadron
NFO—Naval Flight Officer
RIO—Radar Intercept Officer

CHAPTER 39

Cold War Incidents Involving U.S. Navy Aircraft

From 1945 to 1969, U.S. Navy aircraft were involved in a number of aerial incidents with forces of the Soviet Union, People's Republic of China, Democratic People's Republic of Korea (North Korea), and the Czechoslovak Republic (Czechoslovakia). These incidents resulted in the loss of eight Navy and one Coast Guard aircraft; 81 Navy, Marine Corps, and Coast Guard aviators and crewman; and several aircraft damaged and crewmen wounded and injured. The list below, compiled from official and unofficial sources, does not include aircraft lost in direct action in the Korean and Vietnam Wars, nor aircraft shot down by Chinese forces in the vicinity of Vietnam in connection with that war.

Date	Aircraft	Squadron	Remarks
15 Nov 1945	PBM-5		On a routine patrol mission, this Mariner was attacked by a Soviet fighter 25 miles south of Dairen (Port Arthur), Manchuria, while investigating six Soviet transport ships and a beached seaplane in the Gulf of Chihli in the Yellow Sea. No damage inflicted.
20 Feb 1946	PBM-5	VP-26	Based from Tsingtao, China, during a training mission, this aircraft made an unauthorized flight over Dairen (Port Arthur), Manchuria. As a result, it was fired upon by Soviet fighters for 20 minutes. No damage inflicted.
8 Apr 1950	PB4Y-2	VP-26, Det A	Based from Port Lyautey, French Morocco, while on a patrol mission launched from Wiesbaden, West Germany, this Privateer (BuNo 59645) was lost when attacked by Soviet aircraft over the Baltic Sea off the coast of Lepija, Latvia. Wreckage was recovered, but unconfirmed reports stated that the ten missing crewmembers were taken prisoner.
6 Nov 1951	P2V-3W	VP-6	While conducting a weather reconnaissance mission under United Nations Command, this Neptune (BuNo 124284) was shot down by Soviet aircraft over the Sea of Japan off Vladivostok, Siberia. Ten crewmembers reported as missing.
16 Jul 1952	PBM-5S	VP-892	Aircraft attacked by MiG-15 off the coast of Korea. No damage inflicted.
31 Jul 1952	PBM-5S2	VP-731	While conducting a patrol mission, this Mariner (BuNo 59277) based from Iwakuni, Japan, was attacked by two Chinese MiG-15s over the Yellow Sea, resulting in two crewmembers killed and two more seriously wounded. The PBM suffered extensive damage, but was able to make it safely to Paengyong-do, Korea.
20 Sep 1952	P4Y-2S	VP-28	Aircraft attacked by two Chinese MiG-15s off the coast of China, but able to return safely to Naha, Okinawa.
23 Nov 1952	P4Y-2S	VP-28	Attacked without result by a Chinese MiG-15 off Shanghai, China.

Date	Aircraft	Squadron	Remarks
18 Jan 1953	P2V-5	VP-22	This Neptune (BuNo 127744) was shot down by Chinese antiaircraft fire near Swatow, and ditched in the Formosa Strait. Eleven of 13 crewmen were rescued by a Coast Guard PBM-5 under fire from shore batteries on Nan Ao Tao island. Attempting to takeoff in 8- to 12-foot swells, the PBM crashed. Ten survivors out of 19 total (including five from the P2V) were rescued by *Halsey Powell* (DD 686). During the search effort, a PBM-5 from VP-40 received fire from a small-caliber machine gun, and *Gregory* (DD 802) received fire from shore batteries.
19–28 Jun 1953	PBM-5S2, P2V-5(2)	VP-46, VP-1	Fired upon, in separate incidents, by surface ships in the Formosa Strait. No damage inflicted.
8 Jul 1953	P2V-5	VP-1	Fired upon by Chinese antiaircraft artillery (AAA) near Nantien, China. No damage inflicted.
21 Jul 1953	P2V-5	VP-1	Fired upon by Chinese AAA near Amoy Island in the Formosa Strait. No damage inflicted.
2 Oct 1953	PBM-5		Damaged during attack by two Chinese MiGs over the Yellow Sea.
12 Mar 1954	AD-4, AD-4N		Two ADs of VA-145 and VC-35 Det F launched from *Randolph* (CVA 15), on a simulated strike mission against a West German airfield, were attacked over or near the Czech border by a Czech MiG-15. The VA-145 AD sustained tail damage.
9 Apr 1954	P2V-5	VP-2	This Neptune was attacked by a Chinese MiG-15 while on patrol over the Yellow Sea. The MiG made three firing passes and the Neptune's crew returned fire. There was no apparent damage to either aircraft resulting from the encounter.
26 Jul 1954	AD-4, F4U-5N	VF-54, VC-3	While searching for survivors from a Cathay Pacific airliner shot down by Chinese fighters on 22 July, two AD-4s launched from *Philippine Sea* (CVA 47) were attacked by two Chinese LA-7 fighters. During the engagement, the two LA-7s were downed by six ADs and one F4U-5N that came to assist. The ADs encountered fire from a Chinese gunboat, but no damage was sustained in either situation.
4 Sep 1954	P2V-5	VP-19	Operating from NAS Atsugi, Japan, this Neptune ditched in the Sea of Japan, 40 miles off the coast of Siberia after an attack by two Soviet MiG-15s. One crewmen was lost, and the other nine were rescued by a USAF SA-16 amphibian.
Feb 1955	P2V		Aircraft sustained slight wing damage after it was fired on by Chinese AAA while over the Formosa Strait.

Date	Aircraft	Squadron	Remarks
9 Feb 1955	AD-5W	VC-11, Det H	While flying an antisubmarine patrol mission from *Wasp* (CVA 18) covering the evacuation of Chinese Nationalists from the Tachen Islands, this aircraft ditched after sustaining damage from antiaircraft fire when it overflew Chinese territory. The three-man crew was rescued by Nationalist Chinese patrol boats.
22 Jun 1955	P2V-5	VP-9	While flying a patrol mission from Kodiak, Alaska, this Neptune (BuNo 131515) crash-landed on St. Lawrence Island in the Bering Sea after an engine was set afire during an attack by two Soviet MiG-15s. Of the 11 crewmen, four sustained injuries due to gunfire and six were injured during the landing. (This was the only incident in which the Soviet Union admitted any responsibility.)
22 Aug 1956	P4M-1Q	VQ-1	While on a patrol mission from Iwakuni, Japan, this Mercator (BuNo 124362) disappeared at night after reporting an attack by hostile aircraft 32 miles off the coast of China (near Wenchow) and 180 miles north of Formosa. There were no survivors of the 16-man crew. Wreckage and one body were recovered by *Dennis J. Buckley* (DDR 808).
12 Jun 1957	AD-6	VA-145	Four AD-6s launched from *Hornet* (CVA 12) overflew the coast of China and encountered fire from Chinese AAA. One Skyraider sustained slight damage.
16 Jun 1959	P4M-1Q	VQ-1	While flying a patrol mission over the Sea of Japan, this Mercator (BuNo 122209) was attacked 50 miles east of the Korean DMZ by two North Korean MiGs. During the attack, the aircraft sustained serious damage to the starboard engines and the tailgunner was seriously wounded. The P4M made it safely to Miho AFB, Japan.
15 Apr 1969	EC-121M	VQ-1	While flying a patrol mission over the Sea of Japan this Warning Star (BuNo 135749) was attacked 90 miles off the coast of Korea by North Korean fighters. All 31 crewmen were lost during the attack. Two bodies and some wreckage were recovered by search vessels.
1 Apr 2001	EP-3E	VQ-1	While flying a routine surveillance mission in international airspace over the South China Sea, this Aeries II (BuNo 156511) was disabled in a midair collision with a Chinese J-8 fighter. Lt. Shane Osborn, mission commander, recovered and executed an emergency landing at the nearest airfield, Lingshui, a Chinese air base on Hainan Island. The 24 crew members were detained by the Chinese and eventually released. The EP-3E was also eventually returned to the United States.

Made in the USA
Middletown, DE
26 January 2018